# SCIENTIFIC REVOLUTIONS

# SCIENTIFIC REVOLUTIONS

## Primary Texts in the
## History of Science

### Brian S. Baigrie

*University of Toronto*

Upper Saddle River, New Jersey 07458

**Library of Congress Cataloging-in-Publication Data**

Baigrie, Brian S. (Brian Scott)
    Scientific revolutions : primary texts in the history of science /
Brian S. Baigrie.
        p. cm.
Includes bibliographical references and index.
    ISBN 0-13-099091-4
    1. Science--History. I. Title.

    Q125.B23 2004
    509--dc22

2003022463

| | |
|---|---|
| **Editorial Director:** Charlyce Jones-Owen | **Manufacturing Buyer:** Tricia Kenny |
| **Senior Acquisitions Editor:** Charles Cavaliere | **Cover Art Director:** Jayne Conte |
| **Editorial Assistant:** Shannon Corliss | **Cover Design:** Kiwi Design |
| **Executive Marketing Manager:** Heather Shelstad | **Photo Researcher:** Kathy Ringrose |
| | **Image Permission Coordinator:** Frances Toepfer |
| **Senior Marketing Assistant:** Jennifer Bryant | **Composition/Full-Service Project Management:** |
| **Managing Editor (Production):** Joanne Riker | Jessica Balch/Pine Tree Composition |
| **Production Full Service Liaison:** Joanne Hakim | **Printer/Binder:** R.R. Donnelley & Sons |

Credits and acknowledgments for material borrowed from other sources and reproduced, with permission, in this textbook appear on pages xiii–xvi.

Pearson Education LTD., London
Pearson Education Singapore, Pte. Ltd
Pearson Education, Canada, Ltd
Pearson Education–Japan
Pearson Education Australia PTY, Limited

Pearson Education North Asia Ltd
Pearson Educación de Mexico, S.A. de C.V.
Pearson Education Malaysia, Pte. Ltd
Pearson Education, Upper Saddle River,
    New Jersey

10 9 8 7 6 5 4 3 2 1
0-13-099091-4

# CONTENTS

# PREFACE

The production of this anthology has been guided by the conviction that the best introduction to the history and philosophy of science is primary source material that reflects, as well as possible, the richness and diversity of scientific culture and practice. The realization of this conviction called for some difficult decisions. Many of the canonical texts of the natural sciences were forged in the service of a body of well-established theory—Joseph Louis Lagrange's magnificent *Mécanique Analytique* and Ronald Aylmer Fisher's *The Correlation Between Relatives on the Supposition of Mendelian Inheritance*—are uncontroversial instances of the articulation of received theories—respectively, those of Newton and Darwin. The greater part of the scientific literature consists of writings of this sort. The focus of this book, however, is on those extraordinary bursts of scientific activity that propel the culture of science in new and, sometimes unexpected, directions. Repositories of tradition, and their elaboration, have received a great deal of critical attention from professional scholars in recent years but there is a great deal, I believe, that both the introductory and the advanced student can learn from these comparatively rare outbursts of innovation.

The selection of readings gathered here takes no stand on the "essential tension," so masterfully portrayed by Thomas Kuhn, between tradition and innovation in the natural sciences. The title of this volume is merely a gentle reminder that these readings emphasize novelty, including novel device production; it is not meant in any way to diminish the importance of work carried out in the service of a received body of knowledge. The title *Scientific Revolutions* serves here as a label for important *turning points* in the history of science and its philosophical interpretation—it is not to be taken in the general sense of historians and philosophers of science as boundaries for great historical periods, often centuries in length, that were dominated by a particular variety of science, whether the science of Copernicus, Newton, or Darwin. Grand intellectual artifacts like "research programs," "paradigms," and "worldviews," however meaningful as organizational tools for professional scholars, tend to obscure the little revolutions that are occurring in science all the time, and the very diversity that makes the natural sciences an exciting and rewarding field for humanistic exploration and discovery.

A number of these turning points have been documented by their innovators in ways that are invariably daunting to an introductory audience. In these cases, another, less technically demanding reading from the same author has been substituted for those readings that were deemed to be too demanding; cases in point are the selections from J. J. Thomson and Albert Einstein. An accessible alternative proved to be unavailable in a few cases, which narrowed the range of candidates for the anthology, sometimes in unfortunate ways. It was decided in two of these cases—Caroline Herschel and Marie Curie—that the absence of suitable primary source material constituted grounds for exceptions to the principle calling for primary source material. The weakness of primary source material, from the point of view of the historian of science, is that it is invariably geared toward reporting results and supporting evidence, thereby effectively denying the reader any insights into the processes involved in scientific discovery and the conditions—often unpleasant—under which scientists labor. Hence, the inclusion of Eve Curie's recounting of her mother's unbridled passion for the experimental life; and the selection by the American astronomer, Maria Mitchell, reflecting on the larger question of science as a vocation for women. If anything, these readings are important reminders that, even in a course that is grounded in primary source material, secondary sources are still indispensable.

Even after the decision was made to restrict the selections to revolutionary documents (understood now as those that propel the culture of science in new and sometimes unexpected directions) that were not too technically demanding, we still faced a daunting body of literature. This anthology focuses on the physical and life sciences—astronomy, physics, chemistry, biology—with some additional readings drawn from the earth sciences (geology and palaeontology) which dovetail rather nicely with important debates in the selected disciplines. Some obvious candidates were excluded on the grounds that they have been reproduced many times and are still widely available; other things being equal, preference has been given to material that are likely to be the least accessible to university students. Of course, there are limits to the application of this principle: Any historical introduction to science, it goes without saying, would be incomplete without the likes of Copernicus, Bacon, Newton, Lavoisier, Faraday, Lyell, Darwin, and Einstein. However, these "paradigm" names are balanced by the inclusion of three kinds of readings that are designed to instill in the student a sense of the diversity of scientific practice.

First, there are a number of readings that are not as well known as they might be but which, nevertheless, opened up entire new areas of scientific research and study in their day—examples are Leeuwenhoek's discovery of microscopic organisms, Priestley's recounting of his discovery of oxygen, Cavendish's determination of the gravitational constant, Volta's creation of the first electric battery, Oersted's detection of the electromagnetic effect, Röntgen's discovery of X-rays, and De Vries' elaboration of the mutation theory. These readings are powerful antidotes to the temptation to reserve the label "scientific revolution" for the extraordinary upheavals associated with the likes of Newton, Darwin, and Einstein.

Second, a number of dissenting voices are included here to counter any suggestion that the history of science follows a natural trajectory from superstition and error to truth. For example, Priestley invoked an elaborate and, ultimately misguided, theory to explain a piece of observational evidence, and Lowell concocted an entire alien civilization to explain puzzling observations. By the same token, however, both inspired generations of scientists to seek answers to questions that their work placed on the agenda. Extraordinary science need not be synonymous with the creation of a body of truths that gain the allegiance of the scientific community.

Finally, there are a number of readings that vividly recount experiments and the production of novel devices—Harvey's experiments on the circulation of the blood, Leeuwenhoek and Hooke on subvisibilia, Priestley on oxygen, Cavendish on the gravitational constant, Volta on the battery, Oersted on the electromagnetic effect, Schwann on cell theory, Mendel on inheritance, Röntgen on X-rays, Thomson on the electron, De Vries on mutations, and Rutherford on the disintegration of the atom. Scientific revolution is still widely portrayed in purely intellectual terms as the elaboration of the consequences of a novel proposition, theory, set of equations, etc. These readings help to correct this bias toward theory, reminding us that many of the important turning points in the history of science were negotiated by experimental practice and the creation of associated technology.

The cultural and national diversity of the modern classroom called for a final tough decision. In our own multicultural age, students approach their lectures and readings with a more profound sense of their own situatedness, not only in their awareness of their own cultural histories but in their conviction that cultural attachments strongly shape beliefs and values. As much as possible, students quite rightly want to see the richness and diversity of their own cultural situation reflected in the content of university instruction. It is not always possible to satisfy this pluralist urge, especially in courses in the history of science and technology that focus narrowly on scientific achievement in the Western intellectual tradition. The selections on Caroline Herschel and Marie Curie notwithstanding, these readings will regrettably reinforce the familiar portrait of the history of science as the privilege of white, bearded, European males. However, in acknowledging this fact, we are not thereby accepting it. Instead, we are setting boundary conditions for the experiences that we are sampling and giving recognition to those many vocal critics who have chastised the androcentrism of science in the European tradition.

The selections have been arranged in chronological order, according to the date of first publication. My judgment was that this practice would make for the least confusion—exceptions are Thomson's work on the electron (though carried out in 1897, the selection included here was published in 1921), the selection by Einstein, and the reflections on Caroline Herschel by Maria Mitchell and Marie Curie by her daughter Eve Curie. Setting aside four brief background readings from Aristotle, Ptolemy, Lucretius, and Paracelsus, the volume opens with the twin 1543 classics of Vesalius and Copernicus, widely regarded as the year of the birth of modern science. It closes with the birth of atomic physics, Einstein's theory of relativity, and Schrödinger's visionary call for the molecularization of life itself. The aim has been to assemble the material that served as the building blocks for modern science, as it emerged during the Renaissance, and as it was refined during the modern period leading up to the Second World War. Developments in quantum mechanics, molecular biology, and high temperature physics have been left for another day. Although these revolutionary developments have their roots in the past, they depend in many instances upon ideas and technological innovations that were unknown to the scientists whose voices are registered in these pages.

After much discussion with colleagues, at the eleventh hour the decision was made to modernize and standardize the text; an exception was the Lucretius reading, which was left intact so as to preserve its poetic structure. The reasons for this decision were many. The most compelling was that standardizing and modernizing the text would eliminate countless inconsistencies in punctuation and spelling that are not only confusing but also make many of the readings a labor to read. Another consideration was that this decision would make an electronic version of this text, which may be just around the corner, easily searchable. Finally, while we recognized that this decision threatened to strip the majority of the readings of some of their historical flavor, standardizing and modernizing the text would not thereby strip the readings of their historical value as repositories of scientific practice. Indeed, for the majority of the readings, eccentricities in punctuation and spelling do not reflect the originals on which the translations were based, but rather the literary conventions of translators, often removed from the originals by decades and, in some cases, centuries. Of course, there are noteworthy exceptions: Grew's (mis)translations of Leeuwenhoek's original communications to the Royal Society, for example, are important sources of information about the reaction of the learned to Leeuwenhoek's marvelous discoveries. Still, it was our sense that, while unaltered historical documents might be more appropriate for graduate students and scholars, for our anticipated reader the trade-off was well worth the effort.

Each reading is prefaced by an introduction that attempts to provide a rationale for its inclusion in this volume. Biographical information on the author is offered when it is needed to motivate the claim that the reading is extraordinary, but the emphasis of these introductions is the reading itself. The biographies of individual scientists, and the rise of the many movements and schools that were inspired by their achievements, are interesting objects of study in their own right. However, it is the text itself that is the focus of this anthology, and not the great scientists or the icons that so often emerge in the wake of their achievements.

Footnotes from the original publications—either courtesy of the author of the reading or a previous editor—have been preserved as endnotes after the reading. Some of the notes from previous editions are valuable sources of information— Drake's notes on Galileo, Bateson's notes on Mendel, the notes on Copernicus prepared for the Royal Astronomical Society—and I've done my best to preserve them. My own footnotes are indicated in square brackets [B.], though I've added numerous short definitions in the main body of the text, without any indication save for square brackets. Although historians of science have annotated individual texts, to my knowledge this is the first anthology in the history of the natural sciences to receive this level of attention.

My footnotes are of three kinds: First, there are footnotes that are designed to outfit the student with biographical information on the individual scientists mentioned by the authors of the readings. These notes attempt to give the student the minimal material needed to make sense of the reading and, if desired, a starting point for additional research. Biographical information is provided for the vast majority of figures named by the authors of these readings, though it must be admitted that some names do not appear with a corresponding footnote, for the most part because the contributions of these individuals were incidental to an understanding of the reading. So, for example, there are no corresponding footnotes for the many individuals who are cited by the likes of Oersted as witnesses to an experimental demonstration in order to authorize it as knowledge. Witnessing itself is a philosophically interesting historical relic of eighteenth and nineteenth century scientific practice, but the witnesses themselves are sources of confusion to introductory readers who naturally presume that there is more to the name than a mere certification of the authenticity of the report; (2) second, there are footnotes that are designed to outfit the student with technical information needed to make sense of the reading. Since this anthology was designed as a teaching tool, it was my position that the elucidation of technical points should be left with the instructor and, therefore, that these sorts of technical footnotes should be kept to a minimum; and, third, there are footnotes, often lengthy, that provide the student with historical information about the reading as a whole or important aspects of it.

The titles of the vast majority of the readings are my own, and not those of the original authors.

I am the benefactor of the generosity of my colleagues at The Institute for History and Philosophy of Science and Technology—Trevor Levere and Mary P. Winsor, who directed me to a number of the readings that appear in this anthology. A special thanks is owed to Professor Levere—his input will be immediately apparent to those who are familiar with his many contributions to the history of chemistry. Thanks also to Jed Z. Buchwald for discussions many years ago on sources in nineteenth century physics; to Sungook Hong for reading the short introductions appended to the physics readings and many useful suggestions for improvement; to Kenton Kroker and David Topper for lengthy discussions on pedagogical issues associated with the history of science; and to Patricia Kazan for helping me devise a plan for the book as a whole. Thanks also to the librarians and staff of Robarts Library at the University of Toronto for helping me track down original material and to my research assistant, Melissa Nelson, for help preparing the text for publication. Finally, a debt to all students, past and present, of my undergraduate class—Scientific Revolutions—for countless suggestions on how to improve the readings for the course. My hope is that you will feel that I've responded to your concerns.

Grateful acknowledgment is also given to the following reviewers: Michael R. Lynn, Agnes Scott College; Andrew D. Wilson, Keene State College; and one reviewer who wishes to remain anonymous.

*Brian S. Baigrie*
*University of Toronto*

# ACKNOWLEDGMENTS

Aristotle. *The Physics.* Ed. P.H. Wicksteed and F.M. Cornford. Cambridge: Harvard University Press, 1929, vol. 1, pp. 116–135; 191–201.

Avogadro, Amadeo. 1811. "Essay on a Manner of Determining the Relative Masses of the Elementary Molecules of Bodies, and the Proportions in Which They Enter Into These Compounds." *Journal de physique* 73, 58–76. Translation from Alembic Club Reprints, No. 4, "Foundations of the Molecular Theory: Comprising Papers and Extracts by John Dalton, Joseph Louis Gay-Lussac, and Amadeo Avogadro (1808–1811)"

Bacon, Francis. *The New Organon.* Edited by Lisa Jardine and Michael Silverthorne. Cambridge: Cambridge University Press, 2000, pp. 14–24.

Boyle, Robert. "On the Excellency and Grounds of the Corpuscular or Mechanical Philosophy." In Peter Shaw, ed., *Philosophical Works of the Honorable Robert Boyle Esq.* London: W. & J Innys, and J. Osborn, and T. Longman, 1725, volume 2, pp. 187–96.

Brahe, Tycho. "The New Star." From J.A. Walden, trans., *A Source Book in Astronomy.* Cambridge: Harvard University Press, 1929, pp. 233–239.

Cavendish, Henry. "Experiments to Determine the Density of the Earth." *Philosophical Transactions of the Royal Society of London* 88 (1798), 469–526.

Copernicus, Nicolaus. *On the Revolutions of the Heavenly Spheres,* translated by John F. Dobson and Selig Brodetsky, Preface and Book 1. Printed originally as *Occasional Notes of the Royal Astronomical Society.* London: Burlington House, 1947, No. 10, pp. 3–23; 27–32.

Cuvier, Georges. *Essay on the Theory of the Earth.* Trans. Robert Jameson. Fourth edition. Edinburgh: W. Blackwood, and Baldwin, Cradock and Joy, 1817, pp. 7–12; 15–17; 121–122; 149–151; 173–175.

Curie, Eve. *Madame Curie: A Biography by Eve Curie.* New York: Garden City, 1943, pp. 153–164; 166–175.

Dalton, John. *A New System of Chemical Philosophy.* Manchester: S. Russell, 1808, pp. 141–144, 211–220.

Darwin, Charles. *The Variations in Animals and Plants Under Domestication.* London: J. Murray, 1868, pp. 446–447; 448–449; 450–452; 481–483.

Darwin, Charles. *On the Origin of Species by Means of Natural Section.* London: John Murray, Albemarle Street, 1872, pp. 48–51; 52–55; 58–60; 62–65; 69; 84–85; 85–87; 103–105.

Descartes, René. *The World.* In John Cottingham, Robert Stoothoff, and Dugald Murdoch, eds., *The Philosophical Writings of Descartes.* Cambridge: Cambridge University Press, 1985, pp. 85–98.

De Vries, Hugo. *The Mutation Theory: Experiments and Observations on the Origin of Species in the Vegetable Kingdom.* Trans. J.B. Farmer and A.D. Darbishire. Chicago: Open Court Publishing Company, 1909–1910, pp. 3–8; 247–259.

Einstein, Albert. *Essays in Science.* Trans. Alan Harris. New York: Philosophical Library, 1934, pp. 53–60.

Faraday, Michael. "On Electrochemical Decomposition." In *Philosophical Transactions of the Royal Society,* 1834, pp. 118–126. Reprinted in Faraday, *Experimental Researches in Electricity.* London: Taylor & Francis, 1839, vol. 1, pp. 127–164.

Faraday, Michael. "Thoughts on Ray Vibrations." In *Experimental Researches,* 1846, vol. 3, pp. 447–452.

Galilei, Galileo. *Two New Sciences.* Trans. Stillman Drake. Toronto: Wall & Thompson, 1974, pp. 153–167.

Harvey, William. *An Anatomical Disputation Concerning the Movement of the Heart and Blood in Living Creatures.* Trans. Gweneth Whitteridge. London: Blackwell Scientific Publications, 1976, pp. 10–22; 29–30; 32–35; 38–40; 42–47; 50–54; 56–61; 66–68; 70–72; 74–77; 80–83; 86–87; 89–93; 100–102; 103–104; 107–110; 114–117; 120–124; 128–133.

Herschel, William. "Catalogue of a Second Thousand of New Nebulae and Clusters of Stars; with a Few Introductory Remarks on the Construction of the Heavens." Read June 11, 1789 and published originally in the *Philosophical Transactions of the Royal Society, 79* (1789), 212–255.

Hooke, Robert. *Micrographia, or some Physiological Descriptions of Minute Bodies, made by Magnifying Glasses with Observations and Inquiries thereupon.* London: J. Martyn and J. Allestry, 1665, pp. 131–135.

Hutton, James. *Theory of the Earth, with Proofs and Illustrations in 4 Parts.* Edinburgh: Cadell, 1795, volume I, pp. 280–281, volume II, pp. 540–564.

Lamarck, Jean Baptiste. *Zoological Philosophy.* Trans. Hugh Elliot. New York: Hafner Publishing Company, 1963, pp. 107–120; 122; 126–27.

Lavoisier, Antoine-Laurent. *Elements of Chemistry in a New Systematic Order.* Trans. by Robert Kerr. Edinburgh: William Creech, 1790, pp. xii–xxxvii, 175–189, 208–211.

Leeuwenhoek, Antoni van. "A Letter of Mr. Leeuwenhoeck to Dr. G," *Philosophical Collections,* vol. 2 (1681), pp. 3–5;

Leeuwenhoek, Antoni van. "An Abstract of a Letter From Mr. Anthony Leeuwenhoeck to Sir C.W," *Philosophical Transactions of the Royal Society,* vol. 13 (1682–1683), pp. 74–79.

Linnaeus, Carolus von. "The Families of Plants." The Botanical Society at Lichfield, 1787. In W.C. Dampier and M. Dampier, eds., *Readings on the Literature of Science.* New York: Harper Torchbooks, 1924, pp. 188–195.

Lowell, Percival. *Mars.* London: Longmans, Green, 1896, pp. 129–140; 148–155.

Lucretius Carus, Titus. *De Rerum Natura.* Trans. William Ellery Leonard. London: J. M. Dent, 1921.

Lyell, Charles. *Principles of Geology,* vol. 1. London: John Murray, Albemarle-Street, 1830, pp. 83–91; 144–154.

Maxwell, James Clerk. *The Scientific Papers of James Clerk Maxwell.* Cambridge: Cambridge University Press, 1890, vol. II, pp. 241–255.

Mendel, Gregor. "Experiments in Plant Hybridization." In William Bateson, *Mendel's Principles of Heredity.* Cambridge: Cambridge University Press, 1913, pp. 335–364.

Mendeléev, Dmitri. "The Periodic Law of the Chemical Elements," *Chemical News* (1879), 40, pp. 231–232; 243–244; 267–268; (1880), 41, pp. 27–28.

Mitchell, Maria. "Reminiscences of the Herschels." *The New Century Monthly Magazine.* Volume 38, 1889.

Newton, Isaac. *The Mathematical Principles of Natural Philosophy.* Ed. Florian Cajori. Trans. A. Motte. Berkeley: University of California Press, 1934, pp. xvii–xxxiii, 1–8, 398–400, 543–547.

Oersted, John Christian. "Experiments on the Effect of a Current of Electricity on the Magnetic Needle," *Annals of Philosophy* 16 (1820), pp. 273–76.

Osiander, "Preface to *On the Revolutions of the Heavenly Spheres,*" trans. A.M. Duncan. New York: Barnes & Noble Books, 1976, pp. 22–23.

Paracelsus, *The Hermetic and Alchemical Writings of Paracelsus.* Trans. Arthur Edward Waite. Boulder: Shambhala, 1976, pp. 3–11.

Priestley, Joseph. *Experiments and Observations on Different Kinds of Air.* Second edition. London: J. Johnson, 1776, vol. 2, pp. 29–50.

Ptolemy, "Selection from *The Almagest.*" In G. Schwartz and P. Bishop, eds., *Moments of Discovery.* New York: Basic Books, 1958, pp. 174–180.

Röntgen, Wilhelm Conrad. "On a New Type of Rays." Trans. Arthur Stanton. *Nature* 53 (1896), 274–276.

Rutherford, Ernest. "Collisions of $\alpha$ Particles with Light Atoms. IV. An Anomalous Effect in Nitrogen," *The London, Edinburgh and Dublin Philosophical Magazine and Journal of Science* 37 (1919), 581–587.

Schrödinger, Erwin. *What is Life? The Physical Aspect of the Living Cell & Mind and Matter.* Cambridge: Cambridge University Press, 1944, pp. 22–25; 68–70; 73–75; 83–84; 94–96.

Schwann, Theodore. 1839. *Mikroskopische untersuchungen uber die ubereinstimmung in der striker und den wachstum der tiere und pflanzen,* Berlin. Trans. Henry Smith as *Microscopical Researches into the Accordance in the Structure and Growth of Animals and Plants.* London: The Sydenham Society, 1847.

Thomson, Joseph Jon. "Carriers of Negative Electricity," *Nobel Lectures: Physics, 1901–1921*. Amsterdam: Elsevier, 1967, pp. 144–153.

Vesalius, Andreas. "Selection from *De Humani Corporis Fabrica*." In G. Schwartz and P. Bishop, eds., *Moments of Science*. New York: Basic Books, 1958, pp. 517–528.

Volta, Alessandro. "On the Electricity excited by the Mere Contact of Conducting Substances of Different Kinds," *Philosophical Transactions of the Royal Society*, vol. 90 (1800), pp. 403–431.

# LIST OF PLATES

# SCIENTIFIC REVOLUTIONS

# Causation and Movement

## Aristotle (384–322 B.C.)

*The twentieth century philosopher and mathematician, A. N. Whitehead, claimed that Western intellectual history was one extended footnote to Plato. In terms of his influence on the development of scientific ideas and practices, it is arguable that Aristotle was at least the equal of his distinguished teacher. Aristotle developed a systematic philosophy that he applied to the central questions of his day. His system was distinguished by the extent to which it engaged empirical investigation. Aristotle's central ideas acquired a canonical status during the Middle Ages. If not the final word on any subject, his words were invariably taken to be the starting point for any investigation. In the natural sciences, his central doctrines were assailed during the seventeenth century, but his system of logic and his emphasis on purposefulness persisted until well into the twentieth century.*

*This reading, which is taken from Aristotle's* Physics, *addresses the issue of causation. The notion of causation has historically stood front and center in accounts of the aims of science and the character of scientific explanation. For Aristotle, "to know" was to know by means of four causes—the material, formal, efficient, and the final cause. The material cause deals with the substrate, such as the bronze of a statue, while the formal cause is concerned with its shape. The final cause is its end or purpose for the sake of which the process of making the status was commenced, and the efficient cause is that which initiates the process of change. Each of these four causes can be identified in the writings of Plato (c. 427 to 347 BC), but they did not make up a system for Plato, as they did for Aristotle. Many of the revolutionary episodes in the history of scientific ideas have been associated with the rejection of one or other of Aristotle's four causes.*

Now that we have determined the different senses in which "nature" may be understood (as signifying either "material" or "form"),

*Source:* Aristotle. 1929. *The Physics.* P. H. Wicksteed and F. M. Cornford (eds.). Cambridge: Harvard University Press, vol. 1, pp. 116–135; 191–201.

we have next to consider how the mathematician differs from the physicist or natural philosopher; for natural bodies have surfaces and occupy spaces, have lengths and present points, all which are subjects of mathematical study. And then there is the connected question whether astronomy is a separate science from physics or only a special branch of it; for if the student of nature is concerned to know what the Sun and Moon are, it would be strange if he avoided inquiry into their essential properties; especially as we find that writers on nature have, in fact, discoursed on the shape of the Moon and Sun and raised the question whether the Earth, or the cosmos, is spherical or otherwise.

Physicists, astronomers, and mathematicians, then, all have to deal with lines, figures and the rest. But, the mathematician is not concerned with these concepts *qua* boundaries of natural bodies, nor with their properties as manifested in such bodies. Therefore, he abstracts them from physical conditions; for they are capable of being considered in the mind in separation from the motions of the bodies to which they pertain, and such abstraction does not affect the validity of the reasoning or lead to any false conclusions.

Now the exponents of the philosophy of "Ideas"[a] also make abstractions, but in doing so they fall unaware into error; for they abstract physical entities, which are not really susceptible to the process as mathematical entities are. And this would become obvious if one should undertake to define, respectively, the mathematical and the "ideal" entities, together with their properties; for the concepts "odd," "even," "straight," "curved," will be found to be independent of movement; and so too with "number," "line," and "figure." But of "flesh" and "bone" and "man" this is no longer true, for these are in the same case as a "turned-up nose," not in the same case as "curved." The point is further illustrated by those sciences which are rather physical than mathematical, though combining both disciplines, such as optics, harmonics, and astronomy; for the relations between them and geometry are, so to speak, reciprocal; since the geometer deals with physical lines, but not *qua* physical, whereas optics deals with mathematical lines, but *qua* physical not *qua* mathematical.

Since "nature" is used ambiguously, either for the form or for the matter, nature, as we have seen, can be regarded from two points of view; and therefore, our speculations about it may be likened to an inquiry as to what "snubnosed-ness" is; that is to say, it can neither be isolated from the material subject in which it exists, nor is it constituted by it.

At this point, in fact, we may again raise two questions: Which of the two aspects of nature is it that claims the attention of the physicist? Or is his subject the *compositum* that combines the two? In that case, if he is concerned with the *compositum*, he must also inquire into its two factors; and then we must ask further whether this inquiry is the same for both factors or different for each.

In reading the ancients one might well suppose that the physicist's only concern was with the material; for Empedocles[b] and Democritus[c] have remarkably little to say about kinds of things and what is the constituent essence of them. But if art imitates nature, and if in the arts and crafts it pertains to the same branch of knowledge both to study its own distinctive aspect of things and likewise (up to a point) the material in which the same is manifested (as the physician, for instance, must study health and also bile and phlegm, the state of which constitutes health; and the builder must know what the house is to be like and also that it is built of bricks and timber; and so in all other cases), it seems to follow that physics must take cognizance both of the formal and of the material aspect of nature.

---

[a]This passage refers to the views of Plato (c. 428 BC–347 BC) and his disciples. [B.]

[b]Empedocles of Acragas (c. 490 BC–c. 430 BC) is remembered as the author of the four element theory of matter (earth, air, fire, and water), which was authoritative until the rise of modern chemistry in the eighteenth century. [B.]

[c]Democritus of Abdera (c. 460 BC–c. 370 BC) is remembered, chiefly through the writings of Aristotle, as the leading exponent in antiquity of the theory of atoms (from the Greek *atomos*) and the void. [B.]

And, further, the same inquiry must embrace both the purpose or end and the means to that end. And the "nature" is the goal for the sake of which the rest exist; for if any systematic and continuous movement is directed to a goal, this goal is an end in the sense of the purpose to which the movement is a means. (A confusion on this point betrayed the poet into the unintentionally comic phrase in reference to a man's death: "He has reached his end for the sake of which he was born." For the "goal" does not mean any kind of termination, but only the best.) For in the arts, too, it is in view of the end that the materials are either made or suitably prepared, and we make use of all the things that we have at our command as though they existed for our sake; for we too are, in some sort, a goal ourselves. For the expression "that for the sake of which" a thing exists or is done has two senses (as we have explained in our treatise *On Philosophy*). Accordingly, the arts which control the material and possess the necessary knowledge are two: the art which uses the product, and the art of the master-craftsman who directs the manufacture. Hence, the art of the user also may in a sense be called the master-art; the difference is that this art is concerned with knowing the form, the other, which is supreme as controlling the manufacture, with knowing the material. Thus, the helmsman knows what are the distinctive characteristics of the helm as such, that is to say, its form, and gives his orders accordingly; while what the other knows is out of what wood and by what manipulations the helm is produced. In the crafts, then, it is we who prepare the material for the sake of the function it is to fulfill, but in natural products nature herself has provided the material. In both cases, however, the preparation of the material is commanded by the end to which it is directed.

And again, the conception of "material" is relative, for it is different material that is suited to receive the several forms.

How far then, is the physicist concerned with the form and identifying essence of things and how far with their material? With the form primarily and essentially, as the physician is with health; with the material up to a certain point, as the physician is with sinew and the smith with bronze. For his main concern is with the goal, which is formal; but he deals only with such forms as are conceptually, but not factually, detachable from the material in which they occur. In nature man generates man; but the process presupposes and takes place in natural material already organized by the solar heat and so forth. But how we are to take the subject and what it is, is a question for First Philosophy to determine . . .

We have next to consider in how many senses "because" may answer the question "why." For we aim at understanding, and since we never reckon that we understand a thing until we can give an account of its "how and why," it is clear that we must look into the "how and why" of things coming into existence and passing out of it, or more generally into the essential constituents of physical change, in order to trace back any object of our study to the principles so ascertained.

Well then, (1) the existence of *material* for the generating process to start from specifically or generically considered is one of the essential factors we are looking for. Such is the bronze for the statute or the silver for the phial. (Material cause.) Then, naturally, (2) the thing in question cannot be there unless the material has actually received the *form* or characteristics of the *type*, conformity to which brings it within the definition of the thing we say it is, whether specifically or generically. Thus the interval between two notes is not an octave unless the notes are in the ratio of 2 to 1; nor do they stand at a musical interval at all unless they conform to one or other of the recognized ratios. (Formal cause.) Then again (3), there must be something to initiate the process of the change or its cessation when the process is completed, such as the act of a voluntary agent (of the smith, for instance) or the father who begets a child; or more generally the prime, conscious or unconscious, *agent* that produces the effect and starts the material on its way to the product, changing it from what it was to what it is to be. (Efficient cause.) And lastly, (4) there is the *end* or purpose for the sake of which the process is initiated as when a man takes exercise for the sake of his health. "Why does he take exercise?" we ask. And the answer: "Because he thinks it good for his health" satisfies us. (Final cause.) Then there are all the intermediary agents, which are set in motion by the prime agent and make for the goal, as means to the end. Such are the reduction of superfluous flesh and purgation, or drugs and surgical instruments, as means to health. For both actions and tools may be means or "*media,*" through which the efficient cause reaches the end aimed at.

This is a rough classification of the causal determinants of things; but it often happens that, when we specify them we find a number of them coalescing as joint factors in the production of a single effect, and that not merely incidentally; for it is *qua* statue that the statue depends for its existence alike on the bronze and on the statuary. The two, however, do not stand on the same footing for one is required as the material and the other as initiating the change.

Also it can be said of certain things indifferently that either of them is the cause or the effect of the other. Thus, we may say that a man is in fine condition "because" he has been in training or that he has been in training "because" of the good condition he expected as the result. But one is the cause as aim (final) and the other as initiating the process (efficient).

Again, the same cause is often alleged for precisely opposite effects. For if its presence causes one thing we lay the opposite to its account if it is absent. Thus, if the pilot's presence would have brought the ship safe to harbor, we say that he caused its wreck by his absence.

But in all cases the essential and causal determinants we have enumerated fall into four main classes. For letters are the causes of syllables, and the material is the cause of

manufactured articles, and fire and the like are causes of physical bodies, and the parts are causes of the whole, and the premises are causes of the conclusion, in the sense of that [premise, or design] out of which these [final outcomes] are respectively made; but of these things some are causes in the sense of the *substratum* (e.g., the parts stand in this relation to the whole), others in the sense of the *essence*—the whole or the synthesis or the form. And again, the fertilizing sperm, or the physician, or briefly the voluntary or involuntary *agent* sets going or arrests the transformation or movement. And finally, there is the goal or end in view which animates all the other determinant factors as the best they can attain to; for the attainment of that "for the sake of which" anything exists or is done is its final and best possible achievement (though of course "best" in this connection means no more than "taken to be the best").

These are the main classes of determinant factors and causes . . .

Since nature is the principle of movement and change and it is nature that we are studying, we must understand what "movement" is; for if we do not know this, neither do we understand what nature is. When we have defined the meaning of movement or progress from this to that, we must attempt in the same way a discussion of the associated conceptions to which it leads. Now, movement is clearly one of the things we think of as "continuous," and it is in connection with continuity that we first encounter the concept of the "unlimited." And this is why in definitions of continuity this concept of the "illimitable" frequently occurs, as when we say that the continuous is that which is susceptible of division without limit. Further, movement (it is said[d]) cannot occur except in relation to place, void, and time. Evidently, then, for these reasons and because these four things—movement, place, void, and time—are universal conditions common to all natural phenomena, we

[d]The reference is to the followers of Democritus and the doctrine of atoms and the void. [B].

must consider each of them on the threshold of our inquiry; for the treatment of peculiar properties must come after that of properties common to all natural things.

We must begin, then, as already said, with movement in general or progress from this to that. Now, some potentialities never exist apart, but always reveal themselves as actualized; others, while they are something actually, are capable of becoming something else than they are, that is to say, have potentialities not realized at the moment; and these potentialities may concern their substantive being (what they are) or their quantity or their qualities; and so on with the other categories of existence. And under the category of "relation" may be relations between the "more" and the "less," or between that which is active and that which is acted on, and generally between that which "moves" (or changes) something as the agent and that which is moved (or changed) by it as the patient. For that which has the power of producing a change can only act in reference to a thing capable of being changed; and that which is capable of being changed can only suffer change under the action of that which has the power to change it.

Now, motion and change cannot exist in themselves apart from what moves and changes. For, wherever anything changes it always changes either from one thing to another, or from one magnitude to another, or from one quality to another, or from one place to another; but there is nothing that embraces all these kinds of change in common, and is itself neither substantive nor quantitative nor qualitative nor pertaining to any of the other categories, but existing in detachment; so neither can movement or change exist independently of these, for there is nothing independent of them.

Again, in each of these four cases, there are two poles between which the change moves; in substantive existence, for example, [the poles are] form and shortage from form; in quality, white and black; in quantity, the perfectly normal and an achievement short of perfection; and so, too, in the case of

vection, up and down, or the action of levity and gravity. So there are as many kinds of change as there are categories of existence.

Reverting, therefore, to the universal distinction already established between "being-at-the-goal" in actuality and being in potentiality "such-as-is-capable-of-attaining-the-goal," we can now define motion or change as the progress of the realizing of a potentiality, *qua* potentiality, e.g. the actual progress of qualitative modification in any modifiable thing *qua* modifiable; the actual growing or shrinking (for we have no single word to include them both) of anything capable of expanding or contracting; the process of coming into existence or passing out of that which is capable of so coming and passing; the actual moving of the physical body capable of changing its place. That this is what we really mean by motion or change may be shown thus: building material is actualizing the potentialities in virtue of which we call it "building material" when it is in the act of being built into a structure, and this act is the process or "movement" of "building"; and so too with other processes: learning, healing, rolling, jumping, maturing, aging.

And since in certain cases the same thing may have both an actuality and a potentiality (not indeed at the same time or not in the same respect, but potentially hot, for instance, and actually cold) it follows that many things act on and are acted on, by each other; for anything will be at once capable of acting and of being acted upon. And so it happens that every physical body which causes motion must be capable of being moved; for whenever it causes motion it is itself under the action of some other body which is keeping it in motion.[e] But the inference that has sometimes been drawn, that there is *no* cause of a thing being in motion,

[e]Aristotle did not have the modern concept of inertia as the convervation of a body's state of motion or rest, and so he could not offer an explanation for the motion of projectiles; e.g., why a javelin keeps moving once it leaves the hand that is throwing it. [B.]

which cause is not itself in motion, is false. The truth in this matter will be explained later on; suffice it now to say that there is a cause of things being in motion, which cause is itself immovable; but motion is the functioning of a movable thing, all the time that it is bringing its potentiality into act, not *qua* itself, but *qua* movable.

To illustrate what I mean by *"qua"* this or [*"qua"*] that: The bronze is potentially the statue, but neither to be the statue nor to move or change in any respect is the self-realization of the bronze *qua* bronze; for it is not the same thing to be bronze and to be potentially movable or changeable. Were it the same thing, absolutely and by definition, then indeed moving would be its self-realization; but it is not the same. (It is clear in the case of opposites the potentiality of health and the potentiality of disease are different things, otherwise being diseased and being healthy would be identical, but whatever it is, humor or blood, to be subject to the healthy or unhealthy condition is one and the same thing in both cases.) And since it is not the same (any more than color and visibility, for instance, are the same), it is clear that motion must be the realization of the specific potentiality in question and of the subject only *qua* seat of this specific potentiality.

Clearly, then, this is the nature of movement, and a thing is moving just as long as it is actually functioning in this particular way, and neither before nor after. For anything capable of this special kind of functioning may be exercising it at one time, but not at another; for instance, the building materials are functioning *as materials for building only* so long as they are in process of being built with; for as soon as the edifice itself is actually raised, the functioning of what were materials for a house is merged in the functioning of the house itself; but as long as they are being built with, they are functioning as materials for a house. The act of building, then, is the energizing or bringing into actuality of the potentiality of the materials *qua* materials; and the passage of the materials of a house into the texture of the house itself, so long as it is in progress, is their "movement" *qua* materials of building. And this is the theory of all the other "movements" equally.

## FURTHER READING

Judson, Linsay, ed. 1995. *Aristotle's Physics: A Collection of Essays.* Oxford: Clarendon Press.

Lennox, James G. 2001. *Aristotle's Philosophy of Biology: Studies in the Origins of Life Science.* Cambridge: Cambridge University Press.

# Saving the Appearances

## Ptolemy (c. 100–c. 170)

*The cosmology fashioned by the Hellenized Egyptian, Ptolemy (Claudius Ptolemaeus), dominated science for thirteen centuries. The guiding assumption of his seminal work, the* Syntaxis mathematica *(known through Arabian scientists as the* Almagest), *is that all heavenly bodies (the Sun, Moon, planets, and stars) move in uniform, circular motion around a fixed point, situated near a stationary Earth. In order to reconcile the appearances, which are exceedingly irregular, with the supposition of an underlying regularity, Ptolemy invoked a number of sophisticated geometrical devices—the epicycle on deferent construction, the eccentric, and the equant—that remained in widespread use until the late seventeenth century.*

## ON THE ORDER OF THE THEOREMS

The work which we have projected commences with a consideration of the general relation between the Earth as a whole and the heavens as a whole. Of the special treatments that follow, the first part deals with the position of the ecliptic, the places inhabited by the human race, and the differences among the successive places, in each separate horizon, along the curvature of the Earth's surface. The preliminary study of these relations makes easier the examination of the subsequent questions. The second part gives an account of the motion of the Sun and the Moon and of the phenomena that depend on these motions. For without the previous understanding of these matters, it

*Source:* Ptolemy. 1958. "Selection from *The Almagest.*" In G. Schwartz and P. Bishop, eds., *Moments of Discovery.* New York: Basic Books, pp. 174–180.

would be impossible to set forth a complete theory of the stars. Since the theory of the stars is contained, in accordance with the general plan in the concluding portion of this essay, the investigation of the sphere of the so-called fixed stars would properly find its place there, and the material on the five so-called planets would follow. We shall try to set forth all this material using as the basic foundations for knowledge the manifest phenomena themselves and those recorded observations of the ancients and the moderns about which there is no dispute; and we shall seek to fit the propositions together by geometrical proofs.

With respect to the general portion of the treatise the following preliminary assumptions are to be made: (1) that the heaven is spherical in form and rotates as a sphere; (2) that the Earth, too, viewed as a complete whole is spherical in form; (3) that it is situated in the middle of the whole heaven, like a center; (4) that by reason of its size and its distance from the sphere of fixed stars, the Earth bears to this sphere the relation of a point; (5) that the Earth does not participate in any locomotion. We shall say a few words by way of commentary on each of these propositions.

## THAT THE HEAVEN ROTATES AS A SPHERE

It is reasonable to assume that the first ideas on these matters came to the ancients from observations, such as the following: they saw the Sun and the Moon and the other stars moving from east to west in circles always parallel to each other; they saw the bodies begin to rise from below, as if from the Earth itself, and gradually to rise to their highest point, and then, with a correspondingly gradual decline to trace a downward course until they finally disappeared, apparently sinking into the Earth; and then they saw these stars, once more, after remaining invisible for a time, make a fresh start and in rising and setting repeat the same periods of

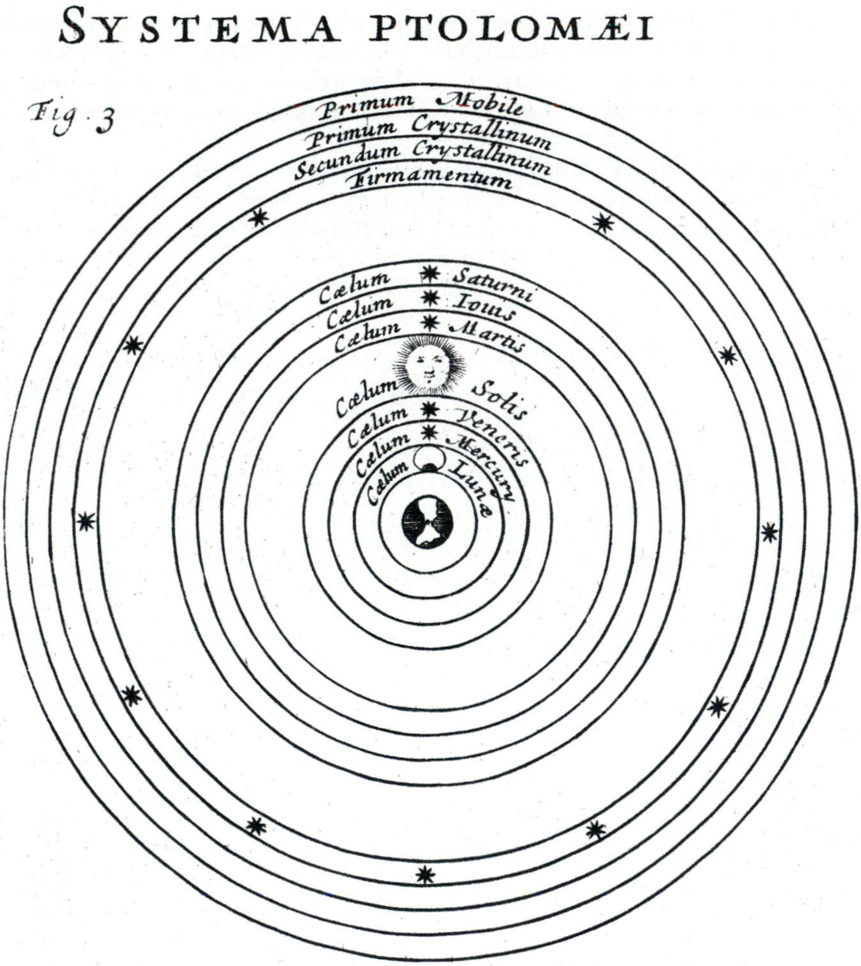

# SYSTEMA PTOLOMÆI

Fig. 3

Primum Mobile
Primum Crystallinum
Secundum Crystallinum
Firmamentum

Cælum ✳ Saturni
Cælum ✳ Iouis
Cælum ✳ Martis
Cælum Solis
Cælum ✳ Veneris
Cælum ✳ Mercurij
Cælum Lunæ

**PLATE 1** The Ptolemaic planetary arrangement, starting at the center: Earth, Moon, Mercury, Venus, Sun, Mars, Jupiter, Saturn, and the sphere of the fixed stars.

time and the same places of rising and setting with regularity and virtual similarity.

They were, however, led to the view of a spherical heaven chiefly by the observed circular motion described about one and the same center by those stars that are always above the horizon. For this point was, necessarily, the pole of the heavenly sphere, since the stars that are nearer this pole revolve in smaller circles, whereas those further away make larger circles, proportionately to their distance, until the distance reaches that of the stars not always visible. And of these latter they observed that those stars nearer the stars that are always visible remained invisible for a shorter time, while those further away remained invisible for a correspondingly longer time. And so, from these phenomena alone they first conceived the aforesaid idea, and then from the consideration of its consequences they adopted the other ideas that follow from it, since all the phenomena without qualification refuted the alternative hypotheses.

For example, if one should suppose, as some have, that the motion of the stars proceeds by a straight line without limit, how could one explain the fact that the daily motion of each star is always seen to begin from the same point? How could the stars in their unlimited motion turn back? And if they did turn back, how could this escape observation? Or how could they fail eventually to become altogether invisible, since they would appear ever smaller and smaller? In point of fact, however, they appear larger when near the region where they disappear [the horizon], and are only gradually occulted and, as it were, cut off by the surface of the Earth.

Again, the suggestion that the stars are kindled when they rise from the Earth and again are snuffed out when they return to the Earth is quite contrary to reason.[a] For even if one should grant that the arrange-ment, size, and number of the stars, and their distances and intervals in space and time could have been the fulfillment of mere random and accidental procedure and that one part of the Earth (the eastern part) had throughout it a kindling force, while the other (the western part) had an extinguishing force, or rather that the same part acted as a kindler from the point of view of some and as an extinguisher from the point of view of others, and that of the stars the very same ones were already kindled or extinguished, as the case might be for some observers, but not yet for others; if, I repeat, one should grant all this, absurd as it is, what of the stars always visible, those that neither rise nor set? Why should the stars that are kindled and extinguished not rise and set everywhere? Why should those not subject to such kindling and extinguishing always be above the horizon in all latitudes? For surely the stars which for some observers are always kindled and extinguished cannot be the same as those which for other observers are never kindled and extinguished. Yet, the proponents of the hypothesis of kindling would have to assume that they are the same for it is quite evident that the same stars rise and set for some observers (i.e., those further south), whereas they neither rise nor set for others (i.e., those further north).

In a word, if one should suppose any other form of motion of the heavens save the spherical, the distances from the Earth to the heavenly bodies would necessarily be unequal, however and wherever the Earth itself might be supposed to be situated. Consequently, the sizes of the stars and their distances from one another would have to appear unequal to the same observers at each return, since the distances from the observers would sometimes be greater and at other times smaller. But this is not seen to be the case. For what makes the apparent size of a heavenly body greater when it is near the horizon is not its smaller distance but the vaporous moisture surrounding the Earth between our eye and the heavenly body. It is the same as when objects immersed in water

[a]This view is often ascribed to Epicurus (c. 341 B.C.–270 B.C.), who is remembered for his revival of Democritean atomism and the founding of a school dedicated to the pursuit of happiness. [B.]

appear larger and, in fact, the more deeply immersed the larger.

The hypothesis of spherical motion finds support also in the fact that on any other hypothesis save this one alone it is impossible that the instruments for measuring hours should be correct. This is also supported by the following fact: just as the motion of the heavenly bodies is completely without hindrance and the smoothest of all motions, and the most easily moved of all shapes is the circular for plane figures and the spherical for solids, so also since the polygon with the greater number of sides is the larger of regular polygons having equal perimeters, it follows that in the case of plane figures the circle is greater than any polygon of equal perimeters, and in the case of solid figures the sphere is greater. And the heaven is greater than all other bodies.

Various physical considerations, too, lead to the same conclusion. Thus the aether[b] consists of finer and more homogeneous parts than does any other body. Now surfaces of bodies of homogeneous parts are themselves of homogeneous parts, and the circular surface in the case of plane figures and the spherical surface in the case of solid figures are the only surfaces that consist of homogeneous parts. The aether not being a plane surface but a solid may therefore be inferred to be of spherical form. A similar inference may be made from the fact that nature has constructed all earthly and destructible bodies entirely of circular forms but forms not having homogeneous parts, while she has constructed the divine bodies in the aether of spherical form having homogeneous parts. For if these bodies were flat

or quoit-shaped [flattened-ring or discus-shaped] their form would not appear circular to all observers at the same time from different places of the Earth. Hence it is reasonable to infer that the aether which encloses the heavenly bodies, being of the same nature, is of spherical form, and because of its composition out of homogeneous parts, moves with uniform circular motion.

## THE ABSOLUTE IMMOBILITY OF THE EARTH

In the same way as before it can be proved that the Earth cannot make any movement whatever in the aforesaid oblique direction, or ever change its position at all from its place at the center, for the same results would in that case have followed as if it had happened to be placed elsewhere than at the center. So I, for one, think it is gratuitous for any one to inquire into the causes of the motion towards the center when once the fact that the Earth occupies the middle place in the universe, and that all weights move towards it, is made so patent by the observed phenomena themselves. The ground for this conviction which is readiest at hand, seeing that the Earth has been proved to be spherical and situated in the middle of the universe, is this simple fact: in all parts of the Earth without exception the tendencies and the motions of bodies which have weight, I mean their own proper motions, always and everywhere operate at right angles to the (tangent) plane drawn evenly through the point of contact where the object falls. That this is so makes it also clear that, if the objects were not stopped by the surface of the Earth, they would absolutely reach the centre itself, since the straight line leading to the center is always at right angles to the tangent-plane to the sphere drawn through the intersection at the point of contact.

All who think it strange that such an immense mass as that of the Earth should neither move itself nor be carried somewhere seem to me to look to their own personal

[b]In physical theory, the aether, as distinct from ordinary matter, was invoked to give a plausible explanation for processes whose mechanisms were not manifest in experience. For Ptolemy, the heavenly bodies are enclosed in an aether which moves in uniform, circular motion, whereas for nineteenth century physicists, the aether transports electromagnetic waves, in much the same way that air carries sound. [B.]

experience, and not to the special character of the universe, and to go wrong through regarding the two things as analogous. They would not, I fancy, think the fact in question to be strange if they could realize that the Earth, great as it is, is nevertheless, when compared with the enclosing body, in the relation of a point to that body. For in this way it will seem to be quite possible that a body relatively so small should be dominated and pressed upon with equal and similarly directed force on all sides by the absolutely greatest body formed of like constituents, there being no up and down in the universe any more than one would think of such things in an ordinary sphere. So far as the composite objects in the universe and their motion on their own account and in their own nature are concerned, those objects which are light, being composed of fine particles, fly towards the outside, that is, towards the circumference, though their impulse seems to be towards what is for individuals "up" because with all of us what is over our heads, and is also called "up," points towards the bounding surface; but all things which are heavy, being composed of denser particles, are carried towards the middle, that is, to the center, though they seem to fall "down," because, again, with all of us the place at our feet, called "down," itself points towards the center of the Earth, and they naturally settle in a position about the center, under the action of mutual resistance and pressure which is equal and similar from all directions. Thus, it is easy to conceive that the whole solid mass of the Earth is of huge size in comparison with the things that are carried down to it, and that the Earth remains unaffected by the impact of the quite small weights (falling on it), seeing that these fall from all sides alike, and the Earth welcomes, as it were, what falls and joins it. But, of course, if as a whole, it had had a common motion, one and the same with that of the weights, it would, as it was carried down, have got ahead of every other falling body, in virtue of its enormous excess of size, and the animals and all separate weights would have been left behind

floating on the air, while the Earth, for its part at its great speed, would have fallen completely out of the universe itself. But indeed this sort of suggestion has only to be thought of in order to be seen to be utterly ridiculous.

Certain thinkers,[c] though they have nothing to oppose to the above arguments, have concocted a scheme which they consider more acceptable, and they think that no evidence can be brought against them if they suggest for the sake of argument that the heaven is motionless, but that the Earth rotates about one and the same axis from west to east, completing one revolution approximately every day,[d] or alternatively that both the heaven and the Earth have a rotation of a certain amount, whatever it is, about the same axis, as we said, but such as to maintain their *relative* situations.

These persons forget, however, that while so far as appearances in the stellar world are concerned, there might, perhaps, be no objection to this theory in the simpler form, yet, to judge by the conditions affecting ourselves and those in the air about us, such a hypothesis must be seen to be quite ridiculous. Suppose we could concede to them such an unnatural thing as that the most rarefied and lightest things either do not move at all or do not move differently from those of the opposite character, when it is clear as day that things in the air and less rarefied have swifter motions than any bodies of

[c]The reference is perhaps to a pupil of Plato— Heracleides of Pontus (c. 390 B.C.–c. 322 B.C.)— who is said to have been the first to state that the Earth rotates. There was little enthusiasm for this view in Antiquity and the Middle Ages. [B.]

[d]When he observed a new star in the constellation of Scorpio in 143 B.C., Hipparchus (c. 190–125 B.C.) decided to create a catalogue of the stars. Comparing his records with observations made 150 years earlier, he found that changes in the distances of the stars from fixed celestial points had occurred during this period. The only explanation was that the axis of the Earth had rotated in the direction of the apparent daily motion of the stars, with the result that the equinoxes fell earlier each year. [B.]

more earthy character, and that (we could further concede that) the densest and heaviest things could have a movement of their own so swift and uniform; when earthy bodies admittedly sometimes do not readily respond even to motion communicated to them by other things; yet they must admit that the rotation of the Earth would be more violent than any whatever of the movements which take place about it, if it made in such a short time such a colossal turn back to the same position again, that everything not actually standing on the Earth must have seemed to make one and the same movement always in the contrary sense to the Earth, and clouds and any of the things that fly or can be thrown could never be seen traveling towards the east, because the Earth would always be anticipating them all and forestalling their motion towards the east, insomuch that everything else would seem to recede towards the west and the parts which the Earth would be leaving behind it.

For, even if they should maintain that the air is carried round with the Earth in the same way and at the same speed, nevertheless the solid bodies in it would always have appeared to be left behind in the motion of the Earth and air together, or, even if the solid bodies themselves were, so to speak, attached to the air and carried round with it, they could no longer have appeared either to move forwards or to be left behind, but would always have seemed to stand still, and never, even when flying or being thrown, to make any excursion or change their position, although we so clearly see all these things happening, just as if no slowness or swiftness whatever accrued to them in consequence of the Earth not being stationary.

## FURTHER READING

Evans, James. 1998. *The History and Practice of Ancient Astronomy.* Oxford: Oxford University Press.

Michael Hoskin, ed. 1997. *The Cambridge Illustrated History of Astronomy.* Cambridge: Cambridge University Press.

# On the Nature of Things

## Lucretius (95–45 B.C.)

*Lucretius occupies a unique position in the history of science. As a poet, he belongs to a small but distinguished group of Roman poets. He has no claim to recognition as a scientist of any significance. Still, the one surviving work,* De rerum natura *(On the Nature of Things), of this poet remains the immortal exposition of ancient atomism.*

*As opposed to Aristotle's philosophy, which was attuned to the appearances of things, atomism contended that the nature of things is radically different from the phenomena by which they are known. Insisting on the atomic structure of all living things, Lucretius dismissed notions of the immortality of humankind, and extended the hypothesis of atomism to the human mind itself.*

*Following the death of Lucretius, atomism disappeared from view for well over a thousand years, until the recovery of Lucretius' poem in 1417, furnishing natural philosophers with an alternative to the prevailing Aristotelian physics. Because of its atheistic basis (compared with the Christianized Aristotle), until the latter portion of the seventeenth century atomism appealed to few philosophers—Thomas Hobbes (1588–1679) was a notable exception—most referring explanations of natural phenomena to "particles" or "corpuscles," rather than to atoms.*

*Character of the Atoms*

           Bodies, again,
Are partly primal germs of things, and partly
Unions deriving from the primal germs.
And those which are the primal germs of things
No power can quench; for in the end they
    conquer
By their own solidness; though hard it be
To think that aught in things has solid frame;
For lightnings pass, no less than voice and shout,
Through hedging walls of houses, and the iron

White-dazzles in the fire, and rock will burn
With exhalations fierce and burst asunder.
Totters the rigid gold dissolved in heat;
The ice of bronze melts conquered in the flame;
Warmth and the piercing cold through silver
    seep,
Since, with the cups held rightly in the hand,
We oft feel both, as from above is poured
The dew of waters between their shining sides:
So true it is no solid form is found.
But yet because true reason and nature of things
Constrain us, come, whilst in few verses now
I distangle how there still exist
Bodies of solid, everlasting frame—
The seeds of things, the primal germs we teach,
Whence all creation around us came to be.
First since we know of a twofold nature exists,

*Source:* Lucretiu Carus, Titus. 1921. *De Rerum Natura.* Trans. William Ellery Leonard. London: J. M. Dent.

Of things, both twain and utterly unlike—
Body, and place in which all things go on—
Then each must be both for and through itself,
And all unmixed: where'er be empty space,
There body's *not;* and so where body bides,
There not at all exists the void inane.
Thus primal bodies are solid, without a void.
But since there's void in all begotten things,
All solid matter must be round the same;
Nor, by true reason canst thou prove aught hides
And holds a void within its body, unless
Thou grant what holds it be a solid. Know,
That which can hold a void of things within
Can be naught else than matter in union knit.
Thus matter, consisting of a solid frame,
Hath power to be eternal, though all else,
Though all creation, be dissolved away.
Again, were naught of empty and inane,
The world were then a solid; as, without
Some certain bodies to fill the place held,
The world that is were but a vacant void.
And so, infallibly, alternative-wise
Body and void are still distinguished,
Since nature knows no wholly full nor void.
There are, then, certain bodies, possessed of
    power
To vary forever the empty and the full;
And these can never be sundered from without
By beats and blows, nor from within be torn
By penetration, nor be overthrown
By any assault so ever through the world—
For without void, naught can be crushed, it
    seems,
Nor broken, nor severed by a cut in twain,
Nor can it take the damp, or seeping cold
Or piercing fire, those old destroyers three;
But the more void within a thing, the more
Entirely it totters at their sure assault.
Thus if first bodies be, as I have taught,
Solid, without a void, they must be then
Eternal; and, if matter ne'er had been
Eternal, long ere now had all things gone
Back into nothing utterly, and all
We see around from nothing had been born—
But since I taught above that naught can be
From naught created, nor the once begotten
To naught be summoned back, these primal
    germs
Must have an immortality of frame.

And into these must each thing be resolved,
When comes its supreme hour, that thus there be
At hand the stuff for plenishing the world.

So primal germs have solid singleness,
Nor otherwise could they have been conserved
Through aeons and infinity in time
For the replenishment of wasted worlds.
Once more, if nature had given a scope for things
To be forever broken more and more,
By now the bodies of matter would have been
So far reduced by breakings in old days
That from them nothing could, at season fixed,
Be born, and arrive its prime and top of life.
For, lo, each thing is quicker marred than made;
And so whate'er the long infinitude
Of days and all fore-passed time would now
By this have broken and ruined and dissolved,
That same could ne'er in all remaining time
Be builded up for plenishing the world
But mark: infallibly a fixed bound
Remaineth stablished 'gainst their breaking
    down;
Since we behold each thing so ever renewed,
And unto all, their seasons, after their kind,
Wherein they arrive the flower of their age.
Again, if bounds have not been set against
The breaking down of this corporeal world,
Yet must all bodies of whatever things
Have still endured from everlasting time
Unto this present, as not yet assailed
By shocks of peril. But because the same
Are, to thy thinking, of a nature frail,
It ill accords that thus they could remain
(As thus they do) through everlasting time,
Vexed through the ages (as indeed they are)
By the innumerable blows of chance.
So in our programme of creation, mark
How 'tis that, through the bodies of all stuff
Are solid to the core, we yet explain
The ways whereby some things are fashioned
    soft—
Air, water, earth, and fiery exhalations—
And by what force they function and go on:
The fact is founded in the void of things.
But if the primal germs themselves be soft,
Reason cannot be brought to bear to show
The ways whereby may be created these

Great crags of basalt and the during iron;
For their whole nature will profoundly lack
The first foundations of a solid frame.
But powerful in old simplicity,
Abide the solid, the primeval germs;
And by their combinations more condensed,
All objects can be tightly knit and bound
And made to show unconquerable strength.
Again, since all things kind by kind obtain
Fixed bounds of growing and conserving life;
Since nature hath inviolably decreed
What each can do, what each can never do;
Since naught is changed, but all things so abide
That ever the variegated birds reveal
The spots and stripes peculiar to their kind,
Spring after spring: thus surely all that is
Must be composed of matter immutable.
For if the primal germs in any wise
Were open to conquest and to change 'twould be
Uncertain also what could come to birth
And what could not, and by what law to each
Its scope prescribed, its boundary stone that
    clings
So deep in Time. Nor could the generations
Kind after kind so often reproduce
The nature, habits, motions, ways of life,
Of their progenitors.
                        And then again,
Since there is ever an extreme bounding point
Of that first body which our senses now
Cannot perceive: That bounding point indeed
Exists without all parts, a minimum
Of nature, nor was e'er a thing apart,
As of itself, nor shall hereafter be,
Since 'tis itself still parcel of another,
A first and single part, whence other parts

And others similar in order lie
In a packed phalanx, filling to the full
The nature of the first body: being thus
Not self-existent, they must cleave to that
From which in nowise they can sundered be.
So primal germs have solid singleness,
Which tightly packed and closely joined cohere
By virtue of their minim particles—
No compound by mere union of the same;
But strong in their eternal singleness,
Nature, reserving them as seeds for things,
Permitteth naught of rupture or decrease.
Moreover, were there not a minimum,
The smallest bodies would have infinites,
Since then a half-of-half could still be halved,
With limitless division less and less.
Then what the difference 'twixt the sum and least
None: for however infinite the sum,
Yet even the smallest would consist the same
Of infinite parts. But since true reason here
Protests, denying that the mind can think it,
Convinced though must confess such things
        there are
As have no parts, the minimums of nature.
And since they are, likewise confess thou must
That primal bodies are solid and eterne.
Again, if Nature, creatress of all things,
Were wont to force all things to be resolved
Unto least parts, then would she not avail
To reproduce from out them anything;
Because whate'er is not endowed with parts
Cannot possess those properties required
Of generative stuff—divers connections,
Weights, blows, encounters, motions, whereby
        things
Forevermore have being and go on.

## FURTHER READING

Kennedy, Duncan F. 2002. *Rethinking Reality: Lucretius and the Textualization of Na-
    ture.* Ann Arbor: University of Michigan Press.
Johnson, W. R. 2002. *Lucretius and the Modern World.* London: Duckworth.

# The Copernican Revolution

## Nicolaus Copernicus (1473–1543)

*With the possible exception of Isaac Newton, no figure occupies a more prominent place in accounts of the creation of modern science than Nicolaus Copernicus. His celebrated work,* De revolutionibus orbium coelestium *(On the Revolutions of the Heavenly Spheres) was only published on his death in 1543, thanks to the efforts of George Rheticus (1514–1576), a young Lutheran mathematician from Wittenberg.*

*Responding to rumors of a new heliocentric system, in 1539 Rheticus had made the trip to Frauenberg, where Copernicus served as canon of the local cathedral. So impressed was Rheticus that he composed a substantial monograph of his own called* Narratio prima de libris revolutionibus *(First Account of the Book of Revolutions) which was published the following year. A new appointment at Leipzig prevented Rheticus from seeing the manuscript through the press, and the task fell to Andreas Osiander (1498–1552), a Nuremberg theologian, who added to the work a famous and unauthorized preface, which is reproduced below, asserting that the heliocentric hypothesis was merely a useful supposition, and not intended to be a true description of the universe. The book met with opposition from theologians, Aristotelians, and even professional astronomers like Tycho Brahe (1546–1601) who recognized its dire consequences for the received scientific and theological views of the day. It was finally placed on the Index of books banned by the Catholic Church in 1616 (from which it was not removed until 1835).*

*Copernicus' great work almost single-handedly overthrew the old geocentric cosmology forged by Aristotle, Ptolemy, and their many disciples. Converts to Copernicus' theory recognized that many of his "proofs" were outmoded, chiefly because Copernicus had to rely upon observations and measurements made with the crudest of instruments. Some of his hypotheses, such as his explanation for the precession of the equinoxes, were resisted as well by later generations of astronomers. Even so, this work was regarded as the single most important scientific document by the founders of the new science of the seventeenth century.*

---

*Sources:* "Osiander's Anonymous Preface." In *Copernicus: On the Revolutions of the Heavenly Spheres,* trans. A.M. Duncan. New York: Barnes & Noble Books, 1976, pp. 22–23.

*On the Revolutions of the Heavenly Spheres,* translated by John F. Dobson and Selig Brodetsky, Preface and Book 1. Printed originally as *Occasional Notes of the Royal Astronomical Society.* London: Burlington House, 1947, No. 10, pp. 3–23; 27–32.

*The most intriguing aspect of Copernicus' great work is that the essential elements of the Copernican system—the abolition of epicycles and deferents, the dissolution of the spheres, the Sun as a star, the infinite expansion of the cosmos, easy and accurate computations of planetary position—are not to be found in it. With the striking exception of the Earth's motion, the work echoes ancient texts, especially Ptolemy's* **Almagest.** *Indeed, in his claim that only a uniform circular motion (or a combination of such motions) can account for the celestial phenomena, Copernicus proved to be more devoted to the spirit of Aristotle's teachings than many of Aristotle's sixteenth-century devotees. Even his central argument for a moving Earth, which was not original with Copernicus, had an ancient pedigree—Copernicus suggests that because the Earth is a sphere, it too must participate in the compounded circular motions which, he contends, are natural to a sphere. This is the enduring paradox of Copernicus' great work—it is at once ancient and modern; conservative and revolutionary. Its significance is to be found, not in what it said, but in what it caused others to say. As a revolution-making—rather than a revolutionary—text, it shifted the direction in which scientific thought would develop.*

## TO THE READER ON THE HYPOTHESES IN THIS WORK

I have no doubt that certain learned men, now that the novelty of the hypotheses in this work have been widely reported—for it establishes that the Earth moves, and indeed that the Sun is motionless in the middle of the universe—are extremely shocked, and think that the scholarly disciplines, rightly established once and for all, should not be upset. But if they are willing to judge the matter thoroughly, they will find that the author of this work has committed nothing which deserves censure. For it is proper for an astronomer to establish a record of the motions of the heavens with diligent and skillful observations, and then to think out and construct laws for them, or rather hypotheses, whatever their nature may be, since the true laws cannot be reached by the use of reason; and from those assumptions the motions can be correctly calculated, both for the future and for the past. Our author has shown himself outstandingly skillful in both of these respects. Nor is it necessary that these hypotheses should be true, nor indeed even probable, but it is sufficient if they merely produce calculations which agree with the observations. That is, unless anyone

is so ignorant of geometry and optics that the epicycle of Venus seems to him probable, or he thinks that it is in accordance with its law that it is sometimes ahead of the Sun and sometimes lags behind it by forty degrees or more. For who does not see that from that assumption it necessarily follows that the star's diameter appears more than four times greater, and its area more than sixteen times greater, at perigee than at apogee, to which all the experience of the ages is opposed. There are other things also in this discipline which are no less absurd, which it is quite unnecessary to examine for the present purpose. For it is clear enough that this subject is completely and simply ignorant of the laws which produce apparently irregular motions. And if it does work out any laws—as certainly it does work out very many—it does not do so in any way with the aim of persuading anyone that they are valid, but only to provide a correct basis for calculation. Since different hypotheses are sometimes available to explain one and the same motion (for instance eccentricity or an epicycle for the motion of the Sun) an astronomer will prefer to seize on the one which is easiest to grasp; a philosopher will perhaps look more for probability; but neither will grasp or convey anything certain, unless it has been divinely revealed to him. Let us therefore allow these new hypotheses also to become known beside the older, which are no more probable, especially since they are remarkable and easy; and let them bring with them the vast treasury of highly learned observations. And let no one expect from astronomy, as far as hypotheses are concerned, anything certain, since it cannot produce any such thing, in case if he seizes on things constructed for any other purpose as true, he departs from this discipline more foolish than he came to it. Farewell.

## TO THE MOST HOLY LORD, POPE PAUL III. THE PREFACE OF NICOLAUS COPERNICUS TO THE BOOKS OF THE REVOLUTIONS

I may well presume, most Holy Father,[a] that certain people, as soon as they hear that in this book *On the Revolutions of the Spheres of the Universe* I ascribe movement to the earthly globe, will cry out that, holding such views, I should at once be hissed off the stage. For I am not so pleased with my own work that I should fail duly to weigh the judgment which others may pass thereon; and though I know that the speculations of a philosopher are far removed from the judgment of the multitude—for his aim is to seek truth in all things as far as God has permitted human reason so to do—yet I hold that opinions which are quite erroneous should be avoided.

Thinking, therefore, within myself that to ascribe movement to the Earth must indeed seem an absurd performance on my part to those who know that many centuries have consented to the establishment of the contrary judgment, namely that the Earth is placed immovably as the central point in the middle of the universe, I hesitated long whether, on the one hand, I should give to the light these my Commentaries written to prove the Earth's motion, or whether, on the other hand, it were better to follow the example of the Pythagoreans[b] and others who were accustomed to impart their philosophic mysteries only to intimates and friends, and then not in writing but by word of mouth, as the letter of Lysis to Hipparchus witnesses. In my judgment they did so not, as some would have it, through jealousy of sharing their doctrines, but as fearing lest these so noble and hardly won discoveries of the learned should be despised by such as either care not to study aught save for gain, or—if by the encouragement and example of others they are stimulated to philosophic liberal pursuits—yet by reason of the dullness of their wits are in the company of philosophers as drones among bees. Reflecting thus the thought of the scorn which I had to fear on account of the novelty and incongruity of my theory, almost induced me to abandon my project . . .

That I allow the publication of these my studies may surprise your Holiness the less in that, having been at such travail to attain them, I had already not scrupled to commit to writing my thoughts upon the motion of the Earth. How I came to dare to conceive such motion of the Earth, contrary to the received opinion of the mathematicians and indeed contrary to the impression of the senses, is what your Holiness will rather expect to hear. So I should like your Holiness to know that I was induced to think of a method of computing the motions of the spheres by nothing else than the knowledge

[a]In view of the conflict between Scripture and Copernicus' work, the dedication to Pope Paul III is remarkable, Church authorities in Rome had been aware of Copernicus' central claims for the better part of a decade and actively enouraged their publication. The contrast with the reception accorded to Galileo in the seventeenth century could not be more pronounced. [B.]

[b]Pythagoras (c. 580 B.C.–c. 500 B.C.) established a school dedicated to the importance of numbers, to which he attached mystical qualities. Among other discoveries, Pythagoreans are credited with the discovery of irrational numbers. [B.]

that the mathematicians are inconsistent in these investigations.

For, first, the mathematicians are so unsure of the movements of the Sun and Moon that they cannot even explain or observe the constant length of the seasonal year. Second, in determining the motions of these and of the other five planets, they do not even use the same principles and hypotheses as in their proofs of seeming revolutions and motions. So some use only concentric circles, while others eccentrics and epicycles.[c] Yet even by these means they do not completely attain their ends. Those who have relied on concentrics, though they have proven that some different motions can be compounded therefrom, have not thereby been able fully to establish a system which agrees with the phenomena. Those again who have devised eccentric systems, though they appear to have almost established the seeming motions by calculations agreeable to their assumptions, have yet made many admissions which seem to violate the first principle of uniformity in motion. Nor have they been able thereby to discern or deduce the principal thing—namely, the shape of the universe and the unchangeable symmetry of its parts. With them it is as though an artist were to gather the hands, feet, head and other members for his images from diverse models, each part excellently drawn, but not related to a single body, and since they in no way match each other, the result would be monster rather than man. So in the course of their exposition, which the mathematicians call their system (μέθοδοσ), we find that they have either omitted some indispensable detail or introduced something foreign and

wholly irrelevant. This would of a surety not have been so had they followed fixed principles; for if their hypotheses were not misleading, all inferences based thereon might be surely verified. Though my present assertions are obscure, they will be made clear in due course.

I pondered long upon this uncertainty of mathematical tradition in establishing the motions of the system of the spheres. At last I began to chafe that philosophers could by no means agree on any one certain theory of the mechanism of the universe, wrought for us by a supremely good and orderly Creator, though in other respects they investigated with meticulous care the minutest points relating to its orbits. I therefore took pains to read again the works of all the philosophers on whom I could lay hand to seek out whether any of them had ever supposed that the motions of the spheres were other than those demanded by the mathematical schools. I found first in Cicero[d] that Hicetas of Syracuse had realized that the Earth moved. Afterwards I found in Plutarch[e] that certain others had held the like opinion. I think fit here to add Plutarch's own words, to make them accessible to all:

> The rest hold the Earth to be stationary, but Philolaus the Pythagorean says that she moves around the (central) fire on an oblique circle like the Sun and Moon. Heraclides of Pontus and Ecphantus the Pythagorean also make the Earth to move, not indeed through space but

---

[c]Callipus (fl. 4th c. B.C.), correcting and completing the work of Eudoxus (c. 400 B.C.–c. 347 B.C.), supposed that each planet was attached to a sphere that rotated on poles attached inside another sphere rotating in a different direction at a different rate, and this sphere in another, until the number and motions of concentric spheres could account for the irregularities of the planetary motions. [B.]

[d]A Roman orator and statesman, Cicero (106–43 B.C.) argued that while philosophy may generate knowledge, rhetoric was required to made knowledge effective. Insisting that the application of knowledge to human affairs was the greatest human achievement, he claimed that a great person must master both philosophy and rhetoric. [B.]

[e]An essayist and biographer, Plutarch (c. 46–c. 120) composed a number of works, including the enormously influential *The Parallel Lives*, which features 46 surviving biographies arranged in pairs (one Greek life and one comparable Roman life) and four single biographies. [B.]

by rotating round her own center as a wheel on an axle, from West to East.

Taking advantage of this I too began to think of the mobility of the Earth; and though the opinion seemed absurd, yet knowing now that others before me had been granted freedom to imagine such circles as they chose to explain the phenomena of the stars, I considered that I also might easily be allowed to try whether, by assuming some motion of the Earth, sounder explanations than theirs for the revolution of the celestial spheres might so be discovered.

Thus assuming motions, which in my work I ascribe to the Earth, by long and frequent observations I have at last discovered that if the motions of the rest of the planets be brought into relation with the circulation of the Earth and be reckoned in proportion to the orbit of each planet, not only do their phenomena presently ensue, but the orders and magnitudes of all stars and spheres, indeed, the heavens themselves, become so bound together that nothing in any part thereof could be moved from its place without producing confusion of all the other parts and of the universe as a whole.

In the course of the work, the order which I have pursued is as here follows. In the first book I describe all positions of the spheres together with such movements as I ascribe to Earth; so that this book contains, as it were, the general system of the universe. Afterwards, in the remaining books, I relate the motions of the other planets and all the spheres to the mobility of Earth that we may gather thereby how far the motions and appearances of the rest of the planets and spheres may be preserved, if related to the motions of the Earth.

I doubt not that gifted and learned mathematicians will agree with me if they are willing to comprehend and appreciate, not superficially but thoroughly, according to the demands of this science, such reasoning as I bring to bear in support of my judgment. But [so] that learned and unlearned alike may see that I shrink not from any man's criticism, it is to your Holiness rather than anyone else that I have chosen to dedicate these studies of mine, since in this remote corner of Earth in which I live you are regarded as the most eminent by virtue alike of the dignity of your office and of your love of letters and science. You by your influence and judgment can readily hold the slanderers from biting, though the proverb has it that there is no remedy against a sycophant's tooth. It may fall out, too, that idle babblers, ignorant of mathematics, may claim a right to pronounce a judgment on my work, by reason of a certain passage of Scripture basely twisted to suit their purpose. Should any such venture to criticize and carp at my project, I make no account of them; I consider their judgment rash, and utterly despise it. I well know that even Lactantius,[f] a writer in other ways distinguished but in no sense a mathematician, discourses in a most childish fashion touching the shape of the Earth, ridiculing even those who have stated the Earth to be a sphere. Thus my supporters need not be amazed if some people of like sort ridicule me too . . .

# BOOK I

### 1. *That the universe is spherical.*[1]

In the first place we must observe that the universe is spherical. This is either because that figure is the most perfect,[2] as not being articulated[3] but whole and complete in itself; or because it is the most capacious and therefore best suited for that which is to contain and preserve all things; or again because all the perfect parts of it, namely, Sun, Moon and stars, are so formed; or because all things tend to assume this shape, as is seen in the case of drops of water and liquid bod-

[f]A teacher of rhetoric who converted to Christianity later in life, the writings of Lactantius (fl. 4th c.) are dedicated to the inadequacy of pagan beliefs and the truth of Christianity. Lactantius quoted verses from Isaiah and St. Paul to demonstrate that the Earth was not spherical. [B.]

ies in general if freely formed.[4] No one doubts that such a shape has been assigned to the heavenly bodies.

### 2. *That the Earth also is spherical.*[5]

The Earth also is spherical, since on all sides it inclines toward the center. At first sight, the Earth does not appear absolutely spherical, because of the mountains and valleys; yet these make but little variation in its general roundness, as appears from what follows. As we pass from any point northward, the North Pole of the daily rotation gradually rises, while the other pole sinks correspondingly and more stars near the North Pole[6] cease to set, while certain stars in the South do not rise. Thus, Canopus, invisible in Italy, is visible in Egypt, while the last star of Eridanus, seen in Italy, is unknown in our colder zone. On the other hand, as we southward, these stars appear higher, while those which are high for us appear lower. Further, the change in altitude of the pole is always proportional to the distance traversed on the Earth, which could not be save on a spherical figure.[7] Hence, the Earth must be finite and spherical.

Furthermore, dwellers in the East do not see eclipses of the Sun and Moon which occur in the evening here, nor do they in the West see those which occur here in the morning. Yet mid-day eclipses here are seen later in the day by the eastward dwellers, earlier by the westerners. Sailors too have noted that the sea also assumes the same shape, since land invisible from the ship is often sighted from the mast-head. On the other hand, if some shining object on the mast-head be observed from the shore, it seems gradually to sink as the vessel leaves the land. It is also a sure fact that water free to flow always seeks a lower level, just as Earth does, nor does the sea come higher up the shore than the convexity of the Earth allows. It therefore follows that land, rising above the level of ocean, is by so much further removed from the center.

### 3. *How Earth, with the water on it, forms one sphere.*

The waters spread around the Earth form the seas and fill the lower declivities. The volume of the waters must be less than that of the Earth, else they would swallow up the land (since both, by their weight, press toward the same center). Thus, for the safety of living things, stretches of the Earth are left uncovered, and also numerous islands widely scattered. No, what is a continent, and indeed the whole of the Mainland, but a vast island?

We must pass by certain Peripatetics who claim the volume of the waters to be ten times that of the Earth.[8] They base themselves on a mere guess that in the transmutation of the elements, one part of Earth is resolved into ten of water. They say, in fact, that the Earth rises to a certain height above the water because, being full of cavities, it is not symmetrical as regards weight and therefore the center of weight does not accord with the geometrical center. Ignorance of geometry prevents them from seeing that the waters cannot be even seven times as great if some part of the Earth is to be left dry, unless the Earth, as being heavier, be quite removed from the center of gravity to make room for the waters. For spheres are to each other as the cubes of their diameters. If, therefore, there had been seven parts of water to one of Earth, the Earth's diameter could not be greater than the radius of the waters. Even less is it possible that the waters could be ten times as great as the Earth.[9]

There is, in fact, no difference between the Earth's center of gravity and its geometric center, since the height of the land above the ocean does not increase continuously; for so it would utterly exclude the waters and there could be no great gulfs of seas between parts of the Mainland.[10] Further, the depth of ocean would constantly increase from the shore outwards, and so neither island nor rock nor anything of the nature of land would be met by sailors however far they ventured. Yet, we know that between the Egyptian Sea and the Arabian Gulf, almost in the middle of the great landmass, is a passage barely 15 stades wide. On the other hand, in his *Cosmography* Ptolemy would have it that the habitable land extends to the middle circle[11] with a *terra incognita* beyond where modern discovery has added Cathay and a very extensive region as far as 60° of longitude. Thus, we know now that the Earth is inhabited to a greater longitude than is left for ocean.

This will more evidently appear if we add the islands found in our own time under the Princes of Spain and Portugal, particularly America, a land named after the Captain who discovered it and, on account of its unexplored size, reckoned as another mainland; besides many other islands hitherto unknown.[12] We thus wonder the less at the so-called Antipodes or Antichthones.[13] For geometrical argument demands that the mainland of America on account of its position be diametrically opposite to the Ganges basin in India.

From such considerations then, it is clear that land and water have the same center of gravity, which coincides with the center of the Earth's volume. Yet since earth is the heavier, and its chasms filled with water, therefore the quantity of the water is but moderate as against earth, though, as to the surface, there may perhaps be more water. Moreover, the Earth, with the waters around it, must have a shape conformable with its shadow. Now, at the Moon's eclipse we see a perfect arc of a circle; the Earth therefore is not flat as Empedocles and Anaxagoras would have had it, nor drum-shaped as Leucippus held, nor bowl-shaped as Heraclitus[g]

said, nor yet concave in some other way as Democritus believed; nor again cylindrical as Anaximander maintained, nor yet infinitely thick with roots extending below as Xenophanes represented; but perfectly round, as the Philosophers rightly hold.[14]

*4. That the Motion of the heavenly bodies is uniform, circular, and perpetual, or composed of circular motions.*

We now note that the motion of heavenly bodies is circular. Rotation is natural to a sphere and by that very act is its shape expressed. For here we deal with the simplest kind of body, wherein neither beginning nor end may be discerned nor, if it rotate ever in the same place, may the one be distinguished from the other.

Now in the multitude of heavenly bodies various motions occur. Most evident to sense is the diurnal rotation, the νυχθημερον, as the Greeks call it, marking day and night. By this motion the whole universe, save Earth alone, is thought to glide from East to West.[15] This is the common measure of all motions, since time itself is numbered in days. Next, we see other revolutions in contest, as it were, with this daily motion and opposing it from West to East. Such opposing motions are those of Sun and Moon, and the five planets. Of these the Sun portions out the year, the Moon the month, the common measures of time. In like manner the five planets define each his own independent period.

But these bodies exhibit various differences in their motion. First, their axes are not that of the diurnal rotation, but of the zodiac, which is oblique thereto. Second, they do not move uniformly even in their own orbits; for are not Sun and Moon found now slower, now swifter in their courses? Further, at times the five planets become stationary at one point and another and even go backward. While the Sun ever goes forward unswerving on his own course, they wander in diverse ways, straying now southward, now northward. For this reason they are named *planets*.[16] Furthermore, sometimes they ap-

---

[g]Very little is known about the figures mentioned by Copernicus, except through the writings of others. Anaxagoras (c. 500 B.C.–c. 428 B.C.) gave the modern explanation for eclipses of the sun and moon. Heraclitus (fl. 500 B.C.) is credited with the aphorism "we cannot step twice into the same river," expressing his conviction that nature is in a perpetual state of flux. Leucippus (fl. 500–450 B.C.) is credited (along with his pupil Democritus) with originating the atomic theory of matter. [B.]

proach Earth, being then in *perigee*, while at other times receding they are in *apogee*.

Nevertheless, despite these irregularities, we must conclude that the motions of these bodies are ever circular or compounded of circles. For the irregularities themselves are subject to a definite law and recur at stated times, and this could not happen if the motions were not circular, for a circle alone can thus restore the place of a body as it was. So with the Sun which, by a compounding of circular motions, brings ever again the changing days and nights and the four seasons of the year. Now therein it must be that diverse motions are conjoined, since a simple celestial body cannot move irregularly in a single orbit. For such irregularity must come of unevenness either in the moving force (whether inherent or acquired) or in the form of the revolving body. Both these alike the mind abhors regarding the most perfectly disposed bodies.[17]

It is then generally agreed that the motions of Sun, Moon and planets do but seem

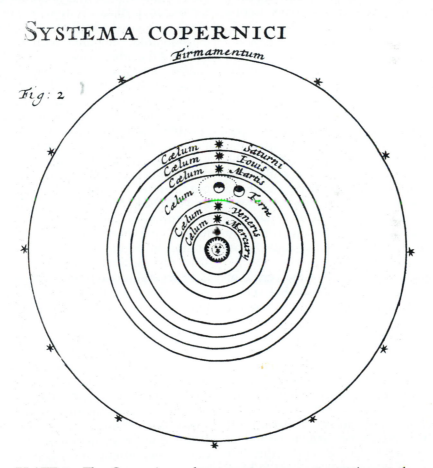

**PLATE 2** The Copernican planetary arrangement, starting at the center: Sun, Mercury, Venus, Earth (with the Moon revolving round it), Mars, Jupiter, Saturn, the fixed stars.

irregular either by reason of the diverse directions of their axes of revolution, or else by reason that Earth is not the center of the circles in which they revolve, so that to us on Earth the displacements of these bodies when near seem greater than when they are more remote, as is shown in the *Optics*.[18] If we then consider equal arcs in the paths of the planets, we find that they seem to describe differing distances in equal periods of time. It is therefore above all needful to observe carefully the relation of the Earth toward the heavens, for fear that, searching out the things on high, we should pass by those nearer at hand, and mistakenly ascribe earthly qualities to heavenly bodies.

*5. Whether circular motion belongs to the Earth; and concerning its position.*

Since it has been shown that Earth is spherical, we now consider whether her motion is conformable to her shape and her position in the universe. Without these we cannot construct a proper theory of the heavenly phenomena. Now authorities agree that Earth holds firm her place at the center of the universe, and they regard the contrary as unthinkable, indeed, as absurd. Yet, if we examine more closely, it will be seen that this question is not so settled, and needs wider consideration.

A seeming change of place may come of movement either of object or of observer, or again of unequal movements of the two (for between equal and parallel motions no movement is perceptible). Now it is Earth from which the rotation of the heavens is seen. If then some motion of Earth be assumed it will be reproduced in external bodies, which will seem to move in the opposite direction.

Consider first the diurnal rotation. By it the whole universe, save Earth alone and its contents, appears to move very swiftly. Yet grant that Earth revolves from West to East, and you will find, if you ponder it, that my conclusion is right. It is the vault of heaven[19] that contains all things, and why should not

motion be attributed rather to the contained than to the container, to the located than the locater?[h] The latter view was certainly that of Heraclides[20] and Ecphantus the Pythagorean[21] and Hicetas of Syracuse (according to Cicero).[22] All of them made the Earth rotate in the midst of the universe, believing that the stars set owing to the Earth coming in the way, and rise again when it has passed on.

There is another difficulty, namely, the position of Earth. Nearly all have hitherto held that Earth is at the center of the universe. Now, grant that Earth is not at the exact center but at a distance from it which, while small compared to the starry sphere, is yet considerable compared with the orbits of Sun and the other planets. Then calculate the consequent variations in their seeming motions, assuming these to be really uniform and about some center other than the Earth's. One may then perhaps adduce a reasonable cause for these variable motions. And indeed since the planets are seen at varying distances from the Earth, the center of Earth is surely not the center of their orbits. Nor is it certain whether the planets move toward and away from Earth, or Earth toward and away from them. It is therefore justifiable to hold that the Earth has another motion in addition to the diurnal rotation. That the Earth, besides rotating, wanders with several motions and is indeed a planet, is a view attributed to Philolaus the Pythagorean, no mean mathematician, and one whom Plato is said to have eagerly sought out in Italy.[23]

Many, however, have thought that Earth could be shown by geometry to be at the center and like a mere point in the vast heavens. They have thought too that Earth, as center, ever remains unmoved, since if the whole system move the center must remain at rest, and the parts nearest the center must move most slowly.

[h]This passage strongly suggests that for Copernicus the universe is bounded by the celestial sphere. [B.]

*6. Of the vastness of the heavens compared with the size of the Earth.*[24]

That the size of Earth is insignificant in comparison with the heavens, may be inferred thus. The bounding circles (interpreting the Greek word *horizons*) bisect the celestial sphere. This could not be if the size of the Earth or its distance from the center were considerable compared with the heavens—for a circle to bisect a sphere it must pass through its center and be in fact a "great circle." Let the circle *ABCD* represent the celestial horizon, and *E* that point of the Earth from which we observe. The "horizon" or boundary line between bodies visible and bodies invisible has its center at this point. Suppose that from point *E* we observe with Dioptra or Astrolabe or Chorobates[25] the first point of the sign Cancer rising at *C* and at the same moment the first point of Capricorn setting at *A. AEC,* since it is observed as a straight line through Dioptra, is a diameter of the ecliptic, for six zodiacal signs form a semicircle and its center *E* coincides with that of the horizon. Next, suppose that after some time the first point of Capricorn rises at *B*; then Cancer will be seen setting at *D*, and *BED* will be a straight line, again a diameter of the ecliptic. Hence, it is clear that *E*, the point of intersection of the two lines, is the center of the horizon. Therefore, the horizon always bisects the ecliptic, which is a great circle on the sphere. But a circle that bisects a great circle must itself be a great circle. Therefore, the horizon is a great circle and its center is that of the ecliptic.

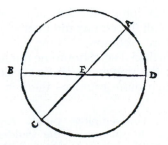

It is true that a line from the surface of Earth cannot coincide with the one from its center. Yet owing to their immense length compared to the size of Earth these lines are practically parallel. Moreover, owing to the great distance of their meeting point they are practically one line—for the distance between them is immeasurably small in comparison with their length—as is shown in the *Optics.*[26] It therefore follows that the heavens are immeasurable in comparison with Earth. Thus, the Earth appears as a mere point compared to the heavens, as a finite thing to the infinite.[27]

Yet it does not follow that the Earth must be at rest at the center of the universe. Should we not be more surprised if the vast universe revolved in twenty-four hours, than that little Earth should do so? For the idea that the center is at rest and the parts nearest it move least does not imply that Earth remains still. It is merely as one should say that the heavens revolve, but the poles are still, and the parts nearest them move least (as *Cynosura* moves slower than *Aquila* or *Procyon*, because, being nearer the pole, it describes a smaller circle). These all belong to the same sphere, whose motion becomes zero at the axis. Such motion does not admit that all the parts have the same rate of motion, since the revolution of the whole brings back each point to the original position in the same time, though the distances moved are unequal.

So too, it may be said, Earth, as part of the celestial sphere, shares in the motion thereof, though being at the center she moves but little. Being herself a body and not a mere point, she will therefore move through the same angle as the heavens but with a smaller radius in any given period of time. The falsity of this is clear, for if true it would always be mid-day in one place and midnight in another, and the daily phenomena of rising and setting could not occur, for the motion of the whole and the part are one and inseparable. A quite different theory is required to explain the various motions observed, namely that bodies moving in smaller paths revolve more quickly than those moving in larger paths. Thus Saturn, most distant of the planets, revolves in 30 years, and Moon, nearest the Earth, compasses her circuit in a month. Lastly, then, the Earth must be taken to go round in the course of a day and a night, and so doubt is again cast on the diurnal rotation of the heavens.

Besides we have not yet fixed the exact position of the Earth, which as shown above, is quite uncertain. For what was proved is only the vast size of the heavens compared with the Earth, but how far this immensity extends is quite unknown.

*7. Why the ancients believed that the Earth is at rest, like a center, in the middle of the universe.*[28]

The ancient philosophers tried by diverse other methods to prove Earth fixed in the midst of the universe. The most powerful argument was drawn from the doctrine of the heavy and the light. For, they argue, Earth is the heaviest element, and all things of weight move towards it, tending to its center. Hence, since the Earth is spherical, and heavy things move vertically to it, they would all rush together to the center if not stopped at the surface. Now those things which move towards the center must, on reaching it, remain at rest. Much more then will the whole Earth remain at rest at the center of the universe. Receiving all falling bodies, it will remain immovable by its own weight.[29]

Another argument is based on the supposed nature of motion. Aristotle says that the motion of a single and simple body is simple. A simple motion may be either straight, or circular. Again a straight motion may be either up or down. So every simple motion must be either toward the center, namely, downward, or away from the center, namely, upward, or round the center, namely, circular. Now it is a property only of the heavy elements—earth and water—t–o move downward; that is, to seek the center. But the light elements—air and fire—move upward away from the center. Therefore, we must ascribe rectilinear motion to these four elements. The celestial bodies however have circular motion. So far Aristotle.[30]

If then, says Ptolemy, Earth moves at least with a diurnal rotation, the result must be the reverse of that described above. For the motion must be of excessive rapidity, since in 24 hours it must impart a complete rotation to the Earth. Now things rotating very rapidly resist cohesion or, if united, are apt to disperse, unless firmly held together. Ptolemy therefore says that Earth would have been dissipated long ago, and (which is the height of absurdity) would have destroyed the heavens themselves; and certainly all living creatures and other heavy bodies free to move could not have remained on its surface, but must have been shaken off. Neither could falling objects reach their appointed place vertically beneath, since in the meantime the Earth would have moved swiftly from under them. Moreover, clouds and everything in the air would continually move westward.[31]

*8. The insufficiency of these arguments, and their refutation.*[i]

For these and like reasons, they say that Earth surely rests at the center of the universe. Now if one should say that the Earth moves, that is as much as to say that the motion is natural, not forced; and things which happen according to nature produce the opposite effects to those due to force. Things subjected to any force, gradual or sudden, must be disintegrated, and cannot long exist. But natural processes being adapted to their purpose work smoothly.

Idle, therefore, is the fear of Ptolemy that Earth and all thereon would be disintegrated by a natural rotation, a thing far different from an artificial act. Should he not fear even more for the universe, whose motion must be as much more rapid as the heavens are

---

[i]Copernicus here employs purely Aristotelian concepts to disarm one of the standard arguments against the motion of the earth. There is no evidence that he was aware that his theory invalidated the foundation of Aristotelian physics. [B.]

greater than the Earth? Have the heavens become so vast because of the centrifugal force of their violent motion, and would they collapse if they stood still? If this were so the heavens must be of infinite size. For the more they expand by the centrifugal force of their motion, the more rapid will become the motion because of the ever increasing distance to be traversed in 24 hours. And in turn, as the motion waxes, must the immensity of the heavens wax. Thus velocity and size would increase each the other to infinity; and as the infinite can neither be traversed nor moved, the heavens must stand still![32]

They say too that outside the heavens is no body, no space, nay not even void, in fact absolutely nothing, and therefore no room for the heavens to expand.[33] Yet, surely it is strange that something can be held by nothing. Perhaps indeed it will be easier to understand this nothingness outside the heavens if we assume them to be infinite, and bounded internally only by their concavity, so that everything, however great, is contained in them, while the heavens remain immovable. For the fact that it moves is the principal argument by which men have inferred that the universe is finite.

Let us then leave to physicists[34] the question whether the universe be finite or no, holding only to this that Earth is finite and spherical.[j] Why then hesitate to grant Earth that power of motion natural to its shape, rather than suppose a gliding round of the whole universe, whose limits are unknown and unknowable? And why not grant that the diurnal rotation is only apparent in the heavens but real in the Earth? It is but as the saying of Aeneas in Virgil—"We sail forth

from the harbor, and lands and cities retire."[35] As the ship floats along in the calm, all external things seem to have the motion that is really that of the ship, while those within the ship feel that they and all its contents are at rest.

It may be asked what of the clouds and other objects suspended in the air, or sinking and rising in it? Surely not only the Earth, with the water on it, moves thus, but also a quantity of air and all things so associated with the Earth. Perhaps the contiguous air contains an admixture of earthy or watery matter and so follows the same natural law as the Earth, or perhaps the air acquires motion from the perpetually rotating Earth by propinquity and absence of resistance. So the Greeks thought that the higher regions of the air follow the celestial motion, as suggested by those swiftly moving bodies, the "comets," or "pogoniae" as they called them,[36] for whose origin they assign this region, for these bodies rise and set just like other stars. We observe that because of the great distance from the Earth that part of the air is deprived of terrestrial motion, while the air nearest Earth, with the objects suspended in it, will be stationary, unless disturbed by wind or other impulse which moves them this way or that; for a wind in the air is as a current in the sea.

We must admit the possibility of a double motion of objects which fall and rise in the universe, namely the resultant of rectilinear and circular motion. Thus heavy falling objects, being especially earthy, must doubtless retain the nature of the whole to which they belong. So also there are objects which by their fiery force are carried up into the higher regions. This terrestrial fire is nourished particularly by earthy matter, and flame is simply burning smoke. Now it is a property of fire to expand that which it attacks, and this so violently that it cannot in any wise be restrained from breaking its prison and fulfilling its end. The motion is one of extension from the center outward, and consequently any earthy parts set on fire are carried to the upper region.[37]

[j]Copernicus' system is bounded by the heavens and so presumably finite. Since the Copernican system did not require the stars to be fastended to the same sphere, it did not rule out a greatly expanded universe. By the sixteenth century, followers of Copernicus, such as Thomas Digges (d. 1595), suggested that the stars were scattered through space. [B.]

but, according to a truer estimate, more than 52 (as will be shown later) yet we are not aware of anything in all that space except air, and, if you will, the so called "fiery element." Besides, the diameter of the orbit of Venus, by which she passes to a distance of 45 degrees more or less on either side of the Sun, must be six times the distance from the Earth's center to her perigee, as will also be shown later. What then will they say is contained in the whole of that space, which is so much bigger than that which could contain the Earth, the Air, the aether, the Moon and Mercury, in addition to the space that the huge epicycle of Venus would occupy if it revolved round the resting Earth?

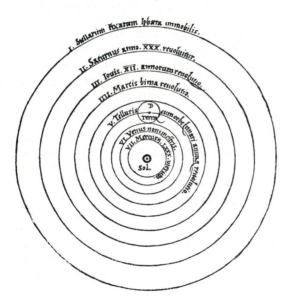

Unconvincing too is Ptolemy's proof that the Sun moves between those bodies that do and those that do not recede from him completely. Consideration of the case of the Moon, which does so recede, exposes its falseness. Again, what cause can be alleged, by those who place Venus nearer than the Sun, and Mercury next, or in some other order? Why should not these planets also follow separate paths, distinct from that of the Sun, as do the other planets? And this might be said even if their relative swiftness and slowness does not belie their alleged order. Either then the Earth cannot be the center to which the order of the planets and their orbits is related, or certainly their relative order is not observed, nor does it appear why a higher position should be assigned to Saturn than to Jupiter, or any other planet.

Therefore I think we must seriously consider the ingenious view held by Martianus Capella, the author of the *Encyclopaedia*[48] and certain other Latins, that Venus and Mercury do not go round the Earth like the other planets but run their courses with the Sun as center, and so do not depart from him further than the size of their orbits allows. What else can they mean than that the center of these orbits is near the Sun? So certainly the orbit of Mercury must be within that of Venus, which, it is agreed, is more than twice as great.

We may now extend this hypothesis to bring Saturn, Jupiter and Mars also into relation with this center, making their orbits great enough to contain those of Venus and Mercury and the Earth; and their proportional motions according to the Table demonstrate this.[49] These outer planets are always nearer to the Earth about the time of their evening rising, that is, when they are in opposition to the Sun, and the Earth between them and the Sun. They are more distant from the Earth at the time of their evening setting, when they are in conjunction with the Sun and the Sun between them and the Earth. These indications prove that their center pertains rather to the Sun than to the Earth, and that this is the same center as that to which the revolutions of Venus and Mercury are related.

But since all these have one center it is necessary that the space between the orbit Venus and the orbit of Mars must also be viewed as a sphere concentric with the others, capable of receiving the Earth with her satellite the Moon and whatever is contained within the sphere of the Moon—for we must not separate the Moon from the Earth, the former being beyond all doubt nearest to the latter, especially as in that space we find suitable and ample room for the Moon.

We therefore assert that the center of the Earth, carrying the Moon's path, passes in a great orbit among the other planets in an annual revolution round the Sun; that near the Sun is the center of the universe; and that whereas the Sun is at rest, any apparent motion of the Sun can be better explained by motion of the Earth. Yet so great is the universe that though the distance of the Earth from the Sun is not insignificant compared with the size of any other planetary path, in accordance with the ratios of their sizes, it is insignificant compared with the distance of the sphere of the fixed stars.

I think it is easier to believe this than to confuse the issue by assuming a vast number of spheres, which those who keep Earth at the center must do. We thus rather follow nature, who producing nothing vain or superfluous often prefers to endow one cause with many effects. Though these views are difficult, contrary to expectation, and certainly unusual, yet in the sequel we shall, God willing, make them abundantly clear at least to mathematicians.

Given the above view—and there is none more reasonable—that the periodic times are proportional to the sizes of the orbits, then the order of the spheres, beginning from the most distant, is as follows. Most distant of all is the sphere of the fixed stars, containing all things, and being therefore itself immovable. It represents that to which the motion and position of all the other bodies must be referred. Some hold that it too changes in some way,[50] but we shall assign another reason for this apparent change, as will appear in the account of the Earth's motion.[51] Next is the planet Saturn, revolving in 30 years. Next comes Jupiter, moving in a 12 year circuit: then Mars, who goes round in 2 years. The fourth place is held by the annual revolution in which the Earth is contained, together with the orbit of the Moon as on an epicycle. Venus, whose period is 9 months, is in the fifth place, and sixth is Mercury, who goes round in the space of 80 days.

In the middle of all sits the Sun enthroned. In this most beautiful temple could we place this luminary in any better position from which he can illuminate the whole at once? He is rightly called the Lamp, the Mind, the Ruler of the Universe; Hermes Trismegistus names him the Visible God,[52] Sophocles' Electra calls him the All-seeing.[53] So the Sun sits as upon a royal throne ruling his children the planets which circle round him. The Earth has the Moon at her service. As Aristotle says, in his *de Animalibus,* the Moon has the closest relationship with the Earth.[54] Meanwhile, the Earth conceives by the Sun, and becomes pregnant with an annual rebirth.

So we find underlying this ordination an admirable symmetry in the universe, and a clear bond of harmony in the motion and magnitude of the orbits such as can be discovered in no other wise. For here we may observe why the progression and retrogression appear greater for Jupiter than Saturn, and less than for Mars, but again greater for Venus than for Mercury; and why such oscillation appears more frequently in Saturn than in Jupiter, but less frequently in Mars and Venus than in Mercury; moreover why Saturn, Jupiter, and Mars are nearer to the Earth at opposition to the Sun than when they are lost in or emerge from the Sun's rays.[55] Particularly Mars, when he shines all night, appears to rival Jupiter in magnitude, being only distinguishable by his ruddy color; otherwise he is scarce equal to a star of the second magnitude, and can be recognized only when his movements are carefully followed. All these phenomena proceed from the same cause, namely, Earth's motion.

That there are no such phenomena for the fixed stars proves their immeasurable distance, compared to which even the size of the Earth's orbit is negligible and the parallactic effect unnoticeable. For every visible object has a certain distance beyond which it can no more be seen (as is proved in the *Optics*).[56] The twinkling of the stars, also, shows that there is still a vast distance between the furthest of the planets, Saturn, and the sphere of the fixed stars, and it is chiefly by this indication that they are distinguished from the planets. Further, there must necessarily be a great difference between moving and non-moving bodies. So great is this divine work of the great and noble Creator!

### 11. *Explanation of the threefold motion of the Earth.*

Since then planets agree in witnessing to the possibility that Earth moves, we shall now briefly discuss the motion itself, in so far as the phenomena can be explained by this hypothesis. This motion we must take to be threefold. The first defines the Greek *nychthemerinon,* the cycle of night and day. It is produced by the rotation of the Earth on its axis from West to East, corresponding to the opposite motion by which the universe appears to move round the equinoctial circle, that is the equator, which some call the "equidial" circle, translating the Greek expression *isémerinos.* The second is the annual revolution of the center of the Earth, together with all things on the Earth. This describes the ecliptic round the Sun, also from West to East, that is, backwards,[57] between the orbits of Venus and Mars. So it comes about that the Sun himself seems to traverse the ecliptic with a similar motion. For instance, when the center of the Earth passes over Capricorn, as seen from the Sun, the Sun appears to pass over Cancer as seen from the Earth; but seen from Aquarius, he would seem to pass over Leo, and so on. The equator and Earth's axis are variably inclined[58] to this circle, which passes through the middle of the Zodiac, and to its plane, since if they were fixed and followed simply the motion of the Earth's center there would be no inequality of days and nights.[59] Then there is a third motion, of declination, which is also an annual revolution, but forwards,

that is, tending in opposition to the motion of the Earth's center; and thus, as they are nearly equal and opposite, it comes about that the axis of the Earth, and its greatest parallel, the equator, point in an almost constant direction, as if they were fixed.[60] But meanwhile, the Sun is seen to move along the oblique direction of the ecliptic with that motion which is really due to the center of the Earth (just as if the Earth were the center of the universe, remembering that we see the line joining Sun and Earth projected on the sphere of the fixed stars).

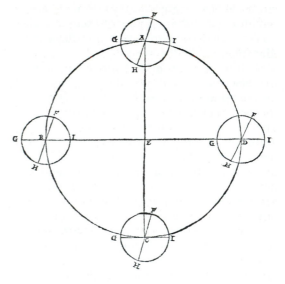

To express it graphically, draw a circle *ABCD* to represent the annual path of Earth's center in the plane of the ecliptic. Let *E* near its center be the Sun. Divide this circle into four equal parts by the diameters *AEC* and *BED*. Let the first point of Cancer be at *A*, of Libra at *B*, of Capricorn at *C* and of Aries at *D*. Now let the center of the Earth be first at *A* and round it draw the terrestrial Equator *FGHI*. This circle *FGHI* however is not in the same plane as the ecliptic but its diameter *GAI* is the line of intersection with the ecliptic.

Draw the diameter *FAH*, at right angles to *GAI*, and let *F* be the point of the greatest declination to the South, *H* to the North.

This being so the inhabitants of the Earth will see the Sun near the center $E$ at its winter solstice in Capricorn, owing to the turning towards the Sun of the point of greatest Northern declination $H$. Hence in the diurnal rotation the inclination of the equator to $AE$ makes the Sun move along the tropic of Capricorn, which is distant from the equator by an angle equal to $EAH$.

Now let the center of the Earth travel forwards and let $F$, the point of greatest declination, move to the same extent backwards until both have completed quadrants of their circles at $B$. During this time the angle $EAI$ remains always equal to the angle $AEB$, on account of the equality of the motions. The diameters $FAH$, $FBH$ and $GAI$, $GBI$ are also always parallel each to each, and the Equator remains parallel to itself. These parallel lines appear coincident in the immensity of the heavens as has often been mentioned. Therefore, from the first point of Libra, $E$ will appear to be in Aries, and the intersection of the planes will be the line $GBIE$, so that the diurnal rotation will give no declination, and all motion of the Sun will be lateral [in the plane of the ecliptic]. The Sun is now at the vernal equinox. Further, suppose that the center of the Earth continues its course. When it has completed a semi-circle at $C$, the Sun will appear to be entering Cancer. $F$, the point of greatest southern declination of the Equator, is now turned towards the Sun, and he will appear to be running along the Tropic of Cancer, distant from the Equator by an angle equal to $ECF$. Again, when $F$ has turned through its third quadrant, the line of intersection $GI$ will once more fall along the line $ED$, and from this position the Sun will be seen in Libra at the autumnal equinox. As the process continues and $HF$ gradually turns towards the Sun, it will produce a return of the same phenomena as we observed at the starting-point.

We can explain it otherwise as follows. Take the diameter $AEC$ in the plane of the paper. $AEC$ is the line of intersection by this plane of a circle perpendicular to it. At points $A$ and $C$, that is at Cancer and

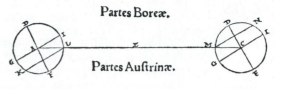

Partes Boreæ.

Partes Auſtrinæ.

Capricorn respectively, describe in this plane a circle of longitude of the Earth $DFGI$. Let $DF$ be the axis of the Earth, $D$ the North Pole, $F$ the South, and $GI$ a diameter of the equator. Since then $F$ turns towards the Sun at $E$, and the northern inclination of the Equator is the angle $IAE$, the rotation round the axis will describe a parallel south of the equator with diameter $KL$ and at a distance from the equator equal to $LI$, the apparent distance from the equator of the Sun in Capricorn. Or better, by this rotation round the axis the line of sight $AE$ describes a conical surface, with vertex at Earth's center and as base a circle parallel to the equator. At the opposite point $C$ the same phenomena occur, but conversely. Thus the contrary effects of the two motions, that of the center and that of declination, constrain the axis of the Earth to remain in a constant direction, and produce all the phenomena of Solar motions.

We were saying that the annual revolution of the center and of declination were *almost* equal. If they tallied exactly the equinoctial and solstitial points and the whole obliquity of the ecliptic with reference to the sphere of the fixed stars would be unchangeable. There is, however, a slight discrepancy, which has only become apparent as it accumulated in the course of ages. Between Ptolemy's time and ours it has reached nearly 21°, the amount by which the equinoxes have precessed. For this reason some have thought that the sphere of the fixed stars also moves, and they have therefore postulated a ninth sphere. This being found insufficient, modern authorities now add a tenth. Yet they have still not attained the result which we hope to attain by the motion of the Earth. We shall assume this motion as a hypothesis and follow its consequences.[61]

## NOTES

1. This title, like that of many other chapters, is taken from the *Almagest* of Ptolemy. The work of Copernicus is so closely bound up with that of Ptolemy that it will be convenient here to review the history of the *Almagest.*

   The *Almagest* of Ptolemy was unknown in the earlier Middle Ages. Its first appearance in the West is in a translation made direct from the Greek in Sicily in the year 1160. Translation direct from the Greek was very unusual at the period. This translation was excessively rare and effectively without influence. About 1170 the Englishman Daniel of Morley was studying the Arabic text of Ptolemy at Toledo with the help of a native Arabic speaking Christian, one Ibn Ghalib. Daniel tells us that he listened to Ibn Ghalib at work with the famous translator Gerard of Cremona (died 1187). Gerard's translation of the *Almagest* was completed about 1175 and was in use in the later Middle Ages. It was made from Arabic and not from Greek. The *Almagest* was again translated from Greek in the fifteenth century by George of Trebizond (1396–1486). In the same century an *Epitome*—also direct from the Greek—was commenced by George Purbach (1423–1461) and completed by his pupil Johann Müller of Königsberg, known as Regiomontanus (1436–1476). The earliest edition of this *Epitome* was printed at Venice in 1496. The first complete Latin edition is that of Liechtenstein, Venice 1515. Liechtenstein used the translation from the Arabic version. George of Trebizond's translation was printed at Venice in 1528 and the Greek text edited by Simon Grynaeus at Basel in 1538. There are many later editions of both Greek and Latin texts.

2. The conception of the sphere as the most perfect of all figures occurs in Plato's *Timaeus.* It became an Aristotelian commonplace which pervades the whole of subsequent Astronomy until Kepler. It is accepted as a matter of course by Copernicus. The locus classicus for the description of the spherical universe is Aristotle's *De Coelo* I, §§ 5–12 and II, §§ I, 4, 5, 6.

3. *Nulla indigens compagine.* The term *compago* is the usual medieval word for the fabric of the human body, *compagines membrorum.* The articulated human body, the *microcosm,* is thus implicitly contrasted with the *macrocosm,* the universe which is not thus articulated. The parallel between macrocosm and microcosm is the commonest basis of the medieval teaching concerning man and the world. It is the key to medieval science in somewhat the same way that evolution is the key to modern science. The work of Copernicus appeared in the same year as the great monograph on the structure of the human body by Vesalius. Thus in 1543 the axe was laid to the tree of Medieval Science from both sides. For science, therefore, that year may be regarded as the opening of the modern period.

4. This idea, the comparison of the spherical world to drops of water, is taken from *Pliny II,* § 65. "As to whether there be *Antipodes* is in dispute between the learned and the vulgar. We maintain that there are men on every part of the Earth. . . . If any should ask why those opposite to us do not fall off, we ask in return why those on the opposite side do not wonder that we do not fall off. . . . But what the vulgar most strenuously resist is the belief that water (which covers the surface of the Earth) is forced into a rounded form. Yet nothing is more obvious. For we see everywhere that hanging drops assume the form of small globes, and are observed to be completely round."

5. *Almagest, 1,* § 4.

6. The word *pole* in the writings of Copernicus and of his predecessors is used for the celestial pole, rather than for the pole of the Earth.

7. The certainty of Copernicus that the form of the Earth is spherical and that the contour of its surface does not correspond to any curve other than that of a circle is of a piece with his general insistence on the sphere and the circle as characteristic of all cosmic form and movement.

8. This view is that of Alexander of Aphrodisias (*c.* 200 A.D.) whose works were very widely read in the north Italian universities.

9. This argument requires little clarification. Assume that the land is in the form of a sphere of volume one seventh that of the waters. Were one to plunge this sphere of land into the sphere of water and to restore the spherical form of the sphere of waters, the whole would be eight times as large as the sphere of land alone, and the sphere of land would in consequence touch the sphere of water only in the interior while the center of the whole sphere would lie only on the circumference of the sphere of land. The sphere of land could thus no longer rise above the circumference of the sphere of water except by ceasing to touch the middle point of the whole water body.

10. The meaning is that there is not one single uniform land mass collected on one side of the Earth, making it lopsided.

11. By "middle circle" Copernicus means the 180th degree of longitude reckoning eastward from the "islands of the blessed" in the Western Ocean. The authority of Copernicus is Ptolemy. In his *Geography* VI, § 16, where the position of Serica is discussed, Ptolemy says "Serica is bounded on the east by the unknown land and is between 35 and 63 degrees broad on a meridian which has a geographical length of 180°." Ptolemy reckons geographical longitude from the "islands of the blessed" (the Canaries). Elsewhere (*Geography* I, § 12) Ptolemy says that "the length (that is measurement from West to East) of the known world from the meridian in the islands of the blessed to (the chief town of) Serica is 177¼°." The latitude of the "Metropolis of Sera" is fixed at 38° 36′ (VI, § 16).

12. The newly discovered land of America was of course first regarded as part of Cathay, of which the West Indies were outlying islands. Early in the sixteenth century it became suspected that America was a separate continent. This was confirmed by Vasco Minez de Balboa (*c.* 1475–1517) when he first sighted the Pacific Ocean (1513), and brought out in many maps, e.g. that of Johan Schöner (1515) in which a clear differentiation is exhibited between Cathay and America. The point was proved by the voyage and circumnavigation (1519–1522) by Ferdinand Magellan (*c.* 1480–1521). The matter became common knowledge with the publication of Antonio Pigafelta's account of the journey in 1524.

13. The *Antichthon* is, strictly speaking, the counter-earth of the Pythagorean system of the Universe. Aristotle *De Coelo* II, § 13, 2, Cicero and later Latin writers, however, use *antichthones* as equivalent to inhabitants of the other hemisphere.

14. In medieval phraseology *the philosopher* is a synonym for Aristotle. The philosophers to whom Copernicus here refers are the followers of Aristotle, the Peripatetics.

15. *Almagest*, I, § 8.

16. Greek πλανήτησ = wanderer.

17. The passage is a remarkable illustration of the very firm hold that Aristotelian conceptions had taken. The incorruptible heavens, the necessity that all perfect movement must be in a circle, the eternal heavenly bodies as contrasted with this changeful, corruptible, temporal Earth are ideas from which Copernicus, like all his contemporaries and predecessors, was quite unable to free himself.

18. For the book on *Optics* ascribed to Euclid and Theon's summary of it (edition by J. L. Heiberg, Leipzig, 1895, p. 41), see T. L. Heath, *Manual of Greek Mathematics,* p. 266, Oxford, 1931.

19. A pun is here involved which cannot be reproduced in English (*caelum caelat*).

20. Heracleides of Heracleia in Pontus was a pupil of Plato and his successor Speusippus and studied also with Aristotle and under the Pythagoreans. On Plato's death, being disappointed in not obtaining the headship of the Academy, he returned to his native town. He wrote many philosophical dialogues on ethical and physical topics which have now disappeared. It seems that he first taught the movement of the planets Venus and Mercury round the Sun and the movement of the Sun round the Earth. Later he showed how by the assumption of a real heliocentric system the celestial phenomena could be explained, but there is no evidence that he finally adopted this as the only possible explanation. Information about him has been collected by O. Voss, *De Heracleidis vita et scriptis,* Rostock, 1896. As regards the works of Heracleides and the other Pythagoreans, the reader is referred to Sir T. L. Heath, *Aristarchus of Samos,* Oxford, 1913.

21. Ecphantus of Syracuse, a Pythagorean, was perhaps a pupil of Hicetas. The few references that survive concerning him are in Hippolytus and Aëtius (Diels, *Vorsokratiker,* I, p. 340, 1920), and all the little that is known of him has been put together by M. Wellmann in Pauly-Wissowa's *Real-Enkyklopädie.*

22. The reference to Cicero is to the *Quaestiones Academicae,* IV, § 29, where we read "Hicetas the Syracusan, so Theophrastus says, regarded the Heavens, the Sun, the Moon and the Stars, in fine all outside the Earth, as standing still, and that nothing in the world moves except the Earth which turns and revolves on its axis with great rapidity and produces exactly the same appearances as if the entire Heavens turned around an immobile Earth. Some think that Plato in his *Timaeus* expresses the same opinion but in more obscure terms."

    This Hicetas was a Pythagorean, the sole remains of whose works is this sentence and a reference to Aëtius (see Diels, *Vorsokratiker,* I, p. 340, 1922). All that we know of Hicetas has been put together by M. Wellmann in Pauly-Wissowa and amounts to hardly more than we have here.

23. The statement that Plato visited Philolaus in Italy rests on the unsupported statement of Diogenes Laertius. It is probable that Philolaus was an older contemporary of Socrates. Substantial fragments of his works have come down to us (see H. Diels, *Vorsokratiker,* I, p. 301, 1922). Copernicus had probably gained his knowledge of Philolaus from Plato and Stobaeus.

24. *Almagest,* I, § 6.

25. The Dioptra was known to Copernicus from works circulating at the time in the names of Euclid and Heron of Alexandria. By *Horoscopium* he means not the familiar plan of astrologers but the instrument or instruments used to obtain it, i.e., an astrolabe or armillary sphere; both these instruments had been familiar since the earlier Middle Ages. The Chorobates is described in *Vitruvius,* VIII, § 5 whose work was accessible to Copernicus.

26. Cf. note 18.

27. The passage resembles one in the work of Archimedes' *The sand reckoner.* See T. L. Heath, *Works of Archimedes,* p. 222, Cambridge, 1897.

28. *Almagest,* I, § 7.

29. The argument is drawn from Aristotle, *De Coelo,* II, § 14; 296b.

30. Aristotle, *De Coelo,* I, §§ 2–3, III, §§ 3–5.

31. *Almagest,* I, § 5.

32. Aristotle, *Phys. Aus.* III, § 4. "First we must determine in how many ways the word infinite is employed. The first meaning is 'that which cannot be traversed.' " See also *De Coelo*, I, § 5, *Phys. Aus.* IV, § 4 and especially *De Coelo*, I, § 7.
33. Aristotle, *De Coelo*, I, § 9.
34. By the *physicists* is meant the commentators on the *Physica* of Aristotle, a book very widely read in the north Italian schools.
35. *Aeneid*, III, 72.
36. Pogoniae = bearded. Comets are spoken of as bearded stars in Aristotle's *Meteorologica*, I, § 7, 4 and elsewhere.
37. Comets, falling stars, and certain other celestial phenomena have, according to Aristotle, a less orderly arrangement than the events in what he regarded as the more distant heavens. They thus partook of a terrestrial nature. Aristotle assumes the existence of exhalations from the Earth which become ignited in consequence of the motions of the upper regions of the Cosmos. *Meteorologica*, I, § 4–5.
38. On this striking passage, Alexander von Humboldt remarks that "even the idea of universal gravitation or attraction toward the Sun as the center of the world seems to have hovered before the mind of this great man." Yet the analog to the Newtonian view, if it exists, is very distant. Copernicus presents us only with the activity of the parts of a single world body and has nothing to say as to the relation of the separate bodies with one another on all sides. Nor is his gravity an essential property of bodies but is present because they are not in the place to which they naturally belong.
39. *Optics*, § 56.
40. The order given in the *Timaeus* is Moon, Sun, Venus, Mercury, Mars, Jupiter, Saturn.
41. *Almagest*, IX, § I.
42. Among the most widely read "moderns" who took this view was the Arabian Astronomer Alfraganus (Ahmed teen Muhammed ben Ketu al Fagani, d. *c.* 880), whose works had been rendered into Latin by Gerard of Cremona (died 1187) by the Jew Johannes Hispalensis (Avendeath *c.* 1150) by Hugo Sanctallensis (fourteenth century) and Bencivenni Zucchero (1313). The work was edited by Melanchthon from the literary remains of Regiomontanus at Nuremberg in 1537.
43. Alpetragius is the Spanish Arab Nured din el Betrugi (fl. *c.* 1180) whose *Liber astronomiae* was translated in 1217 by Michael Scot (d. *c.* 1235) but never printed. It was translated into Hebrew by Moses ben Tibbon in 1259 and retranslated from Hebrew into Latin by the Jew Kolonymus ben David in 1529. This work, to which Copernicus here doubtless refers, was printed at Venice in 1531 along with Sacro Bosco with the following title: Alpetragii Arabis, *Theorica planetarum physicis comm. probata nuperrime ad latinos translata a Calo Calonymo hebraeo Neapolitano.*
44. This computation is attributed to Eratosthenes (276–194 B.C.) by Ptolemy *op. cit.* I, § 12, from whom Copernicus must have taken it, since the works of Eratosthenes were not available to him.
45. The idea was that the orbit of each planet was confined within two spheres, through the apogee and perigee respectively, and that the farther sphere of the planet coincided with the nearer sphere of the next one, thus:

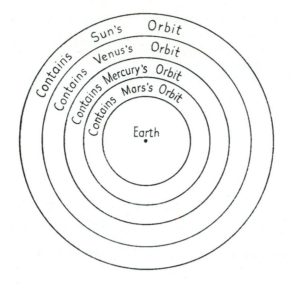

46. By Albategni, Copernicus means Muhammed ben Sabir ben Sinan el Battani (died *c.* 919). Battan is a small place in the Hauran (Artensis) where he was born. Battani, Albattani, Albategni as he was variously known to the West, wrote a work *De motu stellarum* which was known in the Middle Ages by a Latin translation prepared by Plato of Tivoli about 1130. About the same date Robert of Retines translated into Latin the tables which accompanied this work. The translations were printed in 1537 at Nürnberg with the work of Regiomontanus on Alfraganus (see note 42) under the title *Mahometis Albatenii de scientias tellarum liber, cum aliquot additionibus Joannis Regiomantani ex bibliotheca Vaticana transcriptus.*

47. Averroes is the medieval Latin form of the name of the heretical Spanish writer Muhammed ibn Ahmed ibn Muhammed ibn Roschd (1126–1198). Averroes takes a very important part in the history of medieval philosophy by reason of his commentaries on the works of Aristotle, which profoundly influenced the North Italian schools and especially Padua. Averroes wrote little on astronomy, among his few works on this subject being an Epitome of the *Almagest.* This work is not known in Latin but was translated into Hebrew at Naples by Jacob Anatoli in 1231. It is not clear how Copernicus obtained access to this document. It may be that he is not quoting Averroes directly, but from another writer.

48. Martianus Capella was a native of Madaura in Africa, who practiced as a lawyer in Carthage about the beginning of the fifth century. His work *On the marriage of Philology and Mercury and on the Seven Liberal Arts* is a ridiculously strained and heavy allegory in difficult Latin treating of the nature and extent of human knowledge. The work was highly regarded in the Middle Ages during which the "Seven Liberal Arts" (Grammar, Dialectic, Rhetoric, Geometry, Arithmetic, Astronomy and Music) formed the basis of the Academic discipline. The work was frequently printed in the early sixteenth century beginning with 1499. The passage to which Copernicus refers is in Book VIII, Eyssenliant's edition, Leipzig, 1866, p. 317, line 14 ff.

49. The Table is appended to Book V.

50. This refers to the precession of the equinoxes.
51. See Book III.
52. Cf. *Hermetica,* Vol. I, Bk. V. 83, p. 159 (Ed. W. Scott, Oxford 1924). The Hermetic epistles were available to Copernicus, having been edited by Marsilius Ficinus, Treviso, 1472 and J. Schoeffer, 1503.
53. *Electra,* 832–826 is the nearest approach to the reference of Copernicus.
54. Copernicus perhaps means *De generatione animalium,* IV, § 10.
55. Acronyct when the planet rises at sunset and sets at sunrise, being visible all night (Greek "high night").
56. Cf. note 18.
57. Backwards, that is, compared to the diurnal rotation of the stars.
58. *Convertibilem habere inclinationem.*
59. The text here repeats itself by saying that the season would remain unchanged.
60. The "motion of declination" as Copernicus calls it is his own discovery and a matter in which he had no forerunner. The idea follows on the conception of the motion of the Earth as related to the natural attraction of the Sun.
61. In the original manuscript there follow on this chapter two and a half pages which have been heavily scored out. The translation of this section is as follows:

    "Should we allow that the course of Sun and Moon could be diverted with Earth immovable it would yet be less allowable for the other planets. From these and similar causes Philolaus regarded Earth as movable. Some also say that Aristarchus of Samos though not moved by the reasoning that Aristotle advances and rejects (*De Coelo,* II, § 14) was of the same view. But since this cannot be understood, save by the bestowal of wit and industry, it has, as Plato would say, remained hidden from philosophers. There were thus but few who recognized the cause of motion of the stars. Yet if known to Philolaus or any other Pythagorean it is not probable that they would have published it. For it was not the habit of the Pythagoreans to vaunt their philosophical secrets in books nor indeed to reveal them at all but to entrust them to the faith of friends and intimates and so pass it on from hand to hand. In proof thereof is a letter from Lysis to Hipparchus."

    Here Copernicus gives the text of the long and spurious letter of Lysis to Hipparchus which is to be found in *Iamblichus,* V, p. 75. It deals with the custom of the Pythagoreans and is without astronomical bearing.

## FURTHER READING

Koestler, Arthur. 1959. *The Sleepwalkers: A History of Man's Changing Vision of the Universe.* Arkana: Penguin Books.

Kuhn, Thomas S. 1957. *The Copernican Revolution: Planetary Astronomy in the Development of Western Thought.* Cambridge: Harvard University Press.

Dryer, J. L. E. 1963. *History of Astronomy from Thales to Kepler.* New York: Dover.

# The Surgical Art

## Andreas Vesalius (1514–1564)

*The year 1543 can lay claim to marking the birthdate of modern science. In addition to Copernicus' great work, it saw the publication of* De humani corporis fabrica *(On the Fabric of the Human Body, 1543) by Andreas Vesalius. This treatise, with its 250 naturalistic illustrations, is important, not so much for the discoveries that it contains, but for its demonstration of a new method and a bold new conception of the human body as an assemblage of interconnected parts that are utterly indifferent to the operations that are performed on it. As opposed to other anatomists of the day, who sat elevated on a chair reading from a text while a barber surgeon dissected the cadaver, Vesalius carried out his own dissections for his classes. Human anatomy, Vesalius taught, could only be learned from the dissection and observation of the human body. The frontispiece of the* Fabrica—*which depicts Vesalius handling the reproductive organs of a female (who was alleged to have tried to cheat the gallows by declaring herself to be pregnant), visualizes the central tenet of Vesalius' new method—the acquisition of new knowledge demands a collaboration between theory and practice.*

*As for the anatomy itself, Vesalius' book is surprisingly conservative. Commonplace parts of the body (e.g., the parts of the brain and the lymphatic system) are passed over in silence. Although he was vocal in his expressed desire to eradicate the fictions introduced by Galen into human anatomy, the text is guarded: for example, Vesalius concedes his inability to observe the existence of pores in the septum dividing the right and left ventricles of the heart, but suggests that perhaps God's handiwork is so wondrous that the passage escapes human vision. The revolutionary feature of Vesalius' work is to be found, not in the text, but in the illustrations themselves. Vesalius' copper plates were copied and pirated throughout Europe during the following century. Generations of anatomists learned their anatomy from Vesalius, and so these illustrations became the standard for the creation of the standardized anatomical vocabulary that needed to be in place before anatomy could make any real progress.*

*Source:* Andreas Vesalius. 1958. "Selection from *De Humani Corporis Fabrica*." In G. Schwartz and P. Bishop, eds., *Moments of Science.* New York: Basic Books, pp. 517–528.

Those engaged in the arts and sciences, Most Gracious Emperor Charles, find many serious obstacles to the exact study and successful application of them. In the first place, no slight inconvenience results from too great separation between branches of study which serve for the perfection of one art. But much worse is the mischievous distribution among different practitioners of the practical applications of the art. This has been carried so far that those who have set before themselves the attainment of an art embrace one part of it to the neglect of the rest, although they are intimately bound up with it and can by no means be separated from it. Such never achieve any notable result; they never attain their goal or succeed in basing their art upon a proper foundation.

I shall pass over all the other arts in silence and confine myself to a few remarks on that which presides over the health of mankind. This, of all the arts which the mind of man has discovered, is by far the most beneficial, necessary, abstruse, and laborious. But in bygone times, that is to say (in the West) after the Gothic deluge and (in the East) after the reign of Mansur at Bochara in Persia, under whom, as we know, the Arabs still lived as was right on terms of familiarity with the Greeks, medicine began to be sorely distempered. Its primary instrument, the employment of the hand in healing, was so neglected that it was relegated to vulgar fellows with no instruction whatsoever in the branches of knowledge that subserve the art of medicine.

In ancient times there were three medical sects, to wit the Dogmatic, the Empirical, and the Methodical, but the exponents of each of these embraced the whole of the art as the means to preserve health and war against disease. To this end they referred all that they individually thought necessary in their particular sects, and employed the service of a threefold aid to health: first, a

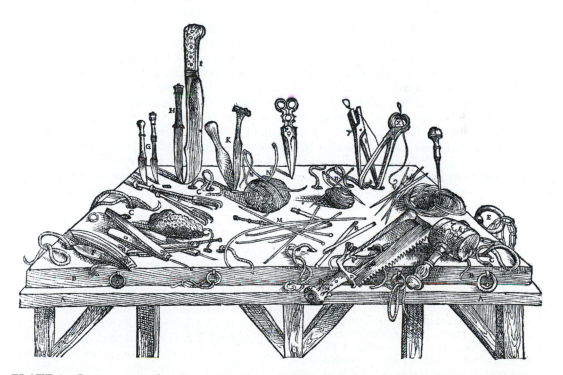

**PLATE 3**  Instruments for dissection. From *De humani corporis fabrica* (Basel, 1543). Courtesy of the Thomas Fisher Rare Book Library, University of Toronto (Toronto, Canada).

theory of diet; second, the whole use of drugs; and third, manual operation [use of the hands]. This last, above the rest, nicely proves the saying that medicine is the addition of that which is lacking, and the removal of that which is in excess; as often as we resort to the art of medicine for the treatment of disease we have occasion to employ it; and time and experience have taught by the benefits it has conferred that it is the greatest aid to human health.

This triple manner of treatment was equally familiar to the doctors of each sect; and those who applied manual operation according to the nature of the affection expended no less care in training their hands than in establishing a theory of diet, or in learning to recognize and combine drugs. This, not to mention his other books, is clearly shown by these most perfect of the compositions of Hippocrates[a]: "On the Function of the Doctor," "On Fractures of Bones," "On Disclocations of Joints and Similar Ailments." Indeed, Galen,[b] after Hippocrates the prince of medicine, in addition to the fact that he boasts from time to time that the care of the gladiators of Pergamon was entrusted to his sole charge, and that when age was now becoming a burden he was reluctant for the monkeys he had for dissection to be skinned by the help of slaves, frequently impresses on us his joy in manual dexterity and how zealously he, in common with the other doctors of Asia, employed it. Indeed, there is not one of the ancients who does not seem as

[a]The *Corpus* of Hippocrates (c. 460–c. 377 B.C.) is widely regarded as the longest surviving scientific text, and the theory of disease advanced therein dominated medicine until the eighteenth century. [B.]

[b]The anatomical and medical ideas of Galen (c. 130–c. 200) dominated medicine for almost fifteen hundred years. His tripartite circulation system was one such idea. According to Galen, the liver produced the natural spirit (blood), which travels through the body via the veins; the heart produced the vital spirit, which travels through the arteries; and the brain the animal spirit, which travels through the nerves. [B.]

solicitous to hand down to posterity the method of cure which is effected by the hand as those methods which depend on diet and drugs.

But it was especially after the ruin spread by the Goths, when all the sciences, which before had flourished gloriously and were practiced as was fitting, went to ruin, that more fashionable doctors, first in Italy, in imitation of the old Romans, despising the work of the hand, began to delegate to slaves the bodily attentions which they judged needful for their patients, and themselves merely to stand over them like master builders. Then, when all the rest also who practiced the true art of healing gradually declined the unpleasant duties of their profession, without however abating any of their claim to money or honor, they quickly fell away from the standard of the doctors of old. Methods of cooking, and all the preparation of food for the sick, they left to nurses; compounding of drugs they left to the apothecaries; manual operation to barbers. Thus in course of time the art of healing has been so wretchedly rent asunder that certain doctors, advertising themselves under the name of physicians, have arrogated to themselves alone the prescription of drugs and diet for obscure diseases, and have relegated the rest of medicine to those whom they call surgeons and scarcely regard as slaves, disgracefully banishing from themselves the chief and most ancient branch of the medical art, and that which principally (if indeed there be any other) bases itself upon the investigation of nature. Yet among the Indians today it is the kings who chiefly exercise this [surgical] art; the Persians hand it down as an obligatory inheritance to their children, as the whole family of the Asclepiads formerly did; the Thracians, with many other nations, cultivate and honor it above other arts, to the neglect almost of that part of the art [the prescription of drugs] which formerly many proscribed from the state, as devised for the deception and destruction of men; for it, refusing the aid of nature, gives no deep relief, but rather, endeavoring to help nature while it is in any case overwrought by the effort to cast off the disease, it often destroys it quite and utterly distracts it from its normal function. Consequently it is to it in particular we owe the fact that so many scoffs are likely to be cast at doctors, and this most holy art is made a mockery, though all the time one part of it, which those trained in liberal studies allow basely to be torn from them, could adorn it forever with peculiar praise.

For when Homer, that wellspring of genius, declares that a man that is a doctor is better than a host, and together with all the poets of Greece celebrates Podalyrius and Machaon, truly these divine sons of Aesculapius are thus praised not for the reason that they banished a touch of fever or other ailments which nature usually cures, unaided, and without the assistance of the doctor more easily than with his aid, nor because they pandered to the appetites of men in obscure and desperate afflictions, but because they devoted themselves in particular to the cure of dislocations, fractures, bruises, wounds, and other branches of continuity, and to the flowing of blood, and because they freed the noble warriors of Agamemnon from javelins, darts, and other evils of that kind, which wars particularly occasion, and which always demand the careful attention of the doctor.

But it was not at all my purpose to set one instrument of medicine above the rest, since the triple art of healing as it is called cannot at all be disunited and wrenched asunder, but belongs in its entirety to the same practitioner; and for the due attainment of this triple art, all the parts of medicine have been established and prepared on an equal footing, so that the individual parts are brought into use with a success proportioned to the degree in which one combines the cumulative force of all. How rarely indeed a disease occurs which does not at once require the triple manner of treatment; that is to say, a proper diet must be prescribed, some service must be rendered by medicine, and some by the hand. Therefore the tyros in this art must by every means be exhorted to follow the Greeks in despising the whisperings of those physicians (save the mark!), and, as the fundamental nature and rational basis of the art prescribes, to apply their hands also to the treatment, for fear that they should rend the body of medicine and make of it a force destructive of the common life of man.

And they must be urged to do this with all the greater earnestness because men today who have had an irreproachable training in the art are seen to abstain from the use of the hand as from the plague, and for this very reason, lest they should be slandered by the masters of the profession as barbers before the ignorant mob, and should henceforth lack equal gain and honor with those less than half doctors, losing their standing both with the uneducated commonality and with princes. For it is indeed above all other things the wide prevalence of this hateful error that prevents us even in our age from taking up the healing art as a whole, makes us confine ourselves merely to the treatment of internal complaints, and, if I may utter the blunt truth once and for all, causes us, to the great detriment of mankind, to study to be healers only in a very limited degree.

For when, in the first place, the whole compounding of drugs was handed over to the apothecaries, then the doctors promptly lost the knowledge of simple medicines which is absolutely essential to them; and they became responsible for the fact that the druggists' shops were filled with barbarous terms and false remedies, and also that so many elegant compositions of the ancients were lost to us, several of which have not yet come to light; and finally, they prepared an endless task for the learned men, not only of our own age, but for those who preceded it by some years, who devoted themselves with indefatigable zeal to research in simple medicines; so much so that they may be regarded as having gone far to restore the knowledge of them to its former brilliance.

But this perverse distribution of the instruments of healing among a variety of craftsmen inflicted a much more odious shipwreck and a far more cruel blow upon the chief branch of natural philosophy [anatomy] to which, since it comprises the natural history of man and should rightly be regarded as the firm foundation of the whole art of medicine and its essential preliminary, Hippocrates and Plato attached so much importance that they did not hesitate to put it first among the parts of medicine. For though, originally, it was the prime object of the doctors' care, and though they strained every nerve to acquire it, it finally began to perish miserably when the doctors themselves, by resigning manual operations to others, ruined anatomy. For when the doctors supposed that only the care of internal complaints concerned them, considering a mere knowledge of the viscera as more than enough for them, they neglected the structure of the bones and muscles, as well as of the nerves, veins, and arteries which run through bones and muscles, as of no importance for them. And further, when the whole conduct of manual operations was entrusted to barbers, not only did doctors lose the true knowledge of the viscera, but the practice of dissection soon died out, doubtless for the reason that the doctors did not attempt to operate, while those to whom the manual skill was relegated were too ignorant to read the writings of the teachers of anatomy.

It is, thus, utterly impossible for this class of men to preserve for us a difficult art which they have acquired only mechanically. And equally inevitably this deplorable dismemberment of the art of healing has introduced into our schools the detestable procedure now in vogue, that one man should carry out the dissection of the human body, and another give the description of the parts. These latter are perched up aloft in a pulpit like jackdaws, and with a notable air of disdain they drone out information about facts they have never approached at first hand, but which they merely commit to memory from the books of others, or of which they have descriptions before their eyes; the former are so ignorant of languages that they are unable to explain their dissections to the onlookers and botch what ought to be exhibited in accordance with the instruction of the physician, who never applies his hand to the dissection, and contemptuously steers the ship out of the manual, as the saying goes. Thus, everything is wrongly taught, days are wasted in absurd questions and in the confusion less is offered to the onlooker than a butcher in his stall could teach a doctor. I omit all mention of those schools in which there is scarcely even a thought of opening a human body to exhibit its structure. So far had ancient medicine fallen some years ago from its pristine glory.

But when medicine in the great blessedness of this age, which the gods will to entrust to the wise guidance of your divine power, had, together with all studies, begun to live again and to lift its head up from its utter darkness (so much so, indeed, that it might without fear of contradiction be regarded in some academies as having nearly recovered its ancient brilliance); and when there was nothing of which the need was now so urgently felt as the resurrection of the science of anatomy, then I, challenged by the example of so many eminent men, insofar as I could and with what means I could command, thought I should lend my aid. And for fear that, when all others for the sake of our common studies were engaged in some attempt and with such great success, I alone should be idle, or for fear that I should fall below the level of my forebears, doctors to be sure not unknown to fame, I thought that this branch of natural philosophy should be recalled from the dead, so that if it did not achieve with us a greater perfection than at any other place or time among the old teachers of anatomy, it might at least reach such a point that one could with confidence assert that our modern science of anatomy was equal to that of old, and that in this age anatomy was unique both in the level to which it had sunk and in the completeness of its subsequent restoration.

But this effort could by no manner of means have succeeded if, when I was studying medicine at Paris, I had not myself applied my hand to this business but had acquiesced in the casual and superficial display to me and my fellow students by certain barbers of a few organs at one or two public dissections. For in such a perfunctory manger was anatomy then treated in the place where we have lived to see medicine happily reborn that I myself, having trained myself without guidance in the dissection of brute creatures, at the third dissection at which it was my fortune ever to be present (this, as was the custom there, was concerned exclusively or principally with the viscera), led on by the encouragement of my fellow students and teachers, performed in public a more thorough dissection than was the custom to be done. Later, I attempted a second dissection, my purpose being to exhibit the muscles of the hand together with a more accurate dissection of the viscera. For except for eight muscles of the abdomen, disgracefully mangled and in the wrong order, no one (I speak the simple truth) ever demonstrated to me any single muscle, or any single bone, much less the network of nerves, veins, and arteries.

Subsequently at Louvain, where I had to return on account of the disturbance of war, because during eighteen years the doctors there had not even dreamed of anatomy, and in order that I might help the students of that academy, and that I myself might acquire greater skill in a matter both obscure and in my judgment of prime importance for the whole of medicine, I did somewhat more accurately than at Paris expound the whole structure of the human body in the course of dissecting, with the result that the younger teachers of that academy now appear to spend great and very serious study in acquiring a knowledge of the parts of man, clearly understanding what invaluable material for philosophizing is presented to them from this knowledge. Furthermore, at Padua, in the most famous gymnasium of the whole world, I had been charged with the teaching of surgical medicine for five years by the illustrious Senate of Venice, which is by far the most liberal in the endowment of the higher branches of learning. And since the carrying out of anatomical inquiry is of importance for surgical medicine, I devoted much effort to the investigation of the structure of man, and so directed my inquiries. And, exploding the ridiculous fashion of the schools, so taught the subject that we could not find in my procedure anything that fell short of the tradition of the ancients.

However, the supineness [apathy] of the medical profession has seen to it only too well that the writings of Eudemus, Herophilus, Marinus, Andreas, Lycus, and other princes of anatomy should not be preserved to us, since not even a fragment of any page has survived of all those famous writers whom Galen mentions, to the number of more than twenty, in his second commentary to the book of Hippocrates on "The Nature of Man." Indeed, even of his own anatomical writings scarcely the half has been saved from destruction. But those who followed Galen, among whom I place Oribasius,[c] Theophilils, the Arabs, and all our own writers whom I have read to date, all of them (and they must pardon me for saying this), if they handed on anything worth reading, borrowed it from him. And, believe me, the careful reader will discover that there is nothing they were further from attempting than the dissection of bodies. They placed an absolute trust in I know not what quality of the writing of their chief, and in the neglect of dissection of the rest, and shamefully reduced Galen to convenient summaries, never departing from him by so much as the breadth of a nail, that is, supposing they succeeded in arriving at his meaning. Indeed, they place it in the forefront of their books that their own writings are pieced together from the teachings of Galen, and that all that is theirs is his. And so completely have all surrendered to his authority

[c]Oribasius (fl. 4th century B.C.) is now remembered principally as a compiler of the contributions of earlier medical writers. Even so, he distinguished himself by correcting Galen's anatomy in several respects. [B.]

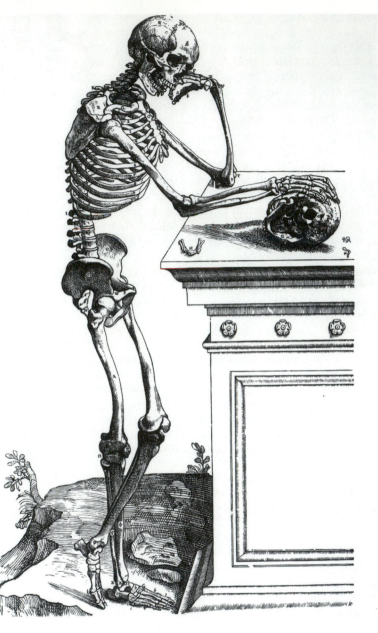

**PLATE 4**    Skeleton from the Side. Andreas Vesalius, *De humani corporis fabrica* (Basil, 1543). Courtesy of the Thomas Fisher Rare Book Library, University of Toronto (Toronto, Canada).

that no doctor has been found to declare that in the anatomical books of Galen even the slightest error has ever been found, much less could now be found; though all the time (apart from the fact that Galen frequently corrects himself, and in later books, after acquiring more experience, removes oversights that he had committed in earlier books, and sometimes teaches contradictory views) it is quite clear to us, from the revival of the art of dissection, from a painstaking perusal of the works of Galen, and from a restoration of them in several places, of which we have no reason to be ashamed, that Galen himself never dissected a human body lately dead.[d] Indeed, more, deceived by his monkeys (although it is admitted that human bodies dried, and prepared as it were for an inspection of the bones, did come under his observation), he frequently wrongly contradicts the ancient doctors who had trained themselves by dissecting human corpses.

And again, how many false observations you will find him to have made even on his monkeys. I shall say nothing about the astonishing fact that in the manifold and infinite divergences of the organs of the human body from those of the monkey Galen hardly noticed anything except the fingers and the bend of the knee—which he would certainly have passed over with the rest, if they had not been obvious to him without dissection. But at the moment I do not propose to criticize the false statements of Galen, easily the foremost among the teachers of anatomy; and much less would I wish to be regarded now in the beginning as disloyal to the author of all good things and lacking in respect for his authority. For, I am not unaware how the medical profession (in this so different from the followers of Aristo-

tle) are likely to be upset when in more than two hundred instances, in the conduct of the single course of anatomy I now exhibit in the schools, they see that Galen has failed to give a true description of the interrelation, use, and, function of the parts of man—how they scowl at times, and examine every inch of the dissection in their determination to defend him. Yet they too, drawn by the love of truth, gradually abandon that attitude and, growing less emphatic, begin to put faith in their own not ineffectual sight and powers of reason rather than in the writings of Galen. These true paradoxes, won not by slavish reliance on the efforts of others, nor supported merely by masses of authorities, they eagerly communicate in their corresponding to their friends; they exhort them so earnestly and so friendly-wise to examine them for themselves, and to come at last to a true knowledge of anatomy, that there is ground for hope that anatomy will here long be cultivated in all our academies as it was of old in Alexandria.

And that the muses might the more smile upon this hope, I have, so far as in me lay, and in addition to my other publications on this subject—which certain plagiarists, thinking me far away from Germany, have put out there as their own—made a completely fresh arrangement in seven books of my information about the parts of the human body in the order in which I am accustomed to lay the same before that learned assembly in this city, as well as at Bologna and at Pisa. Thus, those present at the dissections will have a record of what was there demonstrated, and will be able to expound anatomy to others with less trouble. And also the books will be by no means useless to those who have no opportunity for personal examination, for they relate with sufficient fullness the number, position, shape, substance, connection with other parts, use and function of each part of the human body, together with many similar facts which we are accustomed to unravel during dissection concerning the nature of the parts, and also the method of dissection applicable to dead and

[d]Galen's anatomical views were shaped by the study of the barbary ape, *Macacus innus,* and other animals (pigs, cows, cats, and dogs). As one might expect, errors were incorporated into anatomy, many of which are found in seventeenth century textbooks. [B.]

living animals. Moreover, the books contain representations of all the parts inserted in the text of the discourse, in such a way that they place before the eyes of the student of nature's works, as it were, a dissected corpse.

Thus, in the first book I have described the nature of all bones and cartilages, which, since the other parts are supported by them, and must be described in accordance with them, are the first to be known by students of anatomy. The second book treats of the ligaments by which bones and cartilages are linked one with another, and then the muscles that effect the movements that depend upon our will. The third comprises the close network of veins which carry to the muscles and bones and the other parts the ordinary blood by which they are nourished, and of arteries which control the mixture of innate heat and vital spirit. The fourth treats of the branches not only of the nerves which convey the animal spirit to the muscles, but of all the other nerves as well. The fifth explains the structure of the organs that serve nutrition effected through food and drink; and furthermore, on account of the proximity of their position, it contains also the instrument designed by the Most High Creator for the propagation of the species. The sixth is devoted to the heart, the *somes* of the vital faculty, and the parts that subserve it. The seventh describes the harmony between the structure of the brain and the organs of sense, without, however, repeating from the fourth book the description of the network of nerves arising from the brain . . .

But here there comes into my mind the judgment of certain men who vehemently condemn the practice of setting before the eyes of students, as we do with the parts of plants, delineations, be they never so accurate, of the parts of the human body. These, they say, ought to be learned not by pictures but by careful dissection and examination of the things themselves. As if, in truth my object in adding to the text of my discourse images of the parts, which are most faithful, and which I wish could be free from the risk of being spoiled by the printers, was that students should rely upon them and refrain from dissecting bodies; whereas my practice has rather been to encourage students of medicine in every way I could to perform dissections with their own hands. Assuredly, if the practice of the ancients had lasted down to our day, namely, to train boys at home in carrying out dissections, just as in making their letters and in reading, I would gladly consent to our dispensing not only with pictures but with all commentaries. For the ancients only began to write about dissection when they decided that honor demanded that they should communicate the art not only to their children but to strangers whom they respected for their virtue. For, as soon as boys were no longer trained in dissection, the inevitable consequence at once followed that they learned anatomy less well, since the training had been abolished with which they had been accustomed to begin in youth. So much so that when the art had deserted the family of the Asclepiads, and had been now for many centuries on the decline, books were needed to preserve a view of it. Yet how greatly pictures aid the understanding of these things, and how much more accurately they put the things before the eyes than even the clearest language, which nobody can have failed to experience in geometry and the other mathematical disciplines.

But, however that may be, I have done my best to this single end, namely, in an equally recondite and laborious matter, to aid as many as possible, and truly and completely to describe the structure of the human body—which is built up not of some ten or twelve parts (as seems to those who give it a passing glance) but of some thousands of different parts—and to bring to students of medicine a substantial contribution toward the understanding of those books of Galen treating of this branch of learning, which of all his writings most require the assistance of a teacher.

Moreover, I am aware [first] how little authority my efforts will carry by reason of my youth (I am still in my twenty-eighth year);

and [secondly] how little, on account of the frequency with which I draw attention to the falsity of Galen's pronouncements, I shall be sheltered from the attacks of those who have not—as I have done in the schools of Italy— applied themselves earnestly to anatomy, and who, being now old men devoured by envy at the true discoveries of youths, will be ashamed, together with all the other secretaries of Galen, that they have been hitherto, so blind, failing to notice what I now set forth, yet arrogating to themselves a mighty reputation in the art—(I know, I say, how little authority my efforts will carry) unless they come forth auspiciously into the light, commended by the great patronage of some divine power. And, inasmuch as it cannot be more safely sheltered or more splendidly adorned than by the imperishable name of the Divine Charles, the Most Great and Invincible Emperor, I beseech Your Majesty to allow this useful work of mine, which on many accounts and for many reasons is dangerous to itself, to circulate for a short time under Your Majesty's auspices, glory, and patronage, until through experience of the facts, through judgment which matures with time, and through learning, I may make the fruit of my toil worthy of the Most High and Best Prince, or may offer another gift worthy of acceptance on another subject closed from our art . . .

## FURTHER READING

Brooks, Chandler, and Paul F. Cranefield, eds. 1959. *The Historical Development of Physiological Thought.* New York: Hafner.

O'Malley, C. D. 1964. *Andreas Vesalius of Brussels.* Berkeley: University of California Press.

# The Philosopher's Stone

## Paracelsus (1493–1541)

*Paracelsus (born Theophratus Bombastus von Hohenheim) was a self-described revolutionary. In the presence of his students, he burned the great medieval compilation of medical knowledge, the Canon of Avicenna. Paracelsus looked upon the metals as fundamentally identical with one another, differing only in their degree of maturity. Gold, Paracelsus contended, is the most perfect or mature, as is indicated by its resistance to decay and corruption. It is produced when the natural processes that produce metal in the Earth are carried to their completion. When this process is stopped short for any reason, one of the baser metals is the result. Alchemy was the attempt to carry to fruition the natural processes whereby gold is produced in the Earth. In this approach, its rich vocabulary expressed the organic conception of nature in vivid organic terms— fermentation, vegetation, digestion, generation, maturation.*

*A school known as iatrochemistry, led by Jean Baptiste van Helmont (1579–1644), formed around the writings of Paracelsus. The key was to be alchemy but a reformed alchemy informed by magic and mystical experience. This school regarded chemistry as the servant of medicine. The books that this school sponsored consisted mostly of medical recipes that were usually prefaced by a superficial stab at theory. The theory itself was based on Paracelsus' belief that there are three principles—salt, sulfur, and mercury—out of which all mixed bodies are compounded.*

You who are skilled in alchemy, and as many others as promise yourselves great riches or chiefly desire to make gold and silver, which alchemy in different ways promises and teaches, equally, too, you who willingly undergo toil and vexations, and wish not to be freed from them, until you have attained your rewards, and the fulfillment of the promises made to you; experience teaches this every day, that out of thousands of you not even one accomplishes his desire. Is this a failure of nature or of art? I say no, but it is rather the fault of fate, or of the lack of skill of the operator.

Since, therefore, the characters of the signs, of the stars and planets of heaven, together with the other names, inverted words, recipes, materials, and instruments are thoroughly well-known to such as are

*Source:* Paracelsus. 1976. *The Hermetic and Alchemical Writings of Aureolus Philippus Theophrastus Bombast, of Hohenheim, called Paracelsus the Great: Now for the First Time Faithfully Translated into English.* Trans. Arthur Edward Waite. Boulder, CO: Shambhala, pp. 3–11.

acquainted with this art, it would be altogether superfluous to return to these same subjects in the present book, although the use of such signs, names, and characters at the proper time is by no means without advantage.

But herein will be noticed another way of treating alchemy different from the previous method, and deduced by Seven Canons from the sevenfold series of the metals. This, indeed, will not give scope for a pompous parade of words, but, nevertheless, in the consideration of those Canons, everything which should be separated from alchemy will be treated at sufficient length, and, moreover, many secrets of other things are herein contained. Hence, too, result certain marvelous speculations and new operations which frequently differ from the writings and opinions of ancient operators and natural philosophers, but have been discovered and confirmed by full proof and experimentation.

Moreover, in this art nothing is more true than this, though it be little known and gains small confidence. All the fault and cause of difficulty in alchemy, whereby very many persons are reduced to poverty, and others labor in vain, is wholly and solely lack of skill in the operator, and the defect or excess of materials, whether in quantity or quality, from which it ensues that, in the course of operation, things are wasted or reduced to nothing. If the true process shall have been found, the substance itself while transmuting approaches daily more and more towards perfection. The straight road is easy, but it is found by very few.

Sometimes it may happen that a speculative artist may, by his own eccentricity, think out for himself some new method in alchemy, be the consequence anything or nothing. He need do nothing in order to reduce something into nothing, and again bring back something out of nothing. Yet, this proverb of the incredulous is not wholly false. Destruction perfects that which is good; for the good cannot appear on account of that which conceals it. The good is least good while it is thus, concealed. The concealment must be removed so that the good may be able freely to appear in its own brightness. For example, the mountain, the sand, the earth, or the stone in which a metal has grown is such a concealment. Each one of the visible metals is a concealment of the other six metals.

By the element of fire all that is imperfect is destroyed and taken away, as, for instance, the five metals, Mercury, Jupiter [tin], Mars [iron], Venus [copper], and Saturn [lead]. On the other hand, the perfect metals, Sol [gold] and Luna [silver], are not consumed in that same fire. They remain in the fire; and at the same time, out of the other imperfect ones which are destroyed, they assume their own body and become visible to the eyes. How, and by what method, this comes about can be gathered from the Seven Canons. Hence, it may be learned what are the nature and property of each metal, what it effects with the other metals, and what are its powers when mixed with them.

But this should be noted in the very first place; that these Seven Canons cannot be perfectly understood by every cursory reader at a first glance or a single reading. An inferior intelligence does not easily perceive occult and abstruse subjects. Each one of these Canons demands no slight discussion. Many persons, puffed up with pride, fancy they can easily comprehend all which this book comprises. Thus, they set down its contents as useless and futile, thinking they have something far better of their own, and that, therefore, they can afford to despise what is here contained.

## THE SEVEN CANONS OF THE METALS

1. *Concerning the Nature and Properties of Mercury*

... By the mediation of Vulcan, or fire, any metal can be generated from Mercury. At the same time, Mercury is imperfect as a metal; it is semi-generated and wanting in coagulation, which is the end of all metals.

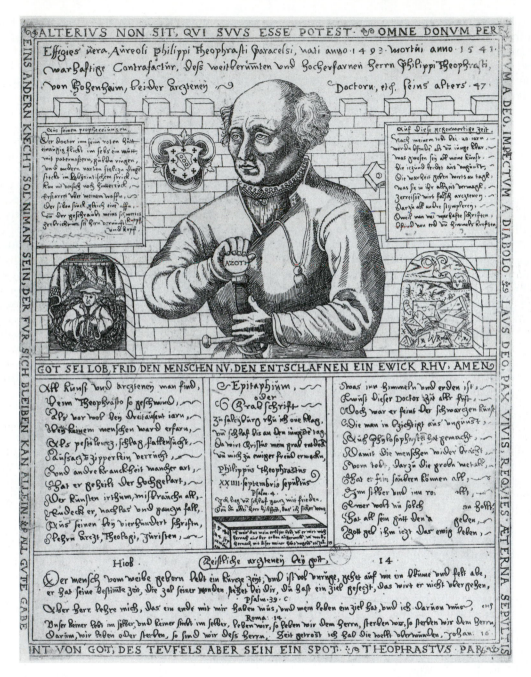

**PLATE 5**   Engraving of Paracelsus.

Up to the halfway point of their generation all metals are Mercury. Gold, for example is Mercury; but it loses the Mercurial nature by coagulation, and although the properties of Mercury are present in it, they are dead, for their vitality is destroyed by coagulation . . .

2. *Concerning the Nature and Properties of Jupiter (Tin)*

In that which is manifest (that is to say, the body of Jupiter) the other six corporeal metals are spiritually concealed, but one more deeply and more tenaciously than another. Jupiter has nothing of a quintessence in his composition, but is of the nature of the four elementaries. On this account his liquefaction is brought about by the application of a moderate fire, and, in like manner, he is coagulated by moderate cold. He has affinity with the liquefactions of all the other metals. For, the more like he is to some nature, the more easily he is united thereto by conjunction. For the operation of those nearly allied is easier and more natural than of those which are remote . . .

The more remote, therefore, Jupiter is found to be from Mars and Venus, and the nearer Sol and Luna, the more "goldness" or "silverness," if I may say so, it contains in his body, and the greater, stronger, more visible, more tangible, more amiable, more acceptable, more distinguished, and more true it is found than in some remote body. . . . This, therefore, is a point which you, as an alchemist, must seriously debate with yourself; how you can relegate Jupiter to a remote and abstruse place, which Sol and Luna occupy, and how, in turn, you can summon Sol and Luna from remote positions to a near place, where Jupiter is corporeally posited; so that, in the same way, Sol and Luna may also be present there corporeally before your eyes. For the transmutation of metals from imperfection to perfection there are several practical recipes. Mix the one with the other. Then, again, separate the one pure from the other. This is nothing else but the process of permutation, set in order by perfect alchemical labor. Note that Jupiter

has much gold and not a little silver. Let Saturn and Luna be imposed on him, and of the rest Luna will be augmented.

3. *Concerning Mars (Iron) and His Properties*

The six occult metals have expelled the seventh from them, and have made it corporeal, leaving it little efficacy, and imposing on it great hardness and weight. This being the case, they have shaken off all their own strength of coagulation and hardness, which they manifest in this other body. On the contrary, they have retained in themselves their color and liquefaction, together with their nobility. It is very difficult and laborious for a prince or a king to be produced out of an unfit and common man. But, Mars acquires dominion with strong and pugnacious hand, and seizes on the position of king. He should, however, be on his guard against snares; that he be not led captive suddenly and unexpectedly. It must also be considered by what method Mars may be able to take the place of king, and Sol and Luna, with Saturn, hold the place of Mars.

4. *Concerning Venus (Copper) and Its Properties*

The other six metals have rendered Venus an extrinsic body by means of all their color and method of liquefaction. It may be necessary, in order to understand this, that we should show, by some examples, how a manifest thing may be rendered occult, and an occult thing rendered materially manifest by means of fire. Whatever is combustible can be naturally transmuted by fire from one form into another, namely, into lime, soot, ashes, glass, colors, stones, and earth. This last can again be reduced to many new metallic bodies. If a metal, too, be burnt, or rendered fragile by old rust, it can again acquire malleability by applications of fire.

5. *Concerning the Nature and Properties of Saturn (Lead)*

Of his own nature Saturn speaks thus; the other six have cast me out as their examiner.

They have thrust me forth from them and from a spiritual place. They have also added a corruptible body as a place of abode, so that I may be what they neither are nor desire to become. My six brothers are spiritual, and thence it ensues that so often as I am put in the fire they penetrate my body and, together with me, perish in the fire, Sol and Luna excepted.

### 6. *Concerning Luna (Silver) and the Properties Thereof*

The endeavor to make Saturn or Mars out of Luna involves no lighter or easier work than to make Luna, with great gain, out of Mercury, Jupiter, Mars, Venus, or Saturn. It is not useful to transmute what is perfect into what is imperfect, but the latter into the former. Nevertheless, it is well to know what is the material of Luna, or where it proceeds. Whoever is not able to consider or find this out will neither be able to make Luna. It will be asked, what is Luna? It is among the seven metals which are spiritually concealed, itself the seventh, external, corporeal, and material. For this seventh always contains the six metals spiritually hidden in itself. And the six spiritual metals do not exist without one external and material metal. So also no corporeal metal can have place or essence without those six spiritual ones. The seven corporeal metals mix easily by means of liquefaction, but this mixture is not useful for making Sol or Luna. For, in that mixture each metal remains in its own nature, or fixed in the fire, or flies from it. For example, mix, in any way you can, Mercury, Jupiter, Saturn, Mars, Venus, Sol, and Luna. It will not from this result that Sol and Luna will so change the other five that, by the agency of Sol and Luna, these will become Sol and Luna. For though all be liquefied into a single mass, nevertheless, each remains in its nature whatever it is. This is the judgment which must be passed on corporeal mixture....

A question may arise: If it be true that Luna and every metal derives its origin and is generated from the other six, what is then its property and its nature? To this we reply:

From Saturn, Mercury, Jupiter, Mars, Venus, and Sol, nothing and no other metal than Luna could be made. The cause is that each metal has two good virtues of the other six, of which altogether there are twelve. These are the spirit of Luna, which thus in a few words may be made known. Luna is composed of the six spiritual metals and their virtues, whereof each possesses two. Altogether, therefore, twelve are thus posited in one corporeal metal... Luna has from the planet Mercury... its liquidity and bright white color. So Luna has from Jupiter... its white color and its great firmness in fire. Luna has from Mars ... its hardness and its clear sound. Luna has from Venus ... its measure of coagulation and its malleability. From Saturn ... its homogeneous body, with gravity. From Sol ... its spotless purity and great constancy against the power of fire. Such is the knowledge of the natural exaltation and of the course of the spirit and body of Luna, with its composite nature and wisdom briefly summarized ...

### 7. *Concerning the Nature of Sol (Gold) and Its Properties*

The seventh after the six spiritual metals is corporeally Sol, which in itself is nothing but pure fire. What in outward appearance is more beautiful, more brilliant, more clear and perceptible, a heavier, colder, or more homogeneous body to see? And it is easy to perceive the cause of this, namely, that it contains in itself the congelations of the other six metals, out of which it is made externally into one most compact body.... The fire of Sol is of itself pure, not indeed alive, but hard, and so far shows the color of sulfur in that yellow and red are mixed therein, in due proportion. The five cold metals are Jupiter, Mars, Saturn, Venus, and Luna, which assign to Sol their virtues; according to cold, the body itself; according to fire, color; according to dryness, solidity; according to humidity, weight; and out of brightness, sound. But that gold is not burned in the element of terrestrial fire, nor is even corrupted, is effected by the firmness of Sol.

For one fire cannot burn another, or even consume it; but rather if fire be added to fire it is increased, and becomes more powerful in its operations. The celestial fire which flows to us on the Earth from the Sun is not such a fire as there is in heaven, neither is it like that which exists upon the Earth, but that celestial fire with us is cold and congealed, and it is the body of the Sun. Wherefore, the Sun can in no way be overcome by our fire. This only happens, that it is liquefied, like snow or ice, by that same celestial Sun. Fire, therefore, has not the power of burning fire, because the Sun is fire, which, dissolved in heaven, is coagulated with us.

## WHAT IS TO BE THOUGHT CONCERNING THE CONGELATION OF MERCURY

To mortify or congeal Mercury, and afterwards seek to turn it into Luna, and to sublimate it with great labor, is labor in vain, since it involves a dissipation of Sol and Luna existing therein. There is another method, far different and much more concise, whereby, with little waste of Mercury and less expenditure of toil, it is transmuted into Luna without congelation. Any one can at pleasure learn this art in alchemy, since it is so simple and easy; and by it, in a short time, he could make any quantity of silver and gold. It is tedious to read long descriptions, and everybody wishes to be advised in straightforward words. Do this, then, proceed as follows, and you will have Sol and Luna, by help whereof you will turn out a very rich man. Wait awhile, I beg, while this process is described to you in a few words, and keep these words well digested, so that out of Saturn, Mercury, and Jupiter you may make Sol and Luna. There is not, nor ever will be, any art so easy to find out and practice, and so effective in itself. The method of making Sol and Luna by alchemy is so prompt that there is no more need of books, or of elaborate instruction, than there would be if one wished to write about last year's snow. . . .

The art is this: After you have made heaven, or the sphere of Saturn, with its life to run over the Earth, place it on all the planets, or such, one or more, as you wish, so that the portion of Luna may be the smallest. Let all run, until heaven, or Saturn, has entirely disappeared. Then, all those planets will remain dead with their old corruptible bodies, having meanwhile obtained another new, perfect and incorruptible body.

That body is the spirit of heaven. From it these planets again receive a body and life, and live as before. Take this body from the life and the Earth. Keep it. It is Sol and Luna. Here you have the art altogether, clear and entire. If you do not yet understand it, or are not practiced therein, it is well. It is better that it should be kept concealed, and not made public.

## FURTHER READING

Debus, Allen G. 1991. *The French Paracelsians: The Chemical Challenge to Medical and Scientific Tradition in Early Modern France.* Cambridge: Cambridge University Press.

Principe, Lawrence M. 2002. "Chemistry: Pre-Eighteenth Century." In *History of Modern Science and Mathematics*, ed. Brian S. Baigrie. New York: Charles Scribner's Sons, volume 2, pp. 142–164.

# The Mutable Heavens

## Tycho Brahe (1546–1601)

*According to Aristotle's principles, change could only take place in the sublunary realm—the heavenly firmament being eternal and incorruptible. Tycho Brahe was able to demonstrate, in his* De nova stella *(The New Star, 1573) that a supernova, which appeared in 1572, showed no sensible parallax and therefore belonged to the sphere of the fixed stars. Brahe's success led to the building of the greatest observatory of his day at Uraniborg, on the Island of Hven. Outfitted with the best instruments and working with enormous quadrants (see Plate 6) and sextants, over a twenty year period, Brahe produced a body of systematic observations, determining the positions of 777 stars with great precision.*

*Though he provided the raw data that Johannes Kepler (1571–1630) would subsequently employ in his defense and elaboration of the Copernican system, Brahe could not accept the heliocentric hypothesis, advancing in its place a compromise system that found limited support among astronomers, in which the planets revolve round the Sun and the Sun and the planets revolve round a stationary Earth. Since his system features more than one center of motion, it was observationally equivalent to the Copernican system.*

## ON A NEW STAR, NOT PREVIOUSLY SEEN WITHIN THE MEMORY OF ANY AGE SINCE THE BEGINNING OF THE WORLD

Last year (1572), in the month of November, on the eleventh day of that month, in the evening, after sunset, when, according to my habit, I was contemplating the stars in a clear sky, I noticed that a new and unusual star, surpassing the other stars in brilliancy, was shining almost directly above my head;

*Source:* Tycho Brahe. 1919. "The New Star." From *A Source Book in Astronomy.* Cambridge: Harvard University Press, pp. 233–239.

and since I had, almost from boyhood, known all the stars of the heavens perfectly (there is no great difficulty in attaining that knowledge), it was quite evident to me that there had never before been any star in that place in the sky, even the smallest, to say nothing of a star so conspicuously bright as this. I was so astonished at this sight that I was not ashamed to doubt the trustworthiness of my own eyes. But when I observed that others, too, on having the place pointed out to them, could see that there was really a star there, I had no further doubts. A miracle indeed, either the greatest of all that have occurred in the whole range of nature since the beginning of the world, or one certainly that is to be classed with those attested by the

Holy Oracles, the staying of the Sun in its course in answer to the prayers of Joshua, and the darkening of the Sun's face at the time of the Crucifixion. For all philosophers agree, and facts clearly prove it to be the case, that in the ethereal region of the celestial world no change, in the way either of generation or of corruption, takes place; but that the heavens and the celestial bodies in the heavens are without increase or diminution, and that they undergo no alteration, either in number, or in size, or in light or in any other respect; that they always remain the same, like unto themselves in all respects, no years wearing them away. Furthermore, the observations of all founders of the science, made some thousands of years ago, testify that all the stars have always retained the same number, position, order, motion, and size as they are found, by careful observation on the part of those who take delight in heavenly phenomena, to preserve even in our own day. Nor, do we read that it was ever before noted by any one of the founders that a new star had appeared in the celestial world, except only by Hipparchus,[a] if we are to believe Pliny.[b] For Hipparchus, according to Pliny (Book II of his *Natural History*), noticed a star different from all others previously seen, one born in his own age.

## ITS POSITION WITH REFERENCE TO THE DIAMETER OF THE WORLD AND ITS DISTANCE FROM THE EARTH, THE CENTER OF THE UNIVERSE

It is a difficult matter, and one that requires a subtle mind, to try to determine the distances of the stars from us, because they are so incredibly far removed from the earth; nor can it be done in any way more conveniently and with greater certainty than by the measure of the parallax (diurnal), if a star have one. For if a star that is near the horizon is seen in a different place than when it is at its highest point and near the vertex, it is necessarily found in some orbit with respect to which the Earth has a sensible size. How far distant the said orbit is, the size of the parallax compared with the semidiameter of the Earth will make clear. If, however, a (circumpolar) star, that is as near to the horizon (at lower culmination) as to the vertex (at upper culmination), is seen at the same point of the *Primum Mobile,* there [is] no doubt that it is situated either in the eighth sphere or not far below it, in an orbit with respect to which the whole Earth is as a point.

In order, therefore, that I might find out in this way whether this star was in the region of the Element, or among the celestial orbits, and what its distance was from the Earth itself, I tried to determine whether it had a parallax, and, if so, how great a one; and this I did in the following way: I observed the distance between this star and Schedir of Cassiopeia (for the latter and the new star were both nearly on the meridian), when the star was at its nearest point to the vertex, being only 6 degrees removed from the zenith itself (and for that reason, though it were near the Earth, would produce no parallax in that place, the visual position of the star and the real position then uniting in one point, since the line from the center of the Earth and that from the surface nearly coincide). I made the same observation when the star was farthest from the zenith and at its nearest point to the horizon, and in each case I found that the distance from the above-mentioned fixed star was exactly the same, without the variation of a minute; namely, 7 degrees and 55 minutes. Then I went through the same process, making numerous observations with other stars. From this I conclude that this new star has no diversity of aspect, even when it is near the horizon. For otherwise in its least altitude it would have been farther away from the above-mentioned

---

[a]The new star was observed by Hipparchus in the constellation Scorpio in 143 B.C. [B.]

[b]The *Natural History* of Pliny (23–79) was a compendium of the knowledge of his day, asserting, for example, the four element theory and the spherical shape of the Earth. [B.]

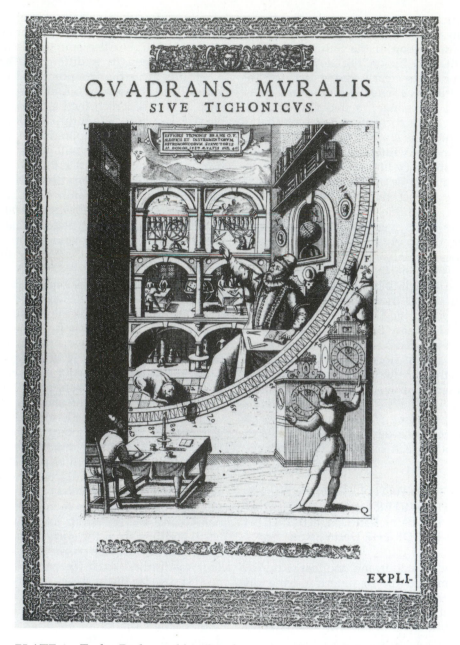

**PLATE 6** Tycho Brahe and his Quadrans muralis or great mural quadrant. From Tycho Brahe, *Astronomiae insturatae mechanica* (1598). Courtesy of the Royal Ontario Museum (Toronto, Ontario).

star in the breast of Cassiopeia than when in its greatest altitude. Therefore, we shall find it necessary to place this star, not in the region of the Element, below the Moon, but far above, in an orbit with respect to which the Earth has no sensible size. For if it were in the highest region of the air, below the hollow region of the Lunar sphere, it would, when nearest the horizon, have produced on the circle a sensible variation of altitude from that which it held when near the vertex.

To make the proof clearer, let a circle be drawn representing the meridian, or some other vertical circle of the *Primum Mobile,* in which the places of all the stars are held to be, and let this circle be *CBDE,* with its center *A.* Let the diameter *BE* indicate the vertex, and *CD* the horizon. Furthermore, let there be described with the same center a circle *MKL,* which shall indicate the circumference of the Earth. Between these let there be drawn another circle *GHFI,* to represent the lowest circle of the lunar sphere and the one nearest the Earth, in which we are to imagine this star to be. And let it first be in its greatest altitude, near the point *G:* it is clear that it is entirely without diversity of aspect; for the two lines one drawn from the center of the Earth, and the other drawn from the eye placed on the surface of the Earth unite in one and the same point of the circle of the *Primum Mobile CBDE,* that is, in the point *B,* or near it if the star is not exactly at *G.* For this star is removed 6 degrees from the vertex, when it is for us at its highest point; which distance, however, produces no sensible variation from the vertex itself. But let this star be placed in the same circle *CHFI* at its lowest altitude, which is the point *O,* and, if the eye is placed at *K* on the surface of the Earth, the star will necessarily be seen in another place on the outermost circle from what it will if the eye is at *A,* the center of the Earth. For, if lines are drawn from *K* on the surface, and *A,* the center of the Earth through *O,* which is the position of the star to the outermost orbit *BDEC,* the line from *A* through *O* will fall in *P,* while the line from *K*

through the same point *O* will fall in *Q. PQ,* therefore is the arc of the *Primum Mobile* showing the diversity of aspect of the star.

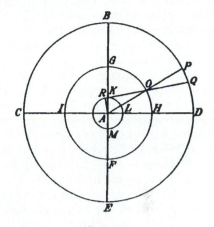

I will try to determine, therefore, the length of the arc *PQ,* so that we may learn how great is the diversity of aspect which this star has when it is at its nearest point to the horizon, if it is placed in the circle *IGHF,* immediately below the orbit of the Moon, at the point *O.* That this may be done more conveniently, let the line *QOK* be produced until another line drawn from the center *A* meets perpendicularly, and let the point of meeting be *R.* Since the angle *BKO* is known by observation—for it is the complement of the least altitude of the star itself namely 62 degrees, 5 minutes—its vertical angle *RKA* will be known, being its equal. Furthermore, the angle *KRA* is by hypothesis a right angle; and the side *KA* is known by some measurement or other, for it is the semi-diameter of the Earth itself. *AR* will be found by Proposition 29 of Regiomontanus[c] concerning plane triangle *ROA,* two sides of which, *RA* and *AO,* are known. For *AO* is the distance from the center of the Earth to the lowest surface

[c]Regiomontanus (1436–1476) translated Ptolemy's *Almagest* from Greek into Latin and assisted with the reform of the Julian calendar. His *On Triangles* (written in 1460, but not published until 1533) introduced modern trigonometry into European scientific circles. [B.]

of the orbit of the Moon, which distance, with Copernicus, I have set at 5,200,000 of the same units in which the semi-diameter of the Earth, *AK*, was reckoned at 100,000 (for I find it best to make use of larger numbers in this computation, that the calculation may be carried on more conveniently and the result be given more exactly); and since in the aforementioned triangle the angle *ORA* is by hypothesis a right angle, the angle *ROA* will be found by the 27th Proposition of Regiomontanus on plane triangles. For by multiplying the side *AR* in to the whole sine, we get 8,863,300,000, which number, being divided by the side *AO*, gives 1699 units, the sine, namely, of the angle *ROA*, whose arc is 0 degrees 58½ minutes; and this number determines the size of the required angle. To this angle *ROA*, the angle *POQ* is equal, since it is its vertical angle, as is manifest from the principles of geometry. Therefore, the arc *PQ*, which is the measure of this angle (for, owing to the immense distance between the lunar sphere and *Primum Mobile*, the arc *PQ* does not differ sensibly from the arc of the circle intercepted by the same lines at the distance *OP*) and indicates the parallax of the star, will be 58½ minutes, which was what we had to find. So great, therefore, would have been the diversity of aspect of this star in the position *O*, as between that place which it held near the vertex and that in which it was seen when nearest the horizon. But after making many careful observations, as I said above, with a most delicate and accurate instrument, I found that this was not the case. From this I conclude that this star which has recently become visible is not in the circle *IGHF*, in the uppermost region, that is, of the air immediately below the orbit of the Moon, nor in any place yet nearer the Earth, for in the latter case the arc *PQ* would have produced a greater length, and the diversity of aspect would be greater; but that it is situated far above the Lunar sphere, in the heaven itself, and in fact in some orbit so far removed from the Earth that the line *KA*, the semi-diameter of the Earth, has no sensible size in

respect to it, but that the whole Earth, when compared to it, is observed to be no more than a point; and this has been found by the founders of the science to be in the eighth sphere or not far from it, in the higher orbits of three superior planets. Therefore, this star will be placed in the heavens themselves, either in the eighth orbit with the other fixed stars or in that of any one of the other planets, is clear from this fact: After the lapse of six months it had not advanced by its own motion a single minute from that place in which I first saw it; and this it must have done if it were in some planetary orbit. For, unlike the *Primum Mobile*, it would be moved by the peculiar motion of the orbit itself, unless it were at rest at one or the other pole of the orbits of the *Secundum Mobile*; from which, however, as I have shown above, it is removed 28 degrees. For the entire orbits, revolving on their own poles, carry along their own stars, or (as I see Pliny and some others hold) are carried along by them; unless, indeed, one would deny the belief accepted by philosophers and mathematicians, and assert (what is absurd) that the stars alone revolve, while the orbits are fixed. Therefore, if this star were placed in some one of the orbits of the seven wandering stars, it would necessarily be carried around with the orbit itself to which it were affixed, in the opposite direction to the daily revolution. And, furthermore, this motion, even in the case of the orbit which moves the slowest, that of Saturn, would, after such a length of time, be noticed, though one were to make his observation without any instrument at all.

Therefore, this new star is neither in the region of the Element, below the Moon, nor among the orbits of the seven wandering stars, but it is in the eighth sphere, among the other fixed stars, which was what we had to prove. Hence it follows that it is not some peculiar kind of comet or some other kind of fiery meteor become visible. For none of these are generated in the heavens themselves, but they are below the Moon, in the upper region of the air, as all philosophers testify; unless one would believe with Albategnius[d] that comets are produced, not in the air, but in the heavens. For he believes that he has observed a comet above the Moon, in the sphere of Venus. That this can be the case, is not yet clear to me. But, please God, sometime, if a comet shows itself in our age, I will investigate the truth of the matter. Even should we assume that it can happen (which I, in company with other philosophers, can hardly admit), still it does not follow that this star is a kind of comet; first, by reason of its very form, which is the same as the form of the real stars and different from the form of all the comets hitherto seen, and then because, in such a length of time, it advances neither latitudinally nor longitudinally by any motion of its own, as comets have been observed to do. For, although these sometimes seem to remain in one place several days, still, when the observation is made carefully by exact instruments, they are seen not to keep the same position for so very long or so very exactly. I conclude, therefore, that this star is not some kind of comet or a fiery meteor, whether these be generated beneath the Moon or above the Moon, but that it is a star shining in the firmament itself; one that has never previously been seen before our time, in any age since the beginning of the world.

[d]Albategnius or Al-Battani (c. 858–929) refined and sometimes improved Ptolemy's measurements, notably, the determination of the equinoxes and the length of the year. His work, which was published in 1537, was widely known during the sixteenth century. [B.]

## FURTHER READING

Christianson, J. R. 2000. *On Tycho's Island: Tycho Brahe and his Assistants, 1570–1601.* Cambridge: Cambridge University Press.

Thoren, Victor E. 1990. *The Lord of Uraniborg: A Biography of Tycho Brahe.* Cambridge: Cambridge University Press.

# A Guide to the Interpretation of Nature

## Francis Bacon (1561–1626)

*The first quarter of the seventeenth century witnessed the appearance of new technical instruments (e.g., the telescope, barometer, thermometer) and the increasing variety of experiments made possible by the flourishing of this new experimental technology. Francis Bacon marks the first systematic attempt to give formal shape to this rapidly emerging experimental science. Indeed, the central feature of his enormously influential philosophy of science is its commitment to the role of observation and experiment as prerequisites for the construction of scientific theory. Where his predecessors regarded experiment as a litmus test of theory that had been derived by a process of deductive reasoning, Bacon took experiment to be the very foundation of science and its generalized methodology. Bacon's work left an indelible imprint on all subsequent philosophical discussions of scientific method.*

*The title of Bacon's work,* Novum Organum, *or* The New Organon *(1620), from which this reading is taken, is based on Aristotle's work on logic, the "Organon" or "Instrument for Rational Thinking." Bacon proposes a new style of reasoning to supplant Aristotle's—one tailored for the pursuit of knowledge in an age of science dominated by the appearance of new instruments and associated experiments. Where Aristotelian science was based on a set of rules that governed the consistency between conclusion and a set of premises accepted unquestioningly as true, Bacon's new experimental style was designed to investigate the soundness of the very foundations of scientific theory—that is, to put nature itself to the test.*

It is part of our plan to set everything out as openly and clearly as possible. For a naked mind is the companion of innocence and simplicity, as once upon a time the naked body was. And therefore we must first lay out the order and plan of our work. It consists of six parts.

---

*Source:* Francis Bacon. 2000. *The New Organon.* Eds. Lisa Jardine and Michael Silverthorne. Cambridge: Cambridge University Press, 14–24.

The first part gives a summary or general description of the science or learning which the human race currently possesses. It seemed good to us to spend some time on what is presently accepted, thinking that this would help the perfection of the old and the approach to the new. We are almost equally eager to develop the old and acquire the new. This also gives us credibility, according to the saying that "an ignorant man will not believe words of knowledge until you have told him what he has in his heart." Therefore, we shall not neglect to sail along the shores of the accepted sciences and arts, importing some useful items into them, in our passage.

However, the divisions of the sciences which we employ include not only things which have been noticed and discovered but also things that until now have been missed but should be there. For in the intellectual as in the physical world, there are deserts as well as cultivated places. And so it is not surprising if we sometimes depart from the customary divisions. An addition not only changes the whole, but necessarily also alters the parts and sections; and the accepted divisions merely reflect the currently accepted outline of the sciences.

In matters which we shall note as missing, we shall be sure to do more than simply suggest a bare title and an outline account of what is needed. For if we report among things missing anything (of some value) whose method seems so obscure that we are justified in suspecting that men will not easily understand what we mean, or what is the task which we imagine and conceive in our mind, we will always take the trouble either to add instructions for carrying out the task or a report of our own performance of a part of it, as an example of the whole; so that we may give some help in each case either by advice or in practice. We feel that our own reputation, as well as the interest of others, requires that no one should suppose that some superficial notions on these matters have simply entered in our heads, and that the things we desiderate and try to grasp are mere wishes. They are such that they are clearly within men's power (unless men fail themselves), and I do have a firm and explicit conception of them. I have undertaken not merely to survey these regions in my mind, like an auger taking the auspices, but to enter them like a general, with a strong will to claim possession. *And this is the first part of the work.*

After coasting by the ancient arts, we will next equip the human understanding to set out on the ocean. We plan therefore, for our second part, an account of a better and more perfect use of reason in the investigation of things and of the true aids of the intellect, so that (despite our humanity and subjection to death) the understanding may be raised and enlarged in its ability to overcome the difficult and dark things of nature. And the art which we apply (which we have chosen to call *Interpretation of Nature*) is an art of logic, though with a great difference, indeed a vast difference. It is true that ordinary logic also claims to devise and prepare assistants and supports for the intellect; in this they are the same. But it differs altogether from ordinary logic in three particular ways: viz., in its end, in its order of demonstration, and in the starting points of its inquiry.

For the end we propose for our science is the discovery of arts, not of arguments, of principles and not of inferences from principles, or signs and indications or works and not probable reasonings. Different results follow from our different design. They defeat and conquer their adversary by disputation; we conquer nature[1] by work.

The nature and order of our demonstration agree with such an end. For in ordinary logic almost all effort is concentrated on the syllogism. The logicians seem scarcely to have thought about induction. They pass it by with barely a mention, and hurry on their formulae for disputation. But we reject proof by syllogism, because it operates in confusion and lets nature slip out of our hands. For, although no one could doubt that things which agree in a middle term, agree also with each other (which has a kind of mathematical certainty), nevertheless, there is a kind of underlying fraud here, in that a syllogism consists of propositions, and propositions consist of words, and words are counters and signs of notions. And therefore if the very notions of the mind (which are like the soul of words, and the basis of every such structure and fabric) are badly or carelessly abstracted from things, and are vague and not defined with sufficiently clear outlines, and thus deficient in many ways, everything falls to pieces. And therefore we reject the syllogism; and not only so far as principles are concerned (they do not use it for that either) but also for intermediate propositions, which the syllogism admittedly deduces and generates in a certain fashion, but without effects, quite divorced from practice and completely irrelevant to the active part of the sciences. For even if we leave to the syllogism and similar celebrated but notorious kinds of demonstration jurisdiction over the popular arts which are based on opinion (for we have no ambitions in this area), still for the nature of things we use induction throughout, and as much for the minor propositions as for the major ones. For we regard *induction* as the form of demonstration which respects the senses, stays close to nature, fosters results and is almost involved in them itself.

And so the order of demonstration also is completely reversed. For the way the thing has normally been done until now is to leap immediately from sense and particulars to the most general propositions, as to fixed poles around which disputations may revolve; then to derive everything else from them by means of intermediate propositions; which is certainly a short route, but dangerously steep, inaccessible to nature and inherently prone to disputations. By contrast, by our method, axioms are gradually elicited step by step, so that we reach the most general axioms only at the very end; and the most general axioms come out not as notional, but as well defined, and such as nature acknowledges as truly known to her, and which live in the heart of things.

By far the biggest question we raise is as to the actual form of induction, and of the judgment made on the basis of induction. For the form of induction which the logicians speak of, which proceeds by simple enumeration, is a childish thing, which jumps to conclusions, is exposed to the danger of instant contradiction, observes only familiar things and reaches no result.

What the sciences need is a form of induction which takes experience apart and analyzes it, and forms necessary conclusions on the basis of appropriate exclusions and rejections. And if the logicians' usual form of judgment has been so difficult and required so much intellectual exertion, how much more effort should we expend on this other judgment, which is drawn not only from the depths of the mind but from the bowels of nature?

And this is not all. For we place the foundations of the sciences deeper and lay them lower, and set our starting points further back than men have ever done before, subjecting them to examination, while ordinary logic accepts them on the basis of others' belief. For logicians borrow (if I may put it this way) the principles of the sciences from the particular sciences themselves; then they pay respect to the first notions of the mind; finally they are happy with the immediate perceptions of healthy senses. But our position is that true logic should enter the provinces of the individual sciences with greater authority than is in our own principles, and compel those supposed principles themselves to give an account as to what extent they are firmly established. As for the first notions of the intellect: not one of the things which the intellect has accumulated by itself escapes our suspicion, and we do not confirm them without submitting them to a new trial and verdict given in accordance with it. Furthermore, we have many ways of scrutinizing the information of the senses themselves. For the senses often deceive, but they also give evidence of their own errors; however the errors are to hand, the evidence is far to seek.

The senses are defective in two ways: They may fail us altogether or they may deceive. First, there are many things which escape the senses even when they are healthy and quite unimpeded; either because of the rarity of the whole body or by the extremely small size of its parts, or by distance, or by its slowness or speed, or because the object is too familiar, or for other reasons. And even when the senses do grasp an object, their apprehensions of it are not always reliable. For the evidence and information given by the senses is always

**PLATE 7**    Portrait of Francis Bacon.

based on the analogy of man not of the universe; it is a very great error to assert that the senses are the measure of things.

So to meet these defects, we have sought and gathered from every side with great and faithful devotion, assistants to the senses, so as to provide substitutes in the case of total failure and correction in the case of distortion. We do this not so much with instruments as with experiments. For the subtlety of experiments is far greater than that of the senses themselves even when assisted by carefully designed instruments; we speak of experiments which have been devised and applied specifically for the question under investigation with skill and good technique. And therefore we do not rely very much upon the immediate and proper perception of the senses, but we bring the matter to the point that the senses judge only of the experiment, the experiment judges of the thing. Hence we believe that we have made the senses (from which, if we prefer not to be insane we must derive everything in natural things) sacred high priests of nature and skilled interpreters of its oracles; while others merely seem to respect and humor the senses, we do so in actual fact. Such are the preparations which we make for the light of nature and its kindling and application; and they would be sufficient in themselves if men's understanding were unbiased, a blank slate. But as men's minds have been occupied in so many strange ways that they have no even, polished surface available to receive the true ray of things, it is essential for us to realize that we need to find a remedy for this, too.

The *Idols*[2] by which the mind is occupied are either artificial or innate. The artificial *idols* have entered men's minds either from the doctrines and sects of philosophers or from perverse rules of proof. The innate idols are inherent in the nature of the intellect itself, which is found to be much more prone to error than the senses. For however much men may flatter themselves and run into admiration and almost veneration of the human mind, it is quite certain that, just as an uneven mirror alters the rays of things from their proper shape and figure, so also the mind, when it is affected by things through the senses, does not faithfully preserve them, but inserts and mingles its own nature of things as it forms and devises its own notions.

The first two kinds of *idols* can be eliminated, with some difficulty, but the last in no way. The only strategy remaining is, on the one hand, to indict them, and to expose and condemn the mind's insidious force, in case after the destruction of the old, new shoots of error should grow and multiply from the poor structure of the mind itself, and the result would be that errors would not be squashed but simply altered; and on the other hand, to fix and establish forever the truth that the intellect can make no judgment except by induction in its legitimate form. Hence the teaching which cleanses the mind to make it receptive to truth consists of three refutations: a refutation of philosophies; a refutation of proofs; and a refutation of natural human reason. When we have dealt with these, and clarified the part played by the nature of things and the part played by the nature of the furnished and adorned the bedchamber for the marriage of the mind and the universe. In the wedding hymn we should pray that men may see born from this union the assistants that they need and a lineage of discoveries which may in some part conquer and subdue the misery and poverty of man. *And this is the second part of the work.*

But we plan not only to show the way and build the roads, but also to enter upon them. And therefore the third part of our work deals with the *Phenomena of the Universe,* that is, every kind of experience, and the sort of natural history which can establish the foundations of philosophy. A superior method of proof or form of interpreting nature may defend and protect the mind from error and mistake, but it cannot supply or provide material for knowledge. But those who are determined not to guess and take omens but to discover and know, and not to make up fairytales and stories about worlds, but to inspect and analyze the nature of this real world, must seek everything from things themselves. No substitute or alternative in the way of intelligence, thought or argument can take the place of hard work and investigation and the visitation of the world, not even if all the genius of all the world worked together. This then we must unfailingly do or abandon the business forever. But to this very day men have acted so foolishly that it is no wonder that nature does not give them access to her.

For in the first place, the information of the senses themselves is defective and deceiving; observation is lazy, uneven and casual; teaching is empty and based on hearsay; practice is slovenly bent on results; experimental initiative is blind, unintelligent, hasty, and erratic; and natural history is shallow and superficial. Between them they have accumulated very poor material for the intellect to construct philosophy and the sciences.

And the tendency to introduce subtle and intricate disputation prematurely comes too late to remedy a situation which is utterly desperate, and does nothing to move on the enterprise or remove error. Thus there is no hope of major development or progress except in a renewal of the sciences.

Its beginnings must come from a natural history, and a natural history of a new kind with a new organization. It would be pointless to polish the mirror if there were no images; and clearly we must get suitable material for the intellect, as well as making reliable instruments. And our history (like our logic) differs from that now in use in many ways: in its purpose or task, in its actual extent and composition, in its subtlety, and also in the selection and arrangement of it in relation to the next stage.

First we propose a natural history which does not so much amuse by the variety of its contents or give immediate profit a first breast to feed philosophy. For although our ultimate aim is works and the active part of science, still we wait for harvest time and do not try to reap moss and the crop while it is still green. We know very well that axioms properly discovered bring whole companies of works with them, revealing them not singly but in quantity. But we utterly condemn and reject the childish desire to take some pledges prematurely, in the form of new works, like an apple of Atalanta which shows the race.[3] Such is the task of our natural history.

And as for its composition, we are making a history not only for nature free and unconstrained (when nature goes its own way and does its own work), such as a history of the bodies of heaven and the sky, of land and sea, or minerals, plants and animals; but much more of nature confined and harassed, when it is forced from its own condition by art and human agency, and pressured and molded. And therefore we give a full description of all the experiments of the mechanical arts, all the experiments of the applied part of the liberal arts, and all the experiments of several practical arts which we have not yet formed a specific art of their own (so far as we have had an opportunity to investigate and they are relevant to our purpose). Moreover (to be plain) we put much more effort and many more resources into this part than into the other, and pay no attention to men's disgust or what they find attractive, since nature reveals herself more through the harassment of art than in her own proper freedom.

And we do not give a history of bodies only; we felt that we should also take the trouble to make a separate history of the powers themselves (which plainly constitute the originals of nature, since they are the material for the first passions and desires, viz., *Dense, Rare, Hot, Cold, Solid, Liquid, Heavy, Light* and many others).

As for subtlety, we are certainly looking for a kind of experience which is far more subtle and simple than those which simply happen. For we bring and draw many things out of obscurity which no one would ever have thought to investigate if he were not following the sure and steady path to the discovery of causes. For in themselves they are of no great use, so that it is quite clear that they have not been sought for themselves. Rather they are to things and works exactly like the letters of the alphabet to speech and words: though useless in themselves, they are still the elements of all discourse.

And in the choice of narratives and experiences we think that we have served men better than those who have dealt with natural history in the past. For we use the evidence of our own eyes, or at least or our own perception, in everything, and apply the strictest criteria in accepting things; so that we exaggerate nothing in our reports for the sake of sensation, and our narrations are free and untouched by fable and foolishness. We also specifically proscribe and condemn many widely accepted falsehoods (which have prevailed for many centuries by a kind of neglect and are deeply engrained), so that they may not trouble the sciences any more. For as someone wisely remarked that the stories and superstitions and trifles which nurses instill into children also seriously deprave their minds,[4] by the same reasoning we feel we must be careful, and even anxious, that philosophy should not at the start get into the habit of any kind of foolishness as we foster and nurture its infancy in the form of natural history. In every experiment which is new and even the least bit subtle, even if (as it seems to us) it is sure and proven, we give a frank account of the method of the experiment we used; so that after we have revealed every move we made men may see any hidden error attached to it, and may be prompted to find more reliable, more meticulous proofs (if any exist); and finally we sprinkle warnings, reservations, and cautions in all directions, with the religious scruple of an exorcist casting out and banishing every kind of fantasy.

Finally, since we have seen how much experience and history distort the sight of the human mind, and how difficult it is (especially for tender or prejudiced minds) at first to get used to nature, we often add our own observations, which are like the first turn or move of history towards philosophy (perhaps one might say, the first glance). They are intended to be like a pledge to men that they will not be forever floundering in the waves of history, and that when we come to the work of the understanding everything will be more ready for action. By such a natural history (as we have outlined) we believe that men may make a safe, convenient approach to nature and supply good, prepared material to the understanding.

After[5] we have surrounded the intellect with the more trustworthy aides and bodyguards, and have used the most stringent selection to build a fine army of divine works, it may seem that nothing remains to be done but to approach philosophy itself. But in such a difficult and doubtful task there are certain points which it seems necessary to introduce first, partly for instruction and partly for their immediate usefulness.

The first point is to give examples of investigation and discovery by our way and method, as exhibited in certain subjects. We particularly choose subjects which are most different from each other; so that in every *genus* we may have an example. We are not speaking of examples added to individual percepts and rules for illustration (these were given in abundance in our second part); we simply mean types and variations, which may bridge before our eyes the whole procedure of the mind and the seamless fabric and order of its discovery of things, in certain subjects, which will be diverse and striking. The analogy that suggests itself in mathematics demonstration is easy and clear when the machine is used, whereas without this convenience everything seems complicated and more subtle than it really is. And so we devote the *fourth part* of our work to such examples, and thus it is truly and simply a particular and detailed application of the second part.

The *fifth part* is useful only for a time until the rest is completed; and is given as a kind of interest until we get the capital. We are not driving blindly towards our goal and ignoring the useful things that come up on the way. For this reason the fifth part of our work consists of things which we have either discovered, demonstrated or added, not on the basis of our methods and instructions for interpretation, but from the same intellectual habits as other people generally employ in investigation and discovery. For while we expect, from our constant converse with nature, greater things from our reflections than our intellectual capacity might suggest, these temporary results in the meantime serve as shelters built along the road for the mind to rest in for a while as it presses on towards more certain things. However, we insist in the meantime that we do not wish to be held to these results themselves, because they have not been discovered or demonstrated by the true form of interpretation. One should not be frightened of such a suspension of judgment in a doctrine which does not assert simply that nothing can be known, but that nothing can be known except in a certain order and by a certain method; and meanwhile it has set up some degrees of certitude for use and comfort until the mind reaches its goal of explanation of its causes. Nor were the schools of philosophers who maintained *lack of conviction*[6] inferior to those who claimed a freedom to make pronouncements. Yet the former did not provide assistance to the sense and understanding, as we have done, but totally undermined belief and authority; which is a very different thing and almost the opposite.

Finally the *sixth* part of our work (which the rest supports and serves) at last reveals and expounds the philosophy which is derived and formed from the kind of correct, pure, strict inquiry which we have already framed and explained. It is beyond our ability and beyond our expectation to achieve this final part and bring it to completion. We have made a start on the task, a start which we hope is not despicable; the end will come from the fortune of mankind, such an end perhaps as in the present condition of things and present state of thought men cannot easily grasp or guess. It is not merely success in speculation which is in question, but the

human situation, human fortune, and the whole potential of works. For man is nature's agent and interpreter; he does and understands only as much as he has observed of the order of nature in works or in inference; he does not know and cannot do more. No strength exists that that can interrupt or break that chain of causes; and nature is conquered only by obedience. Therefore these two goals of man, *knowledge* and *power,* a pair of twins, are really come to the same thing, and works are chiefly frustrated by ignorance of causes.

The whole secret is to never let the mind's eye stray from things themselves, and to take images exactly as they are. May God never allow us to publish a dream of our imagination as a model of the World, but rather graciously grant us the power to describe the true appearance and revelation of the prints and traces of the Creator in his creatures.

And therefore Father, You who have given visible light as the first fruits of creation and, at the summit of Your works, have breathed intellectual light into the face of man, protect and govern this work, which began in Your goodness and returns to Your glory. After You had turned to view the works which Your hand had made, You saw all things were very good and you rested. But man, turning to the works which his hands have made, saw that all things were vanity and vexation of spirit,[7] and has had no rest. Wherefore if we labor in Your works, You will make us to share in Your vision and Your Sabbath. We humbly beseech you that this mind may remain in us; and that you may be pleased to bless the human family with new mercies, through our hands and the hands of those others whom You will give the same.

## NOTES

1. Reading *natura,* for the *natura* of the edition of 1620. This is the reading which Kitchin's translation presupposes. See *The Novum Ogranum; or, A True Guide to the Interpretation of Nature, by Francis Bacon, Lord Verulum* by the Rev. G.W. Kitchin (Oxford University Press, 1855).

2. "Idols" is the usual translation of Bacon's famous *idola*. We too have used it on most occasions, but the meaning of some passages seemed to be better conveyed by the translation "illusion" . . .
3. This was one of the golden balls (or apples) which Milanion threw in front of Atalanta while he was racing her, so that he could win the race and her hand in marriage.
4. Perhaps a reference to Plato, *Republic* 377A, 387B, *Laws* 793D ff., and elsewhere.
5. This is the beginning of the fourth part.
6. Bacon uses the Greek word *acatalepsia,* the mark of the ancient Skeptics.
7. Ecclesiastes, 1:14.

## FURTHER READINGS

Jardine, Lisa and Stewart, A. 1998. *Hostage to Fortune: The Troubled Life of Francis Bacon.* London: Gollancz.

Rossi, P. 1968. *Francis Bacon: From Magic to Science.* Trans. Sacha Rabinovich. London: Routledge & Kegan Paul.

Zagorin, P. 1998. *Francis Bacon.* Princeton: Princeton University Press.

# The Sun of the Microcosm

## William Harvey (1578–1657)

*In 1628, William Harvey announced the circulation of the blood, arguably the most important discovery of the modern period in anatomy and physiology. Galen had elaborated a tripartite system in which the liver, heart, and brain each injected into the body three different spirits and, consequently, that the arteries and veins carried different substances. Drawing on careful experimental calculations of blood flow and the knowledge that the valves in the veins are placed so that blood is allowed to move freely toward the heart but not away from it, Harvey reasoned that blood was pumped to the limbs through the arteries and returned through the veins. Blood passes through the right to the left side of the heart, not via the septum, which was solid, but through the lungs. Observing that the arteries begin to fill at the moment of contraction (systole), it was also clear that blood is pumped from the heart (the sun of the microcosm) into the arteries. Diastole, on the other hand, is related to the filling of the heart.*

*Harvey's critics eagerly pointed out that he failed to specify a connection between the arterial and venous systems, and it was only in 1661 that Marcello Malpighi (1628–1694) first described capillaries from his microscopical observations of lung tissue.* Exercitatio anatomica de motu cordis et sanguinis in animalibus *(1628: Anatomical Treatise on the Movement of the Heart and Blood in Animals)—from which this reading is taken—remains a monument to the style of the natural philosophy of the seventeenth century: the rejection of traditional authority, the emphasis on first-hand experience, and the use of analogies with mechanical devices to make sense of natural systems.*

*Source:* William Harvey. 1976. *An Anatomical Disputation Concerning the Movement of the Heart and Blood in Living Creatures.* Trans. Gweneth Whitteridge. London: Blackwell Scientific Publications, pp. 10–22; 29–30; 32–35; 38–40; 42–47; 50–54; 56–61; 66–68; 70–72; 74–77; 80–83; 86–87; 89–93; 100–102; 103–104; 107–110; 114–117; 120–124; 128–133.

Seeing that we are thinking of the movement, pulse, action, use and usefulness of the heart and arteries, it is of considerable importance first to set forth those things which have been published by others, and to take notice of the things which have been commonly said and taught, so that what has been rightly spoken may be confirmed and what is false corrected in the light of anatomical dissection, personal experience many times repeated, and diligent and precise observation . . .

But since the movement and composition of the heart is different from that of the lungs, and the movement and compositions of the arteries are different from that of the chest, it is probable that different uses and benefits should arise from this, and that the pulse of the heart and its use, and likewise that of the arteries, should differ greatly from that of the chest and the lungs. For, if the pulse and respiration serve the same uses, and if in diastole the arteries draw air into their cavities, as it is commonly said, and in systole send forth fuliginous vapors through the same pores of the flesh and skin, and, furthermore, if in the time between systole and diastole they contain air, at any one time they must contain either air or spirits or fuliginous[a] vapors. What then should these writers reply to Galen, who wrote a book to show that blood was naturally contained in the arteries and nothing but blood, that is, neither spirits nor air, as we can easily conclude from the experiments and arguments in the same book. And if in diastole the arteries are filled with air which they have taken in, in a greater pulse the greater will be the quantity of air entering. Therefore, if, when there is a great pulse, you immerse the whole body in a bath of water or oil, the pulse must needs be immediately either smaller or slower, seeing that it is difficult for the air to permeate into the arteries through the surrounding water of the bath, if not impossible. Moreover, since all the arteries, both the deep and the cutaneous, are distended at the same moment and with the

same speed, how can the air pass through the skin, flesh and whole fabric of the body into its depths, as freely and swiftly as it can through the skin alone? And how do the arteries of the fetus draw air from the outside into their cavities through the mother's belly and the body of the womb? Or again, how do seals, whales, and dolphins, and the whole race of cetaceans and all fish in the bottom of the sea take in air through such a great mass of water, and give it out again by the swift pulse in the systole and diastole of their arteries? But to say that they suck up the air implanted in the water and return their fuliginous vapors into it, is not unlike a fiction. And if in systole the arteries drive out the fuliginous vapors from their cavities through the pores of the flesh and of the skin, why not the spirits likewise, which they say are contained there too, since spirits are much finer than sooty fumes? And if the arteries in their systole and diastole take in air and give it out again, as the lungs do in respiration, why do they not do this when a wound is inflicted by the cutting of an artery? If the trachea is cut by a wound, it is as plain as the noonday sun that the air goes in and comes out in two contrary movements. But when an artery is cut, immediately the blood is driven out by force in one continuous movement, and it is obvious that air does neither go in or come out. If the pulsations of the arteries refrigerate the parts of the body and ventilate them as the lungs do the heart itself, in what way is it commonly said that the arteries carry from the heart to each part of the body the blood crammed full of vital spirits that nourish the heat of the parts, awake this heat from slumber and restore it when it is spent? And how comes it that, if you tie the arteries, the parts are straightway not only numbed and cold, and look pale, but at last, cease to be nourished, which happens, according to Galen, because they are deprived of that heat which previously flowed out through all the parts from the heart, since it is clear from this that arteries carry heat to the parts rather than cooling and ventilation. Besides, how can diastole at

---

[a]In Galenic physiology, fuliginous vapours or "sooty fumes" were the byproduct of a process called "concoction," which took place in the left ventricle. Vital spirits from air were mixed with blood that seeped across the septum from the right ventricle. According to Galen, fuliginous vapors left the body by passing through the pulmonary vein to the lungs. [B.]

one and the same time draw spirits from the heart to warm the parts, and cold from outside the body? Further, although some affirm that the lungs, arteries and heart serve the same uses, yet they say that the heart is the laboratory of the spirits, that the arteries contain spirits and send them abroad, but, contrary to the opinion of Columbus,[b] they deny that the lungs make the spirits or retain them. And yet these same men affirm with Galen against Erasistratus[c] that blood is contained in the arteries and not spirits.

These opinions seem so to war with one another and to refute each other, that all of them are not undeservedly suspect. That blood is contained in the arteries, and that the arteries carry blood only, is obvious from Galen's experiment . . . from arteriotomy and from wounds, and likewise from the fact which Galen also affirms in very many places that from a cut artery in the space of one half hour, the whole mass of blood will be emptied out of every part of the body in a great and forcible profusion. The experiment of Galen is this: "If you bind the artery at both ends with a fine cord and slit it open lengthwise down the middle, you will find that what is contained in the artery between the two ligatures is nothing except blood." And so he proves that it contains only blood. From this we can argue also in the same way: If, after tying and slitting the veins in the same manner, we find in the veins the same blood that is in the arteries (a thing

[b]Matheus Realdus Colombo (1516–1559), a pupil of Vesalius, correctly described in 1559 the pulmonary or lesser circulation—the passage of blood from the right to the left side of the heart via the lungs. Similar views can be found in a number of other sixteenth century writers. Columbo did not recognize the significance of his achievement. [B.]

[c]Erasistratus (c. 304 B.C.–c. 250 B.C.), a late Alexandrian anatomist, contended that the arteries carry air or *pneuma*, a view that was routed by Galen (c. 130–c. 199) who showed that there was a connection between the arterial and venous systems. [B.]

which I have often tried myself in dead men and in living animals), we may conclude likewise by the same reasoning that the arteries contain the same blood as the veins, and nothing but the same blood. Some, while they attempt to resolve this difficulty by affirming that the blood in the arteries is arterial blood, full of spirits, silently concede that it is the function of the arteries to carry the blood from the heart into the whole body, and that the arteries are full of blood, for blood that is full of spirits is nonetheless blood . . .

But the contrary is obvious, both in arteriotomy and in wounds, for the blood comes rushing out of the arteries, leaping violently, sometimes further, sometimes nearer, by fits and starts, but the leaping of it is always in the diastole of the artery and not in the systole. From this it plainly appears that the artery is distended by the impulsion of blood. For while it is being distended, the artery cannot of itself throw out the blood with such force. Instead, according to those things which are commonly related about the use of arteries, it ought to attract air into itself through the wound . . .

These, and other difficulties like them, follow from the opinions that have been set down concerning the pulse and the use of the arteries. Perhaps those things which have been asserted concerning the use and pulse of the heart are no less entangled with very many and inextricable difficulties. Men commonly assert that the heart is the fountain and laboratory of the vital spirits by which it gives life to all the parts, and yet they deny that the right ventricle makes the spirits and say that it only provides nourishment for the lungs. And hence they say that fish have no right ventricle of the heart, and indeed that it is altogether wanting in those creatures that have no lungs, and that the right ventricle of the heart was made for the sake of the lungs.

1. Why then, I ask you, since the constitution of both ventricles is almost the same in that they have the same construction

of fibers, muscular bands, valves, vessels and auricles, and in dissection are both found full of blood that is in both blackish and lumpy, why, I say, should we think that they were appointed to such diverse uses, seeing that their action, motion and pulsation is the same in both? If the three tricuspid valves at the entrance into the right ventricle are a hindrance to the return of blood into the vena cava, and if the three semilunar valves in the orifice of the pulmonary artery are made to impede the regress of blood, why, since things are similarly arranged, should we deny that the valves in the left ventricle were made likewise to hinder the progress and regress of blood?

2. Why, since the valves are almost identical in size, shape and position in the left ventricle as in the right, why do they say that here in the left ventricle they hinder the progress and regress of spirits, and in the right that of blood? It seems unlikely that the same organ can possibly be adapted to hinder the motion of blood and of spirits alike.

3. And why, since the passages and vessels correspond to one another in point of size, that is the pulmonary artery and the pulmonary vein, why should the one be destined to a particular use, namely to nourish the lungs, and the other to a general use?

4. And, as Columbo[d] observed, how is it provable that so much blood is needed to nourish the lungs, for indeed this vessel, the pulmonary artery, is bigger in size than both the branches of the descending vena cava that supply the femoral veins?

5. And lastly I ask why, since the lungs are so near and the vessel so great and the

[d]In addition to his demonstration of the pulmonary circulation, Colombo published detailed descriptions of the pleura, peritoneum, and other organs. [B.]

lungs in continual motion, why is there need for a pulse in the right ventricle, and why is it that nature, for the sake of nourishing the lungs, found it necessary to add a second ventricle to the heart?

When they say that the left ventricle draws material from the lungs and from the right ventricle of the heart, that is to say air and blood, to prepare the spirits, and likewise distributes the spirituous blood into the aorta, and that from this left ventricle fuliginous vapors, on the one hand, are sent back through the pulmonary vein into the lungs, and, on the other, spirits into the aorta, what is it that makes the separation between them, and how is it that spirits and fuliginous vapors pass this way and that without mingling or confusion? If the mitral valves do not hinder the return of fuliginous vapors to the lungs, how can they hinder the return of air? And how do the tricuspid semilunar valves prevent the return of spirits from the aorta in the subsequent diastole of the heart? And by what manner of way do they say that the spirituous blood is distributed from the left ventricle through the pulmonary vein into the lungs, and the mitral valves not hinder it the while, seeing that they affirm that through this same vessel the air enters into the left ventricle from the lungs, the air to whose return they would have these mitral valves to be a hindrance? Good God! How do the mitral valves impede the return of air and not of blood? . . .

But, I beseech you, if the pulmonary vein were made for the conveyance of air, why does it have the constitution of a vein? Nature had need rather of pipes and those annular ones, like those in the bronchi, so that they might always stay open and not collapse, and so that they might remain altogether empty of blood lest its wetness should hinder the passage of air, a thing which is plain enough when we breathe with a whistling and a rumbling noise when the lungs are in trouble, either stuffed with phlegm from the bronchi, or at least laden with a little.

Still less to be tolerated is that opinion which, supposing that two kinds of material, air and blood, are necessary for the making of the vital spirits, does assert that the blood seeps through hidden pores in the septum of the heart, out of the right ventricle into the left, and that the air is drawn in through the great vessel, the pulmonary vein, out of the lungs, and therefore in the septum of the heart there are many pores adapted for the exuding of blood. But, in God's truth, there are no such pores, nor can any be demonstrated.

For the substance of the septum of the heart is thicker and more compact than any part of the body except the bones and sinews. But if there were holes, how was it possible, since both the ventricles are distended and dilated at the same time, for the one to draw anything from the other, or the left draw blood from the right?

When I first applied my mind to observation from the many dissections of living creatures as they came to hand, that by that means I might find out the use and benefits of the motion of the heart through actual inspection with my own eyes, and not from books and the writings of other men, I straightway found it a thing hard to be obtained and full of difficulty, so that I almost believed with Fracastorius[e] that the motion of the heart was known to God alone. For I could rightly distinguish neither how systole nor diastole came to be, nor when nor where the dilatation and the constriction occurred, and that by reason of the quickness of the motion which in many creatures appeared and disappeared in the twinkling of an eye, like the passing of lightning, so that I thought that I sometimes saw systole on this side and diastole on that, sometimes quite the reverse, and sometimes the movements

were changing and without order. And so I was much troubled in mind and did not know what to think, whether what I myself had concluded or whether to believe others, and I did not wonder at that which Andreas Laurentius[f] had written that the motion of the heart was like the ebbing and flowing of Euripus[g] to Aristotle.

At last, using daily more search and diligence, by often looking into many and different sorts of living creatures, by collecting and comparing many observations, I believed that I had hit the nail on the head, unwinded and freed myself from this labyrinth and had gained the knowledge I so much desired, that of the movement and use of the heart and arteries. Since then I have not been afraid both privately to my friends and publicly in my anatomical lectures, after the fashion of the Academy, to deliver my opinion on this matter . . .

First then, in the hearts of all creatures that are still living, after you have opened the chest and cut up the capsule which immediately surrounds the heart, you may observe that the heart moves sometimes, sometimes rests, and that there is a time when it moves and when it moves not.

All this is more evident in the hearts of colder creatures, as toads, snakes, frogs, snails, lobsters, crustaceans, mollusks, shrimps and all manner of little fish. Everything is also more evident in the hearts of warmer animals, like dogs and pigs, if you observe attentively until the heart begins to die and to beat more faintly and, as it were, to be deprived of life. Then you may clearly and plainly see the movements of the heart becoming slower and less frequent and its moments of stillness longer; and you may observe and distinguish more conveniently both the kind of movement that it has and

---

[e] Girolamo Fracastoro (*c.* 1478–1553) authored a book (1530) on syphilis, a disease that he named, which appeared in Europe at the end of the fifteenth century with the Seige of Naples by the French Army of Charles VIII. [B.]

[f] André du Laurens (1558–1609) was the author of *Historia anatomica* (1600), a Galenic medical text widely used in Harvey's time. [B.]

[g] Euripus was a long, narrow channel which was renowned in antiquity for the violent flow and reflow of its tide. [B.]

# Naturally Accelerated Motion

## Galileo Galilei (1564–1642)

*Although he was seventy-six years old at the time, the publication of* Discorsi . . . a due nuove scienze . . . *(1638: Discourse on Two New Sciences) was Galileo's most remarkable scientific achievement. This work introduced an entirely new kind of physics, one that mathematized physical concepts and appealed to careful measurements of natural motions. With his new deductive method, Galileo was able to offer a conclusive mathematical proof for his discovery of the law of free fall three decades previously. In a series of experiments involving rolling balls down inclined planes, he showed that freely falling bodies, whether heavy or light, have the same constant acceleration ($s = \frac{1}{2} at^2$, where s is speed, a acceleration, and t time), and that a body moving on a perfectly smooth surface would neither speed up nor slow down. Where the received Aristotelian science opposed motion and rest, Galileo placed them on the same level as states of matter, thereby providing the critical first step to the law of inertia— the very foundation for the new science that would culminate in the physics of Isaac Newton.*

*Although Galileo is justly regarded as the first modern physicist, his mature treatises are written in dialogue form. More literary than scientific, this style gave full range to Galileo's formidable polemical skills and biting sarcasm. The* Two New Sciences *involves three people—Salviati (who presents Galileo's own views by having him recite passages from a manuscript of an unnamed author), Sagredo (another scholar skilled in mechanics), and Simplicio (the dogged proponent of Aristotelian doctrine). The dialogue is divided into four "days" or parts. This reading is taken from the third day, when the discussion turns to the subject of accelerated motion.*

## ON NATURALLY ACCELERATED MOTION[1]

*Those things that happen which relate to equable motion have been considered in the preceding book; next, accelerated motion is to be treated of.*

And first, it is appropriate to seek out and clarify the definition that best agrees with that [accelerated motion] *which nature employs. Not that there is anything wrong with inventing at pleasure some kind of motion and theorizing about its consequent properties, in the way that some men have derived spiral and conchoidal lines from certain motions, though nature makes no use of these [paths]; and by pretending these, men have laudably demonstrated their essentials from assumptions [ex suppositione]. But since nature does employ a certain kind of acceleration*

*Source:* Galileo. 1974. *Two New Sciences.* Trans. Stillman Drake. Toronto: Wall & Thompson, pp. 153–167.

*for descending heavy things, we decided to look into their properties so that we might be sure that the definition of accelerated motion which we are about to adduce agrees with the essence of naturally accelerated motion. And at length, after continual agitation of mind, we are confident that this has been found, chiefly for the very powerful reason that the essentials successively demonstrated by us correspond to, and are seen to be in agreement with, that which physical experiments [naturalia experimenta] show forth to the senses. Further, it is as though we have been led by the hand to the investigation of naturally accelerated motion by consideration of the custom and procedure of nature herself in all her other works, in the performance of which she habitually employs the first, simplest, and easiest means. And indeed, no one of judgment believes that swimming or flying can be accomplished in a simpler or easier way than that which fish and birds employ by natural instinct.*

*Thus when I consider that a stone, falling from rest at some height, successively acquires new increments of speed, why should I not believe that those additions are made by the simplest and most evident rule?[2] For if we look into this attentively, we can discover no simpler addition and increase than that which is added on always in the same way. We easily understand that the closest affinity holds between time and motion, and thus equable and uniform motion is defined through uniformities of times and spaces; and indeed, we call movement equable when in equal times equal spaces are traversed. And by this same equality of parts of time, we can perceive the increase of swiftness to be made simply, conceiving mentally that this motion is uniformly and continually accelerated in the same way whenever, in any equal times, equal additions of swiftness are added on.*

*Thus, taking any equal particles of time whatever, from the first instant in which the moveable departs from rest and descent is begun, the degree of swiftness acquired in the first and second little parts of time [together] is double the degree that the moveable acquired in the first little part [of time]; and the degree that it gets in three little parts of time is triple; and in four, quadruple that same degree [acquired] in the first particle of time. So, for clearer understanding, if the move-* *able were to continue its motion at the degree of momentum of speed acquired in the first little part of time, and were to extend its motion successively and equably with that degree, this movement would be twice as slow as [that] at the degree of speed obtained in two little parts of time. And thus it is seen that we shall not depart far from the correct rule if we assume that intensification of speed is made according to the extension of time; from which the definition of the motion of which we are going to treat may be put thus:*

## [Definition]

*I say that that motion is equably or uniformly accelerated which, abandoning rest, adds on to itself equal momenta of swiftness in equal times.*

Sagr. Just as it would be unreasonable for me to oppose this, or any other definition whatever assigned by any author, all [definitions] being arbitrary, so I may, without offense, doubt whether this definition, conceived and assumed in the abstract, is adapted to, suitable for, and verified in the kind of accelerated motion that heavy bodies in fact employ in falling naturally. And since it seems that the Author promises us that what he has defined is the natural motion of heavy bodies, I should like to hear you remove certain doubts that disturb my mind, so that I can then apply myself with better attention to the propositions that are expected, and their demonstrations.

Salv. It will be good for you and Simplicio to propound the difficulties, which I imagine will be the same ones that occurred to me when I first saw this treatise, and that our Author himself put to rest for me in our discussions, or that I removed for myself by thinking them out.

Sagr. I picture to myself a heavy body falling. It leaves from rest, that is, from the deprivation of any speed whatever, and enters into motion in which it goes accelerating according to the ratio of increase of time from its first instant of motion. It will have obtained, for example, eight degrees of speed in eight pulse-beats, of which at the fourth beat it will have gained four; at the second [beat], two; and at the first, one. Now, time being infinitely divisible, what follows from this? The speed being always diminished in this ratio, there will be no degree of speed, however small (or we might say, "no degree of slowness, however great"), such that the moveable will not be found to have this [at some time] after its departure from infinite slowness, that is, from rest. Thus, if the degree of speed that it had at four beats of time were such that, maintaining this uniformly, it would run two miles in one hour, while with the degree of speed that it had at the second beat it would have made one mile an hour, it must be said that in instants of time closer and closer to the first [instant] of its moving from rest, it would be found to be so slow that, continuing to move with this slowness, it would not pass a mile in an hour, nor in a day, nor in a year, nor in a thousand [years], and it would not pass even one span[a] in some still longer time. Such events I find very hard to accommodate in my imagination, when our senses show us that a heavy body in falling arrives immediately at a very great speed.

*Salv.*  This is one of the difficulties that gave me pause at the outset; but not long afterward I removed it, and its removal was effected by the same experience that presently sustains it for you.

You say that it appears to you that experience shows the heavy body, having hardly left from rest, entering into a very considerable speed; and I say that this same experience makes it clear to us that the first impetuses of the falling body, however heavy it may be, are very slow indeed. Place a heavy body on some yielding material, and leave it until it has

pressed as much as it can with its mere weight. It is obvious that if you now raise it one or two braccia, and then let it fall on the same material, it will make a new pressure on impact, greater than it made by its weight alone. This effect will be caused by the falling moveable in conjunction with the speed gained in fall, and will be greater and greater according as the height is greater from which the impact is made; that is, according as the speed of the striking body is greater. The amount of speed of a falling body, then, we can estimate without error from the quality and quantity of its impact.

But tell me, gentlemen: if you let a sledge fall on a pole from a height of four braccia, and it drives this, say, four inches into the ground, and will drive it much less from a height of two braccia, and still less from a height of one, and less yet from a span only; if finally it is raised but a single inch, how much more will it accomplish than if it were placed on top [of the pole] without striking it at all? Certainly very little. And its effect would be quite imperceptible if it were lifted only the thickness of a leaf. Now, since the effect of impact is governed by the speed of a given percussent, who can doubt that its motion is very slow and minimal when its action is imperceptible? You now see how great is the force of truth, when the same experience that seemed to prove one thing at first glance assures us of the contrary when it is better considered.

But without restricting ourselves to this experience, though no doubt it is quite conclusive, it seems to me not difficult to penetrate this truth by simple reasoning. We have a heavy stone, held in the air at rest. It is freed from support and set at liberty; being heavier than air, it goes falling downward, not with uniform motion, but slowly at first and continually accelerated thereafter. Now, since speed may be increased or diminished *in infinitum,* what argument can persuade

---

[a]The span of the arms (now the English *fathom*). [B.]

me that this moveable, departing from infinite slowness (which is rest), enters immediately into a speed of ten degrees rather than into one of four, or into the latter before a speed of two, or one, or one-half, or one one-hundredth? Or, in short, into all the lesser [degrees] *in infinitum?*

Please hear me out. I believe you would not hesitate to grant me that the acquisition of degrees of speed by the stone falling from the state of rest may occur in the same order as the diminution and loss of those same degrees when, driven by impelling force, the stone is hurled upward to the same height. But if that is so, I do not see how it can be supposed that in the diminution of speed in the ascending stone, consuming the whole speed, the stone can arrive at rest before passing through every degree of slowness.

*Simp.* But if the degrees of greater and greater tardily are infinite, it will never consume them all, and this rising heavy body will never come to rest, but will move forever while always slowing down—something that is not seen to happen.

*Salv.* This would be so, Simplicio, if the moveable were to hold itself for any time in each degree; but it merely passes there, without remaining beyond an instant. And since in any finite time [*tempo quanto*], however small, there are infinitely many instants, there are enough to correspond to the infinitely many degrees of diminished speed. It is obvious that this rising heavy body does not persist for any finite time in any one degree of speed, for if any finite time is assigned, and if the moveable had the same degree of speed at the first instant of that time and also at the last, then it could likewise be driven upward with this latter degree [of speed] through as much space [again], just as it was carried from the first [instant] to the second; and at the same rate it would pass from the second to a third,

and finally, it would continue its uniform motion *in infinitum.*

*Sagr.* From this reasoning, it seems to me that a very appropriate answer can be deduced for the question agitated among philosophers as to the possible cause of acceleration of the natural motion of heavy bodies. For let us consider that in the heavy body hurled upwards, the force [*virtu*] impressed upon it by the thrower is continually diminishing, and that this is the force that drives it upward as long as this remains greater than the contrary force of its heaviness; then when these two [forces] reach equilibrium, the moveable stops rising and passes through a state of rest. Here the impressed impetus is [still] not annihilated, but merely that excess has been consumed that it previously had over the heaviness of the moveable, by which [excess] it prevailed over this [heaviness] and drove [the body] upward. The diminutions of this alien impetus then continuing, and in consequence the advantage passing over to the side of the heaviness, descent commences, though slowly because of the opposition of the impressed force, a good part of which still remains in the moveable. And since this continues to diminish, and comes to be overpowered in ever-greater ratio by the heaviness, the continual acceleration of the motion arises from there.[3]

*Simp.* The idea is clever, but more subtle than sound; for if it were valid, it would explain only those natural motions which had been preceded by violent motion, in which some part of the external impetus still remained alive. But where there is no such residue, and the moveable leaves from longstanding rest, the whole argument loses its force.

*Sagr.* I believe you are mistaken, and that the distinction of cases made by you is superfluous, or rather, is idle. For tell me: can the thrower impress on the projectile sometimes much force, and sometimes little, so that it may be driven upward a hundred braccia, or twenty, or four, or only one?

*Simp.* No doubt he can.

*Sagr.* No less will the force impressed be able to overcome the resistance of heaviness by so little that it would not raise [the body] more than an inch. And finally, the force of projection may be so small as just to equal the resistance of the heaviness, so that the moveable is not thrown upward, but merely sustained. Thus, when you support a rock in your hand, what else are you doing but impressing on it just as much of that upward impelling force as equals the power of its heaviness to draw it downward? And do you not continue this force of yours, keeping it impressed through the whole time that you support [the rock] in your hand? Does the force perhaps diminish during the length of time that you support the rock? Now, as to this sustaining that prevents the fall of the rock, what difference does it make whether it comes from your hand, or a table, or a rope tied to it? None whatever. You must conclude, then, Simplicio, that it makes no difference at all whether the fall of the rock is preceded by a long rest, or a short one, or one only momentary, and that the rock always starts with just as much of the force contrary to its heaviness as was needed to hold it at rest.

*Salv.* The present does not seem to me to be an opportune time to enter into the investigation of the cause of the acceleration of natural motion, concerning which various philosophers have produced various opinions, some of them reducing this to approach to the center; others to the presence of successively less parts of the medium [remaining] to be divided; and others to a certain extrusion by the surrounding medium which, in rejoining itself behind the moveable, goes pressing and continually pushing it out. Such fantasies, and others like them, would have to be examined and resolved, with little gain. For the present, it suffices our Au-

thor that we understand him to want us to investigate and demonstrate some attributes [passions] of a motion so accelerated (whatever be the cause of its acceleration) that the momenta of its speed go increasing, after its departure from rest, in that simple ratio with which the continuation of time increases, which is the same as to say that in equal times, equal additions of speed are made. And if it shall be found that the events that then shall have been demonstrated are verified in the motion of naturally falling and accelerated heavy bodies,[4] we may deem that the definition assumed includes that motion of heavy things, and that it is true that their acceleration goes increasing as the time and the duration of motion increases.

*Sagr.* By what I now picture to myself in my mind, it appears to me that this could perhaps be defined with greater clarity, without varying the concept [as follows]: Uniformly accelerated motion is that in which the speed goes increasing according to the increase of space traversed. Thus for example, the degree of speed acquired by the moveable in the descent of four braccia would be double that which it had after falling through the space of two, and this would be the double of that resulting in the space of the first braccio.[b] For there seems to me to be no doubt that the heavy body coming from a height of six braccia has, and strikes with, double the impetus that it would have from falling three braccia, and triple that which it would have from two, and six times that had in the space of one.[5]

*Salv.* It is very comforting to have had such a companion in error, and I can tell you that your reasoning has in it so much of the plausible and probable, that our Author himself did not deny to me, when I proposed it to him, that he had labored

[b]The speed in fact is proportional to the square root of the distance, as proved below ($v^2 = 2as$). [B.]

for some time under the same fallacy. But what made me marvel then was to see revealed, in a few simple words, to be not only false but impossible, two propositions which are so plausible that I have propounded them to many people, and have not found one who did not freely concede them to me.

*Simp.*  Truly, I should be one of those who concede them. That the falling heavy body *vires acquirat eundo* [acquires force in going],[6] the speed increasing in the ratio of the space, while the momentum of the same percussent is double when it comes from double height, appear to me as propositions to be granted without repugnance or controversy.

*Salv.*  And yet they are as false and impossible as [it is] that motion should be made instantaneously, and here is a very clear proof of it. When speeds have the same ratio as the spaces passed or to be passed, those spaces come to be passed in equal times;[7] if therefore the speeds with which the falling body passed the space of four braccia were the doubles of the speeds[8] with which it passed the first two braccia, as one space is double the other space, then the times of those passages are equal; but for the same moveable to pass the four braccia and the two in the same time cannot take place except in instantaneous motion. But we see that the falling heavy body makes its motion in time, and passes the two braccia in less [time] than the four; therefore it is false that its speed increases as the space. The other proposition is shown to be false with the same clarity. For that which strikes being the same body, the difference and momenta of the impacts must be determined only by the difference of the speeds;[9] if therefore the percussent coming from a double height delivers a blow of double momentum it must strike with double speed; but double speed passes the double space in the same time, and we see the time of descent to be longer from the greater height.[10]

*Sagr.*  Too evident and too easy is this [reasoning] with which you make hidden conclusions manifest. This great facility renders the conclusions less prized than when they were under seeming contradiction. I think that people generally will little esteem ideas gained with so little trouble, in comparison with those over which long and irresolvable altercations are waged.

*Salv.*  Things would not be so bad if men who show with great brevity and clarity the fallacies of propositions that have commonly been held to be true by people in general received only such bearable injury as scorn in place of thanks. What is truly unpleasant and annoying is a certain other attitude that some people habitually take. Claiming, in the same studies, at least parity with anyone that exists, these men see that the conclusions they have been putting forth as true are later exposed by someone else, and shown to be false by short and easy reasoning. I shall not call their reaction envy, which then usually transforms itself into rage and hatred against those who reveal such fallacies, but I do say that they are goaded by a desire to maintain inveterate errors rather than to permit newly discovered truths to be accepted. This desire sometimes induces them to write in contradiction to those truths of which they themselves are only too aware in their own hearts, merely to keep down the reputations of other men in the estimation of the common herd of little understanding. I have heard from our Academician not a few such false conclusions, accepted as true and [yet] easy to refute; and I have kept a record of some of these.

*Sagr.*  And you must not keep them from us, but must share them with us some time, even if we need a special session for the purpose. But now, taking up our thread again, it seems to me that we have at this point fixed the definition of uniformly accelerated motion, of which we shall treat in the ensuing discussion; and it is this:

### [Definition]

*We shall call that motion equably or uniformly accelerated which abandoning rest adds on to itself equal momenta of swiftness in equal times.*

*Salv.* This definition established, the Author requires and takes as true one single assumption; that is:

### [Postulate]

*I assume that the degrees of speed acquired by the same moveable over different inclinations of planes are equal whenever the heights of those planes are equal.*[11]

He calls the "height" of an inclined plane that vertical from the upper end of the plane which falls on the horizontal line extended through the lower end of the said inclined plane. For an understanding of this, take line *AB* parallel to the horizon, upon which are the two inclined planes *CA* and *CD*; the vertical *CB*, falling to the horizontal *BA*, is called by the Author the height [or altitude, or elevation] of planes *CA* and *CD*. Here he assumes that the degrees of speed of the same moveable, descending along the inclined planes *CA* and *CD* to points *A* and *D*, are equal, because their height is the same *CB*; and the like is also to be understood of the degree of speed that the same body falling from the point *C* would have at *B*.

*Sagr.* This assumption truly seems to me to be so probable as to be granted without

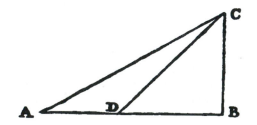

argument, supposing always that all accidental and external impediments are removed, and that the planes are quite solid

and smooth, and that the moveable is of perfectly round shape, so that both plane and moveable alike have no roughness. With all obstacles and impediments removed, my good sense [*il fume naturale*] tells me without difficulty that a heavy and perfectly round ball, descending along the lines *CA*, *CD*, and *CB*, would arrive at the terminal points A D, and *B* with equal impetus.

*Salv.* You reason from good probability. But apart from mere plausibility, I wish to increase the probability so much by an experiment that it will fall little short of equality with necessary demonstration. Imagine this page to be a vertical wall, and that from a nail driven into it, a lead ball of one or two ounces hangs vertically, suspended by a fine thread two or three braccia in length, *AB*. Draw on the wall a horizontal line *DC*, cutting at right angles the vertical *AB*, which hangs a couple of inches out from the wall; then, moving the thread *AB* with its ball to *AC*, set the ball free. It will be seen first to descend, describing the arc *CB*, and then to pass the point *B*, running along the arc *BD* and rising almost up to the parallel marked *CD*, falling short of this by a very small interval and being prevented from arriving there exactly by the impediment of the air and the thread.[12] From this we can truthfully conclude that the impetus acquired by the ball at point *B* in descent through arc *CB* was sufficient to drive it back up again to the same height through a similar arc *BD*. Having made and repeated this experiment several times, let us fix in the wall along the vertical *AB*, as at *E* or *F*, a nail extending out several inches, so that the thread *AC*, moving as before to carry the ball *C* through the arc *CB*, is stopped when it comes to *B* by this nail, *E*, and is constrained to travel along the circumference *BG*, described about the center *E*. We shall see from this that the same impetus can be made that, when reached at *B* before, drove this same moveable through the arc *BD* to the

height of horizontal *CD,* but now, gentle-
men, you will be pleased to see that the
ball is conducted to the horizontal at
point *G.* And the same thing happens if
the nail is placed lower down, as at *F,*
whence the ball will describe the arc *BI,*
ending its rise always precisely at the
same line, *CD.* If the interfering nail is so
low that the thread advancing under it
could not get up to the height *CD,* as
would happen when the nail was closer
to point *B* than to the intersection of *AB*
with the horizontal *CD,* then the thread
will ride on the nail and wind itself
around it.

This experiment leaves no room for
doubt as to the truth of our assumption,

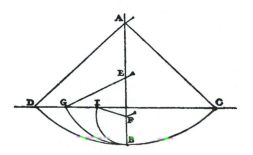

for the two arcs *CB* and *DB* being equal
and similarly situated, the acquisition of
momentum made by descent through the
arc *CB* is the same as that made by descent through the arc *DB;* but the momentum acquired at *B* through arc *CB* is able
to drive the same moveable back up
through arc *BD,* whence also the momentum acquired in the descent *DB* is equal
to that which drives the same moveable
through the same arc from *B* to *D.* So that
in general, every momentum acquired by
descent through an arc equals one which
can make the same moveable rise through
that same arc; and all the momenta that
make it rise through all the arcs *BD, BG,*
and *BI* are equal, because they are created
by the same momentum acquired
through the descent *CB,* as experiment
shows. Hence all the momenta acquired

through descents along arcs *DB, GB,* and
*IB* are equal.

*Sagr.* The argument appears to me conclusive, and the experiment is so well
adapted to verify the postulate that it
may very well be worthy of being con-
ceded as if it had been proved.

*Salv.* I do not want any of us to assume
more than need be, Sagredo; especially
because we are going to make use of this
assumption chiefly in motions made
along straight surfaces, and not curved
ones, in which acceleration proceeds by
degrees very different from those that we
assume it to take when it proceeds in
straight lines.[13] The experiment adduced
thus shows us that descent through arc
*CB* confers such momentum on the moveable as to reconduct it to the same height
along any of the arcs *BD, BG,* or *BI.* But
we cannot show on this evidence that the
same would happen when [even] a most
perfect sphere is to descend along straight
planes inclined according to the tilt of the
chords of those arcs. Indeed, we may believe that since straight planes would
form angles at point *B,* a ball that had descended along the incline through the
chord *CB* would encounter obstruction
from planes ascending according to
chords *BD, BG,* or *BI;* and in striking
against those, it would lose some of its
impetus, so that in rising it could not get
back to the height of line *CD.* But if the
obstacle that prejudices this experiment
were removed, it seems to me that the
mind understands that the impetus,
which in fact takes [its] strength from the
amount of the drop, would be able to
carry the moveable back up to the same
height.

Hence, let us take this for the present
as a postulate, of which the absolute truth
will be later established for us by our seeing that other conclusions, built on this
hypothesis, do indeed correspond with
and exactly conform to experience.[14] This
postulate alone having been assumed by
the Author, he passes on to the proposi-

tions, proving them demonstratively; and the first is this:

## Proposition 1. Theorem 1

*The time in which a certain space is traversed by a moveable in uniformly accelerated movement from rest is equal to the time in which the same space would be traversed by the same moveable carried in uniform motion whose degree of speed is one-half the maximum and final degree of speed of the previous, uniformly accelerated, motion.*[15]

*Let line AB represent the time in which the space CD is traversed by a moveable in uniformly accelerated movement from rest at C. Let EB, drawn in any way upon AB, represent the maximum and final degree of speed increased in the instants of the time AB. All the lines reaching AE from single points of the line AB and drawn parallel to BE will represent the increasing degrees of speed after the instant A. Next, I bisect BE at F, and I draw FG and AG parallel to BA and BF; the parallelogram AGFB will [thus] be constructed, equal to the triangle AEB, its side GF bisecting AE at I.*

*Now if the parallels in triangle AEB are extended as far as IG, we shall have the aggregate of all parallels contained in the the quadrilateral*

*equal to the aggregate of those included in triangle AEB, for those in triangle IEF are matched by*

*those contained in triangle GIA, while those which are in the trapezium AIFB are common. Since each instant and all instants of time AB correspond to each point and all points of line AB, from which points the parallels drawn and included within triangle AEB represent increasing degrees of the increased speed, while the parallels contained within the parallelogram represent in the same way just as many degrees of speed not increased but equable, it appears that there are just as many momenta of speed consumed in the accelerated motion according to the increasing parallels of triangle AEB, as in the equable motion according to the parallels of the parallelogram. GB For the deficit of momenta in the first half of the accelerated motion (the momenta represented by the parallels in triangle AGI falling short) is made up by the momenta represented by the parallels of triangle IEF.*

*It is therefore evident that equal spaces will be run through in the same time by two movables, of which one is moved with a motion uniformly accelerated from rest, and the other with equable motion having a momentum one-half the momentum of the maximum speed of the accelerated motion; which was [the proposition] intended.*

## Proposition II. Theorem II

*If a movable descends from rest in uniformly accelerated motion, the spaces run through in any times whatever are to each other as the duplicate ratio of their times; that is, are as the squares of those times.*

*Let the flow of time from some first instant A be represented by the line AB, in which let there be taken any two times, AD and AE. Let HI be the line in which the uniformly accelerated moveable descends from point H as the first beginning of motion; let space HL be run through in the first time AD, and HM be the space through which it descends in time AE. I say that space MH is to space HL in the duplicate ratio of time EA to time AD. Or let us say that spaces MH and HL have the same ratio as do the squares of EA and AD.*

*Draw line AC at any angle with AB. From points D and E draw the parallels DO and EP, of which DO will represent the maximum degree of speed acquired at instant* D *of time* AD, *and* PE *the maximum degree of speed acquired at instant* E *of time* AE.

*Since it was demonstrated above that as to spaces run through, those are equal to one another of which one is traversed by a moveable in uniformly accelerated motion from rest, and the other is traversed in the same time by a moveable carried in equable motion whose speed is one-half the maximum acquired in the accelerated motion, it follows that spaces* MH *and* LH *are the same that would be traversed in times* EA *and* DA *in equable motions whose speeds are as the halves of* PE *and* OD. *Therefore if it is shown that these spaces* MH *and* LH *are in the duplicate ratio of the times* EA *and* DA, *what is intended will be proved.*

*Now in Proposition IV of Book I [*"On Uniform Motion,"* above] it was demonstrated that the spaces run through by movables carried in equable motion have to one another the ratio compounded from the ratio of speeds and from the ratio of times. Here, indeed, the ratio of speeds is the same as the ratio of times, since the ratio of one-half* PE *to one-half* OD, *or of* PE *to* OD, *is that of* AE *to* AD. *Hence the ratio of spaces run through is the duplicate ratio of the times; which was to be demonstrated.*

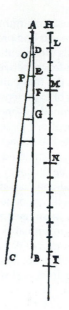

*It also follows from this that this same ratio of spaces is the duplicate ratio of the maximum degrees of speed; that is, of lines* PE *and* OD, *since* PE *is to* OD *as* EA *is to* DA.

## NOTES

1. It is significant that this title refers to natural rather than to uniform acceleration. Galileo's central topic is free fall, and he defines uniformity on the basis of natural phenomena. This reverses the medieval procedure, in which a purely mathematical analysis of accelerated motion was carried out, often illustrated by ingenious examples but never based on reference to free fall.
2. A more ordinary, intuitive view was that the simplest rule was to take the ever changing speeds as proportional to distances traversed from rest . . .
3. What Sagredo presents here was Galileo's own first approach to the question of natural acceleration by seeking its cause; cf. *On Motion.* pp. 89–91 (*Opere*, I, 319–20) . . .
4. . . . Rejection of causal inquiries was Galileo's most revolutionary proposal in physics, inasmuch as the traditional goal of that science was the determination of causes.
5. It is true that impact is proportional to the height of fall, but this does not apply to the speed acquired, as Sagredo assumes . . . Galileo had made this assumption in 1604, in effect using it to define "velocity" physically (*Opere, X,* 115; VIII, 373).
6. Virgil, *Aeneid* iv.175, where the reference is to rumor.

7. . . . The ensuing argument may be an application of this rule to instantaneous velocities, whereas it had previously been proved only for finite motions.

8. The plurals are essential to Galileo's concept, which is that of establishing a one to one correspondence between all possible speeds in the whole motion and all possible speeds in the first half of it. For speeds proportional to distances, this leads to a contradiction of experience, though for speeds proportional to time it does not.

9. If "determined by" means "proportional to," this inference is incorrect, since impact is proportional not to velocity but to its square . . . Fall through doubled height does in fact double the impact, but this results from speed increased as the square root of two, and not from doubled speed. Galileo appears here to believe the apparent doubling of impact to be illusory . . .

10. The logical conclusion here is that the blow delivered is not one of doubled momentum, since it cannot be of doubled speed (denial of consequent). The argument is so elliptical as to suggest a confusion of terminal speed with overall speed, which in the context is improbable. More likely, Galileo expected the reader to review the preceding argument in full.

11. An attempted demonstration of this postulate was added at Galileo's request to editions after 1638, and was placed immediately before Prop. III, below . . .

12. Mention of the thread shows that Galileo continued to adhere to his belief that even in the absence of any medium, a flexible pendulum would eventually stop; see *Dialogue*, pp. 230–231 *(Opere, Vll, 257)*.

13. Galileo had known this as early as 1602 from the fact that a body descends more swiftly along conjugate chords of a circular arc than along its chord, though the latter path is the shorter *(Opere, X, 100)*. Cf. the scholium to Prop. XXXVI . . .

14. The reference here is not to the attempted demonstration preceding Theorem III, below, which was composed later . . . The certainty referred to here derives from observed agreements.

15. Characteristic of Galileo's concern with actual events (note 8, above) is his utilization of one half the terminal speed, which could be measured by observing horizontally deflected bodies. Medieval writers assumed an ideal mean speed to measure every uniformly accelerated motion directly. Galileo's proof matched elements in two infinite aggregates for each instant and all instants, conceiving that in uniform motion there is not one single speed but infinitely many, all equal, and corresponding to the infinitely many speeds, all different, in accelerated motion.

## FURTHER READING

Cohen, I. Bernard. 1991. *Birth of a New Physics.* New York: W. W. Norton & Company.

Drake, Stillman. 2001. *Galileo: A Very Short Introduction.* Oxford: Oxford University Press.

# Causes of Motion

## René Descartes (1596–1650)

*René Descartes' celebrated assertion, "cogito ergo sum" (I think, therefore I am), is widely acknowledged as the starting point of modern philosophy. What is less often recognized is that, in many respects, Descartes was the first modern cosmologist; his scientific writings signify the first attempt to bring a single set of principles to bear on terrestrial and celestial phenomena. Descartes' cosmological speculations have been overshadowed by the dynamical science of motion proposed by Isaac Newton, as well as by his own lasting contributions to modern philosophy. However, he was the architect of a coherent and plausible cosmology that stood at the forefront of natural philosophy for the better part of a century and played a leading role in the demise of the deeply entrenched Scholasticism of the Schools.*

*Descartes' cosmology is founded on the conviction that nature is a machine, an idea that can be traced back to the armillary spheres with which the medieval astronomer imitated the real celestial intelligences that transported the planets through the skies. With Descartes, however, this idea received a new and powerful expression—all natural phenomena, from the motions of celestial bodies to animal and vegetative life, are explicated in terms of the geometrical property of extension and its proper modes (size, shape, position, and the disposition of its parts to be moved). What distinguishes Descartes' mechanical cosmology from similar views advocated by the English philosopher Thomas Hobbes (1588–1679), and the French savant Pierre Gassendi (1592–1656), is that it attempted to restate substantive results in optics, astronomy, and in mathematics in order to forge a foundation in physical theory for the Copernican hypothesis, which Descartes accepted on account of its simplicity and clarity.*

*Descartes spent the period from 1629 to 1633 preparing a comprehensive statement of his mechanical cosmology with the working title,* Le monde. *Upon learning of the condemnation of Galileo's* Dialogue Concerning the Two Chief Systems of the World *in 1633 by the Congregation of the Holy Office for advancing the Copernican hypothesis, Descartes elected to withhold this treatise. The better part of this treatise was published posthumously as two separate works—*Treatise on Man *in 1662 and* The World *(the work from which this reading is taken) in 1664.*

*Source:* Descartes, René. 1985. *The World.* In John Cottingham, Robert Stoothoff, and Dugald Murdoch, eds., *The Philosophical Writings of Descartes.* Cambridge: Cambridge University Press, pp. 85–98.

## DESCRIPTION OF A NEW WORLD; AND THE QUALITIES OF THE MATTER OF WHICH IT IS COMPOSED

For a while, then, allow your thought to wander beyond this world to view another world—a wholly new one which I shall bring into being before your mind in imaginary spaces. The philosophers tell us that such spaces are infinite, and they should certainly be believed, since it is they themselves who invented them. But in order to keep this infinity from hampering and confusing us, let us not try to go right to the end: Let us enter it only far enough to lose sight of all the creatures that God made five or six thousand years ago; and after stopping in some definite place, let us suppose that God creates anew so much matter all around us that in whatever direction our imagination may extend, it no longer perceives any place which is empty.

Even though the sea is not infinite, people on some vessel in the middle of it may stretch their view seemingly to infinity; and yet there is more water beyond what they see. Likewise, although our imagination seems able to stretch to infinity, and this new matter is not supposed to be infinite, yet we can suppose that it fills spaces much greater than all those we have imagined. And just to ensure that this supposition contains nothing you might find objectionable, let us not allow our imagination to extend as far as it could; let us intentionally confine it to a determinate space which is no greater, say, than the distance between the Earth and the principal stars in the heavens, and let us suppose that the matter which God has created extends indefinitely far beyond in all directions. For it is much more reasonable to prescribe limits to the action of our mind than to the works of God, and we are much better able to do so.

Now since we are taking the liberty of fashioning this matter as we fancy, let us attribute to it, if we may, a nature in which there is absolutely nothing that everyone cannot know as perfectly as possible. To this end, let us expressly suppose that it does not have the form of earth, fire, or air, or any other more specific form, like that of wood, stone, or metal. Let us also suppose that it lacks the qualities of being hot or cold, dry or moist, light or heavy, and of having any taste, smell, sound, color, light, or other such quality in the nature of which there might be said to be something which is not known clearly by everyone.

On the other hand, let us not also think that this matter is the "prime matter" of the philosophers, which they have stripped so thoroughly of all its forms and qualities that nothing remains in it which can be clearly understood. Let us rather conceive it as a real, perfectly solid body which uniformly fills the entire length, breadth and depth of this huge space in the midst of which we have brought our mind to rest. Thus, each of its parts always occupies a part of that space which it fits so exactly that it could neither fill a larger one nor squeeze into a smaller; nor could it, while remaining there, allow another body to find a place there.

Let us add that this matter may be divided into as many parts having as many shapes as we can imagine, and that each of its parts is capable of taking on as many motions as we can conceive. Let us suppose, moreover, that God really divides it into many such parts, some larger and some smaller, some of one shape and some of another, however we care to imagine them. It is not that God separates these parts from one another so that there is some void between them: Rather, let us regard the differences he creates within this matter as consisting wholly in the diversity of the motions he gives to its parts. From the first instant of their creation, he causes some to start moving in one direction and others in another, some faster and others slower (or even, if you wish, not at all); and he causes them to continue moving, thereafter, in accordance with the ordinary laws of nature. For God has established these laws in such a marvelous way that even if we suppose he creates nothing beyond what I have mentioned,

**PLATE 10**   Nineteenth century engraving of René Descartes.

and sets up no order or proportion within it but composes from it a chaos as confused and muddled as any the poets could describe, the laws of nature are sufficient to cause the parts of this chaos to disentangle themselves, and arrange themselves in such good order that they will have the form of a quite perfect world; a world in which we shall be able to see not only light but also all the other things, general as well as particular, which appear in the real world.

But before I explain this at greater length, pause again for a bit to consider this chaos, and observe that it contains nothing which you do not know so perfectly that you could not even pretend to be ignorant of it. For, as regards the qualities I have put into it, you may have noticed that I supposed them to be only of such a kind that you could imagine them. And, as regards the matter from which I have composed it, there is nothing simpler or easier to know in inanimate creatures. The idea of this matter is included to such an extent in all the ideas that our imagination can form that you must necessarily conceive it or else you can never imagine anything at all.

Nevertheless, the philosophers are so subtle that they can find difficulties in things which seem extremely clear to other men, and the memory of their "prime matter," which they know to be rather hard to conceive, may divert them from knowledge of the matter of which I am speaking. Thus, I must tell them at this point that, unless I am mistaken, the whole difficulty they face with their matter arises simply from their wanting to distinguish it from its own quantity, and from its external extension, that is, from the property it has of occupying space. In this, however, I am quite willing for them to think they are right, for I have no intention of stopping to contradict them. But they should also not find it strange if I suppose that the quantity of the matter I have described does not differ from its substance any more than number differs from the things numbered. Nor should they find it strange if I conceive its extension, or the property it has of occupying space, not as an accident, but as its true form and essence. For they cannot deny that it can be conceived quite easily in this way. And my purpose is not to explain, as they do, the things which are in fact in the real world, but only to make up, as I please, a world in which there is nothing that the dullest minds are incapable of conceiving, and which nevertheless, could be created exactly as I have imagined it.

Were I to put into this new world the least thing that is obscure, this obscurity might well conceal some hidden contradiction. I had not perceived, and hence, without thinking, I might be supposing something impossible. Instead, since everything I propose here can be distinctly imagined, it is certain that even if there were nothing of this sort in the old world, God can nevertheless create it in a new one. For it is certain that he can create everything we can imagine.

## THE LAWS OF NATURE OF THIS NEW WORLD

But I do not want to delay any longer telling you by what means nature alone can untangle the confusion of the chaos of which I have spoken, and what the laws are that God has imposed on it.

Note, in the first place, that by "nature" here I do not mean some goddess or any other sort of imaginary power. Rather, I am using this word to signify matter itself, in so far as I am considering it taken together with all the qualities I have attributed to it, and under the condition that God continues to preserve it in the same way that he created it. For it follows of necessity, from the mere fact that he continues thus to preserve it, that there must be many changes in its parts which cannot, it seems to me, properly be attributed to the action of God (because that action never changes), and which therefore I attribute to nature. The rules by which these changes take place I call the "laws of nature."

In order to understand this better, recall that among the qualities of matter, we have supposed that its parts have had various different motions from the moment they were created, and furthermore that they are all in contact with each other on all sides without there being any void between any two of them. From this it follows necessarily that from the time they began to move, they also began to change and diversify their motions by colliding with one another. So if God subsequently preserves them in the same way that he created them, he does not preserve them in the same state. That is to say, with God always acting in the same way and consequently always producing substantially the same effect, there are, as if by accident, many differences in this effect. And it is easy to accept that God, who is, as everyone must know, immutable, always acts in the same way. But without involving myself any further in these metaphysical considerations, I shall set out two or three of the principal rules according to which it must be thought that God causes the nature of this new world to operate. These, I believe, will suffice to acquaint you with all the others.

The first is that each individual part of matter continues always to be in the same state so long as collision with others does not force it to change that state. That is to say, if the part has some size, it will never become smaller unless others divide it; if it is round or square, it will never change that shape unless others force it to; if it is brought to rest in some place, it will never leave that place unless others drive it out; and if it has once begun to move, it will always continue with an equal force until others stop or retard it.[a]

There is no one who does not believe that this same rule holds in the old world with respect to size, shape, rest and numerous other such things. But the philosophers have excluded motion from the rule which is just

the thing I most definitely wish to include in it. Do not think, however, that I intend to contradict them: The motion they speak of is so very different from the one I conceive that it may very easily happen that what is true of the one is not true of the other.

They admit themselves that the nature of their motion is very little understood. To render it in some way intelligible they have not yet been able to explain it more clearly than in these terms: *Motus est actus entis in potentia, prout in potentia est.*[b] For me these words are so obscure that I am compelled to leave them in Latin because I cannot interpret them. (And in fact the sentence "Motion is the actuality of a potential being in so far as it is potential" is no clearer for being translated.) By contrast, the nature of the motion I mean to speak of here is so easy to know that the geometers, themselves, who among all men are the most concerned to conceive very distinctly the things they study, have judged it simpler and more intelligible than the nature of their surfaces and lines—as is shown by the fact that they have explained "line" as the motion of a point and "surface" as the motion of a line.

The philosophers also posit many motions which they think can take place without any bodies changing place, like those they call *motus ad formam, motus ad calorem, motus ad quantitatem* ("motion with respect to form," "motion with respect to heat," "motion with respect to quantity") and numerous others. For my part, I am not acquainted with any motion except that which is easier to conceive than the lines of the geometers; the motion which makes bodies pass from one place to another and successively occupy all the spaces which exist in between.

In addition, the philosophers attribute to the least of these motions a being much more solid and real than they attribute to rest, which they say is nothing but the privation of motion. For my part, I conceive of rest as a quality too, which should be

---

[a]This ontological equivalence of rest and motion is the very heart of the new idea of motion fashioned by Descartes. Motion and rest are similarly positive states of bodies that are conserved in the absence of external actions. [B.]

[b]This definition is advanced by Aristotle in his *Physics*, III, 201[a]10. [B.]

*Motion the fundamental feature of cosmology.*

attributed to matter while it remains in one place, just as motion is a quality attributed to matter while it is changing place.

Finally, the motion of which they speak has a very strange nature; for whereas all other things have their perfection as an end and strive only to preserve themselves, it has no other end and no other goal than rest and, contrary to all the laws of nature, it strives of its own accord to destroy itself. By contrast, the motion which I posit follows the same laws of nature as do generally all the dispositions and qualities found in matter—including those which the Schoolmen call *modos et entia rationis cum fundamento in re* ("conceptual modes and entities founded in things") as well as those they call *qualitates reales* (their "real qualities," in which I confess frankly that I can find no more reality than in the others).

I suppose as a second rule that when one body pushes another it cannot give the other any motion unless it loses as much of its own motion at the same time; nor can it take away any of the other's motion unless its own is increased by as much.[c] This rule, together with the preceding, agrees very well with all the observations in which we see one body begin or cease to move because it is pushed or stopped by another one. For, having supposed the preceding rule, we are free from the difficulty in which the Schoolmen find themselves when they wish to explain why a stone continues to move for some time after leaving the hand of the one who threw it. For we should ask, instead, why does the stone not continue to move forever? Yet the reason is easy to give. For who can deny that the air in which it is moving offers it some resistance? We hear it whistle when it cuts through the air; and if a fan, or some other very light and extensive body, is moved through the air, we shall even be able to feel by the weight in our

*impetus*

*Galileo*

hand that the air is impeding its motion rather than keeping it moving, as some have wanted to say. But suppose we refuse to explain the effects of the air's resistance in accordance with our second rule, and we think that the more resistance a body can offer the greater its capacity to check the motion of other bodies (as perhaps we might be persuaded at first). In this case we shall have great difficulty explaining why the motion of the stone is reduced more in colliding with a soft body, which offers moderate resistance than when it collides with a harder body which resists it more. Likewise, we shall find it difficult to explain why, as soon as it has encountered some resistance in the latter, it immediately turns in its tracks rather than stopping or interrupting its motion on that account. On the other hand, if we accept this rule, there is no difficulty at all. For it tells us that the motion of one body is retarded by its collision with another, not in proportion to how much the latter resists it, but only in proportion to how much the latter's resistance is overcome, and to the extent that the latter obeys the rule by taking on the force of motion that the former gives up.

Now, in most of the motions we see in the real world we cannot perceive that the bodies which begin or cease to move are pushed or stopped by some other bodies. But that gives us no reason to think that these two rules are not being followed exactly. For it is certain that such bodies can often receive their agitation from the two elements, air and fire, which are always present among them without being perceivable by the senses (as has just been said), or they may receive it even from the ordinary air, which also cannot be perceived by the senses. It is certain too that they can transfer this agitation sometimes to the ordinary air, and sometimes to the whole mass of the Earth; and when dispersed in the latter, it also cannot be perceived. But even if everything our senses ever experienced in the real world seemed manifestly contrary to what is contained in these two rules, the reasoning

[c] In Descartes' mature *Principa philosophiae* (1644: Principles of Philosophy), part 2, article 40, this statement appears as his third law of nature. [B.]

*Unlike Galileo,
Postulates not
with Solid
equated
evidence—*

*God is Reason?*

which has taught them to me seems so strong that I cannot help believing myself obliged to posit them in the new world I am describing to you. For what more firm and solid foundation could one find for establishing a truth, even if one wished to choose it at will, than the very firmness and immutability which is in God?

So it is that these two rules follow manifestly from the mere fact that God is immutable and that, acting always in the same way, he always produces the same effect. For, supposing that God placed a certain quantity of motion in all matter in general at the first instant he created it, we must either admit that he always preserves the same amount of motion in it, or not believe that he always acts in the same way. Suppose in addition, that from this first instant the various parts of matter, in which these motions are found unequally dispersed, began to retain them or transfer them from one to another, according as they had the force to do so. Then we must necessarily think that God causes them to continue always doing so. And that is what these two rules contain.

I shall add, as a third rule, that when a body is moving, even though its motion for the most part takes place along a curved path and, as we said above, it can never make any movement which is not in some way circular, yet each of its parts individually tends always to continue moving along a straight line.[d] And so the action of these

*Galilean*

parts—i.e., the tendency they have to move—is different from their motion.

For example, if we make a wheel turn on its axle, even though all its parts go in a circle (because, being joined to one another, they cannot do otherwise), their tendency is to go straight ahead. This is obvious if one part happens to get detached from the others, for as soon as it is free its motion ceases to be circular and continues in a straight line.

Likewise, when you swing a stone in a sling, not only does it fly straight out as soon as it leaves the sling, but also while it is in the sling it presses against the middle of it and causes the cord to stretch. This makes it obvious that it always has a tendency to go in a straight line and that it goes in a circle only under constraint.

This rule is based on the same foundation as the other two: It depends solely on God's preserving each thing by a continuous action, and consequently on his preserving it not as it may have been some time earlier but precisely as it is at the very instant that he preserves it. So it is that of all motions, only motion in a straight line is entirely simple and has a nature which may be wholly grasped in an instant. For in order to conceive such motion it suffices to think that a body is in the process of moving in a certain direction, and that this is the case at each determinable instant during the time it is moving. By contrast, in order to conceive circular motion, or any other possible motion, it is necessary to consider at least two of its instants, or rather two of its parts, and the

---

[d]Descartes' version of the law of inertia consists of two separate laws—laws 1 and 3 in *Le Monde* and laws 1 and 2 in the *Principles*. Newton refused to credit Descartes with this law, and arguably for good reasons. First, motion for Descartes in a straight line is not uncaused, as Newton will assert half a century later, but is supported by the conserving activity of God. Second, it is impossible on Descartes' account for any celestial body to move in a straight line since all particles of matter are jostled in the universal plenum. This impossibility is reflected in Descartes' understanding of the mechanics of planetary motion: The planets are carried around by the celestial vortex in great circles, this motion giving rise to a centrifugal tendency that would throw the planets away from the center, save for the counterbalancing pressure of neighboring vortices. The law of inertia plays no role in Descartes' model, except as an unrealized tendency of particles jostling in the universal plenum. Since he did not discern its significance for the developing inertial physics, it's not surprising that Newton refused to credit Descartes with the law of inertia. [B.]

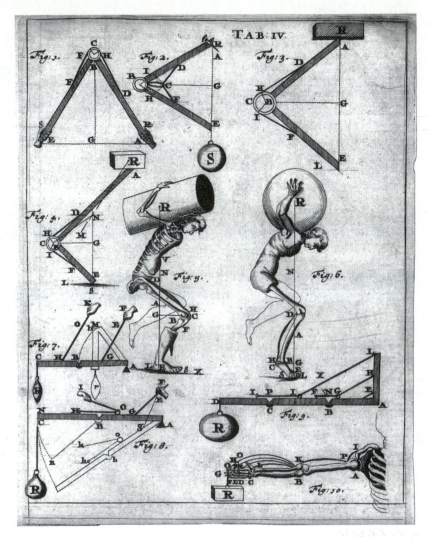

**PLATE 11**   Mechanization of the animal body. In this plate, Figure 1 depicts the conjunction of two levers IFS and HDR at pivot point C. Figure 2 suggests how elastic bands attached to the levers at D and F and to the pivot B might bring the levers closer together. The elastic bands now attached externally to the levers, Figure 3 shows how they might be expanded. Figure 4 outlines an arrangement, featuring levers of different lengths. Levers and elastics are replaced by muscles and bones in Figures 5 and 6, which features arrangements in two people carrying different loads. The vertical line that meets the ground at E is the center of gravity. Figures 7, 8 and 9 are studies of arrangements of pulleys that are then used to demonstrate in Figure 10 how a person can suspend a weight in an outstretched arm. From Giovanni Borelli, *De motu animalium* (Rome, 1680–1681). Courtesy of the Thomas Fisher Rare Book Library, University of Toronto.

relation between them.[e] But so that the philosophers (or rather the sophists) do not find occasion here to exercise their useless subtleties, note that I am not saying that rectilinear motion can take place in an instant, but only that everything required to produce it is present in bodies at each instant which might be determined while they are moving, whereas not everything required to produce circular motion is present . . .

According to this rule, then, it must be said that God alone is the author of all the motions in the world in so far as they exist and in so far as they are rectilinear; but it is the various dispositions of matter which render them irregular and curved. Likewise, the theologians teach us that God is also the author of all our actions, in so far as they exist and in so far as they have some goodness, but it is the various dispositions of our wills that can render them evil.

I could set out many further rules here for determining in detail when, how, and by how much the motion of each body can be changed and increased or decreased by colliding with others—in sum, rules which comprehend in a concise way all the effects of nature. But I shall be content with telling you that apart from the three laws I have ex-pounded, I do not wish to suppose any others but those which follow inevitably from the eternal truths on which mathematicians have usually based their most certain and most evident demonstrations—the truths, I say, according to which God himself has taught us that he has arranged all things in number, weight and measure. The knowledge of these truths is so natural to our souls that we cannot but judge them infallible when we conceive them distinctly, nor doubt that if God had created many worlds, they would be as true in each of them as in this one. Thus those who are able to examine sufficiently the consequences of these truths and of our rules will be able to recognize effects by their causes. To express myself in scholastic terms, they will able to have *a priori* demonstrations of everything that can be produced in this new world.

In order to eliminate any exception that may prevent this, we shall, if you please, suppose in addition that God will never perform any miracle in the new world, and that the intelligences, or the rational souls, which we might later suppose to be there, will not disrupt in any way the ordinary course of nature. In consequence of this, however, I do not promise to set out exact demonstrations of everything I shall say. It will be enough if I open the way which will enable you to discover them yourselves, when you take the trouble to look for them. Most minds lose interest when things are made too easy for them. And to present a picture which pleases you, I need to use shadow as well as bright colors. So I shall be content to continue with the description I have begun, as if my intention was simply to tell you a fable.

[e]Descartes reckoned that God conserves a body just as it is in the moment that it is preserved. If, as Kepler had asserted in his *Astronomia nova* (1609: New Astronomy), curved motions are the privileged paths described by planetary bodies, this would require that God concern himself with two successive moments of time, an implication that conflicts with the conserving action of God. [B.]

## FURTHER READING

Gaukroger, Stephen. 2002. *Descartes' Natural Philosophy*. Cambridge: Cambridge University Press.
Wilson, Margaret. 1999. *Ideas and Mechanism: Ideas on Early Modern Philosophy*. Princeton: Princeton University Press.

# A New Theater of Nature

## Robert Hooke (1635–1702)

*Robert Hooke is one of the great unsung giants of seventeenth science. As a boy he was fascinated with clockwork mechanisms, and his many contributions to the history of science are closely related to his enthusiasm for the mechanical philosophy—an enthusiasm that he shared with Descartes, Boyle, Hobbes, and many others.*

*Hooke served for a time as Robert Boyle's assistant, and his earliest notable achievement was the invention of the air pump, which culminated in the law which bears Boyle's name. A year after the founding of the Royal Society in 1662, Hooke was appointed Curator of Experiments for the Royal Society. Within three years, he published his greatest work, the* Micrographia *(1665: Little Pictures), the first scientific work devoted exclusively to research carried out with one of the great new instruments which fueled the seventeenth century revolution in science—the microscope.*

*In terms of its impact on the public imagination, the* Micrographia *rivaled Galileo's* Sidereus nuncius *(1610: Starry Messenger). In this work, Galileo had marshaled a number of telescopic observations on behalf of the Copernican hypothesis of a moving Earth. In particular, he had taken a familiar object—the Moon—and insisted that the telescope revealed it to be a rugged body, not unlike the Earth. Hooke took familiar things (the eye of a grey drone fly, a louse, a mite, and so forth) and showed that each of these "mechanical contrivances" possessed an intricate structure that flew in the face of received wisdom, which held that such "simple" organisms could be thrown up "spontaneously" through the shuffling of bits and pieces of disorganized matter. Again, in step with Galileo, whose defense of the Copernican system rested heavily on the persuasiveness of engravings of the lunar surface and other stellar objects, Hooke incorporated into the* Micrographia *profuse illustrations made with his own hands. Never one to focus narrowly on a single topic or problem, the book was a feast of observations ranging across the mineral, animal, and vegetable kingdoms. His horrific portrait of the louse, at eighteen inches in length, is as startling today it must have appeared to seventeenth century readers, and it is small wonder that, with the publication of this treatise, insect anatomy emerged as an entirely new field of study. Hooke made it plain just what the microscope could do for the biological sciences.*

*Source:* Robert Hooke. 1665. *Micrographia, or some Physiological Descriptions of Minute Bodies, made by Magnifying Glasses with Observations and Inquiries thereupon.* London: J. Martyn and J. Allestry, pp. 131–135.

Moss is a plant that the wisest of Kings thought neither unworthy of his speculation, nor his pen, and though among plants it be in bulk one of the smallest, it may compare for the beauty of it with any plant that grows and bears a much bigger breadth; it has a root almost like a seedy parsnip, furnished with small strings and suckers, which are all of them finely branched, like those of the roots of much bigger vegetables; out of the springs the stem or the body of the plant, which is somewhat quadrangular rather than cylindrical, most curiously fluted or strung with small creases which run, for the most part, parallel the whole stem; on the sides of the flower are close and thick set, a multitude of fair, large, well-shaped leaves, some of them of a rounder, others of a longer shape, according as they are younger or older when plucked; as I guess by this that those plants that had the stalks growing from the top of them had their leaves of narrow longer shape, all the surface of each side of which is curiously covered with a multitude of little oblong transparent bodies, in the manner you see it expressed in the leaf B, in the XIII. *Scheme* [Plate 12].

This plant, when young and springing up, does much resemble a hollow leek, having thick leaves, almost like that, and seems to be somewhat akin to it in other particulars; although from the top of the leaves, there shoots a small white and transparent hair, or thorn. This stem, in time, comes shooting out in a long, round, and even stalk, which by cutting transversely when dry, I manifestly found to be a stiff, hard, and hollow cane reed, without any kind of knot, or stop, from its bottom, where the leaves encompassed it, to the top, on which there grows a large seed called A, covered with a thin, and more whitish skin, B, terminated in a long thorny top, which at first covers all the case, and by degrees, as they swell, the skin cleaves, and at length falls off, with its thorny top and skin (which is a part of it) and leaves the seed case to ripen, and by degrees to shatter out its seed at a place underneath this cap, B, which before the

seed is ripe, appears like a flat barred button, without any hole in the middle; but as it ripens, the button grows bigger, and a hole appears in the middle of it, E, out of which, in all probability, the seed falls. For as it ripens by a provision of nature that end of the case turns downward after the same manner as the ears of wheat and barley usually do and opening several of their dry red cases, F, I found them to be quite hollow, without anything at all in them; whereas when I cut them asunder with a sharp penknife when green, I found in the middle of this great case, another smaller round case, between which two, the interstices were filled with multitudes of stringy fibers, which seemed to suspend the lesser case in the middle of the other, which (as far as I was able to discern) seemed full of exceedingly small white seeds, much like the seedbag in the knop [flower bud] of a carnation, after the flowers have been two or three days, or a week, fallen off; but this I could not so perfectly discern, and therefore cannot positively affirm it.

After the seed was fallen away, I found both the case, stalk, and plant all grow red and wither, and from other parts of the root continually to spring new branches of slips, which by degrees increased, and grew as big as the former, seeded, ripened, shattered, and withered.

I could not find that it observed any particular seasons for these several kinds of growth, but rather found it to be springing, mature, ripe, seedy, and withered at all times of the year; but I found it most to flourish and increase in warm and moist weather.

It gathers its nourishments, for the most part, out of some *lapidescent* [stony] or other substance corrupted or changed from its former texture, or substantial form, for I have found it to grow on the rotten parts of stone, of bricks, of wood, of bones, of leather, etc.

It often grows on the barks of several trees, spreading itself sometimes from the ground upwards, and sometimes from some chink or cleft of the bark of the tree, which has some putrefied substance in it; but this

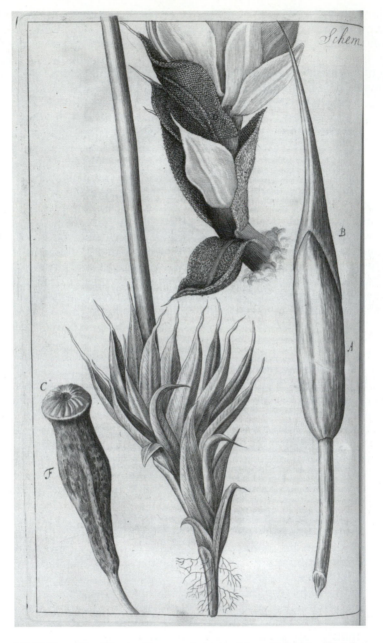

**PLATE 12** Illustration of mould. Robert Hooke, *Micrographia* (London, 1665). Courtesy of the Thomas Fisher Rare Book Library, University of Toronto (Toronto, Canada).

seems of a distinct kind from that which I observed to grow on putrefied inanimate bodies, and rotten earth.

There are also great varieties of other kinds of mosses, which grow on trees, and several other plants, of which I shall here make no mention, nor of the moss growing on the skull of a dead man, which much resembles that of trees.

Whether this plant does sometimes originally spring or rise out of corruption, without any disseminated seed, I have not yet made trials enough to be very much, either positive or negative; for as it seems very hard to conceive how the seed should be generally dispersed into all parts where there is a corruption begun, unless we may rationally suppose, that this seed being so exceedingly small, and consequently exceedingly light, is thereby taken up, and carried to and fro in the air into every place, and by the falling drops of rain is washed down out of it, and so dispersed into all places, and there only takes root and propagates, where it finds a convenient soil or matrix for it to thrive in; so if we will have it to process from corruption, it is not less difficult to conceive.

First, how the corruption of any vegetable, much less of any stone or brick should be the parent of so curiously figured, and so perfect a plant as this is. But here indeed, I cannot but add that is seems rather to be a product of the rain and those bodies where it is stayed [found] than of these very bodies themselves, since I have found it growing on marble, and flint; but always the microscope, if not the naked eye, would discover some little hole of dirt in which it was rooted.

Next, how the corruption of each of those exceedingly differing bodies should all conspire to the production of the same plant, that is, that stones, bricks, wood, or vegetable substances, and bones, leather, horns, or animate substances, unless we may with some plausibility say that air and water are the coadjutors, or *menstruums,* in all kinds of *purifications,* and that thereby the bodies

(though while they retained their substantial forms, were of exceeding differing natures, yet) since they are dissolved and mixed into one another, they may be very *homogenous,* they are almost resolved into air, water, and earth; retaining, perhaps, one part of their vegetative faculty yet entirely, which meeting with congruous assailants such as the heat of the air, and the fluidity of the water, and such like coadjutors and conveniences, acquires a certain vegetation for a time, wholly differing perhaps from the kind of vegetation it had before.

To explain my meaning a little better with a gross similitude: Suppose a curious piece of clockwork that had had several motions and contrivances in it, which, when in order would all have moved in their designed methods and periods. We will further suppose by some means that this clock comes to be broken, bruised, or otherwise disordered, so that several parts of it being dislocated, are impeded, and soft and still, and not only hinder its own progressive motion, and produce not the effect which they were designed for, but because the other parts also have a dependence upon them, put a stop to their motion likewise and so the whole instrument becomes unserviceable, and not fit for any form of life. This instrument afterwards, by some shaking and tumbling, and throwing up and down, comes to have several of its parts shaken out, and several of its curious motions, and contrivances, and particles all fallen asunder; here a pin falls out, and there a pillar, and here a wheel, and there a hammer, and a spring, and the like, and among the rest away falls those parts also which were bruised and disordered, and had all this while impeded the motion of the rest, hereupon several of those other motions that yet remain, whole springs were not quite run down, being now at liberty, begin each of them to move, thus or thus, but quite after another method than before, there being many regulating parts and the like fallen away and lost. Upon this, the owner, who chances to hear and observe some of these effects, being ignorant of the watchmaker's art, wonders what is behind his clock, and presently imagines that some artist had been at work, and has set his clock in order, and made a new kind of instrument of it, but upon examining circumstances, he finds there was no such matter, but that the casual slipping out of a pin has made several parts of his clock fall to pieces, and that thereby the obstacle that all this will hinder his clock, together with other useful parts that have fallen out, and so his clock was set at liberty. And upon winding up those springs again when they run down, he finds his clock to go, but quite after another manner than it was before.

And thus it may be perhaps in the business of moss and mold, and mushrooms, and several other spontaneous kinds of vegetations, which may be caused by a vegetative principle, which was a coadjutor to the life and growth of the greater vegetable, and was by the destroying of the life of it stopped and impeded in performing its office; but afterwards, upon a further corruption of several parts that had all the while impeded it, the heat of the Sun winding up, as it were, the spring, sets it again into a vegetative motion, and this being single, and not at all regulated as it was before (when a part of that greater *machine* the pristine vegetable) is moved after quite a differing manner and produces effects very differing from those it did before.

But this I propose only as a conjecture, not that I am more inclined to this *hypothesis* than the seminal, which upon good reason I guess to be mechanical also, as I may elsewhere more fully show: But because I may, by this, hint a possible way how this appearance may be solved, supposing we should be driven to confess from certain experiments and observations made that such and such vegetables were produced out of the corruptions of another, without any concurrent seminal principle (as I have given some reason to suppose, in the description of a microscopic mushroom) without derogating at all from the infinite wisdom of the Creator. For this accidental production, as I may call

it, does manifest as much, if not very much more, of the excellence of his contrivance as anything in the more perfect vegetative bodies of the world, even as the accidental motion of the *automaton* does make the owner see that there was much more contrivance in it then he first imagined. But of this I have added more in the description of mold, and the vegetables of rose leaves, etc., those being much more likely to have their original from such a cause than this which I have described, in the thirteen scheme, which indeed I cannot conceive otherwise, than as a most perfect conspicuous and vast vegetable in the world, and to be a rank so high as that it may very properly be reckoned with the tall cedar of Lebanon, as that kingly botanist has done.

We know there may be as much curiosity of contrivance, and excellence of forming a very small pocket-clock, that takes not up an inch square of room, as there may be in a church-clock that fills a whole room; and I know not whether all the contrivances and mechanisms requisite to a perfect vegetable may not be crowded into an exceedingly less room than this of moss, as I have heard of a striking watch so small that it served for a pendant in a lady's ear; and I have already given you the description of a plant growing on rose leaves that is abundantly smaller than moss, insomuch that near one-thousand of them would hardly make the bigness of one single plant of moss. And by comparing the bulk of moss with the bulk of the biggest kind of vegetable we meet within story (of which kind we find in some hotter climates, as Guine and Brazil, the stock or body of some trees to be twenty foot in diameter, whereas the body or stem of moss, for the most part, is not above one-sixtieth part of an inch) we shall find that the bulk of one will exceed the bulk of the other, no less than 2,985,984 or 298,958,400,000, and supposing the production on a rose leaf to be a plant, we shall have of those Indian plants to exceed a production of the same vegetable kingdom no less then one-thousand times the former number; so prodigiously various

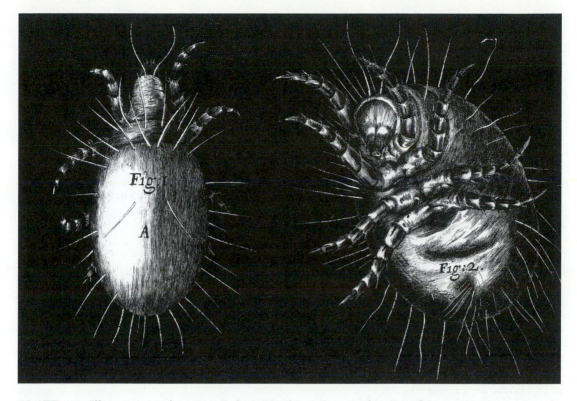

**PLATE 13**   Illustration of a mite. Robert Hooke, *Micrographia* (London, 1665). Courtesy of the Thomas Fisher Rare Book Library, University of Toronto (Toronto, Canada).

are the works of the Creator, and so all-sufficient is he to perform what to men would seem impossible, they being both alike each to him, even as one day, and a thousand year are to him as one and the same time.

I have taken notice of such an infinite variety of those smaller kinds of vegetations that should I have described every one of them, they would almost have filled a volume, and proved big enough to have made a new Herbal, such multitudes are there to be found in moist hot weather, especially in the summer time; on all kinds of putrefying substances, which, whether they do more properly belong to the classes of mushrooms, or molds, or mosses, I shall not now dispute, there being some that seem more properly of one kind, others of another, their colors and

magnitudes being as much differing as their figures and substances. Nay, I have observed that putting fair water (whether rain-water or pump-water, or May-dew, or snow-water, it was almost all one) I have often observed I say that this water would, with a little standing, tarnish and cover all about the sides of the glass that lay under water with a lovely green; but though I have often endeavored to discover with my microscope whether this green were like moss, or long striped sea-weed, or any other peculiar form, yet so ill and imperfect are our microscopes that I could not certainly discriminate any.

Growing trees also, and any kinds of woods, stones, bones, etc., that have been long exposed to the air and rain will be all covered over with a greenish scruff, which will very much soil and green any kind of cloth that is rubbed against it; viewing this, I could not certainly perceive in many parts of it determinate form, though in many I could perceive as a bed as it were of young moss, but in other parts it looked almost like green bushes, and very confused, but always of whatever irregular figures that parts appeared of, they were always green, and seemed to be either some vegetable or to have some vegetating principle.

## FURTHER READING

Inwood, Stephen. 2002. *The Man Who Knew Too Much: The Strange and Inventive Life of Robert Hooke.* London: Macmillan.

Hunter, Michael and Schaffer, Simon, eds. 1989. *Robert Hooke: New Studies.* Woodbridge: Boydell Press.

# Mechanical Chemistry

## Robert Boyle (1627–1691)

*During the second part of the seventeenth century, chemistry was transformed from a purely organic science to one that was mechanistic in outlook. Robert Boyle who, in many ways, is better described as a mechanical philosopher than as a chemist, was the most important figure in this transformation. Boyle was committed to the mechanical philosophy from the very beginning of his scientific career, and his interest in chemistry stems from his conviction that this science was in a unique position to provide the mechanical philosophy with an experimentally based theory of matter.*

*Boyle's scientific reputation was established with his very first publication—The Spring and Weight of the Air (1660). With the aid of the new air pump designed and built with Robert Hooke (1635–1703), Boyle showed that the air has weight. A second edition, which appeared in 1662, announced the famous generalization that bears Boyle's name—the volume occupied by a gas is the reciprocal of its pressure. The appearance of The Sceptical Chemist in 1661 marks the emergence of analytic chemistry out of its alchemical past. Boyle's distinction between a compound and a mixture, and his insistence on precise definitions of chemical terms, set a new standard for chemical practice.*

*Boyle's extraordinary work was never completed but one theme dominates his chemical writings: Chemical reactions are merely the reshuffling of particles and all chemical processes are the products of particles of matter in motion. He also believed, in accordance with the alchemists, that almost anything could be made into anything else. Although experiments did suggest that some substances are durable, Boyle never questioned whether metals were compounds. He continued to look for a way of transmuting gold and exchanged recipes with such well-known alchemists as the philosopher John Locke (1632–1704) and Isaac Newton (1642–1727). Throughout his scientific career, he continued to regard metals as mixed bodies, and substances, such as water and alcohol, as elementary. What he did, however, was undermine the traditional conviction that elements are material carriers of qualities. Where the traditional view was that analysis separates mixed bodies into active principles, Boyle designed chemical tests to show that different bodies yield widely differing substances in analysis.*

---

*Source:* Robert Boyle. 1674. "On the Excellency and Grounds of the Corpuscular or Mechanical Philosophy." In Peter Shaw, ed., *Philosophical Works of the Honorable Robert Boyle Esq.* London: W. & J. Innys, and J. Osborn, and T. Longman, 1725, volume 1, pp. 187–196.

By embracing the corpuscular or mechanical philosophy, I am far from supposing with the Epicureans[a] that atoms, accidentally meeting in an infinite vacuum were able, of themselves, to produce a world and all its phenomena: Nor do I suppose, when God had put into the whole mass of matter an invariable quantity of motion, he needed do no more to make the universe; the material parts being able, by their own unguided motions, to throw themselves into a regular system. The philosophy I plead for reaches but to things purely corporeal; and distinguishing between the first origin of things and the subsequent course of nature, teaches that God indeed gave motion to matter; but that, in the beginning, he so guided the various motions of the parts of it as to contrive them into the world he designed that they should compose; and established those rules of motion, and that order amongst things corporeal, which we call the laws of nature. Thus, the universe was, once framed by God and the laws of motion, settled and everything was upheld by his perpetual concourse and general providence, the same philosophy teaches that the phenomena of the world are physically produced by the mechanical properties of the parts of matter, and that they operate upon one another according to mechanical laws. It is of this kind of corpuscular philosophy that I speak.

And the first thing that recommends it is the intelligibility or clearness of its principles and explanations. Among the Peripatetics[b] there are many intricate disputes about matter, privation, substantial forms, their educa-

tions, etc. And the chemists [alchemists] are puzzled to give such definitions, and accounts, of their hypostatical principles as are consistent with one another, and to some obvious phenomena; and much more dark and intricate are their doctrines about the Archeus, Astral Beings, and other odd notions; which perhaps, have in part occasioned the darkness and ambiguousity of their expressions, which could not be very clear, when the conceptions were obscure. And if the principles of the Aristotelians and chemists are thus obscure, it is not to be expected that the explications made by the help of such principles only should be intelligible. And, indeed, many of them are so general and slight, or otherwise so unsatisfactory, that granting their principles, it is very hard to understand or admit their applications of them to particular phenomena. And, I think, even in some of the more ingenious and subtle of the Peripatetic discourses, the authors, upon their superficial and narrow theories, have acted more like painters than philosophers; and only shown their skill in making men fancy they see castles, cities, and older structures, that appear solid, magnificent, and extensive; when the whole piece is superficial, artificially made up of colors and comprised within a frame. But, as to the corpuscular philosophy, men do so easily understand one another's meaning, when they talk of local motion, rest, magnitude, shape, order, situation, and texture of material substances; and these principles afford such clear accounts of those things that are rightly deduced from them alone; that even such Peripatetics or chemists as maintain other principles, acquiesce in the explications made by these, when they can be had; and seek no further: though, perhaps, the effect be so admirable, as to make it pass for that of a hidden form, or an occult quality. Those very Aristotelians, who believe the celestial bodies to be moved by intelligences, have no recourse to any peculiar agency of theirs to account for eclipses; and we laugh at those East Indians who, to this day, go out in multitudes,

[a]Epicurus (c. 341–c. 270 B.C.) elevated the doctrine of atoms and the void to the centerpiece of his moral philosophy; even free will was explained in terms of the movements of atoms. Epicurean atomism was subsequently popularized by Lucretius in his poem *De rerum natura*. [B.]

[b]The building which housed the school of Aristotle contained a peripatos, or a covered walking place. This architectural feature produced a name for the school itself (the *Peripatos*) and a name for Aristotle's followers—Peripatetics. [B.]

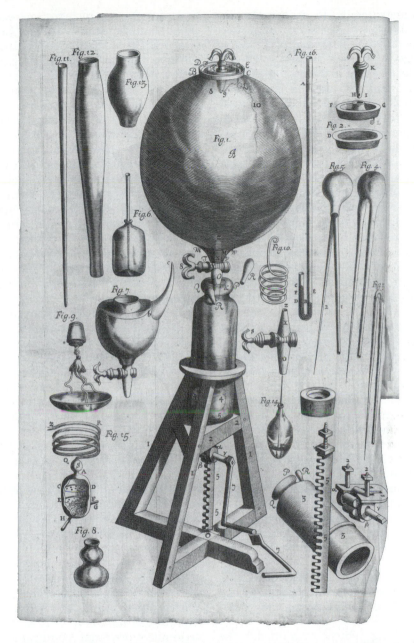

**PLATE 14**   Robert Boyle's first air pump, which was employed in his experiments on animal respiration. From Robert Boyle, *New Experiments Physico-Mechanical, Touching the Spring of the Air.* London: M. Flesher, third edition, 1682. Courtesy of the Thomas Fisher Rare Book Library, University of Toronto (Toronto, Canada).

with some instruments, to relieve the distressed luminary; whose loss of light, they fancy, proceeds from some fainting fit; out of which it must be roused. For no intelligent man, whether chemist or Peripatetic, flies to his peculiar principles, after he is informed that the Moon is eclipsed by the interposition of the Earth between her and it; and the sun, by that of the Moon, between him and the Earth. And, when we see the image of a man cast into the air by a concave spherical speculum; though most men are amazed at it, and some suspect it to be no less than an effect of witchcraft, yet he who is skilled enough in catoptrics will, without consulting Aristotle or Paracelsus or flying to hypostatic principles or substantial forms, be satisfied that the phenomenon is produced by rays of light reflected and made to converge according to optical and mathematical laws.

I next observe that there cannot be fewer principles than the two grand ones of our philosophy, matter and motion; for matter alone, unless it be moved, is wholly inactive; and, while all the parts of a body continue in one state, without motion, that body will not exercise any action, or suffer any alteration; though it may, perhaps, modify the action of other bodies that move against it. Nor can we conceive any principles more primary than matter and motion; for either both of them were immediately created by God; or, if matter be eternal, motion must either be produced by some immaterial supernatural agent; or it must immediately flow, by way of emanation, from the nature of the matter it pertains to.

There cannot be any physical principles more simple than matter and motion; neither of them being resoluble into any other thing.

The next thing which recommends the corpuscular principles is their extensiveness. The genuine and necessary effect of the strong motion of one inert particle of matter against another is either to drive it on, in its entire bulk, or to break and divide it into particles of a determinate motion, figure, size, posture, rest, order or texture. The two

first of these, for instance, are each of them capable of numerous varieties; for the figure of a portion of matter may either be one of the five regular geometrical figures, some determinate species of solid figures, or irregular, as the grains of sand, feathers, branches, files etc. And, as the figure, so the motion of one of these particles may be exceedingly diversified, not only by the determination to a particular part of the world but by several other things; as by the almost infinitely different degrees of celerity; by the manner of its progression, with or without rotation etc., and more yet by the line wherein it moves; as circular, elliptical, parabolical, hyperbolical, spiral, etc. For, as later geometricians have shown that these curves may be compounded of several motions, that is, described by a body whose motion is mixed, and results from two or more simple motions; so, how many more curves may be made by new compositions, and recompositions of motion, is not easy to determine.

Now since a particle of matter, by virtue of only two mechanical properties that belong to it, may be diversified so many ways, what a vast number of variations may we suppose capable of being produced by the compositions, and recompositions of myriads of single invisible corpuscles, that may be contained and concreted in one small body; and each of them are endowed with more than two or three of the fertile, universal principles above-mentioned? And the aggregate of those corpuscles may be further diversified by the texture resulting from their assemblage into a body which, as so made up, has its own magnitude, shape, pores, and many capacities of acting and suffering, upon account of the place it holds among other bodies, in a world constituted like ours so that, considering the numerous diversifications that compositions and recompositions may make of a small number, those who think the mechanical principles may serve, indeed, to account for the phenomena of some particular part of natural philosophy, as statics and the theory of planetary motions, etc., but prove inapplicable to all the phenomena that things corporeal seem to imagine, and that by putting together the letters of the alphabet one may, indeed, make up all the words to be found in Euclid or Virgil, or in the Latin or English language, but that they can by no means supply words to all the books of a great library, much less, to all the languages in the world.

There are other philosophers who, observing the great efficacy of magnitude, situation, motion, and connection in engines are willing to allow those mechanical principles a great share in the operations of bodies of a sensible bulk and manifest mechanism, and, therefore, to be usefully employed in accounting for the effects and phenomena of such bodies; though they will not admit that these principles can be applied to the hidden transactions among the minute particles of bodies; and, therefore, think it necessary to refer these to what they call nature, substantial forms, real qualities, and the like unmechanical agents. But this is not necessary; for the mechanical properties of matter are to be found, and the laws of motion take place, not only in the great masses and the middle-sized lumps, but in the smallest fragments of matter; a lesser portion of it being as much a body as a greater, must as necessarily as the other have its determinate bulk and figure. And whoever views sand through a good microscope will easily perceive that each minute grain has as well its own size and shape as a rock or a mountain. Thus too, when we let fall a large stone, and a pebble, from the top of a high building, they both move in agreement with the laws of acceleration in heavy descending bodies; and the rules of motion are observed, not only in cannon bullets, but in small shot, and the one strikes down a bird, according to the same laws, as the other batters a wall. Nature works with much finer materials, and employs more curious contrivances, than art yet an artist, according to the quantity of the matter he employs, the exigency of the design he undertakes, and the magnitude and shape of the instruments he uses, is able to make pieces of work of the same nature or kind, of extremely different bulks where yet

the like art, contrivance, and motion may be observed. Thus, a smith who with a hammer and other large instruments, can, out of masses of iron, forge great bars or wedges to make strong and ponderous chains to secure streets and gates may, with lesser instruments, make smaller nails, and filings, almost as minute as dust; and with yet finer tools, make links wonderfully light and slender. And therefore, to say that in natural bodies, whose bulk is manifest and their structure visible, the mechanical principles may be usefully admitted but are not to be extended to such portions of matter, whose parts and texture are invisible, is like allowing that the laws of mechanism may take place in a town-clock, and not in a pocket-watch: or, because the terraqueous globe is a vast magnetic body, one should affirm that magnetic laws are not to be expected manifest in a small spherical piece of lodestone; yet experience shows us that, notwithstanding the immense disproportion between these two spheres, the terella as well as the Earth, has its poles, equator, and meridians; and in several other magnetic properties resembles the terrestrial globe.

When to solve the phenomena of nature, agents are made use of which, though they involve no contradiction in their notions, as many think substantial forms and real qualities do, yet are such that we conceive not how they operate to produce effects; such agents I mean, as the soul of the world, the universal spirit, the plastic power, etc., the curiosity of an inquisitive person is not satisfied hereby; who seeks not so much to know what is the general agent that produces a phenomenon, as by what means, and after what manner, it is produced. Daniel Sennertus,[c] and other physicians, tell us of diseases which proceed from incantation; but to be sure, it is very trivial to a sober physician, who comes to visit a patient reported to be

---

[c]A very influential teacher and physician, Daniel Sennert (1572–1637) worked hard to reconcile the theories of Aristotle, Galen, Parcelsus, and the classical atomists. [B.]

bewitched, to hear only that the strange symptoms he meets with, and would have an account of, are produced by a witch or the devil; and he will never be satisfied with so short an answer, if he can by any means reduce those extravagant symptoms to any more known and stated diseases, such as epilepsy, convulsions, hysteric fits, etc., and if he cannot, he will confess his knowledge of this distemper to come far short of what might be expected and attained in other diseases, wherein he thinks himself bound to search into the morbific [disease-causing] matter and will not be satisfied, until he can, probably, deduce from that and the structure of the human body, and other concurring physical causes, the phenomena of the malady. And it would be of little satisfaction to one who desires to understand the causes of the phenomena in a watch, and how it comes to point at and strike the hours to be told that a certain watch-maker so contrived it; or, to him who would know the true causes of an echo, to be answered that it is a man, a vault, or a wood, that makes it.

I come now to consider that which I observe most alienates other sects from the mechanical philosophy; viz., a supposition that it pretends to have principles so universal and mathematical that no other physical hypothesis can be tolerated by it.

This I look upon as an easy, indeed but an important, mistake; for the mechanical principles are so universal, and applicable to so many purposes that they are rather fitted to take in, than to exclude, any other hypothesis founded on nature. And such hypotheses, if prudently considered, will be found, as far as they have truth on their side, to be either legitimately deducible from the mechanical principles or fairly reconcileable to them. For such hypotheses will, probably, attempt to account for the phenomena of nature, either by the help of a determinate number of material ingredients, such as the *tria prima*[d] of the chemists, or else by introducing some general agents, as the Platonic soul of the world, and the universal spirit, asserted by some chemists, or, by both these ways together.

Now, the chief thing that a philosopher should look after, in explaining difficult phenomena, is not so much what the agent is or does as what changes are made in the patient to bring it to exhibit the phenomena proposed and by what means, and after what manner, those changes are effected. So that the mechanical philosopher being satisfied, one part of matter can act upon another, only by virtue of local motion, or the effects and consequences thereof; he considers, if the proposed agent be not intelligible and physical, it can never physically explain the phenomena; and if it be intelligible and physical, it will be reducible to matter and some or other of its universal properties. And the indefinite divisibility of matter, the wonderful efficacy of motion, and the almost infinite variety of coalitions and structures that may be made of minute and insensible corpuscles being duly weighed, why may not a philosopher think it possible to make out, by their help, the mechanical possibility of any corporeal agent, how subtle, diffused, or active whatsoever, that can be solidly proved to have a real existence in nature? Though, the Cartesians are mechanical philosophers, yet their *Materia subtilis* [subtle matter], which the very name declares to be a corporeal substance is, for all I know, little less diffused through the universe, or less active in it, than the universal spirit of some chemists; not to say the *Anima mundi* [world soul] of the Platonists. But whatever be the physical agent, whether it be inanimate, or living, purely corporeal, or united to an intellectual substance, the above-mentioned changes, wrought in the body made to exhibit the phenomena, may be effected by the same, or the like means or

---

[d]Paracelsus conceptualized matter in terms of three elements, or *tria prima*—mercury, sulfur, and salt. When a twig burns, for instance, the presence of sulfur is revealed by the flame, mercury by the smoke, and salt by the ashes (when extracted with water and evaporated). [B.]

after the same, or the like manner: as, for instance, corn may be reduced to meal. The materials and shape of the mill-stones and their peculiar motion and adaptation will be much of the same kind; and, to be sure, the grains of corn will suffer a various attrition, and comminution in their passage to the form of meal, whether the corn be ground by a watermill, or a windmill, a horsemill, or a handmill; that is, a mill, whose stones are turned by inanimate, by brute, or by rational agents. And if an angel himself should work a real change in the nature of a body, it is scarce conceivable to men how he could do it without the assistance of local motion since, if nothing were displaced, or otherwise moved than before it is hardly conceivable how it should be, in itself, different from what it was before.

But if the chemists, or others, who would deduce a complete natural philosophy from salt, sulphur, and mercury, or any determined number of ingredients of things, would well consider what they undertake, they might easily discover that the material parts of bodies can reach but to a few phenomena of nature, while these things [ingredients] are considered but as quiescent things where they would find themselves to suppose them active; and that things purely corporeal cannot but by means of local motion, and the effects that may result from it, be very variously shaped, sized, and combined parts of matter; so that the chemists must leave the greatest part of the phenomena of the universe unexplained, by means of the ingredients of bodies, without taking in the mechanical and more comprehensive properties of matter, especially local motion. I willingly grant that salt, sulfur, and mercury, or some substances analogous to them, are obtainable by the action of the fire, from a very great many dissipable bodies here below. Nor do I deny that in explaining several phenomena of such bodies it may be of use to a naturalist to know and consider that if sulfur, for instance, abounds in the body proposed, it may be, then, probably argued that the qualities usually attending that principle, when predominant, may be also upon

its account found in the body that so largely partakes of it. But, though chemical explications are sometimes the most obvious, yet they are not the most fundamental and satisfactory; for the chemical ingredient itself, whether sulfur or any other, must owe its nature and other qualities to the union of insensible particles, in a convenient size, shape, motion, or rest, and texture; all which are but mechanical properties of convening corpuscles. And this may be illustrated by what happens in artificial fireworks. For, though, in most of those sorts, made either for war, or recreation, gunpowder is a principal ingredient, and many of the phenomena may be derived from the greater or lesser proportion wherein it enters the compositions, yet there may be fireworks made without gunpowder, as appears by those of the ancient Greeks and Romans. And gunpowder owes its aptness to fire, and to be exploded, to the mechanical texture of more simple portions of matter, nitre [potassium nitrate: saltpeter], charcoal, and sulfur. And sulfur itself, though it be by many chemists mistaken for an hypostatical [essential] principle, owes its inflammability to the union of still more simple and primary corpuscles; since chemists confess that it had an inflammable ingredient; and experience shows that it very much abounds with an acid and uninflammable salt and is not destitute of a terrestrial part.

It may, indeed, be here alleged that the productions of chemical analyses are simple bodies; and, upon that account, irresolute; but that several substances, which chemists call the salts, sulfurs, or mercuries of the bodies that afford them, are not simple and homogenous is demonstrable. Nor is their not being easily dissipable, or resoluble, a clear proof of their not being made up of more primitive portions of matter. For compounded bodies may be as difficultly resoluble as most of those that chemists obtain by the fire; witness common greenglass, which is far more durable and irresoluble than many of those which pass for hypostatical substances. And some enamels will, for several times, even vitrify in the forge, without losing their nature or often so much as their color; yet enamel consists of salt, powder of pebbles, or sand, and calcined [oxidized] tin and if not white, usually of some tinging metal or mineral. But, however indestructible the chemical principles are supposed, several of the operations ascribed to them will never be made to appear without the help of local motion; were it not for this, we can but little better solve the phenomena of many bodies by knowing what ingredients compose them than we can explain the operations of a watch by knowing of how many and of what metals, the balance, the wheels, the chain, and older parts consist; or than we can derive the operations of a windmill from barely knowing that it is made up of wood, stone, canvas, and iron. And here let me add that it would not at all overthrow the corpuscularian hypothesis, though, either by more exquisite purifications or by some other operations, than the usual analysis by fire, it should appear that the material principles of mixed bodies are not the *tria prima* of the vulgar chemists; but, either substances of another nature, or fewer in number; or, if it were true that the Helmontians[e] had such a resolving menstruum as their master's alkahest, by which he affirms that he could reduce stones into salt, of the same weight with the mineral and bring both that salt, and all other mixed and tangible bodies, into insipid water. For whatever be the number or qualities of the chemical principles, if they really exist in nature, it may very possibly be shown that they are made up of insensible corpuscles, of determinate bulks and shapes; and by the various coalitions and textures of such corpuscles, many material ingredients may be composed, or made to result. But

though the alkahestical reductions, newly mentioned, should be admitted, yet the mechanical principles might well be accommodated even to them. For the solidity, taste, etc., of salt may be fairly accounted for by the stiffness, sharpness, and other mechanical properties of the minute particles whereof salt consists: and if, by a farther action of the alkahest, the salt, or any other solid body, be reduced into insipid water, this also may be explained by the same principles; supposing a farther comminution of its parts, and such an attrition as wears off the edges and points that enabled them to strike briskly upon the organ of taste: for as to fluidity and firmness, they principally depend upon two of our grand principles, motion and rest. And it is certain that the agitation, or rest, and the looser contact, or closer cohesion of the particles, is able to make the same portion of matter at one time a firm and at another a fluid body. Although future sagacity and industry of chemists should obtain, from mixed bodies, homogeneous substances, different in number, nature, or both, from their vulgar salt, sulfur, and mercury; yet the corpuscular philosophy is so general and fertile as to be fairly reconcilable to such a discovery; and also so useful, that these new material principles will, as well as the old *tria prima,* stand in need of the more universal principles of the corpuscularians, especially of local motion. And, indeed, whatever elements or ingredients men have pitched upon yet, if they take not in the mechanical properties of matter, their principles are so deficient that I have observed both the materialists and chemists not only leave many things unexplained, to which their narrow principles will not extend; but, even in the particulars they presume to give an account of, they either content themselves to assign such common and indefinite causes as are too general to be satisfactory; or, if they venture to give particular causes, they assign precarious or false ones, liable to be easily disproved by circumstances, or instances, whereto their doctrines will not agree. The chemists, however, need

---

[e]The *alkahest,* as elaborated by Johannes Baptista van Helmont (1579–1644), was a solvent that was able to break down any substance into its ingredients and from these into the primordial water that he regarded as the fundamental sustratum of all things. Many seventeenth century chemists dedicated their labors to the preparation of the alkahest. [B.]

not be frightened from acknowledging the prerogative of the mechanical philosophy, since that may be reconcilable with the truth of their own principles, so far as they agree with the phenomena they are applied to; for these more confined hypotheses may be subordinate to those more general and fertile principles; and there can be no ingredient assigned that has a real existence in nature, but may be derived, either immediately or by a row of compositions, from the universal matter, modified by its mechanical properties. For if with the same bricks, differently put together and arranged, several bridges, vaults, houses, and other structures may be raised merely by various contrivances of parts of the same kind, what a great variety of ingredients may be produced by nature from the various coalitions and contextures of corpuscles, that need not be supposed, like bricks, all of the same size and shape but to have, both in the one and the other, as great a variety as could be wished for? And the primary and minute concretions that belong to these ingredients may, without opposition from the mechanical philosophy, be supposed to have their particles so minute and strongly coherent that nature of herself scarcely ever tears them asunder. Thus, mercury and gold may be successively made to put on a multitude of disguises, and yet so retain their nature as to be reducible to their pristine forms.

From here it is probable, if besides rational souls, there be any immaterial substances, such as the heavenly intelligences, and the substantial forms of the Aristotelians that are regularly to be numbered among natural agents, their way of working being unknown to us, they can only help to constitute and effect things, but will very little help us to conceive how things are effects; so that, by whatever principles natural things are constituted, it is by the mechanical principles that their phenomena must be clearly explained. For instance, we take for granted, with the Aristotelians, that the planets are made of a quintessential matter and moved by angels or immaterial intelligences yet, to explain the stations, progressions and retrogradations, and phenomena of the planets, we must have recourse either to eccentrics, epicycles, etc., or to motions, made in elliptical,[f] or other peculiar lines; and, in a word, to theories wherein the motion, figure, situation, and other mathematical, or mechanical properties are chiefly employed. But if the principles proposed be corporeal, they will then be fairly reducible or reconcilable to the mechanical principles; these being so general and fertile that, among real material things, there is none but may be derived from or reduced to them. And when the chemists shall show that mixed bodies owe their qualities to the predominance of any one of their three grand ingredients, the corpuscularians will show that the very qualities of this or that ingredient flow from its peculiar texture, and the mechanical properties of the corpuscles that compose it. And to affirm that because the chemical furnaces afford a great number of uncommon productions, and phenomena, that there are bodies or operations among things purely corporeal not derivable from or reconcilable to the principles of mechanical philosophy is to say, because there are many and various hymns, pavanes, threnodies, courants, gavottes, sarabands, etc. in a music book, many of the tunes, or notes have no dependence on the scale of music; or as if because excepting rhomboids, squares, pentagons, chiliagons,[g] and numerous other polygons, one should affirm there are some rectilineal figures not reducible to triangles, or that have properties which overthrow Euclid's doctrine of triangles and polygons.

[f]The reference to Kepler's ellipse is remarkable given Boyle's focus on chemical phenomena. Kepler's ideas were not widely known. For example, there is no reference to Kepler's ellipse in the writings of Descartes, despite Descartes' expressed interest in the problem of planetary motion. [B.]

[g]A plane figure with 1,000 angles. [B.]

*duction. A critical case was the reproduction of mammals. The ovists thought that the ovary follicle (membrane covering the sac which contains the egg) was in fact the egg, while Leeuwenhoek pointed out that it was impossible for the entire follicle to pass through the narrow fallopian tube to the uterus. The actual mammalian egg was not found until 1832, and the ovist-animalculist controversy persisted until 1875, when it was demonstrated that fertilization represents the fusion of the nuclei of the spermatozoa and the egg.*

## A LETTER OF MR. LEEUWENHOEK TO DR. G.[a] CONTAINING AN ACCOUNT OF HIS OBSERVATIONS LATELY MADE OF VAST NUMBERS OF ANIMALS IN SEMINE ANIMALIUM

Viewing the melt of a live codfish, I found the Succus [juices] thereof, which ran from it full of small live animals, incessantly moving to and fro; these trials I repeated three times with the same success, until I was weary of them. I have also viewed the melt of pikes or jacks, and therein also found an incredible number of small animals. And I judge that there were at least ten thousand of these creatures in the bigness of a small sand. These were smaller than those I observed in beasts, but their tails longer and thinner. I viewed also the matter in the vasa deferentia of a male hare four days after it was killed, and found it full of these small tadpoles swimming in a clear liquor, but they were without motion; the same I found also in the testicle. I examined also the matter in the vasa deferentia of birds, such as cocks and turkey cocks, and found it full of oblong bodies, bigger in the middle than at each end, which I conceived to be animals. I viewed also the testicle of a dog taken out of the second skin, which I have caused to be drawn in the one Figure: *CHID* is the second skin fast to the testicle: *DKLMNO* is the vas deferens, *GP* the vas preparans. Viewing the matter taken from *O* presently after inspection, I discovered a vast number of small creatures. The same thing I also found in the

matter taken out of the vessels crinkled at *G*, but by cutting the vessels some blood mingled with it which was full of globules.

I have also cut the vessels at *E*, *F* and *G* and found these animals there also. After three hours cutting the Vessel at *A*, I found multitudes of animals there also, but most dead.

The semen of a cock about a year old, which had been kept alone in a coop for five days, I found exceedingly full of those animals, at least 50,000 in the bigness of a sand. Those were like river eels, which wriggled very much; these closing together would make a cloud, and separating again make it seem to disperse. I found them also in the vas deferens, in the epididymis, and in the vas preparans: but among these were mingled many globules, and other small oval bodies about the same size, which seemed to maintain life by their motion, but yet I conceived it rather to proceed from the motion of the animals between them. By these observations you may judge that the testicle is made on purpose for the production of these animals, and to keep them until sent off . . .

How vast and almost incredible the number of these creatures are you may somewhat better conceive by the calculation which I have hereunto annexed, depending fundamentally on accurate observation.

I have formerly told you that, in a quantity of the juice of the melt of a male codfish of the size of a small [grain of] sand, there are contained more than 10,000 small living creatures with long tails; and considering how many such quantities (viz., of the size of a sand) might be contained in the whole melt, I was of the opinion that the melt of one single codfish contained more living animals than there

[a]The reference is to Nehemiah Grew (1641–1712), who served in 1677 as secretary of the Royal Society. [B.]

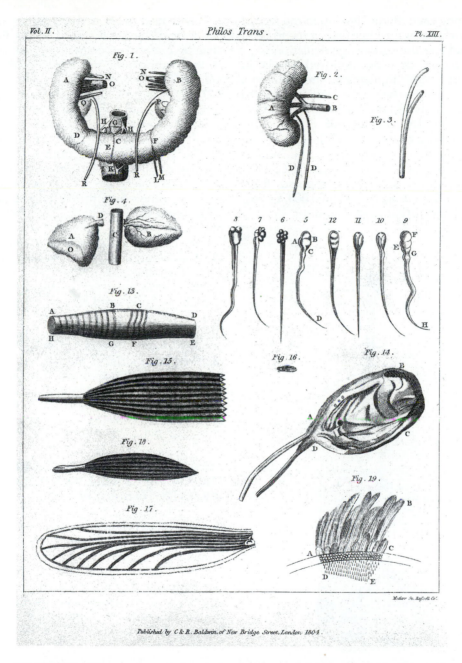

**PLATE 15** Illustration of the various types of "animalcules" observed with the microscope. Spermatozoa collected from different kinds of animals are depicted in Figures 5–12. From *Philosophical Transactions of the Royal Society of London*. Vol. 2, 1672–1683. London: C. & R. Baldwin of New Bridge Street, 1804. Courtesy of the Thomas Fisher Rare Book Library, University of Toronto (Toronto, Canada).

were living men at one time upon the face of the Earth. That which introduced me to be of this belief was this following calculation:

I conceive that one-hundred sands in length will make an inch, and therefore, in a cubic inch there will be a million of such sands. As I have found the melt of a codfish to be about the quantity of fifteen cubic inches, it must therefore contain fifteen-million of quantities as big as a sand. Now if there be ten-thousand animals in each of those quantities, as I have computed, there will be in the whole 150,000,000,000, or one hundred and fifty thousand million.

I will now reckon the number of men which may be on the face of the Earth at once by guess. There are in a great circle, or in the compass of the Earth, 5,400 Dutch miles. Therefore, I imagine there must be 9,276,218 square Dutch miles for the Earth's surface. It is said two thirds of the surface of the Earth is water, and one third only is land; a third therefore of the last number is 3,092,072, which is the number of square miles of dry land on the surface of the Earth. I suppose one third of this uninhabitable, and the other two thirds only inhabited, which two thirds contain 2,061,382 square miles . . .

The number of people in Holland and West Friezland may be about 1,000,000. And if all the rest of the habitable parts of the world were as populous as these (which is very unlikely) there would be 13,385,000,000, thirteen thousand three hundred eighty five millions of men at once on the face of the whole Earth; but in the melt of the codfish I have computed that there are one hundred and fifty thousand millions of animals; the number of these therefore will exceed the number of men more than ten times.[1]

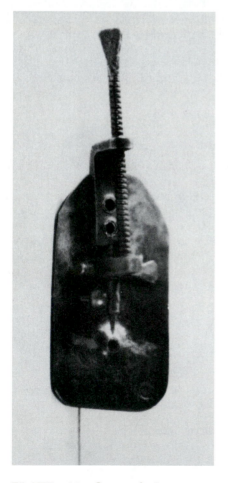

**PLATE 16** One of Leeuwenhoek's simple microscopes.

### AN ABSTRACT OF A LETTER FROM MR. ANTHONY LEEUWENHOEK WRITTEN TO SIR C.W.

Having lately met with a book published by a physician of our country,[b] which treats of human generation, and the egg-branch [ovarium] as it is found in women-kind; and not doubting that what is there said is also applicable to four-footed beasts, I examined (in the presence of a physician and other learned persons, as well as alone) egg-

[b]The reference likely is to Regnier de Graaf's *De mulierum organis generatoni inservientibus* (1672), which describes the minute follicles of the ovary—called Graffian follices by Albtecht von Haller (1708–1777) in the mid-eighteenth century. [B.]

branches of several lambs of a year old that had been several months in the winter kept in a stall for fatting, separated from the rams. From what I have previously found, I cannot but wonder why it should be generally believed that the tuba fallopiana does draw or suck down an egg from the egg-branch, through so narrow a passage, as I showed the tuba fallopiana to have. Considering therewithal that some of the eggs were as big as peas, and others as large as the whole egg-branch; that they were made up of glandulous parts interwoven with blood-vessels, and were shut up so fast in their skins or membranes that I could not with my nails tear one of them from the egg-branch; that some of them consisted of very irregular and unlike parts, which were in some places enclosed in particular skins, and had not at all the shape of an egg; that some of them which stood out beyond the rest were burst open; and yet when I went to pull them off, they stuck so fast that the whole egg-branch came along with them. The smallest eggs, and of a lesser size, were also firmly rooted and fixed in their skins, and had often a waterish substance in them. That besides the supposed eggs of the egg-branch, there were others lying at a distance from it of an inch and more on each side of the womb, and were included in particular skins.

My opinion of these eggs is therefore that they are emunctories, or the emptying of some vessels lying near, such as are often found among the membranes, or adhering to the bowels of animals. But as to generation, though I have formerly been very reserved in declaring my thoughts on this issue, yet being now further instructed by manifold experience, I dare venture to affirm it rather to come from an animalcule (such as I find not only in human seed, but that of all birds, beasts, fishes, and insects) than an egg. And the rather for that I find in the seed of a man, as also of a dog, two different sorts of animalcules, answering the different sexes of male and female.[2]

I know some men will even swear that they have found the aforesaid eggs in the tuba fallopiana of beasts. But I need not be-lieve that these round bodies they have seen in it should be drawn down from the imagined egg-branch, through the long and very narrow passage of the tuba fallopiana, because some of the bodies are as large as a pea (nay as the whole egg-branch), and of a very firm and compacted substance. But the way through which they should pass is no wider than the compass of a small pin. Again, if it were so as is said, these bodies would be found, not by chance, but always when searched for immediately after copulation; but that is so far from being true that it is hardly to be imagined, if we consider how little time is taken up in the copulation of several animals, as a cow, rabbit, etc. In which so short time, nevertheless, ought to be drawn down through a long and narrow passage, a great number of bodies; in some cases two or three, in others six or eight; and more, according to the number of fetuses to be produced.

But supposing such bodies there to be found, why may they not be formed *ex residuo seminis masculi*, gathered together into a ball or globule, as we see several other substances in animals that are neither of too thick nor too thin a consistency, as fat, sanies,[c] etc. Or second, there being no part of the body which is not nourished, and which does not cast off some things that are superfluous, why may there not in the womb or tuba be several excretions made, which by compression on all sides may be brought into a round figure? This supposition being true, it will follow that egg-like bodies are also in the womb or tuba of females that have not been accompanied with the male.

It may be queried, if one animalcule of seed be sufficient to produce a fetus, why are there so many thousands in one drop of it? I answer that in an apple tree (enduring a hundred years and bearing every year a great many thousand blossoms, which may a great part of them be apples, having each of them six or eight seeds) each seed being placed in a

---

[c] A fluid secreted by a wound or ulcer. [B.]

proper soil, and carefully cultivated, is capable of becoming a tree; yet it may happen that nothing grows from all the apples that fall down; whether through want of sun, of grass, seeds, or other accidents. So in the womb, each animalcule might suffice for a generation, if the place where it comes to be nursed be fit for it; but the womb being so large in comparison of so small a creature, and there being so few vessels and places fit to feed it, and bring it up to a fetus; there cannot be too great a number of adventurers, when there is so great a likelihood to miscarry.

It may be asked again, why a woman brings forth only one or two children, since if there were but two proper places in a uterus, several of the animalcules might there be fed. I answer, it may happen to these animalcules, as it does to seven or eight seeds put into a small hole of the ground, that seed which puts out the biggest and strongest root starves all the rest and becomes a tree.

It may be asked me again, why I make the animalcules found in the seed of several animals to be of such different sizes; comparatively to the animals they belong to, viz. in the space of a small sand in the seed of a cock, 50,000; in the roe of a codfish, 10,000; in the roe of a ruff (which fish is 1000 times smaller than a codfish) the animalcules as big as the others. Whereas, it seems reasonable that the animalcules ought to be in size to one another, as the creatures in which they are found, from which it would follow that those animalcules which are in insects would never be capable of being discovered because of their exceeding smallness. I answer that we must satisfy ourselves in these things as well as we can, for (not to speak of a cocoanut) a great walnut with its green shell weighs down 1000 apple tree seeds, and yet the proportion between the trees is not so great.

In my letter of the third of March 1681–82, I described the texture of a flesh and fish muscle; but have since examined that of a flea, judging that if I could find the same filament, I might be positive that the muscles of animals are all of the same make; having therefore several times separated and ex-

posed to view that muscle of the breast to which the leg is partly fastened, I observed the same ring-like indentations in the filaments that I had seen in other places. Some appeared to me thicker in the middle than at the ends, as tab. 2, fig. 1 [Plate 15]. *ABCDEFGH* is the description of the filament of a flea broken out of the breast from which I perceived the filaments of this insect to grow tapering towards the ends, and lose themselves in a membrane or tendon, like the filaments of the muscle of an ox. Some of the indentations were as *CF*, but most throughout were as *ABGH*. Several times I had an appearance as if a filament were constituted of several lesser threads joined together, and lying by the sides of one another.

In pursuing my observations, I took some of the flesh of the legs of the flea, and found it like that of the breast; here I counted 12 of these before named filaments, and some threads without indentations which I conceived might be vessels.[d]

I also with much trouble took out the testicles of a flea, and placed them before my microscope, and drew out the figure as well as I could, as fig. 2. *ABCD* is the testicle, *AF* and *DE* are the vasa deferentia. When the testicles were first taken out, they were of a dark color but in less than 1/10th of a minute their moisture was evaporated, and then they became crumpled, which I have here represented as well as I could.

I also searched for the vessels having as it were rings about them (of which I have formerly spoke) and am satisfied they cannot be air vessels, but rather arteries; for I saw them not only encompass the guts, but spread over and among the eggs.

The sting or snout of the flea, or rather the sheath in which it is kept, had teeth on each side like a saw, and may not fittingly be compared to a quill that is split ragged. When the sting is enclosed in the sheath, the

---

[d]The circulation of the blood in the legs of the flea is open or lacunary; therefore, there are no blood vessels in the legs of the flea. [B.]

teeth on each side go between one another. The length of this sheath is about three diameters of the thickness of hair.

I have made many attempts the last autumn to find out in what time the worm coming from the egg of a flea would become a full grown flea. The eggs of a flea kept in a warm place were hatched in four days and became worms, which I endeavored to bring up, but notwithstanding all my endeavors I could keep them alive no longer than twelve days. When I placed about the half of a small fly in the glass by the worms for their food, the part of the fly caused such steam on the glass that the worms being hairy were entangled in the moisture, and remained immovable until they died. When the worms were twelve days old, they were about the length of four eggs, and the thickness of one. Since I could bring up no worms, I took some which I thought had attained their full growth, and observed the same to spend eight or ten days in spinning their web, and then they stripped off their skin and became nymphae. These nymphae I saw move on the fourth day, though they were clear and white; on the sixth they were red about the head; on the tenth they broke their case, which was a very thin skin, and leaped into the glass, living there without food for the space of seven days.

I also took some flesh from the breast of a louse, and found the flesh threads of the same make as those of the flea.

I took also the flesh from the feet of a gnat, and found that of the same make with the former. But perceiving the legs and body of the gnat to be furnished with very fine feathers.[e] I have caused them to be drawn as fig. 3. The wing also of the gnat being adorned with feathers, I have drawn that too, as fig. 4, which is a wing as it appears to the naked eye, fig. 5. ABC is the same represented in a larger proportion, to show that not only the whole circumference of the wing, as here figure 5. ABC is beset with great and small feathers, as fig. 6. But also the nerves[f] that stiffen the wing as DDDD. The film of the wing which is between the nerves DD, seems by looking under the microscope to be full of a great many small risings, but upon a stricter examination, they are really small hairs, as fig. 7, where a beginning was made to represent the whole wing: ABC are the feathers, and ADEC are the hairs on the film . . .

[e]Perhaps Leeuwenhoek means to say scales. [B.]
[f]What Leeuwenhoek takes to be the nerves are actually the veins. [B.]

## NOTES

1. This very computation ought to have made the author aware of the extreme improbability of his opinion respecting the share which he ascribed to these his animalcula in the work of generation.

2. It is scarcely necessary to remark that this hypothesis of generation is now universally exploded. A living filament furnished by the semen masculinum has been substituted in place of Mr. Leeuwenhoek's animalcula by an ingenious philosopher of this country, now no more; but the theory which at this day has most advocates is that which supposes that the primordium or germ exists in the female before coition, and that during that act it becomes subjected to the influence and actual contact of the semen masculinum, whereby its previously quiescent parts are stimulated into action, and being conveyed, from its former repository (the ovarium) to another receptacle (the uterus) it there undergoes a gradual development, and after a time acquires the contour and resemblance of the parent forms.

## FURTHER READING

Dobell, Clifford. 1932. Antony van *Leeuwenhoek and his "Little animals."* London: J. Bale.

Ford, Brian J. 1985. *Single Lens: The Story of the Simple Microscope.* London: Heinemann.

Ruestow, Edward G. 1996. *The Microscope in the Dutch Republic : The Shaping of Discovery.* Cambridge: Cambridge University Press.

# Newton's Mathematical Principles
# of Natural Philosophy

## Isaac Newton (1642–1727)

*Isaac Newton was unquestionably the most celebrated and influential of the natural philosophers of the seventeenth century, and* Philosophiae naturalis principia mathematica; *Mathematical Principles of Natural Philosophy, 1687), from which this selection is taken, is the most celebrated work in the annals of science. Though Newton's ontology included material corpuscles in motion, it also included the notion of force, which was held to change (or tend to change) the motions of bodies—the measure of the changes of motion serving as the measure of the force. With respect to gravity, he contended that force was empirically quantifiable, in a way that the corpuscular mechanisms (championed by the mechanical philosophers) were not, but Newton also held out the hope that other kinds of force might eventually become equally as well understood as gravity. His approach thus held out the prospect for a truly mathematical physics in which various natural effects would be shown to follow in a rigorously demonstrative and quantitatively exact manner from mathematically expressed laws of force.*

*In light of the eventual triumph of Newtonian science, it is difficult for us to appreciate now just how fierce was the opposition to Newton's scientific views when he first introduced them. Proponents of the views of René Descartes focused on the concept of gravitational attraction. Newton intimated that it acts at a distance—as between the Sun and the Earth, or between the Moon and the sea—in direct violation of Descartes' contention that changes of state are to be explained in terms of innumerable collisions between insensible particles of matter. As a rearguard action, Newton elaborated a philosophical defense on his substantive scientific views in the second (1713) and third (1726) editions of his* Principia. *Newton replied to his critics that he had demonstrated from the phenomena that attraction is a property of some bodies and generalized this claim to include all bodies. Newton recognized that he was not in possession of the cause of gravitation, of whose existence he was convinced. He attempted to forge a mechanical explanation in terms of an ethereal substance pervading all bodies and filling the space between them, but he was never able to demonstrate its existence in the way*

*Source:* Isaac Newton. 1934. *The Mathematical Principles of Natural Philosophy.* Ed. Florian Cajori. Trans. A. Motte. Berkeley: University of California Press, pp. xvii-xviii; 1–14; 398–400; 543–547.

*he thought he had demonstrated the existence of gravitation itself. In the General Scholium, he asserted that experimental philosophy has no room for such "hypotheses." He insisted that, unlike his opponents, he would not invent hypotheses merely to fill an explanatory gap, but he introduced into his natural philosophy concepts of absolute space, time, and motion which he recognized he could not deduce from the phenomena. Finally, Newton in the General Scholium brought God into natural philosophy, as the cause of the order in the world.*

## PREFACE TO THE FIRST EDITION

Since the ancients (as we are told by Pappus[a]) esteemed the science of mechanics of greatest importance in the investigation of natural things, and the moderns, rejecting substantial forms and occult qualities, have endeavored to subject the phenomena of nature to the laws of mathematics, I have in this treatise cultivated mathematics as far as it relates to philosophy. The ancients considered mechanics in a twofold respect: as rational, which proceeds accurately by demonstration, and practical. To practical mechanics all the manual arts belong, from which mechanics took its name. But, as artificers do not work with perfect accuracy, it comes to pass that mechanics is so distinguished from geometry that what is perfectly accurate is called geometrical; what is less so, is called mechanical. However, the errors are not in the art, but in the artificers. He that works with less accuracy is an imperfect mechanic; and if any could work with perfect accuracy he would be the most perfect mechanic of all, for the description of right lines and circles, upon which geometry is founded, belongs to mechanics. Geometry does not teach us to draw these lines, but requires them to be drawn, for it requires that the learner should first be taught to describe these accurately before he enters upon geometry, then it shows how by these operations problems may be solved. To describe right lines and circles are problems, but not geometrical problems. The solution of these problems is required from mechanics, and by geometry the use of them, when so solved, is shown; and it is the glory of geometry that from those few principles, brought from without, it is able to produce so many things. Therefore, geometry is founded in mechanical practice, and is nothing but that part of universal mechanics which accurately proposes and demonstrates the art of measuring. But, since the manual arts are chiefly employed in the moving of bodies, it happens that geometry is commonly referred to their magnitude, and mechanics to their motion. In this sense rational mechanics will be the science of motions resulting from any forces whatsoever, and of the forces required to produce any motions, accurately proposed and demonstrated. This part of mechanics, as far as it extended to the five powers which relate to manual arts, was cultivated by the ancients who considered gravity (it not being a manual power) no otherwise than in moving weights by those powers. But I consider philosophy rather than arts and write not concerning manual but natural powers, and consider chiefly those things which relate to gravity, levity, elastic force, the resistance of fluids, and the like forces, whether attractive or impulsive; and therefore I offer this work as the mathematical principles of philosophy, for the whole burden of philosophy seems to consist in this—from the phenomena of motions

---

[a]In Book VIII of his *Synagoge* or *Collection,* which is devoted to mechanics, Pappus of Alexandria (fl. A.D. 300–350) attempts to justify the thesis that mechanics is a mathematical subject, and not a mere utilitarian one. [B.]

**PLATE 17**  Portrait of Sir Isaac Newton (1689) by Godfrey Kneller. By kind permission of the Trustees of the Portsmouth Estates.

to investigate the forces of nature, and then from these forces to demonstrate the other phenomena; and to this end the general propositions in the first and second Books are directed. In the third Book I give an example of this in the explication of the System of the World; for by the propositions mathematically demonstrated in the former Books, in the third I derive from the celestial phenomena the forces of gravity with which bodies tend to the Sun and the several planets. Then from these forces, by other propositions which are also mathematical, I deduce the motions of the planets, the comets, the Moon, and the sea. I wish we could derive the rest of the phenomena of nature by the same kind of reasoning from mechanical principles, for I am induced by many reasons to suspect that they may all depend upon certain forces by which the particles of bodies, by some causes hitherto unknown, are either mutually impelled towards one another, and cohere in regular figures, or are repelled and recede from one another. These forces being unknown, philosophers have hitherto attempted the search of nature in vain; but I hope the principles here laid down will afford some light either to this or some truer method of philosophy.

In the publication of this work the most acute and universally learned Mr. Edmund Halley[b] not only assisted me in correcting the errors of the press and preparing the geometrical figures, but it was through his solicitations that it came to be published; for when he had obtained of me my demonstrations of the figure of the celestial orbits, he continually pressed me to communicate the same to the Royal Society, who afterwards, by their kind encouragement and entreaties, engaged me to think of publishing them. But after I had begun to consider the inequalities of the lunar motions, and had entered upon some other things relating to the laws and measures of gravity and other forces; and the figures that would be described by bodies attracted according to given laws; and the motion of several bodies moving among themselves; the motion of bodies in resisting mediums; the forces, densities, and motions of mediums; the orbits of the comets, and such like, I deferred that publication until I had made a search into those matters, and could put forth the whole together. What relates to the lunar motions (being imperfect) I have put all together in the corollaries of Prop. LXVI, to avoid being obliged to

---

[b]Halley (1656–1742), who assumed the position of Astronomer Royal of England in 1720, instigated the composition of the *Principia*. By January 1684, Halley (and others) had deduced from Kepler's third law that the Sun's gravitation must vary inversely as the square of the distance. Halley then turned with no success to the more intricate problem of finding the path of a body moving under such an attraction. He visited Newton in Cambridge in August, 1684, and came directly to the point: "What would be the path of a planet under a gravitational attraction varying inversely as the distance"? "An ellipse," Newton replied without hesitation: "I have calculated it." Newton claimed that he could not produce his paper of 1679 in which he had demonstrated the connection of the inverse square relation with elliptical orbits, but promised to reconstruct his proof. A paper was sent to London within three months. Halley was so impressed by the proof that he rushed back to Cambridge in order to persuade Newton to write up his work more fully, so that it could be recorded at the Royal Society. Upon the occasion of visiting Newton once again, Halley discovered that Newton had prepared an account of the motion of a body under a force directed to a fixed center, particularly when the force varies inversely as the square of the distance, in which case the path is a conic with a focus at the center of force. Newton promised to send this short treatise "*De motu*" to the Royal Society, a promise that was communicated to and welcomed by the society on December 10, 1684. Newton indicated that he would prepare a larger treatise on the subject and in April 1685 began the preparation of his celebrated work. Newton probably intended at first to show that an inverse square law of force would account for Kepler's laws of planetary motion. As he succeeded in establishing new theorems, the idea came to him of extending the notion of gravity to all particles in the universe. [B.]

propose and distinctly demonstrate the several things there contained in a method more prolix than the subject deserved and interrupt the series of the other propositions. Some things, found out after the rest, I chose to insert in places less suitable, rather than change the number of the propositions and the citations. I heartily beg that what I have here done may be read with forbearance; and that my labors in a subject so difficult may be examined, not so much with the view to censure, as to remedy their defects ...

## Definition I

*The quantity of matter is the measure of the same, arising from its density and bulk conjointly.*[c]

Thus, air of a double density, in a double space, is quadruple in quantity; in a triple space, sextuple in quantity. The same thing is to be understood of snow, and fine dust or powders, that are condensed by compression or liquefaction, and of all bodies that are by any causes whatever differently condensed. I have no regard in this place to a medium, if any such there is, that freely pervades the interstices between the parts of bodies. It is this quantity that I mean, hereafter, everywhere under the name of body or mass. And the same is known by the weight of each body, for it is proportional to the weight, as I have found by experiments on pendulums, very accurately made, which shall be shown hereafter.

## Definition II

*The quantity of motion is the measure of the same, arising from the velocity and quantity of matter conjointly.*[d]

[c]In step with the modern view, Newton later defines equal densities in terms of inertia, thereby equating mass with inertia. [B.]

[d]By quantity of motion, Newton means momentum, or *mv*. [B.]

The motion of the whole is the sum of the motions of all the parts; and therefore in a body double in quantity, with equal velocity, the motion is double; with twice the velocity, it is quadruple.

## Definition III

*The* vis insita, *or innate force of matter, is a power of resisting, by which every body, as much as in it lies, continues in its present state, whether it be of rest, or of moving uniformly foward in a right line.*

This force is always proportional to the body whose force it is and differs nothing from the inactivity of the mass, but in our manner of conceiving it. A body, from the inert nature of matter, is not without difficulty put out of its state of rest or motion. Upon which account, this *vis insita* may, by a most significant name, be called inertia (*vis inertiae*) or force of inactivity. But a body only exerts this force when another force, impressed upon it, endeavors to change its condition; and the exercise of this force may be considered as both resistance and impulse; it is resistance so far as the body, for maintaining its present state, opposes the force impressed; it is impulse so far as the body, by not easily giving way to the impressed force of another, endeavors to change the state of that other. Resistance is usually ascribed to bodies at rest, and impulse to those in motion; but motion and rest, as commonly conceived, are only relatively distinguished; nor are those bodies always truly at rest, which commonly are taken to be so.

## Definition IV

*An impressed force is an action exerted upon a body, in order to change its state, either of rest, or of uniform motion in a right line.*

This force consists in the action only, and remains no longer in the body when the action is over. For a body maintains every new state it acquires, by its inertia only. But impressed forces are of different origins, as from percussion, from pressure, from centripetal force.

## Definition V

*A centripetal force is that by which bodies are drawn or impelled, or any way tend, towards a point as to a center.*

Of this sort is gravity, by which bodies tend to the center of the Earth; magnetism, by which iron tends to the lodestone; and that force, whatever it is, by which the planets are continually drawn aside from the rectilinear motions, which otherwise they would pursue, and made to revolve in curvilinear orbits. A stone, whirled about in a sling, endeavors to recede from the hand that turns it; and by that endeavor, distends the sling and that with so much the greater force, as it is revolved with the greater velocity, and as soon as it is let go, flies away. That force which opposes itself to this endeavor, and by which the sling continually draws back the stone towards the hand, and retains it in its orbit, because it is directed to the hand as the center of the orbit, I call the centripetal force. And the same thing is to be understood of all bodies, revolved in any orbits. They all endeavor to recede from the centers of their orbits; and were it not for the opposition of a contrary force which restrains them to, and detains them in their orbits, which I therefore call centripetal, would fly off in right lines, with an uniform motion. A projectile, if it was not for the force of gravity, would not deviate towards the Earth, but would go off from it in a right line, and that with an uniform motion, if the resistance of the air was taken away. It is by its gravity that it is drawn aside continually from its rectilinear course, and made to deviate towards the Earth, more or less, according to the force of its gravity, and the velocity of its motion. The less its gravity is, or the quantity of its matter, or the greater the velocity with which it is projected, the less will it deviate from a rectilinear course, and the farther it will go. If a leaden ball, projected from the top of a mountain by the force of gunpowder, with a given velocity, and in a direction parallel to the horizon, is carried in a curved line to the distance of two miles before it falls to the ground; the same, if the resistance of the air were taken away, with a double or decuple [10 times] velocity, would fly twice or ten times as far. And by increasing the velocity, we may at pleasure increase the distance to which it might be projected, and diminish the curvature of the line which it might describe, until at last it should fall at the distance of 10, 30, or 90 degrees, or even might go quite round the whole Earth before it falls; or lastly, so that it might never fall to the Earth, but go forwards into the celestial spaces, and proceed in its motion *in infinitum.* And after the same manner that a projectile, by the force of gravity, may be made to revolve in an orbit, and go round the whole Earth, the Moon also, either by the force of gravity, if it is endued with gravity, or by any other force that impels it towards the Earth, may be continually drawn aside towards the Earth, out of the rectilinear way which by its innate force it would pursue; and would be made to revolve in the orbit which it now describes: nor could the moon without some such force be retained in its orbit. If this force was too small, it would not sufficiently turn the Moon out of a rectilinear course; if it was too great, it would turn it too much, and draw down the Moon from orbit towards the Earth. It is necessary that the force be of a just quantity, and it belongs to the mathematicians to find the force that may serve exactly to retain a body in a given orbit with a given velocity; and vice versa, to determine the curvilinear way into which a body projected from a given place, with a given velocity, may be made to deviate from its natural rectilinear way, by means of a given force . . .

## SCHOLIUM

Hitherto I have laid down the definitions of such words as are less known, and explained the sense in which I would have them to be understood in the following discourse. I do not define time, space, place, and motion, as being well known to all. Only I must observe, that the common people conceive those quantities under no other notions but from the relation they bear to sensible objects. And thence arise certain prejudices, for the removing of which it will be convenient to distinguish them into absolute and relative, true and apparent, mathematical and common.[e]

I. Absolute, true, and mathematical time, of itself, and from its own nature, flows equably without relation to anything external, and by another name is called duration: relative, apparent, and common time, is some sensible and external (whether accurate or unequable) measure of duration by the means of motion, which is commonly used instead of true time; such as an hour, a day, a month, a year.

II. Absolute space, in its own nature, without relation to anything external, remains always similar and immovable. Relative space is some movable dimension or measure of the absolute spaces; which our senses determine by its position to bodies; and which is commonly taken for immovable space; such is the dimension of a subterraneous, an aerial, or celestial space, determined by its position in respect of the Earth. Absolute and relative space are the same in figure and magnitude; but they do not remain always numerically the same. For if the Earth, for instance, moves, a space of our air, which relatively and in respect of the Earth remains always the same, will at one time be one part of the absolute space into which the air passes; at another time it will be another part of the same, and so, ab-

solutely understood, it will be continually changed.

III. Place is a part of space which a body takes up, and is according to the space, either absolute or relative. I say, a part of space; not the situation, nor the external surface of the body. For the places of equal solids are always equal; but their surfaces, by reason of their dissimilar figures, are often unequal. Positions properly have no quantity, nor are they so much the places themselves, as the properties of places. The motion of the whole is the same with the sum of the motions of the parts; that is, the translation of the whole, out of its place, is the same thing with the sum of the translations of the parts out of their places; and therefore the place of the whole is the same as the sum of the places of the parts, and for that reason, it is internal, and in the whole body.

IV. Absolute motion is the translation of a body from one absolute place into another; and relative motion, the translation from one relative place into another. Thus, in a ship under sail, the relative place of a body is that part of the ship which the body possesses; or that part of the cavity which the body fills, and which, therefore, moves together with the ship: and relative rest is the continuance of the body in the same part of the ship, or of its cavity. But real, absolute rest, is the continuance of the body in the same part of that immovable space, in which the ship itself, its cavity, and all that it contains, is moved. Wherefore, if the Earth is really at rest, the body, which relatively rests in the ship, will really and absolutely move with the same velocity which the ship has on the Earth. But if the Earth also moves, the true and absolute motion of the body will arise, partly from the true motion of the Earth, in immovable space, partly from the relative motion of the ship on the Earth; and if the body moves also relatively in the ship, its true motion will arise, partly from the true motion of the Earth, in immovable space, and partly from the relative motions as well of the ship on the earth, as of the body in the ship; and from these relative motions will arise the

[e]These definitions rest on Newton's idea of God, of whom it is impious to think that he did not know where he was or what time it might be. Given Newton's belief that God constitutes duration and space, even without bodies or universes as landmarks, there must be absolute space and time. [B.]

relative motion of the body on the Earth. As if that part of the Earth, where the ship is, was truly moved towards the east, with a velocity of 10,010 parts; while the ship itself, with a fresh gale, and full sails, is carried towards the west, with a velocity expressed by ten of those parts; but a sailor walks in the ship towards the east, with one part of the said velocity; then the sailor will be moved truly in immovable space towards the east, with a velocity of 10,001 parts, and relatively on the Earth towards the west, with a velocity of nine of those parts.

Absolute time, in astronomy, is distinguished from relative [time] by the equation or correction of the apparent time. For the natural days are truly unequal, though they are commonly considered as equal, and used for a measure of time; astronomers correct this inequality that they may measure the celestial motions by a more accurate time. It may be that there is no such thing as an equable motion, whereby time may be accurately measured. All motions may be accelerated and retarded, but the flowing of absolute time is not liable to any change. The duration or perseverance of the existence of things remains the same, whether the motions are swift or slow, or none at all; and, therefore, this duration ought to be distinguished from what are only sensible measures thereof; and from which we deduce it, by means of the astronomical equation. The necessity of this equation, for determining the times of a phenomenon, is evidenced as well from the experiments of the pendulum clock, as by eclipses of the satellites of Jupiter.

As the order of the parts of time is immutable, so also is the order of the parts of space. Suppose those parts to be moved out of their places, and they will be moved (if the expression may be allowed) out of themselves. For times and spaces are, as it were, the places as well of themselves as of all other things. All things are placed in time as to order of succession; and in space as to order of situation. It is from their essence or nature that they are places; and that the primary places of things should be movable is absurd. These are, therefore, the absolute places; and translations out of those places are the only absolute motions.

But because the parts of space cannot be seen, or distinguished from one another by our senses, therefore, in their stead we use sensible measures of them. For from the positions and distances of things from any body considered as immovable, we define all places; and then with respect to such places, we estimate all motions, considering bodies as transferred from some of those places into others. And so, instead of absolute places and motions, we use relative ones; and that without any inconvenience in common affairs; but in philosophical disquisitions, we ought to abstract from our senses, and consider things themselves, distinct from what are only sensible measures of them. For, it may be that there is no body really at rest, to which the places and motions of others may be referred.

But we may distinguish rest and motion, absolute and relative, one from the other by their properties, causes, and effects. It is a property of rest that bodies really at rest do rest in respect to one another. And, therefore, as it is possible that in the remote regions of the fixed stars, or perhaps far beyond them, there may be some body absolutely at rest; but impossible to know, from the position of bodies to one another in our regions, whether any of these do keep the same position to that remote body, it follows that absolute rest cannot be determined from the position of bodies in our regions.

It is a property of motion that the parts, which retain given positions to their wholes, do partake of the motions of those wholes. For, all the parts of revolving bodies endeavor to recede from the axis of motion; and the impetus of bodies moving forwards arises from the joint impetus of all the parts. Therefore, if surrounding bodies are moved, those that are relatively at rest within them will partake of their motion. Upon which account, the true and absolute motion of a body cannot be determined by the translation of it from those which only seem to rest; for the external bodies ought not only to appear at rest, but to be really at rest. For otherwise, all included bodies, besides their translation from near the surrounding ones, partake likewise of their true motions; and though that translation were not made, they would not be really at rest, but only seem to be so. For the surrounding bodies stand in the like relation to the surrounded as the exterior part of a whole does to the interior, or as the shell does to the kernel; but if the shell moves, the kernel will also move, as being part of the whole, without any removal from near the shell.

A property, near akin to the preceding, is this: That if a place is moved, whatever is placed therein moves along with it; and, therefore, a body, which is moved from a place in motion, partakes also of the motion of its place. Upon which account, all motions, from places in motion, are no other than parts of entire and absolute motions; and every entire motion is composed of the motion of the body out of its first place, and the motion of this place out of its place, and so on, until we come to some immovable place, as in the before-mentioned example of the sailor. Wherefore, entire and absolute motions cannot be otherwise determined than by immovable places; and for that reason I did before refer those absolute motions to immovable places, but relative ones to movable places. Now, no other places are immovable but those that, from infinity to infinity, do all retain the same given position one to another; and upon this account must ever remain unmoved; and do thereby constitute immovable space.

The causes by which true and relative motions are distinguished, one from the other, are the forces impressed upon bodies to generate motion. True motion is neither generated nor altered, but by some force impressed upon the body moved; but relative motion may be generated or altered without any force impressed upon the body. For it is sufficient only to impress some force on other bodies with which the former is compared, that by their giving way, that relation may be changed, in which the relative rest or motion of this other body did consist. Again, true motion suffers always some change from any force impressed upon the moving body; but relative motion does not necessarily undergo any change by such forces. For if the same forces are likewise impressed on those other bodies, with which the comparison is made, that the relative position may be preserved, then that condition will be preserved in which the relative motion consists. And, therefore, any relative motion may be changed when the true motion remains unaltered, and the relative may be preserved when the true suffers some change. Thus, true motion by no means consists in such relations.

The effects which distinguish absolute from relative motion are the forces of receding from the axis of circular motion. For there are no such forces in a circular motion purely relative, but in a true and absolute circular motion, they are greater or lesser, according to the quantity of the motion. If a vessel, hung by a long cord, is so often turned about that the cord is strongly twisted, then filled with water, and held at rest together with the water; thereupon, by the sudden action of another force, it is whirled about the contrary way, and while the cord is untwisting itself, the vessel continues for some time in this motion; the surface of the water will at first be plain, as before the vessel began to move; but after that, the vessel, by gradually communicating its motion to the water, will make it begin sensibly to revolve, and recede little by little from the middle, and ascend to the sides of the vessel, forming itself into a concave figure (as I have experienced), and the swifter the motion becomes, the higher the water will rise, until at last, performing its revolutions in the same times with the vessel, it becomes relatively at rest in it. This ascent of the water shows its endeavor to recede from the axis of its motion; and the true and absolute circular motion of the water, which is here directly contrary to the relative, becomes known, and may be measured by this endeavor. At first, when the relative motion of the water in the vessel was greatest, it produced no endeavor to recede from the axis; the water showed no tendency to the circumference, nor any ascent towards the sides of the vessel, but remained of a plain surface, and therefore its true circular motion had not yet begun. But afterwards, when the relative motion of the water had decreased, the ascent thereof towards the sides of the vessel proved its endeavor to recede from the axis; and this endeavor showed the real circular motion of the water continually increasing, until it had acquired its greatest quantity, when the water rested relatively in the vessel. And, therefore, this endeavor does not depend upon any translation of the water in respect to the ambient bodies, nor can true circular motion be defined by such translation. There is only one real circular motion of any one revolving body, corresponding to only one power of endeavoring to recede from its axis of motion, as its proper and adequate effect; but relative motions, in one and the same body, are innumerable, according to the various relations it bears to external bodies, and, like other relations, are altogether destitute of any real effect, any otherwise than they may perhaps partake of that one only true motion. And, therefore, in their system who suppose that our heavens, revolving below the sphere of the fixed stars, carry the planets along with them; the several parts of those heavens, and the planets, which are indeed relatively at rest in their heavens, do yet really move. For they change their position one to another (which never happens to bodies truly at rest), and being carried together with their heavens, partake of their motions, and as parts of revolving wholes, endeavor to recede from the axis of their motions.

Wherefore, relative quantities are not the quantities themselves, whose names they bear, but those sensible measures of them (either accurate or inaccurate), which are commonly used instead of the measured quantities themselves. And if the meaning of words is to be determined by their use, then by the names time, space, place, and motion, their [sensible] measures are properly to be understood; and the expression will be unusual, and purely mathematical, if the measured quantities themselves are meant. On this account, those violate the accuracy of language, which ought to be kept precise, who interpret these words for the measured quantities. Nor do those less defile the purity of mathematical and philosophical truths, who confound real quantities with their relations and sensible measures.

It is indeed a matter of great difficulty to discover and effectually to distinguish the true motions of particular bodies from the apparent; because the parts of that immovable space, in which those motions are performed, do by no means come under the observation of our senses. Yet, the thing is not altogether desperate; for we have some arguments to guide us, partly from the apparent motions, which are the differences of the true motions; partly from the forces, which are the causes and effects of the true motions. For instance, if two globes, kept at a given distance one from the other by means of a cord that connects them, were revolved about their common center of gravity, we might, from the tension of the cord, discover the endeavor of the globes to recede from the axis of their motion, and from this we might compute the quantity of their circular motions. And then, if any equal forces should be impressed at once on the alternate faces of the globes to augment or diminish their circular motions, from the increase or decrease of the tension of the cord, we might infer the increment or decrement of their motions; and from this would be found on what faces those forces ought to be impressed, that the motions of the globes might be most augmented; that is, we might discover their hindmost faces, or those which, in the circular motion, do follow. But the faces which follow being known, and consequently, the opposite ones that precede, we should likewise know the determination of their motions. And thus, we might find both the quantity and the determination of this circular motion, even in an immense vacuum, where there was nothing external or sensible with which the globes could be compared. But now, if in that space some remote bodies were placed that kept always a given position one to another, as the fixed stars do in our regions, we could not indeed determine from the relative translation of the globes among those bodies, whether the motion did belong to the globes or to the bodies. But if we observed the cord, and found that its tension was that very tension which the motions of the globes required, we might conclude the motion to be in the globes, and the bodies to be at rest; and then, lastly, from the translation of the globes among the bodies, we should find the determination of their motions. But, how we are to obtain the true motions from their causes, effects, and apparent differences, and the converse, shall be explained more at large in the following treatise. For to this end it was that I composed it.


## AXIOMS OR LAWS OF MOTION

### Law I

*Every body continues in its state of rest, or of uniform motion in a right line, unless it is compelled to change that state by forces impressed upon it.*

Projectiles continue in their motions, so far as they are not retarded by the resistance of the air, or impelled downwards by the force of gravity. A top, whose parts by their cohesion are continually drawn aside from rectilinear motions, does not cease its rotation, otherwise than as it is retarded by the air. The greater bodies of the planets and comets, meeting with less resistance in freer

spaces, preserve their motions both progressive and circular for a much longer time.


### Law II

*The change of motion[f] is proportional to the motive force impressed; and is made in the direction of the right line in which that force is impressed.*

If any force generates a motion, a double force will generate double the motion, a triple force triple the motion, whether that force be impressed altogether and at once, or gradually and successively. And this motion (being always directed the same way with the generating force), if the body moved before, is added to or subtracted from the former motion, according as they directly conspire with or are directly contrary to each other; or obliquely joined, when they are oblique, so as to produce a new motion compounded from the determination of both.[g]


### Law III

*To every action there is always opposed an equal reaction: or, the mutual actions of two bodies upon each other are always equal, and directed to contrary parts.*

Whatever draws or presses another is as much drawn or pressed by that other. If you press a stone with your finger, the finger is also pressed by the stone. If a horse draws a stone tied to a rope, the horse (if I may so say) will be equally drawn back towards the stone; for the distended rope, by the same endeavor to relax or unbend itself, will draw the horse as much towards the stone as it does the stone towards the horse, and will

---

[f]The alteration of motion Newton has in mind is the rate of change of momentum. For the case of a constant mass, this becomes $F = ma$. Thus, the second law provides a definition of force in terms of the acceleration given to a mass. [B.]

[g]Newton credits Galileo with the first two laws, but the second law is a definition of measurement of kinetic force which Galileo never attained. [B.]

obstruct the progress of the one as much as it advances that of the other. If a body impinge upon another, and by its force change the motion of the other, that body also (because of the equality of the mutual pressure) will undergo an equal change, in its own motion, towards the contrary part. The changes made by these actions are equal, not in the velocities but in the motions of bodies; that is to say, if the bodies are not hindered by any other impediments. For, because the motions are equally changed, the changes of the velocities made towards contrary parts are inversely proportional to the bodies . . .

## RULES OF REASONING IN PHILOSOPHY

### Rule I

*We are to admit no more causes of natural things than such as are both true and sufficient to explain their appearances.*

To this purpose the philosophers say that nature does nothing in vain, and more is in vain when less will serve; for nature is pleased with simplicity, and affects not the pomp of superfluous causes.

### Rule II

*Therefore to the same natural effects we must, as far as possible, assign the same causes.*

As to respiration in a man and in a beast; the descent of stones in Europe and in America; the light of our culinary fire and of the Sun; the reflection of light in the Earth, and in the planets.

### Rule III

*The qualities of bodies, which admit neither intensification nor remission of degrees, and which are found to belong to all bodies within the reach of our experiments, are to be esteemed the universal qualities of all bodies whatsoever.*

For, since the qualities of bodies are only known to us by experiments, we are to hold for universal all such as universally agree with experiments; and such as are not liable to diminution can never be quite taken away. We are certainly not to relinquish the evidence of experiments for the sake of dreams and vain fictions of our own devising; nor are we to recede from the analogy of nature, which is want to be simple, and always consonant to itself. We [in] no way know the extension of bodies than by our senses, nor do these reach it in all bodies; but because we perceive extension in all that are sensible, therefore, we ascribe it universally to all others also. That abundance of bodies are hard, we learn by experience; and because the hardness of the whole arises from the hardness of the parts, we, therefore, justly infer the hardness of the undivided particles not only of the bodies we feel but of all others.[h] That all bodies are impenetrable, we gather not from reason, but from sensation. The bodies which we handle we find impenetrable, and on this basis conclude impenetrability to be a universal property of all bodies whatsoever. That all bodies are movable, and endowed with certain powers (which we call the inertia) of persevering in their motion, or in their rest, we only infer from the like properties observed in the bodies which we have seen. The extension, hardness, impenetrability, mobility and inertia of the whole, result from the extension hardness impenetrability mobility, and inertia of the parts; and hence we conclude the least particles of all bodies to be also all extended, and hard and impenetrable, and movable, and endowed with their proper inertia. And this is the foundation of all philosophy. Moreover, that the divided but contiguous particles of bodies may be separated from one another, is matter of observation; and, in

---

[h]This claim is rejected by modern physics: if we change the state of a substance, say, from solid to liquid, we do not thereby alter its parts but the forces acting between these parts. [B.]

the particles that remain undivided, our minds are able to distinguish yet lesser parts, as is mathematically demonstrated. But, whether the parts so distinguished, and not yet divided, may, by the powers of nature, be actually divided and separated from one another, we cannot certainly determine. Yet, had we the proof of but one experiment that any undivided particle, in breaking a hard and solid body, suffered a division, we might by virtue of this rule conclude that the undivided as well as the divided particles may be divided and actually separated to infinity.

Lastly, if it universally appears, by experiments and astronomical observations that all bodies about the Earth gravitate towards the Earth, and that in proportion to the quantity of matter which they severally contain; that the Moon likewise, according to the quantity of its matter, gravitates towards the Earth; that, on the other hand, our sea gravitates towards the Moon; and all the planets one towards another; and the comets in like manner towards the Sun; we must, in consequence of this rule, universally allow that all bodies, whatsoever, are endowed with a principle of mutual gravitation. For, the argument from the appearances concludes with more force for the universal gravitation of all bodies than for their impenetrability; of which, among those in the celestial regions, we have no experiments, nor any manner of observation. Not that I affirm gravity to be essential to bodies: By their *vis insita* I mean nothing but their inertia. This is immutable. Their gravity is diminished as they recede from the Earth.

### Rule IV

*In experimental philosophy we are to look upon propositions inferred by general induction from phenomena as accurately or very nearly true, not withstanding any contrary hypotheses that may be imagined, until such time as other phenomena occur, by which they may either be made more accurate, or liable to exceptions.*

This rule we must follow, that the argument of induction may not be evaded by hypotheses . . .

### GENERAL SCHOLIUM

The hypothesis of vortices is pressed with many difficulties.[i] That every planet by a radius drawn to the sun may describe areas proportional to the times of description, the periodic times of the several parts of the vortices should observe the square of their distances from the Sun; but that the periodic times of the planets may obtain the ³⁄₂th power of their distances from the sun, the

---

[i]The second book of Newton's great work features a sustained examination of the dynamical conditions of René Descartes' theory of vortex motion. A number of arguments are generated against the possibility of vortices; in particular, Newton argues that the vortex theory cannot be reconciled with Kepler's laws of planetary motion. The problem stems from the incompatibility between the velocity relations in Kepler's second and third laws. Applied to a single vortex, Kepler's second law requires the speeds of its layers to vary inversely as the distances; whereas the third law of periodic times demands that the speeds vary inversely as the square of the distances. The consequence is that the visible center of a vortex—any planet will do nicely—would have two different speeds at the same time.

After reading a review of the *Principia* printed in the influential *Acta Eruditorum* in 1688, the German philosopher and mathematician, G. W. Leibniz, immediately countered what he perceived to be a damaging blow to the vortex theory with his "Essay on the Causes of the Motions of the Heavenly Bodies," which appeared in the February 1689 issue of the *Acta*. Leibniz's "Essay" set a precedent for Cartesian science by investigating the soundness of Kepler's laws in a world of vortices; i.e., in a world where motion encounters resistance as a matter of course. By 1700, many of the more distinguished Cartesians were struggling to reconcile the vortex hypothesis with Kepler's laws of planetary motion and by 1750 all but the most vociferous Cartesians had admitted defeat. [B.]

periodic times of the parts of the vortex ought to be as the ³⁄₂th power of their distances. That the smaller vortices may maintain their lesser revolutions about Saturn, Jupiter, and other planets, and swim quietly and undisturbed in the greater vortex of the Sun, the periodic times of the parts of the Sun's vortex should be equal; but the rotation of the Sun and planets about their axes, which ought to correspond with the motions of their vortices, recede far from all these proportions. The motions of the comets are exceedingly regular, are governed by the same laws with the motions of the planets, and can by no means be accounted for by the hypothesis of vortices; for comets are carried with very eccentric motions through all parts of the heavens indifferently, with a freedom that is incompatible with the motion of a vortex.

Bodies projected in our air suffer no resistance but from the air. Withdraw the air, as is done in Mr. Boyle's vacuum, and the resistance ceases; for in this void a bit of fine down and a piece of solid gold descend with equal velocity. And the same argument must apply to the celestial spaces above the Earth's atmosphere; in these spaces, where there is no air to resist their motions, all bodies will move with the greatest freedom; and the planets and comets will constantly pursue their revolutions in orbits given in kind and position, according to the laws above explained; but though these bodies may, indeed, continue in their orbits by the mere laws of gravity, yet they could by no means have at first derived the regular position of the orbits themselves from those laws.

The six primary planets are revolved about the sun in circles concentric with the Sun, and with motions directed towards the same parts, and almost in the same plane. Ten moons are revolved about the Earth, Jupiter, and Saturn, in circles concentric with them, with the same direction of motion, and nearly in the planes of the orbits of those planets; but it is not to be conceived that mere mechanical causes could give birth to so many regular motions, since the comets range over all parts of the heavens in very eccentric orbits; for by that kind of motion they pass easily through the orbs of the planets, and with great rapidity; and in their aphelions, where they move the slowest, and are detained the longest, they recede to the greatest distances from each other, and hence suffer the least disturbance from their mutual attractions. This most beautiful system of the Sun, planets, and comets, could only proceed from the counsel and dominion of an intelligent and powerful Being. And if the fixed stars are the centers of other like systems, these, being formed by the like wise counsel, must be all subject to the dominion of One; especially since the light of the fixed stars is of the same nature with the light of the Sun, and from every system light passes into all the other systems: and lest the systems of the fixed stars should, by their gravity, fall on each other, he has placed those systems at immense distances from one another.

This Being governs all things, not as the soul of the world, but as Lord over all; and on account of his dominion he is wont to be called *Lord God* παντοκράτωρ, or *Universal Ruler;* for *God* is a relative word, and has a respect to servants; and *Deity* is the dominion of God not over his own body, as those imagine who fancy God to be the soul of the world, but over servants. The Supreme God is a Being eternal, infinite, absolutely perfect; but a being, however perfect, without dominion, cannot be said to be Lord God; for we say, my God, your God, the God of *Israel,* the God of Gods, and Lord of Lords; but we do not say, my Eternal, your Eternal, the Eternal of *Israel,* the Eternal of Gods; we do not say, my Infinite, or my Perfect: these are titles which have no respect to servants. The word God usually signifies *Lord;* but every lord is not a God. It is the dominion of a spiritual being which constitutes a God: a true, supreme, or imaginary dominion makes a true, supreme, or imaginary God. And from his true dominion it follows that the true

God is a living, intelligent, and powerful Being; and, from his other perfections, that he is supreme, or most perfect. He is eternal and infinite, omnipotent and omniscient; that is, his duration reaches from eternity to eternity; his presence from infinity to infinity; he governs all things, and knows all things that are or can be done. He is not eternity and infinity, but eternal and infinite; he is not duration or space, but he endures and is present. He endures forever, and is everywhere present; and, by existing always and everywhere, he constitutes duration and space. Since every particle of space is *always,* and every indivisible moment of duration is *everywhere,* certainly the Maker and Lord of all things cannot be *never* and *nowhere.* Every soul that has perception is, though in different times and in different organs of sense and motion, still the same indivisible person. There are given successive parts in duration, coexistent parts in space, but neither the one nor the other in the person of a man, or his thinking principle; and much less can they be found in the thinking substance of God. Every man, so far as he is a thing that has perception, is one and the same man during his whole life, in all and each of his organs of sense. God is the same God, always and everywhere. He is omnipresent not *virtually* only, but also *substantially;* for virtue cannot subsist without substance. In him are all things contained and moved; yet neither affects the other: God suffers nothing from the motion of bodies; bodies find no resistance from the omnipresence of God. It is allowed by all that the Supreme God exists necessarily; and by the same necessity He exists *always* and *everywhere.* By reason of which also he is all similar, all eye, all ear, all brain, all arm, all power to perceive, to understand, and to act; but in a manner not at all human, in a manner not at all corporeal, in a manner utterly unknown to us. As a blind man has no idea of colors, so have we no idea of the manner by which the all-wise God perceives and understands all things. He is utterly void of all body and bodily figure, and can therefore neither be seen, nor heard, nor touched; nor ought he to be worshiped under the representation of any corporeal thing. We have ideas of his attributes, but what the real substance of anything is we know not. In bodies, we see only their figures and colors, we hear only the sounds, we touch only their outward surfaces, we smell only the smells, and taste the savors; but their inward substances are not to be known either by our senses, or by any reflex act of our minds: much less, then, have we any idea of the substance of God. We know him only by his most wise and excellent contrivances of things, and final causes; we admire him for his perfections; but we reverence and adore him on account of his dominion: for we adore him as his servants; and a god without dominion, providence, and final causes, is nothing else but Fate and Nature. Blind metaphysical necessity, which is certainly the same always and everywhere, could produce no variety of things. All that diversity of natural things which we find suited to different times and places could arise from nothing but the ideas and will of a Being necessarily existing. But, by way of allegory, God is said to see, to speak, to laugh, to love, to hate, to desire, to give, to receive, to rejoice, to be angry, to fight, to frame, to work, to build; for all our notions of God are taken from the ways of mankind by a certain similitude, which, though not perfect, has some likeness, however. And thus much concerning God; to discourse of whom from the appearances of things, does certainly belong to Natural Philosophy.[j]

[j]When the second edition of the *Principia* appeared in 1713, Newton's confidence in the capacity of an experimental outlook was boundless. Even discourse on God, he asserted, fell within the province of experimental science. This passage "experimental philosophy" would be withdrawn in the 1726, English-language edition prepared under the guidance of Henry Pemberton, and replaced with "natural philosophy." [B.]

Hitherto we have explained the phenomena of the heavens and of our sea by the power of gravity, but have not yet assigned the cause of this power. This is certain that it must proceed from a cause that penetrates to the very centers of the Sun and planets, without suffering the least diminution of its force; that operates not according to the quantity of the surfaces of the particles upon which it acts (as mechanical causes used to do), but according to the quantity of the solid matter which they contain, and propagates its virtue on all sides to immense distances, decreasing always as the inverse square of the distances. Gravitation towards the Sun is made up out of the gravitations towards the several particles of which the body of the Sun is composed; and in receding from the Sun decreases accurately as the inverse square of the distances as far as the orbit of Saturn, as evidently appears from the quiescence of the aphelion of the planets; indeed, and even to the remotest aphelion of the comets, if those aphelions are also quiescent. But, hitherto, I have not been able to discover the cause of those properties of gravity from phenomena, and I frame no hypothesis; for whatever is not deduced from the phenomena is to be called an hypothesis; and hypotheses, whether metaphysical or physical, whether of occult qualities or mechanical, have no place in experimental philosophy.[k] In this philosophy particular propositions are inferred from the phenomena, and afterwards rendered general by induction. Thus, it was that the impenetrability, the mobility, and the impulsive force of bodies, and the laws of motion and of gravitation, were discovered. And to us it is enough that gravity does really exist, and act according to the laws which we have explained, and abundantly serves to account for all the motions of the celestial bodies, and of our sea.

And now we might add something concerning a certain most subtle spirit which pervades and lies hid in all gross bodies; by the force and action of which spirit the particles of bodies attract one another at near distances, and cohere, if contiguous; and electric bodies operate to greater distances, as well repelling as attracting the neighboring corpuscles; and light is emitted, reflected, refracted, inflected, and heats bodies; and all sensation is excited, and the members of animal bodies move at the command of the will, namely, by the vibrations of this spirit, mutually propagated along the solid filaments of the nerves, from the outward organs of sense to the brain, and from the brain into the muscles. But these are things that cannot be explained in few words, nor are we furnished with that sufficiency of experiments which is required to an accurate determination and demonstration of the laws by which this electric and elastic spirit operates.

[k]Newton's attack on hypotheses was part of a long-running methodological strategy, which was initially fashioned to buttress his early optical theories, and which was later smuggled into the second edition of the *Principia* (1713), to safeguard it against the objections raised against the first edition (1687). The expression "hypothesis" has many meanings—a conjecture that one examines in its consequence and implications; a proposition that one advances to deduce its logical consequences; etc. The relevant sense for Newton is a proposition that one employs to deduce the celestial phenomena, without affirming that the confirmation of this proposition by observed data implies the ontological truth of the hypothesis. It is in this sense that Andreas Osiander's anonymous preface to *De Revolutionibus* portrays the Copernican system as a mere hypothesis or as a mathematical device that makes no pretensions that the Earth actually moves around the Sun. By asserting "I frame no hypothesis," Newton means generally that he will frame no hypothesis that he knows to be false but, in particular, that his hypotheses are established experimentally, i.e., they are situated in experience and not behind it. [B.]

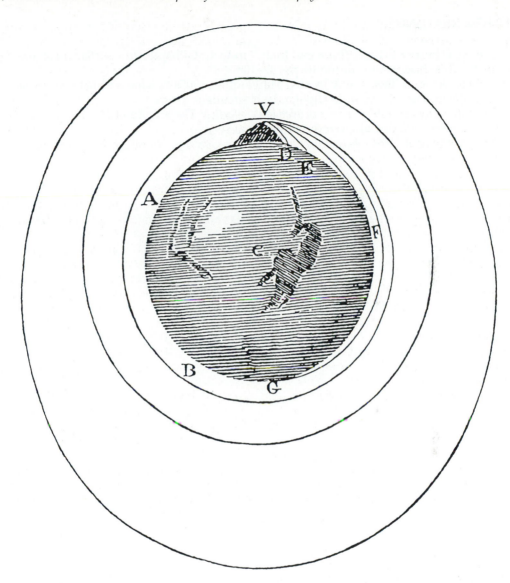

**PLATE 18**   Newton's illustration of the action of centripetal forces: "For a stone that is projected is by the pressure of its own weight forced out of the rectilinear path, which by the initial projection alone it should have pursued, and made to describe a curved line in the air; and though that crooked way is at last brought down to the ground; and the greater the velocity is with which it is projected, the farther it goes before it falls to the Earth. We may therefore suppose the velocity to be so increased, that it would describe an arc of 1, 2, 5, 10, 100, 1000 miles before it arrived at the Earth, until at last, exceeding the limits of the Earth, it should pass into space without touching it." Isaac Newton, *Mathematical Principles of Natural Philosophy*. Trans. A. Motte; revised by F. Cajori. Berkeley: University of California Press, 1934.

## FURTHER READINGS

Cohen, I. Bernard. 1971. "Newton, Isaac." In C. C. Gillispie, ed., *Dictionary of Scientific Biography*, volume 10, pp. 42–103.

Dobbs, Betty Jo Teeter and Jacobs, Margaret C. 1995. *Newton and the Culture of Newtonianism*. Atlantic Highlands: Humanities Press.

Westfall, Richard. 1971. *Force in Newton's Physics: The Science of Dynamics in the Seventeenth Century*. London: Macdonald.

White, Michael. 1997. *Isaac Newton: The Last Sorcerer*. Reading, MA: Addison-Wesley.

# The Sexual System

## Carolus Linnaeus (1707–1778)

*As a youth, Carl Linnaeus composed a remarkable poem on the marriage of plants, in which he maintained that plants reproduced in the same manner as animals—via female and male organs. The idea that plants are given to sexuality was already a staple in biological treatises, thanks to the work of Nehemiah Grew (1641–1712) and Rudolph Camerarius (1665–1721), but this idea was first elaborated by Linnaeus in a biological system. As early as 1730, he announced that the stamens and pistils were none other than the sexual organs of plants, which could serve as the basis for a new biological system.*

*The mature form of this system was presented in his* Systema naturae *(1735: Natural System), from which this reading is taken. The various plants are grouped by Linnaeus into twenty-four classes, according to the number of stamens and their relative order. Each class is then divided into certain orders, mostly according to the number of pistils. The practical applicability of this system made botany a pleasurable and easy science. After one look at the organs or fertilization, any plant could be quickly placed in the proper class and order. Linnaeus was aware that the sexual system was an artificial structure. It was rigorously erected on a single principle of division, and so represented the natural affinities only partially. He worked hard to replace the sexual system with a natural system, which would express the natural relations.*

*His lasting contribution was his creation in 1749 of binomial nomenclature, which he introduced in* Species plantarum *(1753) by giving each plant a generic name and a specific name. Until then, scientific plant names were polynomial—a short Latin description of the distinguishing feature. This combination of name and description was unsatisfactory, being too long for the name and too brief for the description. Linnaeus' innovation, separating the two functions, is the basis of modern nomenclature.*

1. All the real knowledge which we possess depends on *method,* by which we distinguish the similar from the dissimilar. The greater number of natural distinctions this method comprehends, the clearer becomes our idea of the things. The more numerous the objects which employ our attention, the more difficult it becomes to form such a method and the more necessary. The great Creator has in no part of his works presented a greater variety to the human mind than in the vegetable kingdom, which covers the whole globe that we inhabit; by reason of

*Source:* "The Families of Plants," *Genera Plantarum.* The Botanical Society at Lichfield, 1787. In *Readings on the Literature of Science,* eds. W. Dampier and M. Dampier, pp. 188–195.

which, if a distinct method is ever necessary, it is necessary here; if we hope to gain a distinct knowledge of vegetables . . .

2. To him therefore vegetables are known who can join the similar to the similar, and can separate the dissimilar from the dissimilar.

3. The *botanist* is he who can affix similar names to similar vegetables, and different names to different ones, so as to be intelligible to every one.

4. The *names* of plants are *generic*, and (where there are any species), *specific*. These

should be certain and well-founded, not vague, evasive, or variously applicable. Before they can be such, it is necessary that they should have been affixed to certain, not to vague, genera for if this foundation be unsteady, the names also, and in consequence the doctrine of the botanist, crumbles into ruin.

5. The *species* are as numerous as the different and constant forms of vegetables which exist upon this globe; which forms, according to instinctive laws of generation, produce others similar to themselves, but in

**PLATE 19**   Noah's Ark. Painting by Edward Hicks. Courtesy of the Philadelphia Museum of Art.

greater numbers. Hence there are as many species as there are different forms or structures of plants now existing; excepting such less-different *varieties*, which situation or accident has occasioned.

6. The *genera* are as numerous as the common proximate attributes of the different species, as they were created in the beginning; this is confirmed by revelation, discovery, observation; hence the genera are all natural.

For we must not join in the same genus the horse and the swine, though both species had been one-hoofed, nor separate in different genera the goat, the reindeer, and the elk, though they differ in the form of their horns. We ought therefore by attentive and diligent observation to determine the limits of the genera, since they cannot be determined a priori . . .

7. That it has pleased Infinite Wisdom to distinguish the genera of plants by their *fructification* was discovered in the last age; and first indeed by Conradus Gesner,[a] the ornament of his time, as appears from his posthumous epistles, and from the plates published by Camerarius,[b] although the first, who introduced this great discovery into use, was Andreas Cesalphinus,[c] which would nevertheless have shortly expired in its cradle, unless it had been recalled into life by the care of Robert Morison, and nourished by Joseph P. Tournefort[d] with pure systematic

rules. This was at length confirmed by all the great men, then existing, in the science.

8. This foundation being given, this point fixed, immediately every one capable of such researches joined their labors to turn it into use, to build a system; all with the same inclination, and to the same purpose, but not all with equal success. Because the fundamental rule was known but to few, which if the builders did not observe, quickly fell to the ground with the first tempest the insubstantial edifice, however splendid; Boerhave (Instit. 31) well observes, that *"a teacher, as he explains discoveries, may proceed from generals to particulars, but an inventor on the contrary must pass from particulars to generals."*[e]

For some assuming the different parts of fructification as the principle of their system, and descending according to the laws of division from classes through orders even to species, broke and dilacerated the natural genera and did violence to nature by their hypothetical and arbitrary principles. For example, one from the *Fruit* denies that the peach and almond can be joined in the same genus, another from the *regularity of the Petals* denies that Valerian and Valerianoides; another from their *number* that flax and radiola; another from their *sex* that the urtica androgyna, and dioica, etc. can be combined under the same genus; for, say they, if these cannot be conjoined in the same class, much less in the same genus; not having observed, that themselves have contrived the classes, but that the Creator himself made the genera. Hence arose so many false genera; such controversy among authors; so many bad names, and such confusion! Such, indeed, was the state of things that as often as a new system-maker arose the whole botanic world was thrown into a panic. And for my part I do not know whether these system-builders produced

[a]Gesner (1516–1565) collected more than 500 plant species not described in ancient texts. His planned encyclopedia of plants was not published due to his untimely death from the plague. His notes and engravings were used by botanists for the following 200 years. [B.]

[b]Rudolph Jacob Camerarius (1665–1721) produced the first clear experimental evidence for the sexuality of plants in his *De sexu plantarum* (1694: On the Sex of Plants). [B.]

[c]In his work *De plantis* (1583: On Plants), Andrea Cesalphino (1519–1603) classified plants according to fruit and seed characteristics. [B.]

[d]Joseph Pitton de Tournefort (1656–1708) is regarded as the first botanist to define a genus as a cluster of species. [B.]

[e]Herman Boerhave (1668–1738)—a scholar of immense learning and a gifted teacher—was compared to Newton by his peers, though he is associated with no major contribution. [B.]

more evil than good to the science; this is certain, if the unlearned be compared with the learned, they much surpass them in number; physicians, apothecaries, gardeners lamented this misfortune, and with reason. I confess their theory had been excellent had it pleased the great Creator to have made all the fructifications of the same genus of plants equally similar amongst themselves; as are the individuals of the same species. As this is not so, we have no resource, since we are not the governors of nature, nor can create plants according to our own conceptions, but to submit ourselves to the laws of nature, and learn by diligent study to read the characters inscribed on plants. If every different mark of the fructification be adjudged sufficient for distinguishing the genus, why should we a moment hesitate to proclaim nearly as many genera as species? We are scarcely acquainted with any two flowers so similar to each other, but that some difference of their parts may be discerned; I also once endeavored from the flower alone to determine all the specific differences, but frequently with less success, since there is an easier method. I wish it, therefore, to be acknowledged by all true botanists, if they ever expect any certainty in the science, that the *genera and species must be all natural*; without which assumed principle there can be nothing excellent done in the science . . .

9. I do not deny that natural classes may not be given as well as natural genera. I do not deny that a natural method ought much to be preferred to ours, or those of other discoverers; but I laugh at all the natural methods hitherto cried up; and provoked in my own defense I venture to affirm that not a single class before given, in any system, is natural; so long as those genera, and those characters, which at present exist, are arranged under it. It is easy to distribute the greatest part of the known genera into their natural classes, but so much the greater difficulty attends the arrangement of the rest. And I can not persuade myself that the present age will see a natural system, nor per-

haps our latest posterity. Let us nevertheless study plants, and in the mean time content ourselves with artificial and succedaneous classes [substitutes for natural classes] . . .

10. These natural genera assumed two things are required to preserve them pure: First, that the true species, and no others, be reduced to their proper genera. Secondly, that all the genera be circumscribed by true limits or boundaries, which we term *generic characters*.

11. These characters, as I turn over the authors, I find uncertain and unfixed before Tournefort—to him, therefore, we ought deservedly to ascribe the honor of this discovery of ascertaining the genera. Indeed, other systematists of other sects have given characters, but I can understand none of them, who preceded Tournefort, or who did not tread in his steps. . . . Tournefort assumed the petals and the fruit, as diagnostic marks of the genera, and no other parts; so did almost all his followers; but the moderns, oppressed by the quantity of new and lately detected genera, have supposed that these parts alone are insufficient for distinguishing all the genera; and have since believed themselves necessitated to have recourse to the habit and appearance of plants, as the leaves, situation of the flowers, stem, root, etc., that is to recede from the steady foundation of the fructification, and to relapse into the former barbarism; with what ill omen this is done, it would be easy to demonstrate, if this were the time and place for such a talk; whatever may be the event, I acknowledge the parts described by Tournefort to be insufficient, if the petals alone or the fruit were to be used for this purpose. But I ask: for what reason should these characters alone be used? Does inspection show this or revelation, or any arguments either a priori, or posteriori? Certainly, it is none of these. I acknowledge no authority but inspection alone in botany. Are there not many more parts of the fructification? Why should those only be acknowledged and no others? Did not the same Creator make the latter, as well as the former? Are all the parts not

equally necessary to the fructification? We have described of the calyx: 1, the involucre; 2, the spathe; 3, the perianth; 4, the ament; 5, the glume; 6, the calyptre of the corol; 7, the tube or claws; 8, the border; 9, the nectory of the stamens; 10, the filaments; 11, the anthers of the pistil; 12, the germ; 13, the style; 14, the stigma of the pericarp; 15, the capsule; 16, the silique; 17, the legume; 18, the nut; 19, the drupe; 20, the berry; 21, the pome the seed; 22, 23, and its crown the receptacle; 24, of the fructification; 25, of the flower; 26, of the fruit. Thus are there more parts, more letters here, than in the alphabets of languages. These marks are to us as so many vegetable letters, which, if we can read, will teach us the characters of plants: they are written by the hand of God; it should be our study to read them.

12. Tournefort did wonders with his characters, but since so many and such new genera have been since discovered, it should be our business to adhere indeed to his principles, but to augment them with new discoveries, as the science increases.

13. *Figures* alone for determining the genera I do not recommend; before the use of letters was known to mankind, it was necessary to express everything by picture, where it could not be done by word of mouth, but on the discovery of letters the more easy and certain way of communicating ideas by writing succeeded. . . .

(a) From a figure alone who could ever argue with any certainty, but most easily from written words.

(b) If I wish to bring into use, or quote in any work the characters of a genus; I cannot always easily paint the figure of it, nor etch or engrave it, or print it off, but can easily copy the description.

(c) If in the same genus, as happens in many, some of the parts should differ in respect to number or figure in some of the species or individuals, yet I am expected to note the situation and proportion of these parts; it be-

comes impossible to express these by a print, unless I should give a number of figures. Hence, if there should be fifty species, I must exhibit as many prints, and who would be able to extract any certainty from such a variety? But in a description the parts are omitted, which differ; and the labor is much less to describe, those which agree, and much more easy to be understood.

14. We have therefore endeavored to express by words all the marks or distinctions as clearly, if not more so, than others have done by their expensive prints . . .

19. I have selected the *marks* in describing every part of the fructification, which are certain and real, not those which are vague and fluctuating. Others have frequently assumed the taste, the odor, the size (without the proportion); these you will never find adduced by me, but only these four certain immutable mechanical principles: *number, figure, situation*, and *proportion*. These four attributes, with those twenty-six letters, above-mentioned, distinguish the genera so certainly from each other, that nothing more is wanted. There are other marks for distinguishing genera, but these alone considered, the rest become superfluous, nor is there any necessity to fly to the habit of the plant . . .

22. I am confident the *flower* is much to be preferred to the fruit in determining the genera, though others have been of a quite different opinion; and that the nectaries are of greater advantage in determining the genera, than almost any other part; although so much neglected and overlooked by others, that they even had not a name given to them . . .

29. The use of some botanic system I need not recommend even to beginners, since without system there can be no certainty in botany. Let two enquirers, one a systematic, and the other an empiric, enter a garden filled with exotic and unknown plants, and at the same time furnished with the best botanic library; the former will easily seduce the plants by studying the letters inscribed

on the fructification, to their class, order, and genus; after which there remains but to distinguish a few species. The latter will be necessitated to turn over all the books, to read all the descriptions, to inspect all the figures with infinite labor; nor unless by accident can be certain of his plant . . .

## FURTHER READING

Blunt, Wilfrid. 2001. *Linnaeus: The Complete Naturalist.* Princeton: Princeton University Press.

Farber, Paul Lawrence. 2000. *Finding Order in Nature: The Naturalist Tradition from Linnaeus to E. O. Wilson.* Baltimore: Johns Hopkins University Press, ch. 1.

# The Principle of Fire

## Joseph Priestley (1733–1804)

*A non-conformist minister who was introduced to the world of science by Benjamin Franklin (1706–1790), Priestley carried out experiments on "airs"—nitrous air (nitric oxide), phlogisticated air (nitrogen), nitrous vapor (nitrogen dioxide), acid air (hydrochloric acid), and many others. He designed a simple apparatus, consisting of a mercury-filled trough over which glass vessels could be inverted to collect gas. The substance to be heated was placed in another glass vessel on the surface of the mercury, and Priestley focused the Sun's rays on it using a twelve-inch lens.*

*To test his airs, Priestley employed mice that he caught in wire traps and introduced into the gas-filled vessels. When a substance, which he called mercurius calcinatus per se (the oxide of mercury), was heated using his apparatus, it was found to give off a colorless gas that made a candle burn brightly. Priestley believed that all combustible materials contained a "principle of fire" called phlogiston (from the Greek phlogistos), which was given off when they burned. Air in which things had been burned became less able to support combustion because it was saturated with phlogiston. Priestley called his gas in which a candle flame burned brightly "dephlogisticated air." This was the air that Antoine-Laurent Lavoisier was later to call oxygen. Priestley's theoretical understanding of his results did not keep pace with his gifts as an experimenter. Although the evidence continued to mount against phlogiston, Priestley defended the existence of this entity until the end of his life.*

The contents of this section will furnish a very striking illustration of the truth of a remark, which I have more than once made in my philosophical writings, and which can hardly be too often repeated, as it tends greatly to encourage philosophical investigations; viz., that more is owing to what we call chance, that is, philosophically speaking, to the observation of events arising from unknown causes, than to any proper design, or pre-conceived theory in this business. This does not appear in the works of those who write synthetically upon these subjects; but would, I doubt not, appear very strikingly in those who are the most celebrated for their philosophical acumen, did they write analytically and ingenuously.

For my own part, I will frankly acknowledge, that, at the commencement of the experiments recited in this section, I was so far from having formed any hypothesis that led to the discoveries I made in pursuing them,

*Source:* Joseph Priestley. 1776. *Experiments and Observations on Different Kinds of Air.* Second edition. London: J. Johnson, vol. 2, pp. 29–50.

that they would have appeared very improbable to me had I been told of them; and when the decisive facts did at length obtrude themselves upon my notice, it was very slowly, and with great hesitation, that I yielded to the evidence of my senses. And yet, when I reconsider the matter, and compare my last discoveries relating to the constitution of the atmosphere with the first, I see the closest and the easiest connection in the world between them, so as to wonder that I should not have been led immediately from the one to the other. That this was not the case, I attribute to the force of prejudice, which, unknown to ourselves, biases not only our judgments, properly so called, but even the perceptions of our senses; for we may take a maxim so strongly for granted, that the plainest evidence of sense will not entirely change, and often hardly modify our persuasions; and the more ingenious a man is, the more effectually he is entangled in his errors; his ingenuity only helping him to deceive himself, by evading the force of truth.

There are, I believe, very few maxims in philosophy that have laid firmer hold upon the mind than that air, meaning atmospherical air (free from various foreign matters, which were always supposed to be dissolved, and intermixed with it) is a simple elementary substance, indestructible, and unalterable, at least as much so as water is supposed to be. In the course of my inquiries, I was, however, soon satisfied that atmospherical air is not an unalterable thing; for that the phlogiston with which it becomes loaded from bodies burning in it, and animals breathing it, and various other chemical processes, so far alters and deprives it, as to render it altogether unfit for inflammation, respiration, and other purposes to which it is subservient; and I had discovered that agitation in water, the process of vegetation, and probably other natural processes, by taking out the superfluous phlogiston, restore it to its original purity. But, on my own, I had no idea of the possibility of going any farther in this way, and thereby, procuring air purer than the

best common air. I might, indeed, have naturally imagined that such would be air that should contain less phlogiston than the air of the atmosphere; but I had no idea that such a composition was possible.[a]

It will be seen in my last publication that, from the experiments which I made on the marine acid air [gaseous hydrogen chloride], I was led to conclude that common air consisted of some acid (and I naturally inclined to the acid that I was then operating upon) and phlogiston; because the union of this acid vapor and phlogiston made inflammable air [hydrogen]; and inflammable air, by agitation in water, ceases to be inflammable, and becomes respirable. And though I could never make it quite so good as common air, I thought it very probable that vegetation, in more favorable circumstances than any in which I could apply it, or some other natural process, might render it more pure.

Upon this, which no person can say was an improbable supposition, was founded my conjecture of volcanoes having given birth to the atmosphere of this planet, supplying it with a permanent air, first inflammable, then deprived of its inflammability by agitation in water, and further purified by vegetation.

Several of the known phenomena of the nitrous acid might have led me to think that this was more proper for the constitution of the atmosphere than the marine acid; but my thoughts had got into a different train, and nothing but a series of observations, which I shall now distinctly relate, compelled me to adopt another hypothesis, and brought me, in a way of which I had then no idea, to the solution of the great problem, which my reader will perceive I have had in view ever since my discovery that the atmospheric air is alterable, and therefore, that it is not an elementary substance, but a composition, viz., what this composition is, or what is the

[a]In terms of the phlogiston theory, mercury had already lost phlogiston when it had been heated to form *mercurius calcinatus per se,* and so the evolution of anything else on heating to a higher temperature was completely unexpected. [B.]

thing that we breathe, and how is it to be made from its constituent principles.

At the time of my former publication, I was not possessed of a burning lens of any considerable force; and for want of one, I could not possibly make many of the experiments that I had projected, and which, in theory, appeared very promising. I had, indeed, a mirror of force sufficient for my purpose. But the nature of this instrument is such that it cannot be applied, with effect, except upon substances that are capable of being suspended or resting on a very slender support. It cannot be directed at all upon any substance in the form of a powder, nor hardly upon any thing that requires to be put into a vessel of quicksilver; which appears to me to be the most accurate method of extracting air from a great variety of substances, as was explained in the Introduction to this volume. But having afterwards procured a lens of twelve inches diameter, and twenty inches focal distance, I proceeded with great alacrity to examine, by the help of it, what kind of air a great variety of substances, natural and factitious, would yield, putting them into the vessels represented in fig. a [Plate 20], which I filled with quicksilver, and kept inverted in a basin of the same. Mr. Warltire,[b] a good chemist, and lecturer in natural philosophy, happening to be at that time in Calne, I explained my views to him, and was furnished by him with many substances, which I could not otherwise have procured.

With this apparatus, after a variety of other experiments, an account of which will be found in its proper place, on the First of August, 1774, I endeavored to extract air from mercurius calcinatus per se[c] [mercuric oxide]; and I presently found that, by means of this lens, air was expelled from it very readily. Having got about three or four times as much as the bulk of my materials, I ad-

mitted water to it, and found that it was not imbibed by it. But what surprised me more than I can well express, was that a candle burned in this air with a remarkably vigorous flame, very much like that enlarged flame with which a candle burns in nitrous air [nitric oxide], exposed to iron or liver of sulfur [various compounds of potassium and sulfur]; but as I had got nothing like this remarkable appearance from any kind of air besides this particular modification of nitrous air, and I knew no nitrous acid was used in the preparation of mercurius calcinatus, I was utterly at a loss how to account for it.

In this case, also, though I did not give sufficient attention to the circumstance at that time, the flame of the candle, besides being larger, burned with more splendor and heat than in that species of nitrous air; and a piece of red-hot wood sparkled in it exactly like paper dipped in a solution of nitre [potassium nitrate], and it consumed very fast; an experiment which I had never thought of trying with nitrous air.

At the same time that I made the above mentioned experiment, I extracted a quantity of air, with the very same property, from the common red precipitate, which being produced by a solution of mercury in spirit of nitre [nitric acid], made me conclude that this peculiar property, being similar to that of the modification of nitrous air above mentioned, depended upon something being communicated to it by the nitrous acid; and since the mercurius calcinatus is produced by exposing mercury to a certain degree of heat, where common air has access to it, I likewise concluded that this substance had collected something of nitre, in that state of heat, from the atmosphere.

This, however, appearing to me much more extraordinary than it ought to have done, I entertained some suspicion that the mercurius calcinatus, on which I had made my experiments, being bought at a common apothecary's, might, in fact, be nothing more than red precipitate; though had I been anything of a practical chemist, I could not have entertained any such suspicion. However,

[b]Warltire was a friend of Priestley's and a traveling lecturer in natural philosophy. [B.]

[c]A calx was a metal oxide produced by the roasting of metal. [B.]

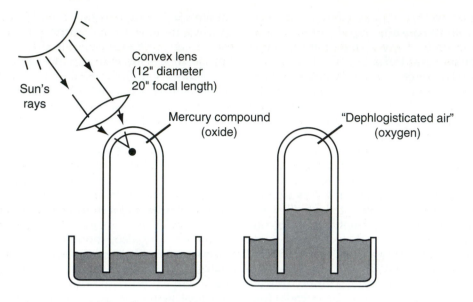

**PLATE 20**    Illustration of Priestley's experiment.

mentioning this suspicion to Mr. Warltire, he furnished me with some that he had kept for a specimen of the preparation, and which, he told me, he could warrant to be genuine. This being treated in the same manner as the former, only by a longer continuance of heat, I extracted much more air from it than from the other.

This experiment might have satisfied any moderate skeptic; but, however, being at Paris in the October following, and knowing that there were several very eminent chemists in that place, I did not omit the opportunity, by means of my friend Mr. Magellan, to get an ounce of mercurius calcinatus prepared by Mr. Cadet[d], of the genuineness of which there could not possibly be any suspicion; and at the same time, I frequently mentioned my surprise at the kind of air which I had got from this preparation to Mr. Antoine-Laurent Lavoisier, Mr. le Roy, and several other philosophers, who honor me

with their notice in that city; and who, I dare say, cannot fail to recollect the circumstance.

At the same time, I had no suspicion that the air which I had got from the mercurius calcinatus was even wholesome, so far was I from knowing what it was that I had really found; taking it for granted, that it was nothing more than such kind of air as I had brought nitrous air to be by the processes above mentioned; and in this air I have observed that a candle would burn sometimes quite naturally, and sometimes with a beautiful enlarged flame, and yet remain perfectly noxious.

At the same time that I had got the air above mentioned from mercurius calcinatus and the red precipitate, I had got the same kind from red lead or minium [red lead oxide]. In this process, that part of the minium on which the focus of the lens had fallen, turned yellow. One third of the air, in this experiment, was readily absorbed by water, but, in the remainder, a candle burned very strongly, and with a crackling noise.

That fixed air [carbon dioxide] is contained in red lead I had observed before; for

[d]A chemist of repute, Louis-Claude Cadet (1731–1799) collaborated with Lavoisier. [B.]

I had expelled it by the heat of a candle, and had found it to be very pure. I imagine it requires more heat than I then used to expel any of the other kind of air.

This experiment with red lead confirmed me more in my suspicion, that the mercurius calcinatus must get the property of yielding this kind of air from the atmosphere, the process by which that preparation, and this of red lead is made, being similar. As I never make the least secret of anything I observe, I mentioned this experiment also, as well as those with the mercurius calcinatus, and the red precipitate, to all my philosophical acquaintances at Paris, and elsewhere; having no idea, at that time, to what these remarkable facts would lead.

Presently, after my return from abroad, I went to work upon the mercurius calcinatus, which I had procured from Mr. Cadet; and, with a very moderate degree of heat, I got from it about one fourth of an ounce of it, an ounce measure of air, which I observed to be not readily imbibed, either by the substance itself from which it had been expelled (for I suffered them to continue a long time together before I transferred the air to any other place) or by water, in which I suffered this air to stand a considerable time before I made any experiment upon it.

In this air, as I had expected, a candle burned with a vivid flame; but what I observed new at this time (Nov. 19), and which surprised me no less than the fact I had discovered it before, was that, whereas a few moments agitation in water will deprive the modified nitrous air of its property of admitting a candle to burn in it; yet, after more than ten times as much agitation as would be sufficient to produce this alteration in the nitrous air, no sensible change was produced in this. A candle still burned in it with a strong flame; and it did not, in the least, diminish common air, which I have observed that nitrous air, in this state, in some measure, does.

But I was much more surprised, when, after two days, in which this air had continued in contact with water (by which it was diminished about one twentieth of its bulk) I agitated it violently in water about five minutes, and found that a candle still burned in it as well as in common air. The same degree of agitation would have made phlogisticated nitrous air fit for respiration indeed, but it would certainly have extinguished a candle.

These facts fully convinced me, that there must be a very material difference between the constitution of the air from mercurius calcinatus, and that of phlogisticated nitrous air, notwithstanding their resemblance in some particulars. But, though I did not doubt that the air from mercurius calcinatus was fit for respiration, after being agitated in water, as every kind of air without exception, on which I had tried the experiment, had been, I still did not suspect that it was respirable in the first instance; so far was I from having any idea of this air being, what it really was, much superior, in this respect, to the air of the atmosphere.

In this ignorance of the real nature of this kind of air, I continued from this time (November) to the first of March following; having, in the meantime, been intent upon my experiments on the vitriolic acid air above recited, and the various modifications of air produced by spirit of nitre, an account of which will follow. But in the course of this month, I not only ascertained the nature of this kind of air, though very gradually, but was led by it to the complete discovery of the constitution of the air we breathe.

Until this first of March, 1775, I had so little suspicion of the air from mercurius calcinatus, etc., being wholesome that I had not even thought of applying to it the test of nitrous air; but thinking (as my reader must imagine I frequently must have done) on the candle burning in it after long agitation in water, it occurred to me at last to make the experiment; and putting one measure of nitrous air to two measures of this air, I found, not only that it was diminished, but that it was diminished quite as much as common air, and that the redness of the mixture was likewise equal to that of a similar mixture of nitrous and common air.

After this, I had no doubt but that the air from mercurius calcinatus was fit for respiration, and that it had all the other properties of genuine common air. But I did not take notice of what I might have observed, if I had not been so fully possessed by the notion of there being no air better than common air, that the redness was really deeper, and the diminution something greater than common air would have admitted.

Moreover, this advance in the way of truth, in reality, threw me back into error, making me give up the hypothesis I had first formed, viz., that the mercurius calcinatus had extracted spirit of nitre from the air; for I now concluded, that all the constituent parts of the air were equally, and in their proper proportion, imbibed in the preparation of this substance, and also in the process of making red lead. For at the same time that I made the above-mentioned experiment on the air from mercurius calcinatus, I likewise observed that the air which I had extracted from red lead, after the fixed air was washed out of it, was of the same nature, being diminished by nitrous air like common air; but, at the same time, I was puzzled to find that air from the red precipitate was diminished in the same manner, though the process for making this substance is quite different from that of making the two others. But to this circumstance I happened not to give much attention.

I wish my reader be not quite tired with the frequent repetition of the word surprise, and others of similar import; but I must go on in that style a little longer. For the next day I was more surprised than ever I had been before, with finding that, after the above-mentioned mixture of nitrous air and the air from mercurius calcinatus, had stood all night (in which time the whole diminution must have taken place; and, consequently, had it been common air, it must have been made perfectly noxious, and entirely unfit for respiration or inflammation) a candle burned in it, and even better than in common air.

I cannot, at this distance of time, recollect what it was that I had in view in making this experiment; but I know I had no expectation of the real issue of it. Having acquired a considerable degree of readiness in making experiments of this kind, a very slight and evanescent motive would be sufficient to induce me to do it. If, however, I had not happened for some other purpose, to have had a lighted candle before me, I should probably never have made the trial; and the whole train of my future experiments relating to this kind of air might have been prevented.

Still, however, having no conception of the real cause of this phenomenon, I considered it as something very extraordinary; but as a property that was peculiar to air extracted from these substances, and adventitious; and I always spoke of the air to my acquaintance as being substantially the same thing with common air. I particularly remember my telling Dr. Price, that I was myself perfectly satisfied of its being common air, as it appeared to be so by the test of nitrous air; though, for the satisfaction of others, I wanted a mouse to make the proof quite complete.

On the eighth of this month I procured a mouse, and put it into a glass vessel, containing two ounce-measures of the air from mercurius calcinatus. Had it been common air, a full-grown mouse, as this was, would have lived in it about a quarter of an hour. In this air, however, my mouse lived a full half hour; and though it was taken out seemingly dead, it appeared to have been only exceedingly chilled; for, upon being held to the fire, it presently revived, and appeared not to have received any harm from the experiment.

By this I was confirmed in my conclusion, that the air extracted from mercurius calcinatus, etc., was, at least, as good as common air; but I did not certainly conclude that it was any better; because, though one mouse would live only a quarter of an hour in a given quantity of air, I knew it was not impossible that another mouse might have lived in it half an hour; so little accuracy is there in this method of ascertaining the goodness of air: and indeed I have never had recourse to it for my own satisfaction, since the discovery of that most ready, accurate, and elegant test that nitrous air furnishes. But in this case I had a view to publishing the most generally-satisfactory account of my experiments that the nature of the thing would admit of.

This experiment with the mouse, when I had reflected upon it some time, gave me so much suspicion that the air into which I had put it was better than common air, that I was induced, the day after, to apply the test of nitrous air to a small part of that very quantity of air which the mouse had breathed so long; so that, had it been common air, I was satisfied it must have been very nearly, if not altogether, as noxious as possible, so as not to be affected by nitrous air; when, to my surprise again, I found that though it had been breathed so long, it was still better than common air. For after mixing it with nitrous air, in the usual proportion of two to one, it was diminished in the proportion of four and a half to three and a half; that is, the nitrous air had made it two ninths less than before, and this in a very short space of time; whereas I had never found that, in the longest time, any common air was reduced more than one fifth of its bulk by any proportion of nitrous air, nor more than one fourth by any phlogistic process whatever. Thinking of this extraordinary fact upon my pillow, the next morning I put another measure of nitrous air to the same mixture, and, to my utter astonishment, found that it was farther diminished to almost one half of its original quantity. I, then, put a third measure to it; but this did not diminish it any farther but, however, left it one measure less than it was even after the mouse had been taken out of it.

Being now fully satisfied that this air, even after the mouse had breathed it half an hour, was much better than common air; and having a quantity of it still left, sufficient for the experiment, viz., an ounce measure and a half, I put the mouse into it; when I observed that it seemed to feel no shock upon being put into it, evident signs of which would have been visible, if the air had not been very wholesome; but that it remained

perfectly at its ease another full half hour, when I took it out quite lively and vigorous. Measuring the air the next day, I found it to be reduced from one and a half to two-thirds of an ounce measure. And after this, if I remember well (for in my register of the day I only find it noted, that it was considerably diminished by nitrous air) it was nearly as good as common air. It was evident, indeed, from the mouse having been taken out quite vigorous, that the air could not have been rendered very noxious.

For my further satisfaction I procured another mouse, and putting it into less than two ounce measures of air extracted from mercurius calcinatus and air from red precipitate (which, having found them to be of the same quality, I had mixed together) it lived three-quarters of an hour. But not having had the precaution to set the vessel in a warm place, I suspect that the mouse died of cold. However, as it had lived three times as long as it could probably have lived in the same quantity of common air, and I did not expect much accuracy from this kind of test, I did not think it necessary to make any more experiments with mice.[e]

Being now fully satisfied of the superior goodness of this kind of air, I proceeded to measure that degree of purity, with as much accuracy as I could, by the test of nitrous air; and I began with putting one measure of nitrous air to two measures of this air, as if I had been examining common air; and now I observed that the diminution was evidently greater than common air would have suffered by the same treatment. A second measure of nitrous air reduced it to two thirds of its original quantity, and a third measure to one half. Suspecting that the diminution could not proceed much farther, I then added only half a measure of nitrous air, by which it was diminished still more; but not

[e]Scientists had experimented on animal subjects for centuries, but the use of animals as allies (as qualitative assays) in experimental practice was a new and important development with Priestley. [B.]

much, and another half measure made it more than half of its original quantity; so that, in this case, two measures of this air took more than two measures of nitrous air, and yet remained less than half of what it was. Five measures brought it pretty exactly to its original dimensions.

At the same time, air from red precipitate was diminished in the same proportion as that from mercurius calcinatus, five measures of nitrous air being received by two measures of this without any increase of dimensions. Now as common air takes about one half of its bulk of nitrous air, before it begins to receive any addition to its dimensions from more nitrous air, and this air took more than four half-measures before it ceased to be diminished by more nitrous air, and even five half-measures made no addition to its original dimensions, I conclude that it was between four and five times as good as common air. It will be seen that I have since procured air better than this, even between five and six times as good as the best common air that I have ever met with.

## FURTHER READING

Brock, W. H. 1992. *The Fontana History of Chemistry.* London: Fontana.

Crosland, Maurice P. 2002. "Chemistry: Eighteenth Century." In Brian S. Baigrie, ed., *History of Modern Science and Mathematics.* New York: Charles Scribner's Sons, vol. 2, pp. 164–185.

Weeks, Mary E., revised by Henry M. Leicester. 1968. *Discovery of the Elements.* Easton, PA: Journal of Chemical Education.

# The Elements of Chemistry

## Antoine-Laurent Lavoisier (1743–1794)

*Antoine-Laurent Lavoisier utterly changed the direction and content of chemistry. Opposed to the unbridled speculations of the supporters of phlogiston, he attempted to bring chemistry closer to the spirit of Newton's methodological prohibition against framing hypotheses. His greatness consisted in being able to clarify the experimental work of others, and to place their results into a new chemical context of his own devising. The work of Joseph Black (1728–1799), Joseph Priestley, and Henry Cavendish (1731–1810) was completed in this manner by Lavoisier's providing a new interpretation of their experimental results.*

*The turning point in Lavoisier's scientific career was a visit by Priestley to Paris in 1774. Over dinner, he was informed by Priestley of his discovery of dephlogisticated air using red precipitate of mercury and red lead. Lavoisier repeated Priestley's experiment and reached different conclusions, based on identical bits of information. He showed that when mercury was heated in air and turned red and earthy it gained weight; and that, at the same time, the air in which it was being heated had lost weight. By something more than a coincidence, the weight gained by mercury was identical to that lost by the air. What's more, when the red earth was heated, Lavoisier found that he could break it down and recover from it a gas that weighed exactly what the air had lost originally. Phlogiston did not square with this picture, which seemed to be a case of simple combination. Mercury and air combine when heated. Heat them some more and they revert to their original states. Weigh them. Measure them. It was this straightforward.*

*Lavoisier performed additional experiments. All pointed to the fact that in any reaction between matter the combined weight of the substances was exactly equal to the combined weight of the substances used up. Matter was never created nor destroyed. It did not change its chemical properties unless it was broken down into simpler forms of matter, or combined or reacted with other forms of matter to form new substances. Changes in the properties of matter were due to definite chemical reactions, not to the gain or loss of some quality such as phlogiston.*

*In 1783, Lavoisier formally announced the new chemistry, based on the concept of the chemical element. The elements were substances not susceptible to decomposition.*

---

*Source:* Antoine-Laurent Lavoisier, 1790. *Elements of Chemistry in a New Systematic Order.* Trans. Robert Kerr. Edinburgh: William Creech, pp. xii–xxxvii; 175–179.

*Lavoisier compiled a list of thirty-three elements. In addition to oxygen, hydrogen, mercury, and others, his list included light and calorique (the substance of heat). These names were as new as the concept of the element, representing a new nomenclature that keyed on the properties of the elements and chemicals themselves. The known facts about the characteristics of chemical reactions became the basis for the new chemistry. Oxygen meant "acid former," and hydrogen meant "water former." These properties were determined by experiment and observation, eliminating the speculations on "the principles of activity" prevalent in the chemistry of Paracelsus.*

When I began the following work, my only object was to extend and explain more fully the Memoir which I read at the public meeting of the Academy of Sciences in the month of April 1787, on the necessity of reforming and completing the Nomenclature of Chemistry. While engaged in this employment, I perceived, better than I had ever done before, the justice of the following maxims of the Abbé de Condillac,[a] in his "System of Logic", and some other of his works.

> We think only through the medium of words. Languages are true analytical methods. Algebra, which is adapted to purpose in every species of expression, in the most simple, most exact, and best manner possible, is at the same time a language and an analytical method. The art of reasoning is nothing more than a language well arranged.

Thus, while I thought myself employed only in forming a nomenclature, and while I proposed to myself nothing more than to improve the chemical language, my work transformed itself by degrees, without my being able to prevent it, into a treatise upon the Elements of Chemistry.

The impossibility of separating the nomenclature of a science from the science itself, is owing to this, that every branch of physical science must consist of three things: the series of facts which are the objects of the science, the ideas which represent these facts, and the words by which these ideas are expressed. Like three impressions of the same seal, the word ought to produce the idea, and the idea to be a picture of the fact. And, as ideas are preserved and communicated by means of words, it necessarily follows that we cannot improve the language of any science without at the same time improving the science itself; neither can we, on the other hand, improve a science, without improving the language or nomenclature which belongs to it. However certain the facts of any science may be, and, however just the ideas we may have formed of these facts; we can only communicate false impressions to others, while we want words by which these may be properly expressed.

To those who will consider it with attention, the first part of this treatise will afford frequent proofs of the truth of the above observations. But, as in the conduct of my work, I have been obliged to observe an order of arrangement essentially differing from what has been adopted in any other chemical work yet published, it is proper that I should explain the motives which have led me to do so. It is a maxim universally admitted in geometry, and indeed in every branch of knowledge, that, in the

[a]The reference is perhaps to *La logique* (1780) by Condillac (1714–1780). A follower of Newton's conception of scientific methodology, and enamored of the variety of empiricism advanced by John Locke (1632–1704) in his *Essay Concerning Human Understanding* (1690), Condillac developed a theory of language as the cause of intellectual functions. His suggestion that scientific explanation calls for a method of analysis geared toward classifying the elements of a subject according to the logical relations discerned beneath the phenomena exerted a powerful influence on scientists at the end of the eighteenth century. [B.]

progress of investigation, we should proceed from known facts to what is unknown. In early infancy, our ideas spring from our wants; the sensation of want excites the idea of the object by this manner, from a series of sensations, observations, and analyses, a successive train of ideas arises, so linked together, that an attentive observer may trace back to a certain point the order and connection of the whole sum of human knowledge.

When we begin the study of any science, we are in a situation, respecting that science, similar to that of children; and the course by which we have to advance is precisely the same which nature follows in the formation of their ideas. In a child, the idea is merely an effect produced by a sensation; and, in the same manner, in commencing the study of a physical science, we ought to form no idea but what is a necessary consequence, and immediate effect, of an experiment or observation. Besides, he that enters upon the career of science, is in a less advantageous situation than a child who is acquiring his first ideas. To the child, nature gives various means of rectifying any mistakes he may commit respecting the salutary or hurtful qualities of the objects which surround him. On every occasion his judgments are corrected by experience; want and pain are the necessary consequences arising from false judgment; gratification and pleasure are produced by judging aright. Under such masters, we cannot fail to become well informed; and we soon learn to reason justly, when want and pain are the necessary consequences of a contrary conduct.

In the study and practice of the sciences it is quite different; the false judgments we form neither affect our existence nor our welfare; and we are not forced by any physical necessity to correct them. Imagination, on the contrary, which is ever wandering beyond the bounds of truth, joined to self-love and that self-confidence we are so apt to indulge, prompt us to draw conclusions which are not immediately derived from facts; so that we become in some measure interested in deceiving ourselves. Hence, it is by no

means to be wondered, that, in the science of physics in general, men have often made suppositions, instead of forming conclusions. These suppositions, handed down from one age to another, acquire additional weight from the authorities by which they are supported, until at last they are received, even by men of genius, as fundamental truths.

The only method of preventing such errors from taking place, and of correcting them when formed, is to refrain and simplify our reasoning as much as possible. This depends entirely upon ourselves, and the neglect of it is the only source of our mistakes. We must trust to nothing but facts. These are presented to us by nature, and cannot deceive. We ought, in every instance, to submit our reasoning to the test of experiment, and never to search for truth but by the natural road of experiment and observation. Thus, mathematicians obtain the solution of a problem by the mere arrangement of data, and by reducing their reasoning to such simple steps, to conclusions so very obvious, as never to lose sight of the evidence which guides them.

Thoroughly convinced of these truths, I have imposed upon myself, as a law, never to advance but from what is known to what is unknown; never to form any conclusion which is not an immediate consequence necessarily following from observation and experiment; and always to arrange the facts, and the conclusions which are drawn from them, in such an order as shall render it most easy for beginners in the study of chemistry thoroughly to understand them. Hence, I have been obliged to depart from the usual order of courses of lectures and of treatises upon chemistry, which always assume the first principles of the science, as known, when the pupil or the reader should never be supposed to know them until they have been explained in subsequent lectures. In almost every instance, these begin by treating of the elements of matter, and by explaining the table of affinities, without considering, that, in so doing, they must bring the principal phenomena of chemistry into view at the very outset; they make use of terms which have not been defined, and suppose the science to be understood by the very persons they are only beginning to teach. It ought likewise to be considered, that very little of chemistry can be learned in a first course, which is hardly sufficient to make the language of the science familiar to the ears, or the apparatus familiar to the eyes. It is almost impossible to become a chemist in less than three or four years of constant application.

These inconveniences are occasioned not so much by the nature of the subject, as by the method of teaching it; and, to avoid them I was chiefly induced to adopt a new arrangement of chemistry, which appeared to me more consonant to the order of nature. I acknowledge, however, that in thus endeavoring to avoid difficulties of one kind, I have found myself involved in others of a different species, some of which I have not been able to remove; but I am persuaded, that such as remain do not arise from the nature of the order I have adopted, but are rather consequences of the imperfection under which chemistry still labors. This science still has many chasms, which interrupt the series of facts, and often render it extremely difficult to reconcile them with each other. It has not, like the elements of geometry, the advantage of being a complete science, the parts of which are all closely connected together. Its actual progress, however, is so rapid, and the facts, under the modern doctrine, have assumed so happy an arrangement that we have ground to hope, even in our own times, to see it approach near to the highest state of perfection of which it is susceptible.

The rigorous law from which I have never deviated, of forming no conclusions which are not fully warranted by experiment, and of never supplying the absence of facts, has prevented me from comprehending in this work the branch of chemistry which treats of affinities, although, it is perhaps the best calculated of any part of chemistry for being re-

duced into a completely systematic body. Messrs. Etienne-Francois Geoffroy,[b] Gellert, Torbern Bergman,[c] Carl Willheim Scheele (1742–1786),[d] Louis B. G. de Morveau,[e] Richard Kirwan,[f] and many others, have collected a number of particular facts upon this subject, which only wait for a proper arrangement; but the principal data are still wanting or at least, those we have are either not sufficiently defined, or not sufficiently proved, to become the foundation upon which to build so very important a branch of

[b]Inspired by Newton's concept of universal gravitation, chemists attempted to explain chemical reactions in terms of attractions between the particles of the reagents. Tables of affinity or, in modern terms, "displacements," were prepared to visualize the relative strength of the these attractive forces. In 1718, Etienne-Francois Geoffroy (1672–1731) produced the first systematization of chemical facts by mean of tables of affinity. [B.]

[c]An ardent proponent of the phlogiston theory, Torbern Bergman (1735–1784) was the first to draw a distinction between organic and inorganic bodies. In 1775, he produced two sets of tables of affinity, one for reactions at low temperatures with reagents in solution, and another for reactions at high temperature when the reagents were in the dry fused state. [B.]

[d]The pneumatic chemist Carl Wilhelm Scheele (1742–1786) prepared oxygen before Priestley but his results were not published until 1777, by which time Priestley's work was well known. [B.]

[e]Louis Bertrand Guyton de Morveau (1737–1816) was an early convert to Lavoisier's new theory. He had suggested in 1782 that chemical names be systematized in a manner similar to that employed by Linnaeus in his botanical nomenclature. A substance should have one fixed name which should be chosen from Greek or Latin roots. This name should reflect its composition, if known. The reformed chemical nomenclature of Lavoisier, de Morveau, and their collaborators was published in 1787 under the title *Méthode de Nomenclature Chimique*. [B.]

[f]The Irish chemist Richard Kirwan (1733–1812) composed a stout defense of the phlogiston theory in 1787, which was published in France the following year. Kirwan endosed Lavoisier's new chemistry in 1791. [B.]

chemistry. This science of affinities, or elective attractions holds the same place with regard to the other branches of chemistry, as the higher or transcendental geometry does with respect to the simpler and elementary part; and I thought it improper to involve those simple and plain elements, which I flatter myself the greater part of my readers will easily understand, in the obscurities and difficulties which still attend that other very useful and necessary branch of chemical science. Perhaps a sentiment of self-love may, without my perceiving it, have given additional force to these reflections. Mr de Morveau is at present engaged in publishing the article *Affinity* in the Methodical Encyclopedia; and I had more reason than one to decline entering upon a work in which he is employed.

It will, no doubt, be a matter of surprise, that in a treatise upon the elements of chemistry, there should be no chapter on the constituent and elementary parts of matter; but I shall take occasion, in this place, to remark, that the fondness for reducing all the bodies in nature to three or four elements, proceeds from a prejudice which has descended to us from the Greek Philosophers. The notion of four elements, which, by the variety of their proportions, compose all the known substances in nature, is a mere hypothesis, assumed long before the first principles of experimental philosophy or of chemistry had any existence. In those days, without possessing facts, they framed systems; while we, who have collected facts, seem determined to reject them, when they do not agree with our prejudices. The authority of these fathers of human philosophy still carry great weight, and there is reason to fear that it will even bear hard upon generations yet to come.

It is very remarkable that, notwithstanding the number of philosophical chemists who have supported the doctrine of the four elements, there is not one who has not been led by the evidence of facts to admit a greater number of elements into their theory. The first chemists that wrote after the revival of letters, considered sulfur and salt as elementary substances entering into the composition of a great number of substances; hence, instead of four, they admitted the existence of six elements. Johann Joachim Becher[g] assumes the existence of three kinds of earth, from the combination of which, in different proportions, he supposed all the varieties of metallic substances to be produced. Georg Ernst Stahl[h] gave a new modification to this system; and succeeding chemists have taken the liberty to make or to imagine changes and additions of a similar nature. All these chemists are carried along by the innocence of the genius of the age in which they lived, which contented itself with assertions without proofs; or, at least, once admitted as proofs the slightest degrees of probability, unsupported by that strictly rigorous analysis required by modern philosophy.

All that can be said upon the number and nature of elements is, in my opinion, confined to discussions entirely of a metaphysical nature. The subject only furnishes us with indefinite problems, which may be solved in a thousand different ways, not one of which, in all probability, is consistent with nature. I shall, therefore, only add upon this subject, that if, by the term *elements*, we mean to express those simple and indivisible atoms of which matter is composed, it is extremely probable we know nothing at all about them; but, if we apply the term *elements*, or *principles of bodies,* to express our idea of the last point which analysis is capable of reaching, we must admit, as elements, all the substances into which we are capable, by any means, to reduce bodies by decomposition.

[g]Johann Joachim Becher (1635–1682) claimed that all inorganic bodies were a mixture of three earthly principles: vitreous earth; combustible earth; and mercurial earth. [B.]

[h]The combustible earth of Becher's theory became phlogiston, or the combustible element in substances, at the hands of Georg Ernst Stahl (1660–1734). [B.]

Not that we are entitled to affirm that these substances we consider as simple may not be compounded of two, or even of a greater number of principles; but, since these principles cannot be separated, or rather since we have not hitherto discovered the means of separating them, they act with regard to us as simple substances, and we ought never to suppose them compounded until experiment and observation has proved them to be so.

The foregoing reflections upon the progress of chemical ideas naturally apply to the words by which these ideas are to be expressed. Guided by the work which, in the year 1787, Messrs de Moreau, Claude-Louis Berthollet,[i] Antoine Francois de Fourcroy,[j] and I composed upon the Nomenclature of Chemistry, I have endeavored, as much as possible, to denominate simple bodies by simple terms and I was naturally led to name the first. It will be recollected that we were obliged to retain that name of any substance by which it had been long known in the world, and that in two cases only we took the liberty of making alterations; first, in the case of those which were but newly discovered, and had not yet obtained names, or at least which had been known but for a short time, and the names of what had not yet received the sanction of the public; and, second, when the names which had been adopted, whether by the ancients or the moderns, appeared to us to express evidently false ideas, when they confounded the substances, to which they were applied, with others possessed of different, or per-

haps opposite qualities. We made no scruple, in this case, of substituting other names in their room, and the greatest number of these were borrowed from the Greek language. We endeavored to frame them in such a manner as to express the most general and the most characteristic quality of the substances; and this was attended with the additional advantage both of assisting the memory of beginners, who find it difficult to remember a new word which has no meaning, and of accustoming them early to admit no word without connecting with it some determinate idea.

To those bodies which are formed by the union of several simple substances we gave new names, compounded in such a manner as the nature of the substances directed; but, as the number of double combinations is already very considerable, the only method by which we could avoid confusion, was to divide them into classes. In the natural order of ideas, the name of the class or genus is that which expresses a quality common to a great number of individuals: The name of the species, on the contrary expresses a quality peculiar to certain individuals only. These distinctions are not, as some may imagine, merely metaphysical, but are established by nature. "A child," says the Abbé de Condillac, "is taught to give the name tree to the first one which is pointed out to him. The next one he sees presents the same idea, and he gives it the same name. This he does likewise to a third and a fourth, until at last the word tree, which he first applied to an individual, comes to be employed by him as the name of a class or a genus, an abstract idea, which comprehends all trees in general. But, when he learns that all trees serve not the same purpose, that they do not all produce the same fruit, he will soon learn to distinguish them by specific and particular names." This is the logic of the sciences, and is naturally applied to chemistry.

The acids, for example, are compounded of two substances, of the order of those which we consider as simple; the one constitutes acidity, and is common to all acids,

---

[i]Claude-Louis Berthollet (1748–1822) was the first French chemist to accept Lavoisier's new system and a collaborator with him on the new chemical nomenclature. His magnum opus, the *Essai de statique chimique* (1803) advanced his theory of indefinite proportions, which was routed by the work of John Dalton. [B.]

[j]Antoine Francois de Fourcroy (1755–1809) was an important proponent of Lavoisier's new system, teaching it at the Jardin de Roi, where he was a professor of chemistry. [B.]

and, from this substance, the name of the class or the genus ought to be taken; the other is peculiar to each acid, and distinguishes it from the rest, and from this substance is to be taken the name of the species. But, in the greatest number of acids, the two constituent elements, the acidifying principle and that which it acidifies may exist in different proportions, constituting all the possible points of equilibrium or of saturation. This is the case in the sulfuric and the sulfurous acids [sulfur dioxide]; and there two states of the same acid we have marked by varying the termination of the specific name.

Metallic substances which have been exposed to the joint action of the air and of fire, lose their metallic luster, increase in weight, and assume an earthy appearance. In this state, like the acids, they are compounded of a principle which is common to all, and one which is peculiar to each. In the same way, therefore, we have thought proper to class them under a generic name, derived from the common principle; for which purpose, we adopted the term *oxyd*; and we distinguish them from each other by the particular name of the metal to which each belongs. Combustible substances, which in acids and metallic oxides are a specific and particular principle, are capable of becoming, in their turn, common principles of a great number of substances. The sulfurous combinations have been long the only known ones in this kind. Now, however, we know, from the experiments of Messrs. Vandermonde, Gaspard Monge,[k] and Berthollet, that charcoal may be combined with iron, and perhaps with several other metals; and that, from this combination, according to the proportions, may be produced steel, plumbago [lead ore], etc. We know likewise, from the experiments

of M. Pierre-Joseph Pelletier[l] that phosphorus may be combined with a great number of metallic substances. These different combinations we have classed under generic names taken from the common substance, with a termination which marks this analogy, specifying them by another name taken from that substance which is proper to each.

The nomenclature of bodies compounded of three simple substances was attended with still greater difficulty, not only on account of their number, but, particularly, because we cannot express the nature of their constituent principles without employing more compound names. In the bodies which form this class, such as the neutral salts, for instance, we had to consider, first, the acidifying principle, which is common to them all; second, the acidifiable principle which constitutes their peculiar acid; third, the saline, earthy, or metallic basis, which determines the particular species of salt. Here we derived the name of each class of salts from the name of the acidifiable principle common to all the individuals of that class; and distinguished each species by the name of the saline, earthy, or metallic basis, which is peculiar to it.

A salt, though compounded of the same three principles, may nevertheless by the mere difference of their proportion, be in three different states. The nomenclature we have adopted would have been defective, had it not expressed these different states; and this we attained chiefly by changes of termination uniformly applied to the same state of the different salts.

In short, we have advanced so far that from the name alone may be instantly found what the combustible substance is which

---

[k]Gaspard Monge (1746–1818) made important contributions to mathematics, notably his application of the techniques of analysis to the theory of curvature. [B.]

[l]Pierre-Joseph Pelletier (1788–1842) extracted a large number of biologically active compounds from plants (caffeine, strychnine, veratrine, and colchicine), founding the chemistry of the alkaloids. His most important discoveries were quinine, used against malaria, and chlorophyll, the green pigment in plants. [B.]

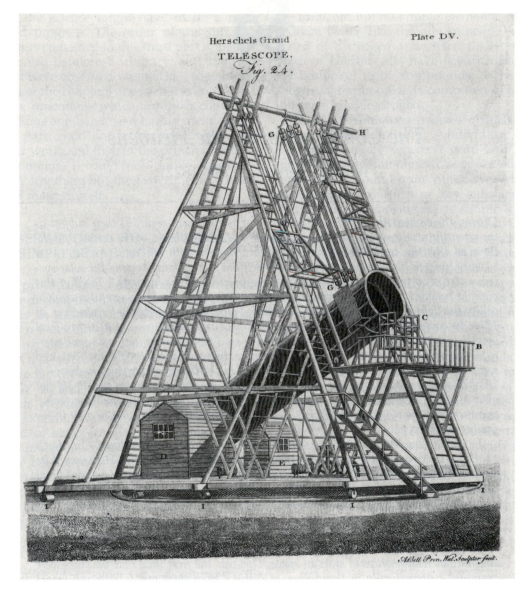

**PLATE 22**   Engraving of William Herschel's giant 40-foot telescope. When completed, the latticework of poles and ladders that supported the main tube and observing galleries was 50 feet high. Regarded as one of the wonders of the day, the telescope was cumbersome and Herschel reverted to a much more manageable 20-foot telescope.

*Until the end of the century, Herschel's work was geared toward determining parallax by the differential method. Galileo had proposed that parallax of a star could be detected, not by measuring its angular distance from standard points on the celestial sphere such as the pole or its zenith, but by observing the variations in its distance from some star close to it, which from its faintness or for some other reason might be supposed to be much further away and therefore less affected by the Earth's motion. In 1782, Herschel presented to the Royal Society a catalogue of 269 doublets. This was followed by a second in 1784 of 434 doublets. A third in 1821 listed 145 more.*

*Returning to his inventory of stellar doubles in 1802, Herschel made a startling discovery: Instead of finding an alternate annual increase and decrease of their distance and angle of position, which the parallax of the Earth's annual motion would have produced, Herschel observed a regular progressive change, which produced a parallax of a higher order than would arise from a systematic parallax occasioned by the Earth's annual motion. Herschel observed a steady advance in one direction which indicated either a real motion of the stars themselves or a general rectilinear motion of the Sun and the whole solar system. This startling discovery persuaded Herschel that often pairs of stars revolve round one another and therefore that they are physically connected in some way. Herschel's observations of binary systems only sufficed to show that a motion of revolution of some kind appeared to be taking place; they were not sufficient to determine with any precision the law of the motion.*

---

By the continuation of a review of the heavens with my 20-foot reflector, I am now furnished with a second thousand of new nebulae.

These curious objects, not only on account of their number, but also in consideration of their great consequence, as being no less than whole sidereal systems, we may hope, will in future engage the attention of astronomers. With a view to induce them to undertake the necessary observations, I offer them the following catalogue, which, like my former one, of which it is a continuation, contains a short description of each nebula or cluster of stars, as well as its situation with respect to some known object.

The form of this work, it will be seen, is exactly that of the former part, the classes and numbers being continued, and the same letters used to express, in the shortest way, as many essential features of the objects as could possibly be crowded into so small a compass as that to which I thought it expedient to limit myself.

The method I have taken of analyzing the heavens, if I may so express myself, is per-

haps the only one by which we can arrive at a knowledge of their construction. In the prosecution of so extensive an undertaking, it may well be supposed that many things must have been suggested, by the great variety in the order, the size, and the compression of the stars, as they presented themselves to my view, which it will not be improper to communicate.

To begin our investigation according to some order, let us depart from the objects immediately around us to the most remote that our telescopes of the greatest power to penetrate into space, can reach. We shall touch but slightly on things that have already been remarked . . .

These suns [stars], every one of which is probably of as much consequence to a system of planets, satellites, and comets, as our own Sun, are now to be considered, in their turn, as the minute parts of a proportionally greater whole. I need not repeat that by my analysis it appears that the heavens consist of regions where suns are gathered into separate systems, and that the catalogues I have given comprehend a list of such systems; but may we not hope that our knowledge will not stop short at the bare enumeration of phenomena capable of giving us so much instruction? Why should we be less inquisitive than the natural philosopher, who sometimes, even from an inconsiderable number of specimens of a plant, or an animal, is enabled to present us with the history of its rise, progress, and decay? Let us then compare together, and class some of these numerous sidereal groups, that we may trace the operations of natural causes as far as we can perceive their agency. The most simple form, in which we can view a sidereal system, is that of being globular. This also, very favorably to our design, is that which had presented itself most frequently, and of which I have given the greatest collection.

But, first of all, it will be necessary to explain what is our idea of a cluster of stars, and by what means we have obtained it. For an instance, I shall take the phenomenon which presents itself in many clusters: It is that of a number of lucid spots, of equal luster, scattered over a circular space, in such a manner as to appear gradually more compressed towards the middle; and which compression, in the clusters to which I allude, is generally carried so far, as, by imperceptible degrees, to end in luminous center, of a resolvable blaze of light. To solve this appearance, it may be conjectured, that stars of any given, very unequal magnitudes, may easily be so arranged, in scattered, much extended, irregular rows, as to produce the above described picture; or, that stars, scattered about almost promiscuously within the frustum of a given cone, may be assigned of such properly diversified magnitudes as also to from the same picture. But who, that is acquainted with the doctrine of chances, can seriously maintain such improbable conjectures? To consider this only a coarse way, let us suppose a cluster to consist of 5,000 stars, and that each of them may be put into one of 5,000 places, and have one of 5,000 assigned magnitudes. Then, without extending our calculation any further, we have five and twenty millions of chances, out of which only one will answer the above

improbable conjecture, while all the rest were against it. When we now remark that this relates only to the given places within the frustum of a supposed cone, whereas these stars might have been scattered all over the visible space of the heavens; that they might have been scattered, even within the supposed cone, in a million places different from the assumed ones, the chance of this apparent cluster's not being a real one, will be rendered so highly improbable that it ought to be entirely rejected.

Mr. Mitchell[a] computes, with respect to the six brightest stars of the Pleiades only, that the odds are near 500,000 to 1 that no six stars, out of the number of those which are equal in splendor to the faintest of them, scattered at random in the whole heavens, would be within so small a distance from each other as the Pleiades are.[1]

Taking it for granted that the stars which appear to be gathered together in a group are in reality thus accumulated, I proceed to prove also that they are nearly of an equal magnitude.

The cluster itself, on account of the small angle it subtends to the eye, we must suppose to be very far removed from us. For, were the stars which compose it at the same distance from one another as Sirius is from the Sun; and supposing the cluster to be seen under an angle of ten minutes, and contain fifty stars at one of its diameters, we should have the mean distance of such stars twelve seconds; and therefore, the distance of the cluster from us about seventeen thousand times greater than the distance of Sirius. Now, since the apparent magnitude of these

[a]John Michell, "An Inquiry into the probable Parallax, and Magnitude of the fixed Stars, from the Quantity of Light which they afford us, and the particular Circumstances of their Situation." *Philosophical Transactions of the Royal Society,* 57 (1767): 234–264. Best known as the founder of seismology, none of the values Michell (1724–1793) used in his famous paper—apparent diameters, periods, brightness, total light received, etc.—were then measured, and some were not measurable. [B.]

stars is equal, and their distance from us is also equal—because we may neglect the diameter of the cluster, which, if the center be seventeen thousand times the distance of Sirius from us, will give us seventeen thousand and twenty-five for the nearest star of the cluster—it follows that we must either give up the idea of a cluster, and recur to the above refuted supposition, or admit the equality of the stars that compose these clusters. It is to be remarked that we do not mean entirely to exclude all variety of size; for the very great distance, and the consequent smallness of the component clustering stars, will not permit us to be extremely precise in the estimation of their magnitudes; though, we have certainly seen enough of them to know that they are not contained within pretty narrow limits; and do not, perhaps, exceed each other in magnitude more than in some such proportion as one full-grown plant of a certain species may exceed another full-grown plant of the same species.

If we have drawn proper conclusions relating to the size of stars, we may with still greater safety speak of their relative situations, and affirm that in the same distances from the center an equal scattering takes place. If this were not the case, the appearance of a cluster could not be uniformly increasing in brightness towards the middle, but would appear nebulous in those parts which were more crowded with stars; but, as far as we can distinguish, in the clusters of which we speak, every concentric circle maintains an equal degree of compression, as long as the stars are visible; and when they become too crowded to be distinguished, an equal brightness takes place, at equal distances from the center, which is the most luminous part.

The next step in my argument will be to show that these clusters are of a globular form. This again we rest on the sound doctrine of chances. Here, by way of [adding] strength to our argument, we may be allowed to take in all round nebulae, though the reasons we have for believing that they consist of stars have not yet been entered

into. For, what I have to say concerning their spherical figure will equally hold good whether they be groups of stars or not. In my catalogs we have, I suppose, not less than one-thousand of these round objects. Now, whatever may be the shape of a group of stars, or of a Nebula, which we would introduce instead of a spherical one, such as a cone, an ellipsis, a spheroid, a circle or a cylinder, it will be evident that out of a thousand situations, which the axes of such forms may have, there is but one that can answer the phenomenon for which we want to account; and that is, when those axes are exactly in a line drawn from the object to the place of the observer. Here again, we have a million of chances of which all but one are against any other hypothesis than that which we maintain, and which, for this reason, ought to be admitted. . . .

We may now venture to raise a superstructure upon the arguments that have been drawn from the appearance of clusters of stars and nebulae of the form I have been examining, which is that of which I have made mention in my *"Theoretical view—Formation of Nebulae—Form I.*[2] It is to be remarked that when I wrote the paragraph I refer to, I delineated nature as well as I do now; but, as I there gave only a general sketch without referring to particular cases, what I then delivered may have been looked upon as little better than hypothetical reasoning, whereas in the present instance this objection is entirely removed, since actual and particular facts are brought to vouch for the truth of every inference.

Having then established that the clusters of stars of the first form, and round nebulae, are of a spherical figure, I think myself plainly authorized to conclude that they are thus formed by the action of central powers. To manifest the validity of this inference, the figure of the Earth may be given as an instance; whose rotundity, setting aside small deviations, the causes of which are well known, is without hesitation allowed to be a phenomenon decisively establishing a centripetal force. Nor do we stand in need of the revolving satellites of Jupiter, Saturn, and the Georgium Sidus,[b] to assure us that the same powers are likewise lodged in the masses of these planets. Their globular figure alone must be admitted as a sufficient argument to render this point incontrovertible. We also apply this inference with equal propriety to the body of the Sun, as well as to that of Mercury, Venus, Mars, and the Moon; as owing their spherical shape to the same cause. And how can we avoid inferring that the construction of the clusters of stars, and nebulae likewise, of which we have been speaking, as is evidently owing to central powers?

Besides, the step that I here make in my inference is in fact a very easy one, and such as ought freely to be granted. Have I not already shown that these clusters cannot have come to their present formation by any random scattering of stars? The doctrine of chance, by exposing the very great odds against such hypotheses may be said to demonstrate that the stars are thus assembled by some power or other. Then, what do I attempt more than merely to lead the mind to the conditions under which this power is seen to act?

In a case of such consequences I may be permitted to be a little more diffuse, and draw additional arguments from the internal construction of spherical clusters and nebulae. If we find that there is not only a general form, which, as has been proved, is a sufficient manifestation of a centripetal force, what shall we say when the accumulated condensation, which everywhere follows a direction towards a center, is even visible to the very eye? Were we not already acquainted with attraction, this gradual condensation would point out a central power, by the remarkable disposition of the stars tending towards a center. In consequence of this visible accumulation, whether it may be owing to attraction only, or whether other

powers may assist in the formation, we ought not to hesitate to ascribe the effect to such as are *central*; no phenomena being more decisive in that particular, than those of which I am treating . . .

I am fully aware of the consequences I shall draw upon myself in but mentioning other powers that might contribute to the formation of clusters. A mere hint of this kind, it will be expected, ought not to be given without sufficient foundation; but let it suffice at present to remark that my arguments cannot be affected by my terms: whether I am right to use the plural number, central powers, or whether I ought only to say, the known force of gravity, my conclusions will be equally valid. I will, however, add that the idea of other central powers being concerned in the construction of the sidereal heavens, is not one that has only lately occurred to me. Long ago I have entertained a certain theory of diversified central powers of attractions and repulsions; an exposition of which I have been delivered in the years 1780, and 1781, to the Philosophical Society, then existing at Bath, in several mathematical papers upon that subject. I shall, however, set aside an explanation of this theory, which would not only exceed the intended limits of this paper, but is moreover not required for what remains at present to be added, and therefore may be given some other time, when I can enter more fully into the subject of the interior construction of sidereal systems.

To return, then, to the case immediately under our present consideration, it will be sufficient that I have abundantly proved that the formation of round clusters of stars and nebulae is either owing to central powers, or at least to one such force as refers to a center.

I shall now extend the weight of my argument by taking in likewise every cluster of stars or nebula that shows a gradual condensation, or increasing brightness, towards a center or certain point; whether the outward shape of such clusters or nebulae be round, extended, or any other given form. What has been said with regard to the doctrine of chance, will of course apply to every cluster,

[b]Until 1850 or so, the planet Uranus, which Herschel had discovered and which he named after King George III, was often referred to as "Georgium Sidus" or as "Herschel." [B.]

and more especially to the extended and irregular shaped ones, on account of their greater size: It is among these that we find the largest assemblages of stars, and most diffusive nebulosities; and therefore the odds against such assemblages happening without some particular power to gather them, increase exceedingly with the number of the stars that are taken together. But if the gradual accumulation either of stars or increasing brightness has before been admitted as a direction to the seat of power, the same effect will equally point out the same cause in the cases now under consideration. There are besides some additional circumstances in the appearance of extended clusters and nebulae that very much favor the idea of a power lodged in the brightest part. Although the form of them be not globular, it is plainly to be seen that there is a tendency towards sphericity, by the swell of the dimensions the nearer we draw towards the most luminous place, denoting as it were a course, or tide of stars, setting towards a center. And, if allegoric expressions be allowed, it should seem as if the stars thus flocking towards the seat of power were stemmed by the crowd of those already assembled, and that while some of them are successful in forcing their predecessors sideways out of their places, other are themselves obliged to take up with lateral situations, while all of them seem equally to strive for a place in the central swelling, and generating spherical figure.

Since, then, almost all the nebulae and clusters of stars I have seen, the number of which is not less than three and twenty hundred, are more condensed and brighter in the middle; and since, from every form, it is now equally apparent that the central accumulation of brightness must be the result of central powers, we may venture to affirm that this theory is no longer an unfounded hypothesis, but is fully established on grounds which cannot be overturned.

Let us endeavor to make some use of this important view of the constructing cause, which can thus model sidereal systems. Perhaps, by placing before us the very extensive and varied collection of clusters, and nebulae furnished by my catalogues, we may be able to trace the progress of its operation, in the great laboratory of the universe.

If these clusters and nebulae were all the same shape, and had the same gradual condensation, we should make but little progress in this inquiry; but, as we find so great a variety in their appearances, we shall be much sooner at a loss how to account for such various phenomena, than be in want of materials upon which to exercise our inquisitive endeavors.

Some of these round clusters consist of stars of a certain magnitude, and given degree of compression, while the whole cluster itself takes up a space of perhaps ten minutes; others appear to be made up of stars that are much smaller, and much more compressed, when at the same time the cluster itself subtends a much smaller angle, such as five minutes. This diminution of the apparent size, and compression of stars, as well as diameter of the cluster to four, three, two minutes, may very consistently be ascribed to the different distances of these clusters from the place in which we observe them; in all which cases we may admit a general equality of the sizes, and compression of the stars that compose them, to take place. It is also highly probable that a continuation of such decreasing magnitudes, and increasing compression, will justly account for the appearance of round, easily resolvable, nebulae; where there is almost a certainty of their being clusters of stars. And no astronomer can hesitate to go still farther, and extend his surmises by imperceptible steps to other nebulae, that still preserve the same characteristics, with the only variations of vanishing brightness, and reduction of size.

Other clusters there are that, when they come to be compared with some of the former, seem to contain stars of an equal magnitude, while their compression appears to be considerably different. Here the supposition of their being at different distances will either not explain the apparently greater compression, or if admitted to do this, will convey to us a very instructive consequence, which is that the stars which are thus supposed not to be more compressed than those in the former cluster, but only to appear so on account of their greater distance, must needs be proportionally larger, since they do not appear of less magnitude than the former. As therefore, one or other of these hypotheses must be true, it is not at all improbable but that, in some instances, the stars may be more compressed; and in others of a greater magnitude. This variety of size, in different spherical clusters, I am, however, inclined to believe may not go farther than the difference in size found among the individuals belonging to the same species of plants, or animals, in their different states of age, or vegetation, after they are come to a certain degree of growth. A farther inquiry into the circumstances of the extent, both in condensation and variety of size, that may take place in the stars of different clusters, we shall postpone until other things have been previously discussed.

Let us then continue to turn our view to the power which is molding the different assortment of stars into spherical clusters. Any force, that acts without interruption, must produce effects proportional to the time of its action. Now, as it has been shown that the spherical figure of a cluster of stars is so owing to central powers, it follows that those clusters which, *ceteris paribus,* are the most complete in this figure, must have been the longest exposed to the action of these causes. This will admit to various points of view. Suppose, for instance, that 5,000 stars had been once in a certain scattered situation, and that another 5,000 equal stars had been in the same situation, then that of the two clusters which had been longest exposed to the action of the modeling power, we suppose, would be most condensed, and more advanced to the maturity of its figure. An obvious consequence that may be drawn from this consideration is that we are enabled to judge of the relative age, maturity, or climax of a sidereal system from the disposition of its component parts; and making the degrees of brightness in nebulae stand

for the different accumulation of stars in clusters, the same conclusions will stand equally to them all. But we are not to conclude from what has been said that every spherical cluster is of an equal standing in regard to absolute duration, since one that is composed of a thousand stars only, must certainly arrive to the perfection of its form sooner than another, which takes in a range of a million. Youth and age are comparative expressions; and an oak of a certain age may be called very young, while a contemporary shrub is already on the verge of its decay. The method of judging with some assurance of the condition of any sidereal system may perhaps not improperly be drawn from the standard laid down; so that, for instance, a cluster or nebula which is very gradually more compressed, such as the nebulae I have called *planetary* seem to present us with, may be looked upon as very aged, and drawing on towards a period of change, or dissolution. This has been before surmised, when, in a former paper, I considered the uncommon degree of compression that must prevail in a nebula to give it a planetary aspect; but the argument, which is now drawn from the powers that have collected the formerly scattered stars to the form we find they have assumed, must greatly corroborate that sentiment.

This method of viewing the heavens seems to throw them into a new kind of light. They now are seen to resemble a luxuriant garden, which contains the greatest variety of productions, in different flourishing beds; and one advantage we may at least reap from it is, that we can, as it were, extend the range of our experience to an immense duration. For, to continue the simile I have borrowed from the vegetable kingdom, is it not almost the same thing, whether we live successively to witness the germination, blooming, foliage, fecundity, fading, withering, and corruption of a plant, or whether a vast number of specimens, selected from every stage through which the plants passes in the course of its existence, be brought at once to our view?

**NOTES**

1. *Phil. Trans.* Vol. LVII, p. 246.
2. *Phil. Trans.* Vol. LXXV, p. 214.

**FURTHER READINGS**

Crawford, Deborah. 1968. *The King's Astronomer, William Herschel.* New York: J. Messner.

Hoskin, Michael A. 1963. *William Herschel and the Construction of the Heavens.* London: Oldbourne.

King, Henry. 1979. *History of the Telescope.* New York: Dover Publications.

North, John. 1994. *The Fontana History of Astronomy and Cosmology.* London: Fontana Press.

# A Portrait of Caroline Herschel

## Maria Mitchell (1818–1889)

*Maria Mitchell, Professor of Science and Director of the Observatory at Vassar College, was the first professional female astronomer in the United States, and the first female member of the American Academy of Arts and Science (1848). A gifted astronomer, she is credited with the discovery of a comet (1847), and for her advocacy of the removal of all barriers to the full participation of women in science.*

*In this reading, excerpted from an article published in 1894, Mitchell recalls a trip to England and time spent with John Herschel (1792–1871), son of William Herschel, and his family. Her reflections on William's sister, Caroline Herschel (1750–1848), are reminders that, prior to the late nineteenth century, it was exceedingly difficult for women to receive recognition for their contributions to science; women were active contributors to science, but invariably they were relegated to a secondary role and their contributions regarded as comparatively unimportant.*

*Caroline Herschel was an exception to this marginalization. Early in her career, her work as a scientist was primarily that of assisting her brother by note-taking and making routine (and laborious) calculations. However, as time passed, her work became increasingly autonomous. Between the years 1786 and 1797, she was credited with the discovery of eight comets. She published her own catalog of stars and another catalog of 2500 nebulae, for which she received the Gold Medal of the Royal Astronomical Society. In 1835, Herschel and Mary Somerville (1780–1872), the astronomer and physical geographer, were made the first honorary female members of the Royal Society.*

---

Most astronomers come to astronomy through mathematics, or come to mathematics through astronomy. The Herschels were a musical family; music was their vocation: Science was their recreation. Although of Jacob Herschel's children, Sir William and

*Source:* Maria Mitchell. 1889. Reminiscences on the Herschels. *The New Century Monthly Magazine* 38.

Caroline are the only ones who are known to science, it is evident that the taste for science belonged to the whole family, as Caroline Herschel in her autobiography speaks of lying awake and listening to discussions between the father and the elder brothers in which the names of Newton, Leibniz, and Euler frequently occurred.

William Herschel considered himself very fortunate when he was engaged as musician to an English regiment. Growing in reputation, he was appointed organist in a church, studied Italian, Latin, and Greek by himself, and read mathematical works on music. Thus music led him to mathematics, and from there to optics, to astronomy, to discoveries, to reputation. He became known to George III, was pensioned, gave himself wholly to astronomy, was knighted, and soon became a member of all the learned societies of Europe . . .

I arrived at the Herschels' just at dinner time. While the servant was gone to announce me, I looked around the large hall, and the first thing that caught my eye was Borden's map of Massachusetts. I felt at home at once, for that map hung in the room most familiar to me in America.

The servant returned and asked me into the drawing-room, and Sir John Herschel came in at once. He reached both hands to me very cordially and said, "We did not receive your letter, but you are always welcome in this house." Lady Herschel followed, also with a very kind welcome.

I found a cheery fire awaiting me in my room, and after a few minutes I was asked down to dinner, only Sir John and Lady Herschel being present.

After dinner the family assembled in the drawing-room, and the elder daughters were introduced to me. There were twelve children, although Lady Herschel seemed young and was still handsome; she must have been fifty years old. Sir John was at that time sixty-six years old, but he looked much older, being lame and much bent in his figure . . .

On Sunday morning Lady Herschel went to church, and I with her. The Herschels, like all the country gentry whom I knew in England, attended service in a little old stone church, with no style about it; this had not even an organ. Miss Herschel told me that a good deal of effort had been made to raise money enough to purchase one, but it had failed. In the afternoon I remained at home and looked over the manuscripts of Sir William Herschel and his sister, Sir John pointing out the interesting parts. They were very carefully preserved, and were kept with a system, which was in itself a science. The great astronomer wrote his notes on slips of paper at different times; these slips were afterward compared, the results obtained from them were recorded, and indices to the manuscripts made. The first notes on the planet Uranus, which he discovered, speak of it as a comet—he dared not call it a planet—and as a comet it continues for some time to be spoken of in the notes, probably after he knew it to be a planet.[1]

Several of the manuscripts are devoted to the methods of polishing specula; several to observations on light. One of the notes is: "Observed my sister's comet of August 1."

The copies of letters were in themselves numerous and very interesting. The loss of the planet Ceres is mentioned in one to Piazzi.[a] One is to Sir William Watson to ask for a term for the asteroids—what to call them *as a group*. He suggests that more may be discovered. A most remarkable one is to a French gentleman about a chemical discovery, which seems to have been a foreshadowing of photography.

Caroline Herschel followed Sir William to England when he was appointed astronomer to the King, and remained there until his death. She shared in all the nightwatches of her brother, and with pencil in hand and eye on the clock recorded what he saw, made the calculations, registered, coordinated, classed, and analyzed them.

As a gift for the present Lady Herschel, Caroline Herschel prepared her own biography after she was ninety years of age. It is written in a very clear hand, and although English was not her native tongue, the language is good. The sentences are long, but never obscure. Lady Herschel read some passages to me. She says, "My father told me that as I had neither beauty nor riches, no

---

[a]Giuseppe Piazzi (1746–1826) discovered the asteroid Ceres in 1801. He became embroiled in a debate with William Herschel about the appropriate name for his discovery, preferring the term "planetoid" to Herschel's "asteroid." [B.]

man would be likely to make me an offer until I was old, when some one might like, on account of my worth, to marry me."

When I mingled with English scientists, I was not prepared for so much lore of poetry as I found. Mr. Airy,[b] the Astronomer Royal, could repeat the whole of the "Lady of the Lake." Dr. Whewell,[c] the master of Trinity, was a great lover of poetry, and wrote verses himself, though Sir John Herschel was more particularly the poet of science . . .

Sir John's mind was full of vigor at the time of my visit. He was then engaged in rewriting his *Outlines of Astronomy,* but was no longer an active astronomer. He talked with great enthusiasm of the Cape observatory, and described in a very interesting manner the peculiar appearance of a twisted nebula on the larger of the "Magellan Patches."

I went over the grounds the last day, rainy though it was, to get to the barn to see the remains of the telescope used by Sir William: Only the tube was left. It was forty feet long, and the diameter was so great that one could

sit comfortably within it. Arago says that "in 1840 the family, then residing at Slough, formed in procession and walked around this telescope, then, seated on benches within the tube, sang the song written by Sir John and sealed up the tube—its work was over."[2]

Sir John was said to be a man of no wealth. The family, including the servants, numbered some twenty persons; and when I asked, "What is meant in England by a person of no wealth?" I was told that it meant one who could not portion his daughters when they married.

It was the period of our distressing financial crisis of 1857, and English as well as American families were ruined. I asked of an English lady, "What will become of the daughters of an English family in which there is no property?" She replied, "They will live on their brother." And the question was asked of me, "What will become of the daughters of an American family in which there is no money?" "They will *earn* money," I replied. The answer was, "You Americans are a sensible people."

The house was very extensive, the grounds proportionately so: the table was to me, as all English tables seemed, over-bountiful; but in style of furniture and of dress I know no merchant's family in Boston so simple.

English habits may have changed since 1857, but at that time I saw no young ladies in silk. The plain print for morning and simple white for evening were all that the daughters of the astronomer royal or those of Sir John Herschel wore; and yet in the family of the astronomer royal, as in that of Sir John Herschel, a ring of the door-bell might announce not only the highest potentate of science in England, but the highest representative of any social circle—even the Queen herself.

You would say, in looking at Caroline Herschel's portrait, which hung in the drawing-room, "she must have been handsome when she was young." Her ruffled cap

---

[b]George Biddell Airy (1801–1892) was appointed Astronomer Royal in 1835, a post that he held for forty-six years. Although Royal Greenwich Observatory benefited from his organizational abilities, Airy is now remembered for lapses of judgment, first for ignoring John Couch Adams (1819–1892), when he informed Airy in 1845 that he had calculated the elements and position of a hitherto unseen planet (Neptune), and second for dismissing Faraday's field theory. [B.]

[c]One of the pivotal figures of Victorian science, William Whewell's (1794–1866) scholarly and scientific interests included poetry, German literature, Greek philosophy, theology, architecture, political economy, and education. He introduced many scientific terms: "ion," "anode," and "cathode," to physics; and "eocene," "miocene," and "pliocene," to geology. He even introduced the terms "physicist" and "scientist." He is now chiefly remembered for his contributions to history and philosophy of science, especially for his attempt to extract a philosophy of science from a consideration of its historical development. [B.]

shades a mild face, whose blue eyes were even then full of animation. But it was merely the beauty of age. I suspect that this is often the case, especially when the life has been such as to develop the soul, which overcomes ugliness of feature and coarseness of complexion.

If you had asked Caroline Herschel after ten years of labor what good had come of it, she would probably have answered, with the extreme simplicity of her nature, that she had relieved her brother of a good deal of wearisome labor and perhaps kept up his vigor and prolonged his life. Probably it never entered her thoughts to be other than the patient and self-sacrificing assistant to a truly great man.

The woman who has peculiar gifts has a definite line marked out for her, and the call from God to do his work in the field of scientific investigation may be as imperative as that which calls the missionary into the moral field, or the mother into the family: As missionary, or as scientist, as sister, or as mother, no woman has the right to lose her individuality. To discuss the question whether women have the capacity for original investigation in science is simply idle until equal opportunity is given them. We cannot overrate the consequences of such lives, whether it be Mrs. Somerville translating Laplace, Harriet Hosmer modeling her statues, Mrs. Browning writing her poems, or Caroline Herschel spending nights under the open canopy; in all it is the devotion to idea, the loyalty to duty, which reaches to all ages.

One of Caroline Herschel's strong characteristics was the carefulness with which everything was done. We are apt to hurry in everything, as if railroad-speed were the law of daily life—as if our hearts did not beat fast enough. She worked slowly, as if she knew that she had ninety-eight years of this life and all eternity in the next. When she worked in the little observatory at Slough, where the first observations were made, she not only worked in every observatory of the world, but she reached to every school for girls.

If what Caroline Herschel did is a lesson and a stimulus to all women, what she did not do is a warning. Has any being a right not to be? When Caroline Herschel so devoted herself to her brother that on his death her own self died, and her life became comparatively useless, she did, all unconsciously, a wrong, and she made the great mistake of her life.

The fault was only in part her fault. She was honored—late in life—as few women have been, by her family, by her sovereign, by the savants of all Europe. It was too late. It seems probable that her gifts were as fully bestowed as those of her brother; she was left uneducated and undeveloped. It was the English way; it is still the way of the world. Living on more than twenty years after his death, she needed for her own comfort pursuits and avocations outside the life that she had given him, and throughout her nearly one hundred years the world needed all that she could do.

When she kept the records, so systematically and so scientifically that after nearly one hundred years they are still valuable, every line that she wrote was an argument for the higher education of women; when she wrapped herself in innumerable wrappings and took care of the body that the mind might do its duty, she gave a lesson which every girl ought to follow.

She showed also the lesson of the usefulness of the unmarried woman. In England much more than in our country the unmarried woman holds a secondary place—unless she has some title. She even enters the dining-room after every married woman. I would in no way underrate the higher value of the wife and the mother and the blessedness of those whom God has placed in families, but life need not be a failure and a blank when this position is denied. The family is only a larger one; the usefulness is not so intense, but it may be wider spread.

*A second strategy, geared toward measuring the mutual attraction of two artifi-
cially prepared masses in a laboratory setting proved to be much more successful. The
experiment that we really associate with the measurement of the gravitational constant
was carried out in 1798 by Henry Cavendish, who has been widely regarded as the
greatest experimental scientist of the eighteenth century. In addition to his determination of the gravitational constant, which is reproduced here, Cavendish made important contributions to the study of gases (he was the first to weigh gases accurately) and
to the study of electricity.*

Many years ago, the late Rev. John Michell,[a] of this Society, contrived a method of determining the density of the Earth, by render-
ing sensible the attraction of small quantities
of matter; but, as he was engaged in other
pursuits, he did not complete the apparatus
until a short time before his death, and did
not live to make any experiments with it.
After his death, the apparatus came to the
Rev. Francis John Hyde Wollaston,[b] Jackson-
ian Professor at Cambridge, who, not having
conveniences for making experiments with
it, in the manner he could wish, was so good
as to give it to me.

The apparatus is very simple; it consists
of a wooden arm, six feet long, made so as to
unite great strength with little weight. This
arm is suspended in an horizontal position,
by a slender wire forty inches long, and to
each extremity is hung a leaden ball, about
two inches in diameter; and the whole is enclosed in a narrow wooden case, to defend it
from the wind.

As no more force is required to make this
arm turn round on its center, than what is

necessary to twist the suspending wire, it is
plain that if the wire is sufficiently slender,
the most minute force, such as the attraction
of a leaden weight a few inches in diameter,
will be sufficient to draw the arm sensibly
aside. The weights which Mr. Michell intended to use were 8 inches diameter. One of
these was to be placed on one side of the
case, opposite to one of the balls, and as near
it as could conveniently be done, and the
other on the other side, opposite to the other
ball, so that the attraction of both these
weights would conspire in drawing the arm
aside; and, when its position, as affected by
these weights, was ascertained the weights
were to be removed to the other side of the
case; so as to draw the arm the contrary way,
and the position of the arm was to be again
determined; and, consequently, half the difference of these positions would show how
much the arm was drawn aside by the attraction of the weights.

In order to determine from this the density of the Earth, it is necessary to ascertain
what force is required to draw the arm aside
through a given space.

This Mr. Michell intended to do by
putting the arm in motion, and observing
the time of its vibrations, from which it may
easily be computed.[1]

Mr. Michell had prepared two wooden
stands, on which the leaden weights were to
be supported, and pushed forwards, until
they came almost in contact with the case;
but he seems to have intended to move them
by hand.

As the force with which the balls are attracted by these weights is excessively
minute, not more than 1/50,000,000 of their

[a]Michell (1724–1793) was Woodwardian Professor
of Geology at Cambridge (1762–1764), and subsequently Rector of Thornhill. He is remembered
for his defense of Boscovich point-particles
against Newton's atoms, as well as a treatise on
magnets published in 1750. [B.]

[b]Wollaston (1766–1828) introduced the term
"equivalent" into chemistry. He computed a table
with oxygen = 10 as the unit, the system that sur-
vives today in the form of the chemical slide rule.
In its day, many chemists preferred Wollaston's
system to Dalton's because it did not depend on
the existence of such suspect entities as atoms. [B.]

weight, it is plain that a very minute disturbing force will be sufficient to destroy the success of the experiment; and, from the following experiments, it will appear that the disturbing force most difficult to guard against is that arising from the variations of heat and cold; for, if one side of the case is warmer than the other, the air in contact with it will be rarefied, and, in consequence, will ascend, while that on the other side will descend, and produce a current which will draw the arm sensibly aside.[2]

As I was convinced of the necessity of guarding against this source of error, I resolved to place the apparatus in a room which should remain constantly shut, and to observe the motion of the arm from without

by means of a telescope; and to suspend the leaden weights in such a manner that I could move them without entering into the room. This difference in the manner of observing, rendered it necessary to make some alteration in Mr. Michell's apparatus; and as there were some parts of it which I thought not so convenient as could be wished, I chose to make the greatest part of it afresh.

Fig. 1 [Plate 23] is a longitudinal vertical section through the instrument, and the building in which it is placed. *ABCDDCBAEFFE*, is the case; $x$ and $x$ are the two balls, which are suspended by the wires $bx$ from the arm $gbmb$, which is itself suspended by the slender wire $gl$. This arm consists of a slender deal (fir or pine) rod $bmb$, strengthened by a

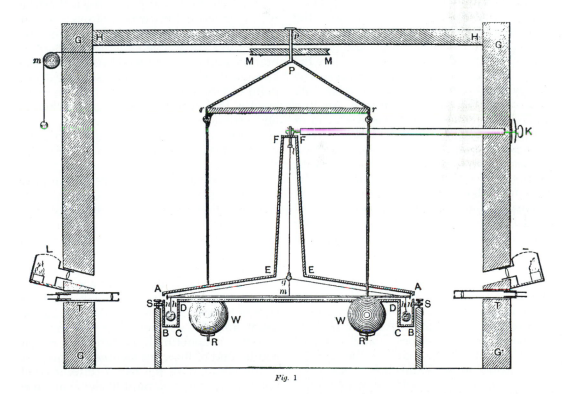

*Fig.* 1

**PLATE 23** Longitudinal vertical section through Cavendish's instrument and the building in which it is placed. From Cavendish, "Experiments to Determine the Density of the Earth," *Philosophical Transactions of the Royal Society* (1798).

silver wire *bgb;* by which means it is made strong enough to support the balls, though very light.[3]

The case is supported, and set horizontal, by four screws, resting on posts fixed firmly into the ground: two of them are represented in the figure by *S* and *S;* the two others are not represented to avoid confusion. *GG* and *GG* are the end walls of the building. *W* and *W* are the leaden weights; which are suspended by the copper rods *RrPrR,* and the wooden bar *rr,* from the center pin *Pp.* This pin passes through a hole in the beam *HH,* perpendicularly over the center of the instrument, and turns round in it, being prevented from falling by the plate *p. MM* is a pulley, fastened to this pin; and *Mm,* a cord wound round the pulley, and passing through the end wall; by which the observer may turn it round, and thereby, move the weights from one situation to the other. . . .

In order to determine the situation of the arm, slips of ivory are placed within the case, as near to each end of the arm as can be done without danger of touching it, and are divided into twentieths of an inch. Another small slip of ivory is placed at each end of the arm, serving as a vernier, and subdividing these divisions into five parts; so that the position of the arm may be observed with ease to hundredths of an inch, and may be estimated to less. These divisions are viewed by means of the short telescopes *T* and *T* (fig. 1.), through slits cut in the end of the case and stopped with glass; they are enlightened by the lamps *L* and *L,* with convex glasses, placed so as to throw the light on the divisions, no other light being admitted into the room.

The divisions on the slips of ivory run in the direction *Ww* so that, when the weights are placed in the positions *w* and *w,* represented by the dotted circles, the arm is drawn aside, in such direction as to make the index point to a higher number on the slips of ivory; for which reason, I call this the positive position of the weights.

*FK* (fig. 1.) is a wooden rod, which, by means of an endless screw, turns round the support to which the wire *gl* is fastened, and

thereby, enables the observer to turn round the wire, until the arm settles in the middle of the case, without danger of touching either side. The wire *gl* is fastened to its support at top, and to the center of the arm at bottom, by brass clips, in which it is pinched by screws. . . .

Before I proceed to the account of the experiments, it will be proper to say something of the manner of observing. Suppose the arm to be at rest, and its position to be observed, let the weights then be moved, the arm will not only be drawn aside thereby, but it will be made to vibrate, and its vibrations will continue a great while; so that, in order to determine how much the arm is drawn aside, it is necessary to observe the extreme points of the vibrations, and from this to determine the point which it would rest at if its motion was destroyed, or the point of rest, as I shall call it. To do this, I observe three successive extreme points of vibration, and take the mean between the first and third of these points, as the extreme point of vibration in one direction, and then assume the mean between this and the second extreme, as the point of rest; for, as the vibrations are continually diminishing, it is evident, that the mean between two extreme points will not give the true point of rest . . .

From this table [see facing page] it appears that, though the experiments agree pretty well together, yet the difference between them, both in the quantity of motion of the arm and in the time of vibration, is greater than can proceed merely from the error of observation. As to the difference in the motion of the arm, it may very well be accounted for from the current of air produced by the difference of temperature; but whether this can account for the difference in the time of vibration is doubtful. If the current of air was regular and of the same swiftness in all parts of the vibration of the ball, I think it could not; but, as there will most likely be much irregularity in the current, it may very likely be sufficient to account for the difference.

By a mean of the experiments made with the wire first used, the density of the Earth comes out 5.48 times greater than that of

*The following Table contains the Result of the Experiments.*

| Exper. | Mot. weight | Mot. arm | Do. corr. | Time vib. | Do. corr. | Density. |
|---|---|---|---|---|---|---|
| 1 { | m. to + | 14,32 | 13,42 | ′ ″ | - | 5,5 |
|  { | + to m. | 14,1 | 13,17 | 14,55 | - | 5,61 |
| 2 { | m. to + | 15,87 | 14,69 | - | - | 4,88 |
|  { | + to m. | 15,45 | 14,14 | 14,42 | - | 5,07 |
| 3 { | + to m. | 15,22 | 13,56 | 14,39 | - | 5,26 |
|  { | m. to + | 14,5 | 13,28 | 14,54 | - | 5,55 |
| 4 ⎨ | m. to + | 3,1 | 2,95 |  | 6,54 | 5,36 |
|  ⎬ | + to − | 6,18 | - | 7,1 | - | 5,29 |
|  ⎨ | − to + | 5,92 | - | 7,3 | - | 5,58 |
| 5 { | + to − | 5,9 | - | 7,5 | - | 5,65 |
|  { | − to + | 5,98 | - | 7,5 | - | 5,57 |
| 6 { | m. to − | 3,03 | 2,9 | ⎫ | - | 5,53 |
|  { | − to + | 5,9 | 5,71 | ⎪ | - | 5,62 |
| 7 { | m. to − | 3,15 | 3,03 | 7,4 | 6,57 | 5,29 |
|  { | − to + | 6,1 | 5,9 | by mean. | - | 5,44 |
| 8 { | m. to − | 3,13 | 3,00 | ⎪ | - | 5,34 |
|  { | − to + | 5,72 | 5,54 | ⎭ | - | 5,79 |
| 9 | + to − | 6,32 | - | 6,58 | - | 5,1 |
| 10 | + to − | 6,15 | - | 6,59 | - | 5,27 |
| 11 | + to − | 6,07 | - | 7,1 | - | 5,39 |
| 12 | − to + | 6,09 | - | 7,3 | - | 5,42 |
| 13 { | − to + | 6,12 | - | 7,6 | - | 5,47 |
|  { | + to − | 5,97 | - | 7,7 | - | 5,63 |
| 14 { | − to + | 6,27 | - | 7,6 | - | 5,34 |
|  { | + to − | 6,13 | - | 7,6 | - | 5,46 |
| 15 | − to + | 6,34 | - | 7,7 | - | 5,3 |
| 16 | − to + | 6,1 | - | 7,16 | - | 5,75 |
| 17 { | − to + | 5,78 | - | 7,2 | - | 5,68 |
|  { | + to − | 5,64 | - | 7,3 | - | 5,85 |

water; and by a mean of those made with the latter wire, it comes out the same. The extreme difference of the results of the twenty-three observations made with this wire, is only .75; so that the extreme results do not differ from the mean by more than .38, or $\frac{1}{14}$ of the whole, and therefore, the density should seem to be determined hereby to great exactness. It, indeed, may be objected that as the result appears to be influenced by the current of air, or some other cause, the laws of which we are not well acquainted with. This cause may perhaps act always, or commonly, in the same direction, and thereby make a considerable error in the result. But yet, as the experiments were tried in various weathers, and with considerable variety in the difference of temperature of the weights and air, and with the arm resting at different distances from the sides of the case, it seems very unlikely that this cause should act so uniformly in the same way, as to make the error of the mean result nearly equal to the difference between this and the extreme; and, therefore, it seems very unlikely that the density of the Earth should differ from 5.48 by so much as 1¼ of the whole.

Another objection, perhaps, may be made to these experiments, namely, that it is uncertain whether, in these small distances, the force of gravity follows exactly the same law as in greater distances. There is no reason, however, to think that any irregularity of this kind takes place, until the bodies come within the action of what is called the attraction of cohesion, and which seems to extend only to very minute distances . . .

According to the experiments made by Dr. Maskelyne[c] on the attraction of the hill Schiehallion, the density of the Earth is 4½ times that of water; which differs rather more from the preceding determination than I should have expected. But I forbear entering into any consideration of which determination is most to be depended on until I have examined more carefully how much the preceding determination is affected by irregularities whose quantity I cannot measure.

[c]Nevil Maskelyne, fifth Astronomer Royal, began publication in 1766 of the *Nautical Almanac*, which contained navigational aids and astronomical tables. Cavendish is here referring to Maskelyne's attempt to measure the deflection of a plumb bob suspended near Schiehallion. [B.]

## NOTES

1. Mr. Coulomb has, in a variety of cases, used a contrivance of this kind for trying small attractions; but Mr. Michell informed me of his intention of making this experiment, and of the method he intended to use, before the publication of any of Mr. Coulomb's experiments.

2. M. Cassini, in observing the variation compass placed by him in the Observatory (which was so constructed so as to make very minute changes of position visible, and in which the needle was suspended by a silk thread) found that standing near the box, in order to observe, drew the needle sensibly aside; which I have no doubt was caused by this current of air. It must be observed, that his compass box was of metal, which transmits heat faster than wood, and also was many inches deep; both which causes served to increase the current of air. To diminish the effect of this current, it is by all means advisable to make the box, in which the needle plays, not much deeper than is necessary to prevent the needle from striking against the top and bottom.

3. Mr. Michell's rod was entirely of wood, and was much stronger and stiffer than this, though not much heavier; but as it had warped when it came to me, I chose to make another, and preferred this form, partly as being easier to construct and meeting with less resistance from the air, and partly because, from its being of a less complicated form, I could more easily compute how much it was attracted by the weights.

## FURTHER READINGS

Berry, Arthur John. 1960. *Henry Cavendish: His Life and Scientific Work.* London: Hutchinson & Co.

Jungnickel, Crista and McCormmach, Russell K. 1999. *Cavendish: The Experimental Life.* Lewisburg: Bucknell.

McCormmach, Russell K. 1968. "John Mitchell and Henry Cavendish: Weighing the Stars," *British Journal for the History of Science* 4: 126–155.

Poynting, J. H. 1894. *The Mean Density of the Earth.* London: Charles Griffon and Company.

# The Artificial Electric Organ

## Alessandro Volta (1745–1827)

*After the invention of the Leyden jar, scientists began to wonder about the relationship between the physiological effect of its discharge and that of shocks given off by electrical eels and the torpedo fish. In a famous series of experiments, Luigi Galvani (1737–1798), an anatomist at the University of Bologna, found that dissected frogs legs twitched as though in spasm or convulsion on contact with a spark from an electric machine. Conceiving a living creature as a fleshy kind of Leyden jar, he conjectured that the motion was caused by a vital force he termed "animal electricity." When the outer surface of the muscles receives an electrical charge (like the outer surface of the Leyden jar), the nerve and inner muscular surface would then become oppositely charged and muscular contraction would follow.*

*Skeptical about the notion of "animal electricity," Alessandro Volta, professor of physics at Pavia, repeated Galvani's experiments, but he concentrated the metallic probes on the nerves only, thereby taking the muscles out of the picture and creating an experimental arrangement that no longer functioned like a Leyden jar. The redesigned apparatus produced the same results. Volta was struck by the fact that electricity was produced only if two different metals were used. He also noticed that some combinations of metals produced more twitching than others. He tried placing a piece of tinfoil and a silver coin in his mouth, one on top of the tongue, the other touching his tongue's lower surface. When the foil was pressed to the coin, he found that this apparatus produced a sour taste in his mouth, which he interpreted as indicating the presence of an electrical discharge. The taste lasted so long as the tin and silver were in contact with one another, showing that the flow of electricity from one place to another was continuous. The metals, he concluded, were not mere conductors but were actually responsible for the production of electricity.*

*Continuing his experiments, Volta realized that the electricity might be conducted from one metal to the other by the fluid in his saliva. When he placed disks of silver, tin or zinc on moist cloth, clay or wood, and then separated them and brought them to the electrometer, a negative electrification resulted. He showed further that improved*

---

*Source:* Alessandro Volta. 1800. "On the Electricity excited by the Mere Contact of Conducting Substances of Different Kinds." *Philosophical Transactions of the Royal Society,* Vol. 90, pp. 403–431.

*results were produced when a circuit was formed by two different metals separated by a moist element, and that their effectiveness was added together when such combinations of metals and moist element were stacked in a repeating pattern. In this way, Volta succeeded in building his column or pile of electric generating elements, described in this letter dated March 1800 to the President of the Royal Society, Sir Joseph Banks.*

*Volta's new device, which he called "the artificial electric organ," was the first continuous source of electric current. With his electric battery, there was no instantaneous flash, as seen in a frictional electric discharge through an air gap. Compared with the older frictional electricity having high potential or driving force (voltage) and very little current (amperage), the new galvanic current possessed low pressures but enormous quantities of electric current at the same time.*

*Volta's experiments were immediately replicated by scientists on both sides of the Atlantic, who recognized that a source of constant-current electricity not only opened up entirely new avenues of research but would ultimately transform other established disciplines in ways that had been unthinkable. The discipline that reaped the greatest immediate benefit from Volta's battery was chemistry, which now possessed a powerful new tool for tracking down new elements and for understanding the nature of chemical bonding.*

---

After a long silence, for which I shall offer no apology, I have the pleasure of communicating to you,[a] and through you to the Royal Society, some striking results I have obtained in pursuing my experiments on electricity excited by the mere mutual contact of different kinds of metal, and even by that of other conductors, also different from each other, either liquid or containing some liquid, to which they are properly indebted for their

[a]Volta's letter to Joseph Banks (1743–1820), president of the Royal Society, was dispatched in two sections due to ongoing military conflict between France and England. Even before the second part of Volta's historic announcement reached the Royal Society, the chemist William Nicholson (1809–1845) and the English surgeon Anthony Carlisle (1768–1840) had constructed a voltaic pile to be placed in the service of chemistry. The first notable result, reported in Nicholson's journal for July 1800, was that water was decomposed by their pile which consisted of 17 large silver coins separated by an equal number of copper disks. Each such pair was separated from the adjoining pairs by bits of cloth soaked in a weak brine solution. [B.]

conducting power. The principal of these results, which comprehends nearly all the rest, is the construction of an apparatus having a resemblance in its effects (that is to say, in the shock it is capable of making the arms, etc., experience) to the Leyden flask, or, rather, to an electric battery weakly charged acting incessantly, which should charge itself after each explosion; and, in a word, which should have an inexhaustible charge, a perpetual action or impulse on the electric fluid; but which differs from it essentially both by this continual action, which is peculiar to it; and because, instead of consisting, like the common electric jars and batteries, of one or more insulating plates or thin strata of those bodies which are alone thought to be *electric*, armed with conductors, or bodies called *non-electric*, this new apparatus is formed merely of several of the latter bodies, chosen from among those which are the best conductors, and therefore the most remote, as has hitherto been believed, from the electric nature. The apparatus to which I allude, and which will, no doubt, astonish you, is only the assemblage of a number of good conductors of different kinds arranged in a certain manner. Thirty, forty, sixty, or more pieces of copper, or rather silver, applied each to a piece of tin, or zinc, which is much better, and as many strata of water, or any other liquid which may be a better conductor, such as salt water, ley, etc., or pieces of paste board, skin, etc., well soaked in these liquids; such strata interposed between every pair or combination of two different metals in an alternate series, and always in the same order of these three kinds of conductors, are all that is necessary for constituting my new instrument, which, as I have said, imitates the effects of the Leyden flask, or of electric batteries, by communicating the same shock as these do; but which, indeed, is far inferior to the activity of these batteries when highly charged, either in regard to the force and noise of the explosions, the spark, the distance at which the discharge may be effected, etc., as it equals only the effects of a battery very weakly charged, though of immense capacity; in other respects, however, it far surpasses the virtue and power of these batteries, as it has no need, like these, of being previously charged by means of foreign electricity, and as it is capable of giving a shock every time it is properly touched, however often it may be.

To this apparatus, much more similar at bottom, as I shall show, and even such as I have constructed it, in its form to the *natural electric organ* of the torpedo or electric eel, etc., than to the Leyden flask and electric batteries, I would wish to give the name of the *artificial electric organ* and, indeed, is it not, like it, composed entirely of conducting bodies? Is it not also active of itself without any previous charge, without the aid of any electricity excited by any of the means hitherto known? Does it not act incessantly, and without intermission? And, in the last place, is it not capable of giving at every moment shocks of greater or lesser strength, according to circumstances, which are renewed by each new touch, and which, when thus repeated or continued for a certain time, produce the same torpor in the limbs as is occasioned by the torpedo, etc.?

I shall now give a more particular description of this apparatus and of others analogous to it, as well as of the most remarkable experiments made with them.

I provide a few dozen of small round plates or disks of copper, brass, or rather silver, an inch in diameter more or less (pieces of coin for example), and an equal number of plates of tin, or, what is better, of zinc, nearly of the same size and figure. I make use of the term *nearly,* because great precision is not necessary, and the size in general, as well as the figure of the metallic pieces, is merely arbitrary; care only must be taken that they may be capable of being conveniently arranged one above the other, in the form of a column. I prepare also a pretty large number of circular pieces of paste board, or any other spongy matter capable of imbibing and retaining a great deal of water or moisture, with which they must be well impregnated in order to insure success to the experiments. These circular pieces of paste board, which I shall call moistened disks, I make a little smaller than the plates of metal, in order that, when interposed between them, as I shall hereafter describe, they may not project beyond them.

Having all these pieces ready in a good state, that is to say, the metallic disks very clean and dry, and the non-metallic ones well moistened with common water, or, what is much better, salt water, and slightly wiped that the moisture may not drop off, I have nothing to do but to arrange them, a matter exceedingly simple and easy.

I place then horizontally, on a table or any other stand, one of the metallic pieces, for example one of silver, and over the first I adapt one of zinc; on the second I place one of the moistened disks, then another plate of silver followed immediately by another of zinc, over which I place another of the moistened disks. In this manner I continue coupling a plate of silver with one of zinc, and always in the same order, that is to say, the silver below and the zinc above it, or vice versa, according as I have begun, and interpose between each of these couples a moistened disk. I continue to form, of several of these stories, a column as high as possible without any danger of its falling.

But, if it contain about twenty of these stories or couples of metal, it will be capable not only of emitting signs of electricity by Cavallo's electrometer,[b] assisted by a condenser, beyond ten or fifteen degrees, and of charging his condenser by mere contact so as to make it emit a spark, etc., but of giving to the fingers with which its extremities (the bottom and top of the column) have been touched several small shocks, more or less frequent, according as the touching has been repeated. Each of these shocks has a perfect resemblance to that slight shock experienced from a Leyden flask weakly charged, or a battery still more weakly charged, or a torpedo in an exceedingly languishing state, which imitates still better the effects of my apparatus by the series of repeated shocks which it can continually communicate.

To obtain such slight shocks from this apparatus which I have described, and which is still too small for great effects, it is necessary that the fingers, with which the two extremities are to be touched at the same time, should be dipped in water, so that the skin, which otherwise is not a good conductor, may be well moistened. To succeed with more certainty, and receive stronger shocks, a communication must be made by means of a metallic plate sufficiently large, or a large metallic wire, between the bottom of the column (that is to say, the lower piece of metal) and water contained in a basin or large cup, in which one, two, or three fingers, or the

whole hand is to be immersed, while you touch the top or upper extremity (the uppermost or one of the uppermost plates of the column) with the clean extremity of another metallic plate held in the other hand, which must be very moist, and embrace a large surface of the plate held very fast. By proceeding in this manner, I can obtain a small pricking or slight shock in one or two articulations of a finger immersed in the water of the basin, by touching, with the plate grasped in the other hand, the fourth or even third pair of metallic pieces. By touching then the fifth, the sixth, and the rest in succession until I come to the last, which forms the head of the column, it is curious to observe how the shocks gradually increase in force. But this force is such that I receive from a column formed of twenty pairs of pieces (not more) shocks which affect the whole finger with considerable pain if it is immersed alone in the water of the basin, which extend (without pain) as far as the wrist and even to the elbow, if the whole hand, or the greater part of it, is immersed; and are felt also in the wrist of the other hand.

I still suppose that all the necessary attention has been employed in the construction of the column, and that each pair or couple of metallic pieces, resulting from a plate of silver applied over one of zinc, is in communication with the following couple by a sufficient stratum of moisture, consisting of salt water rather than common water, or by a piece of pasteboard, skin or any thing of the same kind well impregnated with this salt water. The disk must not be too small, and its surface must adhere closely to those of the metallic plates between which it is placed. This exact and extensive application of moistened disks is very important, whereas the metallic plates of each pair may only touch each other in a few points, provided that their contact is immediate.

All this shows that, if the contact of the metals with each other in some points only be sufficient (as they are excellent conductors) to give a free passage to a moderately

[b]Tiberius Cavallo's (1749–1809) reputation as a physicist was established by his most important work, *A Complete Treatise of Electricity in Theory and Practice* (1777)—a work that contained in its appendixes a rich storehouse of information on the design and operation of instruments. His electrometer was discussed in "New Electrical Experiments and Observations, With an Improvement of Mr. Canton's Electrometer," *Philosophical Transactions of the RoyalSociety* 67:1 (1777), 48–55. [B.]

strong current of electricity, the case is not the same with liquids, or bodies impregnated with moisture, which are conductors much less perfect; and which, consequently, have need of more ample contact with metallic conductors, and still more with each other, in order that the electric fluid may easily pass, and that it may not be too much retarded in its course, especially when it is moved with very little force, as in the present case.

In a word, the effects of my apparatus, that is to say, the shocks felt, are considerably more sensible in proportion as the temperature of the ambient air, or that of the water or moistened disks which enter into the composition of the column, and that of the water even in the basin, is warmer, as heat renders the water a better conductor. But almost all the salts, and particularly common salt, will render it a still better conductor. This is one of the reasons, if not the only one, why it is so advantageous that the water of the basin, and, above all, that interposed between each pair of metallic plates, as well as the water with which the circular pieces of pasteboard are impregnated, etc., should be salt water, as was already observed.

But all these means and all these attentions have only a limited advantage, and will never occasion your receiving very strong shocks as long as the apparatus consists but of one column. Formed only of twenty pair of plates, even though they consist of the two metals most appropriate for these experiments, viz., silver and zinc; for if they were silver and lead, or tin, or copper and tin, the half of the effect would not be produced, unless the weaker effect of each pair were supplied by a much greater number. What really increases the electric power of this apparatus, and to such a degree as to make it equal or surpass that of the torpedo or electric eel, is the number of plates arranged in such a manner and with the attention before mentioned. If, in addition to the twenty pairs above described, twenty or thirty others are added disposed in the same order, the shocks which may be communicated by a column lengthened in this manner will be much stronger, and extend to both arms as far as the shoulder; and especially of that, the hand of which has been immersed in the water; this hand, with the whole arm, will remain more or less benumbed, if by frequently renewing the touches these shocks are made to succeed each other rapidly, and without intermission. This will be the case if the whole hand, or the greater part of it, is immersed in the water of the basin; but if only one finger is immersed, either wholly or in part, the shocks being almost entirely concentrated in it alone, will become so much the more painful, and so acute as to be scarcely supportable.

It may readily be conceived that this column, formed of forty or fifty couples of metals, which gives shocks more than moderate to both the arms of one person, is capable of giving sensible shocks also to several persons, holding each other by the hands (sufficiently moist) so as to form an uninterrupted chain.

I shall now return to the mechanical construction of my apparatus, which is susceptible of several variations, and describe not all those which I have invented or made, either on a small or a large scale, but only a few, which are either curious or useful, which exhibit some real advantage as being easier or sooner constructed, and which are certain in their effects, or can be longer preserved in good order.

I shall begin by one which, uniting nearly all these advantages, differs most in its figure from the columnar apparatus above described, but which is attended with the inconvenience of being much more voluminous. This new apparatus, which I shall call a *couronne de tasses* (a chain of cups) is represented is figure 1 [Plate 24].

I dispose, therefore, a row of several basins or cups of any matter whatever, except metal, such as wood, shell, earth, or rather glass (small tumblers or drinking glasses are the most convenient), half-filled

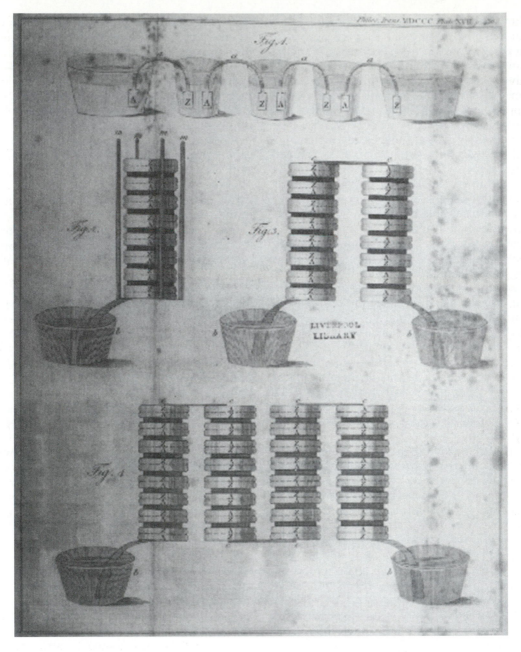

**PLATE 24** Volta's pile or electric battery. From Allesandro Volta, "On the Electricity Excited by the Mere Contact of Conducting Substances of Different Kinds." *Philosophical Transactions of the Royal Society,* vol. 90 (London, 1800). Courtesy of the Thomas Fisher Rare Book Library, University of Toronto (Toronto, Canada).

with pure water, or rather salt water or ley; they all are made to communicate by forming them into a sort of chain, by means of so many metallic arcs, one arm of which, *Sa*, or only the extremity *S*, immersed in one of the tumblers, is of copper or brass, or rather of copper plated silver: and the other, *Za*, immersed into the next tumbler, is of tin, or rather of zinc. I shall here observe, that ley and other alkaline liquors are preferable when one of the metals to be immersed is tin: Salt water is preferable when it is zinc. The two metals of which each arc is composed are soldered together in any part above that which is immersed in the liquor, and which must touch it with a surface sufficiently large. It is necessary, therefore, that this part should be a plate of an inch square, or very little less; the rest of the arc may be as much narrower as you choose, and even a simple metallic wire. It may also consist of a third metal different from the two immersed into the tumblers, since the action of the electric fluid which results from all the contacts of several metals that immediately succeed each other, or the force with which this fluid is at last impelled, is absolutely the same, or nearly so, as that which it would have received by the immediate contact of the first metal with the last without any intermediate metals, as I have ascertained by direct experiments, of which I shall have occasion to speak hereafter.

A series of 30, 40, or 60 of these tumblers connected with each other in this manner, and ranged either in a straight or curved line, or bent in every manner possible, forms the whole of this new apparatus which at bottom and in substance is the same as the other columnar one above described; as the essential part, which consists in the immediate communication of the different metals which form each couple and the mediate communication of one couple with the other, viz., by the intervention of a humid conductor, exist in the one as well as the other.

In regard to the manner of trying these tumblers and the different experiments for which they may be employed, there is no need of saying a great deal after the ample explanation I have already given respecting the columnar apparatus. It may be readily comprehended that to obtain a shock it will be sufficient to immerse one hand into one of the tumblers, and a finger of the other hand into another of the tumblers at a considerable distance from the former, that this shock will be stronger the further these glasses are from each other; that is to say, in proportion to the number of the intermediate glasses, and consequently, that the strongest shock will be received when you touch the first and last end of the chain. It will be readily comprehended also how and why the experiments will succeed much better by grasping and holding fast on one hand, well moistened, a pretty large plate of metal (in order that the communication may be more perfect, and formed in a great number of points), and touching with this plate the water in the tumbler, or rather the metallic arc, while the other is immersed in the other distant tumbler, or touches with a plate, grasped in the like manner, the arc of the latter. In a word, one may comprehend and even foresee the success of a great variety of experiments which may be made with this apparatus or chain of cups much more easily, and in a manner more evident, and which, if I may be allowed the expression, speak more to the eyes than those with the columnar apparatus. I shall therefore forbear from describing a great number of these experiments, which may be easily guessed, and shall relate only a few which are no less instructive than amusing.

Let three twenties of these tumblers be ranged, and connected with each other by metallic arcs, but in such a manner, that, for the first twenty, these arcs shall be turned in the same direction, for example, the arm of silver turned to the left, and the arm of zinc to the right: and for the second twenty in a contrary direction, that is to say, the zinc to the left, and the silver to the right: in the last place, for the third twenty, the silver to the left, as is the case in regard the first. When everything is thus arranged, immerse one finger in the water of the first tumbler, and, with the plate grasped in the other hand, as above directed, touch the first metallic arc (that which joins the first tumbler to the second), then the other arc which joins the second and third tumbler, and so on, in succession, until you have touched them all. If the water be very salt and lukewarm, and the skin of the hands well moistened and softened, you will already begin to feel a slight shock in the finger when you have touched the fourth or fifth arc (I have experienced it some times very distinctly by touching the third), and by successively proceeding to the sixth and the seventh, etc., the shocks will gradually increase in force to the twentieth arc, that is to say, to the last of those turned in the same direction: But by proceeding onwards to the 21st, 22nd, 23rd, or 1st, 2nd, 3rd, of the second twenty, in which they are all turned in a contrary direction, the shocks will each time become weaker, so that at the 36th or 37th, they will be imperceptible, and be entirely null at the 40th, beyond which (and beginning the third twenty, opposed to the second and analogous to the first) the shocks will be imperceptible to the 44th or 45th arc, but they will begin to become sensible, and to increase gradually, in proportion as you advance to the 60th, where they will have attained the same force as that of the 20th arc.

If the twenty arcs in the middle were all turned in the same direction as the preceding twenty and the following twenty, that is to say, if the whole sixty conspired to impel the electric fluid in the same direction, it may readily be comprehended how much greater the effect will be at the end, and how much stronger the shock; and it may be comprehended, in general, to what point it must be weakened in all cases where a greater or smaller number of these forces act contrary to each other by an inverted position of metals.

If the chain be in any part interrupted, either by one of the tumblers being empty of water, or one of the metallic arcs being removed or divided into two pieces, you will receive no shock when you immerse your finger into the water of the first and another into that of the last vessel; but you will have it strong or weak, according to circumstances (leaving these fingers immersed), at the moment when the interrupted communication is restored; at the moment when another person shall immerse into the two tumblers, where the arc is wanting, two of his fingers (which will also receive a slight shock), or rather, when he shall immerse the same arc which has been taken away, or any other; and in the case of the arc separated into two pieces, at the moment which these pieces are again brought into mutual contact (in which case the shock will be stronger than in any other); and, lastly, in the case of the empty tumbler at the moment when water poured into it shall rise to the two metallic arms immersed in this cup which before were dry.

When the chain of cups is of sufficient length, and capable of giving a strong shock, you will experience one, though much weaker, even though you keep immersed two fingers, or the two hands, in one basin of water of pretty large size, in which the first and last metallic arcs are made to terminate provided that either of these hands thus immersed, or rather both of them, be kept respectively in contact, or nearly in contact, with these arcs, you will, I say, experience a shock at the moment when (the chain being interrupted in any part) the communication is restored, and the circle completed in any of the ways before mentioned. One might be surprised that in this circle the electric current having a free passage through an uninterrupted mass of water that which fills the basin, should quit this good conductor to throw itself and pursue its course through the body of the person who holds his hands immersed in the same water, and thus to take a longer passage. But the surprise will cease if we reflect, that living and warm animal substances, and above all, their humors, are, in general, better conductors than water. As the body, then, of the person who immerses his hands in the water, affords an easier passage than this water does to the electric current, the latter must prefer it though a little longer. In a word, the electric fluid, when it must traverse imperfect conductors in a large quantity, and particularly moist conductors, has a propensity to extend itself in a larger stream, or to divide itself into several, and even to pursue a winding course, as it thereby finds less resistance than by following one single channel, though shorter; in the present case, it is only a part of the electric current, which, leaving the water, pursues this new route through the body of the person, and traverses it from the one arm to the other; a greater or less part passes through the water in the vessel. This is the reason why the shock experienced is much weaker than when the electric current is not divided when the person alone forms the communication between one arc and another.

From these experiments one might believe that when the torpedo wishes to communicate a shock to the arms of a man or to animals which touch it, or which approach its body under the water (which shock is much weaker than what the fish can give out of the water) it has nothing to do but to bring together some of the parts of its electric organ in that place, where, by some interval, the communication is interrupted, to remove the interruptions from between the columns of which the said organ is formed, or from between its membranes in the form of thin disks, which lie one above the other from the bottom to the summit of each column, it has, I say, nothing to do but to remove these interruptions in one or more places, and to produce there the requisite contact, either by compressing these columns, or by making some moisture to flow in between the pellicles or diaphragms which have been separated. This is what may be, and what I really conclude to be, the task of the torpedo when it gives a shock; for all the rest, the impulse and movement communicated to the electric fluid, is only a necessary effect of its singular organ, formed, as is seen, of a very numerous series of conduc-

tors, which I have every reason to believe sufficiently different from each other to be *exciters* of the electric fluid by their mutual contacts; and to suppose them ranged in a manner proper for impelling that fluid with a sufficient force from top to bottom, or from the bottom to the top, and for determining a current capable of producing the shock, etc., as soon and as often as all the necessary contacts and communications take place.

But let us now leave the torpedo, and its *natural electric organ,* and return to the *artificial electric organ* of my invention, and particularly to my first *columnar apparatus,* that which imitates the first even in its form (for that composed of tumblers is different in that respect). I might say something also in regard to the construction of the said apparatus with tumblers or *a chain of glasses;* for example, that the first and last tumbler should be of such a size that, when necessary, the whole hand might be immersed in it, but to enter into all these details, would require too much time.

In regard to the columnar apparatus, I endeavored to discover the means of lengthening it a great deal by multiplying the metallic plates in such a manner as not to tumble down: and I discovered, besides others, the following which are represented in the annexed figures (Plate 24, Figs. 2, 3, 4).

In Fig. 2, *mmmm* are rods, three, four, or more in number, which rise from the bottom of the column, and confine, as in a cage, the plates or disks, placed each above the other in such numbers and to such a height as you choose, and which thus prevent them from falling. The rods may be of glass, wood, or metal, only that, in the last case, you must prevent them from coming into immediate contact with the plates: which may be done either by covering each of them with a glass tube, or interposing between them and the column a few stripes of wax cloth, oiled paper, or even plain paper, and, in a word any other body that may either be a *co-hibent* or a bad conductor: wood or paper will be sufficiently so for our purpose, provided only that they are not very damp or moist.

But the best expedient, when you wish to form an apparatus to consist of a great number of plates, above 60, 80, or 100 for example, is, to divide the column into two or more, as seen Figs. 3 and 4 (Plate 24), where the pieces all have their respective positions and communication as if there were only one column. Fig. 4, as well as Fig. 3, may indeed be considered as a bent column.

In all these figures the different metallic plates are denoted by the letters *S* and *Z* (which are the initials of silver and zinc); and the *moistened disks* (of paste board, skin, etc. interposed between each pair of metals), are represented by a black stratum. The plates of metal may either be laid simply upon each other and so brought into union in an indefinite number of points, or they may be soldered together. It is altogether indifferent whichever of these methods be followed. *cc, cc, cc,* are the metallic plates which form a communication between each column, or section of a column, and another; and *bb, bb, bb,* are the basins of water in communication with the lower part or extremities of these columns.

An apparatus thus prepared is exceedingly convenient without being bulky; and it might be rendered portable, with still more ease and safety, by means of circular cases or tubes, in which each column might be enclosed and preserved. It is only to be regretted that it does not long continue in a good state; the moistened disks become dry in one or two days to such a degree that they must be again moistened which, however, may be done without taking to pieces the whole apparatus, by immersing the columns completely in water, and wiping them, when taken out some time after, with a cloth, or in any other manner.

The best method of making an instrument as durable as can be wished, would be to enclose and confine the water interposed between each pair of metals, and to fix these metallic plates in their places by enveloping the whole column with wax or pitch, but this would be somewhat difficult in the execution, and would require a great deal of patience. I have, however, succeeded; and have formed in this manner two cylinders consisting of twenty pairs of metals which can still be employed though made several weeks ago, and which, I hope, will be serviceable for months.

These cylinders are attended with this advantage, that they may be employed for experiments either in an erect, inclined, or lying position, according as you choose, or even immersed in water, provided the top of it be above the surface of the fluid; they might also give a shock when entirely immersed if they contained a greater number of plates, or if several of these cylinders were joined together, and if there were any interruptions that could be removed at pleasure, etc., by which means these cylinders would have a pretty good resemblance to the electric eel, and to have a better resemblance to it even externally, they might be joined together by pliable metallic wires or screw-springs, and then covered with a skin terminated by a head and tail properly formed.

The effects sensible to our organs produced by an apparatus formed of 40 or 50 pair of plates (and even by a smaller, if one of the metals be silver or copper and the other zinc), are reduced merely to shocks, the current of the electric fluid, impelled and excited by such a number and variety of different conductors, silver, zinc, and water, disposed alternately in the manner above described, excites not only contractions and spasms in the muscles, convulsions more or less violent in the limbs through which it passes in its course, but it irritates also the organs of taste, sight, hearing, and feeling, properly so called, and produces in them sensations peculiar to each.

And first, in regard to the sense of feeling; if by means of an ample contact of the hand (well moistened) with a plate of metal, or rather, by immersing the hand to a considerable depth in the water of the basin, I establish on one side a good communication with one of the extremities of my *electromotive* apparatus (we must give new names to instruments that are new not only in their form, but in their effects or the principle on which they depend); and on the other I apply the forehead, eye-lid, tip of the nose, also well moistened, or any part of the body where the skin is very delicate if I apply, I say with a little pressure, any one of these delicate parts, well moistened, to the point of a metallic wire, communicating properly with the other extremity of the said apparatus, I experience, at the moment that the conducting circle is completed, at the place of the skin touched, and a little beyond it, a blow and a prick, which suddenly passes, and is repeated as many times as the circle is interrupted and restored, so that, if these alternations be frequent, they occasion a very disagreeable quivering and pricking. But, if all these communications continue without these alternations, without the least interruption of the circle, I feel nothing for some moments; afterwards, however, there begins at the part applied to the end of the wire, another sensation, which is a sharp pain (without shock), limited precisely by the points of contact, a quivering, not only continued, but which always goes on increasing to such a degree, that in a little time it becomes insupportable, and does not cease until the circle is interrupted.

What proof is more evident of the continuation of the electric current as long as the communication of the conductors forming the circle is continued? And that such a current is only suspended by interrupting that communication? This endless circulation of the electric fluid (this *perpetual* motion) may appear paradoxical and even inexplicable, but it is no less true and real; and you feel it, as I may say, with your hands. Another evident proof may be drawn from this circumstance, that in such experiments you often experience at the moment when the circle is suddenly interrupted, a shock, a pricking, an agitation, according to circumstances, in the same manner as at the moment when it is completed; with this only difference, that these sensations, occasioned by a kind of reflux of the electric fluid, or by the shock

which arises from the sudden suspension of its current, are of less strength. But I have no need, and this is not the place to bring forward proofs of such an endless circulation of the electric fluid in a circle of conductors, where there are some, which, by being a different kind, perform by their mutual contact, the office of exciters or *movers:* This proposition, which I advanced in my first researches and discoveries on the subject of galvanism, and always maintained by supporting them with new facts and experiments, will, I hope, meet with no opposers . . .

In regard to the sense of taste I had before discovered, and published in these first memoirs, where I found myself obliged to combat the pretended animal electricity of Galvani,[c] and to declare it an external electricity moved by the mutual contact of metals of different kinds,—I had discovered, I say, in consequence of this power which I

---

[c]"If the spark from an electric machine caused a frog's legs to twitch as though in spasm or convusion, Galvani reckoned that he could confirm the suspicion of Benjamin Franklin (1706–1790) that lightning was indeed electricity. To test Franklin's hypothesis, he hung frog's legs by their nerves from brass hooks against an iron latticework. The lower tip of the suspended member was connected to a grounded wire. He found that the legs twitched when thunderclouds appeared but he also found that they also twitched when there were no thunderstorms. He noticed that when a copper or brass hook had been pressed into the frog's marrow and hung from an iron trellis, twitching would be seen even when the weather was pleasant. The twitching occurred, he discovered, whenever the muscles came into contact with two different metals at the same time. Atmospheric conditions were clearly not the main cause of the muscular contractions. To confirm this suspicion, he brought the specimen indoors. Using an iron plate instead of the trellis, the same twitching was again observed. Galvani concluded that the animal muscles retained some sort of innate electricity even after the animal had died. Conceiving a living creature as a fleshy kind of Leyden jar, he decided that the motion was caused by a vital force he termed "animal electricity." [B.]

ascribed to metals, that two pieces of these different metals, and particularly one of silver and one of zinc, applied in a proper manner, excited at the tip of the tongue very sensible sensations of taste; that the taste was decidedly acid, if, the tip of the tongue being turned towards the zinc, the electric current proceeded against it, and entered it; and that another taste, less strong but more disagreeable, acrid, and inclining to alkaline, was felt, if (the position of the metals being reversed) the electric current issued from the tip of the tongue; that these sensations continued and received even an increase for several seconds, if the mutual contact of the two metals was maintained, and if the conducting circle was nowhere interrupted. But when I have said here, that exactly the same phenomena take place when you try, instead of one pair of these metallic pieces, an assemblage of several of them ranged in the proper manner; and that the said sensations of taste, whether acid or alkaline, increase but a little with the number of these pairs, I have said the whole. It only remains for me to add that, if the apparatus put in play for these experiments on the tongue be formed of a sufficiently large number of metallic pairs of this kind, for example, if it contain 30, 40, or more, the tongue experiences not only the sensation of taste already mentioned, but, besides that, a blow which it receives at the moment when the circle is completed, and which occasions in it a pricking more or less painful, but fleeting, followed some moments after by a durable sensation of taste. This blow even produces a convulsion or agitation of a part or of the whole of the tongue, when the apparatus, formed of a still greater number of pairs of the said metals, is more active, and if, by means of good communicating conductors, the electric current which it excites must be able to pass every where with perfect freedom.

I must often return to, and insist on, this last condition, because it is essential in all experiments when you wish to obtain sensible effects on the body, or commotions in the limbs, or sensations in the organs of the senses. It is necessary, therefore, that the non-metallic conductors which enter into the circle should be as good conductors as possible, well moistened (if they are not themselves liquid) with water, or with any other liquid that may be a better conductor than pure water; and it is necessary, besides, that the well-moistened surfaces, by which they communicate with the metallic conductor, should be sufficiently large. The communication ought to be confined or reduced to a small number of points of contact only in that place where you wish to concentrate the electric action on one of the most sensible parts of the body, on any of the sensitive nerves, etc., as I have already remarked in speaking of the experiments on feeling, viz., those by which acute pains are excited in different parts. The best method which I have found for producing on the tongue all the sensations above described is to apply the tip of it to the pointed extremity (which, however, must not be too much so) of a metallic rod, which I make to communicate properly, as in the other experiments, with one of the extremities of my apparatus, and to establish a good communication between the hand, or, what is better, both the hands together, and the other extremity. This application of the tip of the tongue to the end of the metallic rod, may either exist already, when you are going to make the other communication to complete the circle (when you are going to immerse your hand into the water of the basin), or be made after the establishment of this communication, while the hand is immersed; and in the latter case I think I feel the pricking and shock in the tongue, a very short time before actual contact. Yes, it always appears to me, particularly if I advance the tip of my tongue gradually that, when it has arrived within a very small distance of the metal, the electric fluid (I would almost say spark), overcoming this interval, darts forward to strike it.

In regard to the sense of sight, which I also found might be affected by the weak current of the electric fluid, arising from the mutual contact of two different metals in general, and in particular, of a piece of silver and one of zinc, it was natural to expect that the sensation of light, excited by my new apparatus, would be stronger in proportion as it contained a greater number of pieces of these metals; each pair of which, arranged in the proper manner, adds a degree of force to the said electric current, as all the other experiments show, and particularly those with the electrometer assisted by the condenser, which I have only mentioned, and which I shall describe on another occasion. But I was surprised to find that, with 10, 20, 30 pairs and more, the flash produced neither appeared longer and more extended, nor much brighter than with one pair. It is true, however, that this sensation of weak and transient light, is excited by such an apparatus much easier and in different ways. To succeed, indeed, with one pair, the following are almost the only methods; viz., that one of the metallic pieces should be applied to the ball of the eye, or the eye-lid well moistened and that it should be made to touch the other metal applied to the other eye, or held in the mouth, which produces a flash much more beautiful; or, that this second metallic piece should be held in the moistened hand and then brought into contact with the former; or, in the last place, that these two plates should be applied to certain parts of the inside of the mouth, making them communicate with each other. But with an apparatus of 20 or 30 pairs, etc., the same flash will be produced by applying the end of a metallic plate or rod, placed in communication with one of the extremities of the apparatus, to the eye, while with one hand you form a proper communication with the other extremity; by bringing, I say, this plate into contact not only with the eye or any part of the mouth, but even the forehead, the nose, the cheeks, lips, chin, and even the throat; in a word, every part and point of the visage, which must only be well moistened before they are applied to the metallic plate. The form as well as the force of this transient light which is perceived varies a little, if the

places of the face to which the action of the electric current is applied, be varied: If it be on the forehead, for example, this light is moderately bright, and appears like a luminous circle, under which figure it presents itself also in several other experiments.

But, the most curious of all these experiments is to hold the metallic plate between the lips, and in contact with the tip of the tongue; since, when you afterwards complete the circle in the proper manner, you excite at once, if the apparatus be sufficiently large and in good order, and the electric current sufficiently strong and in good order, a sensation of light in the eyes, a convulsion in the lips, and even in the tongue, and a painful prick at the tip of it, followed by a sensation of taste.

I have now only to say a few words on hearing. This sense, which I had in vain tried to excite with only two metallic plates, though the most active of all the *exciters* of electricity, viz., one of silver or gold, and the other of zinc, I was at length able to affect it with my new apparatus, composed of 30 or 40 pairs of these metals. I introduced, a considerable way into both ears, two probes or metallic rods with their ends rounded, and I made them to communicate immediately with both extremities of the apparatus. At the moment when the circle was thus completed I received a shock in the head, and some moments after (the communication continuing without any interruption) I began to hear a sound, or rather noise, in the ears, which I cannot well define, it was a kind of crackling with shocks, as if some paste or tenacious matter had been boiling. This noise continued incessantly, and without increasing, all the time that the circle was complete, etc. The disagreeable sensation, and which I apprehended might be dangerous, of the shock in the brain, prevented me from repeating this experiment.

There still remains the sense of smelling, which I have hitherto tried in vain with my apparatus. The electric fluid, which, when made to flow in a current in a complete circle of conductors, produces in the limbs and parts of the living body effects correspondent to their excitability, which stimulating in particular the organs or nerves of touch, taste, sight, and hearing, excite in them some sensations peculiar to each of these senses, as I have found, produces in the interior of the nose only a pricking more or less painful, and commotions more or less extensive, according as the said current is weaker or stronger. And whence comes it, then, that it does not excite any sensation of smell, though, as appears, it stimulates the nerves of that sense? It cannot be said that the electric fluid of itself is not proper for producing odorous sensations, since, when it diffuses itself through the air in the form of aigrettes, etc., in the common experiments made with electric machines, it conveys to the nose a very sensible smell resembling that of phosphorus. Taking similitude into consideration, and reasoning from its analogy with other odoriferous matters, I will say that it must completely diffuse itself throughout the air to excite smell; that it has need, like other effluvia, of the vehicle of the air to affect that sense in such a manner as to excite the sensations of smell. But in the experiments of which I speak, that is to say, of an electric current in a circle of conductors, all contiguous, and without the least interruption, this absolutely cannot take place.

All the facts which I have related in this long paper in regard to the action which the electric fluid excited, and when moved by my apparatus, exercises on the different parts of our body which the current attacks and passes through—an action which is not momentous, but which lasts, and is maintained during the whole time that this current can follow the chain not interrupted in its communications in a word, an action the effects of which vary according to the different degrees of excitability in the parts, as has been seen—all these facts, sufficiently numerous, and others which may be still discovered by multiplying and varying the experiments of this kind, will open a very wide field for reflection, and of views not only curious, but particularly interesting to medicine. There will be a great deal to occupy the anatomist, the physiologist, and the practitioner . . .

To what electricity then, or to what instrument ought the organ of the torpedo or electric eel, etc., to be compared? To that which I have constructed according to the new principle of electricity, discovered by me some years ago, and which my successive experiments, particularly those with which I am at present engaged, have so well confirmed, viz., that conductors are also, in certain cases, exciters of electricity in the case of the mutual contact of those of different kinds, etc., in that apparatus which I have named the *artificial electric organ,* and which being at bottom the same as the natural organ of the torpedo, resembles it also in its form, as I have advanced.

## FURTHER READING

Pera, Marcello. 1992. *The Ambiguous Frog: The Galvani-Volta on Animal Electricity.* Trans. Jonathan Mandelbaum. Princeton: Princeton University Press.

Diber, Bern. 1964. *Alessandro Volta and the Electric Battery.* New York: F. Watts.

# The World Machine

## James Hutton (1726–1797)

*James Hutton described the Earth as a very special kind of machine, one which works in a way that prevents any aging. As envisioned by Hutton, the world machine operates on an endlessly repeating, three-stage cycle. In the first stage, the Earth's topographical features decay as rivers and waves break down rocks, form soils on the continents, and wash the products of erosion into the oceans. In the second stage, the broken down bits of old continents are deposited as horizontal strata in the ocean basins. As the strata build up, their own weight generates pressure and enough heat to mobilize the lower layers. In the third and final stage, matter is expanded by the heat of melting sediments and intruding magmas, resulting in extensive uplift and new continents at the sites of old oceans, while the eroded areas of old continents become new oceans.*

*The distinguishing feature of Hutton's theory of the Earth is that each stage automatically flows into the next one. So long as the current order of nature's laws continue in operation, continents and oceans continually change places in a never-ending mechanical process. The idea of deep geological time (there is "no vestige of a beginning,—no prospect of an end") is a straightforward consequence of the operation of the world machine.*

*Hutton is still widely portrayed as the first real empiricist in geology—i.e., as having induced his theory of the world machine from field observations on granite and unconformities—but this portrait does not square with Hutton's own labors. For Hutton, the most important force was the heat of the Earth that caused sedimentary rocks to fuse into granites and flints. His theory of the Earth was first presented in outline before the Royal Society of Edinburgh on March 7 and April 4, 1785. At this time, Hutton had observed granite at only one inconclusive outcrop. Indeed, Hutton himself seemed to indicate that his theory has been derived by reason from key premises that play no role in the traditional inductivist portrait of Hutton's discovery of deep geological time. His observations are then presented as subsequent confirmations of these ideas.*

*The idea of a world machine, presented in Hutton's* Theory of the Earth *(1795), marked a turning point in geology, though initially it made only a marginal impact on*

Source: James Hutton. 1795. *Theory of the Earth, With Proofs and Illustrations in 4 Parts.* Edinburgh: Cadell, volume I, pp. 280–281; volume II, pp. 540–564.

*geologists. Georges Cuvier gave Hutton a passing glance. A detailed account of Hutton's theory only reached a wide audience when John Playfair (1748–1819), professor of natural philosophy at Edinburgh University, edited it and summarized it as* Illustrations of the Huttonian Theory of the Earth *(1802).*

In examining things which actually exist, and which have proceeded in a certain order, it is natural to look for that which had been first; man desires to know what had been the beginning of those things which now appear. But when, in forming a theory of the Earth,[a] a geologist shall indulge his fancy in framing, without evidence, that which had preceded the present order of things, he then either misleads himself, or writes a fable for the amusement of his reader. A theory of the Earth, which has for [its] object truth can have no retrospect to that which had preceded the present order of this world; for this order alone is what we have to reason upon, and to reason without data is nothing but delusion. A theory, therefore, which is limited to the actual constitution of this Earth cannot be allowed to proceed one step beyond the present order of things . . .

The system of this Earth appears to comprehend many different operations; and it exhibits various powers co-operating for the production of those effects which we perceive. Of this we are informed by studying natural appearances; and in this manner we are led to understand the nature of things, in knowing causes.

That our land, which is now above the level of the sea, had been formerly under water, is a fact for which there is everywhere the testimony of a multitude of observations. This indeed is a fact which is admitted upon all hands; it is a fact upon which the speculations of philosophers have been already much employed; but it is a fact still more important, in my opinion, than it has been ever yet considered. It is not, however, as a solitary fact that any rational system may be founded upon this truth that the Earth had been formerly at the bottom of the sea; we must also see the nature and constitution of this Earth as necessarily subsisting in continual change; and we must see the means employed by nature for constructing a continent of solid land in the fluid bosom of the deep. It is then that we may judge of that design, by finding ends and means contrived in wisdom, that is to say, properly adapted to each other . . .

If it should be admitted that this Earth had been formed by the collection of materials deposited within the sea, there will then appear to be certain things which ought to be explained by a theory, before that theory can be received as belonging to this Earth. These are as follows:

First, we ought to show how it came about that this whole Earth, or by far the greatest part in all the quarters of the globe had been formed of transported materials collected together in the sea. It must be here remembered that the highest of our mountainous countries are equally formed of those traveled materials as are the lowest of our plains; we are not therefore to have recourse to any thing that we see at present for the origin of those materials which actually compose the Earth; and we must show from where had come those traveled materials, manufactured by water, which were employed in composing the highest places of our land.

Second, we must explain how those loose and incoherent materials had been consolidated, as we find they are at present. We are not here to allow ourselves the liberty, which naturalists have assumed without the least

---

[a]Hutton's theory was first published as a paper in 1788 and later extended into a two-volume work, *Theory of the Earth,* which was published in 1795. [B.]

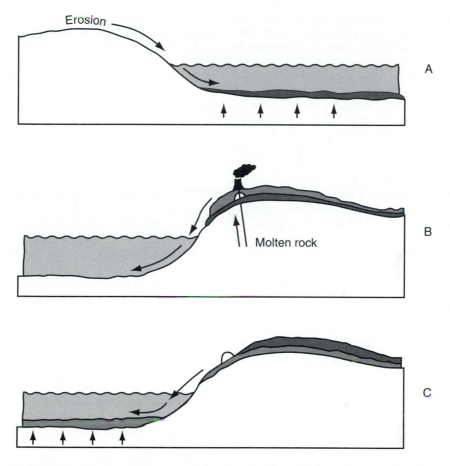

**PLATE 25** Hutton's theory of the Earth. The Earth's topography decays (A) as rivers and waves break down rocks, leading to the formation of soils on continents and the accumulation of eroded material in the oceans. The broken down pieces of continents are deposited as strata in ocean basins (B). Over time, the weight of these strata produces enough heat and pressure to mobilize the lower layers (C). Extensive uplift, produced by the heat of melting sediments and intruding magmas, generates new continents at the sites of old oceans, while new oceans appear at the eroded sites of old oceans.

foundation, of explaining everything of this sort by *infiltration*, a term in this case expressing nothing but our ignorance.

Third, the strata are not always equally consolidated. We often find contiguous strata in very different states with respect to solidity; and sometimes the most solid masses are found involved in the most porous substance. Some explanation surely would be expected for this appearance, which is of a nature so conclusive as ought to attract the attention of a theorist.

Fourth, it is not sufficient to show how the Earth in general had been consolidated;

we must also explain how it comes to pass that the consolidated bodies are always broken and intersected by veins and fissures. In this case, the reason commonly given, that the Earth exposed to the atmosphere had shrunk like moist clay, or contracted by the operation of drying, can only show that such naturalists have thought but little upon the subject. The effect in no shape or degree corresponds to that cause; and veins and fissures, in the solid bodies, are no less frequent under the level of the sea, than on the summits of our mountains.

Fifth, having found a cause for the fracture and separation of the solid masses, we must also tell from where the matter with which those chasms are filled, matter which is foreign both to the earth and to the sea, had been introduced into the veins that intersect the strata. If we fail in this particular, what credit could be given to such hypotheses as are contrived for the explanation of more ambiguous appearances, even when those suppositions should appear most probable?

Sixth, supposing that, hitherto, everything had been explained in the most satisfactory manner, the most important appearances of our Earth still remain to be considered. We find those strata that were originally formed continuous in their substance, and horizontal in their position, now broken, bended, and inclined, in every manner and degree; we must give some reason in our theory for such a general state and disposition of things; and we must tell by what power this event, whether accidental or intended, had been brought about.

Lastly, whatever powers had been employed in preparing land, while situated under water, or at the bottom of the sea, the most powerful operation yet remains to be explained: This is the means by which the lowest surface of the solid globe was made to be the highest upon the Earth. Unless we can show a power of sufficient force, and placed in a proper situation for that purpose, our theory would go for nothing, among people who investigate the nature of things, and who, founding on experience, reason by induction from effect to cause.

Nothing can be admitted as a theory of the Earth which does not, in a satisfactory manner, give the efficient causes for all these effects already enumerated. For, as things are universally to be acknowledged in the Earth, it is essential in a theory to explain those natural appearances.

But this is not all. We live in a world where order everywhere prevails, and where final causes are as well known, at least, as those which are efficient. The muscles, for example, by which I move my fingers when I write, are no more the efficient cause of that motion than this motion is the final cause for which the muscles had been made. Thus, the circulation of the blood is the efficient cause of life; but life is the final cause, not only for the circulation of the blood, but for the revolution of the globe. Without a central luminary, and a revolution of the planetary body, there could not have been a living creature upon the face of this Earth; and, while we see a living system on this Earth, we must acknowledge, that in the solar system, we see a final cause.

Now, in a theory which considers this Earth as placed in a system of things where ends are at least attained, if not contrived in wisdom, final causes must appear to be an object of consideration, as well as those which are efficient. A living world is evidently an object in the design of things, by whatever being those things had been designed, and however, either wisdom or folly may appear in that design. Therefore, the explanation which must be given of the different phenomena of the Earth, must be consistent with the actual constitution of this Earth as a living world, that is, a world maintaining a system of living animals and plants.

Not only are no powers to be employed that are not natural to the globe, no action to be admitted of except those of which we know the principle, and no extraordinary events to be alleged in order to explain a common appearance. The powers of nature are not to be employed in order to destroy the very object of those powers; we are not to make nature act in violation to that order which we actually observe, and in subversion of that end which is to be perceived in the system of created things. In whatever manner, therefore, we are to employ the great agents, fire and water, for producing those things which appear, it ought to be in such a way as is consistent with the propagation of plants and the life of animals upon the surface of the Earth. Chaos and confusion are not to be introduced into the order of nature because certain things appear to our partial views as being in some disorder. Nor are we to proceed in feigning causes, when those seem insufficient which occur in our experience . . .

In examining the structure of our Earth, we find it no less evidently formed of loose and incoherent materials than that those materials had been collected from different parts, and gathered together at the bottom of the sea. Consequently, if this continent of land, first collected in the sea, and then raised above its surface, is to remain a habitable Earth, and to resist the moving waters of the globe, certain degrees of solidity or consolidation must be given to that collection of loose materials; and certain degrees of hardness must be given to bodies which were soft or incoherent, and consequently so extremely perishable in the situation where they now are placed.

But at the same time that this Earth must have solidity and hardness to resist the sudden changes which its moving fluids would occasion, it must be made subject to decay and waste upon the surface exposed to the atmosphere; for, such an Earth as were made incapable of change, or not subject to decay, could not afford that fertile soil which is required in the system of this world, a soil on which depends the growth of plants and life of animals; the end of its intention.

Now, we find this Earth endowed precisely with that degree of hardness and consolidation as qualifies it at the same time to be a fruitful Earth, and to maintain its sta-

tion with all the permanency compatible with the nature of things, which are not formed to remain unchangeable. . . .

We are thus led to inquire into the efficient causes of this constitution of things, by which solidity and stability had been bestowed upon a mass of loose materials, and by which this solid earth, formed first at the bottom of the sea, had been placed in the atmosphere, where plants and animals find the necessary conditions of their life.

Now, we have shown that subterraneous fire and heat had been employed in the consolidation of our Earth, and in the erection of that consolidated body into the place of land. The prejudices of mankind, who cannot see the steps by which we come at this conclusion, are against the doctrine; but prejudice must give way to evidence. No other theory will in any degree explain appearances, while almost every appearance is easily explained by this theory.

We do not dispute the chemical action and efficacy of water, or any other substance which is found among the materials collected at the bottom of the sea; we only mean to affirm that every action of this kind is incapable of producing perfect solidity in the body of the Earth in that situation of things, whatever time should be allowed for that operation, and that whatever may have been the operations of water, aided by fire, and evaporated by heat, the various appearances of mineralization (everywhere presented to us in the solid earth, and the most perfect objects of examination), are plainly inexplicable upon the principle of aqueous solution. On the other hand, the operation of heat, melting incoherent bodies, and introducing softness into rigid substances which are to be united, is not only a cause which is proper to explain the effects in question, but also appears, from a multitude of different circumstances, to have been actually exerted among the consolidated bodies of our Earth, and in the mineral veins with which the solid bodies of the Earth abound.

The doctrine, therefore, of our theory is briefly this: That whatever may have been the operation of dissolving water, and the chemical action of it upon the materials accumulated at the bottom of the sea, the general solidity of that mass of Earth, and the placing of it in the atmosphere above the surface of the sea, has been the immediate operation of fire or heat melting and expanding bodies. Here is a proposition which may be tried, in applying it to all the phenomena of the mineral region; so far as I have seen, it is perfectly verified in that application.

We have another proposition in our theory, one which is still more interesting to consider. It is this, that as, in the mineral regions, the loose or incoherent materials of our land had been consolidated by the action of heat, so upon the surface of this Earth exposed to the fluid elements of air and water there is a necessary principle of dissolution and decay, for that consolidated Earth which from the mineral region is exposed to the day. The solid body being thus gradually impaired, there are moving powers continually employed, by which the summits of our land are constantly degraded, and the materials of this decaying surface traveled towards the coast. There are other powers which act upon the shore, by which the coast is necessarily impaired, and our land subjected to the perpetual encroachment of the ocean. . . .

We have now seen that in every quarter of the globe, and in every climate of the Earth, there is formed, by means of the decay of solid rocks, and by the transportation of those movable materials, that beautiful system of mountains and valleys, of hills and plains, covered with growing plants, and inhabited by animals. We have seen that with this system of animal and vegetable economy, which depends on soil and climate, there is also a system of moving water, poured upon the surface of the Earth, in the most beneficial manner possible for the use of vegetation, and the preservation of our soil; and that this water is gathered together again by running to the lowest place, in order to avoid accumulation of water upon the surface, which would be noxious.

It is in this manner that we first have streams or torrents, which only run in times of rain. But the rain water absorbed onto the Earth is made to issue out in springs, which run perpetually, and which, gathering together as they run, form rivulets, watering valleys, and delighting the various inhabitants of this Earth. The rivulets again are united in their turn, and form those rivers which overflow our plains, and which alternately bring permanent fertility and casual devastation to our land. Those rivers, augmenting in their volume as they unite, pour at last their mighty waters into the ocean; and thus is completed that circulation of wholesome fluids, which the Earth requires in order to be a habitable world.

Our theory further shows, that in the ocean there is a system of animals which have contributed so materially to the formation of our land. These animals are necessarily maintained by the vegetable provision, which is returned in the rivers to the sea, and which the land alone or principally produces. Thus, we may perceive the mutual dependence upon each other of those two habitable worlds—the fluid ocean and the fertile Earth.

The land is formed in the sea, and in great part by inhabitants of that fluid world. But those animals, which form with their *exuviae* such a portion of the land, are maintained, like those upon the surface of the Earth, by the produce of that land to which they formerly had contributed. Thus the vegetable matter, which is produced upon the surface of the Earth in such abundance for the use of animals, and which, in such various shapes, is carried by the rivers into the sea, there sustains that living system which is daily employed to make materials for a future land. . . .

Our solid Earth is everywhere wasted, where exposed to the day. The summits of the mountains are necessarily degraded. The solid weighty materials of those mountains are everywhere urged through the valleys, by the force of running water. The soil, which is produced in the destruction of the solid earth, is gradually traveled by the moving water, but is constantly supplying vegetation with its necessary aid. This traveled soil is at last deposited upon the coast, where it forms most fertile countries. But the billows of the ocean agitate the loose materials upon the shore, and wear away the coast, with the endless repetitions of this act of power, or this imparted force. Thus the continent of our Earth, sapped in its foundation, is carried away into the deep, and sunk again at the bottom of the sea, from where it had originated.

We are, thus, led to see a circulation in the matter of this globe, and a system of beautiful economy in the works of nature. This Earth, like the body of an animal, is wasted at the same time that it is repaired. It has a state of growth and augmentation; it has another state, which is that of diminution and decay. This world is, thus, destroyed in one part, but it is renewed in another; and the operations by which this world is thus constantly renewed, are as evident to the scientific eye, as are those in which it is necessarily destroyed. The marks of the internal fire, by which the rocks beneath the sea are hardened, and by which the land is produced above the surface of the sea, have nothing in them which is doubtful or ambiguous. The destroying operations again, though placed within the reach of our examination, and evident almost to every observer, are no more acknowledged by mankind, than is that system of renovation which philosophy alone discovers.

It is only in science that any question concerning the origin and end of things is formed; and it is in science only that the resolution of those questions is to be attained. The natural operations of this globe, by which the size and shape of our land are changed, are so slow as to be altogether imperceptible to men who are employed in pursuing the various occupations of life and literature. We must not ask the industrious inhabitant, for the end or origin of this Earth; he sees the present, and he looks no farther into the works of time than his experience can supply his reason. We must not ask the statesman, who looks into the history of time past, for the rise and fall of empires; he proceeds upon the idea of a stationary Earth, and most justly has respect to nothing but the influence of moral causes. It is in the philosophy of nature that the natural history of this Earth is to be studied; and we must not allow ourselves ever to reason without proper data, or to fabricate a system of apparent wisdom in the folly of a hypothetical delusion.

When, to a scientific view of the subject, we join the proof which has been given, that in all the quarters of the globe, in every place upon the surface of the Earth, there are the most undoubted marks of the continued progress of those operations which wear away and waste the land, both in its height and width, its elevation and extension, and that for a space of duration in which our measures of time are lost, we must sit down contented with this limitation of our retrospect, as well as prospect, and acknowledge, that it is in vain to seek for any computation of the time, during which the materials of this Earth had been prepared in a preceding world, and collected at the bottom of a former sea.

## FURTHER READING

Gould, Stephen Jay. 1987. *Time's Arrow, Time's Cycle: Myth and Metaphor in the Discovery of Geological Time.* Cambridge: Harvard University Press.

Laudan, Rachel. 1987. *From Mineralogy to Geology: The Foundations of a Science, 1650–1830.* Chicago: The University of Chicago Press.

Playfair, John and Ferguson, Adam. 1997. *James Hutton and Joseph Black: Biographies.* Edinburgh: RSE Scotland Foundation.

# Directed Variation

## Jean Baptiste Lamarck (1744–1829)

*At the advanced age of fifty, Jean Baptiste Lamarck was appointed professor of "zoology, insects, worms and microscopic animals" at the Museum of Natural History in Paris. His great work* Histoire naturelle des animaux sans vertèbres *(1815–1822: Natural History of Invertebrate Animals) reformed the study of invertebrates. His other great work,* Philosophie zoologique *(1809: Zoological Philosophy), from which this reading is taken, propounded a theory of evolution half a century before Darwin's* On the Origin of Species *(1859). Animals, birds, and fishes, Lamarck insisted, exercise willpower to adapt themselves to their living conditions. Some organs are thereby strengthened by use and others weakened by underuse. In this way, acquired characteristics are passed along to subsequent generations.*

*Lamarck has come in for much unfair treatment—first, for opposing the authority of the leading scientists of his day who embraced the idea that species are fixed and immutable; and second, for elaborating an evolutionary theory of directed variation that did not stand up to Darwin's theory of evolution in terms of random variation and natural selection.*

We are not here concerned with an argument, but with the examination of a positive fact; a fact which is of more general application than is supposed, and which has not received the attention that it deserves, no doubt because it is usually very difficult to recognize. This fact consists in the influence that is exerted by the environment on the various living bodies exposed to it.

It is indeed long since the influence of the various states of our organization on our character, inclinations, activities and even ideas has been recognized, but I do not think that anyone has yet drawn attention to the influence of our activities and habits even on our organization. Now since these activities and habits depend entirely on the environment in which we are habitually placed, I shall endeavor to show how great is the influence exerted by that environment on the general shape, state of the parts and even organization of living bodies . . .

The influence of the environment as a matter of fact is in all times and places operative on living bodies, but what makes this influence difficult to perceive is that its effects only become perceptible or recognizable (especially in animals) after a long period of time.

Before setting forth to examine the proofs of this fact, which deserves our attention and

*Source:* Lamarck, J. B. 1963. *Zoological Philosophy.* Trans. Hugh Elliot. Chicago: The University of Chicago Press, pp. 107–120; 122; 126–127.

is so important for zoological philosophy, let us sum up the thread of the discussions that we have already begun.

In the preceding chapter we saw that it is now an unquestionable fact that on passing along the animal scale in the opposite direction from that of nature, we discover the existence, in the groups composing this scale, of a continuous, but irregular degradation in the organization of animals, an increasing simplification in their organization, and, lastly, a corresponding diminution in the number of their faculties.

This well ascertained fact may throw the strongest light over the actual order followed by nature in the production of all the animals that she has brought into existence, but it does not show us why the increasing complexity of the organization of animals from the most imperfect to the most perfect exhibits only an *irregular gradation,* in the course of which there occur numerous anomalies or deviations with a variety in which no order is apparent.

Now on seeking the reason of this strange irregularity in the increasing complexity of animal organization, if we consider the influence that is exerted by the infinitely varied environments of all parts of the world on the general shape, structure and even organization of these animals, all will then be clearly explained.

It will in fact become clear that the state in which we find any animal is, on the one hand, the result of the increasing complexity of organization tending to form a regular gradation; and, on the other hand, of the influence of a multitude of very various conditions ever tending to destroy the regularity in the gradation of the increasing complexity of organization.

I must now explain what I mean by this statement; *the environment affects the shape and organization of animals,* that is to say, that when the environment becomes very different, it produces in course of time corresponding modifications in the shape and organization of animals.

It is true if this statement were to be taken literally, I should be convicted of an error;

for, whatever the environment may do, it does not work any direct modification whatever in the shape and organization of animals.

But great alterations in the environment of animals lead to great alterations in their needs, and these alterations in their needs necessarily lead to others in their activities. Now, if the new needs become permanent, the animals then adopt new habits which last as long as the needs that evoked them. This is easy to demonstrate, and indeed requires no amplification.

It is then obvious that a great and permanent alteration in the environment of any race of animals induces new habits in these animals.

Now, if a new environment, which has become permanent for some race of animals, induces new habits in these animals, that is to say, leads them to new activities which become habitual, the result will be the use of some one part in preference to some other part, and in some cases the total disuse of some part no longer necessary.

Nothing of all this can be considered as hypothesis or private opinion; on the contrary, they are truths which, in order to be made clear, only require attention and the observation of facts.

We shall shortly see by the citation of known facts in evidence, in the first place, that new needs which establish a necessity for some part really bring about the existence of that part, as a result of efforts; and that subsequently its continued use gradually strengthens, develops and finally greatly enlarges it; in the second place, we shall see that in some cases, when the new environment and the new needs have altogether destroyed the utility of some part, the total disuse of that part has resulted in its gradually ceasing to share in the development of the other parts of the animal; it shrinks and wastes little by little, and ultimately, when there has been total disuse for a long period, the part in question ends by disappearing. All this is positive; I propose to furnish the most convincing proofs of it . . .

Among individuals of the same species, some of which are continually well fed and in an environment favorable to their development, while others are in an opposite environment, there arises a difference in the state of the individuals which gradually becomes very remarkable. How many examples I might cite both in animals and plants which bear out the truth of this principle! Now if the environment remains constant, so that the condition of the ill-fed, suffering or sickly individuals becomes permanent, their internal organization is ultimately modified, and these acquired modifications[a] are preserved by reproduction among the individuals in question, and finally give rise to a race quite distinct from that in which the individuals have been continuously in an environment favorable to their development.

A very dry spring causes the grasses of a meadow to grow very little, and remain lean and puny; so that they flower and fruit after accomplishing very little growth.

A spring intermingled with warm and rainy days causes a strong growth in this same grass, and the crop is then excellent.

But if anything causes a continuance of the unfavorable environment, a corresponding variation takes place in the plants—first in their general appearance and condition, and then in some of their special characters.

Suppose, for instance, that a seed of one of the meadow grasses in question is transported to an elevated place on a dry, barren and stony plot much exposed to the winds, and is there left to germinate. If the plant can live in such a place, it will always be badly nourished, and if the individuals reproduced from it continue to exist in this bad environment, there will result a race funda-

mentally different from that which lives in the meadows and from which it originated. The individuals of this new race will have small and meager parts; some of their organs will have developed more than others, and will then be of unusual proportions.

Those who have observed much and studied large collections, have acquired the conviction that according as changes occur in environment, situation, climate, food, habits of life, etc., corresponding changes in the animals likewise occur in size, shape, proportions of the parts, color, consistency, swiftness and skill.

What nature does in the course of long periods we do every day when we suddenly change the environment in which some species of living plant is situated.

Every botanist knows that plants which are transported from their native places to gardens for purposes of cultivation gradually undergo changes which ultimately make them unrecognizable. Many plants, by nature hairy, become glabrous or nearly so; a number of those which used to lie and creep on the ground become erect; others lose their thorns or excrescences; others again whose stem was perennial and woody in their native hot climates, become herbaceous in our own climates and some of them become annuals; lastly, the size of their parts itself undergoes very considerable changes. These effects of alterations of environment are so widely recognized that botanists do not like to describe garden plants unless they have been recently brought into cultivation.

Is it not the case that cultivated wheat (*Triticum sativum*) is a plant which man has brought to the state in which we now see it? I should like to know in what country such a plant lives in nature, otherwise than as the result of cultivation.

Where in nature do we find our cabbages, lettuces, etc., in the same state as in our kitchen gardens? And is it not the same with regard to many animals which have been altered or greatly modified by domestication?

How many different races of our domestic fowls and pigeons have we obtained by

[a]The hypothesis that acquired characteristics or modifications are heritable was held almost universally for well over two thousand years. Lamarck's contribution was to bring this hypothesis to bear on the problem of the diversity of species. [B.]

rearing them in various environments and different countries; birds which we should now vainly seek in nature?

Those which have changed the least, doubtless because their domestication is of shorter standing, and because they do not live in a foreign climate, none the less display great differences in some of their parts, as a result of the habits which we have made them contract. Thus, our domestic ducks and geese are of the same type as wild ducks and geese; but ours have lost the power of rising into high regions of the air and flying across large tracts of country; moreover, a real change has come about in the state of their parts, as compared with those of the animals of the race from which they come.

Who does not know that if we rear some bird of our own climate in a cage and it lives there for five or six years, and if we then return it to nature by setting it at liberty, it is no longer able to fly like its fellows, which have always been free? The slight change of environment for this individual has indeed only diminished its power of flight and doubtless has worked no change in its structure; but if a long succession of generations of individuals of the same race had been kept in captivity for a considerable period, there is no doubt that even the structure of these individuals would gradually have undergone notable changes. Still more, if instead of a mere continuous captivity, this environmental factor had been further accompanied by a change to a very different climate; and if these individuals had by degrees been habituated to other kinds of food and other activities for seizing it, these factors when combined together and become permanent would have unquestionably given rise imperceptibly to a new race with quite special characters.

Where in natural conditions do we find that multitude of races of dogs which now actually exist, owing to the domestication to which we have reduced them ? Where do we find those bulldogs, greyhounds, water spaniels, spaniels, lapdogs, etc.; races which show wider differences than those which we call specific when they occur among animals of one genus living in natural freedom?

No doubt a single, original race, closely resembling the wolf, if indeed it was not actually the wolf, was at some period reduced by man to domestication. That race, of which all the individuals were then alike, was gradually scattered with man into different countries and climates; and after they had been subjected for some time to the influences of their environment and of the various habits which had been forced upon them in each country, they underwent remarkable alterations and formed various special races. Now man travels about to very great distances, either for trade or any other purpose; and thus, brings into thickly populated places, such as a great capital, various races of dogs formed in very distant countries. The crossing of these races by reproduction then gave rise in turn to all those that we now know . . .

Now, the true principle to be noted in all this is as follows:

1. Every fairly considerable and permanent alteration in the environment of any race of animals works a real alteration in the needs of that race.
2. Every change in the needs of animals necessitates new activities on their part for the satisfaction of those needs, and hence new habits.
3. Every new need, necessitating new activities for its satisfaction, requires the animal, either to make more frequent use of some of its parts which it previously used less, and thus greatly to develop and enlarge them; or else to make use of entirely new parts, to which the needs have imperceptibly given birth by efforts of its inner feeling; this I shall shortly prove by means of known facts.

Thus in order to obtain a knowledge of the true causes of that great diversity of shapes and habits found in the various known animals, we must reflect that the infinitely diversified but slowly changing environment in which the animals of each race have successively been placed has involved each of them in new needs and corresponding alterations in their habits. This is a truth which, once recognized, cannot be disputed. Now we shall easily discern how the new needs may have been satisfied, and the new habits acquired, if we pay attention to the two following laws of nature, which are always verified by observation.

### First Law

*In every animal which has not passed the limit of its development, a more frequent and continuous use of any organ gradually strengthens, develops and enlarges that organ, and gives it a power proportional to the length of time it has been so used; while the permanent disuse of any organ imperceptibly weakens and deteriorates it, and progressively diminishes its functional capacity, until it finally disappears.*

### Second Law

*All the acquisitions or losses wrought by nature on individuals, through the influence of the environment in which their race has long been placed, and hence, through the influence of the predominant use or permanent disuse of any organ; all these are preserved by reproduction to the new individuals which arise, provided that the acquired modifications are common to both sexes, or at least to the individuals which produce the young.*

Here we have two permanent truths, which can only be doubted by those who have never observed or followed the operations of nature, or by those who have allowed themselves to be drawn into the error which I shall now proceed to combat.

Naturalists have remarked that the structure of animals is always in perfect adaptation to their functions, and have inferred that the shape and condition of their parts have determined the use of them. Now this is a mistake; for it may be easily proved by observation that it is on the contrary the needs and uses of the parts which have caused the development of these same parts, which have even given birth to them when they did not exist, and which consequently have given rise to the condition that we find in each animal.

If this were not so, nature would have had to create as many different kinds of structure in animals, as there are different kinds of environment in which they have to live; and neither structure nor environment would ever have varied.

This is indeed far from the true order of things. If things were really so, we should not have race horses, shaped like those in England; we should not have big draught horses so heavy and so different from the former, for none such are produced in nature; in the same way we should not have basset hounds with crooked legs, nor greyhounds so fleet of foot, nor water spaniels, etc.; we should not have fowls without tails, fantail pigeons, etc.; finally, we should be able to cultivate wild plants as long as we liked in the rich and fertile soil of our gardens, without the fear of seeing them change under long cultivation.

A feeling of the truth in this respect has long existed; since the following maxim has passed into a proverb and is known by all, *Habits form a second nature.*

Assuredly, if the habits and nature of each animal could never vary, the proverb would have been false and would not have come into existence, nor been preserved in the event of any one suggesting it.

If we seriously reflect upon all that I have just set forth, it will be seen that I was entirely justified when in my work entitled *Recherches sur les corps vivants* (p. 50),[b] I established the following proposition:

> It is not the organs, that is to say, the nature and shape of the parts of an animal's body that have given rise to its special habits and faculties;

[b]In the *Recherches,* which was published in 1802, Lamarck sketched his doctrine of evolution, which was followed by the fully developed theory offered here. [B.]

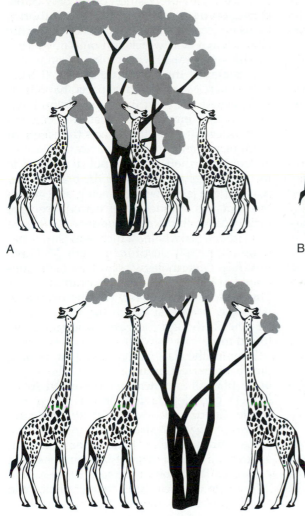

A

B

C

**PLATE 26**   Illustration of Lamarck's theory of the inheritance of acquired characteristics. In response to a change in their environment, ancient giraffes (A) stretched their short necks to reach foliage in the trees. As trees grew taller and leaves moved out of easy access (B), later generations of giraffes stretched their already-lengthened necks. Over the course of many generations, this process of stretching and passing along the acquired characteristic produced the modern long-necked giraffe (C).

but it is, on the contrary, its habits, mode of life and environment that have in course of time controlled the shape of its body, the number and state of its organs and, lastly, the faculties which it possesses.

If this proposition is carefully weighed and compared with all the observations that nature and circumstances are incessantly throwing in our way, we shall see that its importance and accuracy are substantiated in the highest degree.

Time and a favorable environment are as I have already said nature's two chief methods of bringing all her productions into existence: for her, time has no limits and can be drawn upon to any extent.

As to the various factors which she has required and still constantly uses for introducing variations in everything that she produces, they may be described as practically inexhaustible.

The principal factors consist in the influence of climate, of the varying temperatures of the atmosphere and the whole environment, of the variety of localities and their situation, of habits, the commonest movements, the most frequent activities, and, lastly, of the means of self-preservation, the mode of life and the methods of defense and multiplication.

Now as a result of these various influences, the faculties become extended and strengthened by use, and diversified by new habits that are long kept up. The conformation, consistency and, in short, the character and state of the parts, as well as of the organs, are imperceptibly affected by these influences and are preserved and propagated by reproduction.

These truths, which are merely effects of the two natural laws stated above, receive in every instance striking confirmation from facts; for the facts afford a clear indication of nature's procedure in the diversity of her productions.

But instead of being contented with generalities which might be considered hypothetical, let us investigate the facts directly, and consider the effects in animals of the use or disuse of their organs on these same organs, in accordance with the habits that each race has been forced to contract.

Now I am going to prove that the permanent disuse of any organ first decreases its functional capacity, and then gradually reduces the organ and causes it to disappear or even become extinct, if this disuse lasts for a very long period throughout successive generations of animals of the same race.

I shall then show that the habit of using any organ, on the contrary, in any animal which has not reached the limit of the decline of its functions, not only perfects and increases the functions of that organ, but causes it in addition to take on a size and development which imperceptibly alter it; so that in course of time it becomes very different from the same organ in some other animal which uses it far less.

*The permanent disuse of an organ, arising from a change of habits, causes a gradual shrinkage and ultimately the disappearance and even extinction of that organ.*

Since such a proposition could only be accepted on proof, and not on mere authority, let us endeavor to make it clear by citing the chief known facts which substantiate it.

The vertebrates, whose plan of organization is almost the same throughout, though with much variety in their parts, have their jaws armed with teeth; some of them, however, whose environment has induced the habit of swallowing the objects they feed on without any preliminary mastication, are so affected that their teeth do not develop. The teeth then remain hidden in the bony framework of the jaws, without being able to appear outside; or indeed they actually become extinct down to their last rudiments.

In the right-whale, which was supposed to be completely destitute of teeth, M. Geoffroy[c] has nevertheless discovered teeth concealed in the jaws of the fetus of this animal. The professor, moreover, has discovered in birds the groove in which the teeth should be placed, though they are no longer to be found there.

Even in the class of mammals comprising the most perfect animals, where the vertebrate plan of organization is carried to its highest completion, not only is the right-whale devoid of teeth, but the anteater *(Myrmecophaga)* is also found to be in the same condition, since it has acquired a habit of carrying out no mastication, and has long preserved this habit in its race.

Eyes in the head are characteristic of a great number of different animals, and essentially constitute a part of the plan of organization of the vertebrates.

Yet the mole, whose habits require a very small use of sight, has only minute and hardly visible eyes because it uses that organ so little . . .

[c]Etienne Geoffroy St. Hilaire (1772–1844) was a professor of zoology at the Museum of Natural History in Paris, and a close friend of Lamarck's. Geoffroy and Lamarck opposed their colleague Georges Cuvier, who believed in the fixity of species. Geoffroy made a vast contribution to descriptive zoology and classification during his lifetime. [B.]

Light does not penetrate everywhere; consequently animals which habitually live in places where it does not penetrate have no opportunity of exercising their organ of sight, if nature has endowed them with one. Now animals belonging to a plan of organization of which eyes were a necessary part, must have originally had them. Since, however, there are found among them some which have lost the use of this organ and which show nothing more than hidden and covered up vestiges of them, it becomes clear that the shrinkage and even disappearance of the organ in question are the results of a permanent disuse of that organ.

This is proven by the fact that the organ of hearing is never in this condition, but is always found in animals whose organization is of the kind that includes it, and for the following reason.

The substance of sound, that which, when set in motion by the shock or the vibration of bodies transmits to the organ of hearing the impression received, penetrates everywhere and passes through any medium, including even the densest bodies. It follows that every animal, belonging to a plan of organization in which hearing is an essential part, always has some opportunity for the exercise of this organ wherever it may live. Hence among the vertebrates we do not find any that are destitute of the organ of hearing; and after them, when this same organ has come to an end, it does not subsequently recur in any animal of the posterior classes.

It is not so with the organ of sight; for this organ is found to disappear, reappear and disappear again according to the use that the animal makes of it.

In the acephalic mollusks, the great development of the mantle would make their eyes and even their head altogether useless. The permanent disuse of these organs has thus brought about their disappearance and extinction, although mollusks belong to a plan of organization which should comprise them.

Lastly, it was part of the plan of organization of the reptiles, as of other vertebrates, to have four legs in dependence on their skeleton. Snakes ought consequently to have four legs, especially since they are by no means the last order of the reptiles and are farther from the fishes than are the batrachians (frogs, salamanders, etc.).

Snakes, however, have adopted the habit of crawling on the ground and hiding in the grass; so that their body, as a result of continually repeated efforts at elongation for the purpose of passing through narrow spaces, has acquired a considerable length, quite out of proportion to its size. Now, legs would have been quite useless to these animals and consequently unused. Long legs would have interfered with their need of crawling, and very short legs would have been incapable of moving their body, since they could only have had four. The disuse of these parts thus, became permanent in the various races of these animals, and resulted in the complete disappearance of these same parts; although, legs really belong to the plan of organization of the animals of this class . . .

But it is not enough to give an explanation of the cause which has brought about the present condition of the organs of the various animals; a condition that is always found to be the same in animals of the same species; we have in addition to cite instances of changes wrought in the organs of a single individual during its life, as the exclusive result of a great mutation in the habits of the individuals of its species. The following very remarkable fact will complete the proof of the influence of habits on the condition of the organs, and of the way in which permanent changes in the habits of an individual lead to others in the condition of the organs, which come into action during the exercise of these habits . . .

It is known that great drinkers, or those who are addicted to drunkenness, take very little solid food, and eat hardly anything; since the drink which they consume so copiously and frequently is sufficient to feed them.

Now since fluid foods, especially spirits, do not long remain either in the stomach or intestine, the stomach and the rest of the intestinal canal lose among drinkers the habit of being distended, just as among sedentary persons, who are continually engaged on mental work and are accustomed to take very little food; for in their case also the stomach slowly shrinks and the intestine shortens.

This has nothing to do with any shrinkage or shortening due to a binding of the parts which would permit of the ordinary extension, if instead of remaining empty these viscera were again filled; we have to do with a real shrinkage and shortening of considerable extent, and such that these organs would burst rather than yield at once to any demand for the ordinary extension.

Compare two men of equal ages, one of whom has contracted the habit of eating very little, since his habitual studies and mental work have made digestion difficult, the other habitually takes much exercise, is often out-of-doors, and eats well; the stomach of the first will have very little capacity left and will be filled up by a very small quantity of food, while that of the second will have preserved and even increased its capacity.

Here, then, is an organ which undergoes profound modification in size and capacity, purely on account of a change of habits during the life of the individual.

*The frequent use of any organ, when confirmed by habit, increases the functions of that organ, leads to its development and endows it with a size and power that it does not possess in animals which exercise it less.*

We have seen that the disuse of any organ modifies, reduces and finally extinguishes it. I shall now prove that the constant use of any organ, accompanied by efforts to get the most out of it, strengthens and enlarges that organ, or creates new ones to carry on functions that have become necessary.

The bird which is drawn to the water by its need of finding there the prey on which it lives separates the digits of its feet in trying to strike the water and move about on the surface. The skin which unites these digits at their base acquires the habit of being stretched by these continually repeated separations of the digits; thus, in [the] course of time there are formed large webs which unite the digits of ducks, geese, etc., as we actually find them. In the same way efforts to swim, that is to push against the water so as to move about in it, have stretched the membranes between the digits of frogs, sea tortoises, the otter, beaver, etc.

On the other hand, a bird which is accustomed to perch on trees, and which springs from individuals all of whom had acquired this habit, necessarily has longer digits on its feet and differently shaped from those of the aquatic animals that I have just named. Its claws in time become lengthened, sharpened and curved into hooks, to clasp the branches on which the animal so often rests.

We find in the same way that the bird of the waterside which does not like swimming, and yet is in need of going to the water's edge to secure its prey, is continually liable to sink in the mud. Now this bird tries to act in such a way that its body should not be immersed in the liquid, and hence makes its best efforts to stretch and lengthen its legs. The long-established habit acquired by this bird and all its race of continually stretching and lengthening its legs results in the individuals of this race becoming raised as though on stilts, and gradually obtaining long, bare legs, denuded of feathers up to the thighs and often higher still . . .

It is interesting to observe the result of habit in the peculiar shape and size of the giraffe (*Camelo-pardalis*): this animal, the largest of the mammals, is known to live in the interior of Africa in places where the soil is nearly always arid and barren, so that it is obliged to browse on the leaves of trees and to make constant efforts to reach them. From this habit long maintained in all its race, it has resulted that the animal's front legs have become longer than its hind legs, and that its neck is lengthened to such a degree that the giraffe, without standing up on its hind legs, attains a height of six meters (nearly 20 feet) . . .

It is a fact that all animals have special habits corresponding to their genus and species, and always possess an organization that is completely in harmony with those habits.

It seems from the study of this fact that we may adopt one or other of the two following conclusions, and that neither of them can be verified.

*Conclusion adopted hitherto:* Nature (or her Author) in creating animals foresaw all the possible kinds of environment in which they would have to live, and endowed each species with a fixed organization and with a definite and invariable shape, which compel each species to live in the places and climates where we actually find them, and there to maintain the habits which we know in them.

*My individual conclusion:* Nature has produced all the species of animals in succession, beginning with the most imperfect or simplest, and ending her work with the most perfect, so as to create a gradually increasing complexity in their organization; these animals have spread at large throughout all the habitable regions of the globe, and every species has derived from its environment the habits that we find in it and the structural modifications which observation shows us.

The former of these two conclusions is that which has been drawn hitherto, at least by nearly everyone; it attributes to every animal a fixed organization and structure which never have varied and never do vary; it assumes, moreover, that none of the localities inhabited by animals ever vary; for if they were to vary, the same animal could no longer survive, and the possibility of finding other localities and transporting themselves thither would not be open to them.

The second conclusion is my own; it assumes that by the influence of environment on habit, and thereafter, by that of habit on the state of the parts and even on organization, the structure and organization of any animal may undergo modifications, possibly very great, and capable of accounting for the actual condition in which all animals are found.

## FURTHER READING

Bowler, Peter. 1989. *Evolution: The History of an Idea.* Berkeley: University of California Press.

Burkhardt, Richard Wellington. 1977. *The Spirit of System: Lamarck and Evolutionary Biology.* Cambridge: Harvard University Press.

Corsi, Pietro. 1988. *The Age of Lamarck: Evolutionary Theories in France 1790–1830.* Berkeley: University of California Press.

# The Chemical Atom

## John Dalton (1766–1844)

*The Earth's atmosphere is composed of a mixture of several gases of different density (oxygen, nitrogen and water vapor). Assuming that differing specific gravities among gases indicate differing particle weights, John Dalton, who recorded some two hundred thousand meteorological observations in his journals, wondered why was it so homogeneous. Why didn't the heavier gas, oxygen, sink to the bottom of a container or to the lower region of the atmosphere? Samples taken at differing altitudes had the same proportion of chemical elements, though one might expect that nitrogen gas, which is lighter per unit volume, would separate out and float, like oil on water, on the heavier oxygen.*

*Dalton weighed the different elements of air using a home-built apparatus. He discovered that a mixture of gases weighed the same as the combined weight of the gases taken separately. Known as Dalton's law of partial pressures, it states that different gases in a mixture do not attract each other; i.e., the total pressure of a mixture of gases is the sum of the pressures of each gas taken singly. On Dalton's model, different types of particles had different sizes, and that in consequence no equilibrium could be established between particles of different sizes exerting different forces. Therefore, the constituents of a gaseous mixture would not separate into layers.*

*What if all matter, not just gases, were made up of tiny particles? Proust had pointed out in 1788 that substances always combine in whole units. Chemicals might combine by a ratio of four to three or eight to one, but the reaction would not take, say, 8.767 grams of oxygen and 1.16 grams of hydrogen. One way to explain this law of definite proportions, as it was called, was to assume that each element was composed of small, unsplittable particles.*

*The first full account of the chemical atomic theory was given by Dalton in his* A New System of Chemical Philosophy *(1808). All matter, he insisted, is made up of tiny unsplittable particles which, in honor of Democritus, he named atoms. All the atoms are identical in size, shape and weight and possess the characteristic properties of the element. The atoms of one element differ from the atoms of all other elements and this difference between atoms accounts for the differences between the elements themselves. Chemical reactions do not cause any changes in the nature of the atoms but only result in changes in their combinations.*

*Source:* Dalton, John. 1808–1811. *A New System of Chemical Philosophy.* Manchester: S. Russell, pp. 141–44; 211–20.

*Dalton went further, claiming that it was possible for one element to combine with another element in more than one ratio, thus giving rise to more than one compound formed of the two elements. Hydrogen and oxygen, for example, can combine to form water but in other proportions they can combine as hydrogen peroxide. But, when this was the case, since the combinations were between discrete, indivisible particles, such combinations could only take place in simple ratios as 1:1; 1:2; 1:3; etc. For example, one part of A might combine with 1, 2, 3, etc., parts of B to form a series of different compounds composed of A and B; AB1, AB2, AB3, etc. Thus the ratio of B to A in the more complex compounds is simply a small, whole multiple of that ratio in the simple compound. This is known as the law of multiple proportions, and again would seem to follow from the discrete, indivisible nature of the atom.*

## ON THE CONSTITUTION OF BODIES

There are three distinctions in the kinds of bodies, or three states, which have more especially claimed the attention of philosophical chemists; namely, those which are marked by the terms elastic fluids, liquids, and solids. A very famous instance is exhibited to us in water, of a body, which, in certain circumstances, is capable of assuming all the three states. In steam we recognize a perfectly elastic fluid, in water a perfect liquid, and in ice a complete solid. These observations have tacitly led to the conclusion which seems universally adopted that all bodies of sensible magnitude, whether liquid or solid, are constituted of a vast number of extremely small particles, or atoms of matter bound together by a force of attraction, which is more or less powerful according to circumstances, and which as it endeavors to prevent their separation, is very properly called in that view, attraction of cohesion; but as it collects them from a dispersed state (as from steam into water) it is called attraction of aggregation, or more simply affinity. Whatever names it may go by, they still signify one and the same power. It is not my design to call in question this conclusion, which appears completely satisfactory; but to show that we have hitherto made no use of it, and that the consequence of this neglect has been a very obscure view of chemical agency, which is daily growing more so in proportion to the new lights attempted to be thrown upon it.

The opinions I more particularly allude to are those of Berthollet on the Laws of chemical affinity; such as that chemical agency is proportional to the mass, and that in all chemical unions, there exist insensible gradations in the proportions of the constituent principles. The inconsistence of these opinions, both with reason and observation, cannot, I think, fail to strike every one who takes a proper view of the phenomena.

Whether the ultimate particles of a body, such as water, are all alike, that is, of the same figure, weight, etc. is a question of some importance. From what is known, we have no reason to apprehend a diversity in the particulars; if it does exist in water, it must equally exist in the elements constituting water, namely, hydrogen and oxygen. Now it is scarcely possible to conceive how the aggregates of dissimilar particles should be so uniformly the same. If some of the particles of water were heavier than others, if a parcel of the liquid on any occasion were constituted principally of these heavier particles, it must be supposed to affect the specific gravity of the mass, a circumstance not known. Similar observations may be made on other substances. Therefore, we may conclude that *the ultimate particles of all homogeneous bodies are perfectly alike in weight, figure, etc.* In other words, every particle of water is like every other particle of water; every particle of hydrogen is like every other particle of hydrogen, etc.

Besides the force of attraction, which, in one character or another, belongs universally to ponderable bodies, we find another force that is likewise universal, or acts upon all matter which comes under its cognizance, namely, a force of repulsion. This is now generally, and I think properly, ascribed to the agency of heat. An atmosphere of this subtle fluid constantly surrounds the atoms of all bodies, and prevents them from being drawn into actual contact. This appears to be satisfactorily proved by the observation that the bulk of a body may be diminished by abstracting some of its heat. But from what has been stated in the last section it should seem that enlargement and diminution of bulk depend perhaps more on the arrangement than on the size of the ultimate particles. Be this as it may, we cannot avoid inferring from the preceding doctrine on heat, and particularly from the section on the natural zero of temperature, that solid bodies, such as ice, contain a large portion, perhaps $\frac{4}{5}$th of the heat which the same are found to contain in an elastic state, as steam.

We are now to consider how these two great antagonist powers of attraction and repulsion are adjusted, so as to allow the three different states of *elastic, fluids,* and *solids.* We shall divide this subject into four sections; namely, first, *on the constitution of pure elastic fluids;* second, *on the constitution of mixed elastic fluids;* third, *on the constitution of liquids,* and fourth, *on the constitution of solids.*

## ON CHEMICAL SYNTHESIS

When any body exists in the elastic state, its ultimate particles are separated from each other to a much greater distance than in any other state; each particle occupies the center of a comparatively large sphere, and supports its dignity by keeping all the rest, which by their gravity, or otherwise are disposed to encroach up it, at a respectful distance. When we attempt to conceive the *number* of particles in an atmosphere, it is somewhat like attempting to conceive the number of stars in the universe; we are confounded with the thought. But if we limit the subject, by taking a given volume of any gas, we seem persuaded that, let the divisions be ever so minute, the number of particles must be finite; just as in a given space of the universe, the number of stars and planets cannot be infinite.

Chemical analysis and synthesis go no farther than to the separation of particles one from another, and to their reunion. No new creation or destruction of matter is within the reach of chemical agency. We might as well attempt to introduce a new planet into the solar system, or to annihilate one already in existence, as to create or destroy a particle of hydrogen. All the changes we can produce consist in separating particles that are in a state of cohesion or combination, and joining those that were previously at a distance.

In all chemical investigations, it has justly been considered an important object to ascertain the relative *weights* of the simples which constitute a compound. But unfortunately the inquiry has terminated here; whereas from the relative weights in the mass, the relative weights of the ultimate particles or atoms of the bodies might have been inferred, from which their number and weight in various other compounds would appear, in order to assist and to guide future investigations, and to correct their results. Now it is one great object of this work to show the importance and advantage of ascertaining *the relative weights of the ultimate particles, both of simple and compound bodies, the number of simple elementary particles which constitute one compound particle, and the number of less compound particles which enter into the formation of one more compound particle.*

If there are two bodies, *A* and *B,* which are disposed to combine, the following is the order in which the combinations may take place, beginning with the most simple: namely,

1 atom of A + 1 atom of B = 1 atom of C, binary.

1 atom of A + 2 atoms of B = 1 atom of D, ternary.

2 atoms of A + 1 atom of B = 1 atom of E, ternary.

1 atom of A + 3 atoms of B = 1 atom of F, quarternary.

3 atoms of A + 1 atom of B = 1 atom of G, quarternary.

etc. etc.

The following general rules may be adopted as guides in all our investigations respecting chemical synthesis:

1. When only one combination of two bodies can be obtained, it must be presumed to be a *binary* one, unless some other cause appear to the contrary.

2. When two combinations are observed, they must be presumed to be a *binary* and a *ternary*.

3. When three combinations are observed, they must be presumed to be a *binary*, and the other two *ternary*.

4. When four combinations are observed, we should expect one *binary*, two *ternary*, and one *quaternary*, etc.

5. A *binary* compound should always be specifically heavier than the mere mixture of its two ingredients.

6. A *ternary* compound should be specifically heavier than the mixture of a binary and a simple, which would, if combined, constitute it; etc.

7. The above rules and observations equally apply, when two bodies, such as *C* and *D*, *D* and *E*, etc. are combined.

From the application of these rules, to the chemical facts already well ascertained, we deduce the following conclusions: First,

water is a binary compound of hydrogen and oxygen,[a] and the relative weights of the two elementary atoms are as 1:7, nearly; second, ammonia is a binary compound of hydrogen and azote, and the relative weights of the two atoms are as 1:5, nearly; third, nitrous gas is a binary compound of azote and oxygen, the atoms of which weigh 5 and 7 respectively; that nitric acid is a binary or ternary compound according as it is derived, and consists of one atom of azote and two of oxygen, together weighing 19; that nitrous oxide is a compound similar to nitric acid, and consists of one atom of oxygen and two of azote, weighing 17; that nitrous acid is a binary compound of nitric acid and nitrous gas, weighing 31; that oxynitric acid is a binary compound of nitric acid with oxygen, weighing 26; and fourth, carbonic oxide [carbon monoxide] is a binary compound, consisting of one atom of charcoal, and one of oxygen, together weighing nearly 12; that carbonic acid [carbon dioxide] is a ternary compound, (but sometimes binary) consisting of one atom of charcoal, and two of oxygen, weighing 19; etc. etc. In all these cases the weights are expressed in atoms of hydrogen, each of which is denoted by unity.

In the sequel, the facts and experiments from which these conclusions are derived, will be detailed; as well as a great variety of others from which are inferred the constitution and weight of the ultimate particles of the principal acids, the alkalis, the earths, the metals, the metallic oxides and sulfurets [sulfides], the long train of neutral salts, and

---

[a]Dalton gave NH as the formula for ammonia, but unless one knew how much heavier one atom of nitrogen was than one atom of hydrogen (its atomic weight), it was impossible to establish its atomic constitution. Lacking accurate atomic weights, Dalton created his own atomic weight rules. Where only one compound was known between two elements, Dalton assumed that this compound must contain one atom of each. In this way, he arrived at the formula HO for water ($H_2O$). [B.]

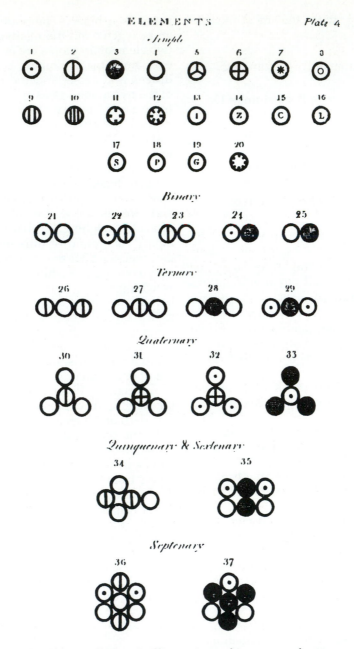

**PLATE 27** Dalton's illustration of a range of atoms, each with its own symbol and atomic weight. From John Dalton, *A New System of Chemical Philosophy,* vol. 1 (1808–1811).

This plate contains the arbitrary marks or signs chosen to represent the several chemical elements or ultimate particles.

| Fig. | | | Fig. | | |
|------|------|------|------|------|------|
| 1. | Hydrog. its ref. weight | 1 | 11. | Strontites | 46 |
| 2. | Azote | 5 | 12. | Barytes | 68 |
| 3. | Carbone or charcoal | 5 | 13. | Iron | 38 |
| 4. | Oxygen | 7 | 14. | Zinc | 56 |
| 5. | Phosphorus | 9 | 15. | Copper | 56 |
| 6. | Sulphur | 13 | 16. | Lead | 95 |
| 7. | Magnesia | 20 | 17. | Silver | 100 |
| 8. | Lime [calcium oxide] | 23 | 18. | Platina | 100 |
| 9. | Soda | 28 | 19. | Gold | 140 |
| 10. | Potash | 42 | 20. | Mercury | 167 |

| | | |
|---|---|---|
| 21. | An atom of water or steam, composed of 1 of oxygen and 1 of hydrogen, retained in physical contact by a strong affinity, and supposed to be surrounded by a common atmosphere of heat; its relative weight = | 8 |
| 22. | An atom of ammonia, composed of 1 of azote and 1 of hydrogen | 6 |
| 23. | An atom of nitrous gas, composed of 1 of azote and 1 of oxygen | 12 |
| 24. | An atom of olefiant gas [ethene], composed of 1 of carbone and 1 of hydrogen | 6 |
| 25. | An atom of carbonic oxide composed of 1 of carbone and 1 of oxygen | 12 |
| 26. | An atom of nitrous oxide, 2 azote + 1 oxygen | 17 |
| 27. | An atom of nitric acid, 1 azote + 2 oxygen | 19 |
| 28. | An atom of carbonic acid, 1 carbone + 2 oxygen | 19 |
| 29. | An atom of carburetted hydrogen [methane], 1 carbone + 2 hydrogen | 7 |
| 30. | An atom of oxynitric acid, 1 azote + 3 oxygen | 26 |
| 31. | An atom of sulphuric acid, 1 sulphur + 3 oxygen | 34 |
| 32. | An atom of sulphuretted hydrogen, 1 sulphur + 3 hydrogen | 16 |
| 33. | An atom of alcohol, 3 carbone + 1 hydrogen | 16 |
| 34. | An atom of nitrous acid, 1 nitric acid + 1 nitrous gas | 31 |
| 35. | An atom of acetous acid, 2 carbone + 2 water | 26 |
| 36. | An atom of nitrate of ammonia, 1 nitric acid + 1 ammonia + 1 water | 33 |
| 37. | An atom of sugar, 1 alcohol + 1 carbonic acid | 35 |

**PLATE 27**   (continued)

in short, all the chemical compounds which have hitherto obtained a tolerably good analysis. Several of the conclusions will be supported by original experiments.

From the novelty as well as importance of the ideas suggested in this chapter, it is deemed expedient to give plates, exhibiting the mode of combination in some of the more simple cases. A specimen of these accompanies this first part [Plate 27]. The elements or atoms of such bodies, as are conceived at present to be simple, are denoted by a small circle, with some distinctive mark; and the combinations consist in the juxtaposition of two or more of these; when three or more particles of elastic fluids are combined together in one, it is supposed that the particles of the same kind repel each other, and therefore take their stations accordingly.

Enough.has been given to show the method; it will be quite unnecessary to devise characters and combinations of them to exhibit to view in this way all the subjects that come under investigation; nor is it necessary to insist upon the accuracy of all these compounds, both in number and weight; the principle will be entered into more particularly hereafter, as far as respects the individual results. It is not to be understood that all those articles marked as simple substances, are necessarily such by the theory; they are only necessarily of such weights. Soda and Potash, such as they are found in combination with acids, are 28 and 42 respectively in weight; but according to Mr. Davy's very important discoveries, they are metallic oxides; the former then must be considered as composed of an atom of metal, 21, and one of oxygen, 7; and the latter, of an atom of metal, 35, and one of oxygen, 7. Or, soda contains 75 percent metal and 25 oxygen; potash, 83.3 metal and 16.7 oxygen. It is particularly remarkable, that according to the above-mentioned gentleman's essay on the Decomposition and Composition of the fixed alkalies, in the *Philosophical Transactions* (a copy of which essay he has just favored me with) it appears that "the largest quantity of oxygen indicated by these experiments was, for potash 17; and for soda, 26 parts in 100, and the smallest 13 and 19."

## FURTHER READING

Cardwell, D. S. L., ed. 1968. *John Dalton and the Progress of Science.* Manchester: Manchester University Press.

Patterson, Elizabeth Chambers. 1970. *John Dalton and the Atomic Theory: The Biography of a Natural Philosopher.* Garden City, NY: Doubleday.

Russell, Colin A. 2002. "Chemistry: Nineteenth Century." In Brian Baigrie, ed., *History of Modern Science and Mathematics.* New York: Charles Scribner's Sons, vol. 2, pp. 185–210.

# Distinguishing an Atom from a Molecule

## Amadeo Avogadro (1776–1856)

*The reputation of Amadeo Avogadro as professor of physics at the University of Turin rests on the famous essay that is reprinted here, which advances the hypothesis that equal volumes of gases at the same temperature and pressure contain equal numbers of the particles of the gas. Avogadro called these particles of gas "molecules." It follows from this hypothesis that the relative molecular weights can be obtained from vapor densities and that the proportion by volume in which gases combine reflects the combining ratio of the molecules.*

*Avogadro was able to show in 1811 that simple gases, such as hydrogen and oxygen, are diatomic and assigned the formula $H_2O$ to water, furnishing an important correction to Dalton's new atomic theory. His work was unappreciated in his day. Only in 1860 did Stanislao Cannizzaro (1826–1910) demonstrate that Avogadro's hypothesis was the key to the problem of atomic and molecular weights—that it furnished a vital link between Gay-Lussac's law of combining volumes and Dalton's atomic theory.*

M. Gay-Lussac[a] has shown in an interesting memoir that gases always unite in a very simple proportion by volume, and that when the result of the union is a gas, its volume also is very simply related to those of its components. But the quantitative proportions of substances in compounds seem only to depend on the relative number of molecules which combine, and on the number of

*Source:* Avogadro, Amadeo. 1811. "Essay on a Manner of Determining the Relative Masses of the Elementary Molecules of Bodies, and the Proportions in Which They Enter Into These Compounds." *Journal de physique* 73: 58–76. Translation from Alembic Club Reprints, No. 4, "Foundations of the Molecular Theory: Comprising Papers and Extracts by John Dalton, Joseph Louis Gay-Lussac, and Amedeo Avogadro (1808–1811)."

[a]In 1805, M. Gay-Lussac (1778–1850) discovered that one volume of oxygen combined with two volumes of hydrogen to form water. Three years later, he formulated his famous law of combining volumes—when gases combine their relative volumes bear a simple numerical relation to each other (e.g., 1:1, 2:1) and to the volumes of their gaseous product, provided pressure and temperature remain constant. John Dalton also was interested in this law, insisting that it was mistaken because it conflicted with his theory of the indivisibility of atoms: One volume of nitrogen (x atoms) plus one volume of nitric oxide (two x atoms) yield two volumes of nitric oxide (two x atoms), instead of one volume = one atom (or molecule, as we now know). As Avogadro points out in this reading, when hydrogen and oxygen unite, the unit of hydrogen, as well as the unit of oxygen in the free state (i.e., as gases) is not the atom but the molecule. The law connecting the atomic weights with the volume of gases is therefore not "equal volumes of gases contain equal

composite molecules which result.[b] It must then be admitted that very simple relations also exist between the volumes of gaseous substances and the numbers of simple or compound molecules which form them. The first hypothesis to present itself in this connection, and apparently even the only admissible one, is the supposition that the number of integral molecules in any gases is always the same for equal volumes, or always proportional to the volumes. Indeed, if we were to suppose that the number of molecules contained in a given volume were different for different gases, it would scarcely be possible to conceive that the law regulating the distance of molecules could give in all cases relations so simple as those which the facts just detailed compel us to acknowledge between the volume and the number of molecules. On the other hand, it is very well conceivable that the molecules of gases being at such a distance that their mutual attraction cannot be exercised, their varying attraction for caloric may be limited to condensing a greater or smaller quantity around them, without the atmosphere formed by this fluid having any greater extent in the one case than in the other, and, consequently, without the distance between the molecules varying; or, in other words, without the number of molecules contained in a given volume being different. Dalton, it is true, has proposed a hypothesis directly opposed to this, namely, that the quantity of caloric is always the same for the molecules of all bodies whatsoever in the gaseous state, and that the greater or less attraction for caloric only results in producing a greater or less condensation of this quantity around

the molecules, and thus varying the distance between the molecules themselves. But in our present ignorance of the manner in which this attraction for the molecules for caloric is exerted, there is nothing to decide us a priori in favor of the one of these hypotheses rather than the other; and we should rather be inclined to adopt a neutral hypothesis, which would make the distance between the molecules and the quantities of caloric vary according to unknown laws, were it not that the hypothesis we have just proposed is based on that simplicity of relation between the volumes of gases on combination, which would appear to be otherwise inexplicable. Setting out from this hypothesis, it is apparent that we have the means of determining very easily the relative masses of the molecules of substances obtainable in the gaseous state, and the relative number of these molecules in compounds; for the ratios of the masses of the molecules are then the same as those of the densities of the different gases at equal temperature and pressure, and the relative number of molecules in a compound is given at once by the ratio of the volumes of the gases that form it. For example, since the numbers 1.10359 and 0.07321 express the densities of the two gases oxygen and hydrogen compared to that of atmospheric air as unity, and the ratio of the two numbers consequently represents the ratio between the masses of equal volumes of these two gases, it will also represent on our hypothesis the ratio of the masses of their molecules. Thus, the mass of the molecule of oxygen will be about 15 times that of the molecule of hydrogen, or more exactly, as 15.074 to one. In the same way the mass of the molecule of nitrogen will be to that of hydrogen as 0.96913 to 0.07321, that is, as 13, or more exactly 13.238 to 1. On the other hand, since we know that the ratio of the volumes of hydrogen and oxygen in the formation of water is two to one, it follows that water results from the union of each molecule of oxygen with two molecules of hydrogen. Similarly, according to the proportions by volume established by M. Gay-Lussac for the elements of ammonia,

---

numbers of atoms," as Dalton supposed, but "equal volumes of gases contain equal numbers of molecules." [B.]

[b]The words "atom" and "molecule" did not yet have their modern meaning. By "integral molecule" Avogadro meant one molecule of a compound; by "constituent molecule" a molecule of a gaseous element; and by "elementary molecule" (or "half molecule") an atom. [B.]

nitrous oxide, nitrous gas, and nitric acid, ammonia will result from the union of one molecule of nitrogen with three of hydrogen, nitrous oxide from one molecule of oxygen with two of nitrogen, nitrous gas from one molecule of nitrogen with one of oxygen, and nitric acid from one of nitrogen with two of oxygen.

There is a consideration which appears at first sight to be opposed to the admission of our hypothesis with respect to compound substances. It seems that a molecule composed of two or more elementary molecules should have its mass equal to the sum of the masses of those molecules; and that in particular, if in a compound one molecule of one substance unites with two or more molecules of another substance, the number of compound molecules should remain the same as the number of molecules of the first substance. Accordingly, on our hypothesis when a gas combines with two or more times its volume of another gas, the resulting compound, if gaseous, must have a volume equal to that of the first of these gases. Now, in general, this is not actually the case. For instance, the volume of water in the gaseous state is, as M. Gay-Lussac has shown, twice as great as the volume of oxygen which enters into it, or, what comes to the same thing, equal to that of the hydrogen instead of being equal to that of the oxygen.[c] But a means of explaining facts of this type in conformity with our hypothesis presents itself naturally enough; we suppose, namely, that the constituent molecules of any simple gas whatever (i.e., the molecules which are at such a distance from each other that they cannot exercise their mutual action) are not formed of a solitary elementary molecule, but are made up of a certain number of these molecules united by attraction to form a single one; and further, that when molecules of another substance unite with the former to form a compound molecule, the integral molecule which should result splits up into two or more parts (or integral molecules) composed of half, quarter, etc., the number of elementary molecules going to form the constituent molecule of the first substance, combined with half, quarter, etc., the number of constituent molecules of the second substance that ought to enter into combination with one constituent molecule of the first substance (or, what comes to the same thing, combined with a number equal to this last of half-molecules, quarter-molecules, etc., of the second substance); so that the number of integral molecules of the compound becomes double, quadruple, etc., what it would have been if there had been no splitting-up, and exactly what is necessary to satisfy the volume of the resulting gas.

On reviewing the various compound gases most generally known, I only find examples of duplication of the volume relatively to the volume of that one of the constituents which combines with one or more volumes of the other. We have already seen this for water. In the same way, we know that the volume of ammonia gas is twice that of the nitrogen which enters into it. M. Gay-Lussac has also shown that the volume of nitrous oxide is equal to that of the nitrogen which forms part of it, and consequently is twice that of the oxygen. Finally, nitrous gas, which contains equal volumes of nitrogen and oxygen, has a volume equal to the sum of the two constituent gases, that is to say, double that of each of them. Thus in all these cases there must be a division of the molecule into two; but it is possible that in other cases the division might be into four, eight, etc. The possibility of this division of compound molecules might have been conjectured a priori; for otherwise the integral

---

[c] If every water molecule contains one oxygen and two hydrogen atoms, it is not clear why one unit of oxygen and two units of hydrogen result in two, and not just one, unit of water vapor. Avogadro realized that the molecules of oxygen and hydrogen contain two atoms each, which doubles the number of water molecules and the volume of water vapor produced from given units of hydrogen and oxygen. The chemical reaction for the production of water reads $2H_2 + O_2 \rightarrow 2H_2O$. For the production of ammonia, the chemical reaction reads $N_2 + 3H_2 \rightarrow 2NH_3$. [B.]

molecules of bodies composed of several substances with a relatively large number of molecules, would come to have a mass excessive in comparison with the molecules of simple substances. We might therefore imagine that nature had some means of bringing them back to the order of the latter, and the facts have pointed out to us the existence of such means. Besides, there is another consideration which would seem to make us admit in some cases the division in question; for how could one otherwise conceive a real combination between two gaseous substances uniting in equal volumes without condensation, such as takes place in the formation of nitrous gas? Supposing the molecules to remain at such a distance that the mutual attraction of those of each gas could not be exercised, we cannot imagine that a new attraction could take place between the molecules of one gas and those of the other. But on the hypothesis of division of the molecule, it is easy to see that the combination really reduces two different molecules to one, and that there would be contraction by the whole volume of one of the gases if each compound molecule did not split up into two molecules of the same nature. M. Gay-Lussac clearly saw that, according to the facts, the diminution of volume on the combination of gases cannot represent the approximation of their elementary molecules. The division of molecules on combination explains to us how these two things may be made independent of each other.

Dalton, on arbitrary suppositions as to the most likely relative number of molecules in compounds, has endeavored to fix ratios between the masses of the molecules of simple substances. Our hypothesis, supposing it well-founded, puts us in a position to confirm or rectify his results from precise data, and, above all, to assign the magnitude of compound molecules according to the volumes of the gaseous compounds, which depend partly on the division of molecules entirely unsuspected by this physicist.

Thus Dalton supposes (in what follows I shall make use of the exposition of Dalton's ideas given in Thomson's "System of Chemistry") that water is formed by the union of hydrogen and oxygen, molecule to molecule. From this, and from the ratio by weight of the two components, it would follow that the mass of the molecule of oxygen would be to that of hydrogen as $7\frac{1}{2}$ to 1 nearly, or, according to Dalton's evaluation, as 6 to 1. This ratio on our hypothesis is, as we saw, twice as great, namely, as 15 to 1. As for the molecule of water, its mass ought to be roughly expressed by $15 + 2 = 17$ (taking for unity that of hydrogen), if there were no division of the molecule into two; but on account of this division it is reduced to half, $8\frac{1}{2}$ or more exactly 8.537, as may also be found directly by dividing the density of aqueous vapor 0.625 (Gay-Lussac) by the density of hydrogen 0.0732. This mass only differs from 7, that assigned to it by Dalton, by the difference in the values for the composition of water; so that in this respect Dalton's result is approximately correct from the combination of two compensating errors; the error in the mass of the molecule of oxygen, and his neglect of the division of the molecule.

Dalton supposes that in nitrous gas the combination of nitrogen and oxygen is molecule to molecule; we have seen on our hypothesis that this is actually the case. Thus Dalton would have found the same molecular mass for nitrogen as we have, always supposing that of hydrogen to be unity, if he had not set out from a different value for that of oxygen, and if he had taken precisely the same value for the quantities of the elements in nitrous gas by weight. But by supposing the molecule of oxygen to be less than half what we find, he has been obliged to make that of nitrogen also equal to less than half the value we have assigned to it, viz., 5 instead of 13. As regards the molecule of nitrous gas itself, his neglect of the division of the molecule again makes his result approach ours; he has made it $6 + 5 = 11$, while according to us it is about $(15 + 13)/2 = 14$, or more exactly $(15.074 + 13.238)/2 = 14.156$, as we also find by dividing 1.03636, the density of nitrous gas according to Gay-Lussac, by

0.07321. Dalton has likewise fixed in the same manner as the facts have given us, the relative number of molecules in nitrous oxide and in nitric acid, and in the first case the same circumstance has rectified his result for the magnitude of the molecule. He makes it 6 + (2 × 5) = 16, while according to our method it should be (15.074 + 2 × 13.238)/2 = 20.775, a number which is also obtained by dividing 1.52092, Gay-Lussac's value for the density of nitrous oxide, by the density of hydrogen.

In the case of ammonia, Dalton's supposition as to the relative number of molecules in its composition is on our hypothesis entirely at fault. He supposes nitrogen and hydrogen to be united in it molecule to molecule, whereas we have seen that one molecule of nitrogen unites with three molecules of hydrogen. According to him the molecule of ammonia would be 5 + 1 = 6; according to us it should be (13 + 3)/2 = 8, or more exactly 8.119, as may also be deduced directly from the density of ammonia gas. The division of the molecule, which does not enter into Dalton's calculations, partly corrects in this case also the error which would result from his other suppositions.

All the compounds we have just discussed are produced by the union of one molecule of one of the components with one or more molecules of the other. In nitrous acid we have another compound of two of the substances already spoken of, in which the terms of the ratio between the number of molecules both differ from unity. From Gay-Lussac's experiments, it appears that this acid is formed from 1 part by volume of oxygen and 3 of nitrous gas, or, what comes to the same thing, of 3 parts of nitrogen and 5 of oxygen; from this it would follow, on our hypothesis, that its molecules should be composed of 3 molecules of nitrogen and 5 of oxygen, leaving the possibility of division out of account. But this mode of combination can be referred to the preceding simpler forms by considering it as the result of the union of 1 molecule of oxygen with 3 of nitrous gas, i.e., with 3 molecules, each composed of a half-molecule of oxygen and a half-molecule of nitrogen, which thus already includes the division of some of the molecules of oxygen which enter into that of nitrous acid. Supposing there to be no other division, the mass of this last molecule would [be] 57.542, that of hydrogen being taken as unity, and the density of nitrous acid gas would be 4.21267, the density of air being taken as unity. But it is probable that there is at least another division into two, and consequently a reduction of the density to half: We must wait until this density has been determined by experiment[d] . . .

It will have been in general remarked on reading this Memoir that there are many points of agreement between our special results and those of Dalton, although we set out from a general principle, and Dalton has only been guided by considerations of detail. This agreement is an argument in favor of our hypothesis, which is at bottom merely Dalton's system furnished with a new means of precision from the connection we have found between it and the general fact established by M. Gay-Lussac. Dalton's system supposes that compounds are made in general in fixed proportions, and this is what experiment shows with regard to the more stable compounds and those most interesting to the chemist. It would appear that it is only combinations of this sort that can take place amongst gases, on account of the enormous size of the molecules which would result from ratios expressed by larger numbers, in spite of the division of the molecules, which is in all probability confined within narrow limits. We perceive that the close packing of the molecules in solids and in liquids, which only leaves between the

[d]Avogadro deduced chemical formulas from his hypothesis to ascertain a number of atomic weights with fairly good accuracy. His pioneering work was taken up by J. J. Berzelius (1779–1848), professor of chemistry at the University of Stockholm, who published tables in 1814, 1818, and 1826, which provided good values of the atomic weights of many elements. [B.]

integral molecules distances of the same order as those between the elementary molecules, can give rise to more complicated ratios, and even to combinations in all proportions; but these compounds will be so to speak of a different type from those with which we have been concerned, and this distinction may serve to reconcile M. Berthollet's ideas as to compounds with the theory of fixed proportions.

## FURTHER READING

Morselli, Mario. 1984. *Amadeo Avogadro, A Scientific Biography.* Dordrecht: D. Reidel.

# Geology and Genesis

## Georges Cuvier (1769–1832)

*By the early decades of the nineteenth century, it was widely accepted that fossils were the organic remains of animals and that most, if not all, fossil animals were extinct. These conclusions were unassailable largely as a result of the field work conducted in the Paris Basin by Georges Cuvier, the creator of paleontology and modern comparative anatomy. His predecessors had emphasized the explanatory power of comparative methods, but they compared species, where Cuvier compared the organs of all vertebrates.*

*Cuvier's classification of form was based on the Aristotelian principle of the subordination of the parts to the whole, or what Cuvier called his principle of organic correlation. It was his crowning achievement. This principle enabled Cuvier to make sensational discoveries based on findings of just a few fossil fragments, such as the fossil marsupial found in the gypsum of Montmarte, which he recognized by its jaw bones. Cuvier isolated the skeleton from the gangue in the presence of his colleagues, who were highly sceptical until the marsupial's pelvis bones were subsequently uncovered, providing a stunning confirmation that Cuvier's interpretation was correct. He worked mainly with the fossils of mammals and reptiles, which were sent to him from all over Europe, thanks to the reputation of his studies and the important offices he held under both Napoleon Bonaparte (1766–1821) and King Louis XVIII.*

*One of his particular paleontological merits was that he definitely demonstrated that the remains he studied belonged to species that had been extinct at various moments in the Earth's history and were no longer found among present-day fauna. The fossil record also placed Cuvier's pronounced religious beliefs at risk. If fossil animals were extinct, and if species were immutable, as mandated by the Book of Genesis, where did the present fauna of the earth come from? They could not be descended from the fossil species, nor was there any evidence for more than one set of animals created by God. In his* Essay on the Theory of the Earth *(1817)—the source of this reading—Cuvier suggested that God, when he revealed himself through Scripture, had held back the whole truth from the primitive Hebrew tribes. His mission was to teach them*

*Source:* Georges Cuvier. 1817. *Essay on the Theory of the Earth.* Fourth Edition. Trans. Robert Jameson. Edinburgh: W. Blackwood, and J. Murray and R. Baldwin, pp. 7–12; 15–17; 121–122; 149–151; 173–175.

*morality, and not paleontology, and so Scripture was not literally true. There had been not one, but a series of creations in which God filled the Earth with animals and then destroyed them in sudden cataclysms. The fossil record bears witness to these successive catastrophes. Scripture records only the last creation, when God created the world as we presently know it.*

## FIRST PROOF OF REVOLUTIONS ON THE SURFACE OF THE GLOBE

The lowest and most level parts of the Earth, when penetrated to a very great depth, exhibit nothing but horizontal strata composed of various substances, and containing almost all of them innumerable marine productions. Similar strata, with the same kind of productions, compose the hills even to a great height. Sometimes the shells are so numerous as to constitute the entire body of the stratum. They are almost everywhere in such a perfect state of preservation that even the smallest of them retain their most delicate parts, their sharpest ridges, and their finest and most tender processes. They are found in elevations far above the level of every part of the ocean, and in places to which the sea could not be conveyed by any existing cause. They are not only enclosed in loose sand, but are often encrusted and penetrated on all sides by the hardest stones. Every part of the Earth, every hemisphere, every continent, every island of any size, exhibits the same phenomenon. We are therefore forcibly led to believe not only that the sea has at one period or another covered all our plains, but that it must have remained there for a long time, and in a state of tranquility; which circumstance was necessary for the formation of deposits so extensive, so thick, in part so solid, and containing exuviae so perfectly preserved.

The time is past for ignorance to assert that these remains of organized bodies are mere *lusus naturae*—productions generated in the womb of the Earth by its own creative powers. A nice and scrupulous comparison of their forms, of their structure, and frequently even of their composition, cannot detect the slightest difference between these shells and the shells which still inhabit the sea. They have therefore once lived in the sea, and been deposited by it. The sea consequently must have rested in the places where the deposition has taken place. Hence, it is evident that the basin or reservoir containing the sea has undergone some change at least, either in extent, or in situation, or in both. Such is the result of the very first search, and of the most superficial examination.

The traces of revolutions become still more apparent and decisive when we ascend a little higher, and approach nearer to the foot of the great chains of mountains. There are still found many beds of shells; some of these are even larger and more solid; the shells are quite as numerous and as entirely preserved; but they are not of the same species with those which were found in the less elevated regions. The strata which contain them are not so generally horizontal; they have various degrees of inclination, and are sometimes situated vertically. While in the plains and low hills it was necessary to dig deep in order to detect the succession of the strata, here we perceive them by means of the allies which time or violence has produced, and which disclose their edges to the eye of the observer. At the bottom of these declivities, huge masses of their debris are collected, and form round hills, the height of which is augmented by the operation of every thaw and of every storm.

These inclined or vertical strata, which form the ridges of the secondary mountains, do not rest on the horizontal strata of the hills which are situated at their base, and serve as their first steps; but, on the contrary, are situated underneath them. The latter are placed upon the declivities of the former. When we dig through the horizontal strata in the neighborhood of the inclined strata, the inclined strata are invariably found below. Indeed, sometimes, when the inclined strata are not too much elevated, their summit is surmounted by horizontal strata. The inclined strata are therefore more ancient than the horizontal strata. And as they must necessarily have been formed in a horizontal position, they have been subsequently shifted into their inclined or vertical position, and that too before the horizontal strata were placed above them.

Thus the sea, previous to the formation of the horizontal strata, had formed others, which, by some means, have been broken, lifted up, and overturned in a thousand ways. There had therefore been also at least one change in the basin of that sea which preceded ours; it had also experienced at least one revolution; and as several of these inclined strata which it had formed first are elevated above the level of the horizontal strata which have succeeded and which surround them, this revolution, while it gave them their present inclination, had also caused them to project above the level of the sea, so as to form islands, or at least rocks and inequalities; and this must have happened whether one of their edges was lifted up above the water, or the depression of the opposite edge caused the water to subside. This is the second result, not less obvious, nor less clearly demonstrated, than the first, to every one who will take the trouble of studying carefully the remains by which it is illustrated and proved.

## PROOFS THAT SUCH REVOLUTIONS HAVE BEEN NUMEROUS

If we institute a more detailed comparison between the various strata and those remains of animals which they contain, we shall soon discover still more numerous differences among them, indicating a proportional number of changes in their condition.

The sea has not always deposited stony substances of the same kind. It has observed a regular succession as to the nature of its deposits; the more ancient the strata are, so much the more uniform and extensive are they; and the more recent they are, the more limited are they, and the more variation is observed in them at small distances. Thus, the great catastrophes which have produced revolutions in the basin of the sea, were preceded, accompanied, and followed by changes in the nature of the fluid and of the substances which it held in solution; and when the surface of the seas came to be divided by islands and projecting ridges, different changes took place in every separate basin.

Among these changes of the general fluid, it must have been almost impossible for the same kind of animals to continue to live; nor did they do so in fact. Their species, and even their genera, change with the strata; and although the same species occasionally recur at small distances, it is generally the case that the shells of the ancient strata have forms peculiar to themselves; that they gradually disappear, until they are not to be seen at all in the recent strata, still less in the existing seas, in which, indeed, we never discover their corresponding species and where several even of their genera are not to be found, that, on the contrary, the shells of the recent strata resemble, as it respects the genus, those which still exist in the sea; and that in the last formed and most loose of these strata, there are some species which the eyes of the most expert naturalist cannot distinguish from those which at present inhabit the ocean.

In animal nature, therefore, there has been a succession of changes corresponding to those which have taken place in the chemical nature of the fluid; and when the sea last receded from our continent, its inhabitants were not very different from those which it still continues to support.

Finally, if we examine with greater care these remains of organized bodies, we shall discover, in the midst even of the most ancient secondary strata, other strata that are crowded with animal or vegetable productions, which belong to the land and to fresh water; and among the more recent strata, that is, the strata which are nearest the surface, there are some of them in which land animals are buried under heaps of marine productions. Thus, the various catastrophes of our planet have not only caused the different parts of our continent to rise by degrees from the basin of the sea, but it has also frequently happened that lands which had been laid dry have been again covered by the water, in consequence either of these lands sinking down below the level of the sea, or of the sea being raised above the level of the lands. The particular portions of the Earth also which the sea has abandoned by its last retreat, had been laid dry once before, and had at that time produced quadrupeds, birds, plants, and all kinds of terrestrial productions; it had then been inundated by the sea, which has since retired from it and left it to be occupied by its own proper inhabitants.

The changes which have taken place in the productions of the shelly strata have not, therefore, been entirely owing to a gradual and general retreat of the waters, but to successive eruptions and retreats, the final result of which, however, has been a universal depression of the level of the sea.

not been frozen as soon as killed they must quickly have been decomposed by putrefaction. But this eternal frost could not have taken possession of the regions which these animals inhabited except by the same cause which destroyed them;[1] this cause, therefore, must have been as sudden as its effect. The breaking to pieces and overturnings of the strata, which happened in former catastrophes, show plainly enough that they were sudden and violent like the last; and the heaps of debris and rounded pebbles which are found in various places among the solid strata, demonstrate the vast force of the motions excited in the mass of waters by these overturnings. Life, therefore, has been often disturbed on this Earth by terrible events—calamities which, at their commencement, have perhaps moved and overturned to a great depth the entire outer crust of the globe, but which, since these first commotions, have uniformly acted at less depth and less generally. Innumerable living beings have been the victims of these catastrophes; some have been destroyed by sudden inundations, others have been laid dry in consequence of the bottom of the seas being instantaneously elevated. Their races even have become extinct, and have left no memorial of them, except some small fragment which the naturalist can scarcely recognize.

## PROOFS THAT THE REVOLUTIONS HAVE BEEN SUDDEN

These repeated eruptions and retreats of the sea have neither been slow nor gradual; most of the catastrophes which have occasioned them have been sudden; and this is easily proved, especially with regard to the last of them, the traces of which are most conspicuous. In the northern regions it has left the carcasses of some large quadrupeds which the ice had arrested, and which are preserved even to the present day with their skin, their hair, and their flesh. If they had

## PROOFS THAT THE EXTINCT SPECIES OF QUADRUPEDS ARE NOT VARIETIES OF THE PRESENTLY EXISTING SPECIES

The following objection has already been started against my conclusions. Why may not the presently existing races of mammiferous land-quadrupeds be mere modifications or varieties of those ancient races which we now find in the fossil state, which modifications may have been produced by change of climate and other local circumstances, and since raised to the present excessive difference, by the operation of similar causes during a long succession of ages?

This objection may appear strong to those who believe in the indefinite possibility of change of forms in organized bodies, and think that during a succession of ages, and by alterations of habitats, all the species may change into each other, or one of them give birth to all the rest. Yet, to these persons the following answer may be given from their own system. If the species have changed by degrees, as they assume, we ought to find traces of this gradual modification.[a] Thus, between the *palaeotherium* and the species of our own days, we should be able to discover some intermediate forms; and yet no such discovery has ever been made. Since the bowels of the Earth have not preserved monuments of this strange genealogy, we have a right to conclude that the ancient and now extinct species were as permanent in their forms and characters as those which exist at present; or at least that the catastrophe which destroyed them did not leave sufficient time for the production of the changes that are alleged to have taken place.

In order to reply to those naturalists who acknowledge that the varieties of animals are restrained by nature within certain limits, it would be necessary to examine how far these limits extend. This is a very curious in-

quiry, and in itself exceedingly interesting under a variety of relations, but has been hitherto very little attended to. It requires that we should define accurately what is, or ought to be, understood by the word *species*, which may be thus expressed: A *species comprehends all the individuals which descend from each other, or from a common parentage, and those which resemble them as much as they do each other.* Thus, the different races which they have generated from them are considered as varieties but of one species. Our observations, therefore, respecting the differences between the ancestors and the descendants, are the only rules by which we can judge on this subject; all other considerations being merely hypothetical, and destitute of proof. Taking the word *variety* in this limited sense, we observe that the differences which constitute this variety depend upon determinate circumstances, and that their extent increases in proportion to the intensity of the circumstances which occasion them.

Upon these principles it may be observed that the most superficial characters are the most variable. Thus, color depends much upon light; thickness of hair upon heat; size upon abundance of food, etc. In wild animals, however, even these varieties are greatly limited by the natural habits of the animal, which does not willingly migrate from the places where it finds in sufficient quantity what is necessary for the support of its species, and does not even extend its haunts to any great distances, unless it also finds all these circumstances conjoined. Thus, although the wolf and the fox inhabit all the climates from the torrid to the frigid zone, we hardly find any other differences among them, through the whole of that vast space, than a little more or a little less beauty in their furs. I have compared the skulls of foxes from the most northern regions and from Egypt with those of France, and found no differences but what might naturally be expected in different individuals. The most savage animals, especially those which are carnivorous, being confined within narrower

[a]Cuvier's debt to Aristotle's teleological view of the organic world was reflected in his belief that all the parts of organisms—like the parts of a machine—serve some particular purpose. Any drastic alteration in one part, he claimed, will result in violent deleterious effects in other parts. Given his teleological views, Cuvier could only be an opponent of an evolutionary hypothesis. Although he was prepared to grant a certain amount of intra-specific change, his correlation of parts doctrine implied that only certain basic forms are possible. If one altered the basic form of any species beyond a certain limit, its essential harmony would be so severely disrupted that the organism would no longer be viable. The transitional forms, which Lamarck regarded as linking species in a seamless chain, were therefore impossible. [B.]

limits, vary still less; and the only difference between the hyena of Persia and that of Morocco, consists in a thicker or a thinner mane.

Animals which subsist upon herbage feel the influence of climate a little more extensively because there is added to it the influence of food, both in regard to its abundance and its quality. Thus, the elephants of one forest are larger than those of another; their tusks also grow somewhat longer in places where their food may happen to be more favorable for the production of the substance of ivory. The same may take place in regard to the horns of stags and reindeer. But, let us examine two elephants the most dissimilar that can be conceived, [and] we shall not discover the smallest difference in the number and articulations of the bones, the structure of the teeth, etc.

Besides, the species of herbivorous animals, in their wild state, seem more restrained from migrating and dispersing than the carnivorous species, being influenced both by climate and by the kind of nourishment which they need. Nature appears also to have guarded against the alterations of species which might proceed from mixture of breeds, by influencing the various species of animals with mutual aversion from each other. Hence, all the cunning and all the force that man is able to exert is necessary to accomplish such unions, even between species that have the nearest resemblances. And when the mule breeds that are thus produced by these forced conjunctions happen to be fruitful, which is seldom the case, this fecundity never continues beyond a few generations, and would not probably proceed so far without a continuance of the same cares which excited it at first. Thus, we never see in a wild state intermediate productions between the hare and the rabbit, between the stag and the doe, or between the martin and the weasel. But the power of man changes this established order, and contrives to produce all these intermixtures of which the various species are susceptible, but which they would never produce if left to themselves . . .

The most remarkable effects of the influence of man are produced upon that animal which he has reduced most completely under subjection. Dogs have been transported by mankind into every part of the world, and have submitted their actions to his entire direction. Regulated in their sexual unions by the pleasure or caprice of their masters, the almost endless variety of dogs differ from each other in color; in length and abundance of hair, which is sometimes entirely wanting; in their natural instincts; in size, which varies in measure as one to five, amounting, in some instances to more than a hundred fold in bulk; in the forms of their ears, noses, and tails; in the relative length of their legs; in the progressive development of the brain in several of the domesticated varieties, occasioning alterations, even in the form of the head; some of them having long slender muzzles with a flat forehead; others having short muzzles, with the forehead convex, etc., insomuch that the apparent differences between a mastiff and a water spaniel, and between a greyhound and a pug dog, are even more striking than between almost any of the wild species of a genus. Finally, and this may be considered as the maximum of known variation in the animal kingdom, some races of dogs have an additional claw on each hind foot, with corresponding bones of the tarsus, as there sometimes occur in the human species some families that have six fingers on each hand. Yet, in all these varieties, the relations of the bones with each other remain essentially the same, and the form of the teeth never changes in any perceptible degree, except that in some individuals one additional false grinder occasionally appears, sometimes on the one side, and sometimes on the other.

It follows from these observations, that animals have certain fixed and natural characters, which resist the effects of every kind of influence, whether proceeding from natural causes or human interference; and we have not the smallest reason to suspect that time has any more effect upon them than climate . . .

## PROOFS, FROM TRADITIONS, OF A GREAT CATASTROPHE, AND SUBSEQUENT RENEWAL OF HUMAN SOCIETY

From all that has been said, it may be seen that nature everywhere distinctly informs us that the commencement of the present order of things cannot be dated at a very remote period; and it is very remarkable that mankind everywhere speak the same language with nature, whether we consult their natural traditions on this subject, or consider their moral and political state, and the intellectual attainments which they had made at the time when they began to have authentic historical monuments. For this purpose we may consult the histories of nations in their most ancient books, endeavoring to discover the real facts which they contain, when disengaged from the interested fictions which often render the truth obscure. The Pentateuch has existed in its present form at least ever since the separation of the ten tribes under Jeroboam, since it was received as authentic by the Samaritans as well as by the Jews; and this assures us of the actual antiquity of that book being not less than two thousand eight hundred years. Besides this, we have no reason to doubt of the book of Genesis having been composed by Moses, which adds five hundred years to its antiquity.

Moses and his people came out of Egypt, which is universally allowed by all the nations of the West to have been the most anciently civilized kingdom on the borders of the Mediterranean. The legislator of the Jews could have no motive for shortening the duration of the nations, and would even have disgraced himself in the estimation of his own, if he had promulgated a history of the human race contradictory to that which they must have learned by tradition in Egypt. We may therefore conclude that the Egyptians had at this time no other notions respecting the antiquity of the human race than are contained in the book of Genesis. And, as Moses establishes the event of a universal catastrophe, occasioned by an eruption of the waters, and followed by an almost entire renewal of the human race, and as he has only referred it to an epoch fifteen or sixteen hundred years previous to his own time, even according to those copies which allow the longest interval, it must necessarily have occurred rather less than five thousand years before the present day . . .

If there is any circumstance thoroughly established in geology, it is that the crust of our globe has been subjected to a great and sudden revolution the epoch of which cannot be dated much farther back than five or six thousand years ago; that this revolution had buried all the countries which were before inhabited by men and by the other animals that are now best known; that the same revolution had laid dry the bed of the last ocean, which now forms all the countries at present inhabited; that the small number of individuals of men and other animals that escaped from the effects of that great revolution have since propagated and spread over the land then newly laid dry; and consequently, that the human race has only resumed a progressive state of improvement since that epoch by forming established societies, raising monuments, collecting natural facts, and constructing systems of science and of learning.

Yet further, that the countries which are now inhabited, and which were laid dry by this last revolution, had been formerly inhabited at a more remote era, if not by man, at least by land animals; that, consequently, at least one previous revolution had submerged them under the waters; and that, judging from the different orders of animals of which we discover the remains in a fossil state, they had probably experienced two or three eruptions of the sea.

These alternate revolutions form, in my opinion, the problem in geology that is most important to be solved, or rather to be accurately defined and circumscribed; for in order to solve it satisfactorily and entirely, it were requisite that we should discover the cause of these events, an enterprise involving difficulties of a very different nature.

## NOTES

1. The two most remarkable phenomena of this kind, and which must forever banish all idea of a slow and gradual revolution, are the rhinoceros discovered in 1771 in the banks of the *Vilhoui,* and the elephant recently found by M. Adams near the mouth of the *Lena.* This last retained its flesh and skin, on which was hair of two kinds; one short, fine, and crisped, resembling wool, and the other like long bristles. The flesh was still in such high preservation that it was eaten by dogs.

## FURTHER READING

Gillispie, Charles Coulston. 1951. *Genesis and Geology: A Study in the Relations of Science.* Cambridge: Harvard University Press.

Rudwick, Martin J. S. 1985. *The Meaning of Fossils: Episodes in the History of Paleontology.* Second edition. Chicago: The University of Chicago Press.

Rudwick, Martin J. S. 1998. *Georges Cuvier, Fossil Bones, and Geological Catastrophes: New Translations & Interpretations of the Primary Texts.* Chicago: The University of Chicago Press.

# The Electromagnetic Effect

## Hans Christian Oersted (1777–1851)

*By the end of the eighteenth century, it was known that thunderstorms often affect the direction that a magnetic compass needle points. Drawing on the suggestion of Benjamin Franklin (1706–1790) that lightning is an electric current, Hans Christian Oersted suspected that it was lightning that was responsible for this effect. He reckoned that a wire which glowed from an electrical current passing through it would act like lightning, and disturb a magnetic needle. During a private lecture before a group of students in the spring of 1820, he placed a conducting wire over and parallel to a magnetic needle. The compass needle moved, not in the direction of the current but instead into a position at a right angle to the current, as though a magnet had been moved close to it. He reversed the direction of the current. The compass needle swung again, this time in the opposite direction, again at a right angle. Oersted had demonstrated for the first time that two different forces of nature (electricity and magnetism) could interact.*

*The way in which the magnetic needle and current interacted seemed quite different from the Newtonian manner of central attraction or repulsion—an electric current in a conductor created a circular magnetic field around the conductor. With this experiment, which was reported in Oersted's celebrated paper, the study of electromagnetism was born, which was to be one of the most fruitful areas of study in nineteenth-century science.*

The first experiments respecting the subject which I mean at present to explain, were made by me last winter, while lecturing on electricity and galvanism in the University.[a] It seemed demonstrated by these experiments that the magnetic needle was moved from its position by the galvanic apparatus, but that the galvanic circle must be complete, and not open, which last method was

*Source:* John Christian Oersted. 1820. "Experiments on the Effect of a Current of Electricity on the Magnetic Needle." *Annals of Philosophy* 16, 273–276. Translated from a printed account drawn up in Latin by Oersted, and transmitted by him to the Editor of *Annals of Philosophy*.

[a]Oersted's paper gives a brief account of the condition under which his experiments were made, as well as the results of these experiments, but no indication as to the history of the discovery and development of electromagnetism. For a historical sketch both of the ideas on the subject and the development of Oersted's ideas, see Oersted's contribution to the article "Thermoelectricity," in *Edinburgh Encyclopedia* (1830), vol. XVIII. [B.]

tried in vain some years ago by very cele-brated philosophers. But, as these experi-ments were made with a feeble apparatus, and were not, therefore, sufficiently conclu-sive, considering the importance of the sub-ject, I associated myself with my friend Esmarck to repeat and extend them by means of a very powerful galvanic battery, provided by us in common. Mr. Wleugel, a Knight of the Order of Danneborg, and at the head of the Pilots, was present at, and as-sisted in, these experiments. There were pre-sent likewise Mr. Hauch, a man very well skilled in the Natural Sciences, Mr. Rein-hardt, Professor of Natural History, Mr. Ja-cobsen, Professor of Medicine, and that very skillful chemist, Mr. Zeise, Doctor of Philos-ophy. I had often made experiments by my-self; but every fact which I had observed was repeated in the presence of these gentle-men.

The galvanic apparatus which we em-ployed consisted of 20 copper troughs, the length and height of each of which was 12 inches; but the breadth scarcely exceeded 2 ½ inches. Every trough is supplied with two plates of copper, so bent that they could carry a copper rod, which supports the zinc plate in the water of the next trough. The water of the troughs contained ⅟₆₀th of its weight of sulfuric acid, and an equal quan-tity of nitric acid. The portion of each zinc plate sunk in the water is a square whose side is about 10 inches in length. A smaller apparatus will answer provided it be strong enough to heat a metallic wire red hot.

The opposite ends of the galvanic battery were joined by a metallic wire, which, for shortness sake, we shall call the *uniting con-ductor,* or the *uniting wire.* To the effect which takes place in this conductor and in the sur-rounding space, we shall give the name of the *conflict of electricity.*

Let the straight part of this wire be placed horizontally above the magnetic needle, properly suspended, and parallel to it. If necessary, the uniting wire is bent so as to assume a proper position for the experiment. Things being in this state, the needle will be moved, and the end of it next to the negative side of the battery will go westward.

If the distance of the uniting wire does not exceed ¾ of an inch from the needle, the declination of the needle marks an angle of about 45°. If the distance is increased, the angle diminishes proportionally. The decli-

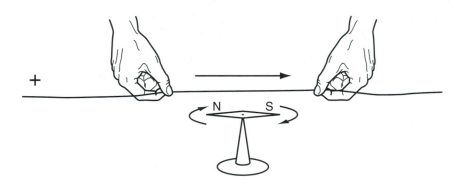

**PLATE 28**   A reconstruction of Oersted's experiment. A copper wire is held above and parallel to a magnetic needle suspended on a pointed pivot. One end of the wire is joined to a battery. The other end of the wire is then brought into contact with the other pole of the battery. As the circuit completes, the needle is turned aside. If the current flowing along the wire above the needle is from north to south, it will cause the north-seeking end of the needle to turn eastwards, and vice versa. If the wire is held below the needle, the directions will be reversed.

nation likewise varies with the power of the battery.[b]

The uniting wire may change its place, either towards the east or west, provided it continue parallel to the needle, without any other change of the effect than in respect to its quantity. Hence the effect cannot be ascribed to attraction; for the same pole of the magnetic needle, which approaches the uniting wire, while placed on its east side, ought to recede from it when on the west side, if these declinations depended on attractions and repulsions. The uniting conductor may consist of several wires, or metallic ribbons, connected together. The nature of the metal does not alter the effect, but merely the quantity.[c] Wires of platinum, gold, silver, brass, iron, ribbons of lead and tin, and a mass of mercury were employed with equal success. The conductor does not lose its effect, though interrupted by water, unless the interruption amounts to several inches in length.

The effect of the uniting wire passes to the needle through glass, metals, wood, water, resin, stoneware, and stones; for it is not taken away by interposing plates of glass, metal or wood. Even glass, metal, and wood, interposed at once, do not destroy and indeed scarcely diminish the effect. The disc of the electrophorus, plates of porphyry, a stone-ware vessel, even filled with water, were interposed with the same result. We found the effects unchanged when the needle was included in a brass box filled with water. It is needless to observe that the transmission of effects through all these matters has never before been observed in electricity and galvanism. The effects, therefore, which take place in the conflict of electricity are very different from the effects of either of the electricities.

If the uniting wire be placed in a horizontal plane under the magnetic needle, all the effects are the same as when it is above the needle, only they are in an opposite direction; for the pole of the magnetic needle next to the negative end of the battery declines to the east.

That these facts may be the more easily retained, we may use this formula—the pole *above* which the negative electricity enters is turned to the *west; under* which, to the *east.*

If the uniting wire is so turned in a horizontal plane as to form a gradually increasing angle with the magnetic meridian, the declination of the needle *increases,* if the motion of the wire is towards the place of the disturbed needle; but it *diminishes* if the wire moves further from that place.

When the uniting wire is situated in the same horizontal plane in which the needle moves by means of the counterpoise, and parallel to it, no declination is produced either to the east or west; but an *inclination* takes place, so that the pole, next which the negative electricity enters the wire, is *depressed* when the wire is situated on the *west* side, and *elevated* when situated on the *east* side.

If the uniting wire be placed perpendicularly to the plane of the magnetic meridian, whether above or below it, the needle remains at rest, unless it be very near the pole; in that case the pole is *elevated* when the entrance is from the *west* side of the wire, and depressed, when from the *east* side.

When the uniting wire is placed perpendicularly opposite to the pole of the magnetic needle, and the upper extremity of the wire receives the negative electricity, the pole is moved towards the east; but when the wire is opposite to a point between the pole and the middle of the needle, the pole is most towards the west. When the upper end of the wire receives positive electricity, the phenomena are reversed.

If the uniting wire is bent so as to form two legs parallel to each other, it repels or attracts the magnetic poles according to the different conditions of the case. Suppose the wire is placed opposite to either pole of the needle, so that the plane of the parallel legs is parallel to the magnetic meridian, and

[b]Oersted is doubtless referring to the fact that the effect depends upon the current in the wire. [B.]

[c]Since the resistance, and hence the current, depends upon the conductor. [B.]

let the eastern leg be united with the negative end, the western leg with the positive end of the battery; in that case the nearest pole will be repelled either to the east or west, according to the position of the plane of the legs. The eastmost leg being united with the positive, and the westmost with the negative side of the battery, the nearest pole will be attracted. When the plane of the legs is placed perpendicular to the place between the pole and the middle of the needle, the same effects recur, but reversed.

A brass needle, suspended like a magnetic needle, is not moved by the effect of the uniting wire. Likewise needles of glass and of gum lac remain unacted upon. We may now make a few observations towards explaining these phenomena.

The electric conflict acts only on the magnetic particles of matter. All non-magnetic bodies appear penetrable by the electric conflict, while magnetic bodies, or rather their magnetic particles, resist the passage of this conflict. Hence they can be moved by the impetus of the contending powers.

It is sufficiently evident from the preceding facts that the electric conflict is not confined to the conductor, but dispersed pretty widely in the circumjacent space.

From the preceding facts we may likewise gather that this conflict performs circles; for without this condition, it seems impossible that the one part of the uniting wire, when placed below the magnetic pole, should drive it towards the east, and when placed above it towards the west; for it is the nature of a circle that the motions in opposite parts should have an opposite direction. Besides, a motion in circles, joined with a progressive motion, according to the length of the conductor, ought to form a conchoidal or spiral line; but this, unless I am mistaken, contributes nothing to explain the phenomena hitherto observed.

All the effects on the north pole above-mentioned are easily understood by supposing that no negative electricity moves in a spiral line bent towards the right, and propels the north pole, but does not act on the south pole. The effects on the south pole are explained in a similar manner, if we ascribe to positive electricity a contrary motion and power of acting on the south pole, but not upon the north. The agreement of this law with nature will be better seen by a repetition of the experiments than by a long explanation. The mode of judging of the experiments will be much facilitated if the course of the electricities in the uniting wire be pointed out by marks or figures.

I shall merely add to the above that I have demonstrated in a book[e] published five years ago that heat and light consist of the conflict of the electricities. From the observations now stated, we may conclude that a circular motion likewise occurs in these effects. This I think will contribute very much to illustrate the phenomena to which the appellation of polarization of light has been given.

[e]Oersted is referring to his *Theory of Light* (1815), the main thesis of which is that heat and light are generated by the union of the opposed electrical forces when this union occurs under resistance. [B.]

## FURTHER READING

Dibner, Bern. 1963. *Oersted and the Discovery of Electro-Magnetism*. New York: Blaisdell.

Williams, L. Pearce. 1981. "Oersted, Hans Christian." In C. C. Gillispie, ed., *Dictionary of Scientific Biography*. New York: Charles Scribner's Sons, vol. 10, pp. 182–186.

point is quite inconclusive, for we know nothing, as yet, of the details of the various classes of the animal kingdom which inhabited the land up to the consolidation of the newest of the secondary strata; and when a large part of the tertiary formations were in progress, the climate does not appear to have been of such a tropical character as seems necessary for the development of the tribe of apes, monkeys, and allied genera. Besides, it must not be forgotten, that almost all the animals which occur in sub-aqueous deposits are such as frequent marshes, rivers, or the borders of lakes, as the rhinoceros, tapir, hippopotamus, ox, deer, pig, and others. On the other hand, species which live in trees are extremely rare in a fossil state, and we have no data as yet for determining how great a number of the one kind we ought to find, before we have a right to expect a single individual of the other. If, therefore, we are led to infer, from the presence of crocodiles and turtles in the London clay, and from the coconuts and spices found in the isle of Sheppey, that at the period when our older tertiary strata were formed, the climate was hot enough for the quadrumanous tribe, we nevertheless could not hope to discover any of their skeletons until we had made considerable progress in ascertaining what were the contemporary pachydermata[14]; and not one of these, as we have already remarked, has been discovered as yet in any strata of this epoch in England.[15]

It is, therefore, clear, that there is no foundation in geological facts, for the popular theory of the successive development of the animal and vegetable world, from the simplest to the most perfect forms; and we shall now proceed to consider another question, whether the recent origin of man lends any support to the same doctrine, or how far the influence of man may be considered as such a deviation from the analogy of the order of things previously established, as to weaken our confidence in the uniformity of the course of nature. We need not dwell on the proofs of the low antiquity of our species, for it is not controverted by any geologist; indeed, the real difficulty which we experience consists in tracing back the signs of man's existence on the Earth to that comparatively modern period when species, now his contemporaries, began to predominate. If there be a difference of opinion respecting the occurrence in certain deposits of the remains of man and his works, it is always in reference to strata confessedly of the most modern order; and it is never pretended that our race co-existed with assemblages of animals and plants, of which *all the species* are extinct. From the concurrent testimony of history and tradition, we learn that parts of Europe, now the most fertile and most completely subjected to the dominion of man, were, within less than three thousand years, covered with forests, and the abode of wild beasts. The archives of nature are in perfect accordance with historical records; and when we lay open the most superficial covering of peat, we sometimes find therein the canoes of the savage, together with huge antlers of the wild stag, or horns of the wild bull. Of caves now open to the day in various parts of Europe, the bones of large beasts of prey occur in abundance; and they indicate, that at periods extremely modern in the history of the globe, the ascendancy of man, if he existed at all, had scarcely been felt by the brutes . . .

## NOTES

1. Playfair, after admitting the extinction of some species, says, "The inhabitants of the globe, then, like all other parts of it, are subject to change. It is not only the individual that perishes, but whole *species,* and even perhaps *genera,* are extinguished."—"A change in the animal kingdom seems to be a *part of the order of nature,* and is visible in

instances to which human power can not have extended."—*Illustrations of the Hutton-ian Theory*, §413.

2. Sir H. Davy, Consolations in Travel, Dialogue 3, "The Unknown." Vol. 1.

3. Plants of an inferior degree of organization to Coniferae, some of which they very much resemble in foliage, but all recent species are infinitely smaller. Many of the fossil species are as gigantic as recent coniferae. Their mode of reproduction is analogous to that of ferns. In English they are called club-mosses, generally found in mountainous heaths in the north of England.

4. Fragments of dicotyledonous wood which have evidently belonged to at least two different species of trees have been obtained from the coal-field of Fife, by Dr. Fleming, of Flisk, and the same gentleman has shown me a large dicotyledonous stem which he procured from the graywacke of Cork. See a memoir by Dr. Fleming on the neighborhood of Cork (Trans. of Wern. Soc. Edin.). I am informed also by Dr. Buckland, that he has received from the coal-field of Northumberland another specimen of dicotyledonous wood, which is now in the Oxford Museum.

5. A German name, generally adopted by geologists for the lowest members of the secondary strata, consisting of sandstone and slate, and which form the chief part of what are termed by some geologists the transition rocks. The rock is very often of a grey color, hence the name, *grau* being German for grey, and *wacke* being a provincial miner's term.

6. Numerous scales of fish have been found by Dr. Fleming in quarries of the old red sandstone at Clashbinnie in Perthshire, where I have myself collected them. These beds are decidedly older than the coal and mountain limestone of Fifeshire.

7. Any animal belonging to the lizard tribe.

8. I do not insist on the abundant occurrence of the scales of a tortoise nearly allied to Trionyx, in the bituminous schists [slate] of Caithness, and in the same formation in the Orkneys in Scotland, as another example of a fossil reptile in rocks as old as the carboniferous series; because the geological position of those schists is not yet determined with precision . . . The numerous fish, and the tortoise of Caithness, are certainly in strata older than the lias [a provincial name . . . for a particular kind of limestone, which being characterized, together with its associated beds, by peculiar fossils, is formed in this work into a particular group of the secondary strata], for that rock rests upon them uncomfortably; but as the strata between the schists and the granite contain no organic remains, and as no fossils of the carboniferous era have yet been found in the Caithness beds, the relative date of the tortoise cannot be determined with confidence. It might possibly be of the age of our magnesian limestone [an extensive series of beds lying in geological position, immediately above the coal-measures, so called because the limestone, the provincial member of the series, contains much of the earth magnesia as a constituent part]. See Geol. Trans. second series, vol. iii., part 1, p. 144, and for a representation of the scales of the Tnionyx, plate 16 of the same part.

9. I have seen in the collection of Dr. Fleming, the teeth of carnivorous fish from the mountain limestone of Fife, which alternates with the coal.

10. A limestone, forming a characteristic feature of a group of the secondary rock . . . so named because it is composed of rounded particles, like the roe or eggs of a fish.

11. On the authority of Dr. Buckland. Trans. Geol. Soc. vol. I, part 2, second series, p. 394.

12. The mammiferous remains of the Stonesfield slate, near Oxford, consist of three or perhaps four jaws, one of which, now in the Oxford Museum, has been examined by M. Cuvier, and pronounced to belong to a species of Didelphis. Another of these

valuable fossils in the possession of my friend Mr. Broderip, appears to be not only specifically, but generically distinct, from that shown to M. Cuvier. See Observations on the Jaw of a fossil Mammiferous Animal found in the Stonesfield Slate, by W. J. Broderip, Esq., Sec. G.S., F.R.S., F.L.S., etc., Zool. Journ., vol. iii. p. 408; 1827.

13. Faluns, in the language of the miners, is the sudden interruption of the continuity of strata in the same place, accompanied by a crack or fissure varying in width from a mere line to several feet, which is generally filled with broken stone, clay, etc., and such a displacement that the separated portions of the once continuous strata occupy different levels.

14. An order of quadrupeds, including the elephant, rhinoceros, horse, pig, etc., distinguished by having thick skins.

15. The only exception of which I have heard is the tooth of an Anoplotherium, mentioned by Dr. Buckland as having been found in the collection of Mr. Allan, labeled "Binstead, Isle of Wight." The quarries of Binstead are entirely in the lower fresh water formation, and such is undoubtedly the geological position in which we might look for the bones of such an animal. My friend Mr. Allan has shown me this tooth, to which, unfortunately, none of the matrix [a portion of rock] is attached, so that it is still open to a captious skeptic to suspect that a Parisian fossil was so ticketed by mistake.

## FURTHER READING

Gould, Stephen Jay. 1987. *Time's Arrow, Time's Cycle: Myth and Metaphor in the Discovery of Geological Time.* Cambridge: Harvard University Press.

Laudan, Rachel. 1982. "The Role of Methodology in Lyell's Science." *Studies in the History and Philosophy of Science* 13: 215–249.

Oldroyd, David R. 1996. *Thinking About the Earth: A History of Ideas in Geology.* Cambridge: Harvard University Press.

Rudwick, Martin. 1988. *The Great Devonian Controversy: The Shaping of Scientific Knowledge Among Gentlemenly Specialists.* Chicago: University of Chicago Press.

# Taking the Measure of Electricity

## Michael Faraday (1791–1867)

*In the wake of Oersted's announcement of the discovery of electromagnetism, editors of scientific journals were inundated with articles on the phenomenon. In particular, scientists were excited about the prospect of using this new effect to obtain continuous rotations from an electric current; that is, to produce an electric motor. Michael Faraday (1791–1867) was carried away by the hubbub surrounding Oersted's experiment. In 1821, he was invited to write a brief historical survey of the evolution of electromagnetism. He used the occasion to repeat systematically almost all of the previous experiments in electromagnetism and to consider the merits of the theories that had been proposed to account for the phenomenon.*

*Oersted's compass showed that electric current was not traversing the wire end to end in a straight line but was instead circling the wire. Faraday set up a simple experiment of his own, showing in September of that year that a wire could be made to move round a fixed magnet through the use of an electric current, and that a magnet could be made to move round a fixed wire. Faraday's electromagnetic rotations quickly swept Europe as a new and important discovery, establishing his reputation as a scientist.*

*Faraday's work occasioned a nasty row with Humphrey Davy, who claimed that Faraday had appropriated the idea for the experiment from him. The allegation was a difficult one Faraday. Davy's public lectures at the Royal Institution had introduced Faraday, at the time an apprenticing book-binder, to the world of science. Davy had taken Faraday on as his assistant at the Royal Institution in March 1813 when Davy had been temporarily blinded by an explosion involving chloride of nitrogen, a very unstable substance. Though Faraday had no formal education, he was invited to travel with Davy on a trip to Europe, where he was introduced to many of the leading scientific figures of his day.*

*Although he was stung by Davy's allegation, it was not damaging, since Faraday's electromagnetic rotations was just one of a series of important contributions to science. In 1833, he embarked on a series of experiments on the conduction of electricity in liquids, which exploited the fact that electric currents flow easily through water solutions*

*Source:* Michael Faraday. 1834. "On Electrochemical Decomposition." In *Philosophical Transactions of the Royal Society,* pp. 118–126. Reprinted in Faraday, *Experimental Researches in Electricity.* London: Taylor & Francis, 1839, vol. 1, pp. 127–164.

*of acids, alkalis, and the salts that they make. No accurate methods were available at the time for measuring how much electricity any given source produced; as one might expect, scientists could not say whether different sources of electricity would produce the same effects.*

*In order to address this issue, Faraday designed a simple apparatus, consisting of a glass tube pierced by two electrodes, terminating in a test tube supported vertically at the top of the globe; in use, the globe and tube would be filled with tap water. When the two terminals on either side of the globe were connected to an electrical source, a current passed through the water, converting it into hydrogen and oxygen, which collected as gases in the top of the test tube. The amount of gas produced was shown by the movement of the water down the tube; assuming that the volume of water electrolyzed was proportional to the amount of electricity passed through it, Faraday was able to compare different sources of electricity. In this way, he developed a more precise definition of the subject of electrochemistry, introducing the terms "electrolysis," "electrolyte," "electrode," "ion," "anode," "cation," and "cathode"—all now household names. He discovered the exact proportions in which various elements were set free in electrolytic decomposition by a standard current, and showed that the amount of each element set free was associated with a precise and constant quantity of electricity.*

## PRELIMINARY

The theory which I believe to be a true expression of the facts of electrochemical decomposition, and which I have therefore detailed in a former series of these Researches, is so much at variance with those previously advanced that I find the greatest difficulty in stating results, as I think, correctly, while limited to the use of terms which are current with a certain accepted meaning. Of this kind is the term *pole,* with its prefixes of positive and negative, and the attached ideas of attraction and repulsion. The general phraseology is that the positive pole *attracts* oxygen, acids, etc., or more cautiously, that it *determines* their evolution upon its surface; and that the negative pole acts in an equal manner upon hydrogen, combustibles, metals, and bases. According to my view, the determining force is *not* at the poles, but within the body under decomposition; and the oxygen and acids are rendered at the *negative* extremity of that body, while hydrogen, metals, etc., are evolved at the *positive* extremity.

To avoid, therefore, confusion and circumlocution, and for the sake of greater precision of expression than I can otherwise obtain, I have deliberately considered the subject with two friends, and with their assistance and concurrence in framing them, I propose henceforward using certain other terms, which I will now define. The *poles,* as they are usually called, are only the doors or ways by which the electric current passes into and out of the decomposing body; and they of course, when in contact with that body, are the limits of its extent in the direction of the current. The term has been generally applied to the metal surfaces in contact with the decomposing substance; but whether philosophers generally would also apply it to the surfaces of air and water, against which I have effected electrochemical decomposition, is subject to doubt. In place of the term *pole,* I propose using that of *electrode,* and I mean thereby that substance, or rather surface, whether of air, water, metal, or any other body, which bounds the extent of the decomposing matter in the direction of the electric current.

The surfaces at which, according to common phraseology, the electric current enters and leaves a decomposing body are most important places of action, and require to be distinguished apart from the poles, with which they are mostly, and the electrodes, with which they are always, in contact . . . The *anode* is therefore that surface at which the electric current, according to our present expression, enters: it is the *negative* extremity of the decomposing body; is where *oxygen*, chlorine, acids, etc., are evolved; and is against or opposite the positive electrode. The *cathode* is that surface at which the current leaves the decomposing body, and is its *positive* extremity; the combustible bodies, metals, alkalies, and bases are evolved there, and it is in contact with the negative electrode.

I shall have occasion in these Researches, also, to class bodies together according to certain relations derived from their electrical actions; and wishing to express those relations without at the same time involving the expression of any hypothetical views, I intend using the following names and terms. Many bodies are decomposed directly by the electric current, their elements being set free; these I propose to call *electrolytes* . . .

Finally, I require a term to express those bodies which can pass to the *electrodes*, or, as they are usually called, the poles. Substances are frequently spoken of as being *electro-negative* or *electro-positive*, according as they go under the supposed influence of a direct attraction to the positive or negative pole. But these terms are much too significant for the use to which I should have to put them; for, though the meanings are perhaps right, they are only hypothetical, and may be wrong; and then, through a very imperceptible, but still very dangerous, because continual, influence, they do great injury to science by contracting and limiting the habitual views of those engaged in pursuing it. I propose to distinguish such bodies by calling those *anions* which go to the anode of the decomposing body; and those passing to the *cathode, cations* and when I have occasion to speak of these together, I shall call them *ions*. Thus, the chloride of lead is an *electrolyte*, and when *electrolyzed* evolves the two *ions*, chlorine and lead, the former being an *anion*, and the latter a *cation*.

These terms, being once well defined, will, I hope, in their use enable me to avoid much paraphrasing and ambiguity of expression. I do not mean to press them into service more frequently than will be required, for I am fully aware that names are one thing and science another.

It will be well understood that I am giving no option respecting the nature of the electric current now, beyond what I have done on former occasions; and that though I speak of the current as proceeding from the parts which are positive to those which are negative, it is merely in accordance with the conventional, though in some degree tacit, agreement entered into by scientific men, that they may have a constant, certain, and definite means of referring to the direction of the forces of that current . . .

## ON A NEW MEASURER OF VOLTA-ELECTRICITY

I have already said, when engaged in reducing common [static] and voltaic electricity to one standard of measurement, and again when introducing my theory of electrochemical decomposition, that the chemical decomposing action of a current *is constant for a constant quantity of electricity*, notwithstanding the greatest variations in its sources, in its intensity, in the size of the electrodes used, in the nature of the conductors (or non-conductors) through which it is passed, or in other circumstances. The conclusive proofs of the truth of these statements shall be given almost immediately.

I endeavored upon this law to construct an instrument which should measure out the electricity passing through it, and which, being interposed in the course of the current used in any particular experiment, should serve at pleasure, either as a *comparative standard* of effect or as a *positive measurer* of this subtle agent.

There is no substance better fitted, under ordinary circumstances, to be the indicating body in such an instrument as water; for it is decomposed with facility when rendered a better conductor by the addition of acids or salt: its elements may in numerous cases be obtained and collected without any embarrassment from secondary action, and, being gaseous, they are in the best physical condition for separation and measurement. Water, therefore, acidulated by sulfuric acid, is the substance I shall generally refer to, although it may become expedient in peculiar cases of forms of experiment to use other bodies.

The first precaution needed in the construction of the instrument was to avoid the recombination of the evolved gases, and effect which the positive electrode has been found so capable of producing. For this purpose various forms of decomposing apparatus were used. The first consisted of straight tubes, each containing a plate and wire of platina [platinum] soldered together by gold, and fixed hermetically in the glass at the closed extremity of the tube (Fig. 1). The tubes were about 8 inches long, 0.7 of an inch in diameter, and graduated. The platina were about an inch long, as wide as the tubes would permit, and adjusted as near to the mouths of the tubes as was consistent with the safe collection of the gases evolved. In certain cases, where it was required to evolve the elements upon as small a surface as possible, the metallic extremity, instead of being a plate, consisted of the wire bent into the form of a ring (Fig. 2). When these tubes were used as measurers, they were filled with dilute sulfuric acid, inverted in a basin of the same liquid (Fig. 3), and placed in an inclined position, with their mouths near to each other, that as little decomposing matter should intervene as possible; and also, in

**PLATE 30** Michael Faraday lecturing at the Royal Institution before members of the Royal family.

such a direction that the platina plates should be in vertical planes.

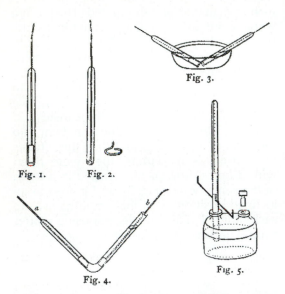

Fig. 1.    Fig. 2.

Fig. 3.

Fig. 4.

Fig. 5.

Another form of apparatus is that delineated (Fig. 4). The tube is bent in the middle; one end is closed; in that end is fixed a wire and plate, *a,* proceeding so far downwards, that, when in the position figured, it shall be as near angle as possible, consistently with the collection at the closed extremity of the tube, of all the gas evolved against it. The plane of this plate is also perpendicular. The other metallic termination, *b,* is introduced at the time decomposition is to be effected, being brought as near the angle as possible, without causing any gas to pass from it towards the closed end of the instrument. The gas evolved against it is allowed to escape.[a]

The third form of apparatus contains both electrodes in the same tube; the transmission, therefore, of the electricity and the consequent decomposition is far more rapid than in the separate tubes. The resulting gas is the sum of the portions evolved at the two electrodes, and the instrument is better adapted than either of the former as a mea-

[a]The gas that is collected in the closed tube is a measure of the total charge. [B.]

surer of the quantity of voltaic electricity transmitted in ordinary cases. It consists of a straight tube (Fig. 5) closed at the upper extremity and graduated, through the sides of which pass platina wires (being fused into the glass), which are connected with two plates within. The tube is fitted by grinding into one mouth of a double-necked bottle. If the latter be one-half or two-thirds full of dilute sulfuric acid, it will, upon an inclination of the whole, flow into the tube and fill it. When an electric current is passed through the instrument, the gases evolved against the plates collect in the upper portion of the tube and are not subject to the recombining power of the platina . . .

I consider the foregoing investigation as sufficient to prove the very extraordinary and important principle with respect to water, *that when subjected to the influence of the electric current, a quantity of it is decomposed exactly proportionate to the quantity of electricity which has passed,* notwithstanding the thousand variations in the conditions and circumstances under which it may at the time be placed. . . .

The instrument offers the only *actual measurer* of voltaic electricity which we at present possess. For without being at all affected by variations in time or intensity, or alterations in the current itself, of any kind, or from any cause, or even of intermissions of action, it takes note with accuracy of the quantity of electricity which has passed through it, and reveals the quantity by inspection; I have therefore named it a VOLTA-ELECTROMETER . . .

In the preceding cases, except the first, the water is believed to be inactive; but to avoid any ambiguity arising from its presence, I sought for substances from which it should be absent altogether; and taking advantage of the law of conduction[1] already developed, I soon found abundance, among which *protochloride of tin* was first subjected to decomposition in the following manner: A piece of platina wire had one extremity coiled up into a small knob, and having been carefully weighed, was sealed hermetically into a piece of bottle glass, so that the knob should be at the bottom of the tube within (Fig. 9). The tube was suspended by a piece

Fig. 9.

of platina wire, so that the heat of a spirit-lamp could be applied to it. Recently fused protochloride of tin was introduced in sufficient quantity to occupy, when melted, about one-half of the tube; the wire of the tube was connected with a volta-electrometer, which was itself connected with the negative end of a voltaic battery: and a platina wire connected with the positive end of the same battery was dipped into the fused chloride in the tube; being, however, so bent that it could not by any shake of the hand or apparatus touch the negative electrode at the bottom of the vessel. The whole arrangement is delineated in Fig. 10.

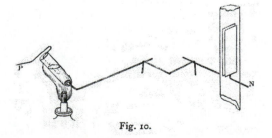

Fig. 10.

Under these circumstances the chloride of tin was decomposed: the chlorine evolved at the positive electrode formed bichloride of tin, which passes away in fumes, and the tin evolved at the negative electrode combined with the platina, forming an alloy, fusible at the temperature to which the tube was subjected, and therefore never occasioning metallic communication through the decomposing chloride. When the experiment had been continued so long as to yield a reasonable quantity of gas in the volta-electrometer, the battery connection was broken, the positive electrode removed, and the tube and remaining chloride allowed to cool. When cold, the tube was broken open, the rest of the chloride and the glass being easily separable from the platina wire and its button of alloy. The latter when washed was then reweighed, and the increase gave the weight of the tin reduced.

I give the particular results of one experiment, in illustration of the mode adopted in this and others, the results of which I shall have occasion to quote. The negative electrode weighed at first 20 grains; after the experiment it, with its button of alloy, weighed 23.2 grains. The tin evolved by the electric current at the *cathode* weighed therefore 3.2 grains. The quantity of oxygen and hydrogen collected in the volta-electrometer = 3.85 cubic inches. As 100 cubic inches of oxygen and hydrogen, in the proportions to form water, may be considered as weighing 12.92 grains, the 3.85 cubic inches would weigh 0.49742 of a grain; that being, therefore, the weight of water decomposed by the same electric current as was able to decompose such weight of protochloride of tin as could yield 3.2 grains of metal. Now 0.49742 : 3.2 :: 9 the equivalent of water is to 57.9, which should therefore be the equivalent of tin, if the experiment had been made without error, and if the electrochemical decomposition *is in this case also definite.* In some chemical works 58 is given as the chemical equivalent of tin, in others 57.9. Both are so near to the result of the experiment, and the experiment itself is so subject to slight causes of variation (as from the absorption of gas in the volta-electrometer), that the numbers leave little doubt of the applicability of the *law of definite action* in this and all similar cases of electro-decomposition.

It is not often I have obtained an accordance in numbers so near as I have just quoted. Four experiments were made on the protochloride of tin; the quantities of gas evolved in the volta-electometer being from 2.05 to 10.29 cubic inches. The average of the four experiments gave 58.43 as the electrochemical equivalent for tin.

The chloride remaining after the experiment was pure protochloride of tin; and no one can doubt for a moment that the equivalent of chlorine had been evolved at the *anode*, and, having formed bi-chloride of tin as a secondary result, had passed away.

*Chloride of lead* was experimented upon in a manner exactly similar, except that a change was made in the nature of the positive electrode; for as the chlorine evolved at the *anode* forms no perchloride of lead, but acts directly upon the platina, it produces, if that metal be used, a solution of chloride of platina in the chloride of lead; in consequence of which a portion of platina can pass to the *cathode,* and would then produce a vitiated result. I therefore sought for, and found in plumbago, another substance which could be used safely as the positive electrode in such bodies as chlorides, iodides, etc. The chlorine or iodine does not act upon it, but is evolved in the free state; and the plumbago has no reaction, under the circumstances, upon the fused chloride or iodide in which it is plunged. Even if a few particles of plumbago should separate by the heat or the mechanical action of the evolved gas, they can do no harm in the chloride.

The mean of three experiments gave the number of 100.85 as the equivalent of lead. The chemical equivalent is 103.5. The deficiency in my experiments I attribute to the solution of part of the gas in the volta-electrometer; but the results leave no doubt on my mind that both the lead and the chlorine are, in this case, evolved in *definite quantities* by the action of a given quantity of electricity.

## NOTES

1. The law referred to asserts "the general assumption of conducting power by bodies as soon as they pass from the solid to the liquid state."

## FURTHER READING

Bowers, Brian. 1974. *Michael Faraday and Electricity.* London: Priority.
Hamilton, James. 2002. *Faraday: The Life.* London: HarperCollins.
Tricker, R. A. R. 1966. *The Contributions of Faraday and Maxwell to Electrical Science.* New York: Pergamon Press.

# Lines of Force

## Michael Faraday (1791–1867)

*Oersted had generated magnetism from electricity and for ten years Faraday dedicated himself to the hunt for the reciprocal condition, namely, the generation of electricity from a magnetic source. Faraday considered carefully what shape an electromagnet should have in order for it to be very strong and to act powerfully on a nearby circuit when it was suddenly magnetized. He settled on a thick ring and had one six inches in diameter and seven-eighths of an inch thick cast in iron. He wound on it two sets of coils, one on each half of the ring. One coil was connected to a galvanometer, the other to a battery. Faraday thought that the current in the first coil of wire might cause a current in the second coil. The galvanometer would measure the presence of the second current and tell the story. The experimental design was sound (it was the first transformer, which is now universally used to convert low voltages to high and vice versa), but it contained a surprise: Despite the steady magnetic force set up in the iron ring, no steady electric current ran through the second coil. Instead, a flash of current ran through the second coil when Faraday closed the circuit, signaled by a feeble jump on the galvanometer. When he opened the circuit again, another flash of current, signaled by a second feeble galvanometer jump. Faraday concluded that the battery current through the one wire induced a similar current through the other wire; but that it continued for an instant only, and partook of the nature more of the electric wave from a Leyden jar than of the current from a voltaic battery.*

*Faraday devised a phenomenological model to explain this result. He had noticed that if iron filings are sprinkled on a paper that is held over a strong magnet, the filings would arrange themselves in distinct patterns, along what Faraday concluded were the magnet's lines of force. He conceived the idea that an electric current forms a kind of magnetic field radiating out in all directions from its source. When he closed the circuit in his experiment, lines of force radiated out, but the second coil of wire cut across them. When that happened, a current was induced in the second coil. When he opened the circuit, the lines of force collapsed back and again the second wire cut through their path and a current was induced.*

*During one of his enormously popular lectures at the Royal Institution in 1831, Faraday demonstrated the lines of force in another way. He took a coil of wire and*

*Source:* M. Faraday. 1846. "Thoughts on Ray Vibrations." In *Experimental Researches,* vol. 3, pp. 447–452.

*moved a magnet into the coil. The needle of the galvanometer attached to the wire swing, then stopped, when the movement of the magnet stopped. When he moved the magnet out of the coil, again the galvanometer registered. If he moved the coil of wire over the magnet, presence of a current showed up. If he let the magnet just sit motionless inside the coil of wire, no action registered on the galvanometer; there was no current. Faraday had discovered the principle of electromagnetic induction. That is, he had discovered the basic principle of the electrical generator or dynamo—the principle on which all modern electrical machines are built. Few discoveries have had a more far-reaching effect.*

*In an extraordinary lecture at the Royal Institution in 1846, Faraday suggested that the lines of force were simply strains in space itself. He even put forward the far-reaching idea that light was nothing but the vibration of electromagnetic lines of force. Faraday was also led to challenge the standard electrical theories of action at a distance. When static electricity was discharged into the air through a piece of blotting paper soaked with an electrolyte, chemical decomposition took place. Where were the "poles" in such a situation which could account for the dissociation of the chemical molecules? All that was necessary was the passage of electricity and this led Faraday to suggest that electricity could not be a material substance. Rather, electricity was a force, which, in an electrolyte, acted by the buildup and breakdown of intramolecular tensions. The "current" was the vibration created by the rupture and re-establishment of chemical bonds caused by the migration of ions through the solution.*

At your request I will endeavor to convey to you a notion of that which I ventured to say at the close of the last Friday evening Meeting, incidental to the account I gave of Wheatstone's[a] electro-magnetic chronoscope; but from first to last understand that I merely threw out as matter for speculation the vague impressions of my mind, for I gave nothing as the result of sufficient consideration, or as the settled conviction, or even probable conclusion at which I had arrived.

The point intended to be set forth for consideration of the hearers was whether it was not possible that the vibrations which in a certain theory are assumed to account for radiation and radiant phenomena may not occur in the lines of force which connect particles, and consequently masses of matter together; a notion which, as far as it is admitted, will dispense with the aether, which, in another view is supposed to be the medium in which these vibrations take place.

You are aware of the speculation which I some time since uttered respecting that view of the nature of matter which considers its ultimate atoms as centers of force, and not as so many little bodies surrounded by forces, the bodies being considered in the abstract as independent of the forces and capable of existing without them. In the latter view, these little particles have a definite form and a certain limited size; in the former view such is not the case, for that which represents size may be considered as extending to any distance to which the lines of force of the particle extend: The particle indeed is supposed to exist only by these forces, and where they are it is. The consideration of matter under this view gradually led me to look at the lines of force as being perhaps the seat of the vibrations of radiant phenomena.

Another consideration bearing conjointly on the hypothetical view both of matter and radiation arises from the comparison of the velocities with which the radiant action and certain powers of matter are transmitted.

[a]A prolific inventor, Charles Wheatstone (1802–1875) built along with William Cooke (1806–1879) the first practical electric telegraph system. His electromagnetic chronoscope was designed to measure the speed of the electric current. [B.]

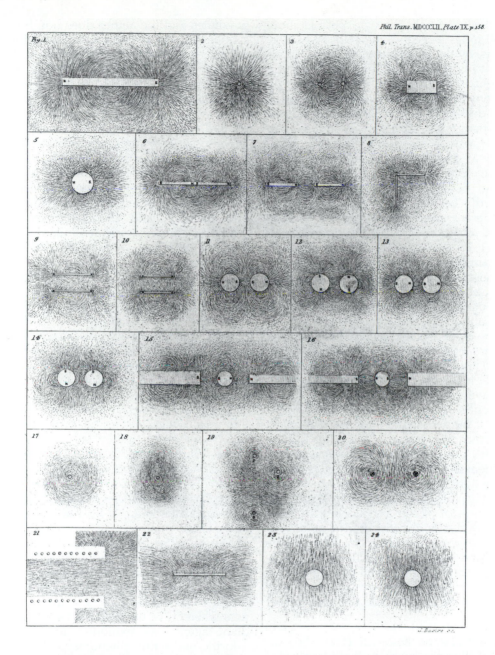

Phil. Trans. MDCCCLII. Plate IX. p 158

**PLATE 31**  Drawing of magnetic lines of force as delineated by iron filings. Figure 1 illustrates the pattern assumed about a bar magnet; figure 2 the pattern over a pole; figure 3 the pattern between contrary poles; figure 4 the pattern with a short magnet; and figure 5 the pattern with a magnetized steel disk. Figures 6 to 13 illustrate the patterns when the magnetizing force is varied. From *Philosophical Transactions of the Royal Society* (London, 1852). Courtesy of the Thomas Fisher Rare Book Library, University of Toronto (Toronto, Canada).

The velocity of light through space is about 190,000 miles a second; the velocity of electricity is, by the experiments of Wheatstone, shown to be as great as this, if not greater: The light is supposed to be transmitted by vibrations through an aether which is, so to speak, destitute of gravitation, but infinite in elasticity; the electricity is transmitted through a small metallic wire, and is often viewed as transmitted by vibrations also. That the electric transference depends on the forces or powers of the matter of the wire can hardly be doubted, when we consider the different conductibility of the various metallic and other bodies; the means of affecting it by heat or cold; the way in which conducting bodies by combination enter into the constitution of non-conducting substances, and the contrary; and the actual existence of one elementary body, carbon, both in the conducting and non-conducting state. The power of electric conduction (being a transmission of force equal in velocity to that of light) appears to be tied up in and dependent upon the properties of the matter, and is, as it were, existent in them.

I suppose we may compare together the matter of the aether and ordinary matter (as, for instance, the copper of the wire through which the electricity is conducted), and consider them as alike in their essential constitution; i.e., either as both composed of little nuclei, considered in the abstract as matter, and of force or power associated with these nuclei, or else both consisting of mere centers of force, according to Boscovich's theory[b] and the view put forth in my speculation; for there is no reason to assume that the nuclei are more requisite in the one case than in the other. It is true that the copper

[b]Ruggero Giuseppe Boscovich (1711–1787) argued that all matter is composed of nonextended mass "points" which exert forces on each other, varying with the distance between them. At very short distances, a strong force of repulsion is in operation. As the distance increases, the force alternates between attraction and repulsion, finally following the inverse square law of attraction for large distances. [B.]

gravitates and the aether does not; but that cannot indicate the presence of nuclei in the copper more than in the aether, for of all the powers of matter gravitation is the one in which the force extends to the greatest possible distance from the supposed nucleus, being infinite in relation to the size of the latter, and reducing that nucleus to a mere center of force. The smallest atom of matter on the Earth acts directly on the smallest atom of matter in the Sun, though they are 95,000,000 miles apart; further, atoms which, to our knowledge, are at least nineteen times that distance, and indeed, in cometary masses, far more, are in a similar way tied together by the lines of force extending from and belonging to each. What is there in the condition of the particles of the supposed aether, if there be even only *one* such particle between us and the Sun, that can in subtlety and extent compare to this?

Let us not be confused by the *ponderability* and *gravitation* of heavy matter, as if they proved the presence of the abstract nuclei; these are due not to the nuclei, but to the force super-added to them, if the nuclei exist at all, and, if the *aether* particles be without this force, which according to the assumption is the case, then they are more material, in the abstract sense, than the matter of this our globe; for matter, according to the assumption, being made up of nuclei and force, the aether particles have in this respect proportionately more of the nucleus and less of the force.

On the other hand, the infinite elasticity assumed as belonging to the particles of the aether, is as striking and positive a force of it as gravity is of ponderable particles, and produces in its way effects as great; in witness whereof we have all the varieties of radiant agency as exhibited in luminous, calorific, and actinic phenomena.

Perhaps I am in error in thinking the idea generally formed of the aether is that its nuclei are almost infinitely small, and that such force as it has, namely its elasticity, is almost infinitely intense. But if such be the received notion, what then is left in the aether but force or centers of force? As gravitation and solidity do not belong to it, perhaps many may admit this conclusion; but what are gravitation and solidity? Certainly not the weight and contact of the abstract nuclei. The one is the consequence of an *attractive* force, which can act at distances as great as the mind of man can estimate or conceive; and the other is the consequence of a *repulsive* force, which forbids forever the contact or touch of any two nuclei; so that these powers or properties should not in any degree lead those persons who conceive of the aether as a thing consisting of force only, to think any otherwise of ponderable matter, except that it has more and other *forces* associated with it than the aether has.

In experimental philosophy we can, by the phenomena presented, recognize various kinds of lines of force; thus there are the lines of gravitating force, those of electro-static induction, those of magnetic action, and others partaking of a dynamic character might be perhaps included. The lines of electric and magnetic action are by many considered as exerted through space like the lines of gravitating force. For my own part, I incline to believe that when there are intervening particles of matter (being themselves only centers of force), they take part in carrying on the force through the line, but that when there are none, the line proceeds through space. Whatever the view adopted respecting them may be, we can, at all events, affect these lines of force in a manner which may be conceived as partaking of the nature of a shake or lateral vibration. For suppose two bodies, A B, distant from each other and under mutual action, and therefore connected by lines of force, and let us fix our attention upon one resultant of force, having an invariable direction as regards space; if one of the bodies move in the least degree right or left, or if its power be shifted for a moment within the mass (neither of these cases being difficult to realize if A and B be either electric or magnetic bodies), then an effect equivalent to a lateral disturbance will take place in the resultant upon which we are fixing our attention; for, either it will increase in force while the neighboring re-sultants are diminishing, or it will fall in force as they are increasing.

It may be asked, what lines of force are there in nature which are fitted to convey such an action and supply for the vibrating theory the place of the aether? I do not pretend to answer this question with any confidence; all I can say is that I do not perceive in any part of space, whether (to use the common phrase) vacant or filled with matter, anything but forces and the lines in which they are exerted. The lines of weight or gravitating force are, certainly, extensive enough to answer in this respect any demand made upon them by radiant phenomena; and so, probably, are the lines of magnetic force: and then who can forget that Mossotti has shown that gravitation, aggregation, electric force, and electro-chemical action may all have one common connection or origin; and so, in their actions at a distance, may have in common that infinite scope which some of these actions are known to possess?

The view which I am so bold as to put forth considers, therefore, radiation as a high species of vibration in the lines of force which are known to connect particles and also masses of matter together. It endeavors to dismiss the aether, but not the vibration. The kind of vibration which, I believe, can alone account for the wonderful, varied, and beautiful phenomena of polarization, is not the same as that which occurs on the surface of disturbed water, or the waves of sound in gases or liquids, for the vibrations in these cases are direct, or to and from the center of action, whereas the former are lateral. It seems to me that the resultant of two or more lines of force is in an apt condition for that action which may be considered as equivalent to a *lateral* vibration; whereas a uniform medium, like the aether, does not appear apt, or more apt than air or water.

The occurrence of a change at one end of a line of force easily suggests a consequent change at the other. The propagation of light, and therefore probably of all radiant action, occupies *time*; and, that a vibration of the line of force should account for the phenomena of radiation, it is necessary that such vibration should occupy time also. I am not aware whether there are any data by which it has been, or could be, ascertained whether such a power as gravitation acts without occupying time, or whether lines of force being already in existence, such a lateral disturbance of them at one end as I have suggested above, would require time, or must of necessity be felt instantly at the other end.

As to that condition of the lines of force which represents the assumed high elasticity of the aether, it cannot in this respect be deficient: The question here seems rather to be whether the lines are sluggish enough in their action to render them equivalent to the aether in respect of the time known experimentally to be occupied in the transmission of radiant force.

The aether is assumed as pervading all bodies as well as space: In the view now set forth, it is the forces of the atomic centers which pervade (and make) all bodies, and also penetrate all space. As regards space, the difference is that the aether presents successive parts or centers of action, and the present supposition only lines of action; as regards matter, the difference is that the aether lies between the particles and so carries on the vibrations, while as respects the supposition, it is by the lines of force between the centers of the particles that the vibration is continued. As to the difference in intensity of action within matter under the two views, I suppose it will be very difficult to draw any conclusion, for when we take the simplest state of common matter and that which most nearly causes it to approximate to the condition of the aether, namely, the state of rare gas, how soon do we find in its elasticity and the mutual repulsion of its particles, a departure from the law, that the action is inversely as the square of the distance!

And now, my dear Phillips, I must conclude. I do not think I should have allowed these notions to have escaped from me had I not been led unaware, and without previous consideration, by the circumstances of the evening on which I had to appear suddenly and occupy the place of another. Now that I have put them on paper, I feel that I ought to have kept them much longer for study, consideration, and, perhaps, final rejection; and it is only because they are sure to go abroad in one way or another, in consequence of their utterance on that evening, that I give them a shape, if shape it may be called, in this reply to your inquiry. One thing is certain, that any hypothetical view of radiation which is likely to be received or retained as satisfactory, must not much longer comprehend alone certain phenomena of light, but must include those of heat and of actinic influence also, and even the conjoined phenomena of sensible heat and chemical power produced by them. In this respect, a view, which is in some degree founded upon the ordinary forces of matter, may perhaps find a little consideration among the other views that will probably arise. I think it likely that I have made many mistakes in the preceding pages, for even to myself, my ideas on this point appear only as the shadow of a speculation, or as one of those impressions on the mind which are allowable for a time as guides to thought and research. He who labors in experimental inquiries knows how numerous these are, and how often their apparent fitness and beauty vanish before the progress and development of real natural truth.

## FURTHER READING

Williams, L. Pearce. 1966. *The Origins of Field Theory*. New York: Random House.

# The Cell Theory

## Theodor Schwann (1810–1882)

*The idea that cellular formation is a universal principle for the formation of organic substances is one of the pillars of modern biology. A fully formed version of this cell theory was first advanced by Theodor Schwann, a zoologist who opposed vitalism, or the view that life involves some special matter or force that is unique to living things, with his materialist hypothesis that the basic unit of life is made out of simple matter.*

*For most writers of the period, the basic units of animals and plants were fibers and/or vessels. The botanist Matthias Jakob Schleiden (1804–1881) had proposed as early as 1838 that all plant tissue is composed of nucleated cells, and not discrete vesicles. Using the newly introduced achromatic microscope, Schwann extended and generalized Schleiden's suggestion through an examination of a variety of animal tissues. He clearly realized that not all parts of the animal body are not actually cellular, but insisted that they are nevertheless produced by cells or develop out of cells.*

*In the wake of Schwann's work, cell theory made remarkable steps forward when Robert Remak (1815–1865) described cell division in 1841. Where Schwann believed that cell formation occurred exogenously (externally), Remak argued that every cell owes its existence to the division of a pre-existing cell. Applying cell theory to the examination of pathological processes, in 1855 Rudolf Virchow (1821–1902) issued the new dogma* omnis cellula e cellula *(all cells come from cells) on the model of William Harvey's "ex ovo omnia" (all [life] from the egg). Schwann's cellular material, cytoblastema, which he regarded as devoid of structure, was renamed protoplasm, and shown in 1861 by Max Schultze (1825–1874) to have a definite structure.*

*Source:* Schwann, Theodor. 1847. *Mikroskopische untersuchungen uber die ubereinstimmung in der striker und den wachstum der tiere und pflanzen,* Berlin, 1839. Trans. by Henry Smith as *Microscopical Researches into the Accordance in the Structure and Growth of Animals and Plants.* London: The Sydenham Society, pp. 161–166.

When organic nature, animals and plants, is regarded as a whole, in contradistinction to the inorganic kingdom, we do not find that all organisms and all their separate organs are compact masses, but that they are composed of innumerable small particles of a definite form. These elementary particles, however, are subject to the most extraordinary diversity of figure, especially in animals; in plants they are, for the most part or exclusively, cells.[a] This variety in the elementary parts seemed to hold some relation to their more diversified physiological function in animals, so that it might be established as a principle that every diversity in the physiological signification or an organ requires a difference in its elementary particles; and on the contrary, the similarity of two elementary particles seemed to justify the conclusion that they were physiologically similar. It was natural that among the very different forms presented by the elementary particles, there should be some more or less alike, and that they might be divided, according to their similarity of figure, into fibers, which compose a great mass of the bodies of animals, into cells, tubes, globules, etc. The division was, of course, only one of natural history, not expressive of physiological idea, and just as a primitive muscular fiber, for example, might seem to differ from one of areolar tissue, or all fibers from cells, so would there be in like manner a difference, however gradually marked between the different kinds of cells. It seemed as if the organism arranged the molecules in the definite forms exhibited by its different elementary particles, in the way required by its physiological function. It might be expected that there would be similar in those structures which were physiologically identical, and such a mode of development was, indeed, already more or less perfectly known with regard to muscular fibers, blood corpuscles, the ovum, and epithelium cells. The only process common to all of them, however, seemed to be the expansion of their elementary particles after had once assumed their proper form. The manner in which their different elementary particles were first formed appeared to vary very much. In muscular fibers there were globules, which were placed together in rows, and coalesced to form a fiber, whose growth proceeded in the direction of its length. In the blood corpuscles it was a globule, around which a vesicle was formed, and continued to grow; in the case of the ovum, it was a globule, around which a vesicle was developed and continued to grow, and around this again a second vesicle was formed.

The formative process of the cells of plants was clearly explained by the researches of Schleiden,[b] and appeared to be the same in all vegetable cells. So that when plants were regarded as something special, as quite distinct from the animal kingdom, one universal principle of development was observed in all the elementary particles of the vegetable organism, and physiological deductions might be drawn from it with regard to the independent vitality of the individual cells of plants, etc. But when the elementary particles of animals and plants were considered from a common point, the vegetable cells seemed to be merely a separate species, co-ordinate with the different species of animal cells, just as the entire class of cells was co-ordinate with the fibers, etc., and the uniform principle of development in vegetable cells might be explained by the slight physiological difference of their elementary particles.

The object, then, of the present investigation was to show that the mode in which the molecules composing the elementary particles of organisms are combined does not vary according to the physiological signification of

[a]The term "cell" was first introduced in the *Micrographia* (1665) by Robert Hooke in reference to the cavities observed in cork. This meaning persisted through the nineteenth century. The term "cellular tissue," for instance, referred to a tissue with holes in it. [B.]

[b]The work of Matthias Jakob Schleiden (1804–1881), professor of botany at the University of Jena, was focused on plant growth and structure as revealed by the microscope. In 1838, he formulated the cell theory for plants, which was subsequently extended to animals and developed into a fully formed cell theory by Schwann. [B.]

those particles, but that they are everywhere arranged according to the same laws; so that whether a muscular fiber, a nerve tube, an ovum, or a blood corpuscle is to be formed, a corpuscle of a certain form, subject only to some modifications, a cell nucleus is universally generated in the first instance; around this corpuscle a cell is developed, and it is the changes which one or more of these cells undergo that determine the subsequent forms of the elementary particles; in short, that there is one common principle of development for all the elementary particles of organisms.

In order to establish this point it was necessary to trace the progress of development in two given elementary parts, physiologically dissimilar, and to compare them with one another. If these not only completely agreed in growth, but in their mode of generation also, the principle was established that elementary parts, quite distinct in a physiological sense, may be developed according to the same laws. This was the same theme of the first section of this work. The course of development of the cells of cartilage and of the cells of the chorda dorsalis was compared with that of vegetable cells. Were the cells of plants developed merely as infinitely minute vesicles which progressively expand, were the circumstances of their development less characteristic than those pointed out by Schleiden, a comparison, in the sense here required, would scarcely have been possible. We endeavored to prove in the first section that the complicated process of development in the cells of plants recurs in those of cartilage and of the chorda dorsalis. We remarked the similarity in the formation of the cell nucleus, and of its nucleolus in all its modifications, with the nucleus of vegetable cells, and the pre-existence of the cell nucleus and the development of the cell around it, the similar situation of the nucleus in relation to the cell, the growth of cells, and the thickening of their wall during growth, the formation of cells within cells, and the transformation of the cell contents just as in the cells of

plants. Here, then, was a complete accordance in every known stage in the progress of development of two elementary parts which are quite distinct, in a physiological sense, and it was established that the principle of development in two such parts may be the same, and so far as could be ascertained in the cases here compared, it is really the same. But regarding the subject from this point of view we are compelled to prove the universality of this principle of development, and such was the object of the second section. For so long as we admit that there are elementary parts which originate according to entirely different laws, and between which and the cells which have just been compared as to the principle of their development there is no connection, we must presume that there may still be some unknown difference in the laws of the formation of the parts just compared, even though they agree in many points. But, on the contrary, the greater the difference of these parts in form and physiological signification, while they agree in the perceptible phenomena of their mode of formation, the more safely may we assume that all elementary parts and have one and the same fundamental principle of development. It was, in fact, shown that the elementary parts of most tissues, when traced backwards from their state of complete development in their primary condition are only developments of cells, which so far as our observations, still incomplete, extend, seemed to be formed in a similar manner to the cells compared in the first section. As might be expected, according to this principle the cells, in their earliest stage, were almost always furnished with the characteristic nuclei, in some the pre-existence of this nucleus, and the formation of the cell around it was proved, and it was then that the cells began to undergo the various modifications, from which the diverse forms of the elementary parts of animals resulted. Thus the apparent difference in the mode of development of muscular fibers and blood corpuscles, the former originating by the arrangement of globules in rows, the latter

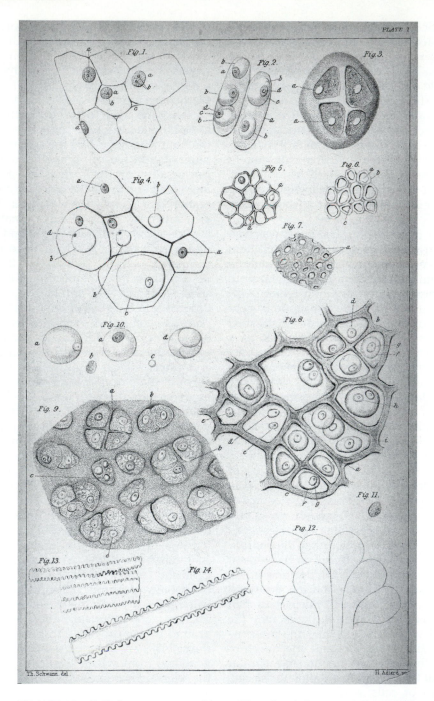

**PLATE 32**   Cellular structures. From Theodor Schwann, *Microscopical Researches into the Accordance in the Structure and Growth of Animals and Plants* (1847).

# EXPLANATION OF THE PLATES.

WHERE no other measurement is given, the figure represents the object magnified about 450 diameters, linear measurement.

## PLATE I.

Fig. 1. Parenchymatous cellular tissue, with cell-nuclei from an onion, magnified 290 times.

2. Matrix of the pollen of Rhipsalis salicornoides.

3. Do. do.

I am indebted to the kindness of Dr. Schleiden for the last two delineations.

4. Cells from the chorda dorsalis of Cyprinus erythrophthalmus.

5. Cartilage from the point of a branchial ray, from the same.

6. Cartilage from the middle of a branchial ray, from the same.

7. Cartilage from the root of a branchial ray, from the same.

8. Branchial cartilage from the larva of Rana esculenta.

9. Cranial cartilage (ethmoid bone) from the larva of Pelobates fuscus.

10. Cells from the crystalline lens of a fœtal pig four inches long.

11. An isolated nucleus of the cells of the crystalline lens.

12. Cells from the crystalline lens of the same fœtus, exhibiting their prolongation into the fibres of the lens.

13. Fibres from the innermost layers of the lens of a pike.

14. Cell from the epidermis of a species of grass.

15

**PLATE 32** Continued.

by the formation of a vesicle around a globule, was reconciled in the fact that muscular fibers are not elementary parts co-ordinate with blood corpuscles, and are like them, vesicles or cells, containing the characteristic cell nucleus, which like the nucleus of the blood corpuscles, is probably formed before the cell. The elementary parts of all tissues are formed of cells in an analogous, though very diversified manner, so that it may be asserted *that there is one universal principle of development for the elementary parts of organisms, however different, and that this principle is the formation of cells.* This is the chief result of the foregoing observations.

The same process of development and transformation of cells within a structureless substance is repeated in the formation of all the organs of an organism, as well as in the formation of new organisms; and the fundamental phenomenon attending the exertion of productive power in organic nature is accordingly as follows: *a structureless substance is present in the first instance, which lies either around or in the interior of cells already existing; and cells are formed in it in accordance with certain laws, which cells become developed in various ways into the elementary parts of organisms.*

The development of the proposition, that there exists one general principle for the formation of all organic productions, and that this principle is the formation of cells, as well as the conclusions which may be drawn from this proposition, may be comprised under the term *cell theory,* using it in its more extended signification, while in a more limited sense, by theory of the cells we understand whatever may be inferred from this proposition with respect to the powers from which these phenomena result.

## FURTHER READINGS

Causey, Gilbert. 1960. *The Cell of Schwann.* Edinburgh: E. & S. Livingstone.

Hughes, Arthur. 1959. *A History of Cytology.* London: Abelard-Schuman.

Gilbert, Scott F., ed. 1991. *A Conceptual History of Modern Embryology.* Cambridge: Cambridge University Press.

# The Survival of the Fittest

## Charles Darwin (1809–1882)

*Armed with a copy of the first volume of Charles Lyell's* Principles of Geology, *in 1831 Charles Darwin boarded HMS* Beagle *and set sail on a five-year voyage of discovery to South America and the Galapagos Islands. He was particularly impressed by the variation found in the finches of the Galapagos Islands, recording fourteen different species, each flourishing in a different region of the islands. After his return to England, Darwin spent the next twenty years assembling a wealth of evidence in favor of an evolutionary account of species. The idea of evolution was not original with Darwin, but he was the first scientist to elaborate a mechanism that was conducive to evolutionary change—the mechanism of natural selection.*

*On his return to England in 1836, Darwin occupied himself with recording his travels and two works in geology that established his reputation as a scientist. Ideas about evolution continued to percolate for more than twenty years. It was only in 1858, however, that Darwin was motivated to place his ideas on evolution before the public, for it was in this year that he received a communication from a comparatively unknown bug-hunter—Alfred Russel Wallace (1823–1913)—that mirrored Darwin's own ideas on the subject. Darwin's celebrated work* On the Origin of Species by Means of Natural Selection of the Preservation of Favored Races in the Struggle for Life *was finally published in 1859, causing a sensation and exhausting its run in a single day. As one might expect, churchmen were deeply opposed to Darwin's theory, but many prominent scientists were disturbed by its implications as well.*

*Darwin continued to publish books that developed his theory of evolution and applied it to new domains, including his* The Descent of Man *(1871), which brought the theory of evolution to bear on the question of human origins. He also prepared five additional editions of the* Origin *over the next fourteen years, making it possible for historians to follow his intellectual development during this period. So extensive were the revisions that only about half of the text from the first edition found its way into the final, sixth edition. The reading here is excerpted from the sixth edition of the* Origin, *in which the term* evolution *and the expression* survival of the fittest *made their appearance.*

---

*Source:* Charles Darwin. 1872. *On The Origin of Species by Means of Natural Selection.* London: John Murray, Albemarle Street, sixth edition, pp. 48–51; 52–55; 58–60; 62–65; 69; 84–85; 85–87; 103–105.

## STRUGGLE FOR EXISTENCE

It has been seen in the last chapter that among organic beings in a state of nature there is some individual variability; indeed I am not aware that this has ever been disputed. It is immaterial for us whether a multitude of doubtful forms be called species or sub-species or varieties; what rank, for instance, the two or three hundred doubtful forms of British plants are entitled to hold, if the existence of any well-marked varieties be admitted. But, the mere existence of individual variability and of some few well-marked varieties, though necessary as the foundation for the work, helps us but little in understanding how species arise in nature. How have all those exquisite adaptations of one part of the organization to another part, and to the conditions of life, and of one organic being to another being, been perfected? We see these beautiful co-adaptations most plainly in the woodpecker and the mistletoe; and only a little less plainly in the humblest parasite which clings to the hairs of a quadruped or feathers of a bird; in the structure of the beetle which dives through the water; in the plumed seed which is wafted by the gentlest breeze; in short, we see beautiful adaptations everywhere and in every part of the organic world.

Again, it may be asked, how is it that varieties, which I have called incipient species, become ultimately converted into good and distinct species which in most cases obviously differ from each other far more than do the varieties of the same species? How do those groups of species, which constitute what are called distinct genera, and which differ from each other more than do the species of the same genus, arise? All these results, as we shall more fully see in the next chapter, follow from the struggle for life. Owing to this struggle, variations, however slight and from whatever cause proceeding, if they be in any degree profitable to the individuals of a species, in their infinitely complex relations to other organic beings and to their physical conditions of life, will tend to

the preservation of such individuals, and will generally be inherited by the offspring. The offspring, also, will thus have a better chance of surviving, for, of the many individuals of any species which are periodically born, but a small number can survive. I have called this principle, by which each slight variation, if useful, is preserved, by the term Natural Selection, in order to mark its relation to man's power of selection. But the expression often used by Mr. Herbert Spencer[a] of the Survival of the Fittest is more accurate, and is sometimes equally convenient. We have seen that man by selection can certainly produce great results, and can adapt organic beings to his own uses, through the accumulation of slight but useful variations, given to him by the hand of Nature. But Natural Selection, as we shall hereafter see, is a power incessantly ready for action, and is as immeasurably superior to man's feeble efforts, as the works of Nature are to those of Art.

We will now discuss in a little more detail the struggle for existence. In my future work this subject will be treated, as it well deserves, at greater length. The elder De Candolle[b] and Lyell have largely and philosophically shown that all organic beings are exposed to severe competition. In regard to plants, no one has treated this subject with more spirit and ability than W. Herbert,[c]

[a]Several years before the publication of the *Origin*, Herbert Spencer (1820–1903) developed an evolutionary theory, which he applied to the development of human societies. He popularized the term "survival of the fittest." [B.]

[b]Augustin Pyrame de Candolle (1778–1841) recognized that soil type profoundly affects the distribution of vegetation. Although he formulated the idea of homologous parts—a concept that supports the idea of evolution—he believed in the immutability of species. [B.]

[c]William Herbert (1778–1847) was an Anglican church minister, and an active member of the Horticultural Society of London, with a keen interest in plant classification and the relationship between hybridization and evolution. Darwin made extensive use of his work to support his arguments for natural selection. [B.]

**PLATE 33** Portrait of Charles Darwin by Julia Margaret Cameron.

Dean of Manchester, evidently the result of his great horticultural knowledge. Nothing is easier than to admit in words the truth of the universal struggle for life, or more difficult—at least I have found it so, than constantly to bear this conclusion in mind. Yet unless it be thoroughly engrained in the mind, the whole economy of nature, with every fact on distribution, rarity, abundance, extinction, and variation, will be dimly seen or quite misunderstood. We behold the face of nature bright with gladness, we often see superabundance of food; we do not see or we forget, that the birds which are idly singing round us mostly live on insects or seeds, and are thus constantly destroying life; or we forget how largely these songsters, or their eggs, or their nestlings, are destroyed by birds and beasts of prey; we do not always bear in mind, that, though food may be now superabundant, it is not so at all seasons of each recurring year.

I should premise that I use this term in a large and metaphorical sense including dependence of one being on another, and including (which is more important) not only the life of the individual, but success in leaving progeny. Two canine animals, in a time of dearth may be truly said to struggle with each other which shall get food and live. But a plant on the edge of a desert is said to struggle for life against the drought, though more properly it should be said to be dependent on the moisture. A plant which annually produces a thousand seeds, of which only one of an average comes to maturity, may be more truly said to struggle with the plants of the same and other kinds which already clothe the ground. The mistletoe is dependent on the apple and a few other trees, but can only in a far-fetched sense be said to struggle with these trees, for, if too many of these parasites grow on the same tree, it languishes and dies. But several seedling mistletoes, growing close together on the same branch, may more truly be said to struggle with each other. As the mistletoe is disseminated by birds, its existence depends on them; and it may methodically be said to struggle with other fruit-bearing plants, in tempting the birds to devour and thus disseminate its seeds. In these several senses, which pass into each other, I use for convenience sake the general term of Struggle for Existence.

A struggle for existence inevitably follows from the high rate at which all organic beings tend to increase. Every being, which during its natural lifetime produces several eggs or seeds, must suffer destruction during some period of its life, and during some season or occasional year, otherwise, on the principle of geometrical increase, its numbers would quickly become so inordinately great that no country could support the product. Hence, as more individuals are produced than can possibly survive, there must in every case be a struggle for existence, either one individual with another of the same species, or with the individuals of distinct species, or with the physical conditions of life. It is the doctrine of Malthus[d] applied

---

[d]As an old man, Darwin claimed that he hit upon the mechanism of natural selection in the fall of 1838 from his reading *An Essay on the Principles of Population* by Malthus.

Indeed, Malthus was a pivotal figure for Darwin, but the road to Malthus was far from direct. He read *On the Life and Writing of Adam Smith* (1793) by Dugald Stewart (1753–1828), assimilating the central tenet of the economist that apparent order arises from the struggle among individuals, and not from principles imposed from above. If the end is an ordered economy, which maximizes benefits for all, the means is a market that encourages individuals to compete and struggle to their own advantages. Then, searching for quantification, Darwin read the lengthy analysis of the work of the Belgian astronomer and statistician Adolphe Quetelet (1796–1874). It was in this work that he found a forceful statement of Malthus' quantitative principle that population would grow geometrically, and food supplies only arithmetically, thus ensuring an intense struggle for existence. [B.]

with manifold force to the whole animal and vegetable kingdoms; for in this case there can be no artificial increase of food, and no prudential restraint from marriage. Although, some species may be now increasing, more or less rapidly, in numbers, all cannot do so, for the world would not hold them.

There is no exception to the rule that every organic being naturally increases at so high a rate, that, if not destroyed, the Earth would soon be covered by the progeny of a single pair. Even slow-breeding man has doubled in twenty-five years, and at this rate, in less than a thousand years, there would literally not be standing-room for his progeny. Linnaeus has calculated that if an annual plant produced only two seeds—and there is no plant so unproductive as this—and their seedlings next year produced two, and so on, then in twenty years there should be a million plants. The elephant is reckoned the slowest breeder of all known animals, and I have taken some pains to estimate its probable minimum rate of natural increase; it will be safest to assume that it begins breeding when thirty years old, and goes on breeding until ninety years old, bringing forth six young in the interval, and surviving until one hundred years old; if this be so, after a period of from 740 to 750 years there would be nearly nineteen million elephants alive, descended from the first pair . . .

In looking at Nature, it is most necessary to keep the foregoing considerations always in mind—never to forget that every single organic being may be said to be striving to the utmost to increase in numbers; that each lives by a struggle at some period of its life; that heavy destruction inevitably falls either on the young or old, during each generation or at recurrent intervals. Lighten any check, mitigate the destruction ever so little, and the number of the species will almost instantaneously increase to any amount.

The causes which check the natural tendency of each species to increase are most obscure. Look at the most vigorous species; by as much as it swarms in numbers, by so much will it tend to increase still further. We know not exactly what the checks are even in a single instance. Nor will this surprise any one who reflects how ignorant we are on this head, even in regard to mankind, although so incomparably better known than any other animal. This subject of the checks to increase has been ably treated by several authors, and I hope in a future work to discuss it at considerable length, more especially in regard to the feral animals of South America. Here I will make only a few remarks, just to recall to the reader's mind some of the chief points. Eggs or very young animals seem generally to suffer most, but this is not invariably the case. With plants there is a vast destruction of seeds, but, from some observations which I have made, it appears that the seedlings suffer most from germinating in ground already thickly stocked with other plants. Seedlings, also, are destroyed in vast numbers by various enemies; for instance, on a piece of ground three feet long and two wide, dug and cleared, and where there could be no choking from other plants, I marked all the seedlings of our native weeds as they came up, and out of 357 no less than 295 were destroyed, chiefly by slugs and insects. If turf which has long been mown, and the case would be the same with turf closely browsed by quadrupeds, be let to grow, the more vigorous plants gradually kill the less vigorous, though fully grown plants; thus out of twenty species growing on a little plot of mown turf (three feet by four) nine species perished, from the other species being allowed to grow up freely.

The amount of food for each species of course gives the extreme limit to which each can increase; but very frequently it is not the obtaining food, but the serving as prey to other animals, which determines the average numbers of a species. Thus, there seems to be little doubt that the stock of partridges, grouse, and hares on any large estate depends chiefly on the destruction of vermin.

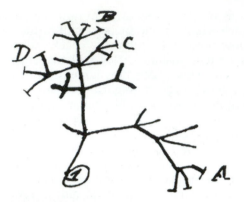

**PLATE 34** Darwin's third tree of nature diagram in his first notebook, ca. 1827–38. The marginal note at the right of the tree diagram states: "Case must be that one generation then should have as many living as now. To do this & to have many species in same genus (as is) *requires* extinction." Used with permission of the Syndics of Cambridge University Library (Trinity Lane, Cambridge, UK).

If not one head of game were shot during the next twenty years in England, and, at the same time, if no vermin were destroyed, there would, in all probability, be less game than at present, although hundreds of thousands of game animals are now annually shot. On the other hand, in some cases, as with the elephant, none are destroyed by beasts of prey; for even the tiger in India most rarely dares to attack a young elephant protected by its dam.

Climate plays an important part in determining the average number of a species, and periodical seasons of extreme cold or drought seem to be the most effective of all checks. I estimated (chiefly from the greatly reduced numbers of nests in the spring) that the winter of 1854–5 destroyed four-fifths of the birds in my own grounds; and this is a tremendous destruction, when we remember that ten percent is an extraordinarily severe mortality from epidemics with man. The action of climate seems at first sight to be quite independent of the struggle for existence; but in so far as climate chiefly acts in reducing food, it brings on the most severe struggle between the individuals, whether of the same or of distinct species, which subsist on the same kind of food. Even when climate, for instance, extreme cold, acts directly, it will be the least vigorous individuals, or those which have got least food through the advancing winter, which will suffer most. When we travel from south to north, or from a damp region to a dry, we invariably see some species gradually getting rarer and rarer, and finally disappearing; and the change of climate being conspicuous, we are tempted to attribute the whole effect to its direct action. But this is a false view; we forget that each species, even where it most abounds, is constantly suffering enormous destruction at some period of its life, from enemies or from competitors for the same place and food; and if these enemies or competitors be in the least degree favored by any slight change of climate, they will increase in numbers; and as each area is already fully stocked with inhabitants, the other species must decrease. When we travel southward and see a species decreasing in numbers, we may feel sure that the cause lies quite as much in other species being favored, as in this one being hurt. So it is when we travel northward, but in a somewhat lesser degree, for the number of species of all kinds and, therefore of competitors, decreases northwards; hence in going northwards, or in ascending a mountain, we far more often meet with stunted forms, due to the directly injurious action of climate, than we do in proceeding southwards or in descending a mountain. When we reach the arctic regions, or snowcapped summits, or absolute deserts, the struggle for life is almost exclusively with the elements.

That climate acts in main part indirectly by favoring other species, we clearly see in the prodigious number of plants which in our gardens can perfectly well endure our climate, but which never become naturalized, for they cannot compete with our native plants nor resist destruction by our native animals.

When a species, owing to highly favorable circumstances, increases inordinately in numbers in a small tract, epidemics—at least, this seems generally to occur with our game animals—often ensue; and here we have a limiting check independent of the struggle for life. But even some of these so-called epidemics appear to be due to parasitic worms, which have from some cause, possibly in part through facility of diffusion amongst the crowded animals, been disproportionately favored; and here comes in a sort of struggle between the parasite and its prey.

On the other hand, in many cases, a large stock of individuals of the same species, relatively to the numbers of its enemies, is absolutely necessary for its preservation. Thus we can easily raise plenty of corn and rapeseed, etc., in our fields, because the seeds are in great excess compared with the number of birds which feed on them; nor can the birds, though having a super-abundance of food at this one season, increase in number proportionally to the supply of seed, as their numbers are checked during the winter; but any one who has tried, knows how troublesome it is to get seed from a few wheat or other such plants in a garden: I have in this case lost every single seed . . .

The dependency of one organic being on another, as of a parasite on its prey, lies generally between beings remote in the scale of nature. This is likewise sometimes the case with those which may be strictly said to struggle with each other for existence, as in the case of locusts and grass-feeding quadrupeds. But the struggle will almost invariably be most severe between the individuals of the same species, for they frequent the same districts, require the same food, and are exposed to the same dangers. In the case of varieties of the same species, the struggle will generally be almost equally severe, and we sometimes see the contest soon decided: for instance, if several varieties of wheat be sown together, and the mixed seed be re-sown, some of the varieties which best suit the soil or climate, or are naturally the most fertile, will beat the others and so yield more seed, and will consequently in a few years supplant the other varieties. To keep up a mixed stock of even such extremely close varieties as the variously-colored sweet peas, they must be each year harvested separately, and the seed then mixed in due proportion, otherwise the weaker kinds will steadily decrease in number and disappear. So again with the varieties of sheep; it has been asserted that certain mountain-varieties will starve out other mountain-varieties, so that they cannot be kept together. The same result has followed from keeping together different varieties of the medicinal leech. It may even be doubted whether the varieties of any of our domestic plants or animals have so exactly the same strength, habits, and constitution, that the original proportions of a mixed stock (crossing being prevented) could be kept up for half-a-dozen generations, if they were allowed to struggle together, in the same manner as beings in a state of nature, and if the seed or young were not annually preserved in due proportion.

As the species of the same genus usually have, though by no means invariably, much similarity in habits and constitution, and always in structure, the struggle will generally be more severe between them, if they come into competition with each other, than between the species of distinct genera. We see this in the recent extension over parts of the United States of one species of swallow having caused the decrease of another species. The recent increase of the missel-thrush in parts of Scotland has caused the decrease of the song-thrush. How frequently we hear of one species of rat taking the place of another species under the most different climates! In Russia the small Asiatic cockroach has everywhere driven before it its great congener. In Australia the imported hive-bee is rapidly exterminating the small, stingless native bee. One species of charlock has been known to supplant another species; and so in other cases. We can dimly see why the competition should be most severe between allied forms, which fill nearly the same place in the economy of nature; but probably in no one case could we precisely say why one species has been victorious over another in the great battle of life.

A corollary of the highest importance may be deduced from the foregoing remarks, namely, that the structure of every organic being is related, in the most essential yet often hidden manner, to that of all the other organic beings, with which it comes into competition for food or residence, or from which it has to escape, or on which it preys. This is obvious in the structure of the teeth and talons of the tiger; and in that of the legs and claws of the parasite which clings to the hair on the tiger's body. But in the beautifully plumed seed of the dandelion, and in the flattened and fringed legs of the water-beetle, the relation seems at first confined to the elements of air and water. Yet the advantage of plumed seeds no doubt stands in the closest relation to the land being already thickly clothed with other plants; so that the seeds may be widely distributed and fall on unoccupied ground. In the water-beetle, the structure of its legs, so well adapted for diving, allows it to compete with other aquatic insects, to hunt for its own prey, and to escape serving as prey to other animals . . .

see that it can act most efficiently. Let the endless number of slight variations and individual differences occurring in our domestic productions, and, in a lesser degree, in those under nature, be borne in mind; as well as the strength of the hereditary tendency. Under domestication, it may be truly said that the whole organization becomes in some degree plastic. But the variability, which we almost universally meet with in our domestic productions, is not directly produced, as Hooker and Asa Gray[e] have well remarked, by man; he can neither originate varieties, nor prevent their occurrence; he can preserve and accumulate such as do occur. Unintentionally he exposes organic beings to new and changing conditions of life, and variability ensues; but similar changes of conditions might and do occur under nature. Let it also be born in mind how infinitely complex and close-fitting are the mutual relations of all organic beings to each other and to their physical conditions of life; and consequently what infinitely varied diversities of structure might be of use to each being under changing conditions of life. Can it, then, be thought improbable, seeing that variations useful to man have undoubtedly occurred, that other variations useful in some way to each being in the great and complex battle of life, should occur in the course of many successive generations? If such do occur, can we doubt (remembering that many more individuals are born than can possibly survive) that individuals having any advantage, however slight, over others, would have the best chance of surviving and of procreating their kind? On the other hand, we may feel sure that any varia-

## NATURAL SELECTION OR THE SURVIVAL OF THE FITTEST

How will the struggle for existence, briefly discussed in the last chapter, act in regard to variation? Can the principle of selection, which we have seen is so potent in the hands of man, apply under nature? I think we shall

[e]Joseph Dalton Hooker (1817–1911) servved as Director of Kew Gardens from 1845. In 1857, Darwin communicated his ideas on evolution to Asa Gray (1810–1888), who became one of Darwin's proponents in America, and authored a number of essays attempting to reconcile Darwin's views with Christian teaching. [B.]

tion in the least degree injurious would be rigidly destroyed. This preservation of favorable individual differences and variations, and the destruction of those which are injurious, I have called Natural Selection, or the Survival of the Fittest. Variations neither useful nor injurious would not be affected by natural selection, and would be left either a fluctuating element, as perhaps we see in certain polymorphic species, or would ultimately become fixed, owing to the nature of the organism and the nature of the conditions.

Several writers have misapprehended or objected to the term Natural Selection. Some have even imagined that natural selection induces variability, whereas it implies only the preservation of such variations as arise and are beneficial to the being under its conditions of life. No one objects to agriculturists speaking of the potent effects of man's selection; and in this case the individual differences given by nature, which man for some object selects, must of necessity first occur. Others have objected that the term selection implies conscious choice in the animals which become modified; and it has even been urged that, as plants have no volition, natural selection is not applicable to them! In the literal sense of the word, no doubt, natural selection is a false term; but who ever objected to chemists speaking of the elective affinities of the various elements?—and yet an acid cannot strictly be said to elect the base with which it in preference combines. It has been said that I speak of natural selection as an active power or Deity; but who objects to an author speaking of the attraction of gravity as ruling the movements of the planets? Everyone knows what is meant and is implied by such metaphorical expressions; and they are almost necessary for brevity. So again it is difficult to avoid personifying the word Nature; but I mean by Nature only the aggregate action and product of many natural laws, and by laws the sequence of events as ascertained by us. With a little familiarity such superficial objections will be forgotten.

We shall best understand the probable course of natural selection by taking the case of a country undergoing some slight physical change, for instance, of climate. The proportional numbers of its inhabitants will almost immediately undergo a change, and some species will probably become extinct. We may conclude, from what we have seen of the intimate and complex manner in which the inhabitants of each country are bound together, that any change in the numerical proportions of the inhabitants, independently of the change of climate itself, would seriously affect the others. If the country were open on its borders, new forms would certainly immigrate, and this would likewise seriously disturb the relations of some of the former inhabitants. Let it be remembered how powerful the influence of a single introduced tree or mammal has been shown to be. But in the case of an island, or of a country partly surrounded by barriers, into which new and better adapted forms could not freely enter, we should then have places in the economy of nature which would assuredly be better filled up, if some of the original inhabitants were in some manner modified; for, had the area been open to immigration, these same places would have been seized on by intruders. In such cases, slight modifications, which in any way favored the individuals of any species, by better adapting them to their altered conditions, would tend to be preserved; and natural selection would have free scope for the work of improvement.

We have good reason to believe . . . that changes in the conditions of life give a tendency to increased variability; and in the foregoing cases the conditions have changed, and this would manifestly be favorable to natural selection, by affording a better chance of the occurrence of profitable variations. Unless such occur, natural selection can do nothing. Under the term of "variations," it must never be forgotten that mere individual differences are included. As man can produce a great result with his domestic animals and plants by adding up in any given direction individual differences, so could natural selection, but far more easily from having incomparably longer time for action. Nor do I believe that any great physical change, as of climate, or any unusual degree of isolation to check immigration, is necessary in order that new and unoccupied places should be left, for natural selection to fill up by improving some of the varying inhabitants. For as all the inhabitants of each country are struggling together with nicely balanced forces, extremely slight modifications in the structure or habits of one species would often give it an advantage over others; and still further modifications of the same kind would often still further increase the advantage, as long as the species continued under the same conditions of life and profited by similar means of subsistence and defense. No country can be named in which all the native inhabitants are now so perfectly adapted to each other and to the physical conditions under which they live, that none of them could be still better adapted or improved; for in all countries, the natives have been so far conquered by naturalized productions, that they have allowed some foreigners to take firm possession of the land. And as foreigners have thus in every country beaten some of the natives, we may safely conclude that the natives might have been modified with advantage, so as to have better resisted the intruders.

As man can produce, and certainly has produced, a great result by his methodical and unconscious means of selection, what may not natural selection effect? Man can act only on external and visible characters. Nature, if I may be allowed to personify the natural preservation or survival of the fittest, cares nothing for appearances, except in so far as they are useful to any being. She can act on every internal organ, on every shade of constitutional difference, on the whole machinery of life. Man selects only for his own good: Nature only for that of the being which she tends. Every se-

lected character is fully exercised by her, as is implied by the fact of their selection. Man keeps the natives of many climates in the same country; he seldom exercises each selected character in some peculiar and fitting manner; he feeds a long and a short beaked pigeon on the same food; he does not exercise a long-backed or long-legged quadruped in any peculiar manner; he exposes sheep with long and short wool to the same climate. He does not allow the most vigorous males to struggle for the females. He does not rigidly destroy all inferior animals, but protects during each varying season, as far as lies in his power, all his productions. He often begins his selection by some half-monstrous form; or at least by some modification prominent enough to catch the eye or to be plainly useful to him. Under nature, the slightest differences of structure or constitution may well turn the nicely balanced scale in the struggle for life, and so be preserved. How fleeting are the wishes and efforts of man! How short his time! And, consequently how poor will be his results, compared with those accumulated by Nature during whole geological periods! Can we wonder, then, that Nature's productions should be far "truer" in character than man's productions; that they should be infinitely better adapted to the most complex conditions of life, and should plainly bear the stamp of far higher workmanship? . . .

## SEXUAL SELECTION

Inasmuch as peculiarities often appear under domestication in one sex and become hereditarily attached to that sex, so no doubt it will be under nature. Thus, it is rendered possible for the two sexes to be modified through natural selection in relation to different habits of life, as is sometimes the case; or for one sex to be modified in relation to the other sex, as commonly occurs. This leads me to say a few words on what I have called Sexual Selection.[f] This form of selection depends, not on a struggle for existence in relation to other organic beings or to external conditions, but on a struggle between the individuals of one sex, generally the males, for the possession of the other sex. The result is not death to the unsuccessful competitor, but few or no offspring. Sexual selection is, therefore, less rigorous than natural selection. Generally, the most vigorous males, those which are best fitted for their places in nature, will leave most progeny. But in many cases, victory depends not so much on general vigor, as on having special weapons, confined to the male sex. A hornless stag or spurless cock would have a poor chance of leaving numerous offspring. Sexual selection, by always allowing the victor to breed, might surely give indomitable courage, length to the spur, and strength to the wing to strike in the spurred leg, in nearly the same manner as does the brutal cockfighter by the careful selection of his best cocks. How low in the scale of nature the law of battle descends, I know not; male alligators have been described as fighting, bellowing, and whirling round, like Indians in a war-dance, for the possession of the females; male salmons have been observed fighting all day long; male stagbeetles sometimes bear wounds from the huge mandibles of other males; the males of certain hymenopterous insects have been frequently seen by that inimitable observer M. Fabre,[g] fighting for a particular female who sits by, an apparently unconcerned beholder of the struggle, and then retires with the conqueror. The war is, perhaps, severest between the males of polygamous animals, and these seem most often provided with special weapons. The males of carnivorous animals are already well armed; though to them and to others, special means of defense may be given through means of sexual selection, as the mane of the lion, and the hooked jaw to the male salmon; for the shield may be as important for victory, as the sword or spear . . .

That natural selection generally acts with extreme slowness I fully admit. It can act only when there are places in the natural polity of a district which can be better occupied by the modification of some of its existing inhabitants. The occurrence of such places will often depend on physical changes, which generally take place very slowly, and on the immigration of better adapted forms being prevented. As some few of the old inhabitants become modified, the mutual relations of others will often be disturbed; and this will create new places, ready to be filled up by better adapted forms, but all this will take place very slowly. Although the individuals of the same species differ in some slight degree from each other, it would often be long before differences of the right nature in various parts of the organization might occur. The result would often be greatly retarded

[f]The mechanism of sexual selection was developed more fully by Darwin in *The Descent of Man.* In an article of 1867, Wallace opposed Darwin's position with his own "pure Darwinism," and a group of strict *selectionists* rallied around Wallace, insisting that all evolutionary change should be attributed to natural selection alone. Though Darwin gave natural selection pride of place among evolutionary forces, since organisms display a range of features that do not promote survival directly, he insisted that other evolutionary forces must have played a role as well. Darwin emphasized two principles leading to non-adaptive change: Adaptive change in one part of an organism can lead to non-adaptive modifications of other features; and an organ constructed under the influence of selection for a specific role may be able, as a consequence of its structure, to perform many other unselected functions as well. [B.]

[g]An entomologist with unmatched observational skills, Jean Henri Fabre (1823–1915) earned his reputation for his observations of parasitic wasps (as well as other insect groups). [B.]

by free intercrossing. Many will exclaim that these several causes are amply sufficient to neutralize the power of natural selection. I do not believe so. But I do believe that natural selection will generally act very slowly, only at long intervals of time, and only on a few of the inhabitants of the same region. I further believe that these slow, intermittent results accord well with what geology[h] tells us of the rate and manner at which the inhabitants of the world have changed . . .

## EXTINCTION CAUSED BY NATURAL SELECTION

Natural selection acts solely through the preservation of variations in some way advantageous, which consequently endure. Owing to the high geometrical rate of increase of all organic beings, each area is already fully stocked with inhabitants; and it follows from this, that as the favored forms increase in number, so, generally, will the less favored decrease and become rare. Rarity, as geology tells us, is the precursor to ex-

---

[h]Lord Kelvin (1824–1907) calculated the age of the Earth from considerations of the time needed to cool from a molten state to the present temperature, the heat, conducted from within, escaping from the surface by radiation. He found that to arrive at the present day temperature between 20 and 40 million years must have elapsed since the Earth was a molten mass, and so the Earth as a habitable planet could not have existed for so long. Geologists who dealt with the evolution of rocks and different forms of life came to very different conclusions. Lyell, for example, calculated a figure of 240 million years as the span of life on Earth. Later, Ernest Rutherford pointed out that if heat was being, and had been, supplied by radioactive transformations taking place within the Earth, the Earth would not have lost heat as quickly as Kelvin had calculated; indeed, that if the heat were bring supplied rapidly enough, the Earth would warm up. [B.]

tinction. We can see that any form which is represented by few individuals will run a good chance of utter extinction, during great fluctuations in the nature of the seasons, or from a temporary increase in the number of its enemies. But we may go further than this; for, as new forms are produced, unless we admit that specific forms can go on indefinitely increasing in number, many old forms must become extinct. That the number of specific forms has not indefinitely increased, geology plainly tells us; and we shall presently attempt to show why it is that the number of species throughout the world has not become immeasurably great.

We have seen that the species which are most numerous in individuals have the best chance of producing favorable variations within any given period. We have evidence of this, in the facts showing that it is the common and diffused or dominant species which offer the greatest number of recorded varieties. Hence, rare species will be less quickly modified or improved within any given period; they will consequently be beaten in the race for life by the modified and improved descendants of the commoner species.

From these several considerations I think it inevitably follows, that as new species in the course of time are formed through natural selection, others will become rarer and rarer, and finally extinct. The forms which stand in closest competition with those undergoing modification and improvement will naturally suffer most. And we have seen in the chapter on the Struggle for Existence that it is the most closely-allied forms,—varieties of the same species, and species of the same genus or of related genera, which, from having nearly the same structure, constitution, and habits, generally come into the severest competition with each other; consequently, each new variety or species, during the progress of its formation, will generally press hardest on its nearest kindred, and tend to exterminate them. We see the same process of extermination among our domesticated productions, through the selection of improved forms by man. Many curious instances could be given showing how quickly new breeds of cattle, sheep, and other animals, and varieties of flowers, take the place of older and inferior kinds. In Yorkshire, it is historically known that the ancient black cattle were displaced by the long-horns, and that these "were swept away by the shorthorns" (I quote the words of an agricultural writer) "as if by some murderous pestilence" . . .

Whether natural selection has really acted thus in adapting the various forms of life to their several conditions and stations, must be judged by the general tenor and balance of evidence given in the following chapters.[i] But we have already seen how it entails extinction; and how largely extinction has acted in the world's history, geology plainly declares. Natural selection also leads to divergence of character; for the more organic beings diverge in structure, habits, and constitution, by so much the more can a large number be supported on the area,—of which we see proof by looking to the inhabitants of any small spot, and to the productions naturalized in foreign lands. Therefore, during the modification of the descendants of any one species, and during the incessant struggle of all species to increase in numbers, the more diversified the descendants become, the better will be their chance of success in the battle for life. Thus the small differences distinguishing varieties of the same species, steadily tend to increase, until they equal the greater differences between species of the same genus, or even of distinct genera.

The affinities of all the beings of the same class have sometimes been represented by a great tree. I believe this simile largely speaks the truth. The green and budding twigs may represent existing species; and those produced during former years may represent the long succession of extinct species. At each period of growth all the growing twigs have tried to branch out on all sides, and to overtop and kill the surrounding twigs and branches, in the same manner as species and groups of species have at all times overmastered other species in the great battle for life. The limbs, divided into great branches, and these into lesser and lesser branches, were themselves once, when the tree was young, budding twigs, and this connection of the former and present buds by ramifying branches may well represent the classification of all extinct and living species in groups subordinate to groups. Of the many twigs which flourished when the tree was a mere bush, only two or three, now grown into great branches, yet survive and bear the other branches; so with the species which lived during long-past geological periods very few have left living and modified descendants. From the first growth of the tree, many a limb and branch has decayed and dropped off; and these fallen branches of various sizes may represent those whole orders, families, and genera which have now no living representatives, and which are known to us only in a fossil state. As we here and there see a thin straggling branch springing from a fork low down in a tree, and which by some chance has been favored and is still alive on its summit, so we occasionally see an animal like the Ornithorhynchus or Lepidosiren, which in some small degree connects by its affinities two large branches of life, and which has apparently been saved from fatal competition by having inhabited a protected station. As buds give rise by growth to fresh buds, and these, if vigorous, branch out and overtop on all sides many a feebler branch, so by generation I believe it has been with the great Tree of Life, which fills with its dead and broken branches the crust of the Earth, and covers the surface with its ever-branching and beautiful ramifications . . .

---

[i]For Darwin's model to work, a number of favorable conditions must be satisfied: The initial variability, the mechanism of natural selection, the tendency for the selected properties to be preserved in breeding, and time. These conditions preoccupied Darwin for the rest of his life. [B.]

## FURTHER READING

Evolution Website. *http://www.bbc.co.uk/education/darwin*

Irvine, William. 1972. *Apes, Angels, and Victorians: The Story of Darwin, Huxley, and Evolution.* New York: McGraw-Hill.

Ruse, Michael. 1999. *The Darwinian Revolution: Science Red in Tooth and Claw.* Chicago: University of Chicago Press.

The Writings of Charles Darwin on the Web. *http://pages.britishlibrary.net/charles.darwin*

Zimmer, Carl. 2002. *Evolution: The Triumph of an Idea.* Harper Perennial Library.

# The Foundations of Genetics

## Gregor Mendel (1822–1884)

*In 1865, Gregor Mendel reported his results of some simple genetic crosses between strains of the garden pea. Working with almost 30,000 pea plants over an eight-year period, Mendel was interested in hybridization as a way of improving cultivation. The key to this problem, he reckoned, was the question of variation. Mendel's work advanced the novel proposition that heredity is particulate, contrary to the blending model of inheritance, favored by Darwin and enshrined in his theory of pangenesis. Characters are transmitted unchanged from one generation to the next, and cannot be modified by changes taking place in the parents' bodies due to new habits or the environment. In the pea plant, hereditary particles are in pairs. Mendel called them "elements" and he attributed them to their respective parents. From one parent comes an element determining round seed shape; from the other parent, another element governing the development of an angular seed shape. In the first generation, all hybrids are alike, exhibiting one of the parental characteristics (round seed shape) in an unchanged form. He called such a characteristic dominant and the other which remains latent he called recessive. The elements determining each paired character pass in the germ cells of the hybrids, without influencing the other, so that one of each pair of elements passes in every pollen (sperm) and in every egg cell.*

*Mendel's work was overlooked for many years only to be "rediscovered" in 1900. Although there was some resistance, the new approach resolved the difficulties inherent in Darwin's original formulation of natural selection, allowing the genetical theory of natural selection to become the dominant view in evolutionary biology. Genetics ushered in a new era in the science of animal and plant breeding, and in the identification of hereditary defects in humans. Once the complexities of the transmission process were understood, the path was cleared for the emergence of molecular biology, a science that would exploit the biochemical and physiological processes by which the hereditary information was coded and then unfolded into living tissue. Recognition of the double helix structure of DNA in 1953 by James Watson (1928–    ) and Francis Crick (1916–    ) opened the way to greater understanding and control of the process of inheritance.*

---

*Source:* Gregor Mendel, "Experiments in Plant Hybridization." In William Bateson, *Mendel's Principles of Heredity.* Cambridge: Cambridge University Press, 1913, pp. 335–364.

*The following translation (along with notes) is taken from* Mendel's Principles of Heredity: A Defence *by William Bateson (1861–1926), who introduced the term "genetics" and contributed enormously toward the establishment of the Mendelian conception of heredity and variation.*

## INTRODUCTORY REMARKS

Experience of artificial fertilization, such as is effected on ornamental plants in order to obtain new variations in color, has led to the experiments which will hereby be discussed. The striking regularity with which the same hybrid forms always reappeared whenever fertilization took place between the same species induced further experiments, the object of which was to follow up the developments of hybrids in their progeny.

To this object, numerous careful observers, such as Kölreuter, Gärtner, Herbert, Lecoq de Boisbauhran, Wichura[a] and others, have devoted a part of their lives with inexhaustible perseverance. Gärtner especially, in his work "Die Bastarderzeugung im Pflanzenreiche" [The Production of Hybrids in the Vegetable Kingdom], has recorded very valuable observations; and quite recently Wichura published the results of some profound investigations into the hybrids of the willow. That so far no generally applicable law governing the formation and development of hybrids has been successfully formulated can hardly be wondered at by anyone who is acquainted with the extent of the task, and can appreciate the difficulties with which experiments of this class have to contend. A final decision can only be arrived at when we shall have before us the results of detailed experiments made on plants belonging to the most diverse orders.

Those who survey the work done in this department will arrive at the conviction that among all the numerous experiments made, not one has been carried out to such an extent and in such a way as to make it possible to determine the number of different forms under which the offspring of the hybrids appear, or to arrange these forms with certainty according to their separate generations, or definitely to ascertain their statistical relations.[1]

It requires indeed some courage to undertake a labor of such far-reaching extent; this appears, however, to be the only right way by which we can finally reach the solution of a question the importance of which cannot be overestimated in connection with the history of the evolution of organic forms.

The paper now presented records the results of such a detailed experiment. This experiment was practically confined to a small plant group, and is now, after eight years' pursuit, concluded in all essentials. Whether the plan upon which the separate experiments were conducted and carried out was the best suited to attain the desired end is left to the friendly decision of the reader.

## SELECTION OF THE EXPERIMENTAL PLANTS

The value and utility of any experiment are determined by the fitness of the material to the purpose for which it is used, and thus in the case before us it cannot be immaterial what plants are subjected to experiment and in what manner such experiment is conducted.

The selection of the plant group which shall serve for experiments of this kind must be made with all possible care if it be desired to avoid from the outset every risk of questionable results.

---

[a]Joseph Gottlieb Kölreuter (1733–1806), Carl Friedrich von Gärtner (1772–1850), and Max Ernst Wichura (1817–1866), are examples of botanists who had carried out systematic investigations of the hybrids of various species. [B.]

The experimental plants must necessarily:

1. Possess constant differentiating characters.
2. The hybrids of such plants must, during the flowering period, be protected from the influence of all foreign pollen, or be easily capable of such protection.
3. The hybrids and their offspring should suffer no marked disturbance in their fertility in the successive generations.[b]

Accidental impregnation by foreign pollen, if it occurred during the experiments and were not recognized, would lead to entirely erroneous conclusions. Reduced fertility or entire sterility of certain forms, such as occurs in the offspring of many hybrids, would render the experiments very difficult or entirely frustrate them. In order to discover the relations in which the hybrid forms stand towards each other and also towards their progenitors it appears to be necessary that all members of the series developed in each successive generations should be, *without exception*, subjected to observation.

At the very outset special attention was devoted to the *Leguminosae*[c] on account of their peculiar floral structure. Experiments which were made with several members of this family led to the result that the genus *Pisum* was found to possess the necessary qualifications.

Some thoroughly distinct forms of this genus possess characters which are constant, and easily and certainly recognizable, and when their hybrids are mutually crossed they yield perfectly fertile progeny. Furthermore, a disturbance through foreign pollen cannot easily occur, since the fertilizing organs are closely packed inside the keel and

the anthers burst within the bud, so that the stigma becomes covered with pollen even before the flower opens. This circumstance is especially important. As additional advantages worth mentioning, there may be cited the easy culture of these plants in the open ground and in pots, and also their relatively short period of growth. Artificial fertilization is certainly a somewhat elaborate process, but nearly always succeeds. For this purpose the bud is opened before it is perfectly developed, the keel is removed, and each stamen carefully extracted by means of forceps, after which the stigma can at once be dusted over with the foreign pollen.

In all, thirty-four more or less distinct varieties of Peas were obtained from several seedsmen and subjected to a two years' trial. In the case of one variety there were noticed, among a larger number of plants all alike, a few forms which were markedly different. These, however, did not vary in the following year, and agreed entirely with another variety obtained from the same seedsman; the seeds were therefore doubtless merely accidentally mixed. All the other varieties yielded perfectly constant and similar offspring; at any rate, no essential difference was observed during two trial years. For fertilization 22 of these were selected and cultivated during the whole period of the experiments. They remained constant without any exception.

Their systematic classification is difficult and uncertain. If we adopt the strictest definition of a species, according to which only those individuals belong to a species which under precisely the same circumstances display precisely similar characters, no two of these varieties could be referred to one species. According to the opinion of experts, however, the majority belong to the species *Pisum sativum*; while the rest are regarded and classed, some as sub-species of *P. sativum*, and some as independent species, such as *P. quadratum*, *P. saccharatum*, and *P. umbellatum*. The positions, however, which may be assigned to them in a classificatory system are quite immaterial for the purposes of the

[b]Bateson does not list this as a third condition. [B.]

[c]*Leguminosae* includes the pea and bean family. With more than 16,000 known species, it is the third largest family of flowering plants. [B.]

experiments in question. It has so far been found to be just as impossible to draw a sharp line between the hybrids of species and varieties as between species and varieties themselves.

## DIVISION AND ARRANGEMENT OF THE EXPERIMENTS

If two plants which differ constantly in one or several characters be crossed, numerous experiments have demonstrated that the common characters are transmitted unchanged to the hybrids and their progeny; but each pair of differentiating characters, on the other hand, unite in the hybrid to form a new character, which in the progeny of the hybrid is usually variable. The object of the experiment was to observe these variations in the case of each pair of differentiating characters, and to deduce the law according to which they appear in successive generations. The experiment resolves itself therefore into just as many separate experiments as there are constantly differentiating characters presented in the experimental plants.

The various forms of Peas selected for crossing showed differences in length and color of the stem; in the size and form of the leaves; in the position, color, size of the flowers; in the length of the flower stalk; in the color, form, and size of the pods; in the form and size of the seeds; and in the color of the seed-coats and of the albumen (cotyledons). Some of the characters noted do not permit of a sharp and certain separation, since the difference is of a "more or less" nature, which is often difficult to define. Such characters could not be utilized for the separate experiments; these could only be applied to characters which stand out clearly and definitely in the plants. Lastly, the result must show whether they, in their entirety, observe a regular behavior in their hybrid unions, and whether from these facts any conclusion can be reached regarding those characters which possess a subordinate significance in the type.

The characters which were selected for experiment relate:

1. To the *difference in the form of the ripe seeds*. These are either round or roundish; the depressions, if any, occur on the surface, being always only shallow; or they are irregularly angular and deeply wrinkled (*P. quadratum*).

2. To the *difference in the color of the seed albumen* (endosperm).[2] The albumen of the ripe seeds is either pale yellow, bright yellow and orange colored or it possesses a more or less intense green tint. This difference of color is easily seen in the seeds as [= if] their coats are transparent.

3. To the *difference in the color of the seed-coat*. This is either white, with which character white flowers are constantly correlated; or it is gray, gray-brown, leather-brown, with or without violet spotting, in which case the color of the standards is violet, that of the wings purple, and the stem in the axils of the leaves is of a reddish tint. The gray seed-coats become dark brown in boiling water.

4. To the *difference in the form of the ripe pods*. These are either simply inflated, not contracted in places; or they are deeply constricted between the seeds and more or less wrinkled (*P. saccharatum*).

5. To the *difference in the color of the unripe pods*. They are either light to dark green, or vividly yellow, in which coloring the stalks, leaf-veins, and calyx participate.[3]

6. To the *difference in the position of the flowers*. They are either axial, that is, distributed along the main stem; or they are terminal, that is, bunched at the top of the stem and arranged almost in a false umbel; in this case the upper part of the stem is more or less widened in section (*P. umbellatum*).[4]

7. To the *difference in the length of the stem*. The length of the stem[5] is very various in some forms; it is, however, a constant character for each, in so far that healthy

plants, grown in the same soil, are only subject to unimportant variations in this character.

In experiments with this character, in order to be able to discriminate with certainty, the long axis of 6 to 7 ft. was always crossed with the short one of ¾ ft. to 1½ ft.

Each two of the differentiating characters enumerated above were united by cross-fertilization. There were made for the

| 1st | trial | 60 | fertilizations on 15 plants. |
|-----|-------|----|----|
| 2nd | " | 58 | " " 10 plants. |
| 3rd | " | 35 | " " 10 plants. |
| 4th | " | 40 | " " 10 plants. |
| 5th | " | 23 | " " 5 plants. |
| 6th | " | 34 | " " 10 plants. |
| 7th | " | 37 | " " 10 plants. |

From a larger number of plants of the same variety only the most vigorous were chosen for fertilization. Weakly plants always afford uncertain results, because even in the first generation of hybrids, and still more so in the subsequent ones, many of the offspring either entirely fail to flower or only form a few and inferior seeds.

Furthermore, in all the experiments reciprocal crossings were effected in such a way that each of the two varieties which in one set of fertilizations served as seed-bearer in the other set was used as the pollen plant.

The plants were grown in garden beds, a few also in pots, and were maintained in their natural upright position by means of sticks, branches of trees, and strings stretched between. For each experiment a number of pot plants were placed during the blooming period in a greenhouse, to serve as control plants for the main experiment in the open as regards possible disturbance by insects.[d] Among the insects[6] which visit Peas,

[d]Mendel seems to have been the first to use controls in botanical practice. These controlled experiments enabled him to discount the significance of poor or unexpected results. [B.]

the beetle *Bruchus pisi* [*Bruchus pisorum*] might be detrimental to the experiments should it appear in numbers. The female of this species is known to lay the eggs in the flower, and in so doing opens the keel; upon the tarsi of one specimen, which was caught in a flower, some pollen grains could clearly be seen under a lens. Mention must also be made of a circumstance which possibly might lead to the introduction of foreign pollen. It occurs, for instance, in some rare cases that certain parts of an otherwise normally developed flower wither, resulting in a partial exposure of the fertilizing organs. A defective development of the keel has also been observed, owing to which the stigma and anthers remained partially covered. It also sometimes happens that the pollen does not reach full perfection. In this event there occurs a gradual lengthening of the pistil during the blooming period, until the stigmatic tip protrudes at the point of the keel. This remarkable appearance has also been observed in hybrids of *Phaseolus* and *Lathyrus*.

The risk of false impregnation by foreign pollen is, however, a very slight one with *Pisum,* and is quite incapable of disturbing the general result. Among more than 10,000 plants which were carefully examined there were only a very few cases where an indubitably false impregnation had occurred. Since in the greenhouse such a case was never remarked, it may well be supposed that *Bruchus pisi,* and possibly also the described abnormalities in the floral structure, were to blame.

## THE FORMS OF THE HYBRIDS[7]

Experiments which in previous years were made with ornamental plants have already afforded evidence that the hybrids, as a rule, are not exactly intermediate between the parental species. With some of the more striking characters, those, for instance, which relate to the form and size of the leaves, the pubescence of the several parts, etc., the intermediate, indeed, is nearly always to be seen; in other cases, however, one of the two parental characters is so preponderant that it is difficult, or quite impossible, to detect the other in the hybrid.[e]

This is precisely the case with the Pea hybrids. In the case of each of the seven crosses the hybrid-character resembles[8] that of one of the parental forms so closely that the other either escapes observation completely or cannot be detected with certainty. This circumstance is of great importance in the determination and classification of the forms under which the offspring of the hybrids appear. Henceforth in this paper those characters which are transmitted entire, or almost unchanged in the hybridization, and therefore in themselves constitute the characters of the hybrid, are termed the *dominant*, and those which become latent in the process *recessive*. The expression "recessive" has been chosen because the characters thereby designated withdraw or entirely disappear in the hybrids, but nevertheless reappear unchanged in their progeny, as will be demonstrated later on.

It was furthermore shown by the whole of the experiments that it is perfectly immaterial whether the dominant character belongs to the seed plant or to the pollen plant; the form of the hybrid remains identical in both cases. This interesting fact was also emphasized by Gärtner, with the remark that even the most practiced expert is not in a position to determine in a hybrid which of the two parental species was the seed or the pollen plant.

Of the differentiating characters which were used in the experiments the following are dominant:

1. The round or roundish form of the seed with or without shallow depressions.
2. The yellow coloring of the seed albumen [cotyledons].

---

[e]Mendel is here attacking the blending theory of inheritance, claiming that his experiments demonstrate that complete dominance of one form is the rule, and perfect blending the exception. [B.]

3. The gray, gray-brown, or leather brown color of the seed-coat, in association with violet-red blossoms and reddish spots in the leaf axils.
4. The simply inflated form of the pod.
5. The green coloring of the unripe pod in association with the same color of the stems, the leaf-veins and the calyx.
6. The distribution of the flowers along the stem.
7. The greater length of stem.

With regard to this last character it must be stated that the longer of the two parental stems is usually exceeded by the hybrid, a fact which is possibly only attributable to the greater luxuriance which appears in all parts of plants when stems of very different lengths are crossed. Thus, for instance, in repeated experiments, stems of 1 ft. and 6 ft. in length yielded without exception hybrids which varied in length between 6 ft. and 7½ ft.

The hybrid seeds in the experiments with seed-coat are often more spotted, and the spots sometimes coalesce into small bluish-violet patches. The spotting also frequently appears even when it is absent as a parental character.

The hybrid forms of the seed-shape and of the albumen [color] are developed immediately after the artificial fertilization by the mere influence of the foreign pollen. They can, therefore, be observed even in the first year of experiment, whilst all the other characters naturally only appear in the following year in such plants as have been raised from the crossed seed.

## THE FIRST GENERATION [BRED] FROM THE HYBRIDS

In this generation there reappear, together with the dominant characters, also the recessive ones with their peculiarities fully developed, and this occurs in the definitely expressed average proportion of three to one, so that among each four plants of this generation three display the dominant character and one the recessive. This relates without exception to all the characters which were investigated in the experiments. The angular wrinkled form of the seed, the green color of the albumen, the white color of the seed-coats and the flowers, the constrictions of the pods, the yellow color of the unripe pod, of the stalk, of the calyx, and of the leaf venation, the umbel-like form of the inflorescence, and the dwarfed stem, all reappear in the numerical proportion given, without any essential alteration. *Transitional forms were not observed in any experiment.*

Since the hybrids resulting from reciprocal crosses are formed alike and present no appreciable difference in their subsequent development, consequently these results [of the reciprocal crosses] can be reckoned together in each experiment. The relative numbers which were obtained for each pair of differentiating characters are as follows:

Expt 1. *Form of seed.* From 253 hybrids 7,324 seeds were obtained in the second trial year. Among them were 5,474 round or roundish ones and 1,850 angular wrinkled ones. Therefrom the ratio 2.96 to 1 is deduced.

Expt 2. *Color of albumen.* 258 plants yielded 8,023 seeds, 6,022 yellow, and 2,001 green; their ratio, therefore, is as 3.01 to 1.

In these two experiments each pod yielded usually both kinds of seed. In well-developed pods which contained on the average six to nine seeds, it often happened that all the seeds were round (Expt. 1) or all yellow (Expt. 2); on the other hand there were never observed more than five wrinkled or five green ones in one pod. It appears to make no difference whether the pods are developed early or later in the hybrid or whether they spring from the main axis or from a lateral one. In some few plants only a few seeds developed in the first formed pods, and these possessed exclusively one of the two characters, but in the

subsequently developed pods the normal proportions were maintained nevertheless.

As in separate pods, so did the distribution of the characters vary in separate plants. By way of illustration the first ten individuals from both series of experiments may serve.

| | Experiment 1. Form of Seed | | Experiment 2. Color of Albumen | |
|---|---|---|---|---|
| *Plants* | *Round* | *Angular* | *Yellow* | *Green* |
| 1 | 45 | 12 | 25 | 11 |
| 2 | 27 | 8 | 32 | 7 |
| 3 | 24 | 7 | 14 | 5 |
| 4 | 19 | 10 | 70 | 27 |
| 5 | 32 | 11 | 24 | 13 |
| 6 | 26 | 6 | 20 | 6 |
| 7 | 88 | 24 | 32 | 13 |
| 8 | 22 | 10 | 44 | 9 |
| 9 | 28 | 6 | 50 | 14 |
| 10 | 25 | 7 | 44 | 18 |

As extremes in the distribution of the two seed characters in one plant, there were observed in Expt. 1 an instance of 43 round and only 2 angular, and another of 14 round and 15 angular seeds. In Expt. 2 there was a case of 32 yellow and only 1 green seed, but also one of 20 yellow and 19 green.

These two experiments are important for the determination of the average ratios, because with a smaller number of experimental plants they show that very considerable fluctuations may occur. In counting the seeds, also, especially in Expt. 2, some care is requisite, since in some of the seeds of many plants the green color of the albumen is less developed, and at first may be easily overlooked. The cause of this partial disappearance of the green coloring has no connection with the hybrid-character of the plants, as it likewise occurs in the parental variety. This peculiarity is also confined to the individual and is not inherited by the offspring. In luxuriant plants this appearance was frequently noted. Seeds which are damaged by insects during their development often vary in color and form, but with a little practice in sorting, errors are easily avoided. It is almost super-fluous to mention that the pods must remain on the plants until they are thoroughly ripened and have become dried, since it is only then that the shape and color of the seed are fully developed.

> *Expt. 3. Color of the seed-coats.* Among 929 plants, 705 bore violet-red flowers and gray-brown seed-coats; 224 had white flowers and white seed-coats, giving the proportion 3.15 to 1.
>
> *Expt. 4. Form of pods.* Of 1,181 plants, 882 had them simply inflated, and in 299 they were constricted. Resulting ratio, 2.95 to 1.
>
> *Expt. 5. Color of the unripe pods.* The number of trial plants was 580, of which 428 had green pods and 152 yellow ones. Consequently these stand in the ratio of 2.82 to 1.
>
> *Expt. 6. Position of flowers.* Among 858 cases 651 had inflorescences axial and 207 terminal. Ratio, 3.14:1.
>
> *Expt. 7. Length of stem.* Out of 1,064 plants, in 787 cases the stem was long, and in 277 short. Hence a mutual ratio of 2.84 to 1. In this experiment the dwarfed plants were carefully lifted and trans-ferred to a special bed. This precaution was necessary, as otherwise they would have perished through being over-grown by their tall relatives. Even in their quite young state they can be eas-ily picked out by their compact growth and thick dark-green foliage.[9]

If now the results of the whole of the ex-periments be brought together, there is found, as between the number of forms with the dominant and recessive characters, an average ratio of 2.98 to 1, or 3 to 1.

The dominant character can have here a *double signification*—viz., that of a parental character or a hybrid-character.[10] In which of the two significations it appears in each sep-arate case can only be determined by the fol-lowing generation. As a parental character it must pass over unchanged to the whole of the offspring; as a hybrid-character, on the other hand, it must maintain the same be-havior as in the first generation.

## THE SECOND GENERATION [BRED] FROM THE HYBRIDS

Those forms which in the first generation ex-hibit the recessive character do not further vary in the second generation as regards this character; they remain *constant* in their off-spring.

It is otherwise with those which possess the dominant character in the first genera-tion. Of these two-thirds yield offspring which display the dominant and recessive characters in the proportion of 3 to 1, and thereby show exactly the same ratio as the hybrid forms, while only one-third remains with the dominant character constant.

The separate experiments yielded the fol-lowing results:

> *Expt. 1.* Among 565 plants which were raised from round seeds of the first generation, 193 yielded round seeds only, and remained therefore constant in this character; 372, however, gave both round and wrinkled seeds, in the proportion of 3 to 1. The number of the hybrids, therefore, as compared with the constants is 1.93 to 1.
>
> *Expt. 2.* Of 519 plants which were raised from seeds whose albumen was of yel-low color in the first generation, 166 yielded exclusively yellow, while 353 yielded yellow and green seeds in the proportion of 3 to 1. There resulted, therefore, a division into hybrid and con-stant forms in the proportion of 2.13 to 1.

For each separate trial in the following ex-periments 100 plants were selected which displayed the dominant character in the first generation, and in order to ascertain the sig-nificance of this, ten seeds of each were culti-vated.

*Expt. 3.* The offspring of 36 plants yielded exclusively gray-brown seed-coats, while of the offspring of 64 plants some had gray-brown and some had white.

*Expt. 4.* The offspring of 29 plants had only simply inflated pods; of the offspring of 71, on the other hand, some had inflated and some constricted.

*Expt. 5.* The offspring of 40 plants had only green pods; of the offspring of 60 plants some had green, some yellow ones.

*Expt. 6.* The offspring of 33 plants had only axial flowers; of the offspring of 67, on the other hand, some had axial and some terminal flowers.

*Expt. 7.* The offspring of 28 plants inherited the long axis, of those of 72 plants some the long and some the short axis.

In each of these experiments, a certain number of the plants came constant with the dominant character. For the determination of the proportion in which the separation of the forms with the constantly persistent character results, the two first experiments are especially important, since in these a larger number of plants can be compared. The ratios 1.93 to 1 and 2.13 to 1 gave together almost exactly the average ratio of 2 to 1. The sixth experiment gave a quite concordant result; in the others the ratio varies more or less, as was only to be expected in view of the smaller number of 100 trial plants. Experiment 5, which shows the greatest departure, was repeated, and then in lieu of the ratio of 60 and 40, that of 65 and 35 resulted. *The average ratio of 2 to 1 appears, therefore, as fixed with certainty.* It is therefore demonstrated that, of those forms which possess the dominant character in the first generation, two-thirds have the hybrid-character, while one-third remains constant with the dominant character.

The ratio 3 to 1, in accordance with which the distribution of the dominant and recessive characters results in the first generation, resolves itself therefore in all experiments into the ratio of 2:1:1, if the dominant charac-

ter be differentiated according to its significance as a hybrid-character or as a parental one. Since the members of the first generation spring directly from the seed of the hybrids, *it is now clear that the hybrids form seeds having one or other of the two differentiating characters, and of these one-half develop again the hybrid form, while the other half yield plants which remain constant and receive the dominant or the recessive characters [respectively] in equal numbers.*

## THE SUBSEQUENT GENERATIONS [BRED] FROM THE HYBRIDS

The proportions in which the descendants of the hybrids develop and split up in the first and second generations presumably hold good for all subsequent progeny. Experiments 1 and 2 have already been carried through six generations; 3 and 7 through five; and 4, 5, and 6 through four; these experiments being continued from the third generation with a small number of plants, and no departure from the rule has been perceptible. The offspring of the hybrids separated in each generation in the ratio of 2:1:1 into hybrids and constant forms.

If *A* be taken as denoting one of the two constant characters, for instance the dominant, *a* the recessive, and *Aa* the hybrid form in which both are conjoined, the expression

$$A + 2Aa + a$$

shows the terms in the series for the progeny of the hybrids of two differentiating characters.

The observation made by Gärtner, Kölreuter, and others, that hybrids are inclined to revert to the parental forms, is also confirmed by the experiments described. It is seen that the number of the hybrids which arise from one fertilization, as compared with the number of forms which become constant, and their progeny from generation to generation, is continually diminishing, but that nevertheless they could not entirely disappear. If an average equality of fertility in all plants in all generations be assumed, and if, furthermore, each hybrid forms seed of which one-half yields hybrids again, while the other half is constant to both characters in equal proportions, the ratio of numbers for the offspring in each generation is seen by the following summary, in which $A$ and $a$ denote again the two parental characters, and $Aa$ the hybrid forms. For brevity's sake it may be assumed that each plant in each generation furnishes only 4 seeds.

| | | | | Ratios |
|---|---|---|---|---|
| *Generation* | *A* | *Aa* | *a* | *A : Aa : a* |
| 1 | 1 | 2 | 1 | 1 : 2 : 1 |
| 2 | 6 | 4 | 6 | 3 : 2 : 3 |
| 3 | 28 | 8 | 28 | 7 : 2 : 7 |
| 4 | 120 | 16 | 120 | 15 : 2 : 15 |
| 5 | 496 | 32 | 496 | 31 : 2 : 31 |
| *N* | | | | $2^n - 1 : 2 : 2^n - 1$ |

In the tenth generation, for instance, $2^n - 1 = 1023$. There result, therefore, in each 2,048 plants which arise in this generation 1,023 with the constant dominant character, 1,023 with the recessive character, and only two hybrids.

## THE OFFSPRING OF HYBRIDS IN WHICH SEVERAL DIFFERENTIATING CHARACTERS ARE ASSOCIATED

In the experiments above described plants were used which differed only on one essential character. The next task consisted in ascertaining whether the law of development discovered in these applied to each pair of differentiating characters when several diverse characters are united in the hybrid by crossing.

As regards the form of the hybrids in these cases, the experiments showed throughout that this invariably more nearly approaches to that one of the two parental plants which possesses the greater number of dominant characters. If, for instance, the seed plant has a short stem, terminal white flowers, and simply inflated pods; the pollen plant, on the other hand, a long stem, violet-red flowers distributed along the stem, and constricted pods; the hybrid resembles the seed parent only in the form of the pod; in the other characters it agrees with the pollen parent. Should one of the two parental types possess only dominant characters, then the hybrid is scarcely or not at all distinguishable from it.

Two experiments were made with a considerable number of plants. In the first experiment the parental plants differed in the form of the seed and in the color of the albumen; in the second in the form of the seed, in the color of the albumen, and in the color of the seed-coats. Experiments with seed characters give the result in the simplest and most certain way.

In order to facilitate study of the data in these experiments, the different characters of the seed plant will be indicated by $A$, $B$, $C$, those of the pollen plant by $a$, $b$, $c$, and the hybrid forms of the characters *by Aa, Bb*, and *Cc*.

Expt. 1.  *AB*, seed parents  *ab*, pollen parents

        *A*, form round  *a*, form wrinkled

        *B*, albumen yellow  *b*, albumen green

The fertilized seeds appeared round and yellow like those of the seed parents. The plants raised therefrom yielded seeds of four sorts, which frequently presented themselves in one pod. In all, 556 seeds were yielded by 15 plants, and of these there were:

315 round and yellow,
101 wrinkled and yellow,
108 round and green,
  32 wrinkled and green.

All were sown the following year. Eleven of the round yellow seeds did not yield plants, and three plants did not form seeds. Among the rest:

| | |
|---|---|
| 38 had round yellow seeds | *AB* |
| 65 round yellow and green seeds | *ABb* |
| 60 round yellow and wrinkled yellow seeds | *AaB* |
| 138 round yellow and green, wrinkled yellow and green seeds | *AaBb* |

From the wrinkled yellow seeds 96 resulting plants bore seed, of which:

| | |
|---|---|
| 28 had only wrinkled yellow seeds | *aB* |
| 68 wrinkled yellow and green seeds | *aBb* |

From 108 round green seeds 102 resulting plants fruited, of which:

| | |
|---|---|
| 35 had only round green seeds | *Ab* |
| 67 round and wrinkled green seeds | *Aab* |

The wrinkled green seeds yielded 30 plants which bore seeds all of like character; they remained constant *ab*.

The offspring of the hybrids appeared therefore under nine different forms, some of them in very unequal numbers. When these are collected and coordinated we find:

| 38 plants with the sign | *AB* |
|---|---|
| 35 " " " | *Ab* |
| 28 " " " | *aB* |
| 30 " " " | *ab* |
| 65 " " " | *ABb* |
| 68 " " " | *aBb* |
| 60 " " " | *AaB* |
| 67 " " " | *Aab* |
| 138 " " " | *AaBb* |

The whole of the forms may be classed into three essentially different groups. The first includes those with the signs *AB*, *Ab*, *aB*, and *ab*: They possess only constant characters and do not vary again in the next generation. Each of these forms is represented on the average thirty-three times. The second group includes the signs *ABb*, *aBb*, *AaB*, *Aab*: These are constant in one character and hybrid in another, and vary in the next generation only as regards the hybrid-character. Each of these appears on any average sixty-five times. The form *AaBb* occurs 138 times: It is hybrid in both characters, and behaves exactly as do the hybrids from which it is derived.

If the numbers in which the forms belonging to these classes appear are compared, the ratios of 1, 2, 4 are unmistakably evident. The numbers 33, 65, 138 present very fair approximations to the ratio numbers of 33, 66, 132.

The development series consists, therefore, of nine classes, of which four appear therein always once and are constant in both characters; the forms *AB*, *ab*, resemble the parental forms, the two others present combinations between the conjoined characters *A*, *a*, *B*, *b*, which combinations are likewise possibly constant. Four classes appear always twice, and are constant in one character and hybrid in the other. One class appears four times, and is hybrid in both characters. Consequently, the offspring of the hybrids, if two kinds of differentiating characters are combined therein, are represented by the expression

$$AB + Ab + aB + ab + 2ABb + 2aBb + 2AaB + 2Aab + 4AaBb$$

This expression is indisputably a combination series in which the two expressions for the characters *A* and *a*, *B* and *b* are combined. We arrive at the full number of the classes of the series by the combination of the expressions:

$$A + 2Aa + a$$
$$B + 2Bb + b$$

Expt. 2　*ABC* seed parents;　*abc*, pollen parents;

　　　　*A*, form round;　*a*, form wrinkled;

　　　　*B*, albumen yellow;　*b*, albumen green;

　　　　*C*, seed-coat gray-brown.　*c*, seed-coat white.

This experiment was made in precisely the same way as the previous one. Among all the experiments it demanded the most time and trouble. From 24 hybrids 687 seeds were obtained in all: These were all either spotted, gray-brown or gray-green, round or wrinkled.[11] From these in the following year 639 plants fruited, and as further investigation showed, there were among them:

| | | | | | |
|---|---|---|---|---|---|
| 8 plants *ABC* | 22 plants *ABCc* | 45 plants *AbbCc* |
| 14 " *ABc* | 17 " *AbCc* | 36 " *aBbCc* |
| 9 " *AbC* | 25 " *aBCc* | 38 " *AaBCc* |
| 11 " *Abc* | 20 " *abCc* | 40 " *AabCc* |
| 8 " *aBC* | 15 " *ABbC* | 49 " *AaBbC* |
| 10 " *aBc* | 18 " *ABbc* | 48 " *AaBbc* |
| 10 " *abC* | 19 " *aBbC* | 78 " *AaBbCc* |
| 7 " *abc* | 24 " *aBbc* | |
| | 14 " *AaBC* | |
| | 18 " *AaBc* | |
| | 20 " *AabC* | |
| | 16 " *Aabc* | |

The whole expression contains 27 terms. Of these 8 are constant in all characters, and each appears on the average 10 times; 12 are constant in two characters, and hybrid in the third; each appears on the average 19 times; 6 are constant in one character and hybrid in the other two; each appears on the average 43 times. One form appears 78 times and is hybrid in all of the characters. The ratios 10:19:43:78 agree so closely with the ratios 10:20:40:80, or 1:2:4:8 that this last undoubtedly represents the true value.

The development of the hybrids when the original parents differ in three characters re-

sults therefore according to the following expression:

$$ABC + ABc + AbC + Abc + aBC + aBc + abC + abc + 2ABCc + 2AbCc + 2aBCc + 2abCc + 2ABbC + 2ABbc + 2aBbC + 2aBbc + 2AaBC + 2AaBc + 2AabC + 2Aabc + 4ABbCc + 4aBbCc + 4AaBCc + 4AabCc + 4AaBbC + 4AaBbc + 8AaBbCc.$$

Here also is involved a combination series in which the expressions for the characters *A* and *a*, *B* and *b*, *C* and *c*, are united. The expressions:

$$A + 2Aa + a$$
$$B + 2Bb + b$$
$$C + 2Cc + c$$

give all the classes of the series. The constant combinations which occur therein agree with all combinations which are possible between the characters *A*, *B*, *C*, *a*, *b*, *c*; two thereof, *ABC* and *abc*, resemble the two original parental stocks.

In addition, further experiments were made with a smaller number of experimental plants in which the remaining characters by twos and threes were united as hybrids: All yielded approximately the same results. There is therefore no doubt that for the whole of the characters involved in the experiments the principle applies *that the offspring of the hybrids in which several essentially different characters are combined exhibit the terms of a series of combinations, in which the developmental series for each pair of differentiating characters are united.* It is demonstrated at the same time that *the relation of each pair of different characters in hybrid union is independent of the other differences in the two original parental stocks.*

If *n* represent the number of the differentiating characters in the two original stocks, $3^n$ gives the number of terms of the combination series, $4^n$ the number of individuals which belong to the series, and $2^n$ the number of unions which remain constant. The series therefore contains, if the original stocks differ in four characters, $3^4 = 81$ classes, $4^4 = 256$ individuals, and $2^4 = 16$ constant forms: or, which is the same, among each 256 offspring of the hybrids are 81 different combinations, 16 of which are constant.

All constant combinations which in Peas are possible by the combination of the said 7 differentiating characters were actually obtained by repeated crossing. Their number is given by $2^7 = 128$. Thereby is simultaneously given the practical proof *that the constant characters which appear in the several varieties of a group of plants may be obtained in all the associations which are possible according to the [mathematical] laws of combination, by means of repeated artificial fertilization.*

As regards the flowering time of the hybrids, the experiments are not yet concluded. It can, however, already be stated that the time stands almost exactly between those of the seed and pollen parents, and that the constitution of the hybrids with respect to this character probably follows the rule ascertained in the case of the other characters. The forms which are selected for experiments of this class must have a difference of at least 20 days from the middle flowering period of one to that of the other; furthermore, the seeds when sown must all be placed at the same depth in the earth, so that they may germinate simultaneously. Also, during the whole flowering period, the more important variations in temperature must be taken into account, and the partial hastening or delaying of the flowering which may result therefrom. It is clear that this experiment presents many difficulties to be overcome and necessitates great attention.

If we endeavor to collate in a brief form the results arrived at, we find that those differentiating characters, which admit of easy and certain recognition in the experimental plants, all behave exactly alike in their hybrid associations. The offspring of the hybrids of each pair of differentiating characters are one-half, hybrid again, while the other half are constant in equal proportions having the characters of the seed and pollen parents respectively. If several differentiating characters are combined by cross-fertilization in a hybrid, the resulting offspring form the terms of a combination series in which the combination series for each pair of differentiating characters are united.

The uniformity of behavior shown by the whole of the characters submitted to experiment permits, and fully justifies, the acceptance of the principle that a similar relation exists in the other characters which appear less sharply defined in plants, and therefore could not be included in the separate experiments. An experiment with peduncles of different lengths gave on the whole a fairly satisfactory results, although the differentiation and serial arrangement of the forms could not be effected with that certainty which is indispensable for correct experiment.

## THE REPRODUCTIVE CELLS OF THE HYBRIDS

The results of the previously described experiments led to further experiments, the results of which appear fitted to afford some conclusions as regards the composition of the egg and pollen cells of hybrids. An important clue is afforded in *Pisum* by the circumstance that among the progeny of the hybrids constant forms appear, and that this occurs, too, in respect of all combinations of the associated characters. So far as experience goes, we find it in every case confirmed that constant progeny can only be formed when the egg cells and the fertilizing pollen are of like character, so that both are provided with the material for creating quite similar individuals, as is the case with the normal fertilization of pure species. We must therefore regard it as certain that exactly similar factors must be at work also in the production of the constant forms in the hybrid plants. Since the various constant forms are produced in *one* plant, or even in *one* flower of a plant, the conclusion appears logical that in the ovaries of the hybrids there are formed as many sorts of egg cells, and in the anthers as many sorts of pollen cells, as there are possible constant combination forms, and that these egg and pollen cells agree in their internal compositions with those of the separate forms.

In point of fact it is possible to demonstrate theoretically that this hypothesis would fully suffice to account for the development of the hybrids in the separate generations, if we might at the same time assume that the various kinds of egg and pollen cells were formed in the hybrids on the average in equal numbers.[12]

In order to bring these assumptions to an experimental proof, the following experiments were designed. Two forms which were constantly different in the form of the seed and the color of the albumen were united by fertilization.

If the differentiating characters are again indicated as *A, B, a, b*, we have:

| | |
|---|---|
| *AB*, seed parent; | *ab*, pollen parents; |
| *A*, form round; | *a*, form wrinkled; |
| *B*, albumen yellow. | *b*, albumen green. |

The artificially fertilized seeds were sown together with several seeds of both original stocks, and the most vigorous examples were chosen for the reciprocal crossing. There were fertilized:

1. The hybrids with the pollen of *AB*.
2. The hybrids " " *ab*.
3. *AB* " " the hybrids.
4. *ab* " " the hybrids.

For each of these four experiments the whole of the flowers on three plants were fertilized. If the above theory be correct, there must be developed on the hybrids egg and pollen cells of the forms *AB, Ab, aB, ab*, and there would be combined:

1. The egg cells *AB, Ab, aB, ab* with the pollen cells *AB*.
2. The egg cells *AB, Ab, aB, ab* with the pollen cells *ab*.

3. The egg cells *AB* with the pollen cells *AB, Ab, aB*, and *ab*.
4. The egg cells *ab* with the pollen cells *AB, Ab, aB*, and *ab*.

From each of these experiments there could then result only the following forms:

1. *AB, ABb, AaB, AaBb*
2. *AaBb, Aab, aBb, ab*
3. *AB, ABb, AaB, AaBb*
4. *AaBb, Aab, aBb, ab*

If, furthermore, the several forms of the egg and pollen cells of the hybrids were produced on an average in equal numbers, then in each experiment the said four combinations should stand in the same ratio to each other. A perfect agreement in the numerical relations was, however, not to be expected since in each fertilization, even in normal cases, some egg cells remain undeveloped or subsequently die, and many even of the well-formed seeds fail to germinate when sown. The above assumption is also limited in so far that while it demands the formation of an equal number of the various sorts of egg and pollen cells, it does not require that this should apply to each separate hybrid with mathematical exactness.[f]

The first and second experiments had primarily the object of proving the composition of the hybrid egg cells, while the third and fourth experiments were to decide that of the pollen cells.[13] As is shown by the above demonstration the first and third experiments and the second and fourth experiments should produce precisely the same

[f]Mendel's disclaimer that the fit of the data and his model ratios will be less than perfect is interesting granted that the fit is remarkably close to the predicted ratio—and certainly closer than the experiments reported in other sections of the paper. The statistician and biometrician R. A. Fisher (1890–1962) went so far as to claim in 1936 that Mendel's data was "too good" (the numbers conforming to the predicted ratios of 1:1:1:1), indicating that the data had been "cooked." [B.]

combinations, and even in the second year the result should be partially visible in the form and color of the artificially fertilized seed. In the first and third experiments the dominant characters of form and color, *A* and *B*, appear in each union, and are also partly constant and partly in hybrid union with the recessive characters *a* and *b,* for which reason they must impress their peculiarity upon the whole of the seeds, all seeds should therefore appear round and yellow, if the theory be justified. In the second and fourth experiments, on the other hand, one union is hybrid in form and in color, and consequently the seeds are round and yellow; another is hybrid in form, but constant in the recessive character of color, whence the seeds are round and green; the third is constant in the recessive character of form but hybrid in color, consequently the seeds are wrinkled and yellow; the fourth is constant in both recessive characters, so that the seeds are wrinkled and green. In both these experiments there were consequently four sorts of seed to be expected; namely, round and yellow, round and green, wrinkled and yellow, wrinkled and green.

The crop fulfilled these expectations perfectly. There were obtained in the

- 1st Experiment, 98 exclusively round yellow seeds;
- 3rd Experiment, 94 exclusively round, yellow seeds;
- In the 2nd Experiment, 31 round and yellow, 26 round and green, 27 wrinkled and yellow, 26 wrinkled and green seeds.
- In the 4th Experiment, 24 round and yellow, 25 round and green, 22 wrinkled and yellow, 27 wrinkled and green seeds.

There could scarcely be now any doubt of the success of the experiment; the next generation must afford the final proof. From the seed sown there resulted for the first experiment 90 plants, and for the third 87 plants which fruited: These yielded for the:

| 1st Expt. | 3rd Expt. | |
|---|---|---|
| 20 | 25 round yellow seeds | *AB* |
| 23 | 19 round yellow and green seeds | *ABb* |
| 25 | 22 round and wrinkled yellow seeds | *AaB* |
| 22 | 21 round and wrinkled green and yellow seeds | *AaBb* |

In the second and fourth experiments the round and yellow seeds yielded plants with round and wrinkled yellow and green seeds, *AaBb.*

From the round green seeds plants resulted with round and wrinkled green seeds, *Aab.*

The wrinkled yellow seeds gave plants with wrinkled yellow and green seeds, *aBb.*

From the wrinkled green seeds plants were raised which yielded again only wrinkled and green seeds, *ab.*

Although in these two experiments likewise some seeds did not germinate, the figures arrived at already in the previous year were not affected thereby, since each kind of seed gave plants which, as regards their seed, were like each other and different from the others. There resulted therefore from the:

| 2nd Expt. | 4th Expt. | | |
|---|---|---|---|
| 31 | 24 | plants of the form *AaBb* | |
| 26 | 25 | " | " *Aab* |
| 27 | 22 | " | " *aBb* |
| 26 | 27 | " | " *ab* |

In all the experiments, therefore, there appeared all the forms which the proposed theory demands, and they came in nearly equal numbers.

In a further experiment the characters of flower-color and length of stem were experimented upon, and selection was so made that in the third year of the experiment each character ought to appear in half of all the plants if the above theory were correct. *A, B, a, b* serve again as indicating the various characters.

*A*, violet-red flowers;    *a*, white flowers;
*B*, axis long.    *b*, axis short.

The form *Ab* was fertilized with *ab*, which produced the hybrid *Aab*. Furthermore, *aB* was also fertilized with *ab*, whence the hybrid *aBb*. In the second year, for further fertilization, the hybrid *Aab* was used as seed parent, and hybrid *aBb* as pollen parent.

Seed parent, *Aab*;    Pollen parent, *aBb*;

Possible egg cells, *Ab, ab*.    Pollen cells, *aB, ab*.

From the fertilization between the possible egg and pollen cells four combinations should result, viz.:

$$AaBb + aBb + Aab + ab$$

From this it is perceived that, according to the above theory, in the third year of the experiment out of all the plants,

| Half should have | Classes |
|---|---|
| violet-red flowers (*Aa*) | 1, 3 |
| white flowers (*a*) | 2, 4 |
| a long axis (*Bb*) | 1, 2 |
| a short axis (*b*) | 3, 4 |

From 45 fertilizations of the second year 187 seeds resulted, of which only 166 reached the flowering stage in the third year. Among these the separate classes appeared in the numbers following:

| Class | Color of flower | Stem | |
|---|---|---|---|
| 1 | Violet-red | Long | 47 times |
| 2 | White | Long | 40 times |
| 3 | Violet-red | Short | 38 times |
| 4 | White | Short | 41 times |

There subsequently appeared,
The violet-red flower color (*Aa*) in 85 plants,
The white flower color (*a*) in 81 plants,

The long stem (*Bb*) in 87 plants,
The short stem (*b*) in 79 plants.

The theory adduced is therefore satisfactorily confirmed in this experiment also.

For the characters of form of pod, color of pod, and position of flowers, experiments were also made on a small scale and results obtained in perfect agreement. All combinations which were possible through the union of the differentiating characters duly appeared, and in nearly equal numbers.

Experimentally, therefore, the theory is confirmed that *the pea hybrids form egg and pollen cells which, in their constitution, represent in equal numbers all constant forms which result from the combination of the characters united in fertilization.*

The difference of the forms among the progeny of the hybrids, as well as the respective ratios of the numbers in which they are observed, find a sufficient explanation in the principle above deduced. The simplest case is afforded by the developmental series of *each pair of differentiating characters.* This series is represented by the expression *A+2Aa+a*, in which *A* and *a* signify the forms with constant differentiating characters, and *Aa* the hybrid form of both. It includes in three different classes four individuals. In the formation of these, pollen and egg cells of the form *A* and *a* take part on the average equally in the fertilization; hence each form [occurs] twice, since four individuals are formed. There participate consequently in the fertilization

The pollen cells *A+A+a+a*,
The egg cells *A+A+a+a*.

It remains, therefore, purely a matter of chance which of the two sorts of pollen will become united with each separate egg cell. According, however, to the law of probability, it will always happen, on the average of many cases, that each pollen form *A* and *a* will unite equally often with each egg cell form *A* and *a*, consequently one of the two pollen cells *A* in the fertilization will meet with the egg cell *A* and the other with the egg cell *a*, and so likewise one pollen cell *a* will unite with an egg cell *A*, and the other with the egg cell *a*.

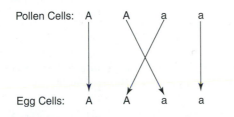

The result of the fertilization may be made clear by putting the signs for the conjoined egg and pollen cells in the form of fractions, those for the pollen cells above and those for the egg cells below the line. We then have

$$\frac{A}{A} \quad + \quad \frac{A}{a} \quad + \quad \frac{a}{A} \quad + \quad \frac{a}{a}$$

In the first and fourth term the egg and pollen cells are of like kind, consequently the product of their union must be constant, viz., *A* and *a*. In the second and third, on the other hand, there again results a union of the two differentiating characters of the stocks, consequently the forms resulting from these fertilizations are identical with those of the hybrid from which they sprang. *There occurs accordingly a repeated hybridization.* This explains the striking fact that the hybrids are able to produce, besides the two parental forms, offspring which are like themselves. *A/a* and *a/A* both give the same union *Aa*, since, as already remarked above, it makes no difference in the result of fertilization to which of the two characters the pollen or egg cells belong. We may write then

$$A/A + A/a + a/A + a/a = A + 2\,Aa + a.$$

This represents the average result of the self-fertilization of the hybrids when two differentiating characters are united in them. In individual flowers and in individual plants, however, the ratios in which the forms of the series are produced may suffer not inconsiderable fluctuations.[14] Apart from the fact that the numbers in which both sorts of egg cells occur in the seed vessels can only be regarded as equal on the average, it remains purely a matter of chance which of the two sorts of pollen may fertilize each separate egg cell. For this reason the separate values must necessarily be subject to fluctuations, and there are even extreme cases possible, as were described earlier in connection with the experiments on the forms of the seed and the color of the albumen. The true ratios of the numbers can only be ascertained by an average deduced from the sum of as many single values as possible; the greater the number the more are merely chance effects eliminated.

The developmental series for hybrids in which two kinds of differentiating characters are united contains among 16 individuals 9 different forms, viz.,

$$AB + Ab + aB + ab + 2ABb + 2aBb + 2AaB + 2Aab + 4AaBb.$$

Between the differentiating characters of the original stocks *A*, *a* and *B*, four constant combinations are possible, and consequently the hybrids produce the corresponding four forms of egg and pollen cells: *AB*, *Ab*, *aB*, *ab*, and each of these will on the average figure 4 times in the fertilization, since 16 individuals are included in the series. Therefore, the participators in the fertilization are

Pollen cells
*AB+AB+AB+AB+Ab+Ab+Ab+Ab+aB+aB+aB*
*+aB+ab+ab+ab+ab.*
Egg cells
*AB+AB+AB+AB+Ab+Ab+Ab+Ab+aB+aB+aB*
*+aB+ab+ab+ab+ab.*

In the process of fertilization each pollen form unites on an average equally often with each egg cell form, so that each of the four pollen cells *AB* unites once with one of the forms of egg cell *AB, Ab, aB, ab.* In precisely the same way the rest of the pollen cells of the forms *Ab, aB, ab,* unite with all the other egg cells. We obtain therefore:

$$\frac{AB}{AB} + \frac{AB}{Ab} + \frac{AB}{aB} + \frac{AB}{ab} + \frac{Ab}{AB} + \frac{Ab}{Ab} + \frac{Ab}{aB} + \frac{Ab}{ab} + \frac{aB}{AB} + \frac{aB}{Ab} + \frac{aB}{aB} + \frac{aB}{ab} + \frac{ab}{AB} + \frac{ab}{Ab} + \frac{ab}{aB} + \frac{ab}{ab}$$

or

$$AB + ABb + AaB + AaBb + ABb + Ab + AaBb + Aab + AaB + AaBb + aB + aBb + AaBb + Aab +$$
$$aBb + ab = AB + Ab + aB + ab + 2ABb + 2aBb + 2AaB + 2Aab + 4AaBb$$

In precisely similar fashion is the developmental series of hybrids exhibited when three kinds of differentiating characters are conjoined in them. The hybrids form eight various kinds of egg and pollen cells: *ABC, ABc, AbC, Abc, aBC, aBc, abC, abc,* and each pollen form unites itself again on the average once with each form of egg cell.

The law of combination of different characters which governs the development of the hybrids finds therefore its foundation and explanation in the principle enunciated, that the hybrids produce egg cells and pollen cells which in equal numbers represent all constant forms which result from the combinations of the characters brought together in fertilization.[g]

[g]Mendel's paper contains two additional sections. Neither section presents new experimental results to support his theories, and they are omitted here. [B.]

## NOTES

1. It is to the clear conception of these three primary necessities that the whole success of Mendel's work is due. So far as I know this conception was absolutely new in his day.
2. Mendel uses the terms "albumen" and "endosperm" somewhat loosely to denote the cotyledons, containing food-material, within the seed.
3. One species possesses a beautifully brownish-red colored pod, which when ripening turns to violet and blue. Trials with this character were only begun last year. Of these further experiments it seems no account was published. Correns has since worked with such a variety.
4. This is often called the Mummy Pea. It shows slight fascination. The form I know has white standard and salmon-red wings.
5. In my account of the these experiments (*R.H.S. Journal,* vol. XXV., p. 54) I misunderstood this paragraph and took "axis" to mean the *floral* axis, instead of the main axis of the plant. The unit of measurement, being indicated in the original by a prime (′), I carelessly took to have been an *inch,* but the translation here given is evidently correct.
6. It is somewhat surprising that no mention is made of Thrips, which swarm in pea flowers. I had come to the conclusion that this is a real source of error and I see Laxton held the same opinion.
7. Mendel throughout speaks of his cross-bred Peas as "hybrids," a term which many restrict to the offspring of two distinct *species.* He, as he explains, held this to be only a question of degree.

8.  Note that Mendel, with true penetration, avoids speaking of the hybrid-character as "transmitted" by either parent, thus escaping the error pervading older views of heredity.
9.  This is true also of the dwarf or "Cupid" Sweet Peas.
10. This paragraph presents the view of the hybrid-character as something incidental to the hybrid, and not "transmitted" to it—a true and fundamental conception here expressed probably for the first time.
11. Note that Mendel does not state the cotyledon-color of the first crosses in this case; for as the coats were thick, it could not have been seen without opening or peeling the seeds.
12. This and the preceding paragraph contain the essence of the Mendelian principles of heredity. [Mendel's account of the production of reproductive cells in hybrids is called the "law of random segregation." Mendel's second law of independent assortment is reflected in his discussion of the production of eggs and pollen in plants hybrid for more than one character. [B.]]
13. To prove, namely, that both were similarly differentiated, and not one or other only.
14. Whether segregation by such units is more than purely fortuitous may perhaps be determined by seriation.

## FURTHER READING

Bowler, Peter. 1989. *The Mendelian Revolution*. Baltimore: Johns Hopkins University. MendelWeb. *http://www.mendelweb.org/*
Olby, Robert C. 1985. *Origins of Mendelism*. Chicago: University of Chicago Press.

# Theory of Pangenes

## Charles Darwin (1809–1882)

*Darwin's theory of evolution by natural selection rests critically on the ability of individuals to transmit valuable traits to subsequent generations. The difficulty was that his theory did not offer an explanation for this process. In* The Variation of Animals and Plants under Domestication *(1868), from which this reading is taken, Darwin returned to this problem, elaborating "his provisional hypothesis of pangenesis," which attempted in one swoop to explain a number of biological phenomena—hereditary resemblance, inheritance of acquired characteristics, atavism (where characteristics skip a generation), prepotency (which is now called "dominance"), where the characteristics of one parent mask those of the other parent, and reversion (the reappearance of ancient characteristics to reappear as though from nowhere).*

*Darwin's hypothesis was based on the assumption that each character able to vary independently of another was linked to a material bearer. Every cell of the developing organism was able to produce tiny gemmules, all different from one another, that were responsible for the formation of individual organs. These gemmules can reproduce independently of one another and in varying degrees of strength. Whenever cell division occurs, they enter into the daughter cells and can freely circulate within the body, passing into the reproductive cells which ensure their transmission to subsequent generations. If certain kinds of gemmules diminish in number as compared with others, the characteristic they determine is weakly developed; if they are reduced still further, it eventually becomes latent.*

*Darwin defended his hypothesis on the grounds that it showed that normal individual differences are random—they are primarily a function of the way that gemmules are altered by external conditions that encroach on an individual's reproductive organs and thereby on the gemmules themselves. Second, he argued that it demonstrates how acquired characteristics can be inherited. When something changes during the life of an organism, such as the strength of a blacksmith's arms, this affects the gemmules given off, and consequently the gemmules can be passed on to the next generation.*

*Although Darwin believed that pangenesis threw light on the problem of heredity and variation, it was widely dismissed by scientists, who remarked that Darwin had merely revived tired old ideas that had appeared in almost every century dating back to Hippocrates (c. 460–370 B.C.). In step with Herbert Spencer (1820–1903), Darwin*

*Source:* Charles Darwin. 1868. *The Variations in Animals and Plants Under Domestication.* London: J. Murray, vol. 2, pp. 446–447; 448–449; 450–452; 481–483.

*believed that the whole body, and not just the sex cells, produces the germ cells. On this basis, Spencer argued that what one puts into reproduction is taken away from the individual. Undue production of sperm cells in males leads first to headaches and then to stupidity, imbecility, and finally, insanity.*

Reversion . . . proves to us that the transmission of a character and its development, which ordinarily go together and thus escape discrimination, are distinct powers; and these powers in some cases are even antagonistic, for each acts alternatively in successive generations. Reversion is not a rare event, depending on some unusual or favorable combination of circumstances; but occurs so regularly with crossed animals and plants, and so frequently with uncrossed breeds, that it is evidently an essential part of the principle of inheritance. We know that changed conditions have the power of evoking long-lost characters, as in the case of some feral animals. The act of crossing in itself possesses this power in a high degree. What can be more wonderful than that characters, which have disappeared during scores, or hundreds, or even thousands of generations, should suddenly reappear perfectly developed, as in the case of pigeons and fowls when purely bred, and especially when crossed; or as with the zebrine stripes on dun-colored horses, and other such cases? Many monstrosities come under this same head, as when rudimentary organs are redeveloped, or when an organ which we must believe was possessed by an early progenitor, but of which not even a rudiment is left, suddenly reappears, as with the fifth stamen in some Scrophulariaceae [a large family of dicotyledonous plants]. We have already seen that reversion acts in bud-reproduction; and we know that it occasionally acts during the growth of the same individual animal, especially, but not exclusively, when of crossed parentage, as in the rare cases described of individual fowls, pigeons, cattle, and rabbits, which have reverted as they advanced in years to the colors of one of their parents or ancestors.

We are led to believe, as formerly explained, that every character which occasionally reappears is present in a latent form in each generation, in nearly the same manner as in male and females animals secondary characters of the opposite sex lie latent, ready to be evolved when the reproductive organs are injured. This comparison of the secondary sexual characters which are latent in both sexes, with other latent characters, is the more appropriate from the case recorded of the hen, which assumed some of the masculine characters, not of her own race, but of an early progenitor; she thus exhibited at the same time the redevelopment of latent characters of both kinds and connected both classes. In every living creature we may feel assured that a host of lost characters lie ready to be evolved under proper conditions. How can we make intelligible, and connect with other facts, this wonderful and common capacity of reversion—this power of calling back to life long-lost characters? . . .

It is almost universally admitted that cells, or the units of the body, propagate themselves by self-division or proliferation, retaining the same nature, and ultimately becoming converted into the various tissues and substances of the body. But besides this means of increase I assume that cells, before their conversion into completely passive or "form-material," throw off minute granules of atoms, which circulate freely throughout the system, and when supplied with proper nutriment multiply by self-division, subsequently becoming developed into cells like those from which they were derived. These granules for the sake of distinctness may be called cell-gemmules, or, as the cellular theory is not fully established, simply gemmules. They are supposed to be transmitted from the parents to the offspring, and are generally developed in the generation which immediately succeeds, but are often transmitted in a dormant state during many generations and are then developed. Their development is supposed to depend on their union with other partially developed cells or gemmules which precede them in the regular course of growth. Why I use the term union will be seen when we discuss the direct action of pollen on the tissues of the mother-plant. Gemmules are supposed to be thrown off by every cell or unit, not only during the adult state, but during all the stages of development. Lastly, I assume that the gemmules in their dormant state have a mutual affinity for each other, leading to their aggregation either into buds or into the sexual elements. Hence, speaking strictly, it is not the reproductive elements, nor the buds, which generate new organisms, but the cells themselves through the body. These assumptions constitute the provisional hypothesis which I have called Pangenesis. Nearly similar views have been propounded, as I find, by other authors, more especially by Mr. Herbert Spencer; but they are here modified and amplified.[a]

It may be useful to give an illustration of the hypothesis. If one of the simplest protozoa be formed, as appears under the microscope, of a small mass of homogeneous gelatinous matter, a minute atom thrown off from any part and nourished under favorable circumstances would naturally reproduce the whole; but if the upper and lower

surfaces were to differ in texture from the central portion, then all three parts would have to throw off atoms or gemmules, which when aggregated by mutual affinity would form either buds or the sexual elements. Precisely the same view may be extended to one of the higher animals; although in this case many thousand gemmules must be thrown off from the various parts of the body. Now, when the leg, for instance, of a salamander is cut off, a slight crust forms over the wound, and beneath this crust the uninjured cells or units of bone, muscle, nerves, etc., are supposed to unite with the diffused gemmules of those cells which in the perfect leg come next in order; and these as they become slightly developed unite with others, and so on until a papilla of soft cellular tissue, the "budding leg," is formed, and in time a perfect leg. Thus, that portion of the leg which had been cut off, neither more nor less, would be reproduced. If the tail or leg of a young animal had been cut off, a young tail or leg would have been reproduced, as actually occurs with the amputated tail of a tadpole; for gemmules of the units which compose the tail are diffused throughout the body at all ages. But during the adult stage the gemmules of the larval tail would remain dormant, for they would not meet with pre-existing cells in a proper state of development with which to unite. If from changed conditions or any other cause any part of the body should become permanently modified, the gemmules, which are merely minute portions of the contents of the cells forming the part, would naturally reproduce the same modification. But gemmules previously derived from the same part before it had undergone any change would still be diffused throughout the organization, and would be transmitted from generation to generation, so that under favorable circumstances they might be redeveloped, and then the new modification would be for a time or forever lost. The aggregation of gemmules derived from every part of the body, through their mutual affinity, would form buds, and their aggregation

[a]In a lengthy footnote, which is not reproduced here, Darwin discusses the views of Georges Louis Leclerc de Buffon (1707–1788), Charles Bonnet, David Owen (1802–1892), and Herbert Spencer as they relate to the doctrine of pangenesis with the aim of distancing his view from those of his predecessors. [B.]

in some special manner, apparently in small quantity, together probably with the presence of gemmules of certain primordial cells, would constitute the sexual elements. By means of these illustrations the hypothesis of pangenesis has, I hope, been rendered intelligible . . .

The hypothesis of pangenesis, as applied to the several great classes of facts just discussed, no doubt is extremely complex; but so assuredly are the facts. The assumptions, however, on which the hypothesis rests cannot be considered as complex in any extreme degree—namely, that all organic units, besides having the power, as is generally admitted, of growing by self-division, throw off free and minute atoms of their contents, that is gemmules. These multiply and aggregate themselves into buds and the sexual elements; their development depends on their union with other nascent cells or units; and they are capable of transmission in a dormant state to successive generations.

In a highly organized and complex animal, the gemmules thrown off from each different cell or unit throughout the body must be inconceivably numerous and minute. Each unit of each part, as it changes during development, and we know that some insects undergo at least twenty metamorphoses, must throw off its gemmules. All organic beings, moreover, include many dormant gemmules derived from their grandparents and more remote progenitors, but not from all their progenitors. These almost indefinitely numerous and minute gemmules must be included in each bud, ovule, spermatozoon, and pollen-grain. Such an admission will be declared impossible; but, as previously remarked, number and size are only relative difficulties, and the eggs or seeds produced by certain animals or plants are so numerous that they cannot be grasped by the intellect.

The organic particles with which the wind is tainted over miles of space by offensive animals must be infinitely minute and numerous; yet they strongly affect the olfactory nerves. An analogy more appropriate is afforded by the contagious particles of certain diseases, which are so minute that they float in the atmosphere and adhere to smooth paper; yet we know how largely they increase within the human body, and how powerfully they act. Independent organisms exist which are barely visible under the highest powers of our recently-improved microscopes, and which probably are fully as large as the cells or units in one of the higher animals; yet these organisms no doubt reproduce themselves by germs of extreme minuteness, relatively to their own minute size. Hence, the difficulty, which at first appears insurmountable, of believing in the existence of gemmules so numerous and so small as they must be according to our hypothesis, has really little weight. The cells or units of the body are generally admitted by physiologists to be autonomous, like the buds on trees, but in a less degree. I go one step further and assume that they throw off reproductive gemmules. Thus an animal does not, as a whole, generate its kind through the sole agency of the reproductive system, but each separate cell generates its kind. It has often been said by naturalists that each cell of a plant has the actual or potential capacity of reproducing the whole plant; but it has this power only in virtue of containing gemmules derived from every part. If our hypothesis be provisionally accepted, we must look at all the forms of asexual reproduction, whether occurring at maturity or as in the case of alternate generation during youth, as fundamentally the same, and dependent on the mutual aggregation and multiplication of the gemmules. The regrowth of an amputated limb of the healing of a wound is the same process partially carried out. Sexual generation differs in some important respects, chiefly, as it would appear, in an insufficient number of gemmules being aggregated within the separate sexual elements, and probably in the presence of certain primordial cells. The development of each being, including all forms of metamorphosis and metagenesis, as well as the so-called growth of the higher animals, in which structure changes though not in a striking manner, depends on the presence of gemmules thrown off at each period of life, and on their development, at a corresponding period, in union with preceding cells. Such cells may be said to be fertilized by the gemmules which come next in the order of development. Thus the ordinary act of impregnation and the development of each being are closely analogous processes. The child, strictly speaking, does not grow into the man, but includes germs which slowly and successively become developed and form the man. In the child, as well as in the adult, each part generates the same part for the next generation. Inheritance must be looked at as merely a form of growth, like the self-division of a lowly-organized unicellular plant. Reversion depends on the transmission from the forefather to his descendants of dormant gemmules, which occasionally become developed under certain known or unknown conditions. Each animal and plant may be compared to a bed of mold full of seeds, most of which soon germinate; some lie for a period dormant, while others perish. When we hear it said that a man carries in his constitution the seeds of an inherited disease, there is much literal truth in the expression. Finally, the power of propagation possessed by each separate cell, using the term in its largest sense, determines the reproduction, the variability, the development and renovation of each living organism. No other attempt, as far as I am aware, has been made, imperfect as this confessedly is, to connect under one point of view these several grand classes of facts. We cannot fathom the marvelous complexity of an organic being; but on the hypothesis here advanced this complexity is much increased. Each living creature must be looked at as a microcosm; a little universe, formed of a host of self-propagating organisms, inconceivably minute and as numerous as the stars in heaven.

## FURTHER READING

Everson, Ted. W. 2002. "Genetics and Molecular Biology." In Brian S. Baigrie, ed., *History of Modern Science and Mathematics.* New York: Charles Scribner's Sons, vol. 3, pp. 93–133.

Carson, E. A. 1966. *The Gene: A Critical History.* Philadelphia: W. B. Saunders.

# Experimental Physics as a University Subject

## James Clerk Maxwell (1831–1879)

*James Clerk Maxwell took up Faraday's electromagnetic discoveries in 1855 and saw that Faraday's conception for describing the interactions of electricity and magnetism was susceptible of precise mathematical description. This monumental work, known as the electromagnetic theory, showed that magnetism and electricity could not exist separately. In support of Faraday's field theory, Maxwell showed that an electromagnetic field was, in fact, created by the oscillation of an electrical current. This field, he claimed, radiated outward from its source at a constant speed, which could be calculated by taking a ratio of certain magnetic units to certain electrical units, which worked out to be approximately 186,000 miles per second. Since this value jibed with the speed of light, Maxwell concluded that light itself must be an oscillating electric charge. Indeed, Maxwell reckoned that light must be just one a large family of radiations caused by charges oscillating at different velocities.*

*In 1871, Maxwell was appointed first Professor of Experimental Physics at Cambridge and he played a leading role in planning and developing the Cavendish Laboratory, opened in 1874 by its patron, the Duke of Devonshire. The creation of the Cavendish marked the beginning of a new era of scientific activity. A characteristic of the experiments carried out under Maxwell's direction was an emphasis on precise measurement, several orders of magnitude higher than anything previously attempted. Although the results achieved in actual research were modest during the first few years of its existence, the indirect effect of the laboratory was very considerable. Nor was this influence confined to Cambridge, for Maxwell's writings inspired Heinrich Hertz (1857–1894) in the work that laid the foundations for a new school of physics in Germany.*

*Source:* James Clerk Maxwell. 1870. "Introductory Lecture on Experimental Physics." From the *Report of the British Association.* Reprinted in James Clerk Maxwell, *The Scientific Papers of James Clerk Maxwell.* Cambridge: Cambridge University Press, 1890, vol. II, pp. 241–255.

The University of Cambridge—in accordance with that law of its evolution, which, while maintaining the strictest continuity between the successive phases of its history, adapts itself with more or less promptness to the requirements of the times—has lately instituted a course of Experimental Physics.

This course of study, while it requires us to maintain in action all those powers of attention and analysis which have been so long cultivated in the University, calls on us to exercise our senses in observation, and our hands in manipulation. The familiar apparatus of pen, ink, and paper will no longer be sufficient for us, and we shall require more room than that afforded by a seat at desk, and a wider area than that of the black board. We owe it to the magnificence of our Chancellor, that, whatever be the character in other respects the experiments which we hope hereafter to conduct, the material facilities for their full development will be upon a scale which has not hitherto been surpassed.

The main feature, therefore, of Experimental Physics at Cambridge is the Devonshire [Cavendish] Physical Laboratory, and I think it desirable that on the present occasion, before we enter on the details of any special study, we should consider by what means we, the University of Cambridge, may, as a living body, appropriate and vitalize this new organ, the outward shell of which we expect soon to rise before us. The course of study at this University has always included Natural Philosophy, as well as Pure Mathematics. To diffuse a sound knowledge of Physics and to imbue the minds of our students with correct dynamical principles have been long regarded as among our highest functions, and very few of us can now place ourselves in the mental condition in which even such philosophers as the great Descartes were involved in the days before Newton had announced the true laws of the motion of bodies. Indeed the cultivation and diffusion of sound dynamical ideas has already effected a great change in the language and thoughts even of those who make no pretensions to science, and we are daily receiving fresh proofs that the popularization of scientific doctrines is producing as great an alteration in the mental state of society as the material applications of science are effecting in its outward life. Such indeed is the respect paid to science that the most absurd opinions may become current, provided they are expressed in language, the sound of which recalls some well-known scientific phrase. If society is thus prepared to receive all kinds of scientific doctrines, it is our part to provide for the diffusion and cultivation, not only of true scientific principles, but of a spirit of sound criticism, founded on an examination of the evidences on which statements apparently scientific depend.

When we shall be able to employ in scientific education, not only the trained attention of the student, and his familiarity with symbols, but the keenness of his eye, the quickness of his ear, the delicacy of his touch, and the adroitness of his fingers, we shall not only extend our influence over a class of men who are not fond of cold abstractions, but, by opening at once all the gateways of knowledge, we shall ensure the association of the doctrines of science with those elementary sensations which form the obscure background of all our conscious thoughts, and which lend a vividness and relief to ideas, which, when presented as mere abstract terms, are apt to fade entirely from the memory.

In a course of Experimental Physics we may consider either the physics or the experiments as the leading feature. We may either employ the experiments to illustrate the phenomena of a particular branch of Physics, or we may make some physical research in order to exemplify a particular experimental method. In the order of time, we should begin, in the lecture room, with a course of lectures on some branch of Physics aided by experiments of illustration, and conclude, in the Laboratory, with a course of experiments of research.

Let me say a few words on these two classes of experiments—experiments of illustration and experiments of research. The aim of an experiment of illustration is to throw light upon some scientific idea so that the student be enabled to grasp it. The circumstances of the experiment are so arranged that the phenomenon which we wish to observe or to exhibit is brought into prominence, instead of being obscured and entangled among other phenomena, as it is when it occurs in the ordinary course of nature. To exhibit illustrative experiments, to encourage others to make them, and to cultivate in way the ideas on which they throw light, forms an important part of our duty.

The simpler the materials of an illustrative experiment, and the more familiar they are to the student, the more thoroughly is he likely to acquire the idea which it is meant to illustrate. The educational value of such experiments is often inversely proportional to the complexity of the apparatus. The student who uses homemade apparatus, which is always going wrong, often learns more than one who has the use of carefully adjusted instruments, to which he is apt to trust, and which he dares not take to pieces.

It is very necessary that those who are trying to learn from books the facts of physical science should be enabled by the help of a few illustrative experiments to recognize these facts when they meet with them out of doors. Science appears to us with a very different aspect after we have found out it is not in lecture rooms only, and by means of the electric light projected on a screen, that we may witness physical phenomena, but that we may find illustrations of the highest doctrines of science in games and gymnastics, in traveling by land and by water, in storms of the air and of the sea, and whether there is matter in motion.

This habit of recognizing principles amid the endless variety of their action never degrade our sense of the sublimity of nature, or mar our enjoyment of its beauty. On the contrary, it tends to rescue our scientific ideas from that vague condition in which we too often leave them, buried among the products of a lazy credulity, and to raise them into their proper position the doctrines in which our faith is so assured, that we are ready at all times to act on them.

Experiments of illustration may be of very different kinds. Some may be adaptations of the commonest operations of ordinary life, others may be carefully arranged exhibitions of some phenomenon which occurs only under peculiar conditions. They all, however, agree in this, that their aim is to present some phenomenon to the senses of the student in such a way that he may associate with it the appropriate scientific idea. When he has grasped this idea, the experiment which illustrates it has served its purpose.

In an experiment of research, on the other hand, this is not the principal aim. It is true that an experiment, in which the principal aim is to see what happens under certain conditions, may be regarded as an experiment of research by those who are not yet familiar with the result, but in experimental researches, strictly so called, the ultimate object is to measure something which we have already seen—to obtain a numerical estimate of some magnitude.

Experiments of this class—those in which measurement of some kind is involved—are the proper work of a Physical Laboratory. In every experiment we have first to make our senses familiar with the phenomenon, but we must not stop here, we must find out which of its features are capable of measurement, and what measurements are required in order to make a complete specification of the phenomenon. We must then make these measurements, and deduce from them the result which we require to find.

This characteristic of modern experiments—that they consist principally of measurements—is so prominent, that the opinion seems to have got abroad, that in a few years all the great physical constants will have been approximately estimated, and that the only occupation which will then be left to men of science will be to carry on these measurements to another place of decimals.

If this is really the state of things to which we are approaching, our Laboratory may perhaps become celebrated as a place of conscientious labor and consummate skill, but it will be out of place in the University, and ought rather to be classed with the other great workshops of our country, where equal ability is directed to more useful ends.

But we have no right to think thus of the unsearchable riches of creation, or of the untried fertility of those fresh minds into which these riches will continue to be poured. It may possibly be true that, in some of those fields of discovery which lie open to such rough observations as can be made without artificial methods, the great explorers of former times have appropriated most of what is valuable, and that the gleanings which remain are sought rather for their abstruseness, than for their intrinsic worth. But the history of science shows that even during that phase of her progress in which she devotes herself to improving the accuracy of the numerical measurement of quantities with which she has long been familiar, she is preparing the material, for the subjugation of new regions, which would have remained unknown if she had been contented with the rough methods of her early pioneers. I might bring forward instances gathered from every branch of science, showing how the labor of careful measurement has been rewarded by the discovery of new fields of research, and by the development of new scientific ideas. But the history of the science of terrestrial magnetism affords us a sufficient example of what may be done by experiments in concert, such as we hope some day to perform in our Laboratory.

That celebrated traveler, Humboldt,[a] was profoundly impressed with the scientific value of a combined effort to be made by the observers of all nations, to obtain accurate measurements of the magnetism of the earth; and we owe it mainly to his enthusiasm for science, his great reputation and his widespread influence, that not only private

men of science, but the governments of most of the civilized nations, our own among the number, were induced to take part in the enterprise. But the actual working out of the scheme, and the arrangements by which the labors of the observers were so directed as to obtain the best results, we owe to the great mathematician Gauss, working along with Weber, the future founder of the science of electromagnetic measurement, in the magnetic observatory of Göttingen, and aided by the skill of the instrument-maker Leyser. These men, however, did not work alone. Numbers of scientific men joined the Magnetic Union, learned the use of the new instruments and the new methods of reducing the observations; and in every city of Europe you might see them, at certain stated times, sitting, each in his cold wooden shed, with his eye fixed at the telescope, his ear attentive to the clock, and his pencil recording in his note-book the instantaneous position of the suspended magnet.

Bacon's conception of "experiments in concert" was thus realized, the scattered forces of science were converted into a regular army, and emulation and jealousy became out of place, for the results obtained by any one observer were of no value until they were combined with those of the others.

The increase in the accuracy and completeness of magnetic observations which was obtained by the new method, opened up fields of research which were hardly suspected to exist by those whose observations of the magnetic needle had been conducted in a more primitive manner. We must reserve for its proper place in our course any detailed description of the disturbances to which the magnetism of our planet is found to be subject. Some of these disturbances are periodic, following the regular courses of the Sun and Moon. Others are sudden, and are called magnetic storms, but, like the storms of the atmosphere, they have their known seasons of frequency. The last and the most mysterious of these magnetic changes is that secular variation by which the whole character of the Earth, as a great magnet, is being

[a] In 1836, Alexander von Humboldt (1769–1859) suggested in a letter to the president of the Royal Society the worldwide establishment of geomagnetic observatories. In 1834 there were twenty-three such observatories, but it was left to Carl Friedrich Gauss (1777–1855), in concert with Wilhelm Eduard Weber (1804–1891), to organize a worldwide network of observatories, the *Magnetische Verein*, and to coordinate the resulting measurements. Their effort set a precedent for international scientific collaboration. [B.]

**PLATE 35**    Ernest Rutherford's laboratory at Cambridge University.

slowly modified, while the magnetic poles creep on, from century to century, along their winding track in the polar regions.

We have thus learned that the interior of the Earth is subject to the influences of the heavenly bodies, but that besides this there is a constantly progressive change going on, the cause of which is entirely unknown. In each of the magnetic observatories throughout the world an arrangement is at work, by means of which a suspended magnet directs a ray of light on a prepared sheet of paper moved by clockwork. On that paper the never-resting heart of the Earth is now tracing, in telegraphic symbols which will one day be interpreted, a record of its pulsations and its flutterings, as well as of that slow but mighty working which warns us that we must not suppose that the inner history of our planet is ended.

But this great experimental research on terrestrial magnetism produced lasting effects on the progress of science in general. I need only mention one or two instances. The new methods of measuring forces were successfully applied by Weber to the numerical determination of all the phenomena of electricity, and very soon afterwards the electric telegraph, by conferring a commercial value on exact numerical measurements, contributed largely to the advancement, as well as to the diffusion of scientific knowledge.

But it is not in these more modern branches of science alone that this influence is felt. It is to Gauss, to the Magnetic Union, and to magnetic observers in general, that

*Widened Circles*

*"Constantly progressive Change".*

*Must have Substance to theory.*

we owe our deliverance from that absurd method of estimating forces by a variable standard which prevailed so long even among men of science. It was Gauss who first based the practical measurement of magnetic force (and therefore of every other force) on those long established principles, which, though they are embodied in every dynamical equation, have been so generally set aside, that these very equations, though correctly given in our Cambridge textbooks, are usually explained there by assuming, in addition to the variable standard of force, a variable, and therefore illegal, standard of mass.

Such, then, were some of the scientific results which followed from bringing together mathematical power, experimental sagacity, and manipulative skill, to direct and assist the labors of a body of zealous observers. If therefore we desire, for our own advantage and for the honor of our University, that the Devonshire Laboratory should be successful, we must endeavor to maintain it in living union with the other organs and faculties of our learned body. We shall therefore first consider the relation in which we stand to those mathematical studies which have so long flourished among us, which deal with our own subjects, and which differ from our experimental studies only in the mode in which they are presented to the mind.

*Exp. is Science only in different form.*

There is no more powerful method for introducing knowledge into the mind than that of presenting it in as many different ways as we can. When the ideas, after entering through different gateways, effect a junction in the citadel of the mind, the position they occupy becomes impregnable. Opticians tell us that the mental combination of the views of an object which we obtain from stations no further apart than our two eyes is sufficient to produce in our minds an impression of the solidity of the object seen; and we find that this impression is produced even when we are aware that we are really looking at two flat pictures placed in a stereoscope. It is therefore natural to expect that the knowledge of physical science obtained by the combined use of mathematical analysis and experimental research will be of a more solid, available, and enduring kind than that possessed by the mere mathematician or the mere experimenter.

But what will be the effect on the University, if men pursuing that course of reading which has produced so many distinguished Wranglers, turn aside to work experiments? Will not their attendance at the Laboratory count not merely as time withdrawn from their more legitimate studies, but as the introduction of a disturbing element, tainting their mathematical conceptions with material imagery, and sapping their faith in the formulae of the textbooks? Besides this, we have already heard complaints of the undue extension of our studies, and of the strain put upon our questions by the weight of learning which they try to carry with them into the Senate-House. If we now ask them to get up their subjects not only by books and writing, but at the same time by observation and manipulation, will they not break down altogether? The Physical Laboratory, we are told, may perhaps be useful to those who are going out in Natural Science, and who do not take in Mathematics, but to attempt to combine both kinds of study during the time of residence at the University is more than one mind can bear.

No doubt there is some reason for this feeling. Many of us have already overcome the initial difficulties of mathematical training. When we now go on with our study, we feel that it requires exertion and involves fatigue, but we are confident that if we only work hard our progress will be certain.

Some of us, on the other hand, may have had some experience of the routine of experimental work. As soon as we can read scales, observe times, focus telescopes, and so on, this kind of work ceases to require any great mental effort. We may perhaps tire our eyes and weary our backs, but we do not greatly fatigue our minds. It is not till we attempt to bring the theoretical part of our training into contact with the practical that we begin to experience the full effect of what Faraday has called "mental inertia"—not only the difficulty of recognizing, among the concrete objects before us, the abstract relation which we have learned from books, but the distracting pain of wrenching the mind away from the symbols to the objects, and from the objects back to the symbols. This however is the price we have to pay for new ideas.

But when we have overcome these difficulties, and successfully bridged over the gulf between the abstract and the concrete, it is not a mere piece of knowledge that we have obtained: We have acquired the rudiment of a permanent mental endowment. When, by a repetition of efforts of this kind, we have more fully developed the scientific faculty, the exercise of this faculty in detecting scientific principles in nature, and in directing practice by theory, is no longer irksome, but becomes an unfailing source of enjoyment, to which we return so often, that at last even our careless thoughts begin to run in a scientific channel.

I quite admit that our mental energy is limited in quantity, and I know that many zealous students try to do more than is good for them. But the question about the introduction of experimental study is not entirely one of quantity. It is to a great extent a question of distribution of energy. Some distributions of energy, we know, are more useful than others, because they are more available for those purposes which we desire to accomplish.

Now in the case of study, a great part of our fatigue often arises, not from those mental efforts by which we obtain the mastery of the subject, but from those which are spent in recalling our wandering thoughts; and these efforts of attention would be much less fatiguing if the disturbing force of mental distraction could be removed.

This is the reason why a man whose soul is in his work always makes more progress than one whose aim is something not immediately connected with his occupation. In the latter case the very motive of which he makes use to stimulate his flagging powers

becomes the means of distracting his mind from the work before him.

There may be some mathematicians who pursue their studies entirely for their own sake. Most men, however, think that the chief use of mathematics is found in the interpretation of nature. Now a man who studies a piece of mathematics in order to understand some natural phenomenon which he has seen, or to calculate the best arrangement of some experiment which he means to make, is likely to meet with far less distraction of mind than if his sole aim had been to sharpen his mind for the successful practice of the Law, or to obtain a high place in the Mathematical Tripos. I have known men, who when they were at school, never could see the good of mathematics, but who, when in after life they made this discovery, not only became eminent as scientific engineers, but made considerable progress in the study of abstract mathematics. If our experimental course should help any of you to see the good of mathematics, it will relieve us of much anxiety, for it will not only ensure the success of your future studies, but it will make it much less likely that they will prove injurious to your health.

But why should we labor to prove the advantage of practical science to the University? Let us rather speak of the help which the University may give to science, when men well trained in mathematics and enjoying the advantage of a well-appointed Laboratory, shall unite their efforts to carry out some experimental research which no solitary worker could attempt.

At first it is probable that our principal experimental work must be the illustration of particular branches of science, but as we go on we must add to this the study of scientific methods, the same method being sometimes illustrated by its application to researches belonging to different branches of science.

We might even imagine a course of experimental study the arrangement of which should be founded on a classification of methods, and not on that of the objects of investigation. A combination of the two plans seems to me better than either, and while we take every opportunity of studying methods, we shall take care not to dissociate the method from the scientific research to which it is applied, and to which it owes its value.

We shall therefore arrange our lectures according to the classification of the principal natural phenomena, such as heat, electricity, magnetism and so on. In the laboratory, on the other hand, the place of the different instruments be determined by a classification according to methods, such as weighing, measuring, observations of time, optical and electrical methods of observation, and so on.

The determination of the experiments to be performed at a particular time end upon the means we have at command, and in the case of experiments, this may imply a long time of preparation, during which the instruments, the methods, and the observers themselves, are being gradually fitted for their work. When we have thus brought together the requisites, both material and intellectual, for a particular experiment, it may sometimes be desirable that before the instruments are dismounted and the observers dispersed, we should make some other experiment, requiring the same method, but dealing perhaps with an entirely different class of physical phenomena.

Our principal work, however, in the Laboratory must be to acquaint ourselves with all kinds of scientific methods, to compare them, and to estimate their value. It will, I think, be a result worthy of our University, and more likely to be accomplished here than in any private laboratory, if, by the free and full discussion of the relative value of different scientific procedures, we succeed in forming a school of scientific criticism, and in assisting the development of the doctrine of method.

But admitting that a practical acquaintance with the methods of physical science is an essential part of a mathematical and scientific education, we may be asked whether we are not attributing too much importance to science altogether as part of a liberal education.

Fortunately, there is no question here whether the University should continue to be a place of liberal education, or should devote itself to preparing young men for particular professions. Hence though some of us may, I hope, see reason to make the pursuit of science the main business of our lives, it must be one of our most constant aims to maintain a living connection between our work and the other liberal studies of Cambridge, whether literary, philological, historical or philosophical. There is a narrow professional spirit which may grow up among men of science, just as it does among men who practice any other special business.[b] But surely a University is the very place where we should be able to overcome this tendency of men to become, as it were, granulated into small worlds, which are all the more worldly for their very smallness. We lose the advantage of having men of varied pursuits collected into one body, if we do not endeavor to imbibe some of the spirit even of those whose special branch of learning is different from our own.

It is not so long ago since any man who devoted himself to geometry or to any science requiring continued application, was looked upon as necessary a misanthrope, who must have abandoned all human interests, and betaken himself to abstractions so far removed from the world of life and action that he has become insensible alike to the attractions of pleasure and to the claims of duty.

[b]The new laboratories demanded role players—theoreticians, technicians, and number crunchers. In the 1830s, John Herschel managed to contribute to chemistry, mathematics, and astronomy, but he was an exception to the widespread flight to specialized vocations. Science had become too complex for a single individual to make significant contributions without going deep into a single area or discipline. Part of the story of the Cavendish Laboratory was the creation of entire new kinds of professionals, who become very good at one particular thing, such as making a counter for tiny particles. This kind of specialization was something new and has been a feature of scientific practice ever since. [B.]

In the present day, men of science are not looked upon with the same awe or with the same suspicion. They are supposed to be in league with the material spirit of the age, and to form a kind of advanced Radical party among men of learning. We are not here to defend literary and historical studies. We admit that the proper study of mankind is man. But is the student of science to be withdrawn from the study of man, or cut off from every noble feeling, so long as he lives in intellectual fellowship with men who have devoted their lives to the discovery of truth, and the results of whose enquiries have impressed themselves on the ordinary speech and way of thinking of men who never heard their names? Or is the student of history and of man to omit from his consideration the history of the origin and diffusion of those ideas which have produced so great a divergence between one age of the world and another?

It is true that the history of science is very different from the science of history. We are not studying or attempting to study the working of those blind forces which, we are told, are operating on crowds of obscure people, shaking principalities and powers, and compelling reasonable men to bring events to pass in an order laid down by philosophers.

The men whose names are found in the history of science are not mere hypothetical constituents of a crowd, to be reasoned upon only in masses. We recognize them as men like ourselves, and their actions and thoughts, being more free from the influence of passion, and recorded more accurately than those of other men, and are all the better materials for the study of the calmer parts of human nature.

But the history of science is not restricted to the enumeration of successful investigations. It has to tell of unsuccessful inquiries, and to explain why some of the ablest men have failed to find the key of knowledge, and how the reputation of others has only given a firmer footing to the errors into which they fell.

The history of the development, whether normal or abnormal, of ideas is of all subjects that in which we, as thinking men, take the deepest interest. But when the action of the mind passes out of the intellectual stage, in which and error are the alternatives, into the more violently emotional states of anger and passion, malice and envy, fury and madness; the student of science, though he is obliged to recognize the powerful influence which these wild forces have exercised on mankind, is perhaps in some measure disqualified from pursuing the study of this part of human nature.

But then how few of us are capable of deriving profit from such studies. We cannot enter into full sympathy with these lower phases of our nature without losing some of that antipathy to them which is our surest safeguard against a reversion to a meaner type, and we gladly return to the company of those illustrious men who by aspiring to noble ends, whether intellectual or practical, have risen above the region of storms into a clearer atmosphere, where there is no misrepresentation of opinion, nor ambiguity of expression, but where one mind comes into closest contact with another at the point where both approach nearest to the truth . . .

## FURTHER READINGS

Harman, P. M. 1998. *The Natural Philosophy of James Clerk Maxwell*. Cambridge: Cambridge University Press.

Hunt, Bruce J. 1991. *The Maxwellians*. Ithaca: Cornell University Press.

No author. 1910. *A History of the Cavendish Laboratory, 1871–1910*. London: Longmans, Green.

# Playing Patience with the Elements

## Dmitri Ivanovitch Mendeléev (1834–1907)

*In 1869, Dmitri Mendeléev predicted the existence of three new elements, boldly fore-casting not only the chemical properties of these hitherto undetected elements, but their atomic weights as well. Predictions were a staple of chemistry, but Mendeléev's were different: In a science that had been erected stone by stone on the bedrock of experiment, his predictions seemed to be deductive consequences of his theory alone. Amazingly, all three elements were isolated within eight years. Was Mendeléev a magician? Chemists had long suspected the existence of natural families of chemical elements. Displaying great inventiveness in tinkering with the idea of order among the elements, some toyed with the idea of triads or small groups of elements, based on similarities of their proper-ties. One industrial chemist had compared the table of the elements to the keyboard of a piano with its eighty-eight notes and divided into periods or octaves of eight.*

*Mendeléev's creative imagination was unmatched. Taking his cue from a type of solitaire called Patience, he played Patience with the known elements. Taking 63 cards and inscribing on them the names and properties of the elements, he posted the cards on the wall of his laboratory. He sorted out the similar elements and pinned the similar cards together. He then arranged the elements into seven groups, starting with lithium, and continuing with beryllium, boron, carbon, nitrogen, oxygen, and, finally, fluorine. The next element in the order of increasing atomic weight was sodium. This element resembled lithium closely both with respect to its physical and chemical prop-erties. It was placed below lithium on the emerging table. Continuing in this manner, when the list was complete, Mendeléev noticed a startling order: When the elements are lined up in the order of increasing atomic weight, similar characteristics repeat every so often. The properties of the elements, Mendeléev discerned, were periodic functions of their atomic weights.*

*Other bombshells followed. The received atomic weight of gold was 196.2 but it was placed in a space which belonged to platinum, with a received atomic weight of 196.7. Critics jumped on this anomaly. Mendeléev replied that it was the measurements, and not his table, that was mistaken. It turned out that gold had an atomic weight greater than platinum. The magician was right, and the empirics mistaken. His creative imag-ination was most evident in his treatment of those elements that would not fit into his*

*Source:* Mendeléev, Dmitri. 1879. "The Periodic Law of the Chemical Elements." *Chemical News*, vol. 40, pp. 231–232; 243–244; 267–268; 1880, vol. 41, pp. 27–28.

*scheme for the table — as a good card player, he realized that some of the playing cards were still in the deck. If a slot called for an element with specific properties, and there was no such element in his hand, he left spaces in his table for the elements still in the deck. In this way, he was led to predict three undiscovered elements, the subsequent discovery of which he left to practicing chemists.*

Although seven years have passed since these thoughts absorbed any attention; although other occupations have drawn my attention from the problem of the elements, which was always getting nearer a solution; in short, although I might wish to put this question otherwise than I did seven years ago, still I keep to the same firm conviction that I formerly had on the importance and value of the theorems on which my memoir is based; and this is why I am so gratified to see my ideas exposed to the appreciation of the learned. Several occurrences have aided to make some of the logical consequences of the periodic law popular.

First, the law I announced has been considered as a repetition in another form of what has already been said by others. The article in the *Berichte der Deutschen Chemischen Gesellschaft* 1874, p. 348, treats only of the question of priority. It is now certain that the periodic law offers consequences that the old system had scarcely ventured to foresee. Formerly it was only a grouping, a scheme, a subordination to a given fact; while the periodic law furnishes the facts, and tends to strengthen the philosophical question, which brings to light the mysterious nature of the elements. This tendency is of the same category as Prout's law,[a] with the essential difference that Prout's law is arithmetical, and that the periodic law exhausts itself in connecting the mechanical and philosophical laws which form the character and glory of the exact sciences. It proclaims loudly that

the nature of the elements depends above all on their mass, and it considers this function as periodic. The formula of the law might be changed; a greater appreciation of this function will be found, but I believe that the original idea of the periodic law will remain because it is opposed to the primitive notion that the nature of elements depends on unknown causes, and not on their mass . . .

Second, the periodic law requires changes in the atomic weights of many elements yet incompletely examined; for example, indium, cerium, yttrium, erbium, didymium,[b] etc. Before the existence of this law there was no reason for doubting the generally accepted atomic weights of these elements. At present, since the researches of Rammelsberg, Roscoe, Clève, Hoglund, Hildebrand, and others, have led to the same conclusion as that which is derived from the periodic law, it becomes incontestable that it shows us the truth, which is in fact its support.

Third, the periodic law has given the first chance of predicting not only unknown elements, but also of determining the chemical and physical properties of simple bodies still to be discovered, and those of their compounds. The discovery of gallium by M. Lecoq de Boisbaudran,[c] whom I have now

[a]William Prout's (1785–1850) law—formulated in 1815—states that the atomic weight of all atoms is an exact multiple of the atomic weights of hydrogen. [B.]

[b]A mixture of praseodymium and neodymium, thought to be an element until 1885. [B.]

[c]Boisbaudran (1838–1912) discovered with the new spectroscopic technology the element gallium in zinc blend extracted from a mine in the Pyrenees. He soon realized that the new element was the "eka-aluminum" predicted by Mendeléev, thereby providing compelling evidence for the soundness of the periodic classification of the elements. [B.]

the honor of counting as a friend, may be considered as the inauguration of the periodic law, and reckoned among the brilliant pages in the annals of science. The properties announced in the *Comptes Rendus*, Nov. 32, 1875, have been confirmed by [study] after study. It will be enough to mention four —the formation of gallium alum, the equivalent of the oxide, the specific gravity of the metal (5.9), and the atomic weight of the element.

It must be admitted that before the periodic law there was no possibility of a similar prediction. It is here to the point to direct attention to the fact that the fusing-point of gallium is so low that it melts at the heat of the hand. This property might be considered as foreseen, but that is not the case; it suffices to look at the following series:

$$\begin{array}{cccccc} Mg & Al & Si & P & S & Cl \\ Zn & Ga & — & As & Se & Br \\ Cd & In & Sn & Sb & Te & I \end{array}$$

It is evident that in the group Mg, Zn, Cd, the most refractory element (Mg) has the lowest atomic weight, but in the groups commencing with S and Cl the most difficultly fusible bodies are the heaviest. In a transitory group, as Al, Ga, In, it is necessary to notice an intermediate fact, the extremes, that is, the heaviest (In) and the lightest (Al) should be less fusible than the middle one, as it is in reality. I would further remark that a property such as the fusion-point is characterized chiefly by the molecular weight and not by the atomic weight. If we had a variation of solid sulfur, not as $S^{VI}$ (or perhaps heavier, as $S^n$) but $S^{II}$ which form it acquires at 800°, its boiling- and fusion-point would have been much lower. In the same way, ozone, $O^{III}$, will condense much more easily than oxygen, $O^{II}$. Experiments made in our laboratory confirm this fact.

The three circumstances mentioned have obliged chemists to direct their attention, distracted by the brilliant material acquisitions which distinguish our epoch, towards the periodic law. I ought now myself to complete what is still wanting on this subject, but for the time being I am occupied with other matters, and I should leave the care of developing this question to the future and to new forces, which will I hope endeavor to bring as the first fruits of the periodic law a new philosophical order, in fixing it by pillars strengthened by new experiments, so as to give greater stability to the edifice already begun. I will add but three brief observations:

First, the best way of drawing up the table of elements, so as to show the periodic relations, will, I think, be:

TYPICAL ELEMENTS.

| I. | II. | III. | IV. | V. | VI. | VII. |
|----|-----|------|-----|-----|-----|------|
| H | | | | | | |
| Li | Be | B | C | N | O | F |
| Na | | | | | | |

EVEN ELEMENTS.                                                  ODD ELEMENTS.

| I. | II. | III. | IV. | V. | VI. | VII. | VIII. | | | | I. | II. | III. | IV. | V. | VI. | VII. |
|----|-----|------|-----|-----|-----|------|-------|---|---|---|----|-----|------|-----|-----|-----|------|
| — | — | — | — | — | — | — | | | | | — | — | — | | — | — | — |
| K | Ca | — | Ti | V | Cr | Mn | Fe | Co | Ni | Cu | Mg | Al | Si | P | S | Cl |
| Rb | Sr | Yt | Zr | Nb | Mo | — | Ru | Rh | Pd | Ag | Zn | Ga | — | As | Se | Br |
| Cs | Ba | La | Ce | — | — | — | — | — | — | — | Cd | In | Sn | Sb | Fe | I |
| — | — | Er | Di (?) | Ta | W | — | Os | Ir | Pt | Au | Hg | Tl | Pb | Bi | — | — |
| — | — | — | Th | — | Ur | — | — | — | — | — | — | — | — | — | — | — |

The Roman figures show the groups or the forms of combination.

Second, with regard to new elements recently discovered, I think it necessary to keep silent. Of late years metals have been born and have died, such as Davyum, Mosandrium, etc.; this shows the necessity of caution. It is only necessary to mention Marignac's ytterbium (*Archives des Sciences Physiques at Naturelles*, 1878, Nov. 15, No. 251), because the name of the investigator[d] is itself sufficient guarantee. But, after announcement of the series of new metals of Delafontaine, he himself asked that someone else should make fresh researches in such an inaccessible region as gadolinite. One can still say the same of oxide of didymium; it should be re-examined. The absorption-bands of solutions and the equivalents of oxides are not sufficiently sure to show the individuality of elements; because, in different degrees of oxidation and in salts of different basicity, the absorption-bands and the equivalents of oxides can be heterogeneous for the same elements, as, for instance, in cerium, uranium, iron, chromium, etc.

Third, I should like to fix the attention of chemists on the three principles which are demonstrated in the last chapter, and also on the consequences which are adduced from their strict application to organic compounds (above all not saturated): By their aid we do without hypotheses, we explain cases of isomerism, and we obtain new consequences as yet unexplained . . .

Even up to the time of Laurent and Gerhardt, the words "molecule," "atom," and "equivalent" were used one for the other indiscriminately in the same manner, so now the terms "simple body" and "element" are often confounded one with the other. They have, however, each a distinct meaning, which it is necessary to point out, so as to prevent confusion of terms in philosophical chemistry.

A "simple body" is something material, metal or metalloid, endowed with physical properties, and capable of chemical reactions. The idea of a molecule corresponds with the expression of a "simple body," a molecule is made up of one atom, as in the case of Hg, Cd, and others; or of several atoms, such as $S_2$, $S_6$, $O_2$, $H_2$, $Cl_2$, $P_4$, etc.

A simple body is able to show itself under isomeric and polymeric modifications, and it is only distinguished from a compound body by the homogeneity of its material parts. But, in opposition to this, the name of "element" must be reserved for characterizing the material particles which form simple and compound bodies, and which determine their behavior from a chemical and physical point of view. The word "element" calls to mind the idea of an atom; carbon is an element; coal, diamond, and graphite are simple bodies.

The principal end of modern chemistry is to extend our knowledge of the relations between the composition, the reactions, and the qualities of simple and compound bodies, on the one hand; and, on the other hand, the intrinsic qualities of elements which are contained in them; so as to be able to deduce from the known character of an element all the properties of all its compounds.

For example, saying that carbon is a tetratomic element is making known a fundamental property which appears in all its combinations.

The elements count among their properties, which can be measured exactly, their atomic weight, and the power of showing themselves under the form of different compounds

Alone amongst their properties, the two above mentioned bring in their train a number of facts. The last has given rise to a special theory on the atomicity (valency) of

---

[d]A chemist with a reputation for analytical accuracy, Jean Charles Galissard de Marignac (1817–1894) accurately determined the atomic weights of nearly thirty elements. In 1878, he showed that the erbia extracted from gadolinite contained a colorless earth, ytterbia, which he claimed was an oxide of a new metal, ytterbium. A year later, scandia was extracted from ytterbia. [B.]

elements. Among the other properties of elements which influence the character of bodies, the physical properties (such as cohesion, capacity for heat, coefficient of refrangibility, spectral phenomena, etc.) have been up to the present time too incompletely studied for us to be able to generalize them in a rigorously philosophical manner. What we know of these properties is still insufficient and defective in comparison with our knowledge on the atomic weights and the atomicity of elements. However, it has already been often noticed that the physical properties depend one on another, that the atomic weights and principally the molecular weights of compounds, are equally in intimate relation with them. It is principally the fact that it is easy to measure these properties exactly that has induced us to make these comparisons. It is by studying them, more than by any other means, that we can conceive the idea of an atom and of a molecule. By this fact alone we are enabled to perceive the great influence that studies carried on in this direction can exercise on the progress of chemistry.

The above-mentioned measurable properties are by no means the only ones possessed by the elements. They have beyond these a series of properties which have not yet been able to be treasured, but which still contribute to their recognition. These last have received the name of chemical properties. Certain elements do not combine with hydrogen; they have, according to the recognized term, a basic character, or, in other words, they absorb oxygen and form bases, they form salts when combining with chlorine, other elements (called acidifying elements) do combine with hydrogen; with oxygen they only form acids, and with chlorine only chloranhydrides. Third, there are elements which form the link between the first and second classes; and fourth, there are elements which in their forms of higher oxidation have an acid character, and when less oxidized a basic character. Science does not as yet possess any process by which these properties can be measured, but still they are

counted among the number of qualitative characteristics which distinguish the elements. Further, these last elements possess properties which determine the greater or less stability of compounds; these, again, are chemical properties. It is in this manner that some elements can unite with all the others in compounds capable of being decomposed with a relative facility, while we cannot obtain analogous decompositions in the corresponding compounds of other elements. Not being susceptible of exact measurement, the above-mentioned chemical properties can hardly serve to generalize chemical knowledge; they alone cannot serve as a basis for theoretical considerations. However, these properties should not be altogether neglected, as they explain a great number of chemical phenomena. It is known that Berzelius[e] and other chemists considered these properties as being among the principal characteristics of elements, and that it is on them that the electro-chemical system was based.

As a general rule when we study the properties of elements, bearing in mind practical conclusions and chemical previsions, it is necessary to give equal attention to the general properties of the other bodies of the group, and to the individual properties of the given element in that group; it is only after such comparative studies, and laying stress on an accurately measurable property, that we can generalize the properties of an element. The atomic weight furnishes us now, and will long continue to furnish us, with a property of this nature; for our conception of the atomic weight has acquired an indestructible solidity, above all latterly, since the use of Avogadro's and Ampere's law[f]: Thanks to the efforts of Laurent, Ger-

[e]An ardent proponent of Dalton's atomic theory, Jöns Jacob Berzelius (1779–1848) carried out an extensive study of combining proportions that placed Dalton's theory on a quantitative basis. [B.]

[f]Ampère showed in 1825 that the force between two current-carrying elements decreases as the

hardt, Regnault, Rose, and Cannizzaro,[g] one can even state boldly that the notion of the atomic weight (considered as the smallest part of an element contained in a molecule of its compounds) will remain without change whatever may be the modifications that the philosophical ideas of chemists may undergo. The expression atomic weight[1] implies, it is true, the hypothesis of the atomic structure of bodies; but, then, we are not here discussing denomination, but a conventional idea. It seems that the best method of extending our chemical knowledge would be to elaborate the correlations between the properties of elements and their atomic weights. It is thus that we should obtain the most natural and most fruitful results in the extension of the study of elements. To determine this dependence seems to me to be one of the principal tasks of future chemists; for this problem has the same philosophical importance as the study of the conditions of isomerism has. In the present memoir I shall try and show the already mentioned relation between the atomic weights of elements and their other properties, particularly the faculty of giving different forms of combination.

square of the distance between the two elements, and is proportional to the product of the two currents. He gave a precise mathematical formulation of this law in his most celebrated work — *Notes on the Mathematical Theory of Electrodynamical Phenomena, Solely Deduced from Experiment* (1827). [B.]

[g]Stanislao Cannizzaro (1826–1910) published a pamphlet *Sunto di un corso di filosofia chimica* (1858: Epitome of a Course of Chemical Philosophy) which settled a controversy about atomic weights that had persisted for more than fifty years. This pamphlet, with its clear statement of Avogadro's hypothesis, definition of atoms and molecules, and demonstration that molecular weights could be ascertained from vapor-density experiments, was circulated by Cannizzaro at a conference that was held at Karlsruhe, Germany, in 1860, and accepted by chemists shortly thereafter. [B.]

This last faculty has already been carefully experimented on; a still more precise expression has recently been found for it, in the theory relative to the limits of chemical combinations, to the atomicity of elements, and to the manner of attachment of atoms in the molecules. It is known that Dalton called combinations in multiple proportions the mode of combination of an ideal element, R, with other elements (of the form RX, $RX_2$, $RX_3$, etc.); Gerhardt called them types; they are now used for fixing the atomicity of elements.

The incompleteness which exists in the theory now accepted, with regard to the atomicity of elements, arises from the fact that the opinions of chemists do not coincide in respect to elements such as Na Cl, S, N, P, Ag; some consider the atomicity as an invariable property of atoms, while others affirm the contrary. The uncertainty in the ideas on atomicity come principally from the novelty of their introduction into science, and from this — that they include the hypothesis of the union of elements by parts of their affinity. It also arises, according to my idea, from the fact that we only study the forms of combination without comparing these forms with the other properties of the elements. The gaps which I have just pointed out in the theory of combinations — gaps produced by the doctrine actually accepted on the subject of the atomicity of elements — are at their widest, as I shall point out further on, if the study of the principal properties of elements is based on the atomic weights.

Since the year 1868, the year in which the first part of my work "Principles of Chemistry" appeared, in the Russian language, I have been endeavoring to solve this problem. In this paper I take the liberty of making known the results obtained up to the present time in my researches in that direction.[2] The formation of natural groups, such as the haloids, the metals of the alkalies and alkaline earths, the bodies analogous to sulfur, to nitrogen, etc., furnished me with the first opportunity of comparing the different

**PLATE 36**   Photograph of Dmitri Mendeléev.

properties of the elements with their atomic weights. In the beginning we only arranged in groups the elements which resemble one another in several respects, but later on several experimentalists—notably Gladstone, Cooke, Pettenkoffer, Kremers, Dumas, Lenssen, Odling, etc., observed that the atomic weights of the different members of these groups had a simple and regular relation to each other. The discovery of these relations led to the comparison of the members of different groups with the homologous series, and, later on, to the conception, in a chemico-mechanical manner, of the complex nature of atoms, which has been held as reasonable by the greater number of chemists, but up to the present time it has not received any definite name.

All the relations observed between the atomic weights of elements have not yet led to any logical conclusion or chemical prevision, on account of the gaps in them. This may be the reason why they have not acquired the right of being generally recognized in science.

*First.* Nobody that I know of has, up to the present, prepared any comparative table of the natural groups, and the observed relations between the different members of groups have remained without any connection or explanation. Concerning this subject, in 1859, Strecker rightly said,[3] "It is hardly possible that the relations noticed between the atomic weights of elements which resemble each other in their chemical properties should be purely accidental. However, we must leave to future research the discovery of the "regular" relations which are betrayed in these numbers."

*Second.* Only small variations in the magnitude of the atomic weights of some analogous elements (Mn, Fe, Co, and Ni—Pd, Rh, Ru—Pt, Os, Ir) have been observed. Therefore, we were only authorized in saying that the analogy of elements was connected either by approximate agreement or by the increasing amount of their atomic weights.

*Third.* Nobody has established any theory of mutual comparison between the atomic weights of unlike elements, although it is precisely in connection with these unlike elements that a regular dependence should be pointed out between the properties and the modifications of the atomic weights. The facts published up to now being too isolated could not cause any progress in the philosophical development of chemistry; however, they contain the germs of important additions to chemical science, especially as concerns the nature, to us mysterious, of elements.

In the term *periodic law,* I designate the reciprocal relations between the properties and the atomic weights of elements. Later on I shall develop the relations that are applicable to all the elements: They are shown in the form of a periodic function . . .

I shall show further, and it can be seen from the accompanying tables, that relations of this kind can be drawn up for *all the elements,* showing that there is an intimate dependence between their properties and their atomic weights.

We could have foreseen this by means of the atomic theory because the atomic weight forms one of the variable magnitudes which determine the functions of atoms. A similar consideration led me to discover the above-mentioned dependence, and this is the reason why I mention it here.

From the preceding, as well as from other relations that I have succeeded in finding, it results that all the functions which show how the properties depend on the atomic weight are periodic functions. First, the properties of elements become modified as the atomic weights increase; then they repeat themselves in a new series of elements, *a new period,* with the same regularity as in the preceding series. The periodic law can therefore be formulated in the following manner: *The properties of simple bodies, the constitution of their compounds, as well as the properties of these last, are periodic functions of the atomic weights of elements. . .*

## THE USE OF THE PERIODIC LAW FOR DETERMINING THE PROPERTIES OF AS YET UNDISCOVERED ELEMENTS

The preceding developments show us that the periodic law renders it possible for us to bring to light the unknown properties of elements whose atom analogs are known to us. Further we can see, by referring to Tables I and II, in which the periodic relations are shown, that many elements are missing, and we can confidently predict their discovery. I am therefore going to describe the properties

TABLE I.

LARGE PERIODS.

| | | | | |
|---|---|---|---|---|
| K  = 39 | Rb = 85 | Cs = 133 | „ | „ |
| Ca = 40 | Sr = 87 | Ba = 137 | „ | „ |
| „ | ? Yt = 88 ? | ? Di = 138 ? | Er = 178 ? | „ |
| Ti = 48 ? | Zr = 90 | Ce = 140 ? | La = 180 ? | Th = 231 |
| V  = 51 | Nb = 94 | „ | Fa = 182 | „ |
| Cr = 52 | Mo = 96 | „ | W  = 184 | Ur = 240 |
| Mn = 55 | „ | „ | „ | |

TYPICAL ELEMENTS.

| | | | | | |
|---|---|---|---|---|---|
| H = 1 | Li = 7 | Na = 23 | | Fe = 56 | Os = 195 ? |
| | Be = 9.4 | Mg = 24 | Cu = 63 | Co = 59 | Ir = 197 |
| | B = 11 | Al = 27.3 | Zn = 65 | Ni = 59 | Pt = 198 ? |
| | C = 12 | Si = 28 | „ | Ag = 108 | Au = 199 ? |
| | N = 14 | P = 31 | „ | Cd = 112 | Hg = 200 |
| | O = 16 | S = 32 | As = 75 | In = 113 | Tl = 204 |
| | F = 19 | Cl = 35.5 | Se = 78 | Sn = 118 | Pb = 207 |
| | | | Br = 80 | Sb = 122 | Bi = 208 |
| | | | | Te = 125 ? | |
| | | | | I = 127 | |

TABLE II.

| SERIES | GROUP I. $R_2O$ | GROUP II. $RO$ | GROUP III. $R_2O_3$ | GROUP IV. $RH_4$ $RO_2$ | GROUP V. $RH_3$ $R_2O_5$ | GROUP VI. $RH_2$ $RO_3$ | GROUP VII. $RH$ $R_2O_7$ | GROUP VIII. $RO_4$ |
|---|---|---|---|---|---|---|---|---|
| 1 | H=1 | „ | „ | „ | „ | „ | | |
| 2 | Li=7 | Be=9.4 | B=11 | C=12 | N=14 | O=16 | Fl=19 | |
| 3 | Na=23 | Mg=24 | Al=27.3 | Si=28 | P=31 | S=32 | Cl=35.5 | |
| 4 | K=39 | Ca=40 | − =44 | Ti=48 | V=51 | Cr=52 | Mn=55 .... | Fe = 56; Co = 59. Ni = 59; Cu = 63 . |
| 5 | (Cu=63) | Zn=65 | − =68 | − =72 | As=75 | Se=78 | Br=80 | |
| 6 | Rb=85 | Sr=87 | ?Yt=88 | Zr=90 | Nb=94 | Mo=96 | − =100 .... | Ru=104; Rh=104 Pd=106; Ag=108. |
| | (Ag=108) | Cd=112 | In=113 | Sn=118 | Sb=122 | Te=125 | I=127 | |
| | Cs=133 | Ba=137 | ?Di=138 | ?Ce=140 | „ | „ | „ | |
| | „ | „ | „ | „ | „ | „ | „ | |
| | „ | „ | ?Er=178 | ?La=180 | Ta=182 | W=184 | „ .... | Os=195; Ir =197; Pt=198; Au=199. |
| | (Au=199) | Hg=200 | Tl=204 | Pb=207 | Bi=208 | „ | „ | |
| 12 | „ | „ | „ | Th=231 | „ | Ur=240 | „ | „  „  „  „ |

of several as yet undiscovered elements: by this means I hope to show, in a new and perfectly clear manner, the exactitude of the law, although the confirmation of these proofs is reserved for the future. Let us add that the previous determination of the properties of unknown elements will facilitate the discovery of these elements, because knowing them we can foretell the reactions of their compounds.

So as to avoid introducing new denominations for the unknown elements into science, I shall designate them by the name of the nearest lower analog of the odd or even elements in the same group, and placing in front of this word one of the Sanskrit numbers (eke, dud, tri, tschatour, etc.). The unknown elements of the first group will be called ekacaesium (Ec=175), duicaesium

(Dc=220), etc. If niobium, for example, were not known we could call it ekavanadium. The denominations will show the analogies very clearly; the names, however, of the fourth series have not this advantage because they ought to be derived from those of the elements of the second series, and we know . . . that this typical series is not in complete atomic analogy with the fourth.

Besides, in this series there is only one missing element; it is in the third group, and is called ekaboron, Eb. As it follows K=39, and Ca=40, while it precedes Ti=48, and V=51, its atomic weight should be about Eb=44; its oxide should be $Eb_2O_3$, but it should not have very characteristic properties; it will form in all respects the transition from CaO to $TiO_2$. In its maximum salts, $EbX_3$, the equivalent of the metal will be about 15 =44/3; it will not, therefore, be lower than the equivalents of bases which are already known; it will be intermediate between the equivalent of Mg=12, and that of Ca=20.

We have seen . . . that Yt=88 (?) Di=138 (?), and Er=178 (?) belong to this same group. However, the position of this latter is still very uncertain and the elements have not been sufficiently studied, therefore, the properties of Eb can only be determined by means of its atom analogy with the elements Ca and Ti of the fourth series. The case of this element is, therefore, more complicated than those of other unknown elements. In consideration of Ca and Ti only giving one stable oxide in the air, we may admit that Eb will only give one stable basic oxide, $Eb_2O_3$. The oxide in its properties ought to be to $Al_2O_3$ what Ca is to MgO, or what $TiO_2$ is to $SiO_2$; consequently it should be a more energetic base than aluminum, and at the same time it ought to agree with Al not only in its forms of corresponding compounds, but also, in many cases, in its properties. Thus, the sulfate $Eb_2(SO_4)_3$ will not be such an easily soluble body as $Al_2(SO_4)_3$ because sulfate of calcium is more difficultly soluble than sulfate of magnesium. The base formed by Ca being more feeble than that formed by Na, and, at the same time $TiO_2$ being a less energetic base than $Al_2O_3$, $Eb_2O_3$ will be weaker than MgO. $Eb_2O_3$ will therefore occupy, in many respects, the place between $Al_2O_3$ and MgO: Numbers of its reactions will be explained by this circumstance.

Duiboron, or yttrium, gives an oxide, in every respect more energetic, as Sr gives a more marked base than Ca; however, even as there exists a great concordance between Ca and Sr, Ti and Zr, so shall we find many analogies between ekaboron and duiboron (yttrium?). If, then, yttrium is veritably duiboron, and ought to be accompanied by ekaboron, the separation of ekaboron from yttrium will be very difficult; in fact it will only be possible by means of excessively delicate differences; for example, in the solubility of the salts, or in the energy of the basic oxides, etc.

Oxide of ekaboron will naturally be insoluble in alkalies, but we are uncertain as to whether it will drive off the ammonia from chlorhydrate of ammonia. The carbonate of ekaboron will be insoluble in water, and it will be precipitated as a basic salt, if we can judge from what we know of the salts of MgO and $Al_2O_3$. Its salts will be colorless, and will give gelatinous precipitates with KHO $K_2CO_3$, $HNa_2PO_4$, etc. Sulfate of potassium will give a double salt with $Eb_2(SO_4)_3$, a sort of alum, which will probably not be isomorphous with alum proper. A few salts only of ekaboron will crystallize well, and they will belong to the double salts. The degree of volatility of $EbCl_3$ will depend on the molecular formula of this compound; $EbCl_3$ will be volatile, but $Eb_2Cl_6$ and the higher molecules will not volatize. Chloride of ekaboron will in all probability, be more difficultly volatized than chloride of aluminum, because $TiC1_4$ boils at a higher temperature than $SiC1_4$; because also $CaCl_2$ is more difficultly volatized than $MgCl_2$. But, we may be permitted to presume that the salts of ekaboron will not be sufficiently volatile to be discovered by means of spectrum analysis. The chloride of ekaboron will naturally be a solid body: Its anhydride will be decomposed by water more easily than $MgCl_2$ with the evolution of HCl.

As the volume of $CaCl_2$=49, and the volume of $TiCl_4$=109, the volume of $EbCl_3$ will be about 78, and its density will be 2.

Oxide of ekaboron will be an infusible powder, which will, after calcination, dissolve in acids, although with difficulty; it will easily give to water its alkaline reactions but it will not completely saturate acid solutions of litmus so as to make the color disappear. The density of the oxide will be about 3.5; the volume about 30, because the volume of $K_2O$=35, of $Cu_2O_2$=36, of $Ti_2O$,=40, of $Cr_2O_6$=72.[4]

Ekaboron, the simple body, will be a light, non-volatile difficultly fusible metal. It will only decompose in water under the influence of heat, and even then incompletely; it will dissolve in acids, with the evolution of hydrogen. Its density will be about 3.0 (apparently higher), because its volume is about 15; for the volumes of metals in the even series diminish constantly from the first group. Thus the volume of K=50, of Ca=25, of Ti and V=about 9, and of Cr, Mn, and Fe=about 7.


## NOTES

1. By replacing the expression of *atomic weight* by that of *elementary weight*, I think we should, in the case of elements, avoid the conception of atoms.
2. In relation to some historical and polemical observations on this question, see the *Berichte der Deutschen Chemischen Gesellschaft*, 1871, p. 348.
3. "Theorien und Experimente zur Bestimmung der Atom gewichte der Elemente," p. 146.
4. Oxide of duiboron (yttria?) should, from an analogical point of view, have for its number 4.8.


## FURTHER READING

Levere, Trevor. 2001. *Transforming Matter: A History of Chemistry from Alchemy to the Buckyball*. Baltimore: Johns Hopkins University Press.

Strathern, Paul. 2000. *Mendeleyev's Dream: The Quest for the Elements*. London: Hamish Hamilton.

# Shadow Pictures

## Wilhelm Conrad Röntgen (1845–1923)

*In the closing months of 1895, the shattering announcement came that a little-known German professor of physics at Würtzburg in Bavaria, Wilhelm Conrad Röntgen, had discovered rays that could make invisible things visible, that could pass through clothes, skin, and flesh, to cast the shadows of human bones on photographic plates. Because of their mysterious nature, Röntgen called them X-rays.*

*The discovery of X-rays was not the culmination of a long-standing research program. Röntgen was fifty years old when he made the discovery that gained for him in 1901 the first Nobel Prize for physics. His lifelong interest was in the physics of solids, and not in gas discharge phenomena; indeed, a review of his forty-nine published papers reveals that none had addressed the subject of gas discharges.*

*The discovery was really a fortunate accident involving a discharge tube. Röntgen was engaged in repeating an experiment on cathode rays carried out by William Crookes, which involved placing a mica shield in the form of a maltese cross in the middle of the tube, between the two electrodes, to see if it would cast a shadow. It did indeed. The shadow of the cross appeared on the wall of the glass tube. But this did not explain the nature of the fluorescence in the tube. Perhaps the greenish rays were ultraviolet rays? A screen coated with a fluorescent material, potassium platinocyanide, happened to be lying nearby on a laboratory table. It lit up. Röntgen put the tube in a box made of thin black cardboard. To make sure that no light came through the box, he switched on the current to his tube. No light came through the box but, to his surprise, he noticed a strange glow in the far corner of his laboratory bench. Thinking that the glow was a figment of his imagination, he turned the switch again. He saw the glow again. Drawing back the curtains of his laboratory window, he found that the glow had come from the small fluorescent screen that he had been placed at the far end of the table.*

*Röntgen knew that the cathode rays would make the screen glow but he also knew that they could not penetrate cardboard. Even if there was a minute leak in the cardboard box, he knew that they could not penetrate more than an inch or two of air. The fluorescent screen indicated that the mysterious rays could travel through the glass of the tube, the cardboard box, and air. He reckoned that they must consist of some unknown kind of invisible light. If so, they must cast a shadow. On a whim, he placed his*

*Source:* Wilhelm Conrad Röntgen. 1896. "On a New Type of Rays." Translated by Arthur Stanton. *Nature* 53, 274–276.

*hand in front of the screen and received the shock of his life. What he saw was not the shadow of his hand but a skeleton of a hand. He could see his own bones, with the flesh and skin forming a faint, grayish fringe around them.*

*This fortunate chain of events revealed to Röntgen an entirely new kind of radiation that could penetrate human flesh, wood and cardboard, metal foil and fabric, but was stopped by bones and stone, thick metal and other material of high density. He also found that the rays affected photographic plates, so that what he had seen on the fluorescent screen could be photographed. It became clear to him that this was a new form of light, invisible to the naked eye and which never had been observed or recorded.*

*The sensation caused by Röntgen's discovery was unprecedented in the annals of science. Over one hundred papers appeared about X-rays in the twelve months after its announcement. More than one thousand books, pamphlets, and articles appeared on X-rays in the public press during this same period. Physicists were besieged by physicians who recognized the great utility of the new rays. Before the end of the nineteenth century, "radiography" was applied in diagnosing lesions of the skull, the heart, and the lungs, and in renal pathology. The power of X-rays to destroy organic cells was noticed as well, but no one appreciated the long-term threat.*

(1) A discharge from a large induction coil is passed through a Hittorf's vacuum tube, or through a well-exhausted Crookes' or Lenard's tube. The tube is surrounded by a fairly close-fitting shield of black paper; it is then possible to see, in a completely darkened room, that paper covered on one side with barium platinocyanide lights up with brilliant fluorescence when brought into the neighborhood of the tube, whether the painted side or the other be turned towards the tube. The fluorescence is still visible at

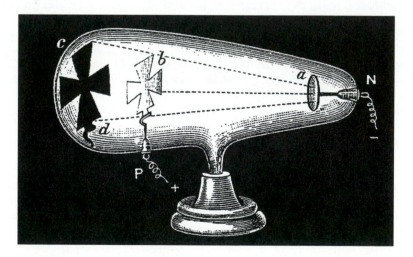

**PLATE 37**   Cathode ray shadows. William Crookes (1832–1919) placed a maltese cross made of Mica at the end of a low-pressure discharge tube facing a silver cathode to see whether it would cast a shadow—an experimental arrangement recreated by Röntgen, which resulted in his discovery of X-rays.

two meters distance. It is easy to show that the origin of the fluorescence lies within the vacuum tube.

(2) It is seen, therefore, that some agent is capable of penetrating black cardboard which is quite opaque to ultra-violet light, sunlight, or arc-light. It is therefore of interest to investigate how far other bodies can be penetrated by the same agent. It is readily shown that all bodies possess this same transparency, but in very varying degrees. For example, paper is very transparent; the fluorescent screen will light up when placed behind a book of a thousand pages; printer's ink offers no marked resistance. Similarly the fluorescence shows behind two packs of cards; a single card does not visibly diminish the brilliancy of the light. So, again, a single thickness of tinfoil hardly casts a shadow on the screen; several have to be superposed to produce a marked effect. Thick blocks of wood are still transparent. Boards of pine two or three centimeters thick absorb only very little. A piece of sheet aluminum, 15 mm thick, still allowed the X-rays (as I will call the rays, for the sake of brevity) to pass, but greatly reduced the fluorescence. Glass plates of similar thickness behave similarly; lead glass is, however, much more opaque than glass free from lead. Ebonite several centimeters thick is transparent. If the hand be held before the fluorescent screen, the shadow shows the bones clearly with only faint outlines of the surrounding tissues.

Water and several other fluids are very transparent. Hydrogen is not markedly more permeable than air. Plates of copper, silver, lead, gold, and platinum also allow the rays to pass, but only when the metal is thin. Platinum .2 mm thick allows some rays to pass; silver and copper are more transparent. Lead 1.5 mm thick is practically opaque.[a] If a square rod of wood 20 mm in the side be painted on one face with white lead, it casts little shadow when it is so turned that the painted face is parallel to the X-rays, but a strong shadow if the rays have to pass through the painted side. The salts of the metals, either solid or in solution, behave generally as the metals themselves.

(3) The preceding experiments lead to the conclusion that the density of the bodies is the property whose variation mainly affects their permeability. At least no other property seems so marked in this connection. But that density alone does not determine the transparency is shown by an experiment wherein plates of similar thickness of Iceland spar, glass, aluminum, and quartz were employed as screens. Then the Iceland spar showed itself much less transparent than the other bodies, though of approximately the same density. I have not remarked any strong fluorescence of Iceland spar compared with glass (see below, No. 4).

(4) Increasing thickness increases the hindrance offered to the rays by all bodies. A picture has been impressed on a photographic plate of a number of superposed layers of tinfoil, like steps, presenting thus a regularly increasing thickness. This is to be submitted to photometric processes when a suitable instrument is available.

(5) Pieces of platinum, lead, zinc, and aluminum foil were so arranged as to produce the same weakening of the effect.[b] The annexed table shows the relative thickness and density of the equivalent sheets of metal.

|  | Thickness (mm) | Relative Thickness | Density |
|---|---|---|---|
| Platinum | 0.018 | 1 | 21.5 |
| Lead | 0.05 | 3 | 11.3 |
| Zinc | 0.10 | 6 | 7.1 |
| Aluminum | 3.5 | 200 | 2.6 |

From these values it is clear that in no case can we obtain the transparency of a body from the product of its density and thickness. The transparency increases much more rapidly than the product decreases.

[a]Röntgen discovered that absorption of X-rays increases with the atomic number. Consequently, lead proved to be a most effective absorber. [B.]

[b]With atomic number 82, lead should have appeared more opaque than platinum, with atomic number 78. [B.]

(6) The fluorescence of barium platino-cyanide is not the only noticeable action of the X-rays. It is to be observed that other bodies exhibit fluorescence, e.g., calcium sulfide, uranium glass, Iceland spar, rock-salt, etc.

Of special interest in this connection is the fact that photographic dry plates are sensitive to the X-rays. It is thus possible to exhibit the phenomena so as to exclude the danger of error. I have thus confirmed many observations originally made by eye observation with the fluorescent screen. Here the power of X-rays to pass through wood or cardboard becomes useful. The photographic plate can be exposed to the action without removal of the shutter of the dark slide or other protecting case, so that the experiment need not be conducted in darkness. Manifestly, unexposed plates must not be left in their box near the vacuum tube.

It seems now questionable whether the impression on the plate is a direct effect of the X-rays, or a secondary result induced by the fluorescence of the material of the plate. Films can receive the impression as well as ordinary dry plates.

I have not been able to show experimentally that the X-rays give rise to any caloric effects. These, however, may be assumed, for the phenomena of fluorescence show that the X-rays are capable of transformation. It is also certain that all the X-rays falling on a body do not leave it as such.

The retina of the eye is quite insensitive to these rays; the eye placed close to the apparatus sees nothing. It is clear from the experiments that this is not due to want of permeability on the part of the structures of the eye.

(7) After my experiments on the transparency of increasing thicknesses of different media, I proceeded to investigate whether the X-rays could be deflected by a prism. Investigations with water and carbon disulfide in mica prisms of 30° showed no deviation either on the photographic or the fluorescent plate. For comparison, light rays were allowed to fall on the prism as the apparatus was set up for the experiment. They were deviated 10 mm and 20 mm respectively in the case of the two prisms.

With prisms of ebonite and aluminum, I have obtained images on the photographic plate, which point to a possible deviation. It is, however, uncertain, and at most would point to a refractive index 1.05. No deviation can be observed by means of the fluorescent screen. Investigations with the heavier metals have not as yet led to any result, because of their small transparency and the consequent enfeebling of the transmitted rays.

On account of the importance of the question, it is desirable to try in other ways whether the X-rays are susceptible of refraction. Finely powdered bodies allow in thick layers but little of the incident light to pass through, in consequence of refraction and reflection. In the case of X-rays, however, such layers of powder are for equal masses of substance equally transparent with the coherent solid itself. Hence we cannot conclude any regular reflection or refraction of the X-rays. The research was conducted by the aid of finely-powdered rock-salt, fine electrolytic silver powder, and zinc dust already many times employed in chemical work. In all these cases the result, whether by the fluorescent screen or the photographic method, indicated no difference in transparency between the powder and the coherent solid.

It is, hence, obvious that lenses cannot be looked upon as capable of concentrating the X-rays; in effect, both an ebonite and a glass lens of large size prove to be without action. The shadow photograph of a round rod is darker in the middle than at the edge; the image of a cylinder filled with a body more transparent than its walls exhibits the middle brighter than the edge.

(8) The preceding experiments, and others which I pass over, point to the rays being incapable of regular reflection. It is, however, well to detail an observation which at first sight seemed to lead to an opposite conclusion.

I exposed a plate, protected by a black paper sheath, to the X-rays, so that the glass side lay next to the vacuum tube. The sensitive film was partly covered with star-shaped pieces of platinum, lead, zinc, and aluminum.

On the developed negative the star-shaped impression showed dark under platinum, lead, and, more markedly, under zinc; the aluminum gave no image. It seems, therefore, that these three metals can reflect the X-rays; as, however, another explanation is possible, I repeated the experiment with this only difference, that a film of thin aluminum foil was interposed between the sensitive film and the metal stars. Such an aluminum plate is opaque to ultra-violet rays, but transparent to X-rays. In the result the images appeared as before, this pointing still to the existence of reflection at metal surfaces.

If one considers this observation in connection with others, namely, on the transparency of powders, and on the state of the surface not being effective in altering the passage of the X-rays through a body, it leads to the probable conclusion that regular reflection does not exist, but that bodies behave to the X-rays as turbid media to light.

Since I have obtained no evidence of refraction at the surface of different media, it seems probable that the X-rays move with the same velocity in all bodies, and in a medium which penetrates everything, and in which the molecules of bodies are embedded. The molecules obstruct the X-rays, the more effectively as the density of the body concerned is greater.

(9) It seemed possible that the geometrical arrangement of the molecules might affect the action of a body upon the X-rays, so that, for example, Iceland spar might exhibit different phenomena according to the relation of the surface of the plate to the axis of the crystal. Experiments with quartz and Iceland spar on this point lead to a negative result.

(10) It is known that Lenard,[c] in his investigations on cathode rays, has shown that they belong to the aether, and can pass

through all bodies. Concerning the X-rays the same may be said.

In his latest work, Lenard has investigated the absorption coefficients of various bodies for the cathode rays, including air at atmospheric pressure, which gives 4.10, 3.40, 3.10 for 1 cm, according to the degree of exhaustion of the gas in discharge tube. To judge from the nature of the discharge, I have worked at about the same pressure, but occasionally at greater or smaller pressures. I find, using a Weber's photometer, that the intensity of the fluorescent light varies nearly as the inverse square of the distance between screen and discharge tube. This result is obtained from three very consistent sets of observations at distances of 100 and 200 mm. Hence air absorbs the X-rays much less than the cathode rays. This result is in complete agreement with the previously described result, that the fluorescence of the screen can still be observed at 2 meters from the vacuum tube. In general, other bodies behave like air; they are more transparent for the X-rays than for the cathode rays.

(11) A further distinction, and a noteworthy one, results from the action of a magnet. I have not succeeded in observing any deviation of the X-rays even in very strong magnetic fields.

The deviation of cathode rays by the magnet is one of their peculiar characteristics; it has been observed by Hertz[d] and Lenard, that several kinds of cathode rays exist

[c]Phillip Eduard Anton Lenard (1862–1947) carried out important work on cathode rays and came close to anticipating the discovery of X-rays. After 1919, he became increasingly hostile to Jewish scientists, contributing greatly to the creation of the racist atmosphere that resulted in the mass exodus of scientists from Germany. [B.]

[d]After his appointment as professor of physics at Karlsruhe Technical College in 1885, Heinrich Hertz (1857–1894) commenced an experimental investigation of the electromagnetic theory of James Clerk Maxwell. After three years, he succeeded in producing electromagnetic waves (the existence of which had been predicted some years before by Maxwell), using an electric current. He detected these waves with a second electric current set up some distance away, thereby demonstrating that these waves were transmitted through air. Hertz showed that they traveled at the same speed as light but that they had a much shorter wavelength. These waves—originally called Hertzian waves—now are known as radio waves. [B.]

which differ by their power of exciting phosphorescence, their susceptibility of absorption, and their deviation by the magnet; but a notable deviation has been observed in all cases which have yet been investigated, and I think that such deviation affords a characteristic not to be set aside lightly.

(12) As the result of many researches, it appears that the place of most brilliant phosphorescence of the walls of the discharge-tube is the chief seat from whence the X-rays originate and spread in all directions; that is, the X-rays proceed from the front where the cathode rays strike the glass. If one deviates the cathode rays within the tube by means of a magnet, it is seen that the X-rays proceed from a new point, i.e., again from the end of the cathode rays.

Also for this reason the X-rays, which are not deflected by a magnet, cannot be regarded as cathode rays which have passed through the glass, for that passage cannot, according to Lenard, be the cause of the different deflection of the rays. Hence I conclude that the X-rays are not identical with the cathode rays, but are produced from the cathode rays at the glass surface of the tube.

(13) The rays are generated not only in glass. I have obtained them in an apparatus closed by an aluminum plate 2 mm thick. I propose later to investigate the behavior of other substances.

(14) The justification of the term "rays," applied to the phenomena, lies partly in the regular shadow pictures produced by the interposition of a more or less permeable body between the source and a photographic plate or fluorescent screen.

I have observed and photographed many such shadow pictures. Thus, I have an outline of part of a door covered with lead paint; the image was produced by the discharge-tube on one side of the door, and the sensitive plate on the other. I have also a shadow of the bones of the hand (Fig. 1), of a wire wound upon a bobbin, of a set of weights in a box, of a compass card and needle completely enclosed in a metal case

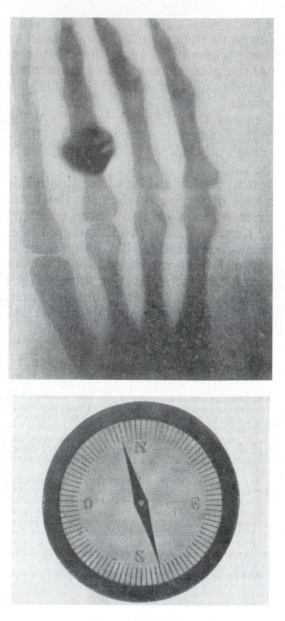

(Fig. 2), of a piece of metal where the X-rays show the want of homogeneity, and of other things.

For the rectilinear propagation of the rays, I have a pin-hole photograph of the discharge apparatus covered with black paper. It is faint but unmistakable.

**PLATE 38**  An illustration of Edison's fluoroscope. The first major improvement on the original Röntgen apparatus was a device to permit direct observation of an object, such as a hand, rather than an image on a photographic plate. This device with its many subsequent improvements was known as the "fluoroscope." Thomas Edison (1847–1931) was one of the first to work at improving this device, though he discontinued his work on X-rays when one of his assistants, who was in charge of the apparatus at the National Electrical Exhibition of 1896, died in 1904 after lengthy exposure to the virulent rays.

(15) I have sought for interference effects of the X-rays, but possibly, in consequence of their small intensity, without result.

(16) Researches to investigate whether electrostatic forces act on the X-rays are begun but not yet concluded.

(17) If one asks, what then are these X-rays; since they are not cathode rays, one might suppose, from their power of exciting fluorescence and chemical action, them to be due to ultra-violet light. In opposition to this view a weighty set of considerations presents itself. If X-rays be indeed ultra-violet light, then that light must posses the following properties:

a.  It is not refracted in passing from air into water, carbon bisulfide, aluminum, rock-salt, glass or zinc.
b.  It is incapable of regular reflection at the surfaces of the above bodies.
c.  It cannot be polarized by any ordinary polarizing media.
d.  The absorption by various bodies must depend chiefly on their density.

That is to say, these ultra-violet rays must behave quite differently from the visible, infra-red, and hitherto known ultra-violet rays.

These things appear so unlikely that I have sought for another hypothesis.

A kind of relationship between the new rays and light rays appears to exist; at least the formation of shadows, fluorescence, and the production of chemical action point in this direction. Now it has been known for a long time that besides the transverse vibrations which account for the phenomena of light, it is possible that longitudinal vibrations should exist in the aether, and, according to the view of some physicists, must exist. It is granted that their existence has not yet been made clear, and their properties are not experimentally demonstrated. Should not the new rays be ascribed to longitudinal waves in the aether?

I must confess that I have in the course of this research made myself more and more familiar with this thought, and venture to put the opinion forward, while I am quite conscious that the hypothesis advanced still requires a more solid foundation.

## FURTHER READING

Dibner, Bern. 1963. *The New Rays of Professor Röntgen*. Norwalk: Burndy Library.

Glasser, Otto. 1934. *Wilhelm Conrad Röntgen and the Early History of the Röentgen Rays*. Springfield, IL: C. C. Thomas.

# Martian Engineers

## Percival Lowell (1855–1916)

*In 1877, Giovanni Schiaparelli (1835–1910), Director of the Brera Observatory in Milan, discovered that Mars' surface was scarred by a series of "canali." He refused to take a stand as to whether these canali were "channels" (natural phenomena) or canals (artifacts produced by Martian engineers). Stimulated by Schiaparelli's discovery, Percival Lowell dedicated fifteen years of his life to the study of Mars. As an astronomer, he made important contributions to planetary astronomy but his name will forever be linked with Mars and the belief that Mars was once home to intelligent life.*

*In 1894, Lowell resolved to study Mars under the best possible conditions. With his own considerable financial resources, he began construction of an observatory at Flagstaff, Arizona, at an altitude of 7,000 feet, far away from the smoke and lights of civilization. Two years later, in 1896, a twenty-four-inch telescope was installed. A series of books appeared on Mars in quick succession that popularized the idea of an inhabited Mars, culminating with the book from which this reading is excerpted—*Mars.

*The hypothesis that the dark areas of the Martian surface are vegetation did not originate with Lowell, but he contributed greatly to the credibility that it enjoyed in the astronomical community and the public. It was only in the late 1950s that scientists began to suspect that the changing patterns of dark and light on the Martian surface are due to light-colored dust being blown across the surface by winds. The idea of Martian engineers was finally discredited with the mapping of the Martian surface by the Mariner and Viking spacecraft in the 1960s and 1970s. The canals exist, but not in the incredible system of hundreds of straight lines envisioned by Lowell; most, in fact, turned out to be chance alignments of dark passages. The seed planted by Lowell, however, was undaunted by the weight of scientific authority: More than a century after Schiaparelli's discovery, the belief that Mars once housed living things is as popular as it was during the first decade of the twentieth century.*

*Source:* Percival Lowell. 1896. *Mars.* London: Longmans, Green, 2nd edition, pp. 129–140; 148–155.

## FIRST APPEARANCES

In the last chapter we saw how badly off for water Mars, to all appearance, is; so badly off that inhabitants of that other world would have to irrigate to live. As to the actual presence there of such folk, the broad physical characteristics of the planet express no opinion beyond the silence of consent, but they have something very vital to say about the conditions under which alone their life could be led. They show that these conditions must be such that in the Martian mind there would be one question perpetually paramount to all the local labor, women's suffrage, and Eastern questions put together—the water question. How to procure water enough to support life would be the great communal problem of the day.

Were Mars like the Earth, we might well despair of detecting signs of any Martians for some time yet. Across the gulf of space that separates us from Mars, an area thirty miles wide would just be perceptible as a dot. It would, in such case, be hopeless to look for evidence of folk. Anything like London or New York, or even Chicago in its own estimation would be too small to be seen, so sorry a figure does man cut upon the Earth he thinks to own. From the standpoint of forty millions of miles distance, probably the only sign of his presence here would be such semi-artificialities as the great grain-fields of the West when their geometric patches turned with the changing seasons from ochre to green, and then from green to gold. By his crops we should know him. A telltale fact this, for it would be still more likely to be the case with Mars. If the surface of the planet were cultivated at all, it would probably be upon a much more thorough plan than is the case with the Earth. Conditions hold there which would necessitate a much more artificial state of things. If cultivation there be, it must be cultivation largely dependent upon a system of irrigation, and therefore much more systematic than any we have as yet been forced to adopt.

Now, at this point in our investigation, when the broad features of Mars disclose conditions which imply irrigation as their organic corollary, we are suddenly confronted on the planet's face with phenomena so startlingly suggestive of this very thing as to seem its uncanny presentment. Indeed, so amazingly lifelike is their appearance that, had we possessed our present knowledge of the planet's physical condition before, we might almost have predicted what we see as criteria of the presence of living beings. What confronts us is this:

When the great continental areas, the reddish-ochre portions of the disk, are attentively examined in sufficiently steady air, their desert-like ground is seen to be traversed by a network of fine, straight, dark lines. The lines start from points on the coast of the blue-green regions, commonly well-marked bays, and proceed directly to what seem centers in the middle of the continent, since most surprisingly they meet there other lines that have come to the same spot with apparently a like determinate intent. And this state of things is not confined to any one part of the planet, but takes place all over the reddish-ochre regions.

The lines appear either absolutely straight from one end to the other, or curved in an equally uniform manner. There is nothing haphazard in the look of any of them. Plotting upon a globe betrays them to be arcs of great circles almost invariably, even the few outstanding exceptions seeming to be but polygonal combinations of the same. Their most instantly conspicuous characteristic is this hopeless lack of happy irregularity. They are, each and all, direct to a degree. The lines are as fine as they are straight. As a rule, they are of scarcely any perceptible breadth, seeming on the average to be less than a Martian degree, or about thirty miles wide. They differ slightly among themselves, some being a little broader than this; some a trifle finer, possibly not above fifteen miles across. Their length, not their breadth, renders them visible; for though at such a distance we could not distinguish a dot less than thirty miles in diameter, we could see a line of much less breadth, because of its

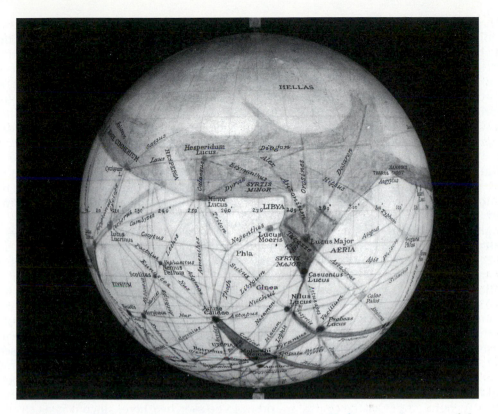

**PLATE 39**   Percival Lowell's Mars Globe 1903 at 270 degrees. *Courtesy of the Lowell Observatory Archives/Coleman Kennedy Collection.*

length. Speaking generally, however, the lines are all of comparable width.

Still greater uniformity is observable in different parts of the same line, for each line maintains its individual width, from one end of its course to the other. Although, at and near the point where it leaves the dark regions, some slight enlargement seems to occur, after it has fairly started on its course, it remains of substantially the same size throughout. As to whether the lines are even on their edges or not, I should not like to say; but the better they are seen, the more even they look. It is not possible to affirm positively on the point, as they are practically nearer one dimension than two.

On the other hand, their length is usually great, and in cases enormous. A thousand or fifteen hundred miles may be considered about the average. The Ganges, for example, which is not a long one as Martian canals go, is about 1,450 miles in length. The Brontes, one of the newly discovered, radiating from the Gulf of the Titans, extends over 2,400 miles; while, among really long ones, the Eumenides, with its continuation the Orcus, the two being in truth one line, measures 3,540 miles from the point where it leaves the Phoenix Lake to the point where it enters the Trivium Charontis, throughout this whole distance, nearly equal to the diameter of the planet, deviating neither to the right nor to the left from the great circle upon which it set out. On the other hand, the shortest line is the Nectar, which is only about 250 miles in length; sweetness being, according to Schiaparelli its christener, as short-lived on Mars as elsewhere.

That, with very few exceptions, the lines all follow arcs of great circles is proved, first, by the fact that, when not too long, they show as straight lines; second, that, when seen near this limb, they appear curved, in keeping with the curvature of a spherical surface viewed obliquely; third, that, when the several parts of some of the longer lines are plotted upon a globe, they turn out to lie in one great circle. Apparent straightness throughout is only possible in comparatively short lines. For a very long arc upon the surface of a revolving globe tilted toward the observer to appear straight, it, or its prolongation, must pass through the center of the disk at the moment. Such, of course, is rarely the case. At times, however, the conditions are strikingly fulfilled by the great canal called the Titan. The Titan starts from the Gulf of the Titans, in south latitude 20°, and runs north almost exactly upon the 169th meridian for an immense distance. I have followed it over 2,300 miles down the disk to about 43° north, as far as the tilt of the planet's axis would permit. As the rotation of the planet swings it round, it passes the central meridian of the disk simultaneously throughout its length, and at that moment comes out so strikingly straight it seems a substantialized meridian itself.

Although each line is the arc of a great circle, the direction taken by this great circle may be any whatsoever. The Titan, as we have seen, runs nearly due north and south; certain canals crossing this run, on the contrary, almost due east and west. There are others again, belting the disk at well-nigh every angle between these two extremes. Nor is there any preponderance, apparently, for one direction as against any other. This indifference to direction is important as showing that the rotation of the planet has no bearing upon the inclination of the canals.

But, singular as each line looks to be by itself, it is the systematic network of the whole that is most amazing. Each line not only goes with wonderful directness from one point to another, but at this latter spot it contrives to

meet, exactly, another line which has come with like directness from quite a different direction. Nor do two only manage thus to rendezvous. Three, four, five, and even seven will similarly fall in on the same spot—a gregariousness which, to a greater or less extent, finds effective possibility all over the surface of the planet. The disk is simply a network of such intersections. Sometimes a canal goes only from one intersection to another; more commonly it starts with right of continuation, and, after reaching the first rendezvous, goes on in unchanged course to several more.

The result is that the whole of the great reddish-ochre portions of the planet is cut up into a series of spherical triangles of all possible sizes and shapes. What their number may be lies quite beyond the possibility of count at present; for the better our own air, the more of them are visible. About four times as many as are down on Schiaparelli's chart of the same regions have been seen at Flagstaff. But, before proceeding further with a description of these Martian phenomena, the history of their discovery deserves to be sketched here, since it is as strange as the canals themselves.

The first hint the world had of their existence was when Schiaparelli saw some of the lines in 1877, now eighteen years ago. The world, however, was anything but prepared for the revelation, and, when he announced what he had seen, promptly proceeded to disbelieve him. Schiaparelli had the misfortune to be ahead of his times, and the yet greater misfortune to remain so; for not only did no one else see the lines at that opposition, but no one else succeeded in doing so at subsequent ones. For many years fate allowed Schiaparelli to have them all to himself, a confidence he amply repaid. While others doubted, he went from discovery to discovery. What he had seen in 1877 was not so very startling in view of what he afterward saw. His first observations might well have been of simple estuaries, long natural creeks running up into the continents, and even cutting them in two. His later observations were too peculiar to be explained, even by so improbable a configuration of the Martian surface. In 1879 the canali, as he called them (channels, or canals, the word may be translated, and it is in the latter sense that he now regards them), showed straighter and narrower than they had in 1877: This not in consequence of any change in them, but from his own improved faculty of detection; for what the eye has once seen it can always see better a second time. As he gazed they appeared straighter, and he made out more. Lastly, toward the end of the year, he observed one evening what struck even him as a most startling phenomenon—the twinning of one of the canals: Two parallel canals suddenly showed where but a single one had showed before. The paralleling was so perfect that he suspected optical illusion. He could, however, discover none by changing his telescopes or eye-pieces. The phenomenon, apparently, was real.

At the next opposition he looked to see if by chance he should mark a repetition of the strange event, and went, as he tells us, from surprise to surprise; for one after another of his canals proceeded startlingly to become two, until some twenty of them had thus doubled. This capped the climax to his own wonderment, and, it is needless to add, to other people's incredulity; for nobody else had yet succeeded in seeing the canals at all, let alone seeing them double. Undeterred by the general skepticism, he confirmed at each fresh opposition his previous discoveries, which, in view of the fact that no one else did, tended in astronomical circles to an opposite result.

For nine years he labored thus alone, having his visions all to himself. It was not till 1886 that any one but he saw the canals. In April of that year Perrotin,[a] at Nice, first did so. The occasion was the setting up of the great Nice glass of twenty-nine inches' aperture. In spite of the great size of the glass,

[a]In addition to work associated with the Martian canals, Henri Joseph Perrotin (1845–1904), Director of the Nice Observatory from 1879, contributed to important projects, notably, on spectroscopy and work on the asteroids. [B.]

however, a first attempt resulted in nothing but failure. So, later, did a second, and Perrotin was on the point of abandoning the search for good, when, on the 15th of the month, he suddenly detected one of the canals, the Phison. His assistant, M. Thollon, saw it immediately afterward. After this they managed to make out several others, some single, some double, substantially as Schiaparelli had drawn them; the slight discrepancies between their observations and his being in point of fact the best of confirmations.

Since then, other observers have contrived to detect the canals, the list of the successful increasing at each opposition, although even now their number might almost be told on one's hands and feet.

The reason that so few astronomers have as yet succeeded in seeing these lines is to be found in our own atmosphere. That in ordinary atmosphere the lines are not easy objects is certain. A moderately good air is essential to their detection; and unfortunately the locations of most of our observatories preclude this prerequisite. Size of aperture of the telescope used is a very secondary matter. That Schiaparelli discovered the canals with an $8\frac{1}{3}$-inch glass, and that the 26-inch glass at Washington has refused to show them to this day, are facts that speak emphatically on the point.

The importance of atmosphere in the study of planetary detail is far from being appreciated. It is not simply question of a clear air, but of a steady one. To detect fine detail, the atmospheric strata must be as evenly disposed as possible.

Next in importance to a steady air comes attentive perception on the part of the observer. The steadiest air we can find is in a state of almost constant fluctuation. In consequence, revelations of detail come only to those who patiently watch for the few good moments among the many poor. Nor do I believe even average air to be entirely without such happy exceptions to a general blur. In these brief moments perseverance will show the canals as faint streaks. To see them as they are, however, an atmosphere pos-

sessing
imperati
their fin
air mus
marking
cut cha
who ha
upon th

Alth
the so-
dispelle
belief s
their p
of their
tional,
nectior
double
make
fore do
jectors
till mc
not ha
in the
ally a
the ca
is like
danci
disad
increa
other
best

It
with
preci
case
and
ring
the
this
alwa
was

**AR'**

It i
are
hac
not
are

---

## INTRODUCTORY

In this lecture I wish to give an account of some investigations which have led to the conclusion that the carriers of negative electricity are bodies, which I have called corpuscles,[a] having a mass very much smaller than that of the atom of any known element, and are of the same character from whatever source the negative electricity may be derived.

The first place in which corpuscles were detected was a highly exhausted tube through which an electric discharge was passing. When an electric discharge is sent through a highly exhausted tube, the sides of the tube glow with a vivid green phosphorescence. That this is due to something proceeding in straight lines from the cathode—the electrode where the negative electricity enters the tube—can be shown in the following way (the experiment is one made many years ago by Sir William Crookes): A Maltese cross made of thin mica is placed between the cathode and the walls of the tube [see Plate 37]. When the discharge is past, the green phosphorescence no longer extends all over the end of the tube, as it did when the cross was absent. There is now a well-defined cross in the phosphorescence at the end of the tube; the mica cross has thrown a shadow and the shape of the shadow proves that the phosphorescence is due to something traveling from the cathode in straight lines, which is stopped by a thin plate of mica. The green phosphorescence is caused by cathode rays and at one time there was a keen controversy as to the nature of these rays. Two views were prevalent: One, which was chiefly supported by English physicists, was that the rays are negatively electrified bodies shot off from the cathode with great velocity; the other view, which was held by the great majority of German physicists,[b] was that the rays are some kind of aethereal vibration or waves.

The arguments in favor of the rays being negatively charged particles are primarily that they are deflected by a magnet in just the same way as moving, negatively electrified particles. We know that such particles, when a magnet is placed near them, are acted upon by a force whose direction is at right angles to the magnetic force, and also at right angles to the direction in which the particles are moving.

Thus, if the particles are moving horizontally from east to west, and the magnetic force is horizontal from north to south, the force acting on the negatively electrified particles will be vertical and downwards.

When the magnet is placed so that the magnetic force is along the direction in which the particle is moving, the latter will not be affected by the magnet.

The next step in the proof that cathode rays are negatively charged particles was to show that when they are caught in a metal vessel they give up to it a charge of negative electricity. This was first done by Perrin.[c] This experiment was made conclusive by placing the catching vessel out of the path of the rays, and bending them into it by means of a magnet, when the vessel became negatively charged.

---

[a]Thomson referred to his fundamental particles as "corpuscles" in honor of Isaac Newton. Some years earlier, George Johnstone Stoney (1826–1911) had proposed that the unit of electricity gained or lost when atoms became electrically charged ions should be called the *electron*. The name *electron* gained currency in the decade or so after Thomson's 1897 experiment as the reality of his fundamental particles became accepted. [B.]

[b]Crookes was convinced that the cathode rays were streams of particles carrying an electric charge. His view was effectively refuted by Eugen Goldstein (1850–1930), who pointed out that, in a cathode ray tube evacuated to 1/100,000 normal air pressure, the rays traveled at least 90 centimeters, whereas the expected free path of an ordinary molecule in air at this pressure would be expected to be only about 0.6 centimeters. [B.]

[c]Jean Baptiste Perrin (1870–1942) showed in 1895 that cathode rays are deflected by a magnetic field and so carry a negative charge. [B.]

## ELECTRIC DEFLECTION OF THE RAYS

If the rays are charged with negative electricity, they ought to be deflected by an electrified body as well as by a magnet. In the earlier experiments made on this point no such deflection was observed. The reason of this has been shown to be that when cathode rays pass through a gas they make it a conductor of electricity, so that if there is any appreciable quantity of gas in the vessel through which the rays are passing, this gas will become a conductor of electricity and the rays will be surrounded by a conductor which will screen them from the effect of electric force, just as the metal covering of an electroscope screens off all external electric effects.

By exhausting the vacuum tube until there was only an exceedingly small quantity of air left in to be made a conductor, I was able to get rid of this effect and to obtain the electric deflection of the cathode rays. This deflection had a direction which indicated a negative charge on the rays.

Thus, cathode rays are deflected by both magnetic and electric forces, just as negatively electrified particles would be.

Hertz showed, however, that cathode particles possess another property which seemed inconsistent with the idea that they are particles of matter, for he found that they were able to penetrate very thin sheets of metal, e.g., pieces of gold leaf, and produce appreciable luminosity on glass behind them. The idea of particles as large as the molecules of a gas passing through a solid plate was a somewhat startling one, and this led me to investigate more closely the nature of the particles which form the cathode rays.

The principle of the method used is as follows: When a particle carrying a charge $e$ is moving with velocity $v$ across the lines of force in a magnetic field, placed so that the lines of magnetic force are at right angles to the motion of the particle, then, if $H$ is the magnetic force, the moving particle will be acted on by a force equal to $Hev$. This force acts in the direction which is at right angles

to the magnetic force and to the direction of the motion of the particle. If also we have an electric field of force $X$, the cathode ray will be acted upon by a force $Xe$. If the electric and magnetic fields are arranged so that they oppose each other, then, when the force $Hev$ due to the magnetic field is adjusted to balance the force due to the electric field $Xe$, the green patch of phosphorescence due to the cathode rays striking the end of the tube will be undisturbed, and we have

$$Hev = Xe$$

or

$$v = X/H.$$

Thus, if we measure, as we can do without difficulty, the values of $X$ and $H$ when the rays are not deflected, we can determine the value of $v$, the velocity of the particles. In a very highly exhausted tube this may be ⅓ the velocity of light, or about 60,000 miles per second; in tubes not so highly exhausted it may not be more than 5,000 miles per second, but in all cases when the cathode rays are produced in tubes their velocity is much greater than the velocity of any other moving body with which we are acquainted. It is, for example, many thousand times the average velocity with which the molecules of hydrogen are moving at ordinary temperatures, or indeed at any temperature yet realized.

## DETERMINATION OF *e/m*

Having found the velocity of the rays, let us now subject them to the action of the electric field alone. Then, the particles forming the rays are acted upon by a constant force and the problem is like that of a bullet projected horizontally with a velocity $v$ and falling under gravity. We know that in time $t$, the bullet will fall a depth equal to $gt^2/2$, where $g$ is the acceleration due to gravity. In our case the acceleration due to the electric field is equal to $Xe/m$, where $m$ is the mass of the particle. The time $t = l/v$, where $l$ is the length of path, and $v$ the velocity of projection.

Thus, the displacement of the patch of phosphorescence where the rays strike the glass is equal to

$$(1/2) \, (Xe/m) \, (l^2, v^2).$$

We can easily measure this displacement $d$, and we can thus find $e/m$ from the equation

$$e/m = (2d/X) \times (v^2/l^2).$$

The results of the determinations of the values of $e/m$ made by this method are very interesting, for it is found that, however the cathode rays are produced, we always get the same value of $e/m$ for all the particles in the rays. We may, for example, by altering the shape of the discharge tube and the pressure of the gas in the tube, produce great changes in the velocity of the particles, but unless the velocity of the particles becomes so great that they are moving nearly as fast as light, when other considerations have to be taken into account, the value of $e/m$ is nearly constant. The value of $e/m$ is not merely independent of the velocity. What is even more remarkable is that it is independent of the kind of electrodes we use and also of the kind of gas in the tube. The particles which form the cathode rays must come either from the gas in the tube or from the electrodes; we may, however, use any kind of substance we please for the electrodes and fill the tube with gas of any kind and yet the value of $e/m$ will remain unaltered.

This constant value, when we measure $e/m$ in the c.g.s. system of magnetic units, is equal to about $1.7 \times 10^7$. If we compare this with the value of the ratio of the mass to the charge of electricity carried by any system previously known, we find that it is of quite a different order of magnitude. Before the cathode rays were investigated, the charged atom of hydrogen met with in the electrolysis of liquids was the system which had the greatest known value of $e/m$, and in this case the value is only $10^4$, hence for the corpuscle

in the cathode rays the value of $e/m$ is 1,700 times the value for the corresponding quantity for the charged hydrogen atom. This discrepancy must arise in one or other of two ways; either the mass of the corpuscle must be very small compared with that of the atom of hydrogen, which until quite recently was the smallest mass recognized in physics, or else the charge on the corpuscle must be very much greater than that on the hydrogen atom. Now, it has been shown by a method which I shall shortly describe, that the electric charge is really the same in the two cases; hence we are driven to the conclusion that the mass of the corpuscle is only about 1/1,700 of that of the hydrogen atom.[d]

[d]Thomson was predisposed to explain his observations in terms of fundamental particles by an atomic tradition extending back to Dalton. In his celebrated paper of 1897, "Cathode Rays" (*Proceedings of the Royal Institution* 15: 419), Thomson quoted with approval the speculations of William Prout, who proposed in 1815 that the few dozen types of atoms that are believed to make up the known chemical elements were composed of one fundamental type of atom. Prout took this to be the atom of hydrogen. Thomson's idea of very light cathode ray particles was supported by Phillip Lenard who reported in 1894 that cathode ray particles could travel thousands of times further through gases than could ordinary atoms or molecules. Since cathode ray particles are much lighter than atoms, the possibility was open that they are constituents of atoms.

This possibility was not open, however, to the Berlin physicist Walter Kaufmann (1871–1947), who produced more accurate measurements of the mass/charge ratio than did Thomson. Kaufmann did not claim to have discovered a fundamental particle. He was strongly influenced by the Viennese physicist and philosopher of science Ernst Mach (1836–1916), who pronounced that it was unscientific to bother oneself with hypothetical entities like atoms that could not be directly observed. Thomson, in contrast, thought that it was part of the business of physics to discover fundamental particles. It is difficult to avoid the conclusion that this philosophical conviction played a central role in his discovery of the electron. [B.]

Thus, the atom is not the ultimate limit to the subdivision of matter; we may go further and get to the corpuscle, and at this stage the corpuscle is the same from whatever source it may be derived.

## CORPUSCLES VERY WIDELY DISTRIBUTED

It is not only from what may be regarded as a somewhat artificial and sophisticated source, viz., cathode rays, that we can obtain corpuscles. When once they had been discovered, it was found that they are of very general occurrence. They are given out by metals when raised to a red heat; indeed any substance when heated gives out corpuscles to some extent. We can detect the emission of them from some substances, such as rubidium and the alloy of sodium and potassium, even when they are cold; and it is perhaps allowable to suppose that there is some emission by all substances, though our instruments are not at present sufficiently delicate to detect it unless it is unusually large.

Corpuscles are also given out by metals and other bodies, but especially by the alkali metals, when these are exposed to light.

They are being continually given out in large quantities and with very great velocities by radioactive substances such as uranium and radium; they are produced in large quantities when salts are put into flames, and there is good reason to suppose that corpuscles reach us from the sun.

The corpuscle is thus very widely distributed, but wherever it is found, it preserves its individuality, $e/m$ being always equal to a certain constant value.

The corpuscle appears to form a part of all kinds of matter under the most diverse conditions; it seems natural, therefore, to regard it as one of the bricks of which atoms are built up . . .

## MAGNITUDE OF THE ELECTRIC CHARGE CARRIED BY THE CORPUSCLE

I shall now return to the proof that the very large value of $e/m$ for the corpuscle, as compared with that for the atom of hydrogen, is due to the smallness of $m$ the mass, and not to the greatness of $e$ the charge. We can do this by actually measuring the value of $e$, availing ourselves for this purpose of a discovery by C. T. R. Wilson,[e] that a charged particle acts as a nucleus round which water vapor condenses and forms drops of water. If we have air saturated with water vapor and cool it, so that it would be supersaturated if there were no deposition of moisture, we know that if any dust is present, the particles of dust act as nuclei round which the water condenses and we get the familiar phenomena of fog and rain. If the air is quite dust-free, we can, however, cool it very considerably without any deposition of moisture taking place. If there is no dust, C. T. R. Wilson has shown that the cloud does not form until the temperature has been lowered to such a point that the super saturation is about eightfold. When, however, this temperature is reached, a thick fog forms even in dust-free air.

When charged particles are present in the gas, Wilson showed that a much smaller amount of cooling is sufficient to produce the fog, a four-fold super saturation being all that is required when the charged particles are those which occur in a gas when it is in a state in which it conducts electricity. Each of the charged particles becomes the center round which a drop of water forms; the drops form a cloud, and thus the charged

---

[e]Thomson had measured the ratio of the electron's mass and charge. The outstanding issue was to measure the mass and charge separately. The cloud chamber, devised by Thomson's student Charles Thomson Rees Wilson (1869–1959), was based on the idea that ions (like grains of dust) could serve to start the growth of droplets of water in humid air. [B.]

particles, however, small to begin with, now become visible and can be observed.

The effect of the charged particles on the formation of a cloud can be shown very distinctly by the following experiment: A vessel which is in contact with water is saturated with moisture at the temperature of the room. This vessel is in communication with a cylinder in which a large piston slides up and down. The piston to begin with is at the top of its travel; by suddenly exhausting the air from below the piston, the air in the vessel will expand very quickly. When, however, air expands, it gets cool; thus the air in the vessel previously saturated is now supersaturated. If there is no dust present, no deposition of moisture will take place, unless the air is cooled to such a low temperature that the amount of moisture required to saturate it is only about ⅛th of that actually present.

Now, the amount of cooling, and therefore of super saturation, depends upon the travel of the piston; the greater the travel the greater the cooling. Suppose the travel is regulated so that the super saturation is less than eightfold and greater than fourfold. We now free the air from dust by forming cloud after cloud in the dusty air; as the clouds fall they carry the dust down with them, just as in nature the air is cleared by showers. We find at last that when we make the expansion no cloud is visible.

The gas is now made in a conducting state by bringing a little radium near the vessel; this fills the gas with large quantities of both positively and negatively electrified particles. On making the expansion now an exceedingly dense cloud is formed. That this is due to the electrification in the gas can be shown by the following experiment: Along the inside walls of the vessel we have two vertical insulated plates which can be electrified. If these plates are charged, they will drag the electrified particles out of the gas as fast as they are formed, so that in this way we can get rid of, or at any rate largely reduce, the number of electrified particles in the gas. If the expansion is now made with the plates charged before bringing up the radium, there is only a small cloud formed.

We can use the drops to find the charge on the particles, for when we know the travel of the piston, we can deduce the amount of super saturation, and hence the amount of water deposited when the cloud forms. The water is deposited in the form of a number of small drops all of the same size; thus the number of drops will be the volume of the water deposited divided by the volume of one of the drops. Hence, if we find the volume of one of the drops, we can find the number of drops which are formed round the charged particles. If the particles are not too numerous, each will have a drop round it, and we can thus find the number of electrified particles.

From the rate at which the drops slowly fall we can determine their size. In consequence of the viscosity or friction of the air small bodies do not fall with a constantly accelerated velocity, but soon reach a speed which remains uniform for the rest of the fall; the smaller the body, the slower this speed. Sir George Stokes[f] has shown that $V$, the speed at which a drop of rain falls, is given by the formula

$$V = (2/9) \times (ga^2/\mu)$$

where $a$ is the radius of the drop, $g$ the acceleration due to gravity, and $\mu$ the coefficient of viscosity of the air.

If we substitute the values of $g$ and $\mu$, we get

$$V = 1.28 \times 10^6 \times a^2$$

[f]The viscous drag of the air depends on both the radius of the droplet and its velocity. George Stokes (1819–1903) showed that this force is given by this formula: drag force of droplet = $6\pi\eta \times$ radius of droplet $\times$ velocity of droplet, where $\eta$ is a numerical quantity that gives the viscosity or stickiness of the air, and is established through various measurements. [B.]

Hence if we measure $V$ we can determine $a$, the radius of the drop.

We can in this way find the volume of a drop, and may therefore, as explained above, calculate the number of drops, and therefore the number of electrified particles.

It is a simple matter to find by electrical methods the total quantity of electricity on these particles; and hence, as we know the number of particles, we can deduce at once the charge on each particle.

This was the method by which I first determined the charge on the particle; H. A. Wilson[g] has since used a simpler method founded on the following principles: C. T. R. Wilson has shown that the drops of water condense more easily on negatively electrified particles than on positively electrified ones. Thus, by adjusting the expansion, it is possible to get drops of water round the negative particles and not round the positive; with this expansion, therefore, all the drops are negatively electrified. The size of these drops and therefore their weight can, as before, be determined by measuring the speed at which they fall under gravity. Suppose now, that we hold above the drops a positively electrified body; then, since the drops are negatively electrified, they will be attracted towards the positive electricity, and thus the downward force on the drops will be diminished and they will not fall so rapidly as they did when free from electrical attraction. If we adjust the electrical attraction so that the upward force on each drop is equal to the weight of the drop, the drops will not fall at all, but will, like Mahomet's coffin, remain suspended between heaven and earth. If then we adjust the electrical force until the drops are in equilibrium and neither fall nor rise, we know that the upward force on each drop is equal to the weight of the drop, which we have already

[g]H.A. Wilson (1874–1964) used ions produced by X-rays, but the resulting cloud of water droplets was subjected to a strong vertical electric field. [B.]

determined by measuring the rate of fall when the drop was not exposed to any electrical force. If $X$ is the electrical force, $e$ the charge on the drop, and $w$ its weight, we have, when there is equilibrium,

$$Xe = w$$

Since $X$ can easily be measured and $w$ is known, we can use this relation to determine $e$, the charge on the drop. The value of $e$, found by these methods, is $3.1 \times 10^{-10}$ electrostatic units, or $10^{-20}$ electromagnetic units. This value is the same as that of the charge carried by a hydrogen atom in the electrolysis of dilute solutions, an approximate value of which has been long known.

It might be objected that the charge measured in the preceding experiments is the charge on a molecule or collection of molecules of the gas, and not the charge on a corpuscle.

This objection does not, however, apply to another form in which I tried the experiment, where the charges on the corpuscles were got, not by exposing the gas to the effects of radium, but by allowing ultraviolet light to fall on a metal plate in contact with the gas. In this case, as experiments made in a very high vacuum show, the electrification, which is entirely negative, escapes from the metal in the form of corpuscles. When a gas is present, the corpuscles strike against the molecules of the gas and stick to them.

Thus, though it is the molecules which are charged, the charge on a molecule is equal to the charge on a corpuscle, and when we determine the charge on the molecules by the methods I have just described, we determine the charge carried by the corpuscle.

The value of the charge when the electrification is produced by ultraviolet light is the same as when the electrification is produced by radium.

We have just seen that $e$, the charge on the corpuscle, is in electromagnetic units equal to $10^{-20}$, and we have previously found that $e/m$, $m$ being the mass of a corpuscle, is equal to $1.7 \times 10^{7}$, hence $m = 6 \times 10^{-28}$ grams.

We can realize more easily what this means if we express the mass of the corpuscle in terms of the mass of the atom of hydrogen.

We have seen that for the corpuscle $e/m = 1.7 \times 10^7$. If E is the charge carried by an atom of hydrogen in the electrolysis of dilute solutions, and M is the mass of the hydrogen atom, $E/M = 10^4$; hence $e/m = 1{,}700\ E/M$.

We have already stated that the value of e found by the preceding methods agrees well with the value of E, which has long been approximately known. Townsend[h] has used a method in which the value of $e/E$ is directly measured, and has shown in this way also that e is equal to E. Hence, since $e/m = 1{,}700\ E/M$, we have $M = 1{,}700\ m$, i.e., the mass of a corpuscle is only about 1/1,700 part of the mass of the hydrogen atom.

In all known cases in which negative electricity occurs in gases at very low pressures, it occurs in the form of corpuscles, small bodies with an invariable charge and mass. The case is entirely different with positive electricity.

## FURTHER READING

Buchwald, J. Z. and Warwick, Andrew. 2001. *Histories of the Electron: The Birth of Microphysics.* Cambridge: MIT Press.

Kim, Dong-Won. 2002. *Leadership and Creativity—A History of the Cavendish Laboratory, 1871–1919.* Boston: Kluwer Academic Publishers.

_. Townsend (1868–1957) passed a cloud of
 s through sulfuric acid, which absorbed
   . He measured the electric charge picked
    acid and the increase in weight due to
    ed water. [B.]

# The Discovery of Radium

## Eve Curie (b. 1904)

*Marie Curie was the very model of the experimental scientist. Her work was characterized by precise measurement, a relentless drive to achieve her goals as a scientist, and an unbridled faith in the power of experiment. Experiment indicated that the radiant activity of uranium, thorium, and radium was constant and, consequently, when she discovered that the activity of polonium diminished over time, Curie regarded the behavior of polonium as the exception to the rule. Her confidence in experiment prevented her from following an important clue furnished by the behavior of polonium. Ernest Rutherford—who would play the role of architect of the atom in the coming decades—would soon suggest, in contrast to Curie, that the decreased activity of radioactive substances over time was the rule, and that uranium only seemed to be stable because it had a very long period of decay.*

*Marie Curie's life labor as a scientist is all the more remarkable because during the most extraordinary and productive period of her scientific career, she was mother to a young daughter—Irène Joliet Curie (1897–1956)—who would follow in her mother's footsteps and make important contributions to chemistry. A second daughter, Eve, was born in 1904, the year after the Curies shared the Nobel Prize in Physics with Henri Becquerel (1852–1908). Eve would later author the autobiography of her mother from which this reading is taken. Cobbled together from letters, diaries and conversations, she chronicles the discovery of radium and polonium in a way that highlights a feature of scientific practice that can easily be overlooked—namely, the sheer difficulty of scientific work. At the same time, she takes the reader into the Curies' ramshackle laboratory, providing precious insights into the process of discovery—insights that are often missing in scientific papers that are geared toward the reporting of positive results.*

*As important as Curie's work was to the age-old philosophical quest for the structure of matter, her discovery of radium was perhaps even more important in its application to medical practice. Aware of its ability to cause blisters and inflammation of the skin, Pierre studied the effects of radium on animals, and found that by destroying diseased cells it could offer a treatment for tumors and certain forms of cancer. Once this therapeutic method (Curietherapy) was made public, the industrial production of radium began, and clinics opened throughout the world. The Curies declined to patent*

*Source:* Curie, Eve. 1943. *Madame Curie: A Biography by Eve Curie.* New York: Garden City Publishing Co., pp. 153–164; 166–175.

*their technique for producing radium, and the ensuing wealth, on the grounds that it would be "contrary to the scientific spirit."*

*The Curies were awarded the Nobel Prize in Physics in 1903, but they shied away from publicity and continued their simple lifestyle. After Pierre's untimely death in 1906, Marie donated the gram of radium they had prepared together — now worth more than a million gold francs — to her laboratory.*

After Röntgen's discovery of X rays, Henri Poincaré[a] conceived the idea of determining whether rays like the X ray were emitted by "fluorescent" bodies under the action of light. Attracted by the same problem, Henri Becquerel examined the salts of a "rare metal," uranium. Instead of finding the phenomenon he had expected, he observed another, altogether different and incomprehensible: He found that uranium salts *spontaneously* emitted, without exposure to light, some rays of unknown nature. A compound of radium, placed on a photographic plate, surrounded by black paper, made an impression on the plate through the paper. And, like the X ray, these astonishing "uranic" salts discharged an electroscope by rendering the surrounding air a conductor.

Henri Becquerel made sure that these surprising properties were not caused by a preliminary exposure to the Sun and that they persisted when the uranium compound had been maintained in darkness for several months. For the first time, a physicist had observed the phenomenon to which Marie Curie was later to give the name of *radioactivity*. But the nature of the radiation and its origin remained the enigma.

Becquerel's discovery fascinated the Curies. They asked themselves where the energy came from—tiny, to be sure—which uranium compounds constantly disengaged in the form of radiation. And what was the nature of this radiation? Here was an engrossing subject of research, a doctor's thesis! The subject tempted Marie most because it was a virgin field: Becquerel's work was very recent and so far as she knew nobody in the laboratories of Europe had yet attempted to make a fundamental study of uranium rays. As a point of departure, and as the only bibliography, there existed some communications presented by Henri Becquerel at the Academy of Science during the year 1896. It was a leap into great adventure, into an unknown realm.

There remained the question of where she was to make her experiments—and here the difficulties began. Pierre made several approaches to the Director of the School of Physics with practically no results: Marie was given the free use of a little glassed-in studio on the ground floor of the school. It was a kind of storeroom, sweating with damp, where unused machines and lumber were put away. Its technical equipment was rudimentary and comfort nil.

Deprived of an adequate electrical installation and of everything that forms material for the beginning of scientific research, she kept her patience, sought and found a means of making her apparatus work in this hole.

It was not easy. Instruments of precision have sneaking enemies—humidity, changes of temperature. Incidentally the climate of this little workroom, fatal to the sensitive electrometer, was not much better for Marie's health. But this had no importance. When she was cold, the young woman took her revenge by noting the degrees of temperature in centigrade in her notebook. On February 6, 1898, we find, among the formulas and figures: "Temperature here 6°25." Six

---

[a] A mathematician of wide-ranging interests, Henri Poincaré (1854–1912) made important contributions to a number of branches of mathematics (e.g., topology, number theory, probability theory). [B.]

**PLATE 41** Photograph of Marie Curie in her laboratory.

degrees! . . .[b] Marie, to show her disapproval, added ten little exclamation points.

The candidate for the doctor's degree set her first task to be the measurement of the "power of ionization" of uranium rays—that is to say, their power to render the air a conductor of electricity and so to discharge an electroscope. The excellent method she used, which was the key to the success of her experiments, had been invented for the study of other phenomenon by two physicists well known to her: Pierre and Jacques Curie. Her technical installation consisted of an "ionization chamber," a Curie electrometer and piezoelectric quartz.[c]

At the end of the several weeks the first result appeared: Marie acquired the cer-

[b]About 44° Fahrenheit.

[c]Curie's apparatus exploits the fact that, when subjected to mechanical stress, some crystals display piezoelectric properties, such as electric polarization. [B.]

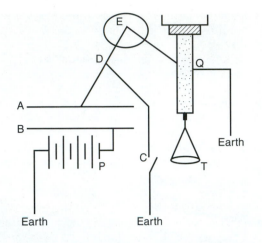

**PLATE 42** Illustration of Marie Curie's method of measuring the conductivity acquired by air under the action of radioactive material. Finely-powdered material was spread on a plate B, making the air between the plates A and B a conductor. In order to measure the conductivity, the plate B was raised to a high potential by connecting it with one pole of a battery of small accumulators P; the other pole was connected to earth. Since plate A was maintained at the potential of the Earth by the connection CD, an electric current was set up between the two plates. The potential of plate A was then recorded by the electrometer, E. If the connection with the Earth connection was broken at C, the plate A was then recorded by the electrometer, E. If the connection with the Earth connection was broken at C, the plate A became charged, causing a deflection of the electrometer.  The velocity of the deflection is proportional to the intensity of the current, and so served as a measure of the latter. Curie's preferred method was to compensate the charge of plate A, so that it would cause no deflection of the electrometer, by means of a quartz electric balance Q, one sheath of which was connected to plate A and the other to the Earth. This had the effect of generating progressively a known quantity of electricity during the time observed. The operation could be regulated such that, at each instant, there was compensation between the quantity of electricity that passed through the condenser and that of the opposite kind furnished by the quartz. In this way, the quantity of electricity passing through the condenser for a given time could be reckoned in absolute units.

tainty that the intensity of this surprising radiation was proportional to the quantity of uranium contained in the samples under examination, and that this radiation, which could be measured with precision, was not affected either by the chemical state of combination of the uranium or by external factors such as lighting or temperature.

These observations were perhaps not very sensational to the uninitiated, but they were of passionate interest to the scientist. It often happens in physics that an inexplicable phenomenon can be subjected, after some investigation, to laws already known, and by this very fact loses its interest for the research worker. Thus, in a badly constructed detective story, if we are told in the third chapter that the woman of sinister appearance who might have committed the crime is in reality only an honest little housewife who leads a life without secrets, we feel discouraged and cease to read.

Nothing of the kind happened here. The more Marie penetrated into intimacy with uranium rays, the more they seemed without precedent, essentially unknown. In spite of their very feeble power, they had an extraordinary individuality.

Turning this mystery over and over in her head, and pointing toward the truth, Marie felt and could soon affirm that the incomprehensible radiation was an *atomic* property. She questioned: Even though the phenomenon had only been observed with uranium, nothing proved that uranium was the only chemical element capable of emitting such radiation. Why should not other bodies possess the same power? Perhaps it was only by chance that this radiation had been observed in uranium first, and had remained attached to uranium in the minds of physicists. Now it must be sought for elsewhere.

No sooner said than done. Abandoning the study of uranium, Marie undertook to examine *all known chemical bodies*, either in the pure state or in compounds. And the result was not long in appearing: Compounds of another element, thorium, also emitted spontaneous rays like those of uranium and of similar intensity. The physicist had been right: The surprising phenomenon was by no means the property of uranium alone, and it became necessary to give it a distinct name. Mme Curie suggested the name of *radioactivity*. Chemical substances like uranium and thorium, endowed with this particular "radiance," were called *radio elements.*

Radioactivity so fascinated the young scientist that she never tired of examining the most diverse forms of matter, always by the same method. Curiosity, a marvelous feminine curiosity, the first virtue of a scientist, was developed in Marie to the highest degree. Instead of limiting her observation to simple compounds, salts and oxides, she had the desire to assemble samples of minerals from the collection at the School of Physics, and of making them undergo almost at hazard, for her own amusement, a kind of customs inspection which is an electrometer test. Pierre approved, and chose with her the veined fragments, hard and crumbly, oddly shaped, which she wanted to examine.

Marie's idea was simple—simple as the stroke of genius. At the crossroads where Marie now stood, hundreds of research workers might have remained, nonplussed, for months or even years. After examining all known chemical substances, and discovering—as Marie had done—the radiation of thorium, they would have continued to ask themselves in vain whence came this mysterious radioactivity. Marie, too, questioned and wondered. But her surprise was translated into fruitful acts. She had used up all evident possibilities. Now she turned toward the unplumbed and the unknown.

She knew in advance what she would learn from an examination of the minerals, or rather she thought she knew. The specimens that contained neither uranium nor thorium would be revealed as totally "inactive." The others, containing uranium or thorium, would be radioactive.

Experiment confirmed this prevision. Rejecting the inactive minerals, Marie applied herself to the others and measured their radioactivity. Then came a dramatic revelation: The radioactivity was a *great deal stronger* than could have been normally foreseen by the quantity of uranium or thorium contained in the products examined!

"It must be an error in experiment," the young woman thought; for doubt is the scientist's first response to an unexpected phenomenon.

She started her measurements over again, unmoved, using the same products. She started over again ten times, twenty times. And she was forced to yield to the evidence: The quantities of uranium and of thorium found in these minerals were by no means sufficient to justify the exceptional intensity of the radiation she observed.

Where did this excessive and abnormal radiation come from? Only one explanation was possible: The minerals must contain, in small quantity, a *much more powerfully radioactive substance* than uranium and thorium.

But what substance? In her preceding experiments, Marie had already examined *all known chemical elements.*

The scientist replied to the question with the sure logic and the magnificent audaciousness of a great mind: The minerals certainly contained a radioactive substance, which was at the same time a chemical element unknown until this day: *a new element.*

A new element! It was a fascinating and alluring hypothesis—but still a hypothesis. For the moment this powerfully radioactive substance existed only in the imagination of Marie and of Pierre. But it did exist there. It existed strongly enough to make the young woman go to see Bronya [Marie's sister] one day and tell her in a restrained, ardent voice:

"You know, Bronya, the radiation that I couldn't explain comes from a new chemical element. The element is there and I've got to find it. We are sure! The physicists we have spoken to believe we have made an error in experiment and advise us to be careful. But I am convinced that I am not mistaken."

These were unique moments in her unique life. The layman forms a theatrical—and wholly false—idea of the research worker and of his discoveries. "The moment of discovery" does not always exist: The scientist's work is too tenuous, too divided, for the certainty of success to crackle out suddenly in the midst of his laborious toil like a stroke of lightning, dazzling him by its fire. Marie, standing in front of her apparatus, perhaps never experienced the sudden intoxication of triumph. This intoxication was spread over several days of decisive labor, made feverish by a magnificent hope. But it must have been an exultant moment when, convinced by the rigorous reasoning of her brain that she was on the trail of a new matter, she confided the secret to her elder sister, her ally always. Without exchanging one affectionate word, the two sisters must have lived again, in a dizzying breath of memory, their years of waiting, their mutual sacrifices, their bleak lives as students, full of hope and faith . . .

In a first communication to the Academy . . . and published in the *Proceedings* on April 12, 1898, "Marie Sklodovska Curie" announced the probable presence in pitchblende ores of a new element endowed with powerful radioactivity. This was the first stage of the discovery of radium.

By the force of her own intuition the physicist had shown to herself that the wonderful substance must exist. She decreed its existence. But its incognito still had to be broken. Now she would have to verify hypothesis by experiment, isolate this material and see it. She must be able to announce with certainty: "It is there."

Pierre Curie had followed the rapid progress of his wife's experiments with passionate interest. Without directly taking part in Marie's work, he had frequently helped her by his remarks and advice. In view of the stupefying character of her results, he did not hesitate to abandon his study of crystals for the time being in order to join his efforts to hers in the search for the new substance.

Thus, when the immensity of a pressing task suggested and exacted collaboration, a great physicist was at Marie's side—a physicist who was the companion of her life. Three years earlier, love had joined this exceptional man and woman together—love, and perhaps some mysterious foreknowledge, some sublime instinct for the work in common.

The available force was now doubled. Two brains, four hands, now sought the unknown elements in the damp little workroom in the Rue Lhomond. From this moment onward it is impossible to distinguish each one's part in the work of the Curies. We know that Marie, having chosen to study the radiation of uranium as the subject of her thesis, discovered that other substances were also radioactive. We know that after the examination of minerals she was able to announce the existence of a new chemical element, powerfully radioactive, and that it was the capital importance of this result which prompted Pierre Curie to interrupt his very different research in order to try to isolate this element with his wife. At the time—May or June 1898—a collaboration began which was to last for eight years, until it was destroyed by a fatal accident.

We cannot and must not attempt to find out what should be credited to Marie and what to Pierre during those eight years. It would be exactly what the husband and wife did not want. The personal genius of Pierre Curie is known to us by the original work he had accomplished before this collaboration. His wife's genius appears to us in the first intuition of discovery, the brilliant start; and it was to reappear to us again, solitary, when Marie Curie the widow unflinchingly carried the weight of a new science and conducted it, through research, step by step, to its harmonious expansion. We therefore have formal proof that in the fusion of their two efforts, in this superior alliance of man and woman, the exchange was equal.

Let this attempt suffice for our curiosity and admiration. Let us not attempt to separate these creatures full of love, whose handwriting alternates and combines in the working notebooks covered with formulae, these creatures who were to sign nearly all their scientific publications together. They were to write "We found" and "We observed"; and when they were constrained by fact to distinguish between their parts, they were to employ this moving location:

Certain minerals containing uranium and thorium (pitchblende, chalcolite, uranite) are very active from the point of view of the emission of Becquerel rays. In a preceding communication, *one of us* showed that their activity was even greater than that of uranium and thorium, and stated the opinion that this effect was due to some other very active substance contained in small quantity in these minerals.

Pierre and Marie Curie,
*Proceedings of the Academy
of Science,* July 18, 1898.

Marie and Pierre looked for this "very active" substance in an ore of uranium called pitchblende, which in the crude state had shown itself to be four times more radioactive than the pure oxide of uranium that could be extracted from it. But the composition of this ore had been known for a long time with considerable precision. The new element must therefore be present in very small quantity or it would not have escaped the notice of scientists and their chemical analysis.

According to their calculations—"pessimistic" calculations, like those of true physicists, who always take the less attractive of two probabilities—the collaborators thought the ore should contain the new element to a maximum quantity of one per cent. They decided that this was very little. They would have been in consternation if they had known that the radioactive element they were hunting down did not count for more than a millionth part of pitchblende ore.

They began their prospecting patiently, using a method of chemical research invented by themselves, based on radioactivity: They separated all the elements in pitchblende by ordinary chemical analysis and then measured the radioactivity of each of the bodies thus obtained. By successive eliminations they saw the "abnormal" radioactivity take refuge in certain parts of the ore. As they went on, the field of investigation was narrowed. It was exactly the technique used by the police when they search the houses of a neighborhood, one by one, to isolate and arrest a malefactor.

But there was more than one malefactor here: The radioactivity was concentrated principally in two different chemical fractions of the pitchblende. For M. and Mme. Curie it indicated the existence of two new elements instead of one. By July 1898 they were able to announce the discovery of one of these substances with certainty.

"You will have to name it," Pierre said to his young wife, in the same tone as if it were a question of choosing a name for little Irène.

The one-time Mlle. Sklodovska reflected in silence for a moment. Then, her heart turning toward her own country which had been erased from the map of the world, she wondered vaguely if the scientific event would be published in Russia, Germany, and Austria—the oppressor countries—and answered timidly:

"Could we call it 'polonium'?"

In the *Proceedings of the Academy* for July 1898 we read:

> We believe the substance we have extracted from pitchblende contains a metal not yet observed, related to bismuth by its analytical properties. If the existence of this new metal is confirmed we propose to call it *polonium,* from the name of the original country of one of us.

The choice of this name proves that in becoming a French woman and a physicist Marie had not disowned her former enthusiasms. Another thing proves it for us: Even before the note "On a New Radioactive Substance Contained in Pitchblende" had appeared in the *Proceedings of the Academy,* Marie had sent the manuscript to her native country, to that Joseph Boguski who directed the little laboratory at the Museum of Industry and Agriculture where she had made the first experiments. The communication was published in Warsaw in a monthly photographic review called *Swiatlo* almost as soon as in Paris.

Life was unchanged in the little flat in the Rue de la Glacière. Marie and Pierre worked even more than usual; that was all. When the heat of summer came, the young wife found time to buy some baskets of fruit in the markets and, as usual, she cooked and put away preserves for the winter, according to the recipes used in the Curie family. Then she locked the shutters on her windows, which gave on burned leaves; she registered their two bicycles at the Orleans station, and, like thousands of other young women in Paris, went off on holiday with her husband and her child.

This year the couple had rented a peasant's house at Auroux, in Auvergne. Happy to breathe good air after the noxious atmosphere of the Rue Lhomond, the Curies made excursions to Mende, Puy, Clermont, Mont-Dore. They climbed hills, visited grottoes,

bathed in rivers. Every day, alone in the country, they spoke of what they called their "new metals," polonium and "the other"— the one that remained to be found. In September they would go back to the damp workroom and the dull minerals; with freshened ardor they would take up their search again . . .

In spite of their prosaic character—or perhaps because of it—some notes written by Mme. Curie in that memorable year 1898 seem to be worth quoting. Some are to be found in the margins of a book called *Family Cooking,* with respect to a recipe for gooseberry jelly:

> I took eight pounds of fruit and the same weight in crystallized sugar. After an ebullition of ten minutes, I passed the mixture through a rather fine sieve. I obtained fourteen pots of very good jelly, nor transparent, which "took" perfectly.

In a school notebook covered with gray linen, in which the young mother had written little Irène's weight day by day, her diet and the appearance of her first teeth, we read under the dates July 20, 1898, some days after the publication of the discovery of polonium:

> Irène says "thanks" with her hand. She can walk very well now on all fours. She says "Gogli, gogli, go." She stays in the garden all day at Sceauux on a carpet. She can roll, pick herself up, and sit down.

On August 15, at Auroux:

> Irène has cut her seventh tooth, on the lower left. She can stand for half a minute alone. For the past three days we have bathed her in the river. She cries, but today (fourth bath) she stopped crying and played with her hands in the water.
>
> She plays with the cat and chases him with war cries. She is not afraid of strangers any more. She sings a great deal. She gets up on the table when she is in her chair.

Three months later, on October 17, Marie noted with pride: "Irène can walk very well, and no longer goes on all fours."

On January 5, 1899: "Irène has fifteen teeth!"

Between these two notes—that of October 17, 1898, in which Irène no longer goes on all fours, and that of January 5 in which Irène has fifteen teeth—and a few months after the note on gooseberry preserve, we find another note worthy of remark.

It was drawn up by Marie and Pierre Curie and a collaborator called G. Bémont. Intended for the Academy of Science, and published in the *Proceedings* of the session of December 26, 1898, it announced the existence of a second new chemical element in pitchblende.

Some lines of this communication read as follows:

> The various reasons we have just enumerated lead us to believe that the new radioactive substance contains a new element to which we propose to give the name of RADIUM.
>
> The new radioactive substance certainly contains a very strong proportion of barium; in spite of that its radioactivity is considerable. The radioactivity of radium therefore must be enormous . . .

The aim was to obtain a pure radium and polonium. In the most strongly radioactive products the scientists had prepared, these substances figured only in imperceptible traces. Pierre and Marie already knew the method by which they could hope to isolate the new metals, but the separation could not be made except by treating very large quantities of crude material.

Here arose three agonizing problems:

How were they to get a sufficient quantity of ore? What premises could they use to effect their treatment? What money was there to pay the inevitable cost of the work?

Pitchblende, in which polonium and radium were hidden, was a costly ore, treated at the St. Joachimsthal mines in Bohemia for the extraction of uranium salts used in the manufacture of glass. Tons of pitchblende would cost a great deal—a great deal too much for the Curie household.

Ingenuity was to make up for wealth. According to the expectation of the two scientists, the extraction of uranium should leave, intact in the ore, such traces of polonium and radium as the ore contains. There was no reason why these traces should not be found in the residue. And, whereas crude pitchblende was costly, its residue after treatment had very slight value. By asking an Austrian colleague for a recommendation to the directors of the mine at St. Joachimsthal would it not be possible to obtain a considerable quantity of such residue for a reasonable price?

It was simple enough, but somebody had to think of it.

It was necessary, of course, to buy this crude material and pay for its transportation to Paris. Pierre and Marie appropriated the required sum from their very slight savings. They were not so foolish as to ask for official credits. . . If two physicists on the scent of an immense discovery had asked the University of Paris or the French government for a grant to buy pitchblende residue they would have been laughed at . . . But at least could there not be found, in the numerous buildings attached to the Sorbonne, some kind of suitable workroom to lend to the Curie couple? Apparently not. After vain attempts, Pierre and Marie staggered back to their point of departure, which is to say to the School of Physics where Pierre taught, to the little room where Marie had done her first experiments. The room gave on a courtyard, and on the other side of the yard there was a wooden shack, an abandoned shed, with a skylight roof in such bad condition that it admitted the rain. The Faculty of Medicine had formerly used the place as a dissecting room, but for a long time now it had not even been considered fit to house the cadavers. No floor: An uncertain layer of bitumen covered the earth. It was furnished with some worn kitchen tables, a blackboard which had landed there for no known reason, and an old cast-iron stove with a rusty pipe.

A workman would not willingly have worked in such a place: Marie and Pierre, nevertheless, resigned themselves to it. The shed had one advantage: It was so untempting, so miserable, that nobody thought of refusing them the use of it . . . The director of the school, had always been very kind to Pierre Curie and no doubt regretted that he had nothing better to offer. However that may be, he offered nothing else; and the couple, very pleased at not being put out into the street with their material, thanked him, saying that "this would do" and that they would "make the best of it."

As they were taking possession of the shed, a reply arrived from Austria. Good news! By extraordinary luck, the residue of recent extractions of uranium had not been scattered. The useless material had been piled up in a no-man's-land planted with pine trees, near the mine at St. Joachimsthal. Thanks to the intercession of Professor Suess and the Academy of Science of Vienna, the Austrian government, which was the proprietor of the State factory there, decided to present a ton of residue to the two French lunatics who thought they needed it. If, later on, they wished to be sent a greater quantity of the material, they could obtain it at the mine on the best terms. For the moment the Curies had to pay only the transportation charges on a ton of ore.

One morning a heavy wagon, like those which deliver coal, drew up in the Rue Lhomond before the School of Physics. Pierre and Marie were notified. They hurried bareheaded into the street in their laboratory gowns. Pierre, who was never agitated, kept his calm; but the more exuberant Marie could not contain her joy at the sight of the sacks that were being unloaded. It was pitchblende, *her* pitchblende, for which she received a notice some days before from the freight station. Full of curiosity and impatience, she wanted to open one of the sacks and contemplate her treasure without further waiting. She cut the strings,

undid the coarse sackcloth and plunged her two hands into the dull brown ore, still mixed with pine needles from Bohemia.

There was where radium was hidden. It was from there that Marie must extract it, even if she had to treat a mountain of this inert stuff like dust on the road . . .

The shed in the Rue Lhomond surpassed the most pessimistic expectations of discomfort. In summer, because of its skylights, it was too stifling as a hothouse. In winter one did not know whether to wish for rain or frost; if it rained, the water fell drop by drop, with a soft nerve-racking noise, on the ground or on the worktables, in places where the physicists had to mark in order to avoid putting apparatus there. If it froze, one froze. There was no recourse. The stove, even when it was stoked white, was a complete disappointment. If one went near enough to touch it one received a little heat, but two steps away and one was back in the zone of ice.

It was almost better for Marie and Pierre to get used to the cruelty of the outside temperature, since their technical installation—hardly existent—possessed no chimneys to carry off noxious gases, and the greater part of their treatment had to be made in open air, in the courtyard. When a shower came in the physicists hastily moved their apparatus inside: To keep on working without being suffocated they set up draughts between the opened door and windows . . .

In such conditions M. and Mme. Curie worked for four year from 1898 and 1902.

During the first year they busied themselves with the chemical separation of radium and polonium and they studied the radiation of the products (more and more active) thus obtained. Before long they considered it more practical to separate their efforts. Pierre Curie tried to determine the properties of radium, and to know the new metal better. Marie continued those chemical treatments, which would permit her to obtain salt of pure radium.

In this division of labor Marie had chosen the "man's job." She accomplished the toil of the day laborer. Inside the shed her husband was absorbed by delicate experiments. In the courtyard, dressed in her old dust-covered and acid-stained smock, her hair blown by the wind, surrounded by smoke which stung her eyes and throat, Marie was a sort of factory all by herself.

I came to treat as many as twenty kilograms of matter at a time [she writes], which had the effect of filling the shed with great jars full of precipitates and liquids. It was killing work to carry the receivers, to pour off the liquids and to stir, for hours at a stretch, the boiling matter in a smelting basin.

Radium showed no intention of allowing itself to be known by human creatures. Where were the days when Marie naively expected the radium content of pitchblende to be *one percent?* The radiation of the new substance was so powerful that a tiny quantity of radium, disseminated through the ore, was the source of striking phenomena, which could be easily observed and measured. The difficult, the impossible thing, was to isolate this minute quantity, to separate it from the gangue in which it was so intimately mixed.

The days of work became months and years: Pierre and Marie were not discouraged. This material that resisted them, which defended its secrets, fascinated them. United by their tenderness, united by their intellectual passions, they had, in a wooden shack, the "anti-natural" existence for which they had both been made, she as well as he.

At this period we were entirely absorbed by the new realm that was, thanks to an unhoped-for discovery, opening before us [Marie was to write]. In spite of the difficulties of our working conditions, we felt very happy. Our days were spent at the laboratory. In our poor shed there reigned a great tranquility: Sometimes, as we watched over some operation, we would walk up and down, talking about work in the present and in the future; when we were cold a cup of hot tea taken near the stove comforted us. We lived in our single preoccupation as if in a dream.

. . . We saw only very few persons at the laboratory; among the physicists and chemists there were a few who came from time to time, either to see our experiments or to ask for advice from Pierre Curie, whose competence in several branches of physics was well-known. Then took place some conversations before the blackboard—the sort of conversation one remembers well because it acts as a stimulant for scientific interest and the ardor for work without interrupting the course of reflection and without troubling that atmosphere of peace and meditation, which is the true atmosphere of a laboratory.

Whenever Pierre and Marie, alone in this poor place, left their apparatus for a moment and quietly let their tongues run on, their talk about their beloved radium passed from the transcendent to the childish.

"I wonder what *It* will be like, what *It* will look like," Marie said one day with the feverish curiosity of a child who has been promised a toy. "Pierre, what form do you imagine *It* will take?"

"I don't know," the physicist answered gently. "I should like it to have a very beautiful color . . ."

It is odd to observe that in Marie Curie's correspondence we find, upon this prodigious effort, none of the sensitive comments, decked out with imagery, which were to flash suddenly amid the familiarity of her letters. Was it because the years of exile had somewhat relaxed the young woman's intimacy with her people? Was she too pressed by work to find time?

The essential reason for this reserve is perhaps to be sought elsewhere. It was not by chance that Mme. Curie's letters ceased to be original at the exact moment when the story of her life became exceptional. As a student, teacher or young wife, Marie could tell her story . . . But now she was isolated by all that was secret and inexpressible in her scientific vocation. Among those she loved there was no longer anybody able to understand, to realize her worries and her difficult design. She could share her obsessions with only one person, Pierre Curie, companion. To him alone could she confide rare thoughts and dreams. Marie, from now on, was to present to all others, however near they might be to her heart, an almost commonplace picture of herself. She was to paint for them only the bourgeois side of her life. She was to find sometimes accents full of contained emotion to express her happiness as a woman. But of her work she was to speak in laconic, inexpressive little phrases: News in three lines, without even attempting to suggest the wonders that work meant to her.

Here we feel an absolute determination not to illustrate the singular profession she had chosen by literature. Through subtle modesty, and also through horror of vain talk and everything superfluous, Marie concealed herself, dug herself in; or rather, she offered only one of her profiles. Shyness, boredom, or reason, whatever it might have been, the scientist of genius effaced and dissimulated herself behind "a woman like all others."

*Marie to Bronya, 1899:*

Our life is always the same. We work a lot but we sleep well, so our health does not suffer. The evenings are taken up by caring for the child. In the morning I dress her and give her her food. Then I can generally go out at about nine. During the whole of this year we have not been either to the theater or a concert, and we have not paid one visit. For that matter, we feel very well . . . I miss my family enormously, above all you, my dears, and Father. I often think of my isolation with grief. I cannot complain of anything else, for our health is not bad, the child is growing well, and I have the best husband one could dream of; I could never have imagined finding one like him. He is a true gift of heaven, and the more we live together the more we love each other.

Our work is progressing. I shall soon have a lecture to deliver on the subject. It should have been last Saturday but I was prevented from giving it, so it will no doubt be this Saturday, or else in a fortnight.

This work, which is so dryly mentioned in passing, was in fact progressing magnificently. In the course of the years 1899 and 1900, Pierre and Marie Curie published a report on the discovery of "induced radioactivity" due to radium, another on the effects of radioactivity, and another on the electric charge carried by the rays. And at last they drew up, for the Congress of Physics of 1900, a general report on the radioactive substances, which aroused immense interest among the scientists of Europe.

The development of the new science of radioactivity was rapid, overwhelming—the Curies needed fellow workers. Up to now they had had only the intermittent help of a laboratory assistant named Petit, an honest man who came to work for them outside his hours of service—working out a personal enthusiasm, almost in secret. But they now required technicians of the first order. Their discovery had important extensions in the domain of chemistry, which demanded attentive study. They wished to associate competent research workers with them.

Our work on radioactivity began in solitude [Marie was to write]. But before the breadth of the task, it became more and more evident that collaboration would be useful. Already in 1898 one of the laboratory chiefs of the school, G. Bémont, had given us some passing help. Toward 1900 Pierre Curie entered into relations with a young chemist, André Debierne, assistant in the laboratory of Professor Friedel, who esteemed him highly. André Debierne willingly accepted work on radioactivity. He undertook especially the research of a new radio element, the existence of which was suspected in the group of iron and rare clays. He discovered this element named "actinium." Even though he worked in the physico-chemical laboratory at the Sorbonne directed by Jean Perrin, he frequently came to see us in our shed and soon became a close friend to us, to Dr. Curie and later to our children.

Thus, even before radium and polonium were isolated, a French scientist, André Debierne,[d] had discovered a "brother," *actinium . . .*

Marie continued to treat, kilogram by kilogram, the tons of pitchblende residue which were sent her on several occasions from St. Joachimsthal. With her terrible patience, she was able to be, every day for four years, a physicist, a chemist, a specialized worker, an engineer and a laboring man all at once. Thanks to her brain and muscle, the old tables in the shed held more and more concentrated products—products more and more in rich in radium. Mme. Curie was approaching the end: She no longer stood in the courtyard, enveloped in bitter smoke, to watch the heavy basins of material in fusion. She was now at the stage of purification and of the "fractional crystallization" of strongly radioactive solutions. But the poverty of her haphazard equipment hindered her work more than ever. It was now that she needed a spotlessly clean workroom and apparatus perfectly protected against the cold, heat and dirt. In this shed, open to every wind, iron and coal dust was afloat which, to Marie's despair, mixed itself in the products purified with so much care. Her heart sometimes constricted before these little daily accidents, which took so much of her time and her strength.

Pierre was so tired of the interminable struggle that he would have been quite ready to abandon it. Of course, he did not dream of dropping the study of radium and of radioactivity. But he would willingly have renounced, for the time being, the special operation of preparing pure radium. The obstacles seemed insurmountable. Could they not resume this work later on, under better conditions? More attached to the meaning of natural phenomena than to their material reality, Pierre Curie was exasperated to see the paltry results to which Marie's exhausting effort had led. He advised an armistice.

He counted without his wife's character. Marie wanted to isolate radium and she would isolate it. She scorned fatigue and difficulties, and even the gaps in her own knowledge, which complicated her task. After all, she was only a very young scientist: She still had not the certainty and great culture Pierre had acquired by twenty years' work, and sometimes she stumbled across phenomena or methods of calculation which she knew very little, and for which she had to make hasty studies.

So much the worse! With stubborn eyes under her great brow, she clung to her apparatus and her tests tubes.

In 1902, forty-five months after the day on which the Curies announced the probable existence of radium, Marie finally carried off the victory in this war of attrition: She succeeded in preparing a decigram of pure radium, and made a first determination of the atomic weight of the new substance, which was 225.

The incredulous chemists—of whom there were still a few—could only bow before the facts, before the superhuman obstinacy of a woman.

Radium officially existed.

[d]After serving as the Curies' assistant, André Louis Debierne (1874–1949) succeeded Marie Curie as Director of the Radium Institute in Paris, only to be succeeded, on his retirement in 1949, by Irène Joliet-Curie. [B.]

## FURTHER READING

Strathern, Paul. 1999. *Curie and Radioactivity*. London: Arrow Books.

dist
O.
mo
this

onl
stu
pla
Or
wa

m
ter
se
p
ri
w
c

w
h
e
fl
v
h
r

# What Is the Theory of Relativity?

## Albert Einstein (1879–1955)

*In 1905, three remarkable papers were published in the journal* Annalen der Physik *by Albert Einstein, then working in a junior position as a technical expert at the Patent Office in Bern. The first paper dealt with the irregular motion of tiny particles in fluid resulting from their bombardment by molecules—the Brownian movement, first described in 1828. Einstein's paper provided one of the most direct pieces of evidence at the time for the existence of molecules. The second paper dealt with the basis of quantum mechanics. Einstein showed that electromagnetic radiation consisted of particles (photons) that carry a discrete amount of energy. This paper was one of the early results introducing the quantum theory into physics, and it won for Einstein the 1921 Nobel Physics Prize.*

*The third paper "Zur Electrodynamik bewegter Korper" (On the Electrodynamics of Moving Bodies) was the most remarkable of this utterly remarkable trio of papers. It first introduced the special theory of relativity into science—a theory that has become in the public mind synonymous with science itself and with genius. Einstein supposed that the speed of light is a constant for all frames of reference that are moving uniformly to each other. At the same time, he asserted the relativity principle, namely, the laws of nature are the same in all frames of reference moving uniformly relative to each other. To reconcile these two principles, he abandoned the Galilean transformations (the equations for changing velocities in one frame of reference to another frame of reference) and, along with these equations, deeply embedded Newtonian convictions of absolute space, time and motion. The paper was breathtaking and the revolutionary implications staggering to scientists who were utterly wed to Newton's cosmology.*

*Einstein's principle of special relativity only applied to systems in relative uniform motion and the laws of nature, as then formulated, did not hold for accelerated systems. For ten years after the publication of his epoch-making paper, he busied himself with generalizing his special theory. In an accelerated system, forces come into play that are similar to the effects of gravitation. Einstein's general theory is based on his principle of equivalence: "a gravitational field of force at any point in space is in every way equivalent to an artificial field of force resulting from acceleration, so that no experiment can possibly distinguish between them." If the occupants of an elevator, for*

*Source:* Albert Einstein. 1934. *Essays in Science.* Trans. Alan Harris. New York: Philosophical Library, pp. 53–60.

*example, were to be transported to outer space and suddenly accelerated by means of a cable attached to the roof, they would find the floor to be suddenly pressing upwards on their feet and unattached bodies to be falling to the floor of the elevator, exactly as though their weight had been restored; the same effect would be produced, in other words, by the acceleration of the elevator as a gravitational field directed downwards from the ceiling to the floor.*

*If a bullet were to be fired through the elevator from the outside as it was accelerating upwards, the bullet would travel in a straight line through space. To the occupants of the elevator, however, it would appear to fall in its trajectory, as a bullet does on Earth, and the hole it makes on leaving the elevator would be nearer to the floor than the hole it made on entry. According to the principle of equivalence, if a beam of light flashed across the elevator, it would follow a curved path as well. By the same token, this bending of light should occur in a gravitational field. Since the path taken by light is that of shortest time, if light is curved, Einstein declared that space must be curved as well.*

*In this way, Einstein replaced the Newtonian idea of gravitational forces by the conception of space which is made non-Euclidean by the presence of matter. For Newton, a planet which moves in a curved path is pulled out of its rectilinear path by a gravitational force. For Einstein, the path of a planet is curved because space itself is curved and no force need be postulated.*

---

I gladly accede to the request of your colleague to write something for *The Times* on relativity. After the lamentable breakdown of the old active intercourse between men of learning, I welcome this opportunity of expressing my feelings of joy and gratitude towards the astronomers and physicists of England. It is thoroughly in keeping with the great and proud traditions of scientific work in your country that eminent scientists should have spent so much time and trouble, and your scientific institutions have spared no expense, to test the implications of a theory which was perfected and published during the War in the land of your enemies. Even though the investigation of the influence of the gravitational field of the sun on lights of rays is a purely objective matter, I cannot forbear to express my personal thanks to my English colleagues for their work; for without it I could hardly have lived to see the most important implication of my theory tested.[a]

We can distinguish various kinds of theories in physics. Most of them are constructive. They attempt to build up a picture of the more complex phenomena out of the materials of a relatively simple formal scheme from which they start out. Thus the kinetic theory of gases seeks to reduce mechanical, thermal and diffusional processes to movements of molecules; i.e., to build them up out of the hypothesis of molecular motion. When we say that we have succeeded in understanding a group of natural processes, we invariably mean that a constructive theory has been found which covers the processes in question.

Along with this more important class of theories there exists a second, which I will call "principle theories." These employ the analytic, not the synthetic, method. The elements which form their basis and starting-point are not hypothetically constructed but

---

[a] Einstein's theory predicted that light rays would be bent near gravitating bodies, a phenomenon first observed with stellar light near the Sun by Arthur Eddington (1882–1944) at Principe in West Africa during an eclipse of 1919. [B.]

empirically discovered ones, general characteristics of natural processes, principles that give rise to mathematically formulated criteria which the separate processes or the theoretical representations of them have to satisfy. Thus the science of thermodynamics seeks by analytical means to deduce necessary connections, which separate events have to satisfy, from the universally experienced fact that perpetual motion is impossible.

The advantages of the constructive theory are completeness, adaptability and clearness; those of the principle theory are logical perfection and security of the foundations.

The theory of relativity belongs to the latter class. In order to grasp its nature, one needs first of all to become acquainted with the principles on which it is based. Before I go into these, however, I must observe that the theory of relativity resembles a building consisting of two separate stories, the special theory and the general theory. The special theory, on which the general theory rests, applies to all physical phenomena with the exception of gravitation; the general theory provides the law of gravitation and its relations to the other forces of nature.[1]

It has, of course, been known since the days of the ancient Greeks that in order to describe the movement of a body, a second body is needed to which the movement of the first is referred. The movement of a vehicle is considered in reference to the Earth's surface, that of a planet to the totality of the visible fixed stars. In physics the body to which events are spatially referred is called the co-ordinate system. The laws of the mechanics of Galileo and Newton, for instance, can only be formulated with the aid of a co-ordinate system.

The state of motion of the co-ordinate system may not, however, be arbitrarily chosen, if the laws of mechanics are to be valid (it must be free from rotation and acceleration). A co-ordinate system which is admitted in mechanics is called an "inertial system." The state of motion of an inertial system is ac-

cording to mechanics not one that is determined uniquely by nature. On the contrary, the following definition holds good: A co-ordinate system that is moved uniformly and in a straight line relatively to an inertial system is likewise an inertial system. By the "special principle of relativity" is meant the generalization of this definition to include any natural event whatever: Thus, every universal law of nature which is valid in relation to a co-ordinate system C, must also be valid, as it stands, in relation to a co-ordinate system C', which is in uniform translatory motion relatively to C.

The second principle, on which the special theory of relativity rests, is the "principle of the constant velocity of light in vacuo." This principle asserts that light in vacuo always has a definite velocity of propagation (independent of the state of motion of the observer or of the source of the light). The confidence which physicists place in this principle springs from the successes achieved by the electro-dynamics of [James] Clerk Maxwell and Lorentz.[b]

Both of the above-mentioned principles are powerfully supported by experience, but appear not to be logically reconcilable. The special theory of relativity finally succeeded in reconciling them logically by a modification of kinematics; i.e., of the doctrine of the laws relating to space and time (from the point of view of physics). It became clear that to speak of the simultaneity of two events had no meaning except in relation to a given co-ordinate system, and that the shape of measuring devices and the speed at which clocks move depend on their state of motion with respect to the co-ordinate system.

---

[b]A pre-eminent theoretical physicist at the turn of the twentieth century, Lorentz recommended amending Maxwell's equations for the propagation of light, when the source emitting the light is moving. [B.]

**PLATE 44**  Photograph of Einstein.

But the old physics, including the laws of motion of Galileo and Newton, did not fit in with the suggested relativist kinematics. From the latter, general mathematical conditions issued, to which natural laws had to conform, if the above-mentioned two principles were really to apply. To these, physics had to be adapted. In particular, scientists arrived at a new law of motion for (rapidly moving) mass points, which was admirably confirmed in the case of electrically charged particles. The most important upshot of the special theory of relativity concerned the inert mass or corporeal systems. It turned out that the inertia of a system necessarily depends on its energy-content, and this led straight to the notion that inert mass is simply latent energy. The principle of the conservation of mass lost its independence and became fused with that of the conservation of energy.

The special theory of relativity, which was simply a systematic development of the electro-dynamics of Clerk Maxwell and Lorentz, pointed beyond itself, however. Should the independence of physical laws of the state of motion of the co-ordinate system be restricted to the uniform translatory motion of co-ordinate system in respect to each other? What has nature to do with our co-ordinate systems and their state of motion? If it is necessary for the purpose of describing nature to make use of a co-ordinate system arbitrarily introduced by us, then the choice of its state of motion ought to be subject to no restriction; the laws ought to be entirely independent of this choice (general principle of relativity).

The establishment of this general principle of relativity is made easier by a fact of experience that has long been known, namely, that the weight and the inertia of a body are controlled by the same constant (equality of inertial and gravitational mass[c]). Imagine a co-ordinate system which is rotating uniformly with respect to an inertial system in the Newtonian manner. The centrifugal forces which manifest themselves in relation to this system must, according to Newton's teaching, be regarded as effects of inertia. But these centrifugal forces are exactly like the forces of gravity, proportional to the masses of the bodies. Ought it not be possible in this case to regard the co-ordinate system as stationary and the centrifugal forces as gravitational forces? This seems the obvious view, but classical mechanics forbid it.

This hasty consideration suggests that a general theory of relativity must supply the laws of gravitation and the consistent following up of the idea has justified our hopes.

But the path was thornier than one might suppose, because it demanded the abandonment of Euclidean geometry.[d] This is to say, the laws according to which fixed bodies may be arranged in space, do not completely accord with the spatial laws attributed to bodies by Euclidean geometry. This is what we mean when we talk of the "curvature of space." The fundamental concepts of the "straight line," the "plane," etc., thereby lose their precise significance in physics.

In the general theory of relativity the doctrine of space and time, or kinematics, no longer figures as a fundamental independent of the rest of physics. The geometrical behavior of bodies and the motion of clocks rather depend on gravitational fields, which in their turn are produced by matter.

The new theory of gravitation diverges considerably, as regards principles, from Newton's theory. But its practical results agree so nearly with those of Newton's theory that it is difficult to find criteria for distinguishing them which are accessible to

---

[c]The numerical equality of the inertial mass of a body (the acceleration it acquires under a given force) and its gravitational mass (the attraction of other bodies) is demonstrated by the fact that all bodies fall to Earth with the same acceleration. [B.]

[d]Einstein relies on the four-dimensional, non-Euclidean geometry developed by Hermann Minkowski (1864–1909). [B.]

experience. Such have been discovered so far:

1. In the revolution of the ellipses of the planetary orbits around the sun (confirmed in the case of Mercury).[e]
2. In the curving of light rays by the action of gravitational fields (confirmed by the English photographs of eclipses).
3. In a displacement of the spectral lines towards the red end of the spectrum in the case of light transmitted to us from stars of considerable magnitude (unconfirmed so far).[2]

[e]The general theory explained a deviation of 42 seconds of arc per century in the orbit of Mercury. [B.]

The chief attraction of the theory lies in its logical completeness. If a single one of the conclusions drawn from it proves wrong, it must be given up; to modify it without destroying the whole structure seems to be impossible.

Let no one suppose, however, that the mighty work of Newton can really be superseded by this or any other theory. His great and lucid ideas will retain their unique significance for all times as the foundation of our whole modern conceptual structure in the sphere of natural philosophy.[f]

[f]The fact that the same facts could be explained by two such different theories as Newton's theory of gravitation and the general theory of relativity sustained Einstein's conviction that scientific theories are creations of the human mind, rather than inductions from experience. [B.]

## NOTES

1. Special theory, 1905; General theory, 1917.
2. This criterion has also been confirmed in the meantime.

## FURTHER READING

Mih, Walter C. 2000. *The Fascinating Life and Theory of Albert Einstein*. Huntington, NY: Kroshka Books.

Friedman, Michael. 1986. *Foundations of Space–Time Theories*. Princeton: Princeton University Press.

# The New Alchemy

### Ernest Rutherford (1871–1937)

*Following the discovery of radioactivity in 1896 by the French physicist Antoine Henri Becquerel (1852–1908), Ernest Rutherford, who spent a number of years at McGill University in Canada before taking up the Cavendish Chair of Physics and the Directorship of the Cavendish Laboratory at Cambridge University, identified the three main components of radiation and named them alpha, beta, and gamma rays. He also showed that alpha particles are helium nuclei. His work on the scattering of α rays resulted in a theory of atomic structure, which was the first to describe the atom as a dense nucleus about which electrons circulate in orbits.*

*In 1919, Rutherford carried out an important series of experiments when he bombarded nitrogen gas with α particles and obtained atoms of an oxygen isotope and protons. These experiments routed the Newtonian belief in the impenetrability of the atom. Rutherford's transmutation of nitrogen into oxygen was the first artificially induced nuclear reaction, inspiring the intensive research of later scientists on other nuclear transformations and on the nature and properties of radiation. The following paper, "Collisions of α Particles with Light Atoms. IV. An Anomalous Effect in Nitrogen," published by Rutherford in 1919, testifies that the alchemists with their dream of the transmutation of matter had not been so wrong after all—the addition or deletion of protons was taking place in nature all the time.*

. . . A metal source, coated with a deposit of radium **C,** always gives rise to a number of scintillations on a zinc sulfide screen far beyond the range of the α particles. The swift atoms causing these scintillations carry a positive charge and are deflected by a magnetic field, and have about the same range and energy as the swift **H** atoms produced by the passage of α particles through hydrogen. These "natural" scintillations are believed to be due mainly to swift **H** atoms from the radioactive source, but it is difficult to decide whether they are expelled from the radioactive source itself or are due to the action of α particles on occluded hydrogen.

The apparatus employed to study these "natural" scintillations is the same as that described in paper I.[a] The intense source of

*Source:* Ernest Rutherford. 1919. "Collisions of α Particles with Light Atoms. IV. An Anomalous Effect in Nitrogen." *The London, Edinburgh and Dublin Philosophical Magazine and Journal of Science* 37, 581–587.

[a]Rutherford's paper "Collisions of α Particles with Light Atoms" was published in four installments of the *Philosophical Magazine*—I. "Hydro-

radium **C** was placed inside a metal box about 3 cm from the end, and an opening in the end of the box was covered with a silver plate of stopping power equal to about 6 cm of air. The zinc sulfide screen was mounted outside, about 1 mm distant from the silver plate, to admit of the introduction of absorbing foils between them. The whole apparatus was placed in a strong magnetic field to deflect the β rays. The variation in the number of these "natural" scintillations with absorption in terms of cms of air is shown in fig. 1,

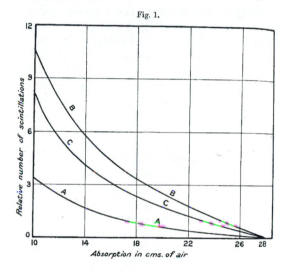

Fig. 1.

*Relative number of scintillations*

*Absorption in cms. of air*

curve *A*. In this case, the air in the box was exhausted and absorbing foils of aluminum were used. Then dried oxygen or carbon dioxide was admitted into the vessel, the number of scintillations diminished to about the amount to be expected from the stopping power of the column of gas.

A surprising effect was noticed, however, when dried air was introduced. Instead of diminishing, the number of scintillations was increased, and for an absorption corresponding to about 19 cm of air the number was about twice that observed when the air

was exhausted. It was clear from this experiment that the α particles in their passage through air gave rise to long-range scintillations which appeared to the eye to be about equal in brightness to **H** scintillations. A systematic series of observations was undertaken to account for the origin of these scintillations. In the first place we have seen that the passage of α particles through nitrogen and oxygen gives rise to numerous right scintillations which have a range of about 9 cm in air. These scintillations have about the range to be expected if they are due to swift **N** or **O** atoms, carrying unit charge, produced by collision with α particles. All experiments have consequently been made with an absorption greater than 9 cm of air, so that these atoms are completely stopped before reaching the zinc sulfide screen.

It was found that these long-range scintillations could not be due to the presence of water vapor in the air; for the number was only slightly reduced by thoroughly drying the air. This is to be expected, since on the average the number of additional scintillations due to air was equivalent to the number of **H** atoms produced by the mixture of hydrogen at 6 cm pressure with oxygen. Since on the average the vapor pressure of water in air was not more than 1 cm, the effects of complete drying would not reduce the number by more than one-sixth. Even when oxygen and carbon dioxide saturated with water vapor at 20°**C** were introduced in place of dry air, the number of scintillations was much less than with dry air. It is well known that the amount of hydrogen or gases containing hydrogen is normally very small in atmospheric air.[b] No difference was observed whether the air was taken directly from the room or from outside the laboratory or was stored for some days over water.

There was the possibility that the effect in air might be due to liberation of **H** atoms from the dust nuclei in the air. No appreciable difference, however, was observed when

---

gen" (pp. 537–561); II. "Velocity of the Hydrogen Atoms" (pp. 562–571); III. "Nitrogen and Oxygen Atoms" (pp. 571–580); and IV. "An Anomalous Effect in Nitrogen" (pp. 581–587). [B.]

[b]Much less than 1 percent. [B.]

the dried air was filtered though long plugs of cotton wool, or by storage over water for some days to remove dust nuclei.

Since the anomalous effect was observed in air, but not in oxygen, or carbon dioxide, it must be due either to nitrogen or to one of the other gases present in atmospheric air. The latter possibility was excluded by comparing the effects produced in air and in chemically prepared nitrogen. The nitrogen was obtained by the well-known method of adding ammonium chloride to sodium nitrite, and stored over water. It was carefully dried before admission to the apparatus. With pure nitrogen, the number of long-range scintillations under similar conditions was greater than in air. As a result of careful experiments, the ratio was found to be 1.25, the value to be expected if the scintillations are due to nitrogen.

The results so far obtained show that the long-range scintillations obtained from air must be ascribed to nitrogen, but it is important, in addition, to show that they are due to collision of α particles with atoms of nitrogen through the volume of the gas. In the first place, it was found that the number of the scintillations varied with the pressure of the air in the way to be expected if they resulted from collision of α particles along the column of gas. In addition, when an absorbing screen of gold or aluminum was placed close to the source, the range of the scintillations was found to be reduced by the amount to be expected if the range of the expelled atom was proportional to the range of the colliding α particles. These results show that the scintillations arise from the volume of the gas and are not due to some surface effect in the radioactive source.

In fig. 1 curve *A*, the results of a typical experiment are given showing the variation in the number of natural scintillations with the amount of absorbing matter in their path measured in terms of centimeters of air for α particles. In these experiments carbon dioxide was introduced at a pressure calculated to give the same absorption of the α rays as ordinary air. In curve *B* the corresponding

curve is given when air at N.T.P.[c] is introduced in place of carbon dioxide. The difference curve *C* shows the corresponding variation of the number of scintillations arising from the nitrogen in the air. It was generally observed that the ratio of the nitrogen effect to the natural effect was somewhat greater for 19 cm than for 12 cm absorption.

In order to estimate the magnitude of the effect, the space between the source and screen was filled with carbon dioxide at diminished pressure and a known pressure of hydrogen was added. The pressure of the carbon dioxide and of hydrogen were adjusted so that the total absorption of α particles in the mixed gas should be equal to that of the air. In this way it was found that the curve of absorption of **H** atoms produced under these conditions was somewhat steeper than curve *C* of fig. 1. As a consequence, the amount of hydrogen mixed with carbon dioxide required to produce a number of scintillations equal to that of air, increased with the increase of absorption. For example, the effect in air was equal to about 4 cm of hydrogen at 12 cm absorption. For a mean value of the absorption, the effect was equal to about 6 cm of hydrogen. This increased absorption of **H** atoms under similar conditions indicated either that (1) the swift atoms from air had a somewhat greater range than the **H** atoms, or (2) that the atoms from air were projected more in the line of flight of the α particles.

While the maximum range of the scintillations from air using radium **C** as a source of α rays appeared to be about the same, viz., 28 cm, as for **H** atoms produced from hydrogen, it was difficult to fix the end of the range with certainty on account of the smallness of the number and the weakness of the scintillations. Some special experiments were made to test whether, under favorable conditions, any scintillations due to nitrogen could be observed beyond 28 cm of air ab-

[c]Normal temperature and pressure—generally 0° and 76 cm Hg. [B.]

sorption. For this purpose a strong source (about 60 mg Ra activity) was brought within 2.5 cm of the zinc sulfide screen, the space between containing dry air. On still further reducing the distance, the screen became too bright to detect very feeble scintillations. No certain evidence of scintillations was found beyond a range of 28 cm. It would therefore appear that (2) above is the more probable explanation.

In a previous paper we have seen that the number of swift atoms of nitrogen or oxygen produced per unit path by collision with α particles is about the same as the corresponding number of **H** atoms in hydrogen. Since the number of long-range scintillations in air is equivalent to that produced under similar conditions in a column of hydrogen at 6 cm pressure, we may consequently conclude that only one long-range atom is produced for every 12 close collisions giving rise to a swift nitrogen atom of maximum range 9 cm.[d]

It is of interest to give data showing the number of long-range scintillations produced in nitrogen at atmospheric pressure under definite conditions. For a column of nitrogen 3.3 cm long, and for a total absorption of 19 cm of air from the source, the number due to nitrogen per milligram of activity is .6 per minute on a screen of 3.14 sq. mm area.

Both as regards range and brightness of scintillations, the long-range atoms from nitrogen closely resemble **H** atoms, and in all probability are hydrogen atoms. In order, however, to settle this important point definitely, it is necessary to determine the deflection of these atoms in a magnetic field. Some preliminary experiments have been made by a method similar to that employed in measuring the velocity of the **H** atom. The main difficulty is to obtain a sufficiently large deflection of the stream of atoms and yet have a sufficient number of scintillations per minute for counting. The rays from a strong source passed through dry air between two parallel horizontal plates 3 cm long and 1.6 mm apart, and the number of scintillations on the screen placed near the end of the plates was observed for different strengths of the magnetic field. Under these conditions, when the scintillations arise from the whole length of the column of air between the plates, the strongest magnetic field available reduced the number of scintillations by only 30 percent. When the air was replaced by a mixture of carbon dioxide and hydrogen of the same stopping power for rays, about an equal reduction was noted. As far as the experiment goes, this is an indication that the scintillations are due to **H** atoms; but the actual number of scintillations and the amount of reduction was too small to place much reliance on the result . . .

## DISCUSSION OF RESULTS

From the results so far obtained it is difficult to avoid the conclusion that the long-range atoms arising from collision of α particles with nitrogen are not nitrogen atoms but probably atoms of hydrogen, or atoms of mass 2. If this be the case, we must conclude that the nitrogen atom is disintegrated[e] under the intense forces developed in a close collision with a swift particle, and that the hydrogen atom which is liberated formed a constituent part of the nitrogen nucleus. We have drawn attention [in another paper] to the rather surprising observation that the range of the nitrogen atoms in air is about the same as the oxygen atoms, although we should expect a difference of about 19 percent. If, in collisions which give rise to swift nitrogen atoms, the hydrogen is at the same time disrupted, such a difference might be accounted for, for the energy is then shared between two systems.

---

[d]The reason is that 6 cm is roughly $\frac{1}{12}$ of an atmosphere. [B.]

[e]The nuclear equation is: $_2\text{He}^4 + _7\text{N}^{14} \rightarrow _8\text{O}^{17} + _1\text{H}^1$. [B.]

It is of interest to note, that while the majority of the light atoms, as is well known, have atomic weights represented by $4n$ or $4n + 3$ where $n$ is a whole number, nitrogen is the only atom which is expressed by $4n + 2$. We should anticipate from radioactive data that the nitrogen nucleus consists of three helium nuclei each of atomic mass 4 and either two hydrogen nuclei or one of mass 2.[f] If the **H** nuclei were outriders of the main system of mass 12, the number of close collisions with the bound **H** nuclei would be less than if the latter were free, for the α particle in a collision comes under the combined field of the **H** nucleus and of the central mass. Under such conditions, it is to be expected that the α particle would only occasionally approach close enough to the **H** nucleus to give it the maximum velocity, although in many cases it may give it sufficient energy to break its bond with the central mass. Such a point of view would explain why the number of swift **H** atoms from nitrogen is less than the corresponding number in free hydrogen and less also than the number of swift nitrogen atoms. The general results indicate that the **H** nuclei, which are released, are distant about twice the diameter of the electron ($7 \times 10^{-13}$ cm) from the center of the main atom. Without a knowledge of the laws of force at such small distances, it is difficult to estimate the energy required to free the **H** nucleus or to calculate the maximum velocity that can be given to the escaping **H** atom. It is not to be expected, *a priori,* that the velocity or range of the **H** atom released from the nitrogen atom should be identical with that due to a collision in free hydrogen.

Taking into account the great energy of motion of the α particle expelled from radium **C,** the close collision of such an α particle with a light atom seems to be the most likely agency to promote the disruption of the latter; for the forces on the nuclei arising from such collisions appear to be greater than can be produced by any other agency at present available. Considering the enormous intensity of the force brought into play, it is not so much a matter of surprise that the nitrogen atom should suffer disintegration as that the α particle itself escapes disruption into its constituents. The results as a whole suggest that, if α particles—or similar projectiles—of still greater energy were available for experiment, we might expect to break down the nucleus structure of many of the lighter atoms[g] . . .

[f]It is worth noting that Rutherford's suggestion that a nucleus can be regarded as consisting of other nuclei was advanced prior to the discovery of the neutron in 1932, by James Chadwick (1891–1974). [B.]

[g]Rutherford restricts his speculation to the lighter atoms for good reason—the electrical repulsion between the positively charged alpha particle and a heavy nucleus like that of gold with a positive charge of 79 electron units was too strong to allow the alpha particle to get close to the nucleus. Neutrons carry no electrical charge, and so, as Otto Hahn (1879–1968) and Fritz Strassmann (1902–    ) discovered in 1938, they are the perfect bullets to cause heavy nuclei to undergo fission. [B.]

## FURTHER READING

Bunge, Mario, and Shea, William R., eds. 1979. *Rutherford and Physics at the Turn of the Century.* New York: Science History Publications.

Oliphant, Mark. 1972. *Recollections of the Cambridge Days.* Amsterdam: Elsevier Publishing Co.

# What Is Life?

## Erwin Schrödinger (1887–1961)

*Erwin Schrödinger, the founder of wave mechanics and one of the towering figures of twentieth-century physics, published a remarkable little book in 1944 that made an indelible impression on many of the scientists who would spearhead the rise of molecular biology—undeniably, the most significant scientific development in the last half of the twentieth century.* What Is Life? *elaborated the provocative thesis that chromosomes are simply bearers of information, and that life itself could fruitfully be regarded in terms of the storage and communication of biological information—so much information, Schrödinger reasoned, that it must be compressed into a "hereditary code-script" that is packed into every cell. What was needed was the identification of these molecules in the cell's nucleus and the key to their code.*

*Schrödinger makes a clear and compelling argument for the inadequacy of classical Newtonian and statistical physics for an explanation of life. Indeed, it is quantum-mechanical rules that are at work in furnishing a discrete coding on the molecular level. The only question is whether the quantum-mechanical laws are themselves adequate for the explanation of life—or are new laws needed to explain life? Schrödinger provided an ambiguous answer to this question. While suggesting that new principles may indeed be needed, his answer is open to the interpretation that what is really needed is a new understanding of quantum mechanics itself.*

## THE HEREDITARY CODE-SCRIPT (CHROMOSOMES)

Let me use the word "pattern" of an organism in the sense in which the biologist calls it "the four-dimensional pattern," meaning not only the structure and functioning of that organism in the adult, or in any other particular stage, but the whole of its ontogenetic development from the fertilized egg cell to the stage of maturity, when the organism begins to reproduce itself. Now, this whole four-dimensional pattern is known to be determined by the structure of that one cell, the fertilized egg. Moreover, we know that it is essentially determined by the structure of only a small part of that cell, its nucleus. This nucleus, in the ordinary "resting state" of the cell, usually appears as a network of chromatine,[a] distributed over the cell. But in

*Source:* Erwin Schrödinger. 1944. *What is Life? The Physical Aspect of the Living Cell & Mind and Matter.* Cambridge: Cambridge University Press, pp. 22–25; 68–70; 73–75; 83–84; 94–96.

[a]The word means "the substance which takes on color," viz., in a certain dyeing process used in microscopic technique. [B.]

401

the vitally important processes of cell division (mitosis and meiosis) it is seen to consist of a set of particles, usually fiber-shaped or rod-like, called the chromosomes, which number eight or twelve or, in man, forty-eight. But I ought really to have written these illustrative numbers as $2 \times 4, 2 \times 6, \ldots 2 \times 24, \ldots$ and I ought to have spoken of two sets, in order to use the expression in the customary meaning of the biologist. For though the single chromosomes are sometimes clearly distinguished and individualized by shape and size, the two sets are almost entirely alike. As we shall see in a moment, one set comes from the mother (egg cell), one from the father (fertilizing spermatozoon). It is these chromosomes, or probably only an axial skeleton fiber of what we actually see under the microscope as the chromosome, that contain in some kind of code-script the entire pattern of the individual's future development and of its functioning in the mature state. Every complete set of chromosomes contains the full code; so there are, as a rule, two copies of the latter in the fertilized egg cell, which forms the earliest stage of the future individual.

In calling the structure of the chromosomes fibers a code-script we mean that the all-penetrating mind, once conceived by LaPlace, to which every causal connection lay immediately open, could tell from their structure whether the egg would develop, under suitable conditions, into a black cock or into a speckled hen, into a fly or a maize plant, a rhododendron, a beetle, a mouse or a woman. To which we may add that that appearance of the egg cells are very often remarkably similar; and even when they are not, as in the case of the comparatively gigantic eggs of birds and reptiles, the difference is not so much in the relevant structures as in the nutritive material which in these cases is added for obvious reasons.

But the term code-script is, of course, too narrow. The chromosome structures are at the same time instrumental in bringing about the development they foreshadow.

They are law-code and executive power—or, to use another simile, they are architect's plan and builder's craft—in one.

## THE GENERAL PICTURE OF THE HEREDITARY SUBSTANCE

From these facts emerges a very simple answer to our question, namely: Are these structures, composed of comparatively few atoms, capable of withstanding for long periods the disturbing influence of heat motion to which the hereditary substance is continually exposed? We shall assume the structure of a gene to be that of a huge molecule, capable only of discontinuous change, which consists in a rearrangement of the atoms and leads to an isomeric[1] molecule. The rearrangement may affect only a small region of the gene, and a vast number of different rearrangements may be possible. The energy thresholds, separating the actual configuration from any possible isomeric ones, have to be high enough (compared with the average heat energy of an atom) to make the charge-over a rare event. These rare events we shall identify with spontaneous mutations.

The later parts of this chapter will be devoted to putting this general picture of a gene and of mutation (due mainly to the German physicist M. Delbrück[b]) to the test,

[b]Working independently, Max Delbrück (1906–1981) and Alfred Hershey (1908–    ) in 1946 found that viruses can recombine genetic material. Delbrück subsequently found that two different types of viruses could reproduce in the same bacterial cell and that the offspring contained characters of both types. He therefore provided the first evidence of recombination in primitive organisms. Hershey would go on in 1952 to design an experiment, in collaboration with Martha Chase (1930–    ), which proved that DNA is the genetic material of bacteriophage (the viruses that infect bacteria).[B.]

by comparing it in detail with genetical facts. Before doing so, we may fittingly make some comment on the foundation and general nature of the theory.

## THE UNIQUENESS OF THE PICTURE

Was it absolutely essential for the biological question to dig up the deepest roots and found the picture on quantum mechanics?

The conjecture that a gene is a molecule is today, I dare say, a commonplace. Few biologists, whether familiar with quantum theory or not, would disagree with it. On p. 50 we ventured to put it into the mouth of a pre-quantum physicist, as the only reasonable explanation of the observed permanence. The subsequent considerations about isomerism, threshold energy, the paramount role of the ratio $W:kT$ in determining the probability of an isomeric transition—all that could very well be introduced on a purely empirical basis, at any rate without drawing on quantum theory. Why did I so strongly insist on the quantum-mechanical point of view, though I could not really make it clear in this little book and may well have bored many a reader?

Quantum mechanics is the first theoretical aspect which accounts from first principles for all kinds of aggregates of atoms actually encountered in nature. The Heitler-London bondage[c] is a unique, singular feature of the theory, not invented for the purpose of explaining the chemical bond. It comes in quite by itself, in a highly interesting and puzzling manner, being forced upon us by entirely different considerations. It proves to correspond exactly with the ob-

[c]Walter Heitler (1904–1981) and Fritz London (1900–1954) applied quantum-mechanical theory to the covalent or electron pair bond in the hydrogen molecule, allowing the calculation of the energy of the covalent bond. [B.]

served chemical facts, and, as I said, it is a unique feature, well enough understood to tell with reasonable certainty that "such a thing could not happen again" in the further development of quantum theory.

Consequently, we may safely assert that there is no alternative to the molecular explanation of the hereditary substance. The physical aspect leaves no other possibility to account for the permanence. If the Delbrück picture should fail, we would have to give up further attempts. That is the first point I wish to make.

## THE DISTINCTION
## THAT REALLY MATTERS

We have thus justified everything in the above scheme, except the main point, namely, that we wish a molecule to be regarded as a solid = crystal.

The reason for this is that the atoms forming a molecule, whether there be few or many of them, are united by forces of exactly the same nature as the numerous atoms which build up a true solid, a crystal. Remember that it is precisely this solidity on which we draw to account for the permanence of the gene!

The distinction that is really important in the structure of matter is whether atoms are bound together by those "solidifying" Heitler-London forces or whether they are not. In a solid and in a molecule they all are. In a gas of single atoms (as, e.g., mercury vapor) they are not. In a gas composed of molecules, only the atoms within every molecule are linked in this way.

## THE APERIODIC SOLID

A small molecule might be called "the germ of a solid." Starting from such a small solid germ, there seem to be two different ways of building up larger and larger associations. One is the comparatively dull way of repeating the same structure in three directions again and again. That is the way followed in a growing crystal. Once the periodicity is established, there is no definite limit to the size of the aggregate. The other way is that of building up a more and more extended aggregate without the dull device of repetition. That is the case of the more and more complicated organic molecule in which every atom, and every group of atoms, plays an individual role, not entirely equivalent to that of many others (as is the case in a periodic structure). We might quite properly call that an aperiodic crystal or solid and express our hypothesis by saying: We believe a gene—or perhaps the whole chromosome fiber[2]—to be an aperiodic solid.

## THE VARIETY OF CONTENTS COMPRESSED IN THE MINIATURE CODE

It has often been asked how this tiny speck of material, the nucleus of the fertilized egg, could contain an elaborate code-script involving all the future development of the organism. A well-ordered association of atoms, endowed with sufficient resistivity to keep its order permanently, appears to be the only conceivable material structure that offers a variety of possible ("isomeric") arrangements, sufficiently large to embody a complicated system of "determinations" within a small spatial boundary. Indeed, the number of atoms in such a structure need not be very large to produce an almost unlimited number of possible arrangements. For illustration, think of the Morse code. The two different signs of dot and dash in well-ordered groups of not more than four allow of thirty different specifications. Now, if you allowed yourself the use of a third sign, in addition to dot and dash, and used groups of not more than ten, you could form 88,752 different "letters"; with five signs and groups up to 25, the number is 372,529,029,846,191,405.

It may be objected that the simile is deficient, because our Morse signs may have different composition (e.g. ·– and ···––) and thus they are a bad analogue for isomerism. To remedy this defect, let us pick, from the third example, only the combinations of exactly twenty-five symbols and those containing five out of each of the supposed five types (five dots, five dashes, etc.). A rough count gives you the number of combinations as 62,330,000,000,000 where the zeros on the right stand for figures which I have not taken the trouble to compute.

Of course, in the actual case, by no means "every" arrangement of the group of atoms will represent a possible molecule; moreover, it is not a question of a code to be adopted arbitrarily, for the code-script must itself be the operative factor bringing about the development. But, on the other hand, the number chosen in the example (25) is still very small, and we have envisaged only the simple arrangements in one line. What we wish to illustrate is simply that with the molecular picture of the gene it is no longer inconceivable that the miniature code should precisely correspond with a highly complicated and specified plan of development and should somehow contain the means to put it into operation . . .

## A REMARKABLE GENERAL CONCLUSION TO THE MODEL

Let me refer to the phrase on p. 66, in which I tried to explain that the molecular picture of the gene made it at least conceivable that the miniature code should be in one-to-one correspondence with a highly complicated and specified plan of development and should somehow contain the means of putting it into operation. Very well then, but how does it do this? How are we going to turn "conceivability" into true understanding?

Delbrück's molecular model, in its complete generality, seems to contain no hint as

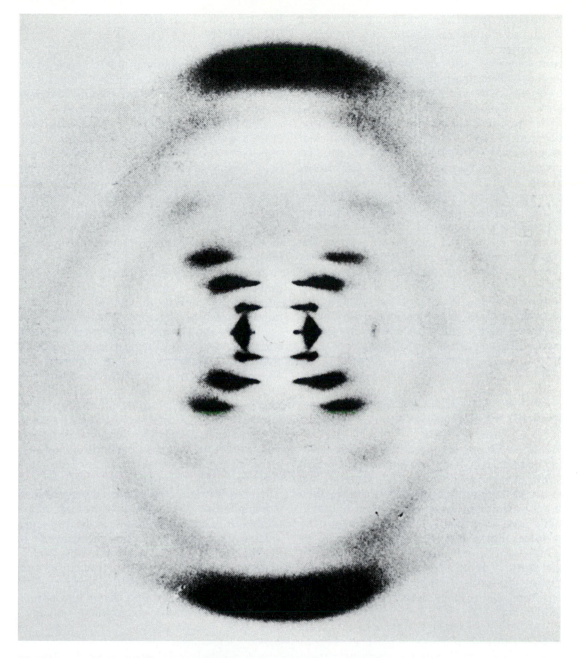

**PLATE 45**  X-ray diffraction photograph of the beta (β-form) of DNA (deoxyribonucleic acid) taken in 1953 by Rosalind Franklin. The image was produced from a beam of x-rays being scattered onto a photographic Figure by the DNA. The resulting cross of bands and spots pointed to DNA having a helical structure.

to how the hereditary substance works. Indeed, I do not expect that any detailed information on this question is likely to come from physics in the near future. The advance is proceeding and will, I am sure, continue to do so, from biochemistry under the guidance of physiology and genetics.

No detailed information about the functioning of the genetical mechanism can emerge from a description of its structure so general as has been given above. That is obvious. But, strangely enough, there is just one general conclusion to be obtained from it, and that, I confess, was my only motive for writing this book.

From Delbrück's general picture of the hereditary substance it emerges that living matter, while not eluding the "laws of physics" as established to date, is likely to involve "other laws of physics" hitherto unknown, which, however, once they have been revealed, will form just as integral a part of this science as the former . . .

## NEW LAWS TO BE EXPECTED IN THE ORGANISM

What I wish to make clear in this last chapter is, in short, that from all we have learnt about the structure of living matter, we must be prepared to find it working in a manner that cannot be reduced to the ordinary laws of physics. And that not on the ground that there is any "new force" or what not, directing the behavior of the single atoms within a living organism, but because the construction is different from anything we have yet tested in the physical laboratory. . . .

## REVIEWING THE BIOLOGICAL SITUATION

The unfolding of events in the life cycle of an organism exhibits an admirable regularity and orderliness, unrivalled by anything we meet with inanimate matter. We find it controlled by a supremely well-ordered group of atoms, which represent only a very small fraction of the sum total in every cell. Moreover, from the view we have formed of the mechanism of mutation we conclude that the dislocation of just a few atoms within the group of "governing atoms" of the germ cell suffices to bring about a well-defined change in the large-scale hereditary characteristics of the organism.

These facts are easily the most interesting that science has revealed in our day. We may be inclined to find them, after all, not wholly unacceptable. An organism's astonishing gift of concentrating a "stream of order" on itself and thus escaping the decay into atomic chaos—of "drinking orderliness" from a suitable environment—seems to be connected with the presence of the "aperiodic solids," the chromosome molecules, which doubtless represent the highest degree of well-ordered atomic association we know of—much higher than the ordinary periodic crystal—in virtue of the individual role every atom and every radical is playing here.

To put it briefly, we witness the event that existing order displays the power of maintaining itself and of producing orderly events. That sounds plausible enough, though in finding it plausible we, no doubt, draw on experience concerning social organization and other events which involve the activity of organisms. And so it might seem that something like a vicious circle is implied.

## NOTES

1. Truly, as light manifests itself and darkness, thus truth is the standard of itself and of error.
2. That it is highly flexible is no objection; so is a thin copper wire.

## FURTHER READING

Watson, James D. and Berry, Andrew. 2003. *DNA: The Secret of Life*. New York: Alfred A. Knopf.

Moore, Walter J. 1989. *Schrödinger: Life and Thought*. Cambridge: Cambridge University Press.

## FURTHER READING

# INDEX